CRIMEWARE

UNDERSTANDING NEW ATTACKS AND DEFENSES

MARKUS JAKOBSSON

ZULFIKAR RAMZAN

 Addison-Wesley

Upper Saddle River, NJ • Boston • Indianapolis • San Francisco
New York • Toronto • Montreal • London • Munich • Paris • Madrid

Many of the designations used by manufacturers and sellers to distinguish their products are claimed as trademarks. Where those designations appear in this book, and the publisher was aware of a trademark claim, the designations have been printed with initial capital letters or in all capitals.

The authors and publisher have taken care in the preparation of this book, but make no expressed or implied warranty of any kind and assume no responsibility for errors or omissions. No liability is assumed for incidental or consequential damages in connection with or arising out of the use of the information or programs contained herein.

The publisher offers excellent discounts on this book when ordered in quantity for bulk purchases or special sales, which may include electronic versions and/or custom covers and content particular to your business, training goals, marketing focus, and branding interests. For more information, please contact: U.S. Corporate and Government Sales, (800) 382-3419, corpsales@pearsontechgroup.com.

For sales outside the United States please contact: International Sales, international@pearsoned.com.

This Book Is Safari Enabled

The Safari® Enabled icon on the cover of your favorite technology book means the book is available through Safari Bookshelf. When you buy this book, you get free access to the online edition for 45 days. Safari Bookshelf is an electronic reference library that lets you easily search thousands of technical books, find code samples, download chapters, and access technical information whenever and wherever you need it.

To gain 45-day Safari Enabled access to this book:

- Go to www.informit.com/onlineedition
- Complete the brief registration form
- Enter the coupon code J6DM-EZRD-F2MK-NEEY-DI7S

If you have difficulty registering on Safari Bookshelf or accessing the online edition, please e-mail customer-service@ safaribooksonline.com.

Visit us on the Web: informit.com/aw

Library of Congress Cataloging-in-Publication Data
Jakobsson, Markus.
  Crimeware : understanding new attacks and defenses / Markus Jakobsson,
    Zulfikar Ramzan. p. cm.
  Includes bibliographical references and index.
  ISBN 978-0-321-50195-0 (pbk. : alk. paper)   1. Computer security.
    2. Internet—Security measures.   3. Computer crimes.   I. Ramzan, Zulfikar.   II. Title.

QA76.9.A25J325 2008
005.8—dc22   2007050736

ISBN-13: 978-0-321-50195-0
ISBN-10:   0-321-50195-0

Text printed in the United States on recycled paper at Courier in Stoughton, Massachusetts.
First printing, April 2008

To Suma and Kabir
and
To A and Art

Contents

2   A Taxonomy of Coding Errors   37

GARY MCGRAW

3   Crimeware and Peer-to-Peer Networks   55

MINAXI GUPTA, MARKUS JAKOBSSON, ANDREW KALAFUT,
AND SID STAMM

6   Crimeware in the Browser   155

DAN BONEH, MONA GANDHI, COLLIN JACKSON, MARKUS JAKOBSSON,
JOHN MITCHELL, ZULFIKAR RAMZAN, JACOB RATKIEWICZ, AND SID STAMM

7   Bot Networks   183

JAMES HOAGLAND, ZULFIKAR RAMZAN, AND SOURABH SATISH

8   Rootkits   229

PRASHANT PATHAK

Preface

Traditionally, malware has been thought of as a purely technical threat, relying principally on technical vulnerabilities for infection. Its authors were motivated by intellectual curiosity, and sometimes by competition with other malware authors.

This book draws attention to the fact that this is all history. Infection vectors of today take advantage of social context, employ deceit, and may use data-mining techniques to tailor attacks to the intended victims. Their goal is profit or political power. Malware become *crimeware*. That is, malware has moved out of basements and college dorms, and is now a tool firmly placed in the hands of organized crime, terror organizations, and aggressive governments. This transformation comes at a time when society increasingly has come to depend on the Internet for its structure and stability, and it raises a worrisome question: *What will happen next?* This book tries to answer that question by a careful exposition of what crimeware is, how it behaves, and what trends are evident.

The book is written for readers from a wide array of backgrounds. Most sections and chapters start out describing a given angle from a bird's-eye view, using language that makes the subject approachable to readers without deep technical knowledge. The chapters and sections then delve into more detail, often concluding with a degree of technical detail that may be of interest only to security researchers. It is up to you to decide when you understand enough of a given issue and are ready to turn to another chapter.

Recognizing that today's professionals are often pressed for time, this book is written so that each chapter is relatively self-contained. Rather than having each chapter be sequentially dependent on preceding chapters, you can safely peruse a specific chapter of interest and skip back and forth as desired. Each chapter was contributed by a different set of authors, each of whom provides a different voice and unique perspective on the issue of crimeware.

This book is meant for anyone with an interest in crimeware, computer security, and eventually, the survivability of the Internet. It is not meant only for people with a technical background. Rather, it is also appropriate for makers of laws and policies, user interface designers, and companies concerned with user education. The book is not intended as a guide to securing one's system, but rather as a guide to determining what the problem really is and what it will become.

Although we often use recent examples of attacks to highlight and explain issues of interest, focus here is on the underlying trends, principles, and techniques. When the next wave of attacks appears—undoubtedly using new technical vulnerabilities and new psychological twists—then the same principles will still hold. Thus, this book is meant to remain a useful reference for years to come, in a field characterized by change. We are proud to say that we think we have achieved this contradictory balance, and we hope that you will agree.

Acknowledgments

We are indebted to our expert contributors, who have helped make this book what it is by offering their valuable and unique insights, and selflessly donated their time to advance the public's knowledge of crimeware. The following researchers helped us provide their view of the problem: Shane Balfe, Jeffrey Bardzell, Shaowen Bardzell, Dan Boneh, Fred H. Cate, David Cole, Vittoria Colizza, Bruno Crispo, Neil Daswani, Aaron Emigh, Peter Ferrie, Oliver Friedrichs, Eimear Gallery, Mona Gandhi, Kourosh Gharachorloo, Shuman Ghosemajumder, Minaxi Gupta, James Hoagland, Hao Hu, Andrew Kalafut, Gary McGraw, Chris J. Mitchell, John Mitchell, Steven Myers, Chris Mysen, Tyler Pace, Kenneth G. Paterson, Prashant Pathak, Vinay Rao, Jacob Ratkiewicz, Melanie Rieback, Sourabh Satish, Sukamol Srikwan, Sid Stamm, Andrew Tanenbaum, Alex Tsow, Alessandro Vespignani, Xiaofeng Wang, Stephen Weis, Susanne Wetzel, Ollie Whitehouse, Liu Yang, and the Google Ad Traffic Quality Team.

In addition, Markus wishes to thank his graduate students, who have helped with everything from performing LaTeX conversions to being experiment subjects, and many of whose research results are part of this book. Zulfikar wishes to thank Oliver Friedrichs and the rest of the Symantec Advanced Threat Research team (as well as his colleagues throughout Symantec) for affording him the opportunity to work on this book and for engaging in countless stimulating discussions on these topics.

We also both want to acknowledge the help and guidance we have received from Jessica Goldstein and Romny French at Addison-Wesley.

Finally, we want to thank our understanding spouses and families, who have seen much too little of us in the hectic months during which we labored on getting the book ready for publication.

Markus Jakobsson
Palo Alto, California
January, 2008

Zulfikar Ramzan
Mountain View, California
January, 2008

About the Authors

Markus Jakobsson, Ph.D., is currently principal scientist at Palo Alto Research Center and an adjunct associate professor at Indiana University. He has previously held positions as principal research scientist at RSA Laboratories, adjunct associate professor at New York University, and was a member of the technical staff at Bell Laboratories. He studies the human factor of security and cryptographic protocols, with a special focus on privacy. Markus has coauthored more than one hundred peer-reviewed articles and is a co-inventor of more than fifty patents and patents pending. He received his Ph.D. in computer science from University of California at San Diego in 1997.

Zulfikar Ramzan, Ph.D., is currently a senior principal researcher with Symantec Security Response. He focuses on improving the security of the online experience, including understanding threats like phishing, online fraud, malicious client-side software, and web security. In general, Zulfikar's professional interests span the theoretical and practical aspects of information security and cryptography. He is a frequent speaker on these issues and has coauthored more than fifty technical articles and one book. Zulfikar received his S.M. and Ph.D. degrees from the Massachusetts Institute of Technology in electrical engineering and computer science (with his thesis research conducted in cryptography and information security).

Chapter 1

Overview of Crimeware

Aaron Emigh and Zulfikar Ramzan

It used to be the case that the authors of malicious code (or malware) were interested primarily in notoriety. However, those days are long gone. The reality is that somewhere along the way, beginning roughly in the very early part of the twenty-first century, a marked shift occurred in the online threat landscape. Cyber-attackers started realizing that they could potentially make serious money from their activities. With more and more people conducting transactions online, malicious code moved away from being simply malicious, and moved toward being criminal. This trend has given rise to a new form of malicious software—namely, *crimeware*.

Crimeware is software that performs illegal actions unanticipated by a user running the software; these actions are intended to yield financial benefits to the distributor of the software. Crimeware is a ubiquitous fact of life in modern online interactions. It is distributed via a wide variety of mechanisms, and attacks are proliferating rapidly.

This book presents material related to crimeware that we hope is of use to people who are interested in information security, whether as researchers or as practitioners. This opening chapter presents a somewhat broad overview of crimeware. It delineates the different types of crimeware seen today and describes how this software arrives on the machine of an end user in the first place and what it does when it gets there. It also describes where opportunities for countermeasures exist. The chapter is peppered with specific real-life examples as well as data about the prevalence of the threats discussed. The remainder of this text will expound upon many of these topics in greater detail and introduce both crimeware concepts that are relevant today and concepts that are either at the bleeding edge of what's possible or even slightly beyond it.

1.1 Introduction

1.1.1 Theft of Sensitive Information

Online identity theft, in which confidential information is illicitly obtained through a computer network and used for profit, is a rapidly growing enterprise. Some estimates of the direct financial losses due to *phishing* alone exceed $1 billion per year [143]. But the losses do not stop here. Additional losses include customer service expenses, account replacement costs, and higher expenses owing to decreased use of online services in the face of widespread fear about the security of online financial transactions. Increasingly, online identity theft is perpetrated using malicious software known as crimeware.

Crimeware can be used to obtain many kinds of confidential information, including usernames and passwords, Social Security numbers, credit card numbers, bank account numbers, and personal information such as birth dates and mothers' maiden names. In addition to online identity theft, crimeware is used in targeted attacks against institutions, such as theft of access credentials to corporate virtual private networks (VPNs) and theft of intellectual property or business data. Crimeware can also be used in distributed denial-of-service attacks, which are used to extort money from businesses, and in *click fraud,* in which online advertisers are cheated into paying criminals who simulate clicks on advertisements they host themselves. Instances of *ransomware* have also occurred, in which data on a compromised machine is encrypted, and the criminal then offers to decrypt the data for a fee.

1.1.2 Crimeware and Its Scope

Crimeware is a subclass of the more broad category of malware, which refers generally to unwanted software that performs malicious actions on a user's computer. In addition to crimeware, malware encompasses (possibly) legal but malicious software, such as adware and spyware, and illegal software without a commercial purpose, such as destructive viruses. Many malware examples straddle the line between being criminal and being malicious. For example, while adware might be a nuisance to some, not all adware is, strictly speaking, criminal. Because adware resides in a gray area and because it is so prevalent, this text discusses adware in more detail in Chapter 12.

Although this text focuses on crimeware, it also discusses issues related to other forms of online malicious activity, such as the broader concepts of malware

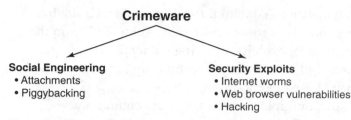

Figure 1.1: Crimeware propagation techniques can be broken up into two broad categories: those based on social engineering and those based on security exploitation.

and phishing attacks. In many cases, these threats have common attributes or share some common solutions. For example, phishing attacks can be used as a social engineering lure to convince users to install crimeware on their machines. Because social engineering is an often-used mechanism for crimeware propagation, and because both phishing and crimeware can serve the ultimate goal of identity theft, it can be difficult to have a detailed exposition of crimeware without reference to phishing. Along similar lines, malware that is not crimeware might have similar propagation and detection mechanisms.

1.1.3 Crimeware Propagation

As shown in Figure 1.1, crimeware is generally spread either by social engineering or by exploiting a security vulnerability. A typical social engineering attack might aim to convince a user to open an email attachment or download a file from a web site, often claiming the attachment has something to do with pornography, salacious celebrity photos, or gossip. Some downloadable software, such as games or video player "accelerators," can also contain malware. According to the twelfth edition of the *Symantec Internet Security Threat Report* (ISTR), 46% of malicious code that propagated during the first half of 2007 did so over the Simple Mail Transfer Protocol (SMTP),[1] making it the most popular means of propagation [401].

Malware is also spread by exploits of security vulnerabilities; as discussed in Chapter 2, these vulnerabilities are often rooted in coding errors. In the first half of 2007, 18% of the 1509 malicious code instances documented by Symantec exploited vulnerabilities [401]. Such malware can propagate using a worm or virus that takes advantage of security vulnerabilities to install the malware, or by making the malware available on a web site that exploits a (web browser or web browser plug-in) security vulnerability. Traffic may be driven to a malicious web site via social engineering, such as spam messages that promise some appealing content

---

1. SMTP is the standard protocol for mail transmission over the Internet.

at the site, or through injecting malicious content into a legitimate web site by exploiting a security weakness such as a cross-site scripting vulnerability on the site. The relatively small percentage of exploits involving vulnerability-oriented malware suggests that attackers find no need to use technically complex methods when simpler social-engineering-based methods will suffice.

Crimeware attacks often span multiple countries, and are commonly perpetrated by organized criminals. Because crimeware is designed with financial gain in mind, the perpetrators often treat their malicious activities as a full-time job rather than as a hobby. They appear to take their work seriously, as indicated by the proliferation of crimeware and the creative and sophisticated mechanisms the attackers have employed. This chapter describes and categorizes the different types of crimeware and discusses the structural elements common to various attacks.

1.2 Prevalence of Crimeware

Information theft via crimeware is a rapidly increasing problem. Phishing scams, for example, are increasingly being performed via crimeware. According to the Anti-Phishing Working Group, both the number of unique key-logging trojans

Month	Applications		URLs	
	2005–2006	2006–2007	2005–2006	2006–2007
May	79	215	495	2100
June	154	212	526	2945
July	174	182	918	1850
August	168	172	958	2303
September	142	216	965	2122
October	154	237	863	1800
November	165	230	1044	1899
December	180	340	1912	2201
January	184	345	1100	1750
February	192	289	1678	3121
March	197	260	2157	1486
April	180	306	2683	1721
May	215	216	2100	3353

Table 1.1: The number of unique password-stealing applications and password-stealing malicious code URLs from May 2005 to 2006 compared with the number from May 2006 to 2007. (*Source:* Anti-Phishing Working Group, Phishing Attack Trends Report, released July 8, 2007. Available from http://www.apwg.org/phishReportsArchive.html.)

and the number of unique URLs distributing such crimeware grew considerably between May 2005 and May 2007, with the bulk of the growth happening between May 2005 and May 2006 [100, 159] (see Table 1.1). Also, according to Symantec, of all threats reported from January to June 2007 that could compromise sensitive information, 88% had keystroke-logging capabilities [401]. This number was up from 76% from the previous reporting period (July to December 2006).

These trends reflect the growing commoditization of crimeware technology and the use of multiple hosts, such as botnets—large networks of compromised computers used together in coordinated attacks—for distribution and data collection.[2] The use of multiple web sites to host the same piece of malicious code makes it more difficult to shut down malicious web sites, thereby stemming the spread and impact of crimeware.

1.3 Crimeware Threat Model and Taxonomy

Crimeware comes in many different flavors. Cybercriminals are technically innovative, and they can afford to invest in technology so long as the investment provides adequate returns. The most dangerous crimeware attacks are carried out as part of professional organized crime. As financial institutions have increased their online presence, the economic value of compromising account information has increased dramatically.

Given the rapid evolution of cybercrime, it is not feasible to provide a comprehensive catalogue of crimeware technologies here. Nevertheless, several types of crimeware are discussed in this section, as representative of the species. The distinctions between crimeware variants are not always clear-cut, because many attacks are hybrids that employ multiple technologies. For example, a deceptive phishing email could direct a user to a site that has been compromised with content injection. The content injection could be used to install a backdoor on the victim's computer via a browser security vulnerability. This backdoor might then be used to install crimeware that poisons the user's hosts file and enables a pharming attack.[3] Subsequent attempts to reach legitimate web sites will then be rerouted to phishing sites, where confidential information is compromised using a man-in-the-middle attack. While this type of example might seem highly involved, it is not uncommon.

---

2. Botnets can be used to carry out a plethora of malicious activities; they are discussed in greater detail in Chapter 7.

3. A more detailed exposition on pharming can be found in the text edited by Jakobsson and Myers [202].

Other malicious software can also be installed using the backdoor, such as a mail relay to transmit spam and a remotely controlled slave that listens over a chat channel and participates in a distributed denial-of-service attack when a command to do so is received.

Notwithstanding the proliferation of various types of crimeware, a crimeware attack on a conventional computing platform without protected data or software can be roughly diagrammed as shown in Figure 1.2. Note that not all stages are

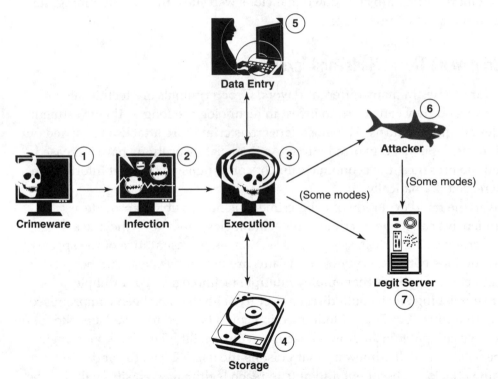

Figure 1.2: The stages of a typical crimeware attack. First, the crimeware (1) is distributed, (2) infiltrates a particular computing platform, and (3) executes. At this point, crimeware can function in multiple ways depending on the nature of the particular crimeware instance. For example, the crimeware instance may (4) scan the user's hard drive for sensitive information or (5) intercept the user's keystrokes. In some modes, the crimeware instance transmits the information it collected (6) directly to the attacker. In other modes, the information is transmitted indirectly to the attacker through an otherwise (7) legitimate server that is being misused. In the case of a man-in-the-middle attack, the information will be sent to (6) the attacker before it is relayed to (7) a legitimate server.

required. In this diagram, the stages of a crimeware attack are categorized as follows:

1. *Crimeware is distributed.* Depending on the particular crimeware attack, crimeware may be distributed via social engineering (as is the case in malicious email attachments and piggyback attacks) or via an exploit of a security vulnerability (as is the case in web browser security exploits, Internet worms, and hacking).

2. *The computing platform is infected.* Infection takes many forms, which are discussed separately later in this chapter. In some cases, the crimeware itself is ephemeral and there may be no executable "infection" stage, as in immediate data theft or system reconfiguration attacks. For example, a crimeware instance might modify a user's hosts file before erasing itself. In such cases, the attack leaves behind no persistent executable code. In other cases, a crimeware instance might be more persistent. For example, a keystroke logger will likely continue to run on the victim's machine.

3. *The crimeware executes,* either as part of a one-time attack such as data theft or system reconfiguration, as a background component of an attack such as that involving a rootkit,[4] or by invocation of an infected component.

4. *Confidential data is retrieved from storage,* in attacks such as those involving data theft. For example, the crimeware can scan the victim's hard drive for sensitive information.

5. *Confidential information is provided by the user,* in attacks such as those involving keyloggers and web trojans. Here the crimeware instance might wait passively until the user visits a particular web site or engages in a particular type of transaction. At that point, the crimeware instance will record whatever information the victim enters.

6. *The attacker misappropriates confidential data.* Data may come from any of several sources (e.g., the victim's hard drive or his or her keystrokes) depending on the type of crimeware involved.

7. *The legitimate server receives confidential data,* either from the executing crimeware (in attacks in which data is explicitly compromised by the crimeware) or from the attacker (in man-in-the-middle attacks).

---

4. A rootkit is a component that uses various stealthing techniques to mask its presence on a machine. Rootkits are discussed in greater detail in Chapter 8.

1.4 A Crimeware Menagerie

Many varieties of crimeware are explored in this section, all of which follow the stages outlined previously. Crimeware species include keyloggers and screenscrapers, redirectors, session hijackers, web trojans, transaction generators, system reconfigurators, and data stealers. In addition, crimeware based on man-in-the-middle attacks is examined, and rootkits that can prevent detection of foreign code are discussed.

1.4.1 Keyloggers and Screenscrapers

Keyloggers are programs that monitor data being input into a machine. They typically install themselves either into a web browser or as a device driver. Keyloggers also send relevant data to a remote server. These programs use a number of different technologies and may be implemented in many ways:

- A *browser helper object* can detect changes to the URL and log information when a URL is affiliated with a designated credential collection site.

- An application-level software package may use a *hooking* mechanism to intercept keystroke data.

- A kernel-level *device driver* can store keyboard and mouse inputs in conjunction with monitoring the user's activities.

- A *screenscraper* monitors both the user's inputs and portions of the display. Screenscrapers can thwart alternate on-screen input security measures. Examples of such on-screen input measures include graphical keyboards where users point and click on the characters in their password, rather than typing the password out explicitly using the physical keyboard.

A keylogger can also be implemented as a hardware device that is physically attached to a machine. Because this book focuses more on the software side, however, such keyloggers fall outside the scope considered by this text. We will not discuss them further here.

Keyloggers may collect credentials for a wide variety of sites. As with many crimeware varieties, configurators are available to automate construction of customized keyloggers (as shown in Figure 1.3). Keyloggers are often packaged to monitor the user's location and to transmit only credentials associated with particular sites back to the attacker. Often, hundreds of such sites are targeted, including financial institutions, information portals, and corporate VPNs. Online poker sites have even been targeted by keylogging trojans (for example, Trojan.checkraise [338]). Similarly, online games such as Lineage and World of

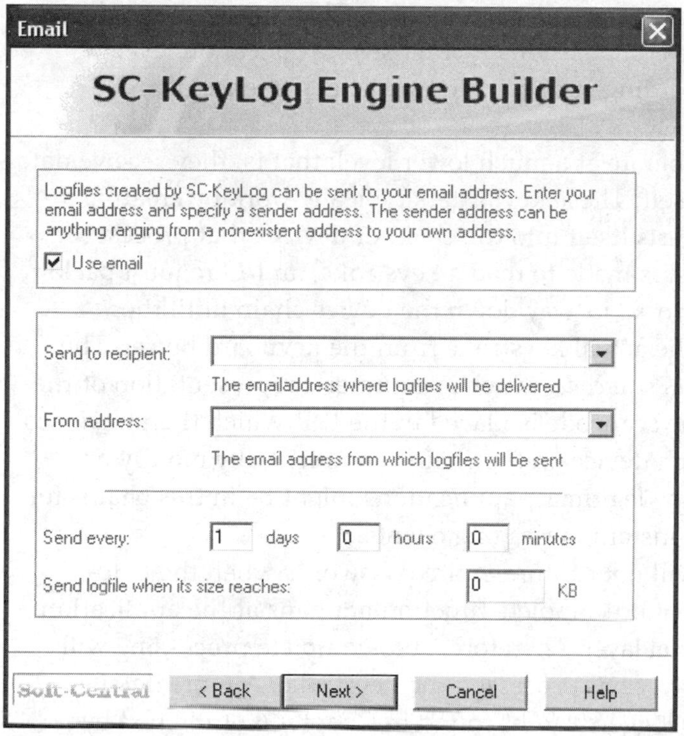

Figure 1.3: An automated keylogger generator. This generator allows the attacker to create a customized keystroke logger. The attacker can specify an email address. The log file that collects the keystrokes is then periodically sent to this particular email address. The user can specify the frequency with which the log file is sent. For example, the user can specify that the file be sent at fixed time intervals or when the file reaches a certain length.

Warcraft have been targeted by malicious code instances (for example, Infostealer.Gampass [335], Infostealer.Lineage [336], and Trojan.Dowiex [339]).

Application-level keyloggers often use some type of system hook (e.g., SetWindowsHook) to monitor keystrokes. A system hook is a mechanism that allows for the interception of Windows messages, commands, or process transactions—including those associated with keyboard events. Keyboard hooks have numerous legitimate purposes. For example, many instant messaging clients use a keyboard hook to determine whether a user is typing a message (and relay that information to whomever the user is communicating with). The actual keylogging application includes a component that initiates the hook as well as a component that logs the data collected. In Windows, the logging functionality might be implemented as a Dynamic Link Library (DLL). Another way to implement an application-level keylogger is by monitoring keyboard requests using, for example, Windows APIs such as `GetAsyncKeyState()` and `GetKeyboardState()`. This approach requires constant polling, so it is more computationally intensive. Application-level keyloggers are capable of recording passwords even in the presence of an auto-complete feature.

Kernel-level keyloggers operate at a much lower level; that is, they receive data directly from the keyboard itself. These keyloggers typically work by creating a layered device driver that inserts itself into the chain of devices that process keystrokes. When any request is made to read a keystroke, an I/O request packet (IRP) is generated. This IRP works its way down the device chain until the lowest-level driver retrieves the actual keystroke from the keyboard buffer. The keystroke is represented by its *scancode*, which is a numeric representation of the key that the user pressed. The scancode is placed in the IRP, which then traverses back up the device chain. Each device on the chain can potentially modify or respond to the scancode. Many legitimate applications might be in this chain—for example, encryption tools or instant messaging clients.

Kernel-level keyloggers will not capture entire passwords when the auto-complete feature is used. The auto-complete function happens at the application layer, which is above the kernel layer. Therefore, auto-complete processing will occur after the keylogging driver has processed the keystroke. A more detailed exposition of kernel-level keyloggers can be found in Chapter 6 of the text by Hoglund and Butler [177].

Various types of secondary damage may follow a keylogger compromise. In one real-world example, a credit reporting agency was targeted by a keylogger spread via pornography spam. This attack led to the compromise of more than 50 accounts with access to the agency; those accounts were, in turn, used to compromise as many as 310,000 sets of personal information from the credit reporting agency's database [219].

1.4.2 Email and Instant Messaging Redirectors

Email redirectors are programs that intercept and relay outgoing emails, in the process sending an additional copy to an unintended address to which an attacker has access. Instant messaging redirectors monitor instant messaging applications and transmit transcripts to an attacker. Email and instant messaging redirectors, examples of which are shown in Figures 1.4 and 1.5, respectively, are used for corporate espionage as well as personal surveillance.

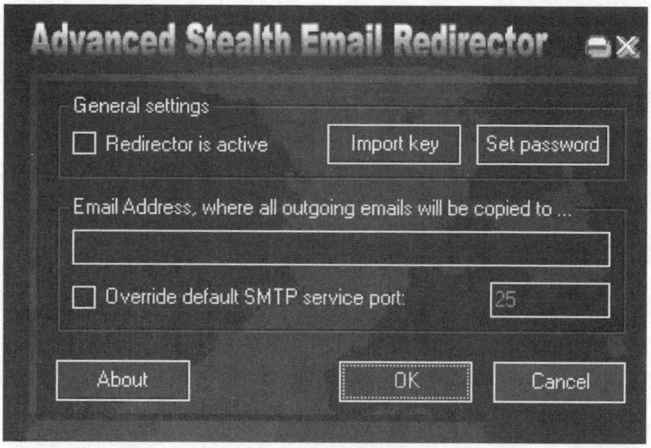

Figure 1.4: An email redirector. Note that the user interface is fairly straightforward and requires the attacker just to specify the email address to which mail should be copied.

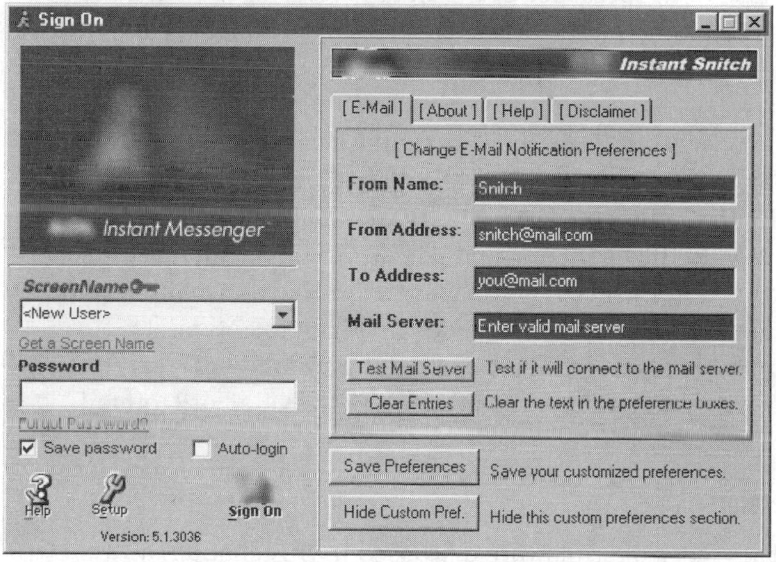

Figure 1.5: An instant messaging redirector. Here instant messaging transcripts are sent to the address specified by the attacker. Although this particular redirector targets the AOL instant messenger, the tool itself is *not* a product developed by AOL.

1.4.3 Session Hijackers

Session hijacking refers to an attack in which a legitimate user session is commandeered. In this kind of attack, a user's activities are monitored, typically by a malicious browser component. When the user logs into his or her account or initiates a transaction, the malicious software "hijacks" the session to perform malicious actions, such as transferring money, once the user has legitimately established his or her credentials. Session hijacking can be performed on a user's local computer by malware, or it can be performed remotely as part of a man-in-the-middle attack. When performed locally by malware, session hijacking can look to the targeted site exactly like a legitimate user interaction that has been initiated from the user's home computer.

1.4.4 Web Trojans

Web trojans are malicious programs that pop up over login screens in an effort to collect credentials. When installed on a machine, the trojan silently waits for the user to visit a particular web site (or set of web sites). When the user visits that site, the trojan places a fake login window on top of the site's actual login window. The user, who is oblivious to the presence of the trojan on his or her machine, then tries to log in normally, thinking that he or she is entering information onto the web site. In reality, the information is being entered locally and then transmitted to the attacker for misuse.

Web trojans do not always duplicate the login window exactly. For instance, they can add extra fields to the log-in window to collect more information. In one example, Infostealer.Banker.D added a field into its fake login window for a victim to enter a PIN (in addition to the username and password) [333]. Along similar lines, some web trojans wait for users to actually log in as they normally would before presenting them with additional form fields in which to enter data.

Figure 1.6 shows a screen shot of a web trojan configurator, which can be used to automatically create a web trojan for either Yahoo!, AOL, MSN, or Hotmail.

1.4.5 Transaction Generators

Unlike many of the other types of crimeware discussed in this chapter, a transaction generator does not necessarily target an end user's computer, but rather typically targets a computer inside a transaction-processing center such as a credit card processor. A transaction generator generates fraudulent transactions for the benefit of the attacker, from within the payment processor. These programs also often intercept and compromise credit card data. Transaction generators are typically installed by attackers who have targeted the transaction-processing center and compromised its security.

Transaction generators could potentially be installed on the end user's machine as well. For example, such a transaction generator could be implemented as some

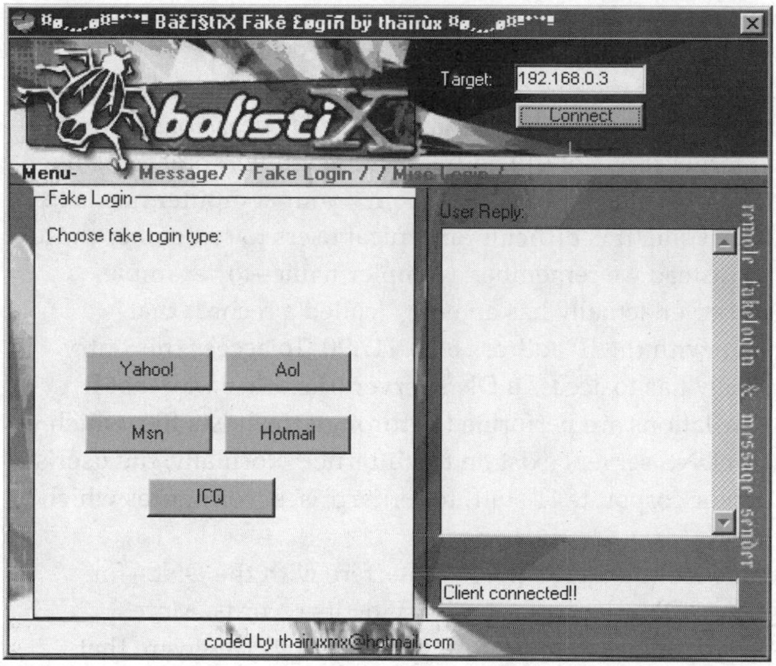

Figure 1.6: A web trojan configurator. This configurator allows the attacker to specify the site for which a fake login is displayed (Yahoo!, AOL, MSN, or Hotmail). When a user visits the site configured by the attacker, the user will be presented with a fake login window that overlays on top of the real login window. Data entered into the fake window will be transmitted to the attacker.

type of web browser extension or plug-in, which then modifies transaction details on the fly. Such transaction generators are discussed in detail in Chapter 6.

1.4.6 System Reconfiguration Attacks

System reconfiguration attacks, such as hostname lookup attacks and proxy attacks, modify settings on a user's computer, which then cause information to be compromised.

Hostname Lookup Attacks

Hostname lookup attacks interfere with the integrity of the *Domain Name System* (DNS). Hostname lookup attacks are commonly referred to as *pharming*. We give a brief description of pharming here; a more extensive treatment can be found in Chapter 4 of the text edited by Jakobsson and Myers [202].

When establishing a connection with a remote computer such as a web server belonging to a bank or other target, a hostname lookup is normally performed to translate a domain name such as "bank.com" to a numeric IP address such as 129.79.78.8. This translation is usually performed by a DNS server.

The DNS is the equivalent of the directory assistance service (or even a giant phone book) for the Internet. Every computer that is directly accessible on the Internet has a unique Internet Protocol (IP) address—for example, something like 129.79.78.8. To access the web site of "www.bank.com", your computer needs to know the IP address of that site. It is difficult for typical users to remember these numerical addresses, so instead we remember a simpler name—for example, www.bank.com. A DNS server actually has an entry (called a record) that associates www.bank.com with the IP address 69.8.217.90. To access this entry, the user's machine typically has to access a DNS server (the other way that IP address-to-hostname translations are performed is through the hosts file, which we discuss later). Many such DNS servers exist on the Internet. Normally, the user's Internet service provider (or corporate IT staff, for enterprises) configures which DNS server to use.

One form of hostname lookup attack tries to interfere with the DNS—for example by compromising a DNS server and modifying its records. More commonly, hostname lookup attacks are performed locally by crimeware that modifies the hosts file on the victim's computer. A computer uses a hosts file to see whether a domain or hostname is known to the local machine with a predetermined address, before it consults DNS. If the domain or hostname appears in the hosts file, the corresponding address will be used, without regard to what a DNS query for that domain might return. If an attacker modifies this file, then, for example, "www.bank.com" might be made to refer to a malicious IP address. When the user goes there, he or she will see a legitimate-looking site and enter confidential information, which actually goes to the attacker.

A second form of hostname lookup attack involves polluting the user's *DNS cache*. The DNS cache is stored on the user's local machine and keeps track of responses provided by DNS servers. This way, if a query for a particular domain name was recently made and a response given, the user's machine does not need to repeat that query. Instead, it can just look up the result in the DNS cache. If the user has a misconfigured DNS cache, however, an attacker might be able to pollute it with incorrect information. Once the cache is polluted, future responses might contain invalid information and lead users to incorrect web sites.

A DNS server also has a cache that can be used to improve its performance; this cache can likewise be polluted if the server is misconfigured. Of course, it might be possible for an attacker to directly compromise a DNS server and modify its records as well. Such attacks that compromise information on the DNS server itself do not fall within the definition of crimeware, as they do not involve software that runs on the victim's computer.

One more way to interfere with hostname lookups is to alter the system configuration of a victim's computer so as to change the DNS server to a malicious server controlled by the attacker. When a user navigates to a correctly named site, such a server might then send the user to a fraudulent site where confidential information is collected. The DNS server settings are often stored in the victim's home broadband router. If an attacker can alter these settings, the victim's machine might be redirected to use the DNS server specified by the router. If this DNS server is controlled by the attacker, he or she can redirect the victim to web sites of the attacker's choice. Unfortunately, an attacker can create a web page that, when simply viewed, will alter the DNS server settings for many popular home broadband routers (so long as the configuration management password on the home router has not been modified from its default setting). This approach is employed in drive-by pharming attacks, as discussed in Chapter 6.

Proxy Attacks

Another type of system reconfiguration attack is to install a proxy through which the user's network traffic will be passed. The attacker can glean confidential information from the traffic while retransmitting it back and forth between the victim and a remote web site. A proxy attack is a form of a man-in-the-middle attack (see Section 1.4.8 for more details).

Proxies come in many types, including HTTP proxies, TCP/IP drivers, and browser helper objects that proxy web traffic from the browser. Many are manageable using a remote interface, such as the one shown in Figure 1.7.

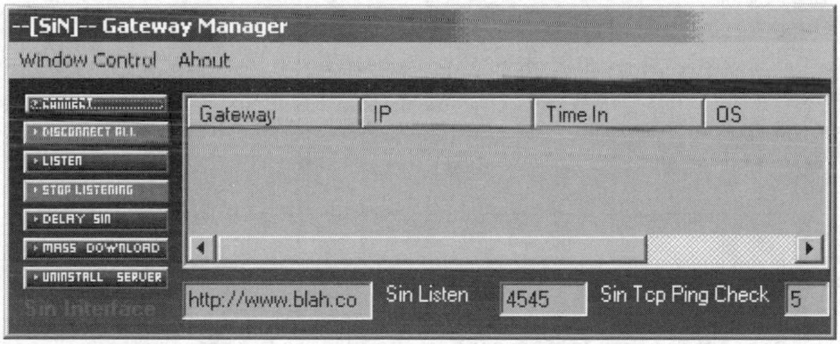

Figure 1.7: A TCP/IP proxy manager. The attacker configures the manager to intercept all traffic between the victim and whatever web site he or she is communicating with.

1.4.7 Data Theft

Once malicious code is running on a user's machine, it can directly steal confidential data stored on the computer. Such data might include passwords, activation keys to software, sensitive correspondence, and any other information that is stored on a victim's computer. Some confidential data, such as passwords stored in browser and email clients, is accessible in standard locations. By automatically filtering data and looking for information that fits patterns such as a Social Security number, a great deal of other sensitive information can also be obtained. Even data the victim thinks he or she has erased could be stolen. When it erases a file, the operating system simply removes references to the file from the file system table. In reality, the underlying content might still reside on the hard disk until it is overwritten by another file, so it remains susceptible to data theft.

Data theft is also commonly performed by crimeware performing corporate (or possibly governmental) espionage, using software such as that shown in Figures 1.8 and 1.9. High-value machines can be targeted, but some espionage may rely on large-scale attacks, because personal computers often contain the same confidential information that is also stored on better-protected enterprise

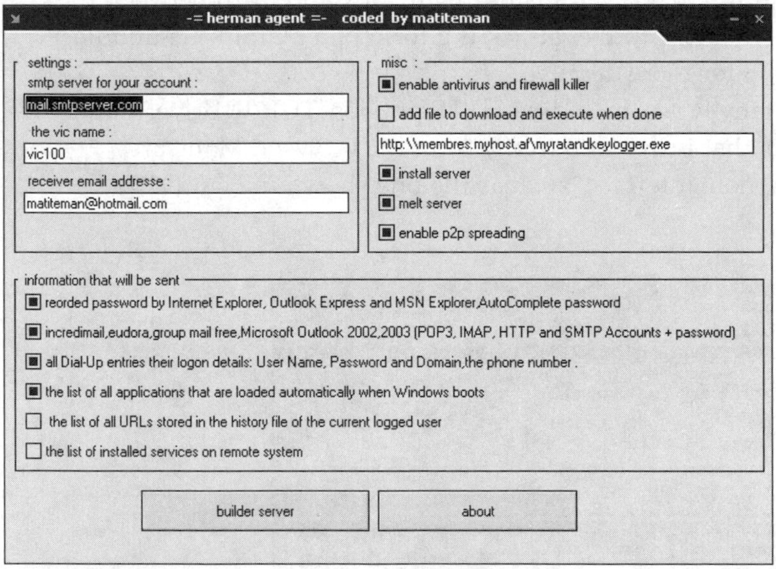

Figure 1.8: A data theft crimeware configuration interface where the files are kept in standard locations. The attacker can specify different types of confidential data to access and an email address to which this information should be sent. Once the configuration tool is run, the attacker will seek to place the resulting crimeware instance on the victim's machine.

Figure 1.9: A data theft crimeware configuration interface where the user can specify any arbitrary file and have it sent over an instant messenger.

Figure 1.10: A man-in-the-middle attack. The attacker intercepts communication from one party and passes it on to the other party, surreptitiously gleaning information along the way. These attacks can be prevented if the data is encrypted end-to-end, and the attacker does not have access to the decryption key, as might happen under the Secure Sockets Layer (SSL) protocol.

computers. In addition to conducting espionage for hire, an attacker might publicly leak confidential memos or design documents, causing their owners economic damage or embarrassment.

1.4.8 Man-in-the-Middle Attacks

A man-in-the-middle attack, schematically illustrated in Figure 1.10, refers to an attack in which the attacker positions himself or herself between two communicating parties and gleans information to which the attacker should not have access or is not entitled. Messages intended for the legitimate site are passed to the attacker instead, who saves valuable information, passes the messages to the legitimate site, and forwards the responses back to the user.

Examples of a man-in-the-middle attack in the context of crimeware-based information theft include the following scenarios:

- A session hijacking attack, in which information is received from a user and passed through to the legitimate site until the desired authentication and/or transaction initiation has been performed, whereupon the session is hijacked.
- A hostname lookup (pharming) attack, in which a web site at the correct host name, but incorrect IP address, relays data between the user and legitimate site, to provide verisimilitude and delay detection.
- A web proxy attack, in which a malicious web proxy receives all web traffic from a compromised computer and relays it to a legitimate site, collecting credentials and other confidential information in the process. The malicious proxy need not be on an external machine, but could be hosted on a victim's home broadband router, which is part of the user's internal network. This concept of hosting such a proxy on the router, which is known as *trawler phishing*, is described in more detail in Chapter 5.

Man-in-the-middle attacks are difficult for a user to detect, because a legitimate site can appear to work properly, and there may be no external indication that anything is wrong. Normally, Secure Sockets Layer (SSL) web traffic will not be vulnerable to a man-in-the-middle attack (assuming the attacker does not possess a decryption key).

The handshake used by SSL ensures that the session is established with the party named in the server's certificate, that an external attacker cannot obtain the session key, and that SSL traffic is encrypted using the session key so it cannot be decoded by an eavesdropper. Proxies normally have provisions for tunneling such encrypted traffic without being able to access its contents. However, browsers and other standard software applications generally silently accept cryptographic certificates from trusted certificate authorities; crimeware can modify this system configuration to install a new trusted certificate authority. Having done so, a proxying intermediary can create its own certificates in the name of any SSL-protected site. These certificates, which appear to come from a "trusted" certificate authority thanks to the altered system reconfiguration, will be unconditionally accepted by the local software. The intermediary is, therefore, able to decrypt the traffic and extract confidential information, and then re-encrypt the traffic to communicate with the other side. In practice, most man-in-the-middle attacks simply do not use SSL, because users do not generally check for its presence [306, 477].

Man-in-the-middle attacks can compromise authentication credentials other than passwords, such as one-time or time-varying passcodes generated by hardware devices. Such stolen credentials can be used by an attacker for authentication as long as they remain valid.

1.4.9 Rootkits

A rootkit is any software that hides the presence and activity of malicious software. Rootkits can be as simple as crude replacements of the administrative software that is commonly used to monitor running processes on a computer, or as complex as sophisticated kernel-level patches that enforce invisibility of protected malicious code, even to detectors with access to kernel-level data structures.

One proposed mechanism for detecting rootkits is to have the core operating system run as a guest *inside* a virtual machine, while security software runs on the *outside* (on the host operating system). This approach provides security software with a bird's-eye view of any malicious software that is running on top of the guest operating system and executing inside the virtual machine. On the flip side, a rootkit can potentially take the existing host operating system and turn it into a guest operating system by running it inside a virtual machine. Any software running on the original host (including security software) will then run inside a virtual machine. Such software will have difficulty detecting the rootkit, which itself runs outside the virtual machine. Such attacks can be aided by modern processor features supporting virtualization. At the same time, if modern processors provide virtualization support, then security software can run in a separate virtual machine, making it difficult to disable [190].

It is theoretically possible for crimeware to install itself not only in the memory and hard drive of an infected computer, but also in nonvolatile storage of hardware devices, such as an ACPI BIOS or a graphics card [167]. Such exploits have been proven possible in laboratory experiments, but have yet to appear in the wild. A more detailed discussion of rootkits can be found in Chapter 8.

1.5 Crimeware Distribution

Crimeware is distributed in many ways: distribution leveraging social engineering (attachment, piggybacking), exploit-based distribution via a server (web browser exploit, including content injection), exploit-based distribution via an infected computer (Internet worms), and distribution via a human (hacking). These distinctions are often blurred, however. For example, a social engineering phishing attack might direct users to a web site that installs crimeware via a web browser exploit.

1.5.1 Attachment

In this mode of distribution, crimeware is sent as an email or instant message attachment. A user is tricked into opening the attachment because it appears to have some value, either salacious (e.g., scandalous pictures or video) or practical (e.g., a security scanning "update" or a video codec "accelerator").

Another form of attachment-based distribution is to distribute crimeware by embedding it in an attractive device such as a USB drive that is "lost" near a target such as a corporation being targeted for corporate espionage. The finders of such devices often attach them to their computers, which can cause software to execute automatically, or may even install their contents out of curiosity. The use of USB drives to propagate crimeware is discussed in more detail in Chapter 4.

1.5.2 Peer-to-Peer Networks

Crimeware can also be distributed over peer-to-peer (P2P) file-sharing networks. Many Internet users, for example, use such networks as a source for MP3 music and other media files. At the same time, these networks are, by definition, decentralized, and there are no real qualifications necessary to join the network. Therefore, there is a risk that some users who join such a network will purposefully (or accidentally) have malicious software running on their machines.

According to the *Symantec Internet Security Threat Report* [401], in the first half of 2007, of all malicious code samples that were propagated, 22% used a P2P file-sharing network. Many of these code samples were not specific to a particular P2P protocol. Instead, they typically copied themselves to any folder on a computer containing the string "shar" on the theory that such a folder might be indicative of a shared folder commonly used in a P2P application. Malicious code, observed by Symantec, used four specific protocols to propagate: Kazaa (used by 18% of code samples), Morpheus (used by 15%), eDonkey (used by 15%), and Winny (used by 5%). These results are summarized in Table 1.2.

The types of malicious code samples that are seen in P2P networks are discussed further in Chapter 3.

1.5.3 Piggybacking

Crimeware can also be distributed within an application that is being downloaded for another purpose. In some cases, the application might actually perform a useful function, but unbeknownst to the user be laced with malicious code. For example, Trojan.checkraise [338] actually has a legitimate function as a rake-back calculator

Propagation Mechanism	Percentage of Threats
General P2P	22%
Kazaa	18%
Morpheus	15%
eDonkey	15%
Winny	5%

Table 1.2: Percentage of malicious code samples analyzed by Symantec that propagated over different specific peer-to-peer file-sharing protocols from January to June 2007. This metric is computed by considering how many malware samples propagated over general peer-to-peer networks, Kazaa, Morpheus, eDonkey, and Winny. The data does not say anything about the percentage of malicious traffic over these channels. Also, a given sample may propagate over several protocols and be counted multiple times. (*Source:* Symantec Internet Security Threat Report [401].)

for poker web sites (see Chapter 17 for a brief explanation of rake-back calculators). Because it ostensibly performs a legitimate function, it might not occur to users that an executable file containing Trojan.checkraise is also recording their keystrokes. Along similar lines, some applications claim to perform a useful function, but actually do not. Such applications are often termed *misleading applications*.

This mode of propagation is a popular choice for software that pops up advertising "adware" and "spyware" protection. In some cases, malicious software can be installed with a user's ostensible consent, by obtaining permission through the use of lengthy and confusing end-user license agreements (EULAs) that make it very difficult to understand what is being authorized. The legal implications of EULAs are discussed further in Chapter 14.

1.5.4 Internet Worms

Crimeware can be spread by *Internet worms* that exploit security vulnerabilities. An infected machine will typically scan other computers in an attempt to find other vulnerable machines, and then infect them as well. Worms usually install a backdoor on infected computers, which allows an attacker (either the worm author or an independent or affiliated attacker) to subsequently install crimeware on them. Infected computers are frequently recruited into a botnet that is controlled by the attacker, typically via an IRC channel or similar means. An example of software for controlling a botnet is shown in Figure 1.11. Crimeware installed through backdoors often includes keyloggers, phishing data collectors, and mail relays used for sending spam.

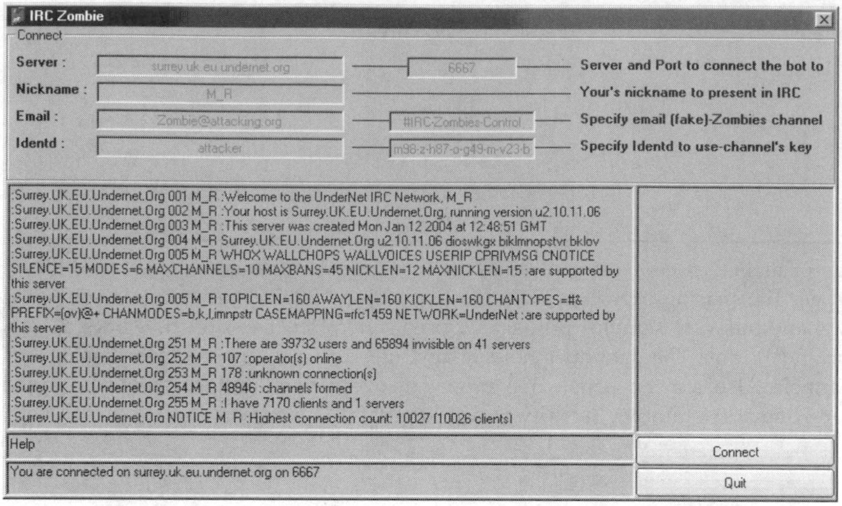

Figure 1.11: A botnet controller interface.

1.5.5 Web Browser Exploits

Web browsers are complex applications that inevitably contain many security vulnerabilities. Such vulnerabilities are a common distribution vector for crimeware. When a user visits a malicious web site, a vulnerability may then be exploited by code on the site. Such vulnerabilities can involve scripting, parsing, processing and displaying content, or any other component that can cause the browser to execute malicious code. In some cases, an exploit is found in the wild even before the vulnerability was known to the browser vendor. Such exploits are called *zero days*.

Not all web browser exploits are disseminated via malicious web sites. A legitimate web site can also distribute a crimeware payload, via a *content injection* attack such as *cross-site scripting*. Content injection refers to the process of inserting malicious content into a legitimate site. In addition to deceptive actions such as redirecting the user to other sites, malicious content can install crimeware on a user's computer through a web browser vulnerability or by a social engineering ruse, such as asking a user to download and install purported antivirus software that actually contains crimeware. Three primary classes of content injection attacks are distinguished, each of which has many possible variations:

- Attackers can compromise a server through a security vulnerability and replace or augment the legitimate content with malicious content.
- Crimeware can be inserted into a site through a cross-site scripting vulnerability. A cross-site scripting vulnerability is a programming flaw involving content coming from an external source, such as a blog, a user's

review of a product on an e-commerce site, an auction, a message in a discussion board, a search term, or a web-based email. Such externally supplied content can consist of a malicious script or other content that is not properly filtered out or encoded by software on the site's server. This content can then run in the context of the web browser of a visitor to the site. The user might think the content was created by the site's owner and, therefore, will be more inclined to trust it.

- Malicious actions can be performed on a site through a SQL injection vulnerability. This approach causes database commands to be executed on a remote server. Such command execution can lead to information leakage, provide a vector for vandalism, or enable injection of malicious content that will subsequently be transmitted to a victim. Like cross-site scripting vulnerabilities, SQL injection vulnerabilities are a result of improper filtering.

Cross-site scripting and SQL injection are propagated through two different primary vectors. In one vector, malicious content is injected into data stored on a legitimate web server, to which a victim is then exposed. In the other vector, malicious content is embedded into a URL, and the user is tricked into clicking on a link pointing to this URL. At this point, the malicious content inside the URL is passed onto the (web) server associated with the domain specified in the URL. The malicious components in the URL might then be displayed on the screen or used as part of a database query, such as an argument to a search function. From the perspective of the user (and the user's browser), this content appears to originate from the web server; in reality, of course, it originated from an attacker.

In addition to distribution via a web browser exploit, another possibility is to take advantage of a vulnerability in a web browser plug-in. Browser plug-ins increase the attack surface[5] of a web browser as well as the complexity of the web browsing environment. As various browser plug-ins increase in popularity, we would expect them to be targeted with increasing frequency.

According to the *Symantec Internet Security Threat Report,* in the first six months of 2007, 237 documented vulnerabilities affected web browser plug-ins [401]. These vulnerabilities could be further broken down as follows: ActiveX components (210 vulnerabilities), Apple QuickTime plug-in (18 vulnerabilities), Sun Java plug-in (4 vulnerabilities), various Mozilla browser extensions (3 vulnerabilities), and Adobe Acrobat plug-in (2 vulnerabilities).

---

5. Informally, the *attack surface* of a system refers to the different mechanisms by which an attacker can attack (and potentially compromise or damage) the system.

Interestingly, during the first half of 2007, Adobe Flash, Microsoft Windows Media Player, and Opera Widgets did not have any documented browser plug-in vulnerabilities. However, some of these applications had documented vulnerabilities during previous reporting periods of the *Symantec Internet Security Threat Report*. For example, from July through December 2006, eight vulnerabilities affected Adobe Flash and three affected Windows Media Player.

1.5.6 Server Compromise

Crimeware can be installed by manually exploiting a security vulnerability or misconfiguration on a server—that is, by breaking into a system. This approach is generally infeasible for large-scale crimeware attacks, but it can be effective against specific targets, such as might be identified in corporate espionage or installation of transaction generators. Specifically, server compromise can play a role in phishing attacks. For example, legitimate sites could be compromised and have malicious content placed on them. Also, attackers might manually compromise a DNS server and configure it to direct DNS queries for targeted domains to phishing servers.

Server-compromise attacks were once the purview of skilled attackers. More recently, the availability of prepackaged port scanners (such as Nmap[6]) and other automated tools have led to a generation of *script kiddies*, who frequently lack the requisite knowledge to find new exploits, but can run the requisite tools to perform the more complex technical functions required to identify and exploit known vulnerabilities. These tools are similar in spirit to the auto-configuration tools shown in Figures 1.3 through 1.9, and Figure 1.11. Such tools remove the need for an attacker to be technically sophisticated. Of course, those auto-configuration tools shown previously are typically designed for client-side attacks, whereas port scanners and similar tools are used to find server-side vulnerabilities.

1.5.7 Affiliate Marketing

Several affiliate marketing programs have sprung up that offer financial rewards for web site operators to install malware on users' computers via security vulnerabilities. One such example is shown in Figure 1.12. With this tactic, web masters are asked to place an HTML <IFRAME> on their web sites that points to a malicious program on the attacker's site. This program, which is downloaded onto the user's web browser when he or she visits the page, is typically designed to exploit particular browser vulnerabilities and to install programs such as adware, spyware, and more general crimeware onto the user's machine. The web site

---

6. http://insecure.org/nmap

Figure 1.12: An affiliate marketing program that provides incentives for web site operators who are able to infect visitors to their sites. Web site operators who sign up as "affiliates" are given a snippet of code to put on their sites. This code snippet is designed to exploit a particular browser vulnerability and can potentially infect the computer of any visitor to the site. For each successful infection, the web site operator will receive an affiliate commission.

operator receives a commission—typically ranging from $0.08 to $0.50—for every "successful" infection. The amount varies on a number of factors, including the country in which the visitor/victim is located.

1.6   Infection and Compromise Points, Chokepoints, and Countermeasures

This chapter has identified several types of crimeware, which can in turn compromise information at different stages specified in Figure 1.2. Each crimeware instance has both an *infection point* and a *data compromise point*. The infection point

Attack Type	Infection Point	Data Compromise Point
Keylogger/screenscraper	2	5 (I/O device)
Email/IM redirector	2	6 (network)
Session hijacker	2	6 (network)
Web trojan	2	5 (I/O device)
Transaction generator	2	5 N/A
Reconfiguration		
Hostname lookup	3 (execution)	5 (web form)
Proxy	3 (execution)	6 (network)
Data theft (proxy)	3 (execution-ephemeral)	4 (storage)

Table 1.3: Infection points and data compromise points for different types of crimeware-based threats. The point numbers correspond to the stages identified in Figure 1.2.

is where the system state is altered (either permanently or ephemerally) to include malicious code or poisoned data. The data compromise point is where the attacker actually obtains sensitive information.

The infection and data compromise points in each of the types of crimeware enumerated in this chapter are described in Table 1.3. The typical infection points occur during the infection (2) and execution (3) stages (where the numbers correspond to the stages in Figure 1.2). The typical compromise points occur in the data storage (4), data entry (5), and network transmission (6) phases.

The infection point and the data compromise point constitute the primary *chokepoints* at which a countermeasure may be applied to thwart each class of crimeware. Any other steps followed by a particular example of malware prior to the data compromise are potential secondary chokepoints at which a countermeasure may also be applied. Examples of countermeasures that can be applied at chokepoints 1 through 6 follow:

1. *Interfere with the distribution of crimeware.* Spam filters can prevent the delivery of deceptive messages. Automated patching can make systems less vulnerable. Improved countermeasures to content injection attacks can prevent cross-site scripting and SQL injection attacks.

2. *Prevent infection of the computing platform.* Signature-based antivirus schemes have problems with reaction time to new attacks, with highly polymorphic code (i.e., code that is distributed in many variants), and with rootkits that obscure crimeware. Behavioral systems can react immediately to new attacks,

although false positives remain a serious problem in such cases. Many legitimate applications have perfectly acceptable functionality that might appear suspicious to a behavior-based system. For example, many instant messaging programs offer a feature that allows one user to see whether another user is typing a message; the mechanism by which this feature is implemented is similar to the mechanism by which a keystroke logger is implemented. More generally, false positives are a concern because consumers are unwilling to tolerate interference with legitimate code (especially given that they may not be able to fully grasp why this interference is happening in the first place). Protected applications that cannot be overwritten or patched except with certified code hold promise as means to prevent infection of existing applications and system files.

3. *Prevent the crimeware from executing.* A low-level mechanism ensuring that only certified code can execute could help prevent attacks, but may prove too restrictive for users, who may have legitimate reasons to run uncertified code.

4. *Prevent the removal of confidential data from storage.* The ability to prevent rogue code from accessing confidential data would be highly useful in preventing access to especially sensitive data, such as signing keys. Specialized hardware is generally required to provide such an assurance. See section 10.3 on trusted computing (written by Angelos Keromytis) of the text edited by Jakobsson and Myers [202]. Also, trusted computing is discussed extensively in Chapter 15 of this text.

5. *Prevent the user from providing confidential information.* Some forms of "white hat keyloggers" can detect when a user is providing credentials to a site that should not receive them. User interfaces need to be vetted to ensure that users can readily provide data to an intended data recipient, even as the entry and transmission of data to an attacker are effectively impeded. A hardware-level trusted path can ensure that keyboard data is appropriately encrypted for the intended data recipient before an attacker could obtain keystrokes. Securely stored credentials can obviate the need for keystrokes in many cases.

6. *Interfere with the ability of the attacker to receive and use confidential data.* Some products sniff traffic to detect a compromise of confidential data. Content-based schemes are suitable for detecting inadvertent compromises, but can be readily overcome by crimeware that employs encryption. Behavior-based systems hold promise as countermeasures in this scenario, but cannot detect all fraudulent use; also, false positives remain an unresolved issue. An effective countermeasure at this step is to ensure that data is encoded

in a form that renders it valueless to an attacker. Such encodings might include encryption that is inextricably bound to a particular communications channel with an authenticated party, and public-key encryption of data that incorporates strict limitations on its use. For example, a piece of sensitive data could be encrypted with the public key of the person to whom that data might be communicated. With this scheme, only that person can decrypt the payload and retrieve the data. Along similar lines, a credential could have its use restricted so that it is valid only when provided from a specific machine. Finally, one other way to limit the usefulness of sensitive credentials is by having them expire quickly. For example, two-factor authentication tokens display passwords that change periodically. The password is valid for only a brief period of time (e.g., a few minutes), after which it can no longer be used for any authentication purpose. While it is possible for an attacker to make use of the current value displayed on the token in real time, such tokens do alter the economics of crimeware. Specifically, constantly changing credentials cannot really be resold in the underground market because they have value only for a brief period of time and only for the specified individual.

In addition to technical considerations, economic considerations arise when pondering crimeware countermeasures. Crimeware is geared toward making the attacker a profit, so a successful countermeasure need not be bulletproof, but merely good enough that it renders the attack unprofitable. Because the attacker is motivated by profit, he or she will likely stop attacking in this manner.

Just because a countermeasure works in a technical sense, however, it may not be practical for other reasons. There are many different types of crimeware and many different ways that crimeware can end up on a machine. The person deploying the countermeasure might require some incentive to take that step. However, such an incentive might not always exist.

Consider the case of a piece of crimeware hosted on a compromised web server. The crimeware will affect the people who view web pages hosted on the web server. The site operator, however, might not have a sufficiently strong incentive to remove the crimeware because it may not target him or her directly (other than, perhaps, tarnishing the site operator's reputation or the popularity of the web site).

Similarly, some types of crimeware infect a machine and then use it to send out spam messages. The "end victim" is the person who receives the spam; the person who owns the infected machine may have less incentive to address the issue because he or she is not the end victim. While we hope most people generally like to be good cyber-citizens, the incentives do not always line up, and technical countermeasures should keep these and similar considerations in mind.

Finally, one often-overlooked countermeasure is to raise users' awareness of the threat posed by crimeware. The hope is that with raised awareness, individuals might engage in less risky behavior and, therefore, be less likely to have their computers become infected. Keep in mind that most crimeware infections propagate through social engineering mechanisms, rather than through exploiting technical vulnerabilities in systems. One approach to raising awareness is via user education. The topic of user education is discussed in greater detail in Chapter 13, which considers some of the challenges in developing user education campaigns.

1.7 Crimeware Installation

A crimeware installation sometimes takes place in two stages. In the first stage, a downloader is executed. In the second stage, the downloader contacts a malicious server and downloads a payload. Crimeware instances employing this two-stage approach are often referred to as *staged downloaders* or *modular malicious code*.

Staged downloaders simplify the malware design and deployment process from the attacker's perspective. First, the downloader portion is typically a smaller file and can easily be sent as an email attachment. Second, the attacker is free to continuously modify and update the malicious payload prior to it being downloaded.

Staged downloaders are quite prevalent. In the first half of 2007, of the top 50 malicious code samples processed by Symantec, 28 included the the ability to download additional components [401]. In many cases, the initial payload (whether loaded directly or by a downloader) is a *backdoor*, like the one shown in Figure 1.13. A backdoor opens up a means for remote control of the victim's computer, usually via a TCP/IP port on which the backdoor listens for commands, either manually sent or sent en masse to a botnet. Most backdoors also include some form of downloader functionality to enable crimeware upgrades.

Crimeware that is not loaded directly can be loaded via a downloader, either as a stand-alone program or as part of a backdoor. The implementation mode of the crimeware varies. Often, it is constructed as a browser helper object (BHO). A BHO is a module that adds functionality to a web browser. In the case of crimeware, additional functionality could be a keylogger that monitors the web site currently being visited and transmits form data on specified sites back to the attacker, or a web proxy that routes traffic through the attacker's server. The extra functionality may also involve a session hijacker that detects a particular page, such as a banking transaction page, and effects a different transaction than the user intended.

One example of a malicious BHO is Infostealer.Banker.D [333], which first waits for the user to log into various web sites and then injects HTML code onto

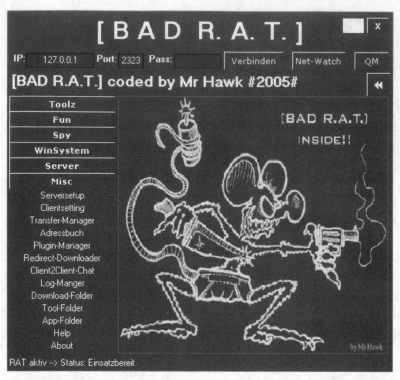

Figure 1.13: A backdoor downloading program.

the subsequent page. The HTML code solicits additional information from the user (e.g., a Social Security or credit card number). Because the HTML injection takes place after the user logs in, the user might think the request for additional information is legitimate, and may be more apt to comply with it. Although this type of attack resembles phishing, it actually arises from malicious code running on the client machine.

Crimeware can also be run as an application program. For example, a web trojan can replace the user's instant messenger application and collect his or her instant messaging password. Data theft programs may look for particular data—such as password data stored in browsers and email clients—and transmit that data back to the attacker. System reconfiguration attacks may change system settings, such as HTTP proxies or hosts files. Alternatively, crimeware can be installed as a device driver. Some keyloggers and TCP/IP proxies, for example, are implemented as drivers [177].

In some cases, the crimeware runs as a separate application and may modify configuration settings to ensure that the crimeware is executed when the computer is rebooted. In other cases, the crimeware embeds itself into legitimate files on a user's computer. Often, such software will be *polymorphically packed,* meaning that some obfuscating transformation will be applied to the involved (binary) files to evade simple signature-based detection by antivirus and anti-malware vendors. In response, some antivirus vendors have developed technologies geared toward behavior-based detection of malicious code [380].

As mentioned earlier, the presence of crimeware can be further obscured by the use of a rootkit, which hides the crimeware to evade detection. Rootkits generally require administrative privileges to install, and they can run in several different ways:

- User-mode rootkits replace administrative applications that can monitor system activities with analogous applications that do not report the presence of the crimeware.
- Kernel-mode rootkits effectively patch the operating system to prevent the crimeware from being visible to detectors that analyze kernel data structures.

1.8 Crimeware Usage

The use of crimeware depends primarily on the type of crimeware that is involved. Such software is typically used for information theft, including identity theft such as phishing; for sending spam; for distributed denial-of-service attacks; for click fraud; or for furthering an information theft attack via information consolidation. Each such application has a different use case. While this chapter primarily discusses crimeware in the context of information compromise, other types of crimeware will also be discussed briefly for completeness.

1.8.1 Information Compromise

Crimeware used for information compromise (such as identity theft) encompasses two basic types: system reconfiguration crimeware and resident crimeware.

System reconfiguration crimeware runs once and modifies a system configuration component such as a hosts file, which will subsequently cause the user's computer to compromise information to a server without the need for resident software. System reconfiguration crimeware can remove itself from the system once the reconfiguration has been performed. For the purposes of this discussion, data theft software is considered to be a variant of reconfiguration crimeware in that the software itself is ephemeral, though in most cases the data theft crimeware does not reconfigure a victim's computer.

Resident crimeware remains on the user's computer, collects confidential information, and transmits it to a location that is accessible to the attacker. Resident crimeware used for identity theft typically has two components: a sending component on a compromised user's computer, and a receiving component on an external server used for data collection.

Resident Crimeware: The Sending Component

A sending component on a user's computer packages data received from a crimeware installation such as a web trojan, keylogger, or screenscraper, and transmits the data to a receiving component. Transmission is performed using one of several different mechanisms:

- Emailing back to a fixed location, typically a free email account, to which the attacker has access.
- Transmitting data over a chat channel, especially an IRC channel that the attacker monitors.
- Transmitting data over TCP/IP (usually via an HTTP POST) to a data collection server to which the attacker has access. Often, many different data collection servers (as many as several thousand) are used in a single attack, to provide resistance to takedowns.

The possibility always exists that attackers may use more sophisticated tactics to transmit data. For example, crimeware could be distributed with an incorporated public cryptographic key, whose corresponding private key is kept secret by the attacker. Any information to be transmitted could be sent using a broadcast mechanism such as posting to a Usenet newsgroup, in which the identity of the attacker among all the potential readers of the newsgroup would be extremely difficult to determine. Data could be further hidden by employing steganographic techniques to embed it within other content, such as photos found on a compromised machine.

Resident Crimeware: The Receiving Component

The receiving components of resident crimeware can run on a remote server and mirror the sending components. In particular, receiving mechanisms include the following options:

- Retrieving email from an email address that is receiving compromised information (typically a free web-based email account).
- Monitoring data appearing on a chat channel, especially an IRC channel, which is receiving compromised information.

- Receiving data over TCP/IP from compromised machines. This action is typically performed by another compromised machine, often one that has been recruited into a botnet.

In all three cases, received data is often repackaged and sent out using different means, with the goal of making the data trail more difficult to follow.

1.8.2 Spam Transmission

Crimeware often attempts to set up an email relay service on a compromised machine. This relaying capability is used by spammers to send spam messages.

Such spamming was historically performed in very high volumes on each compromised machine. Such activity led to poor system performance on the compromised computers, which in turn prompted users to seek remedies to remove the crimeware. More subtle attacks now trickle smaller volumes of spam through many more compromised machines, making detection less trivial and enabling the continued availability of relaying.

Spammers often employ botnets to send spam. Botnets can evade blacklist-based antispam measures because they do not use a small, blockable number of IP ranges to send spam. Some commercial spam-sending software includes the ability to send spam through such botnets, although the spammer carries out the actual recruitment of the spam relay machines.

1.8.3 Denial-of-Service Attacks

Distributed denial-of-service attacks typically involve inundating a computer—or other networked device, such as a router—with more requests (such as SYN or ICMP packets) than it can process. The overload renders the device unable to answer legitimate requests.

Denial-of-service attacks can be used as part of an extortion scheme. In such a scenario, a business is informed that it is subject to a denial-of-service attack, and typically a relatively small-scale attack is mounted to demonstrate that the attacker has the capability to take the business's web site offline for a period of time. An extortion demand is then made, backed by the threat of a larger-scale attack. If the business fails to pay the blackmailer, larger-scale attacks are mounted in conjunction with increasing demands for payment.

The first large-scale denial-of-service attacks were mounted by attackers against high-profile targets such as Yahoo! Since then, attackers have shifted their focus toward trying to achieve financial gain through denial-of-service attacks. Specifically, extortion is particularly prevalent against businesses that lack access to effective legal recourse, such as offshore casinos and betting sites. Such sites are particularly susceptible to extortion because the damages that can be sustained in a single well-chosen day, such as the date of the Super Bowl, the World Cup, or the Kentucky Derby, can account for a very large percentage of the business's annual income.

In the last six months of 2006, Symantec noticed a marked drop in the number of daily observed denial-of-service attacks; this drop has led some to conclude that denial-of-service extortion may no longer be sufficiently profitable to warrant attackers' attention [134]. This trend is not altogether surprising. If the victim refuses to pay the extortionist's fee, then the extortionist is essentially obligated to carry out the denial-of-service attack. Typical attacks are carried out using a botnet and, because of their nature, are highly visible. As a result, the machines on the botnet, as well as the botnet's command and control center, are at risk of being identified (and possibly taken down). The extortionist puts his or her bot army at risk, and may not receive sufficient compensation for that risk. From an economic perspective, the extortioner is likely better off renting the machines he or she controls for the purposes of sending spam. (Not surprisingly, Symantec observed an increase in spam during the last six months of 2006.)

1.8.4 Click Fraud

Online advertising networks offer a web site operator the ability to host third-party advertisements and collect payment for every time a user clicks on an advertisement. The term *click fraud* refers to various schemes in which the number of clicks is artificially inflated. For example, a botnet running crimeware can simulate user visitation of web pages and clicking on advertisements, for which the attacker collects payment. Click fraud is discussed in more detail in Chapter 11.

1.8.5 Data Ransoming

The term *ransomware* refers to crimeware that renders a compromised computer's data unusable, with the attacker subsequently offering to restore use of the data for a fee. Typically, ransomware achieves this aim by encrypting data on a hard drive, with decryption following if the data's owner pays the ransom. Recent examples in the wild have been poorly implemented, using an invariant symmetric key for decryption and receiving payment through inefficient and traceable channels such as purchases at an illicit pharmaceutical site. However, well-implemented ransomware that uses a more robust data-crippling scheme, such as a randomly generated session key encrypted using a public key, could cause significant damage. For more information on ransomware and other types of *crypto-viruses,* refer to the comprehensive text written by Young and Yung [487].

1.8.6 Information Consolidation

Crimeware may be used to collect additional personal information about a person to further identity theft. For example, a keylogger may obtain a bank account number, while other information may be gleaned from compromised files (such as emails and private correspondence) to determine the victim's mother's maiden name or college affiliation, which may be used by the victim's bank as an authentication factor. This authentication factor can then be used to enable high-value fraud. In many cases, searches of public records can yield candidates for such authentication factors, and stolen data from a victim's computer can detect the correct match among several such candidates.

Additionally, crimeware can collect information about a victim's colleagues and acquaintances. This information can be used, in turn, to conduct attacks on those acquaintances. Email can be used to find a circle of friends, and shared email domains may indicate coworkers. Such information can then be used to conduct highly targeted social engineering attacks on people who have a relationship with the first victim. Phishing email recipients, for example, are far more likely to divulge sensitive information if the email appears to come from someone they know [202].

1.9 Organizing Principles for the Remainder of This Text

Crimeware has been crafted using a wide variety of technologies and is an increasingly serious problem. Beyond its use in information theft and aggregation, crimeware is also used in spam transmission, denial-of-service attacks, holding information for ransom, and click fraud. Many of these underlying threats are discussed further throughout this text.

Crimeware used for information compromise follows a seven-part flow, as depicted in Figure 1.2. Each category of crimeware has a characteristic infection point and data compromise point. Each step in the flow represents a chokepoint at which a countermeasure might potentially be applied to the crimeware; chokepoints at which countermeasures to crimeware can be applied correspond to the attack anatomy presented in Figure 1.2.

This text takes a research-oriented view of crimeware. We are interested not only in the current nature of the threat, but also in where it might be going and how we can address it. Crimeware is a complex issue. It encompasses not just technical factors, but also social factors—much of the dissemination of crimeware relies on social trickery and is carried out specifically for financial gain. The remainder of this text explores these crimeware-related topics further.

The individual chapters were independently contributed by different sets of authors whose affiliations range from academic institutions to high-tech companies. Subsequent chapters are designed to be self-contained so that the reader can feel free to peruse them out of order or skip to specific topics of interest. Much of the material presented here is at the bleeding edge of where crimeware is today and where we expect it could go tomorrow.

Acknowledgments

The material in Chapter 1 was adapted in large part from a previous paper written by Emigh [100], which in turn was sponsored by the U.S. Department of Homeland Security Science and Technology Directorate (DHS S&T) and IronKey, Inc. Points of view expressed in this chapter are those of the authors, and do not necessarily represent the official position of the DHS S&T Directorate or IronKey, Inc.

Chapter 2

A Taxonomy of Coding Errors

Gary McGraw

In May 2000, Computer Science Professor Greg Morrisett and I wrote a report for the Infosec Research Council Science and Technology Study Group (ISTSG) focused on malicious code. The purpose of the Malicious Code ISTSG was to develop a national research agenda to address the accelerating threat posed in malicious code. The final report was published in *IEEE Software* [250].

In the course of our work, we identified what has come to be known as the Trinity of Trouble—three factors responsible for the growth of malicious code. The Trinity of Trouble has since been expanded and discussed in *Exploiting Software* [178] and in *Software Security* [249], but it bears repeating here.

The three trends in the Trinity of Trouble are collectively responsible for the increasing number of software vulnerabilities that are exploited by malicious code. Literally thousands of particular coding errors have been identified over the years. Together with Brian Chess and Katerina Tsipenyuk (both of Fortify software), I developed a taxonomy of coding errors called the *Seven Pernicious Kingdoms*. After a brief foray into the underpinnings of the Trinity of Trouble, this chapter introduces the Seven Pernicious Kingdoms.

2.1 The Trinity of Trouble

Complex devices, by their very nature, introduce the risk that malicious functionality may be added (either during creation or afterward) that extends the original device past its primary intended design. An unfortunate side effect of inherent complexity is that it allows malicious subsystems to remain invisible to unsuspecting users until it is too late. Some of the earliest malicious functionality, for example, was associated with complicated copy machines.[1] Extensible systems, including computers, are particularly susceptible to the malicious functionality problem. When extending a system is as easy as writing and installing a program, the risk of intentional introduction of malicious behavior increases drastically.

Any computing system is susceptible to malicious code. Rogue programmers may modify systems software that is initially installed on the machine. Users may unwittingly propagate a virus by installing new programs or software updates from the Internet. In a multiuser system, a hostile user may install a trojan horse to collect other users' passwords. These attack vectors have been well known since the dawn of computing, so why is malicious code a bigger problem now than in the past? Three major trends—connectivity, complexity, and extensibility—have had a large influence on the recent widespread propagation of malicious code.

2.1.1 Connectivity

The growing connectivity of computers through the Internet has increased both the number of attack vectors and the ease with which an attack can be launched. More and more computers—ranging from home PCs to SCADA systems that control critical infrastructures (e.g., the power grid)—are being connected to the Internet. Furthermore, people, businesses, and governments alike increasingly depend on network-enabled communication such as email and web pages provided by information systems. Unfortunately, when these systems are connected to the Internet, they become vulnerable to attacks from distant sources. Put simply, it is no longer the case that an attacker needs physical access to a system to install or propagate malicious code.

Because access through a network does not require human intervention, launching automated attacks from the comfort of one's own living room is relatively easy. Indeed, the recent rise of botnets to carry out distributed denial-of-service attacks is an advance that takes advantage of a number of (previously

---

1. Copy machines were an early target for espionage and, according to tradecraft lore, were easy to compromise owing to their complexity.

compromised) hosts to flood targeted Internet hosts with bogus traffic. The ubiquity of networking means that there are more systems to attack, more attacks, and greater risks from malicious code than in the past.

Directly related to the connectivity trend is the rise of massive distributed systems. These systems, sometimes built according to classic client/server architectures, have grown increasingly larger through the years. Massively multiplayer online role-playing games (MMORPGs) such as Blizzard Entertainment's World of Warcraft are among the largest distributed systems, with millions of subscribers and literally hundreds of thousands of simultaneous users. MMORPGs have become a serious target for malicious hackers, as explained in *Exploiting Online Games* [179]. Similarly crafted SOA systems[2] and Web 2.0 software are susceptible to time and state attacks. Malicious code that takes advantage of overly complicated trust models involved in these massively distributed systems is just around the corner.

2.1.2 Complexity

A second trend that has supported the widespread propagation of malicious code is the growing size and complexity of modern information systems. A desktop system running Windows Vista and associated applications depends on the proper functioning of both the kernel and the applications to ensure that malicious code cannot corrupt the system. However, Vista itself consists of more than 80 million lines of code, and applications are becoming equally, if not more, complex. When systems reach this size, bugs cannot be avoided. The problem is exacerbated by the use of unsafe programming languages (e.g., C or C++) that do not protect against simple kinds of attacks, such as buffer overflows.

Even if the systems and applications code were bug free, their improper configuration by retailers, administrators, or users can open the door to malicious code. In addition to providing more avenues for attack, complex systems make it easier to hide or mask malicious code. In theory, one could analyze and prove that a small program was free of malicious code. In reality, this task is impossible for even the simplest desktop systems today, much less the enterprise-wide systems used by businesses or governments.

---

2. SOA is an acronym for "service-oriented architecture" and has become part of the corporate software lexicon as web services architectures have pushed past the web realm into other kinds of software. See the darkreading article "The Ultimate Insider" at http://www.darkreading.com/ document.asp?doc_id=131477 for more about the relationship between MMORPG security and SOA security.

2.1.3 Extensibility

A third trend enabling malicious code is the degree to which systems have become extensible. An extensible host accepts updates or extensions, sometimes referred to as mobile code, so that the functionality of the system can evolve in an incremental fashion. For example, the JavaScript plug-in architecture of web browsers makes it possible to run client-side AJAX code, extending the capability of the browser. Today's operating systems support extensibility through dynamically loadable device drivers and modules. Today's applications, such as word processors, email clients, spreadsheets, and web browsers, support extensibility through scripting, controls, components, and applets. From an economic standpoint, extensible systems are attractive because they provide flexible interfaces that can be adapted through the inclusion of new components. In today's marketplace, it is crucial that software be deployed as rapidly as possible in order to gain market share. Yet the marketplace also demands that applications provide new features with each release. An extensible architecture makes it easy to satisfy both demands by allowing the base application code to be shipped early and feature extensions shipped later as needed.

Unfortunately, the very nature of extensible systems makes it hard to prevent malicious code from slipping in as an unwanted extension. As a classic example, the Melissa virus took advantage of the scripting extensions of Microsoft's Outlook email client to propagate itself. The virus was coded as a script contained in what appeared to users as an innocuous mail message. When the message was opened, the script was executed; it proceeded to obtain email addresses from the user's contacts database, and then sent copies of itself to those addresses.

Together, connectivity, complexity, and extensibility have made the challenge inherent in writing code that cannot be subverted even more difficult over the years. As a result, today's systems are riddled with coding errors. Understanding these errors is one of the first steps in eradicating them and ridding ourselves of the burden of malicious code. For that reason, describing and discussing a taxonomy of coding errors is a useful exercise.

2.2 The Seven Pernicious Kingdoms

The purpose of any taxonomy (like the one presented here) is to help software developers and security practitioners who are concerned about software understand common coding mistakes that affect security. The goal is to help developers avoid making mistakes and to more readily identify security problems whenever possible. Such a taxonomy is most usefully applied in an automated tool that can spot problems either in real time (as a developer types into an editor) or at compile time using a static analysis tool. When put to work in a tool, a set of security rules organized according to this taxonomy is a powerful teaching mechanism.

This approach represents a striking alternative to taxonomies of attack patterns (see [178]) or simple-minded collections of specific vulnerabilities (e.g., Mitre's CVE; http://www.cve.mitre.org/). Attack-based approaches rely on knowing the enemy and assessing the possibility of similar attack. They represent the "black hat" side of the software security equation (and, therefore, are particularly useful for those people who build malicious code). A taxonomy of coding errors is, strangely, more positive in nature. This kind of thing is most useful to the "white hat" side of the software security world—that is, those who want to prevent the vulnerabilities that lead to malicious code. In the end, both kinds of approaches are valid and necessary.

The goal of the taxonomy presented in this chapter is to educate and inform software developers so that they better understand the way their work affects the security of the systems they build. Developers who know these things (or at the least use a tool that knows this stuff) will be better prepared to build in security than developers who don't. Their code will be less susceptible to malicious-code-related exploits.

Although this taxonomy is incomplete and imperfect, it provides an important start. One problem associated with all categorization schemes (including this one) is their failure to leave room for new (and often surprising) kinds of vulnerabilities. Nor do they take into account higher-level concerns such as the architectural flaws and associated risks described in Chapter 5 of *Software Security* [249].[3] Even when it comes to simple security-related coding issues themselves, this taxonomy is not perfect. Coding problems in embedded control software and common bugs in high-assurance software developed using formal methods are poorly represented here, for example.

The bulk of this taxonomy is influenced by the kinds of security coding problems often found in large enterprise software projects. The taxonomy as it stands is neither comprehensive nor theoretically complete. Instead, it is practical and based on real-world experience. The focus is on collecting common errors and explaining them in such a way that they make sense to programmers.

---

3. This should really come as no surprise. Static analysis for architectural flaws would require a formal architectural description so that pattern matching could occur. No such architectural description exists. (And before you object, UML doesn't cut it.)

The taxonomy is expected to evolve and change as time goes by and coding issues such as platform, language of choice, and so on, change. This version of the taxonomy places greater emphasis on concrete and specific problems than on abstract or theoretical ones. In some sense, the taxonomy may err in favor of omitting "big picture" errors in favor of covering specific and widespread errors.

The taxonomy is made up of two distinct kinds of sets (stolen from biology nomenclature). A *phylum* is a type or particular kind of coding error. For example, **Illegal Pointer Value** is a phylum. A *kingdom* is a collection of phyla that share a common theme; that is, a kingdom is a set of phyla. For example, **Input Validation and Representation** is a kingdom. Both kingdoms and phyla naturally emerge from a soup of coding rules relevant to enterprise software. For this reason, the taxonomy is likely to be incomplete and may be missing certain coding errors.

In some cases, it is easier and more effective to talk about a category of errors than it is to talk about any particular attack. Although categories are certainly related to attacks, they are not the same as attack patterns.

2.2.1 On Simplicity: Seven Plus or Minus Two

Many security taxonomies have come and gone over the years, and all have shared one unfortunate property—an overabundance of complexity. People are good at keeping track of seven things (plus or minus two).[4] In constructing the Seven Pernicious Kingdoms, I used this as a hard constraint and attempted to keep the number of kingdoms down to seven (plus one).

Without further ado, here are the seven kingdoms in order of their importance to software security:

1. Input validation and representation
2. API abuse
3. Security features
4. Time and state
5. Error handling
6. Code quality
7. Encapsulation
* Environment

---

4. The magic number seven plus or minus two comes from George Miller's classic paper "The Magic Number Seven, Plus or Minus Two," *Psychological Review,* vol. 63, pp. 81–97, 1956. See http://www.well.com/user/smalin/miller.html.

A brief explanation of each follows.

1. Input Validation and Representation

Input validation and representation problems are caused by metacharacters, alternate encodings, and numeric representations. Of course, sometimes people just forget to do any input validation at all. If you do choose to do input validation, use a white list, not a black list [178]. Even so, be aware that representation issues are just as important as input validation because "dangerous" content may slip by as an alternate encoding.

Big problems result from trusting input (too much), including buffer overflows, cross-site scripting attacks, SQL injection, cache poisoning, and basically all of the low-hanging fruit that the script kiddies eat. Malicious code often leverages input validation problems to target a particular piece of software.

2. API Abuse

An application programming interface (API) is a contract between a caller and a callee. The most common forms of API abuse are caused by the caller failing to honor its end of this contract. For example, if a program fails to call chdir() after calling chroot(), it violates the contract that specifies how to change the active root directory in a secure fashion. Another good example of library abuse is expecting the callee to return trustworthy DNS information to the caller. In this case, the caller abuses the callee API by making certain assumptions about its behavior (that the return value can be used for authentication purposes). Really bad people also violate the caller–callee contract from the other side. For example, if you subclass SecureRandom and return a not-so-random value, you're not following the rules.

API abuse categories are very common. Malicious code also makes common use of API abuse, especially when such abuse involves network-related functionality. For example, both SYN/ACK attacks and Teardrop attacks involve manipulation of network protocols and packet formation.[5]

3. Security Features

I've said it before, and I'll say it again: Software security is not security software. All of the magic crypto-fairy dust in the world won't make you secure. But it's also true that you can drop the ball when it comes to essential security features. Suppose you decide to use SSL to protect traffic across the network, but you really screw things up. Unfortunately, this happens all the time. Taken collectively, *security features* include topics like authentication, access control, confidentiality,

---

5. For Teardrop, see http://www.cert.org/advisories/CA-1997-28.html. For SYN/ACK, see http://www.cert.org/advisories/CA-1996-21.html.

cryptography, privilege management, and all that other material on the CISSP exam—stuff that is hard to get right.

For the most part, malicious code does not tend to target security features, although some interesting counterexamples to that trend exist. For example, one exception to this general rule is malicious code that attempts to disable antivirus protection—a common tactic.

4. Time and State

Distributed computation is about time and state. That is, for more than one component to communicate, state must be shared (somehow), which takes time. Playing with time and state is the biggest untapped natural attack resource on the planet right now. In particular, time and state errors are proliferating as massively distributed systems such as MMORPGs become more common.

One example from World of Warcraft involves player character location. Instead of tracking the locations of literally millions of objects in the game, game architects chose to ship much of this state information to gamers' PCs and sync it from time to time with game servers. Control over the seemingly innocuous piece of state corresponding to location is given to the game client in the normal course of the game and, therefore, is susceptible to direct tweaking by a malicious gamer bent on cheating. The technique known as telehacking is based on directly changing player location parameters on the client PC and thus teleporting around the game. Malicious code based on such time and state vulnerabilities promises to become more common as systems grow ever larger.

Most programmers anthropomorphize (or, more accurately, only solipsistically ponder) their work. They think about themselves—the single omniscient thread of control manually plodding along, carrying out the entire program in the same way they themselves would do it if forced to do the job manually. That's really quaint. Modern computers switch between tasks very quickly, and in multicore, multi-CPU, or distributed systems, two events may take place at *exactly the same time.* Defects rush to fill the gap between the programmer's model of how a program executes and what happens in reality. These defects are related to unexpected interactions between threads, processes, time, and information. These interactions happen through shared state: semaphores, variables, the file system, the universe, and, basically, anything that can store information.

One day soon, this kingdom will be number one.

5. Error Handling

Want to break software? Throw some junk at a program and see what errors you cause. Errors are not only a great source of "too much information" from a program, but also a source of inconsistent thinking that can be gamed. It gets worse, though. In modern object-oriented systems, the notion of exceptions has brought the once-banned concept of goto back to center stage.

Errors and error handlers represent a class of programming contract. Thus, in some sense, errors represent the two sides of a special form of API. Nevertheless, security defects related to error handling are so common that they deserve a special kingdom all of their own. As with API abuse, there are two ways to blow it here. First comes either forgetting to handle errors at all, or handing them so roughly that they get all bruised and bloody. The second is producing errors that either give out far too much information (to possible attackers) or are so radioactive that no one wants to handle them.

Attackers who build malicious code sometimes resort to fuzzing a target to find a vulnerability that can be exploited. Although fuzzing as a technique is certainly lame, it's also easy. Fuzzing systems often find exploitable conditions in error handing.

6. Code Quality

Security is a subset of reliability, just as all future TV shows are a subset of monkeys banging on zillions of keyboards. If you are able to completely specify your system and all of its positive and negative security possibilities, then security is a subset of reliability. In the real world, security deserves an entire budget of its own. Poor code quality leads to unpredictable behavior. From a user's perspective, that shortcoming often manifests itself as poor usability. For an attacker, bad quality provides an opportunity to stress the system in unexpected ways.

Malicious code that targets poor-quality code is much more common than malicious code that targets high-quality code. This is a fact that should have more effect on purchasing decisions than it seems to have today.

7. Encapsulation

Encapsulation deals with drawing strong boundaries between things and setting up barriers between them. In a web browser, this might mean ensuring that mobile code cannot whack the hard drive arbitrarily (bad applet, kennel up). On a web services server, it might mean differentiating between valid data that has been authenticated and run through the white list and mystery data that was found sitting on the floor in the men's room under the urinal. Boundaries are critical. Some of the most important boundaries today separate classes with various methods. Trust and trust models require careful and meticulous attention to boundaries. Keep your hands off my stuff!

* Environment

Software runs on a machine with certain bindings and certain connections to the bad, mean universe. Getting outside the software is important, however. This kingdom is the kingdom of outside → in. It includes all of the stuff that is outside of your code but is still critical to the security of the software you create.

Administrivia

The next section introduces the phyla that fit under the seven (plus one) kingdoms. To better understand the relationship between kingdoms and phyla, consider a recently found vulnerability in Adobe Reader 5.0.x for UNIX. The vulnerability is present in a function called UnixAppOpenFilePerform() that copies user-supplied data into a fixed-size stack buffer using a call to sprintf(). If the size of the user-supplied data is greater than the size of the buffer it is being copied into, important information—including the stack pointer—is overwritten. By supplying a malicious PDF document, an attacker can execute arbitrary commands on the target system. This attack becomes possible because of a simple coding error—the absence of a check that makes sure the size of the user-supplied data is no greater than the size of the destination buffer.

Developers will associate this check with a failure to code defensively around the call to sprintf(). I classify this coding error according to the attack it enables: "Buffer Overflow." I choose "Input Validation and Representation" as the name of the kingdom to which the "Buffer Overflow" phylum belongs because the lack of proper input validation is the root cause that makes the attack possible. Malicious code writers are making more common use of problems like this one to propagate attacks through documents. By building an attack into a document, they can circumvent many of the usual network-based security mechanisms.

The coding errors represented by phyla can all be detected by static source code analysis tools. Source code analysis offers developers an opportunity to obtain quick feedback about the code that they write. I strongly advocate educating developers about coding errors by having them use a source code analysis tool.

The big list below takes the following form:

Kingdom

- **Phylum.** Explanatory sentence or two

2.3 The Phyla

1. Input Validation and Representation

- **Buffer Overflow.** Writing outside the bounds of allocated memory can corrupt data, crash the program, or cause the execution of an attack payload.

- **Command Injection.** Executing commands from an untrusted source or in an untrusted environment can cause an application to execute malicious commands on behalf of an attacker.

- **Cross-Site Scripting.** Sending unvalidated data to a web browser can result in the browser executing malicious code (usually scripts).

- **Format String.** Allowing an attacker to control a function's format string may result in a buffer overflow.

- **HTTP Response Splitting.** Writing unvalidated data into an HTTP header allows an attacker to specify the entirety of the HTTP response rendered by the browser.

- **Illegal Pointer Value.** This function can return a pointer to memory outside of the buffer to be searched. Subsequent operations on the pointer may have unintended consequences.

- **Integer Overflow.** Not accounting for integer overflow can result in logic errors or buffer overflows.

- **Log Forging.** Writing unvalidated user input into log files can allow an attacker to forge log entries or inject malicious content into logs.

- **Path Traversal.** Allowing user input to control paths used by the application may enable an attacker to access otherwise protected files.

- **Process Control.** Executing commands or loading libraries from an untrusted source or in an untrusted environment can cause an application to execute malicious commands (and payloads) on behalf of an attacker.

- **Resource Injection.** Allowing user input to control resource identifiers may enable an attacker to access or modify otherwise protected system resources.

- **Setting Manipulation.** Allowing external control of system settings can disrupt service or cause an application to behave in unexpected ways.

- **SQL Injection.** Constructing a dynamic SQL statement with user input may allow an attacker to modify the statement's meaning or to execute arbitrary SQL commands.

- **String Termination Error.** Relying on proper string termination may result in a buffer overflow.

- **Struts: Duplicate Validation Forms.** Multiple validation forms with the same name indicate that validation logic is not up-to-date.

- **Struts: Erroneous validate() Method.** The validation form defines a validate() method but fails to call super.validate().

- **Struts: Form Bean Does Not Extend Validator Class.** All Struts forms should extend a Validator class.

- **Struts: Form Field Without Validator.** Every field in a form should be validated in the corresponding validation form.

- **Struts: Plug-in Framework Not in Use.** Use the Struts Validator to prevent vulnerabilities that result from unchecked input.

- **Struts: Unused Validation Form.** An unused validation form indicates that validation logic is not up-to-date.

- **Struts: Unvalidated Action Form.** Every Action form must have a corresponding validation form.

- **Struts: Validator Turned Off.** This Action form mapping disables the form's validate() method.

- **Struts: Validator Without Form Field.** Validation fields that do not appear in forms they are associated with indicate that the validation logic is out-of-date.

- **Unsafe JNI.** Improper use of the Java Native Interface (JNI) can render Java applications vulnerable to security flaws in other languages. Language-based encapsulation is broken.

- **Unsafe Reflection.** An attacker may be able to create unexpected control flow paths through the application, potentially bypassing security checks.

- **XML Validation.** Failure to enable validation when parsing XML gives an attacker the opportunity to supply malicious input.

2. API Abuse

- **Dangerous Function.** Functions that cannot be used safely should never be used.

- **Directory Restriction.** Improper use of the chroot() system call may allow attackers to escape a chroot jail.

- **Heap Inspection.** Do not use realloc() to resize buffers that store sensitive information.

- **J2EE Bad Practices: getConnection().** The J2EE standard forbids the direct management of connections.

- **J2EE Bad Practices: Sockets.** Socket-based communication in web applications is prone to error.

- **Often Misused: Authentication.** [*See complete sample entry on page 54.*]

- **Often Misused: Exception Handling.** A dangerous function can throw an exception, potentially causing the program to crash.

- **Often Misused: Path Manipulation.** Passing an inadequately sized output buffer to a path manipulation function can result in a buffer overflow.

- **Often Misused: Privilege Management.** Failure to adhere to the principle of least privilege amplifies the risk posed by other vulnerabilities.

- **Often Misused: String Manipulation.** Functions that manipulate strings encourage buffer overflows.

- **Unchecked Return Value.** Ignoring a method's return value can cause the program to overlook unexpected states and conditions.

3. **Security Features**

- **Insecure Randomness.** Standard pseudo-random-number generators cannot withstand cryptographic attacks.

- **Least Privilege Violation.** The elevated privilege level required to perform operations such as chroot() should be dropped immediately after the operation is performed.

- **Missing Access Control.** The program does not perform access control checks in a consistent manner across all potential execution paths.

- **Password Management.** Storing a password in plaintext may result in a system compromise.

- **Password Management: Empty Password in Configuration File.** Using an empty string as a password is insecure.

- **Password Management: Hard-Coded Password.** Hard-coded passwords may compromise system security in a way that cannot be easily remedied.

- **Password Management: Password in Configuration File.** Storing a password in a configuration file may result in system compromise.

- **Password Management: Weak Cryptography.** Obscuring a password with a trivial encoding does not protect the password.

- **Privacy Violation.** Mishandling private information, such as customer passwords or Social Security numbers, can compromise user privacy and is often illegal.

4. **Time and State**

- **Deadlock.** Inconsistent locking discipline can lead to deadlock.

- **Failure to Begin a New Session Upon Authentication.** Using the same session identifier across an authentication boundary allows an attacker to hijack authenticated sessions.

- **File Access Race Condition: TOCTOU.** The window of time between when a file property is checked and when the file is used to launch a privilege escalation attack.

- **Insecure Temporary File.** Creating and using insecure temporary files can leave application and system data vulnerable to attack.

- **J2EE Bad Practices: System.exit( ).** A web application should not attempt to shut down its container.

- **J2EE Bad Practices: Threads.** Thread management in a web application is forbidden in some circumstances and is always highly error prone.

- **Signal-Handling Race Conditions.** Signal handlers may change a shared state relied upon by other signal handlers or application code, causing unexpected behavior.

5. Error Handling

- **Catch NullPointerException.** Catching `NullPointerException` should not be used as an alternative to programmatic checks to prevent dereferencing a null pointer.

- **Empty Catch Block.** Ignoring exceptions and other error conditions may allow an attacker to induce unexpected behavior unnoticed.

- **Overly Broad Catch Block.** Catching overly broad exceptions promotes complex error-handling code that is more likely to contain security vulnerabilities.

- **Overly Broad Throws Declaration.** Throwing overly broad exceptions promotes complex error-handling code that is more likely to contain security vulnerabilities.

- **Unchecked Return Value.** Ignoring a method's return value can cause the program to overlook unexpected states and conditions.

6. Code Quality

- **Double Free.** Calling free() twice on the same memory address can lead to a buffer overflow.

- **Inconsistent Implementations.** Functions with inconsistent implementations across operating systems and operating system versions may cause portability problems.

- **Memory Leak.** Memory is allocated but never freed, leading to resource exhaustion.

- **Null Dereference.** The program can potentially dereference a null pointer, thereby raising a `NullPointerException`.

- **Obsolete.** The use of deprecated or obsolete functions may indicate neglected code.

- **Undefined Behavior.** The behavior of this function is undefined unless its control parameter is set to a specific value.

- **Uninitialized Variable.** The program can potentially use a variable before it has been initialized.

- **Unreleased Resource.** The program can potentially fail to release a system resource.

- **Use After Free Referencing.** Memory, after it has been freed, can cause a program to crash.

7. **Encapsulation**
   - **Comparing Classes by Name.** Comparing classes by name can lead a program to treat two classes as the same when they are actually different.

   - **Data Leaking Between Users.** Data can "bleed" from one session to another through member variables of singleton objects, such as servlets, and objects from a shared pool.

   - **Leftover Debug Code.** Debug code can create unintended entry points in an application.

   - **Mobile Code: Object Hijack.** Attackers can use cloneable objects to create new instances of an object without calling its constructor.

   - **Mobile Code: Use of Inner Class.** Inner classes are translated into classes that are accessible at package scope and may expose code that the programmer intended to keep private to attackers.

   - **Mobile Code: Nonfinal Public Field.** An attacker can manipulate nonfinal public variables to inject malicious values.

   - **Private Array-Typed Field Returned from a Public Method.** The contents of a private array may be altered unexpectedly through a reference returned from a public method.

   - **Public Data Assigned to Private Array-Typed Field.** Assigning public data to a private array is equivalent to giving public access to the array.

   - **System Information Leak.** Revealing system data or debugging information helps an adversary learn about the system and form an attack plan.

   - **Trust Boundary Violation.** Commingling trusted and untrusted data in the same data structure encourages programmers to mistakenly trust unvalidated data.

* **Environment**

- **ASP .NET Misconfiguration: Creating Debug Binary.** Debugging messages help attakers learn about the system and plan a form of attack.

- **ASP .NET Misconfiguration: Missing Custom Error Handling.** An ASP .NET application must enable custom error pages to prevent attackers from mining information from the framework's built-in responses.

- **ASP .NET Misconfiguration: Password in Configuration File.** Do not hard-wire passwords into your software.

- **Insecure Compiler Optimization.** Improperly scrubbing sensitive data from memory can compromise security.

- **J2EE Misconfiguration: Insecure Transport.** The application configuration should ensure that SSL is used for all access-controlled pages.

- **J2EE Misconfiguration: Insufficient Session-ID Length.** Session identifiers should be at least 128 bits long to prevent brute-force session guessing.

- **J2EE Misconfiguration: Missing Error Handling.** A web application must define a default error page for 404 and 500 errors and to catch `java.lang.Throwable` exceptions to prevent attackers from mining information from the application container's built-in error response.

- **J2EE Misconfiguration: Unsafe Bean Declaration.** Entity beans should not be declared remotely.

- **J2EE Misconfiguration: Weak Access Permissions.** Permission to invoke EJB methods should not be granted to the ANYONE role.

2.4 More Phyla Needed

This taxonomy includes coding errors that occur in a variety of programming languages. The most important among them are C and C++, Java, and the .NET family (including C# and ASP). Some of the phyla are language specific, because the types of errors they represent are applicable only to specific languages. One example is the "Double Free" phylum. This phylum identifies incorrect usage of low-level memory routines and is specific to C and C++ because neither Java nor the managed portions of the .NET languages expose low-level memory APIs.

In addition to being language specific, some of the phyla are framework specific. For example, the "Struts" phyla apply only to the Struts framework, and the "J2EE" phyla are applicable only in the context of the J2EE applications. "Log Forging," by contrast, is a more general phylum.

The phylum list presented in this chapter is certainly incomplete, but it is adaptable to changes in trends and discoveries of new defects that are bound to happen over time. The current list reflects a focus on finding and classifying security-related defects rather than more general quality or reliability issues. The "Code Quality" kingdom could potentially contain many more phyla, but the ones that are currently included are those most likely to affect software security directly. Finally, classifying errors that are most important to real-world enterprise developers is the most important goal of this taxonomy—most of the information here is derived from the literature, various colleagues, and hundreds of customers.

2.4.1 A Complete Example

Each phylum in the taxonomy is associated with a nice number of clear, fleshed-out examples similar in nature to the rules that a static analysis program uses to find security bugs. An example of the phylum "Often Misused: Authentication," in the kingdom "API Abuse," is included in the sidebar on page 54 to give you some idea of the form that a complete entry takes. For more, see <http://vulncat.fortifysoftware.com>.

2.4.2 Go Forth (with the Taxonomy) and Prosper

The Seven Pernicious Kingdoms are a simple, effective organizing tool for software security coding errors. With more than 60 clearly defined phyla, this taxonomy is both powerful and useful. Detailed descriptions of the phyla with examples can be found on the web at <http://vulncat.fortifysoftware.com>.

The classification scheme given here is designed to organize security rules and, therefore, to help software developers who are concerned with writing secure code and being able to automate detection of security defects. These goals make the taxonomy

- Simple,
- Intuitive to a developer,
- Practical (rather than theoretical) and comprehensive,
- Amenable to automatic identification of errors with static analysis tools, and
- Adaptable with respect to changes in trends that happen over time.

To counter the trends found in the Trinity of Trouble and make progress against malicious code, developers must learn to avoid common coding errors. The taxonomy presented in this chapter should help.

API Abuse: Often Misused: Authentication

(getlogin)

ABSTRACT

The `getlogin()` function is easy to spoof. Do not rely on the name it returns.

EXPLANATION

The `getlogin()` function is supposed to return a string containing the name of the user currently logged in at the terminal, but an attacker can cause `getlogin()` to return the name of any user logged in to the machine. Do not rely on the name returned by `getlogin()` when making security decisions.

Example 1: The following code relies on `getlogin()` to determine whether a user is trusted. It is easily subverted.

```
pwd = getpwnam(getlogin());
if (isTrustedGroup(pwd->pw_gid)) {
 allow();
} else {
 deny();
}
```

RECOMMENDATIONS

You should rely on a user's ID, not the username, for identification. The previous example can be rewritten as follows:

```
pwd = getpwuid(getuid());
if (isTrustedGroup(pwd->pw_gid)) {
 allow();
} else {
 deny();
}
```

If multiple users are allowed to share the same user ID (a dubious proposition from a security standpoint), a bit more care is required. The following example checks whether the username returned by `getlogin()` matches the username associated with the user ID; the check ensures that if two users share the same ID, one user cannot act on behalf of the other.

```
pwd = getpwuid(getuid());
pwdName = pwd->pw_name;
/* Bail out if the name associated with the uid does not
  match the name associated with the terminal. */
if (strncmp(pwdName, getlogin(), MAX_NAM_LEN)) {
 printf("shared uid not supported\n");
 deny();
 return;
}
if (isTrustedGroup(pwd->pw_gid)) {
 allow();
} else {
 deny();
}
```

Note: If the process is not being run from a terminal, `getlogin()` returns NULL.

Example: The phylum "Often Misused: Authentication" in the kingdom "API Abuse."

Chapter 3

Crimeware and Peer-to-Peer Networks

Minaxi Gupta, Markus Jakobsson, Andrew Kalafut,
and Sid Stamm

This chapter contains two sections on the spread of malware over peer-to-peer networks. The bulk of the chapter is devoted to traditional peer-to-peer file-sharing networks, which are considered in the first section. The second section considers the propagation of malware among social networks. In a sense, these are also peer-to-peer networks, but here a peer is not just an adjacent node in an overlay network, but rather a friend or colleague to whom the malware is transmitted.

3.1 Malware in Peer-to-Peer Networks*

The peer-to-peer (P2P) technology offers a unique way for user machines across the Internet to connect to each other and form large networks. These networks can be harnessed for sharing various kinds of resources, including content, processing power, storage, and bandwidth. Among the most popular uses of P2P networks are sharing and distribution of files. Accordingly, various software implementations of the P2P technology specializing in file sharing are available, including Limewire [238]. Unfortunately, the popularity of these networks also

---

*This section is by Minaxi Gupta and Andrew J. Kalafut.

makes them attractive vehicles for spreading various kinds of malware, including crimeware, which is often used for financial gain. As we will see in this section, hundreds of different types of malware have invaded these networks, including worms, viruses, downloaders, backdoors, dialers, adware, and keyloggers. Fortunately, our research also shows that most of it can be defended against using clever filtering techniques involving names and sizes of files containing malware.

3.1.1 Introduction

Peer-to-peer networks specializing in file sharing fall in two broad categories: centralized P2P networks such as Napster [267] and decentralized unstructured networks such as Limewire [238]. Irrespective of flavor, getting a file from a P2P network involves two distinct phases: the *query phase* and the *download phase*. In the case of centralized P2P networks, the content search is facilitated by (replicated) central servers. All participants of such networks know the whereabouts of these servers. The servers keep track of which user has which file and use this information to direct querying users to the IP (Internet Protocol) addresses of holders of the content that they desire. Upon receiving the reply from the server, the querying peer can directly download the content from one or more sources.

Decentralized P2P networks differ from centralized P2P networks in the manner in which the content search is conducted. Peers in such networks stay connected to each other for content search purposes. When a peer wants to search for a file, it sends a request with *keywords* to all nodes to which it is connected. Given that a peer typically connects to four to seven other peers, this implies that the content search request is seen by four to seven directly connected peers. They respond positively if they have the desired content. In addition, they forward the query to the peers to which they are connected. These recipients also respond positively if they have what the querier is looking for. In addition, they forward the query further.

This process continues until the number of hops, or *hopcount*, specified by the original querier is exhausted. To ensure that a content search query is forwarded only as many hops as the querier specifies, each peer that sees the query decrements the hopcount before forwarding the query to its neighbors. When the hopcount reaches zero, the query is dropped.

Upon receiving all responses for its query, the querier picks who it is going to download the file from and downloads the material as it would in the case of centralized P2P networks, by connecting directly. Most popular decentralized P2P networks today are variants of the basic content search and download functionality described here.

Two options for defending against malware in P2P networks are available. The first option relies on identifying malware through antivirus tools after the content has been downloaded. This approach is versatile, in that it protects users' machines from incoming malware irrespective of its source. However, it also has several shortcomings:

- An actual download of the entire file must occur before the antivirus software can scan it. Users on slow connections or those downloading from other users with slow connections may end up spending several hours on a download, only to find that it contains malware.

- While antivirus software may prevent a user from running downloaded malware, it does nothing to prevent the *spread* of malware, via P2P networks or otherwise. Thus the files containing malware will continue to be served through the shared P2P directories even after the antivirus software has identified the malware.

- This approach is effective only on known malware.

- Although simple in theory, this approach is not practical because it relies on users' diligence in keeping their antivirus software running and up-to-date.

The second option is to filter potentially malicious responses in the query phase itself. This approach is efficient because it prevents an actual download of malware-containing files. By not downloading malicious files, it also prevents the spread of malware to the rest of the population. Additionally, it does not require user intervention. However, the filtering must be done only with knowledge about information contained in query responses—namely, the query string itself, file name, size, and the IP address of the offering peer.

The Limewire [238] Gnutella [146] client takes this approach to filter malicious responses. Specifically, Limewire flags the responses returned as the result of a query as malicious if (1) the file name or metadata does not match the words contained in the query; (2) the extension of the returned file is not considered by Limewire to match the file type asked for; or (3) Limewire believes the response contains the Mandragore worm.[1] Such responses are not shown to the user. Although this approach seems promising, the criteria used by Limewire fail to produce the desired results. In fact, our tests show that Limewire detects only 8.8% of malicious responses, with a very high false-positive rate of 40.8%.

---

1. Limewire determines whether a response is the Mandragore worm by checking if the file size is 8192 bytes and the file name is the same as the query string with the addition of `.exe`.

The rest of this section focuses on two P2P networks, Limewire and OpenFT [294]. For both of these networks, we study how much malware is present in these networks. We also investigate practical methods by which malware in P2P networks can be filtered in the query phase itself.

3.1.2 Data Collection

Several considerations drove the choice of these two P2P networks as targets for study. First, to record queries and responses generated in a P2P network, we needed decentralized P2P networks in which queries and their responses are visible to all peers that route the query. This ruled out Napster [267], Bittorrent [41], and distributed hash table-based P2P networks. Also, the chosen P2P networks had to have a mature open-source implementation to allow instrumentation. This precluded the use of closed-source P2P networks such as KaZaa and the eDonkey 2000 network, which is used by eMule [102]. Accordingly, we chose Gnutella [146] as the first P2P network, which is among the top 10 most popular file-sharing programs. We also chose OpenFT, which is another P2P file-sharing network whose structure and operation are similar to the structure and operation of the Gnutella network. We now outline the basic functionality of Gnutella and OpenFT.

Limewire

Gnutella is a popular P2P file-sharing protocol with many available client implementations, of which Limewire [238] is one. In older versions of the Gnutella protocol, all nodes were equal. In the current version of the Gnutella protocol, nodes in the system can operate in two different modes: as a *leaf* or as an *ultrapeer*. Leafs connect to a small number of ultrapeers, and see very little query traffic because ultrapeers do not pass most queries on to leafs. The ultrapeers pass queries on to the leaf nodes only if they believe the leaf has a matching file. Ultrapeers connect to other ultrapeers and legacy nodes not implementing the ultrapeer system. These connections are used for forwarding search queries. Responses to these searches may be sent back along the reverse path through the ultrapeer, or they may be sent out-of-band directly to the originator of the query.

OpenFT

OpenFT is a P2P file-sharing protocol that is very similar in operation to Gnutella. In OpenFT, a node can run in three different modes. A *user* node is similar to a Gnutella leaf, and a *search* node is similar to a Gnutella ultrapeer. A third type of node, an *index* node, maintains a list of search nodes and collects statistics. We use the OpenFT plug-in to the giFT file transfer program, which is the original OpenFT client.

P2P Software Instrumentation

To collect the necessary data for our study, we made several modifications to both Limewire and OpenFT.

First, in both systems, we disabled the normal mechanisms for choosing the node type, and instead forced our Limewire node to connect as an ultrapeer and our OpenFT node to connect as a search node.

Second, we made our modified Limewire client alter all queries passing through our node to disable out-of-band replies, as this option is set by default in many clients to reduce the amount of traffic to nodes in the P2P network but would prevent us from detecting the query responses. These modifications should have had little externally visible impact on the P2P networks.

Third, to identify malware, we added to these programs the ability to automatically download files seen in query responses and scan them for malware.

Finally, we modified Limewire and OpenFT to store the queries and their replies in a database. This allowed us to infer query strings, file names and sizes, and IP addresses of the responding hosts. The database also stored information about the files we downloaded, including the file name, the file size, and whether it contained malware.

Malware Identification

To identify malware, we scanned all downloaded files with a popular open-source antivirus software, ClamAV [405]. We aggressively updated our local copy of the ClamAV signature database, downloading a new copy if it had been modified every 2 hours.

On average, we saw 792,066 responses per day in Limewire and 675,141 responses per day in OpenFT. This made it necessary to be clever in file downloading strategies. First, we leveraged the common belief that most malware attaches itself to nonmedia files and that even the malware believed to accompany media files actually comes with codecs that the media files require, which are executable files. Thus we downloaded with a 100% probability if the file extension contained in a response was one considered to be a program file, archive file, or a Microsoft Office file. The extensions corresponding to these formats are ace, arj, awk. bin, bz2, cab, csh, cue, deb, doc, dmg, exe, gz, gzip, hqx, iso, jar, jnlp, lzh, lha, mdb, msi, msp, nrg, pl, ppt, rar, rpm, sh, shar, sit, tar, taz, tgz, xls, z, zip, zoo, and 7z, a total of 37 different ones. All other files, including the more popular media files, were downloaded with a 1% probability in Limewire. Given that we did not find any malware in any of the files downloaded with a 1% probability, we concluded that this was a reasonable strategy. In fact, the file extension can be used as a first-order filter, in that responses containing file names with extensions outside of this list do not have to be subject to filtering tests. Subsequently in this section, we refer to the file extensions we downloaded files for as the *nonmedia file extensions*.

To further keep the number of downloads manageable, we considered files to be identical if their names and sizes matched, and we did not download files considered to be identical more than once. We took several steps to confirm that we did not miss new malware because of this strategy. First, if we downloaded a file and did not find malware in it, we waited until seven days from the time we first saw the file and then attempted to download it again. This allowed us to catch malware that may not have had signatures in the system yet when first seen. This strategy detected a small number of additional malware not detected on the first scan. Second, we attempted to re-download a malware-containing file again with a 5% probability. Out of 11,534 unique files classified as malware that were re-downloaded, all were classified as the same malware when re-downloaded, indicating that our criterion for considering files to be identical was reasonable.

3.1.3 Malware Prevalence

Data collection on Limewire and OpenFT ran for more than seven months, in two separate periods of approximately three months each, with a break in between of approximately six weeks where no data was collected. Table 3.1 presents an overview of the collected data. OpenFT was a much less popular P2P system, as evidenced by the one order of magnitude less search and response traffic. Also noteworthy is the percentage of responses that corresponded to the nonmedia file extensions. They were two orders of magnitude less than the total number of responses witnessed in each of the two networks. Additionally, although the number of successful downloads was much less than the number of attempted

	Limewire	OpenFT
Start date	4/1/2006	4/10/2006
Data collection days	187	149
Total queries	248,856,923	84,142,530
Total responses	149,418,445	100,596,112
% Responses for nonmedia file extensions	6.37%	1.32%
Unique clients serving nonmedia file extensions	961,312	49,476
Attempted downloads	7,041,812	108,095
Successful downloads	187,683	47,776
% Nonmedia responses represented in downloads	50%	60%

Table 3.1: Aggregate statistics of collected data.

downloads, many files were seen several times and we had to successfully download them only once to know whether they were malicious. The files we were able to download correspond in this way to more than half of the nonmedia responses seen.

Overall, we found 170 distinct pieces of malware in Limewire, including worms, viruses, downloaders, backdoors, dialers, adware, and keyloggers. Of these, 94 were seen only in the first data collection period, and 23 were seen only in the second half. The remaining 53 existed throughout the data collection period. OpenFT also witnessed a similar trend, with 106 distinct pieces seen over the entire course of data collection. Of these, 27 were seen only in the first half of our data collection, 42 were seen only in the second half, and 37 persisted through both. This finding emphasizes the longetivity of malware present in P2P networks.

Figure 3.1 shows the breakdown of malicious responses corresponding to the top malware. These programs contributed at least 1% of the malicious responses in each system. Figure 3.1(a) shows that in Limewire, a large proportion of malicious responses—more than 98%—came from just four distinct malware, with the top one contributing 72% itself. Even though no one malware dominated as dramatically as the top one in Limewire, the story was the same in OpenFT. According to Figure 3.1(b), the top individual malware in OpenFT accounted for about 25% of malicious responses seen. The 13 malware samples shown in the figure together account for 90% of the malicious responses seen in the system. Overall, a small number of distinct malware contributed to 90% or more of the malicious responses in both Limewire and OpenFT. Further, all of the top four malware samples in Limewire and 7 of the 13 malware samples in OpenFT persisted throughout the data collection period.

Breaking malicious responses down by file type, we found that an alarming number of downloadable responses containing zip files contained malware in Limewire. In particular, 88.5% of responses containing zip files were infected. Three other file formats also contained malware: rar (16.7% of responses containing rar files), exe (12.0% of responses containing exe files), and one response containing a doc file. In comparison, we found five file types infected in OpenFT, the same as those on Limewire, with the addition of sit. Also, the percentage of infected responses for all file types was smaller in OpenFT.

3.1.4 Filtering Malware

We tested a range of filters to explore the extent to which P2P networks can be defended against malware. The filters were based on information available during the query phase—namely, query strings, file names and sizes contained in

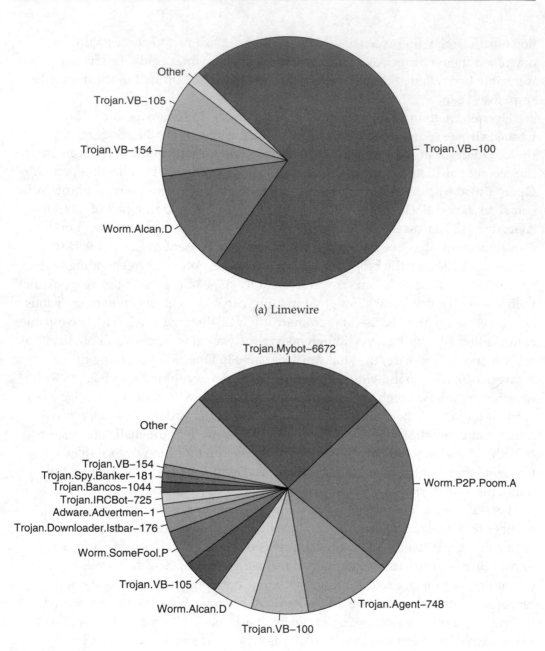

(a) Limewire

(b) OpenFT

Figure 3.1: Proportion of malicious responses from distinct malware accounting for more than 1% of malicious responses.

responses, and IP addresses of hosts that responded. Each of these pieces of information forms a *criterion*. As an example, a filter based on the file size criterion maintained the percentage of "good" and malicious files seen at each file size and started filtering responses when the percentage of malicious files exceeded a certain *threshold*. Although each peer could independently perform the filtering, a more efficient mechanism would be for ultrapeers to filter responses on behalf of the leaf nodes that connect to it. This avoids having the leaf nodes download files and scan them for viruses.

We designed filters by considering each criterion both individually and in combination with other criteria. The composite filters were created in two ways. The first type of filters were *OR-based filters*; they combined multiple single-criterion filters with a logical OR. If a response would be filtered by either of the single-criterion filters, it was filtered by the composite OR-based filter. The second type were *AND-based filters*; they tracked the amount of malware meeting the filtering criteria for each pair of values of the two criteria involved. For example, a composite AND-based filter based on file size and host IP address filtered responses based on the percentage of past responses containing malware for each file size/host IP pair. Note the difference between this and a simple logical AND of two single-criterion filters, which could not be expected to perform better than the single-criterion filters it is composed of.

Two terms are used throughout the rest of this section. The first, *sensitivity*, is a measure of how effective a particular filter was in blocking malicious responses. The second, *false-positive rate*, is a measure of how many *clean* responses the filter blocked incorrectly. Our goal was to achieve the highest possible sensitivity while keeping the false-positive rate low. Formally, sensitivity and false-positive rate as used in this work are defined as follows:

$$\text{Sensitivity} = \frac{\text{Number of malicious responses detected as malicious}}{\text{Total number of malicious responses}}$$

$$\text{False-Positive Rate} = \frac{\text{Number of clean responses detected as malicious}}{\text{Total number of clean responses}}$$

The effect of each filter was simulated with a set threshold percentage X. If more than X percent of responses satisfied the criterion for the filter at any point of time in our data, we blocked that response from the user. By using such percentage-based thresholds, the filters could adapt on their own to the content on the system. For example, if the filters were blocking files of a specific size when a good file started appearing at that size more often than the malicious one did, that size eventually became unfiltered. For each criterion, we experimented with a range of threshold percentages, between 10% and 95%, in 5% increments. At each threshold, the sensitivity and false-positive rate produced by each filter were recorded. Each filter was tested for both Limewire and OpenFT, as well as using the data from one network to make filtering decisions in the other network.

3.1.5 Single-Criterion Filters

We now describe the results obtained for filters based on a single criterion. Specifically, we tested the efficacy of filtering based on file names, file sizes contained in the responses, IP addresses of hosts sending the responses, and query strings that yielded those responses.

File Size–Based Filters

A file size–based filter filters malicious responses based on the file size contained in the response. An ultrapeer could identify sizes of files contained in malicious responses and leaf nodes could filter based on that information. Although simple in theory, two questions needed to be answered to judge the practicality of this filter.

- What if "good" files also share the filtered sizes?
- What happens if malware is polymorphic?

We answer these questions in the context of top malware in Limewire and OpenFT, which accounted for 98% and 90%, respectively, of total malicious responses in each system. Tables 3.2 and 3.3 provide data to answer these questions. The first observation we make from these tables is that malware came in multiple sizes in all but one case. This could be a result of polymorphism or perhaps because malware attached itself to files of various sizes. However, in all cases in Limewire and most cases in OpenFT, most of the malicious responses attributable to a particular malware showed up at one particular size. We also notice that in

Malware Name	Sizes	Sizes with >15% Clean Responses	% Responses at Common Size	% Responses Clean at Common Size
Trojan.VB-100	11	0	99.96%	0.12%
Worm.Alcan.D	9	0	99.86%	0.00%
Trojan.VB-154	14	12	93.71%	75.66%
Trojan.VB-105	5	0	99.69%	0.12%

Table 3.2: Malware returning more than 1% of malicious responses in Limewire, with number of file sizes this malware was seen at, number of these with more than 15% of responses clean, percentage of responses containing this malware at its most common file size, and percentage of all responses at this size clean.

Malware Name	Sizes	Sizes with >15% Clean Responses	% Responses at Common Size	% Responses Clean at Common Size
Trojan.Mybot-6672	1	0	100%	0.00%
Worm.P2P.Poom.A	15	2	96.34%	0.00%
Trojan.Agent-748	241	180	2.00%	28.13%
Trojan.VB-100	3	0	99.33%	0.08%
Worm.Alcan.D	3	1	96.46%	1.85%
Trojan.VB-105	3	1	94.08%	0.08%
Worm.SomeFool.P	2	1	98.83%	0.00%
Trojan.Downloader.Istbar-176	85	2	6.57%	0.00%
Adware.Advertmen-1	162	1	3.66%	0.00%
Trojan.IRCBot-725	22	3	61.74%	12.80%
Trojan.Bancos-1044	20	1	15.41%	0.00%
Trojan.Spy.Banker-181	43	0	10.55%	0.00%
Trojan.VB-154	3	3	88.53%	69.60%

Table 3.3: Malware returning more than 1% of malicious responses in OpenFT, with file size statistics. Column descriptions are the same as in Table 3.2.

only a few cases, the most common size for top malware was also a popular size for good files. Collectively, these observations lead us to believe that a file size–based filter is likely to have a high sensitivity and low false positives for the most common sizes of malware. The major exception to this belief is Trojan.VB-154, for which the most common size accounted for 70% to 76% of clean responses as well.

Another observation from Tables 3.2 and 3.3 is that at most file sizes that the top malware came in, the percentage of malicious responses heavily dominated the clean ones. The exceptions to this were Trojan.VB-154 and Trojan.Agent-748, the latter only in Limewire. For all the others, even if a significant percentage of their sizes encountered a large proportion of clean responses at those sizes, it did not happen for the malware size that dominated. Overall, this implies that irrespective of whether the malware is polymorphic, it is possible to filter it based on file size alone as long as a relatively smaller percentage of good files show up at those sizes. This also leads to the interesting observation that polymorphism may not be the best strategy for an adversary to defeat this filter. As long as a much smaller percentage of good file sizes appears at those sizes, the malicious responses can always be filtered. Further, defeating the filter by monitoring the sizes of popular good files and producing malware at those exact sizes would entail a constant supervision of the P2P networks, for popular files change often per our observation of Limewire and OpenFT.

Filter Performance. The filter maintained the percentage of good and malicious responses seen at every file size. It filtered responses when this percentage exceeded a certain threshold. We tested a range of thresholds, between 10% and 95%, in increments of 5%. Overall, this filter performed remarkably well at all thresholds in both systems, as expected. Its sensitivity ranged from 98% to 92% in Limewire. The corresponding false positives ranged from 7% to 0.14%. The trends were the same for OpenFT, in that the sensitivity ranged from 94% to 82% and the corresponding false positives ranged from 0.5% to 0.01%. Figures 3.2(a) and 3.2(b) show the receiver operating characteristic (ROC) curves for Limewire and OpenFT, respectively. These curves show the trade-off between sensitivity and false-positive rate as we varied the threshold. Clearly, the file size–based filter offered high sensitivity at very low false-positive rates for the entire range of thresholds. (We discuss the ROC curves for other filters laterly.)

Previously Unknown Malware. Given that the file size–based filter performed so well for known malware, it is natural to wonder how it would do for previously unknown malware. To get an intuitive feel for how the filter would perform without being bootstrapped with sizes of malware, we looked at the sizes and frequencies of malware and compared them to the corresponding numbers for good files. In our data, malware came in many different sizes, ranging from 5.7KB to 824MB in Limewire and 7.3KB to 206MB in OpenFT. In comparison, the smallest and largest good file sizes, respectively, in these systems were 3 bytes and 1.91GB in Limewire and 1 byte and 1.94GB in OpenFT. This implies that the malware file sizes were a subset of those of the good files. The frequencies with which each file size showed up share this feature as well. On the days that a good file was returned in a response, its accesses might range from 1 per day to 1242 per day in Limewire and from 1 per day to 82 per day in OpenFT. In comparison, malware frequencies ranged from 1 per day to 451 per day in Limewire and 1 per day to 36 per day in OpenFT. Both of these sets of numbers point to the similarity in accesses of malware and good files, which may imply that malware in P2P networks today does not exhibit remarkably different characteristics that the filter could exploit. Indeed, we found this result in our tests to see whether malware could be filtered by simply observing swings in accesses to files of certain sizes.

This observation has several potential implications. First, malware currently spreads relatively slowly and persists in the P2P networks for a long time, which justifies the feasibility of using file size–based filters. Second, by taking into account the frequency of a file being seen, it is possible to adapt this filter for fast-spreading zero-day malware[2] which will exhibit different access patterns from

---

2. Zero-day worms are the ones for which no signatures are available yet.

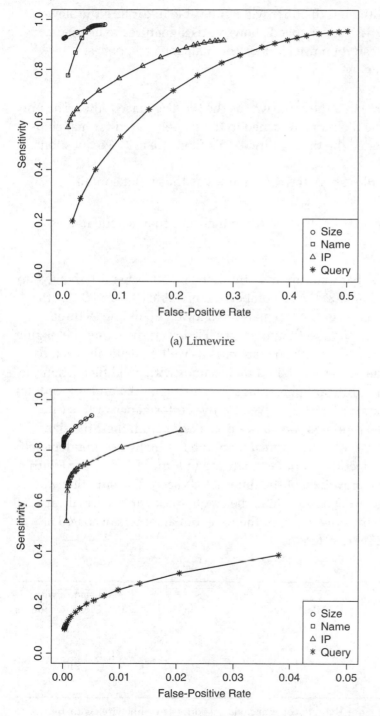

(a) Limewire

(b) OpenFT

Figure 3.2: ROC curves for single-criterion filters.

other good files. Finally, although the filter will not be able to capture the slower zero-day malware initially, its slower speed allows virus signatures to be made available, which the filter can then use to block the malicious responses.

File Name–Based Filters

The file name–based filter works the same way as the file size–based filter. The only difference is that it uses the file name returned in the response to filter malicious responses. As before, to judge the practicality of this filter, we ask two questions:

- How often do good files share the same names as those that contain malware?
- How effective is the filter likely to be when malware changes file names frequently?

The first observation is that malware in both Limewire and OpenFT showed up in many more file names than sizes. As a comparison of Tables 3.4 and 3.5 with Tables 3.2 and 3.3 reveals, most of the top malware showed up in one to three orders of magnitude more file names than file sizes. However, file names belonging to malware were rarely witnessed in clean responses as well. Specifically, in most cases, less than 10% of malicious files shared their names with good files when the good files accounted for a significant percentage (15% in Tables 3.4 and 3.5) of total responses for those file names. This bodes well for the performance of this filter.

Another thing that differentiated file names of malware from their file sizes was the fact that hardly any file names were among the top malware. Not depicted in Tables 3.4 and 3.5 is the fact that topmost malware in Limewire appeared with its most common file name only 2.2% of the times it was seen. The situation was similar, but not as extreme, in OpenFT. Here, the single most common malware occurred with the same name only 0.62% of the time, but all others occurred at their most common name more often.

Malware Name	File Names	File Names with >15% Clean Responses
Trojan.VB-100	25,153	1572
Worm.Alcan.D	7574	827
Trojan.VB-154	5436	216
Trojan.VB-105	4167	51

Table 3.4: Malware returning more than 1% of malicious responses in Limewire, with file name statistics.

Malware Name	File Names	File Names with >15% Clean Responses
Trojan.Mybot-6672	346	1
Worm.P2P.Poom.A	119	0
Trojan.Agent-748	354	1
Trojan.VB-100	361	11
Worm.Alcan.D	194	12
Trojan.VB-105	315	8
Worm.SomeFool.P	44	0
Trojan.Downloader.Istbar-176	88	2
Adware.Advertmen-1	164	0
Trojan.IRCBot-725	132	2
Trojan.Bancos-1044	31	10
Trojan.Spy.Banker-181	59	30
Trojan.VB-154	111	1

Table 3.5: Malware returning more than 1% of malicious responses in OpenFT, with file name statistics.

Filter Performance. Just as we did for the file size–based filter, we tested the file name–based filter on a range of threshold percentages, from 10% to 95%, in increments of 5%. This filter also performed remarkably well, and expectedly so. The only difference was that at higher thresholds, especially at the 90% and 95% thresholds in Limewire, the sensitivity fell off more quickly and the false positives did not fall off as quickly as they did for the file size–based filter. In particular, the sensitivity for this filter ranged from 98% to 78% in Limewire. The corresponding range for false positives was 7% to 1%. The corresponding numbers for OpenFT were 85% to 83% and 0.05% to 0.01%. We note that for the same thresholds, OpenFT experienced a lower false positive rate and sensitivity than Limewire. Finally, the ROC curves for this filter exhibited similar trends as for the file size–based filter, as depicted in Figures 3.2(a) and 3.2(b). (In the case of OpenFT, the curve for name is obscured from view by the curve for size.)

Previously Unknown Malware. The issues in detecting previously unknown malware through this filter remain the same as for the file size–based filter. We do not repeat the discussion in the interest of brevity.

Host IP–Based Filters

Next, we considered filtering malicious responses based on identifying the IP addresses of hosts serving that malware. Similar to the file size–based and file

Malware Name	IPs	IPs with >15% Clean Responses
Trojan.VB-100	131871	6942
Worm.Alcan.D	44544	2856
Trojan.VB-154	24652	14909
Trojan.VB-105	28904	2143

Table 3.6: Malware returning more than 1% of malicious responses in Limewire, with host IP statistics.

Malware Name	IPs	IPs with >15% Clean Responses
Trojan.Mybot-6672	10	4
Worm.P2P.Poom.A	32	8
Trojan.Agent-748	7	4
Trojan.VB-100	352	136
Worm.Alcan.D	346	182
Trojan.VB-105	326	103
Worm.SomeFool.P	92	1
Trojan.Downloader.Istbar-176	130	74
Adware.Advertmen-1	125	47
Trojan.IRCBot-725	102	40
Trojan.Bancos-1044	11	2
Trojan.Spy.Banker-181	18	3
Trojan.VB-154	91	36

Table 3.7: Malware returning more than 1% of malicious responses in OpenFT, with host IP statistics.

name–based filters, we tested the feasibility of using host IPs for filtering malicious responses. Tables 3.6 and 3.7 show the number of unique IP addresses serving the top malware and the percentage of those IPs that offered good files more than 15% of the time. In Limewire, 6% to 60% of IPs serving malware were also serving good files more than 15% of the time. The range was 1% to 57% for OpenFT.

Both of these observations do not seem to bode well for the host IP–based filter. Further, a filter based on the host IP faces other issues unrelated to P2P networks: The use of network address translation (NAT) and Dynamic Host Configuration Protocol (DHCP) make it hard to be certain that the same IP denotes the same host, especially over a long time scale, such as that of the data collected here.

Filter Performance. We tested this filter on the same range of thresholds as the file size–based and file name–based filters. As expected, this filter performed poorly. The best sensitivity it offered was less than 50% for both Limewire and

OpenFT. As the sensitivity approached acceptable ranges, the false-positive rate increased, hitting as high as 30% for Limewire. The false-positive rate for OpenFT remained low, closer to 2%, and some thresholds offered sensitivity as high as 90%. The reason this filter performed reasonably well in OpenFT had to do with the total percentage of infected hosts in OpenFT. Specifically, only 5.4% of hosts in OpenFT were infected with any malware. By comparison, 52% of hosts in Limewire were infected. The ROC curves depicted in Figures 3.2(a) and 3.2(b) show the range of sensitivity and thresholds experienced at various thresholds.

Query String–Based Filters

The last filter we tested based on information available during the query phase involved query strings. We tested this filter in the same way we tested the file size–, file name–, and host IP–based filters. Tables 3.8 and 3.9 contain information

Malware Name	Query Strings	Query Strings with >15% Clean Responses
Trojan.VB-100	80,539	26,858
Worm.Alcan.D	34,391	16,100
Trojan.VB-154	14,899	8581
Trojan.VB-105	16,519	6969

Table 3.8: Malware returning more than 1% of malicious responses in Limewire, with query string statistics.

Malware Name	Query Strings	Query Strings with >15% Clean Responses
Trojan.Mybot-6672	112	94
Worm.P2P.Poom.A	164	136
Trojan.Agent-748	206	163
Trojan.VB-100	426	328
Worm.Alcan.D	284	246
Trojan.VB-105	314	260
Worm.SomeFool.P	93	80
Trojan.Downloader.Istbar-176	104	90
Adware.Advertmen-1	93	78
Trojan.IRCBot-725	131	112
Trojan.Bancos-1044	68	60
Trojan.Spy.Banker-181	50	49
Trojan.VB-154	105	88

Table 3.9: Malware returning more than 1% of malicious responses in OpenFT, with query string statistics.

with which to judge the expected performance of this filter. Specifically, for both Limewire and OpenFT, a large number of query strings ended up returning the top malware. Limewire, being the more popular system, exhibited at least two orders of more queries than OpenFT that returned malware. In both systems, however, a significant percentage of queries that returned malware, ranging from about 33% to as high as 98%, also returned at least 15% good files—indicating that this filter was unlikely to fare well.

Filter Performance. This filter performed the worst of the four filters explored. The trade-offs between sensitivity and false positives remained unacceptable for the entire range of thresholds tested. As an example, when the false-positive rate was less than 5%, the sensitivity was a mere 30% in Limewire. Similarly, when the sensitivity approached 90%, the false-positive rate was close to 50%. At all thresholds, the false-positive rate continued to be low for OpenFT, less than 5%. However, the maximum sensitivity achieved by this filter was a mere 40%. The ROC curves in Figures 3.2(a) and 3.2(b) depict these observations.

3.1.6 Single-Criterion Filters Across Networks

In this section, we discuss our tests of whether the filters developed for one P2P network could be used in another network. If so, then information from one system could be used for filtering in another, or information from multiple systems could be used to increase the effectiveness of filters in any of them.

First, we observed that 57 malware samples were common to both Limewire and OpenFT, or 34% of distinct malware in Limewire and 54% in OpenFT. In fact, in terms of responses containing these malware, these samples accounted for 99.9% of the malicious responses in Limewire and 71.2% in OpenFT. The main reason the number was lower for OpenFT was because the most commonly seen malware in OpenFT, `Trojan.Mybot-6672`, was never seen in Limewire. Still, this commonality was high enough that we expected a reasonably good chance that information from one system would be useful in filtering in the other.

Next, we looked at commonality specifically regarding the criteria we attempted to filter on. We focused only on file size and file names here owing to their performance in each system. Table 3.10 shows that although the commonality in file sizes was not very high across Limewire and OpenFT, the common file sizes accounted for a large proportion of the malicious responses. Using file names from Limewire in OpenFT also holds promise. However, the reverse does not look promising.

Filter Performance Across Systems. The filters we simulated here were similar to those used in Section 3.1.5. The only difference is that here the decision to filter

	Limewire		OpenFT	
Criterion	% Common	% Common Responses	% Common	% Common Responses
File size	7.83%	99.82%	13.84%	51.85%
File name	1.46%	3.02%	25.07%	39.31%

Table 3.10: Commonality of malicious file sizes and names across Limewire and OpenFT and the percentage of responses they accounted for.

a response was based on what was seen previously in the other system. Overall, we found that in both directions, both filters performed close to how they were expected to perform based on the commonality. Thus filtering malware in one network can be bootstrapped with information from the other. Specifically, using OpenFT data in Limewire yielded sensitivities for the file size–based filter in the range of 95% to 88% when thresholds varied between 10% to 95%. The false-positive rates were less than 1% at higher thresholds. Using file names from OpenFT produces poor filtering results, because the commonality was low to begin with. Irrespective of the threshold, using Limewire file sizes in OpenFT produced a sensitivity of 46% to 49%, which mimics the commonality. The false-positive rate was less than 0.5% in all cases. The sensitivities using file names from Limewire to filter in OpenFT also mimicked the commonality

3.1.7 Composite Filters

Next, we investigated the possibility of combining multiple criteria to generate better filters that would produce high sensitivity while keeping the false-positive rate low.

Composite Filters for Individual Networks

We began with the OR-based filters. These filters are combinations of two individual filters joined with a logical OR. If a response matches either of the individual filters, it matches the OR-based filter.

We tested all combinations of OR filters that could be composed using each of the filtering criteria—namely, file size, file name, host IP, and query strings. In general, the OR-based filters performed quite well, improving upon the results produced with the filters based on individual criteria. For the sake of brevity, here we present only the results of the filter composed of file size and file name, *file size OR file name*, because each of these individual criteria performed the best.

For all ranges of thresholds tested, the file size OR file name filter had a sensitivity of more than 99% for Limewire, which is several percentage points higher than any of the individual filters for all false positives. The false-positive rate was higher at lower thresholds but dropped down to 1% at a threshold of 95%. The trend was the same for OpenFT, where this composite filter improved the sensitivity of the best individual filter by several percentage points. The sensitivity for this filter in OpenFT ranged from 93% to 95%. All of the false-positive rates were less than 0.5%.

We next explored the AND-based filters. These filters filter based on how many malicious responses have been previously seen as matching on both criteria they are composed of. By being more precise in adding and removing filters only from the pairs of values that need them, instead of adding and removing filters based on individual values of one criterion, it should be possible to filter more effectively than with single-criterion filters.

While not performing extremely poorly, all of the AND composite filters, with the exception of the *file size AND file name* filter, performed somewhat worse than we intuitively expected. Even this filter only marginally improved the results of the individual filters. To keep the discussion concise, we omit the details of these results.

Investigating why the performance was worse than expected, we found that this result was mainly attributable to the number of combinations of values. No matter what the threshold, the first time we saw a pair of values, the filter was never able to identify it as malicious. With enough pairs of values actually present in the system, this shortcoming can bring down the amount we are able to detect. By comparing the number of these value pairs occurring in malicious responses to the number of malicious responses seen, we determined the maximum percentage detectable after accounting for these. We found that this flaw was, indeed, the cause of the poorer-than-expected performance of these filters. In all cases, the sensitivity we actually achieved was lower than the maximum possible by no more than 3%.

Composite Filters Across Networks

We also investigated whether composite filters could be used to achieve better results when filtering across systems. We tested the entire range of both OR-based and AND-based composite filters from one network into the other. To keep the discussion concise, here we briefly mention the performance of the best composite filter, *file size OR file name*, across the two networks. For this filter, we saw a marginal improvement over what the file size–based filter could achieve across systems on its own, 92.0% sensitivity compared to 91.9% in Limewire, and 50.4% compared to 48.8% in OpenFT. For the AND-based composite filters, the results did not approach those indicated by the commonality of the individual criteria. This finding shows that the commonality of these values in the two systems did not extend to commonality in which values appear together.

Conclusion

In this section, we looked at malware prevalence in the Limewire P2P network using query-response data collected over a period of seven months. We found that even though a wide variety of malware pervaded these systems, only a handful of programs were behind most of the malicious responses. In fact, many were common across Limewire and OpenFT and persisted throughout the data collection period. We used these observations in devising practical filtering criteria to defend against malware in these systems. Our approach to filtering detected malicious responses without requiring a download of the actual file. This saved time that would otherwise have been wasted downloading malicious files, and it prevented the spread of such files.

Our filters were based on information available during the query phase, including file sizes, file names, host IP addresses, and query strings. The filters based on file size and file name performed remarkably well, filtering 94% to 98% of responses in OpenFT and Limewire. Their success resulted from the rarity of "good" files sharing their names and sizes with malware. This relationship held even when the malware was polymorphic and changed its name and size upon execution. We also found that it was possible to filter malicious responses in one system using information from the other system, because Limewire and OpenFT often encounter the same files. Further, combining multiple filtering criteria boosted the filtering capabilities of single-criterion filters, allowing them to filter 95% to 99% of malware-containing responses without penalizing the clean responses.

As described, our filters relied on the presence of malware signatures to bootstrap themselves. This raises questions about how to counter the previously unknown, (i.e., zero-day worms). While the filters are unlikely to know how to distinguish between good files and zero-day worms if the propagation of worms is similar to good files, they should be able to identify high-speed zero-day worms by monitoring the frequency of file names and sizes and by flagging unusually "active" files as malware.

Finally, our filters could be implemented simply on a real system. In ultrapeer-based P2P networks such as Limewire or OpenFT, an ultrapeer would run and download all of the files indicated by responses with file extensions considered to be at high risk for malware. It would scan those files for malware and track the necessary percentages of malicious responses at various file sizes, file names, query strings, or host IP addresses to determine what to filter. The threshold percentage used in determining what to filter can be automatically adjusted over time by tracking false-positive rates. Such a node on the system could then block the malicious responses. For greater effectiveness, implementing ultrapeers could trade information on what to block. Alternatively, to put more control at the end systems, other P2P users could periodically be updated on these filters and would choose what to block based on them.

3.2 Human-Propagated Crimeware*

People are naturally drawn to web sites containing fun content or something humorous, and they generally want to share that experience with their friends. In turn, their friends generally enjoy the site and will often share it with their friends, too. This scheme is considered human propogation: referral to a location based on recommendation of peers. This method of propogation cannot be stopped by any packet-inspecting firewall, email server, or virus detection engine. It has, and always will be, a reliable method of disseminating information.

3.2.1 The Problem

One morning, Alice is checking her email. Among the large number of junk email messages, she notices one with a subject of "Help Find Ashley Flores!" Curious, she opens the email. Alice is greeted with a picture of a 16-year-old girl and a note from her mother begging for help finding Ashley. The message asks two things: (1) If you've seen her, let me know; and (2) send this message to all of your friends to spread the word. Alice feels really bad about the missing girl, especially because she has a daughter of her own, so she forwards the message to as many people as she can find in her address book.

What Alice doesn't know is that Ashley Flores is not lost—this is a hoax. Alice was captivated by the email, however, and felt compelled to share it with everyone she could. This is an exemplary case of human-propogated information. Of course, people share more than just details about lost girls. They also share videos, links to funny web sites, and many other types of data that could be infected with viruses.

3.2.2 Infection Vectors

The fact that Alice forwarded the hoax to all of her friends is, in itself, not a problem. Dangerous situations pop up when the information that is the subject of

---

*This section is by Sid Stamm and Markus Jakobsson.

discussion has the ability to infect its viewers' computers. Most of these infection vectors share one feature: They quickly draw immense numbers of people to the site, and they are forgotten after a while. These characteristics are ideal for spreading malware, because a drawn-out, gradual propogation may more easily be detected.

Viral videos. YouTube and Google Video are just two examples of sites where one can find videos that captivate their viewers, and anyone can share material. Many other web sites also host this kind of material, and it circulates widely. Oftentimes, these popular videos are displayed through proprietary media players (e.g., Flash, Java applet, ActiveX controls)—all of which have the potential to do more than just display video. Knock-off sites of these popular content distribution sites could have the potential to serve infecting content.

Games and fads. The number of online game web sites attests to the fact that people enjoy playing games while on the web. Every once in a while, a new game emerges whose popularity grows like wildfire—and, of course, appears somehow on the web. In 2005, sudoku grew in popularity and has popped up in many forms on the web. When people discover new immersive games (such as sudoku or online chess), they often share them with their friends; this is especially the case with multiplayer games such as go, chess, or checkers.

Besides videos and games, many other web fads are shared among friends. Any website that is shared among friends is given an unwarranted trust. The rationale is akin to this: "If my friend Bob thinks the site is safe, it must be." Unfortunately, Bob may have misjudged the site, and it may actually be an infection vector for malware.

3.2.3 Case Study: Signed Applets

In mid-2005, Carlton Draught let loose on the Internet an impressive advertisement—its "Big Ad." Served up by a web site, visitors could watch the video as it streamed to their computers, even in full-screen mode. The video was constructed in an "epic" style (very big, looked very expensive and impressive), and the advertisement's site was received by Internet patrons impressively fast; after being online for only one day, the advertisement had been viewed 162,000 times [131]. Two weeks later, when the advertisement made its debut on television, the online version had been viewed more than 1 million times, from 132 countries [131].

The success of socio-viral marketing is evident in the case of Carlton Draught's brilliant move. Thanks to a custom video-streaming technology built by Vividas, the popular advertisement was disseminated across the globe with a blistering speed and breadth. This word-of-mouth content delivery mechanism could also easily be adopted by crimeware-possessing hackers, who often see opportunity where others do not.

Distributing Full-Screen Video. The distribution of the Big Ad was shared among Internet users mostly by word-of-mouth (or email, blog, and so on). Meanwhile, the customized video-streaming software on the Big Ad web site used widely available technologies—namely, Java applets and binary executables. This allowed the ad to be displayed as "streamed" content on the web while full screen—a feature usually reserved for desktop applications.

A visitor to the Carlton Draught web site is prompted by his or her browser about a signed Java applet that is being served. An applet is a compiled Java program that, when signed and authorized by a user, has more access to the user's computer than standard parts of web pages such as JavaScript or HTML. This prompt asks the visitor if he or she would like to trust the applet. The prompt displayed by Firefox 1.5 is shown in Figure 3.3. Once its applet is authorized, the Carlton Draught site uses the applet to download and install the Vividas media player onto the visitor's computer. This executable program is then run to provide access to streaming media that is presented in full screen. The result is a video that starts to play immediately.

Making It a Truly Viral Video. The web site can install programs on the client's computer only because the Java applets used are signed; signed applets are given more access to users' computers in the belief that people will properly authenticate a signed applet—by checking the certificate—before running it. Many people, however, ignore the content of the "Want to trust this applet?" dialog that is

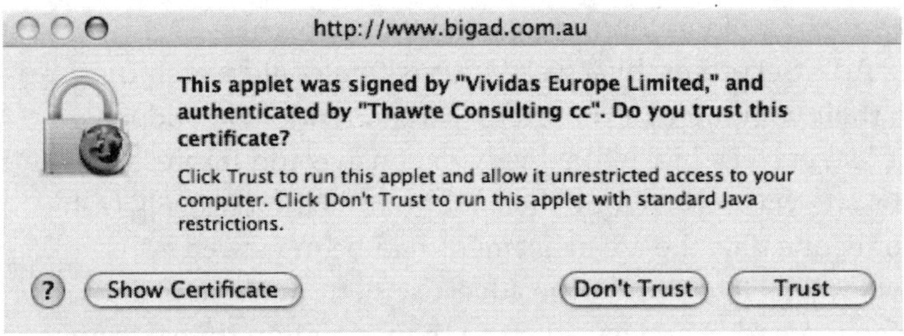

Figure 3.3: The prompt Firefox 1.5 provides before running a signed (trusted) Java applet. It shows who signed the applet and who issued the certificate. Once the certificate is accepted by the visitor, the associated signed applet has elevated access on the user's computer, such as access to the file system.

displayed by their browsers and simply click the "Trust" button. This check is performed so users can decide whether to trust an applet and thus give it more access to their PCs.

A malicious person could make a copy of the web site (by downloading all of the files and putting them on the user's own web server), and then modify the signed applet files to do what he or she wants. Of course, the user is required to re-sign the applet files before deploying augmented copies (the old signature will be invalid owing to the changed content), but browsers still allow people to "trust" any signed applet, whether it is authenticated with an authority-issued certificate or a *self-signed* certificate that anyone can create. These self-signed certificates can easily be created without help from an authority (such as Verisign or Thawte). Although these certificates provide the same functionality to applets, the owner of the certificate has not been deemed "trusted" by any authority. As mentioned before, many people don't know or care about the difference between the two types of certificates and will allow any signed applet to run on their machines.

The ability to download and install arbitrary executables onto a computer would allow an evil person to install malware instead of a media player. An even more malicious person could do both, making it seem as if all that was run was a media player, when, in fact, other software was installed in the background. People who visit the evildoer's copy of a signed-applet deploying site could then become infected with malware while having the same experience as visitors who visit the legitimate site.

Getting In on the Action. An attacker with a mirrored (but infected) copy of this popular advertisement could draw people to his or her site by using many different techniques. For example, in the case of Carlton Draught, the domain www.bigad.com.au was registered to host the advertisement. A similar domain could be registered and used by the contact (e.g., bigad.net, bigad.com, verybigad.com.au, verybigad.com). This tactic capitalizes on people who do not remember the web site's real address properly, but only the content of the advertisement. People recall that it was a very big ad and, therefore, may mistakenly "remember" the address as verybigad.com. This mechanism is similar to the one used in cousin-domain phishing attacks [202]. Cousin-domain attacks rely on using a domain similar to a legitimate one (for example, bonkofamerica.com versus bankofamerica.com) to fool visitors into trusting the phishing site. They may mimic target domains in a conceptual manner, as democratic-party.us mimics democrats.org, or rely on typos, as is described in Chapter 10.

Additionally, an attacker may spread the word by getting listed in search engines such that people who type "very big ad" are drawn to the attacker's site.

This takes a significant effort, but can be sped up by participating in a web ring or other heavily linked network (because many search engines rank sites based on the number of links to a page).

A third method to spread the word about the attacker's look-alike site is to send spam. The attacker could obtain a mail list in the same way spammers do, and then circulate a very simple email linking to his or her copy of the site. The email circulated would be spoofed, or appear to come from a legitimate authority instead of the attacker himself. It is straightforward to spoof an email: One simply needs to provide a false sender to the mail relay server. These spoofed emails can seem especially credible to recipients if the original has received media coverage, so the email sent by the attacker could resemble something like this:

```
To:       xxxx@xxxxxx.xxx
From:     Carlton Draught (press@carltonbeer.com.au)
Subject:  Success

For Immediate Release:

Carlton Draught is proud to announce one million hits to its
latest advertisement. As covered by USA Today (link), the site is
an extraordinary adventure into new marketing techniques and
proves to be very successful.

The advertisement can be viewed by clicking on
http://www.verybigad.com.
```

Involuntary assistance (luck) might also be a factor in the success of an attacker's mirror site. After two weeks of Internet buzz surrounding the bigad.com.au site, the advertisement was aired on television. This airing increased exposure to more people who may have not known about the ad, and some of them probably sought a copy of the advertisement online. These people (who had not seen the original site) would be most vulnerable to spam messages mentioning the attacker's copy as well as to search engines that index the attacker's site above the real one.

Experimental Evidence

In 2006, an experiment [388] was conducted to assess the effect of human-propogated malware that could be delivered from a web site mirroring the Carlton Draught Big Ad site. A copy of the bigad.com.au site was erected at verybigad.com, and then its URL was circulated to a few people. After a few weeks, people from all over the globe had accessed the simulated attack site. The researchers modified the signed applets, re-signed them with an untrusted certificate, and then served the modified copies to see whether people would trust modified, signed Java applets. This was done to simulate the steps an attacker would take in to place malware into the copied and signed applet.

Erecting a Mirror. A copy of the `bigad.com.au` site was created in a very simple fashion: All of the files served by the main site were downloaded and assembled onto a second web server referred to by the address registered by the researchers, `verybigad.com`. The HTML files, Java applets, and streamed media files were all copied.

To simulate an attack, the Java applet JAR files housing the streaming media playing software were decompressed, and their signatures were removed. A self-signed certificate was created and signed by an unknown entity that the researchers called "Key Authority." Next, the applet's code files were augmented to write the remote user's IP address to a log file, thereby recording who allowed the applet to execute. The researchers then re-created and signed with the new, self-signed certificate. The modified JAR files took the place of the legitimate ones on the `verybigad.com` copy of the web site.

When visiting the new `verybigad.com` web site, a visitor's experience would mimic exactly a visit to the legitimate `bigad.com.au` web site except for different certificate information in the browser's "Would you like to run this applet" prompt (Figure 3.4). This slight difference is not necessarily enough to prevent people from trusting the evil copy of the big advertisement.

Figure 3.4: The prompt Firefox 1.5 provides before running a signed (trusted) Java applet. The applet referenced in the top dialog is verified with an authoritative certificate issued by Thawte and should be trusted. The bottom one, signed by "Key Authority," is self-signed and should not be trusted.

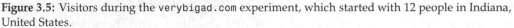

Figure 3.5: Visitors during the `verybigad.com` experiment, which started with 12 people in Indiana, United States.

Results. The researchers found that roughly 70% of the visitors to the copy site loaded the self-signed applet. They suggest that this result is a low estimate, owing to some difficulties encountered in deploying the site; clients with some versions of Internet Explorer were not properly delivered the applet, so they could not run it. This added to the number of hits to the site that did not load the applet (though not necessarily due to conscious choice).

Spreading through word of mouth (or email, instant message, and so forth), the experimental copy of the big advertisement was viewed by people from all over the globe (Figure 3.5).

Chapter 4

Crimeware in Small Devices

Bruno Crispo, Melanie Rieback, Andrew Tanenbaum,
Ollie Whitehouse, and Liu Yang

This chapter considers the potential for crimeware in small devices, including USB drives, radio frequency identification (RFID) tags, and general mobile devices. These devices can and often do contain important data. As these devices continue to proliferate, crimeware authors may turn their attention to them.

4.1 Propagation Through USB Drives*

Not counting built-in hardware, USB flash drives are probably the most popular storage devices today. They are small, lightweight, fast, portable, rewritable, and reliable. In 2007, the largest-capacity USB flash drive had a storage size of 64GB [436]. USB flash drives are supported by all modern operating systems. Besides being used in data storage and transfer, these drives find use in a variety of other applications. In particular, they can be used by system administrators to load configuration information and software tools for system maintenance, troubleshooting, and recovery. In case of system failure or emergency, a bootable USB flash drive can be used to launch an operating system [439]. These drives are also used in audio players, such as the iPod produced by Apple, Inc.

---

*This section is by Liu Yang.

While USB flash drives certainly offer convenience in our lives, they also pose security challenges to computer users and organizations. For example, they can be used as carriers of viruses, spyware, and crimeware [431, 432]. Computers and other electronic devices are vulnerable to attackers connecting a flash drive to a free USB port and installing crimeware to retrieve confidential information from the systems. One common feature of USB flash drives is that they are small in size and, therefore, can be easily disguised. For example, they can be integrated into a watch or a pen. This feature helps in information stealing by USB flash drives. In 2006, for example, a man in England was convicted of using an MP3 player to compromise ATMs; he stole roughly $400,000 of other people's money [434]. The criminal plugged his MP3 player into the back of free-standing cash machines, and the MP3 player then recorded the customer details as they were transmitted over the phone lines to the bank. The recorded information was used to clone cards for taking money from the ATMs.

Crimeware can be propagated by USB flash drives in a variety of ways. The propagator may distribute it intentionally or unintentionally, locally or remotely (e.g., selling USB drives preloaded with crimeware at a very low price on eBay, as in the case involving the sale of wireless routers with malicious firmware described by Tsow et al. [426]). Alternatively, the attacker may intentionally drop USB flash drives containing crimeware in places where they are sure to be found (e.g., bathroom, elevator, and sidewalk)—and simply wait.

In 2006, Stasiukonis and his colleagues were hired by a credit union to evaluate the security of its network system [383]. Instead of using a traditional approach, Stasiukonis and his colleagues prepared some USB flash drives imprinted with a trojan that, when run, would collect passwords, logins, and machine-specific information from a user's computer, and then email the findings back to them. They scattered these drives in the parking lot, smoking areas, and other areas that employees frequently visited. Most employees who found the USB drives plugged the drives into their computers immediately after they sat down in front of their computers. The collected confidential information was then mailed back to the researchers. Among the 20 distributed USB flash drives, 15 were found by credit union employees and all had been plugged into the company's computers. The harvested data helped Stasiukonis and his colleagues to compromise additional systems of the company.

Many portable media players (PMPs) have their data saved on USB flash drives. Like the common USB drives used for data transfer, these players pose potential threats to the computers to which they are connected for power recharging and music downloading. Apart from being infected by crimeware stored on a connected computer, some media players based on USB flash drives have inborn threats before they are shipped out from the manufacturers. For example, some of the fifth-generation iPods made by Apple were reported to contain a trojan named RavMonE.exe, a variant of the W32/RJump worm [433, 445]. Upon the iPod being connected to a computer with its auto-run option enabled, the crimeware was installed to the connected computer if the user agreed to the auto-run prompt [452]. The crimeware opened a backdoor providing the attacker with unauthorized remote access to the compromised computer [445, 448]. Imagine that a user connects such an iPod on his company's computer for downloading music; the crimeware may be propagated to the company's entire network in just a few seconds. That will allow the attacker to remotely access the company's computer systems.

In November 2006, Microsoft released Zune [455], a digital audio player. The device plays music and videos, displays images, receives FM radio, and shares files wirelessly with other Zunes. Like the Bluetooth malware, the wireless feature of Zune presents an extra challenge for security forces. For example, Zune will be able to transmit corporate data outside the building without going through the company's networks.

4.1.1 Example: Stealing Windows Passwords

An example will suffice to show how easy it is to steal the passwords of a Windows system with a USB flash drive. In Microsoft Windows systems, users' accounts, which also contain usernames and passwords, are kept in the Windows registry and in the SAM (Secure Account Manager) file. The SAM file keeps usernames and hash values of the corresponding passwords. This file is located under the %SystemRoot%\system32\config directory for the Windows 2000 and Windows XP operating systems and under a slightly different directory for the Windows 9X and Windows NT systems.

One approach to obtain the usernames and the corresponding passwords is to access the SAM file. It is impossible to access the SAM file while the Windows operating system is running, because this file is used by the operating system. However, if an attacker has physical access to the machine, it is possible to copy the SAM file by booting the machine with another operating system. A bootable USB flash drive [439] can be used to accomplish this task. After the machine is booted up, the hard drive containing the SAM file can be mounted to the file system of the running system. Then the SAM file can be copied to a directory of the connected USB drive.

The newly obtained SAM file can be processed offline by using a password recovery tool such as LCP [438], SAMDump [449], SAMinside [450], or

pwdump [442, 443, 444]. For example, LCP can extract the usernames and
corresponding password hashes from the imported SAM file and then retrieve the
passwords of users by using any of three approaches: the dictionary attack, the
brute force attack, and the hybrid attack (which combines the former two
strategies). Usually, the LCP will find the passwords of the target users in a short
time, sometimes within a few minutes. In cases where the password hashes of
users are encrypted by the SYSKEY tool of the operating system, a file named
system, which contains the ciphertext of the encrypted password hashes, needs to
be copied as well to recover the passwords of the target users. The system file is
located in the same directory as the SAM file.

The preceding approach may retrieve the passwords of users without their
awareness, because the attacker does not make any change to the target system.
The only requirement for an attacker is to gain the physical access to a target
machine for a few minutes. The copied files can be hidden in the USB flash drive
as "deleted" files and recovered later by using some tools.

Another way to compromise a Windows system running on FAT/FAT32 file
systems is to boot the system using a USB drive, move the logon.scr file to a
backup directory, and change the cmd.exe file name to logon.scr. After that
change, the rebooted Windows system will enter the DOS interface directly
without asking for a username and password. This approach allows an attacker to
change the password of the administrator by using a command such as net user
admin mypass [454]; the attacker can then do whatever he or she wants. The
compromise may be detected by the administrator soon, once he or she realizes
that the administrator password has been changed.

Besides the previously mentioned methods, some tools may be used to reset
the accounts and passwords for Windows systems. For example, Windows
Key [446, 447] can be installed on a bootable USB flash drive and then used to
reset usernames and passwords for a Windows system in a few minutes.

4.1.2 Example: Let's Go Further

The emergence of the U3 smart drive [451], which allows applications to be
executed directly on a specially formatted USB flash drive, has raised even more
concern among members of the security community. In September 2006, an instant
USB password recovery tool—USB Switchblade [432, 437]—was demonstrated as
part of Hak5, an online technology show. USB Switchblade consists of a U3 USB
flash drive with a payload capable of installing backdoors and extracting
confidential information from a connected system [440]. Unlike the traditional USB
flash drives, U3 flash drives are self-activating and can auto-run applications when

inserted into a system. Upon being inserted into a machine running Microsoft Windows system, USB Switchblade silently recovers information from the system such as password hashes, IP addresses, browser history, auto-fill information, and AIM and MSN Messenger passwords, as well as creating a backdoor to the target system for later access. This tool takes advantage of a feature in U3 to create a virtual CD-ROM drive on the USB flash drive, allowing the Windows auto-run function to work. In case the auto-run option is disabled, or if U3 is not used, USB Switchblade can be started by executing a single script on the drive. The tool has evolved to circumvent the antivirus protection of some systems that would usually detect malicious executables.

Another U3-based malware—USB Hacksaw [431]—has been developed as an extension of USB Switchblade. Once installed on a system, it will run a process in the background whenever the computer starts, waiting for a USB flash drive to be connected. When a USB flash drive is inserted into the system, its contents are automatically copied and sent through an encrypted SMTP connection to a remote email account controlled by an attacker. Both USB Switchblade and USB Hacksaw are available on public web sites.

4.1.3 DMA Vulnerability

Direct memory access (DMA) is a feature of modern computers that use bulk data transfers to copy blocks of memory from the system RAM to or from a buffer on a device without subjecting the CPU to a heavy overhead. With DMA, a CPU would initialize the data transfer, then do other operations as the transfer is in progress, and receive an interrupt from the DMA controller once the transfer has been completed. Many types of hardware use DMA for data transfer, including disk drives, graphics cards, and networks cards. The specifications for both Firewire and USB, for example, have provisions for DMA. That means under many circumstances a device plugged into a Firewire or USB port has the ability to read and write the physical memory of the connected computer. Such access bypasses the control of the operating system for security check.

Becher, Dornseif, and Klein have demonstrated how to exploit the DMA feature of a system by plugging an iPod running Linux into the Firewire port of a target machine [122]. The iPod successfully grabbed a screenshot of the connected machine without the computer's permission. Actually, the authors claim that they can read and write arbitrary data from and to an arbitrary location of the memory. Thus they can scan the memory for key material and inject malicious code to the memory. For example, the malicious code may scan the hard drive of the target machine for confidential documents and copy them to the iPod.

4.1.4 Gauging the Risk

One feature of USB-based crimeware is its low propagation cost. All an attacker needs is a bunch of USB flash drives, on which the attacker installs the crimeware. Because the size of crimeware is small, it can be loaded onto almost any USB flash drive. In mid-2007, the cost for a 1GB USB flash drive was approximately $10.

Another feature of USB-based crimeware is its high hit rate, based on the statistics that 15 out of 20 scattered USB flash drives had been found and plugged into a company's computers by the firm's employees [383]. This hit rate is much higher than that of traditional phishing emails. By using state-of-the-art techniques, more than 99% of phishing emails can be filtered by the mail servers before they can reach the recipients [13, 14]. According to a phone survey conducted by Pew Internet & American Life Project in 2005, 2% of people who received phishing emails admitted to providing the requested information [113]. Hence the hit rate of phishing emails is expected to be $0.01 \times 0.02 = 0.02\%$, much lower than that of USB-based crimeware. An important factor responsible for the high hit rate of USB-based crimeware is that few people will refuse to take a free USB flash drive given its convenience for data storage and transportation. If it is an iPod, people will like it even more.

Statistics show that the total financial loss attributed to phishing was $2.8 billion in 2006 [252], and the average loss per victim was $1244 [441]. We believe that USB-based crimeware may cause a higher loss than the traditional phishing emails, owing to its much higher hit rate. A person having a USB flash drive loaded with crimeware may share the drive with family members, friends, or colleagues. Thus, USB-based crimeware will hit at least one victim if the crimeware is not detected by the antivirus software. Assume such an attack causes the same amount of average loss (i.e., $1244) to a victim as phishing does. Then a $10 investment in a USB flash drive will make a profit of $1244 for the attacker. What else can be more profitable than this business? The loss will be worse if one USB flash drive harvests information from more than one victim. While a victim is not likely to fall prey twice to the same phishing attack, he or she will not escape the attack of the crimeware unless it is removed by the antivirus software from the system.

Attackers may also design crimeware that propagates through the USB port. In other words, the program can "infect" any USB storage device that is inserted into the machine. If a USB device becomes infected, it can spread the crimeware to other machines it plugs in. In countries where pirated software is popular, computer users may not be able to update their antivirus software in time to avoid the attack. The USB-based crimeware in such systems is expected to survive longer than usual because of the out-of-date virus database used by the systems. That will cause more damage to both individuals and society.

The storage size of USB flash drives has increased rapidly, going from the initial 8MB [453] to 64GB in 2006 [349]. This huge capacity provides convenience when the goal is theft of bulk information. For example, a thief could steal all of a server's or PC's data, take it home, and crack the security at the attacker's leisure.

4.1.5 Countermeasures

Several techniques can be used to reduce the threats posed by USB-based crimeware. First, all users should keep their antivirus software up-to-date. This will make it more difficult for the crimeware to circumvent the security check of the system.

A lot of USB-based crimeware takes advantage of the auto-run feature of Windows system, so disabling the auto-run feature of the Windows system will help to reduce the likelihood of being automatically infected by crimeware contained in a connected USB flash drive. Organizations such as financial institutions may also need to disable the USB ports of the computers used by their employees.

Some administration tools [435] can be used to control the use of USB devices, to track information as it is read from or written to the USB devices, and to log every event and attempt to access the USB devices. The logs will help to trace the attacker in case some information has been stolen or suspicious accesses have been performed.

Because a lot of crimeware steals information and communicates with remote attackers, it is very important to keep computers behind the protection of the firewall and to make sure the firewall is working well. In case a computer has been infected by USB-based crimeware, stop using that machine and cut off its network connection before taking further actions to clean the crimeware.

Fortunately, USB-based crimeware has aroused public attention. Both industries and researchers are making valiant efforts to mitigate the threats posed by it. The good news is that some manufacturers of USB drives have begun to let their products be shipped with built-in antivirus protection [193]. Nevertheless, we need to recognize that the built-in antivirus software must be updated the first time the USB drives are used. As time goes on, the regular USB drives without protection will be gradually replaced by the new ones with antivirus protection.

4.2 Radio Frequency ID Crimeware*

Radio frequency identification (RFID) technology is on the verge of exciting times: Standards are solidifying, RFID tag prices have hit an all-time low, and the mandates of the two largest proponents of RFID—the U.S. government and

---

*This section is by Melanie Rieback, Bruno Crispo, and Andrew Tanenbaum.

Wal-Mart—have motivated RFID trials on a global scale. By 2015, the total market for RFID is predicted to soar to $24.5 billion [78]. *InformationWeek* dubbed RFID as one of the "Five Disruptive Technologies to Watch in 2007" [394].

But as RFID's growth attracts more media attention, undesirable characters may also begin to take notice of this technology. Big money tends to mobilize criminals, who are creative in finding ways to steal it. RFID's main security defense is its learning curve, but deployers should not assume that criminals will be technophobic. Financially motivated attackers have long embraced the Internet, along with other emerging technologies such as instant messaging and MySpace, using them to extort large sums of money from companies and individuals alike. In fact, financially motivated, technologically based attacks are on the rise: According to a Symantec study [209], more than half of recent major Internet threats tried to harvest personal information—a sign that financial gain is likely behind the attacks (i.e., through spam, phishing, and botnets). Trojans, worms, and viruses often steal usernames and passwords for financial web sites. Identity theft features were found in 54% of the top-50 malicious code samples detected by Symantec in 2005.

These trends suggest that RFID technology may also become a popular target, once criminals determine that it is profitable. The upcoming paragraphs will ponder the logical but unexplored concept of RFID crimeware—attacks focused on obtaining financial returns in the context of RFID technology.

4.2.1 Radio Frequency Identification

RFID tags are remotely powered computer chips that augment physical objects with computing capabilities. RFID blurs the boundaries between the online and physical worlds, giving physical objects a "virtual" presence, thus increasing their visibility and efficiency in a wide range of automated processes. More abstractly, RFID tags also serve as an enabler for ubiquitous [473] or invisible [474] computing, allowing individuals to manage hundreds of wirelessly interconnected real-world objects, as if an intuitive extension of their own physical bodies.

RFID tags may be as small as a grain of rice (or smaller), and have built-in logic (microcontroller or state machine), a coupling element (analog front end with antenna), and memory (pre-masked or EEPROM). Passive tags (such as the tracking device shown in Figure 4.1) are powered exclusively by their reading devices, whereas active tags also contain auxiliary batteries on board. Under ideal conditions, passive low-frequency (LF) tags (125–135 kHz) can be read up to 30 cm away, high-frequency (HF) tags (13.56 MHz) up to 1 m away, ultra-high-frequency (UHF) tags (2.45 GHz) up to 7 m away, and active tags 100 m or more away [120].

Figure 4.1: Typical RFID usage: compact discs.

RFID deployments also employ a wide variety of physically distributed RFID readers, access gateways, management interfaces, and databases. A typical example of RFID back-end architecture is the Electronic Product Code (EPC) network. Its consists of RFID tags, RFID readers, data filtering/correlation servers, object name (ONS) resolvers, and EPC Information Service (EPCIS) databases.

RFID Applications

RFID promises to unleash a flood of new applications, forever banishing wires, lines at the grocery store, and pocket change from our daily lives. RFID proponents also extol its commercial uses for asset tracking and supply chain management. Contactless access passes help us police our residential, industrial, and national borders, while consumers have embraced RFID-based retail systems such as PayPass and SpeedPass and automatic toll payment systems such as EZ-Pass, IPass, and SunPass. RFID-based personal applications are also proliferating, ranging from "smart" refrigerators, to interactive children's toys, to domestic assistance facilities for the elderly. RFID tags can identify lost house pets [279] and even keep tabs on people; the data carriers have assisted with surgeries [248], prevented the abduction of babies, and tracked teenagers on their way to school. Subdermal RFID chips have even become hip accessories for patrons of some European nightclubs. They have also been (less glamorously) deployed for tracing the origins of cadavers donated to the medical school at the University of California [319].

Why RFID Is Big Money

The RFID industry is growing. In 2005, the global market for RFID technologies was $1.94 billion. By 2015, it is predicted to reach $24.5 billion [78]. However, despite the value of RFID itself, the application domains that use RFID equipment are worth even more. One type of frequently RFID-tagged objects, shipping containers, carry $185,000 worth of cargo on average, and sometimes up to $2 million to $3 million each [243]. Pharmaceuticals are also big-ticket RFID-tagged items; Trizivir, a three-in-one HIV drug from GlaxoSmithKline (one of the 32 most commonly counterfeited drugs [280]), costs $825 per month [11]. But most importantly, the retail economy (and its frequently tagged supply chain) involves more than $1845 trillion in transactions annually [457]. With these amounts of money at stake, it is easy to see how the success of RFID in any given application depends on having a reliable and secure environment for operations.

4.2.2 RFID Security Problems

RFID's association with big-ticket physical objects could make even nontechnically savvy criminals take note of this technology. This section discusses the major classes of attacks against RFID systems as well as the attacker model.

Major Classes of RFID Attacks

- *Skimming.* RFID tags are designed to be readable by any compliant reader. Unfortunately, this allows any compatible reader to scan tagged items unbeknownst to the bearer. Attackers can also collect RFID information from greater distances by eavesdropping on the more powerful outbound RFID queries.

- *Tracking.* RFID technology could facilitate the monitoring of individuals' whereabouts and actions. RFID readers placed in strategic locations (such as doorways) can record RFID tags responses, which can be persistently associated with an individual person. Also, RFID tags with non-unique identifiers can enable tracking by forming *constellations*, or recurring groups of tags that are associated with an individual.

- *Tag cloning.* Tag cloning produces unauthorized copies of legitimate RFID tags. Attackers in a supermarket, for example, might write appropriately formatted data on blank RFID tags, identifying the products as similar, but cheaper versions. A real-world example of tag cloning occurred when researchers from Johns Hopkins University and RSA Security cloned a cryptographically protected Texas Instruments digital signature transponder, which they used to buy gasoline and unlock a digital signal transponder (DST)–based car immobilizer [44].

- *Relay Attacks.* Attackers can use relay devices, which intercept and retransmit RFID reader queries and/or RFID tag responses, to carry out man-in-the-middle attacks on RFID deployments. RFID relay devices have been independently implemented by at least three researchers: Ziv Kfir [213], Jonathan Westhues [476], and Gerhard Hancke [165].

- *Tag spoofing.* Attackers can use actively powered devices to emulate one or more RFID tags. Tag emulators can create fake tag responses by synchronizing themselves with the querying RFID reader's clock signal and then using either a passive load resistor [475] or actively transmittted sideband frequencies [351] to send data in accordance with higher-level RFID standards.

- *Denial of service.* Attackers can exploit RFID systems by preventing either the RFID tags or back-end RFID middleware from functioning. For example, thieves could steal RFID-tagged items by deactivating/removing tags or by placing them in a Faraday cage. An attacker could also engage in a denial-of-service attack by using the opposite approach: flood an RFID system with more data than it can handle.

- *Malware.* Attackers can also use RFID malware—that is, traditional "hacking" attacks condensed down so that they fit onto (and can be launched from) RFID tags. RFID malware encompasses three distinct categories: RFID exploits, RFID worms, and RFID viruses [350]. RFID exploits can take the form of buffer overflows, code insertion, and SQL injection attacks. RFID worms and viruses are simply RFID exploits that copy the original exploit to newly appearing RFID tags. The main difference between the two is that RFID worms rely on network connections to propagate, whereas RFID viruses do not.

Attacker Model

So far, the most prominent RFID attackers have been graduate students. That's not a problem, because grad students have good intentions and a limited profit motive. However, the attacker model might not remain that way: Profit-driven attackers are likely to appear, once RFID becomes sufficiently pervasive. Parallel to the current situation with Internet malware, RFID may then face attackers who range from bored kids to organized crime.

Low-stakes attackers (also known as script kiddies) are likely to appear once simple (or fully automated) RFID attacks have proven to be profitable. Internet lore has provided many historical examples of such attackers. For example, in 2001–2002, JuJu Jiang planted a commercial keylogger at 13 Kinko's stores in Manhattan [316]. Over the course of nearly two years, he collected more than 450 online banking usernames and passwords from Kinko's customers. The hijinks ended when investigators discovered and traced Jiang's IP address back to his mother's apartment.

RFID technology is also likely to face challenges from profit-driven attackers who focus on low-risk, easily exploitable targets. The simplest RFID-based attacks are physical attacks (i.e., Faraday cages, tag swapping) or unauthorized tag querying/rewriting using a standard OEM RFID reader. Ultimately, more sophisticated attacks (i.e., tag spoofing, selective tag jamming) will likely come within reach of the low-skill attackers, as inexpensive RFID tag emulation devices should soon be appearing on the commercial market (i.e., OpenPICC [475]).

High-stakes attackers are more worrisome. Focusing on broader-scale, high-profit operations, organized criminals could adopt RFID as a shiny new tool to enhance their preexisting criminal activities. Criminals have never proven to be technophobic; the Internet has already become a playground for their extortion and identity theft activities. Furthermore, if RFID is used to identify and secure big-ticket articles such as bulk pharmaceuticals, passports, money, and cars, organized crime will surely embrace the use of RFID crimeware.

Nontraditional attackers could also emerge, in the form of businesses and governments. These entities could (perhaps inadvertently) abuse the capabilities of RFID-enhanced data collection, thus blurring the line between attackers and "the establishment." To avoid such missteps, the RFID-enabled collection of personal data must be regulated and monitored for legal compliance.

4.2.3 Types of RFID Crimeware

Traditional crimeware takes several forms. Similarly, RFID crimeware manifests itself in multiple variations, including RFID-enabled vandalism (of data or physical objects), RFID-enabled identity theft (of personal/financial information), and RFID-enabled theft (of data or physical objects).

RFID-Enabled Vandalism

Not everyone considers digital vandalism to be a serious crime. Think about a defaced website: Is it lighthearted and amusing? An act of self-expression? Political activism? Or is the defacement just plain criminal? One thing is certain: No matter how frivolous such acts may seem, digital vandalism is definitely not harmless. Security software firm McAfee estimates that cybertheft and vandalism cost the U.S. economy $20 billion per year [328].

Worse yet, criminals perform other acts of vandalism on the Internet, such as distributed denial-of-service (DDoS) attacks, that cause monetary losses and public embarassment. For example, in 2000, the DDoS attacks on Yahoo!, eBay, Amazon.com, and other prominent web portals led to approximately $1.2 billion in lost revenues. Digital vandalism is a convenient weapon for competitors and enemies. However, profit-driven criminals have also discovered the utility of vandalism; they use DDoS attacks (via botnets) to extort money from web sites, offering "protection" from the attacks if they are paid a fee.

Vandalism of this kind is likely to cross over into the RFID domain. Criminals could vandalize high-value databases (such as the EPC Information Service databases) for the purposes of extortion or to cripple competition. For example, RFID-wielding crooks could use a technique similar to cryptoviruses [487] to aid their extortion attempts. First demonstrated in 1989, a cryptovirus employs military-grade cryptography to take data hostage. The attacker could encrypt data in the victim's database (perhaps using an RFID worm) and then send a ransom note, demanding that a specific sum of money be sent to an e-payment account maintained by the remote malicious user (e.g., EGold, Webmoney) in exchange for the key enabling decryption of the "kidnapped" data.

Unfortunately, RFID merely makes this situation worse, by enabling criminals to vandalize tagged physical objects via their corresponding RFID tag data. This is most vividly illustrated with an example. Ford Motor Company uses reusable active RFID transponders on every vehicle at its manufacturing facilities in the United States. When a car enters a painting booth, the RFID transponder queries the database to find the correct paint code; it then routes this information to a robot, which selects the correct paint and spray-paints the vehicle [154]. It takes only a small bit of imagination and a back-of-the-envelope calculation to realize how serious the financial consequences of vandalism would be in this scenario. Thus, not only does RFID give computer criminals an unprecedented ability to cause financial damage, but it also increases their leverage when performing high-stakes extortion.

RFID-Enabled Identity Theft

Unbeknownst to many, the Internet is a classroom, meeting place, and bazaar for thieves of personal/financial data. Identity theft is lucrative—stolen personal or financial data can readily be resold on the black market. For example, stolen Visa Gold or Mastercard details sell for $100 apiece [492]. Criminals use the stolen information to make online purchases, having the goods delivered to a drop. The illicit goods are then resold through online auctions. Lists of 30 million email addresses can also be purchased for less than $100 [398]. According to the Federal Trade Commission, approximately 10 million Americans have their personal information abused every year, costing consumers $5 billion and businesses $48 billion annually [492].

Identity theft is so lucrative that it is likely to be carried over into the RFID arena. There are several ways that criminals can perform RFID-enabled theft of personal/financial information; one vivid example is skimming attacks against

RFID credit cards. Two researchers from University of Massachusetts at Amherst, Tom Heydt-Benjamin and Kevin Fu, recently demonstrated the skimming of cleartext information from RFID-enabled credit cards [172], including the cardholder name and credit card number. They dubbed it the "Johnny Carson attack," after Carson's "Carnac the Magnificent" sketches, in which he divined answers without physically opening an envelope containing the questions. Heydt-Benjamin and Fu hypothesize that, in a similar way, criminals could bribe post office employee to harvest credit card information from sealed envelopes.

Criminals could also adopt RFID malware [350] as a tool for identity theft. RFID malware is composed of RFID exploits (buffer overflows, code insertion, SQL injection), RFID worms (RFID exploits that download and execute remote malware), and RFID viruses (RFID exploits that leverage back-end software to copy the original exploit to newly appearing RFID tags). Attackers could thus use RFID tags as a low-risk way to install remote malware, perhaps to harvest personal/financial data from the back-end database.

To continue the analogy, criminals looking for vulnerable RFID readers could perform "RFID wardriving" (modeled after WiFi wardriving [36] or warkitting [426]), where criminals wander the streets looking for exploitable RFID readers. Or perhaps, if they seek a vulnerability in specific RFID middleware, criminals could try their hand at RFID "fuzzing"; this involves the use of RFID emulators to randomly send partially invalid RFID data to RFID middleware, with the purpose of elucidating automated vulnerablity.

Spamming (i.e., sending scores of unwanted emails) is another frustrating practice that criminals use to turn a profit on the Internet. A common misperception is that spammers earn money from product sales; the reality is that spammers primarily get their revenue from other sources. These ventures may include banner ads (which pay the spammer per click), the covert downloading of a program that dials a premium-rate toll number, accepting payment for nonexistent items, and "pump and dump" stock schemes, which encourage people to buy (thus raise the price of) a certain stock, so spammers can then sell it for a profit [232]. RFID tags could also be enlisted for "spamming" purposes. For example, an EPC Gen2 tag could have a bogus URI that points to a banner ad instead of an ONS server, thus earning revenue for the spammer for each tag read.

RFID-Enabled Physical Theft

Even in the digital age, both high- and low-stakes criminals still pursue the theft of physical objects. Cars make an especially attractive target. According to the National Insurance Crime Bureau (NICB), the total losses from vehicle theft are more than $8 billion annually in the United States [221]. Identification (fake or not) is also worth a fair amount on the black market: Stolen passports are worth $7500, and counterfeit ones are worth $1500 each [149]. Gadgets and commercial items also attract thievery. The U.S. retail industry loses $46 billion annually to retail and supply chain theft [488], and losses from cargo stolen "in transport" have been estimated to be as high as $12 billion [180].

RFID is now hyped as a tool to secure these big-ticket items—from cars, passports, and retail items to 40-foot shipping containers. Of course, traditional security procedures and tools will remain available. Nevertheless, if RFID proves to be the "weakest link," making the theft of big-ticket physical items any easier, even criminals who are not technically savvy will start to take notice.

RFID-specific attacks can facilitate the theft of services (from usage of ski lifts, or public transportation, to cheating highway toll payment systems) or the theft of physical objects. One of the most obvious methods of RFID-specific theft is to deactivate or swap RFID tags on retail objects. However, RFID technology can also allow criminals to steal larger-ticket items. A classic example was the 2005 Johns Hopkins University/RSA Security attack against the Texas Instruments Digital Signal Transponder (TI-DST) [44]. During their security analysis, the JHU/RSA team reverse-engineered the details of TI's proprietary cipher, and then used an array of 16 FPGAs to crack the 40-bit cryptographic keys on DST tags in just under an hour. These keys were then used to create cloned DST tags, which allowed the group to disable a vehicle immobilizer in a 2005 Ford automobile and to purchase gas at various Exxon–Mobil locations.

Perhaps surprisingly, the JHU/RSA Security attack was not as academic as some people might think. There are documented cases of real-world car thieves stealing cars via wireless attacks on keyless entry and ignition systems [12]. In one case, thieves stole two of soccer star David Beckham's BMW X5 SUVs in six months by using laptops to wirelessly break into the car's computer. It takes as long as 20 minutes to crack the encryption, so the thieves followed Beckham to the mall where he had a lunch appointment, and attacked the car after it was parked [12].

Regardless of the antitheft technology used, expensive physical objects will attract high-stakes attackers. Despite the learning curve, criminals will inevitably evolve their techniques to adapt to technological advances. And if it proves to be sufficiently profitable, criminals will learn how to attack RFID technology.

4.2.4 Countermeasures and Other Considerations

RFID deployers can take a number of countermeasures to protect individuals and businesses from RFID crimeware. Like with many other systems, RFID security requires a combination of policy-level, procedural, and technological controls.

Policy-level controls may include high-level RFID/IT security policies, interorganizational security policies (i.e., EPCglobal), and high-level privacy policies for RFID-collected data. Deployers also have the obligation to raise public awareness about the inherent dangers of their RFID systems, so as to help prevent the users from being exploited.

Procedural controls come in many forms, but primarily entail the use of other kinds of security controls to supplement those provided by RFID. For example, physical access control is a critical security measure for many high-stakes applications; random inspection can help to ensure that RFID tags belong to their corresponding physical objects. Such spot checks can help to protect objects ranging from transport containers to e-Pedigreed drugs.

Auditing is another tool that RFID system operators can use to verify the behavior of their systems. Also, RFID system architects should devote attention to providing security awareness training courses for RFID operators and must explicitly outline procedures for secure tag disposal. For more examples of practical, common-sense advice on how to secure RFID systems, the reader is advised to check out the National Institute of Standards and Technology (NIST) RFID Security Guidelines (NIST SP 800-98) [284].

Technological controls for RFID have prompted a considerable body of media coverage and research. Researchers have developed a range of technological RFID security tools and techniques, including permanent tag deactivation (RFID tag removal/destruction, SW-based tag "killing"), temporary tag deactivation (Faraday cages, sleep/wake modes), on-tag crytography (stream/block ciphers, public-key algorithms), off-tag cryptography (external re-encryption), on-tag authentication (lightweight protocols, e-Pedigrees), on-tag access control (hash locks [365]/ pseudonyms), and off-tag access control (Blocker Tag [205], RFID Enhancer Proxy). There are entire dedicated survey papers available [204] that discuss the breadth and scope of the options that are available. The reader is highly recommended to consult such sources [25].

System deployers must also adhere to best-practice RFID tag security principles, such as limiting read/write access to RFID tag data, using non-informative tag ID formats, and using strong on-tag cryptography, when appropriate. RFID middleware also has its own security demands. Best practices for RFID middleware include bounds checking, sanitizing input data, eliminating unnecessary features, limiting permissions/access, parameter binding, code auditing, and following secure programming practices.

In summary, system designers must assume that RFID is the weakest link of the security within a larger application, and then design their systems accordingly. Considering the amount of money at stake, and the evolution toward an increasingly hostile and financially motivated breed of attacker, RFID system architects and operators need to be increasingly proactive in defending against threats to their systems.

4.3 Mobile Crimeware*

Today, mobile devices are quickly becoming an important part of our daily computing experience. Over the last 10 years, we have seen the introduction of cross-platform sandboxed[1] code execution environments such as J2ME,[2] as well as native yet multiplehandset-supported (i.e., develop one, run on many) systems such as BREW.[3] This fueled the initial wave of application development on mobile handsets. In addition, we have seen a movement in part by handset manufacturers away from proprietary operating systems to documented and extensible platforms such as Symbian,[4] Windows Mobile,[5] and Mobile Linux. With the ability to develop code for handsets and platforms on an after-market basis, there is the risk that—as occurred with the desktop—mobile crimeware will appear.

Mobile platforms lend themselves to mobile crimeware in a number of ways that are quite unique when compared to the desktop. The first of these aspects is the "premium" services that exist in modem telecommunications. Some premium-rate numbers require the calling of a number; this is similar to the old dialers that were seen on the desktop when modems were the most prevalent means of achieving connectivity. Another unique aspect of mobile platforms is the practice of either sending or receiving SMS or MMS messages to a premium number. The result is a set of direct methods for obtaining a financial benefit from crimeware without having a long and protracted set of hoops through which to jump to extract the cash. To establish one of these premium-rate numbers is a trivial matter. A number of Internet-based services offer such solutions,[6] placing the onus on the purchaser (the purchaser of the service, not the end user) of such services to play by the rules and within any applicable laws.

The other unique element with regard to mobile devices is simply the sheer number[7] of different vectors through which malicious code can be introduced.

---

*This section is by Ollie Whitehouse.

1. http://en.wikipedia.org/wiki/Sandbox_(computer_security)

2. http://en.wikipedia.org/wiki/J2ME

3. http://en.wikipedia.org/wiki/BREW

4. http://en.wikipedia.org/wiki/Symbian

5. http://en.wikipedia.org/wiki/Windows_Mobile

6. http://www.csoft.co.uk/nox8/shortcode_premium_index.pl

7. http://www.symantec.com/enterprise/security_response/weblog/2007/02/a_picture_is_worth_a_thousand.html

While mobile devices inherit all the means that exist on the desktop, they also introduce a number of unique vectors through their extensive communications capabilities.

Today we have only one known example of crimeware on mobile devices, RedBrowser.[8] RedBrowser is a trojan written in Java (MIDP[9]/CLDC[10]) and executed within the J2ME environment. Once executed, it attempts to send premium-rate SMS messages, thus causing the user direct fiscal loss and potentially leading to disputed billing with the user's carrier (mobile service provider). Because RedBrowser was developed in Java, it executed not only on smart-phone operating systems but also on any proprietary platform or handset that implemented J2ME and MIDP/CLDC support. However, things are not all bad: By default, the MIDP security model states that if the code is not signed and attempts to send an SMS, then the user should be prompted. This prompting does not occur if the code is signed and, therefore, trusted. Some vendors, such as RIM in the BlackBerry, have extended this security model further with their own security controls.

In the case of RedBrowser, which wasn't signed, the user was continually prompted so that RedBrowser could send messages. While it is a proof of concept, this program does not pose a significant threat to users. Even so, this requirement on signing should be seen as a hurdle that will be overcome by determined attackers if it becomes cost-effective. There have already been several examples of malicious code being signed by valid certificates; the process simply requires the registration of a company and the appropriate amount of money being paid to the certificate-signing authorities.

While the MIDP specification provides a degree of protection, there is no such protection afforded to Windows Mobile devices currently. Conversely, Symbian 9 introduced a fine-grained capabilities model that affords similar protection as MIDP against such threats. However, as a result, it is also open to the same attack vector of obtaining a valid signing certificate.

This type of crimeware (i.e., one that causes financial loss) can be expected to become more prevalent in the future as the benefits to the attacker can be obtained relatively quickly (i.e., receiving the money 10 days after revenue is received from the operator). In terms of mobile devices' susceptibility to other classes of crimeware, such as theft of personal information, the story is also similar. J2ME (and thus Java) by its nature is a sandbox and so only has limited access to user

---

8. http://www.symantec.com/security_response/writeup.jsp?docid=2006-022814-5027-99

9. http://java.sun.com/products/midp/

10. http://java.sun.com/products/cldc/

data outside this sandbox. Windows Mobile, on the other hand, provides some protection from untrusted applications—that is, those unsigned applications whether or not in a two-tier device—through the restriction of trusted APIs. Symbian 9 utilizes its fine-grained capabilities model to provide protection from applications that are not signed with the appropriate capabilities (permissions). Even with these protections from malicious code such as trojans, other avenues for attack will continue to exist. Thus, as the sensitivity of the data we store on these devices increases, along with the many methods of transmitting the data out of the device, the likelihood that attackers will start to target these devices will also grow.

Another example of malicious code that may be used for nefarious purposes, such as the extraction of personal of sensitive information, is spyware. Numerous examples of spyware can be cited for mobile platforms ranging from Windows Mobile to Symbian, although compared to their desktop counterparts, they remain rudimentary. Nevertheless, their ability to obtain valid signing certificates is extremely worrisome. We have already seen one example for the Symbian 9 platform that managed to obtain such a signing certificate. Today's spyware requires an attacker to have physical access to a device to install the application initially, and it typically focuses on logging call, SMS, and email data as opposed to keystrokes, web history, and content from the device. Over time, however, we can expect this situation to change. It is not inconceivable that these early incarnations will eventually lead to more aggressive spyware that is installed in drive-by, download-style situations and that targets the user-supplied data and the data held on the device. When will this occur? To be fair, only when the data on mobile devices increases sufficiently (i.e., when these devices become the weapon of choice in Internet banking or payment), when users' computer usage patterns change enough that they move away from the desktop, and when the desktop becomes significantly more difficult to attack. Only then will attackers have the incentive to research, develop, and deploy their weapons of mass infiltration.

In summary, mobile crimeware is not a major issue at the present time, but there definitely exist opportunities for it to become one. Users typically don't see their mobile devices as computers, the security is a generation or two behind that seen on the desktop, the security solutions are not as evolved, there is a larger attack surface than with any other platform, mobile devices are increasingly holding sensitive personal information, and there are quick and direct means to directly cause fiscal loss. These facts do not paint a pretty picture, but the security industry at least has the opportunity to raise these issues today in the hope that through collaboration with operators, operating system vendors, and key industry players we can address these issues before they become a problem.

Chapter 5

Crimeware in Firmware

*Vittoria Colizza, Hao Hu, Steven Myers, Sid Stamm,
Alex Tsow, and Alessandro Vespignani*

Crimeware is traditionally thought of as running inside a personal computing device, such as a desktop or laptop. Of course, malicious code can, in principle, be executed on any type of device. This first part of this chapter considers the execution of malicious code in firmware, specifically the possibility that a home broadband router can be infected. Beyond just infecting a single router, it is entirely conceivable that the malicious code can propagate to other routers wirelessly. This propagation is considered in more detail in the second part of this chapter, where it is modeled as an epidemic.

5.1 Propagation by Firmware Updates*

The overwhelming majority of crimeware targets conventional computer systems—for example, desktops, laptops, and network servers. However, embedded computers are essential components to a growing number of electronics—including cell phones, video game consoles, and digital music players—whose primary tasks are outside general computing. As these application-specific devices gain connectivity to the Internet and manage sensitive information, they become attractive targets for malicious activity. With these new devices come new channels of infection. Wireless devices such as Bluetooth-enabled cell phones and WiFi access points face threats from local malicious agents in addition to the Internet.

---

*This section is by Alex Tsow and Sid Stamm.

103

An attacker within radio range can apply malicious alterations to an unsecured device. Retailers and resellers, and particularly those with ephemeral online venues, have an opportunity to replace manufacturer firmware with potentially invisible crimeware.

This section presents the general challenge and risks of malicious firmware (Section 5.1.1) and then examines detailed vulnerabilities of a particularly dangerous special case, consumer-oriented wireless routers, in the remaining subsections. They are attractive targets because of their computational versatility, their continual access to the Internet, and the services they provide in a small network (Section 5.1.2). Their vulnerability stems from the confluence of several factors: the burden of managing configuration on a device to which many clients have access (Section 5.1.3); an array of misunderstood security features that are ineffective, broken, or hampered by legacy requirements (Section 5.1.4); and the consequences of open-access default settings combined with the pandemic failure to change them (Section 5.1.5). Section 5.1.6 surveys some of the abuses that can occur with malicious firmware replacements in wireless routers. Section 5.1.7 presents the ways in which the malicious firmware can infect a wireless router. The section closes with a look at countermeasures and risk mitigation techniques (Section 5.1.8).

5.1.1 Embedded Control Systems: Ubiquitous and Mutable

As consumer electronics become more sophisticated, they depend more heavily on embedded control systems to manage their functionality. Their application ranges from the seemingly mundane—the timer and exposure control in a microwave oven—to the obviously complex—the underlying computer in a video gaming console. These control systems can be decomposed into hardware and software components, although in many cases the software is invisible to the end user. This embedded software, or *firmware,* can reside on immutable readonly memory (ROM), on electronically erasable programmable readonly memory (EEPROM), or (more commonly) on flash memory when the software component is large. Because these last two media are rewritable, manufacturers can create interfaces for changing the firmware after the devices have been purchased by customers.

Manufacturers frequently allow end users to install official updates to their firmware. This is common practice among producers of digital cameras, portable music players, cell phones, wireless routers, and many other kinds of consumer electronics. User applied firmware patches give manufacturers flexibility: They can bring devices to market with less testing, they can fix security errors, and they can add new functionality.

For example, Apple has raised the maximum output resolution of its fifth-generation video iPod with a firmware update. Updates to previous models had expanded the *codec*s that the iPod plays, altered its digital rights management (DRM), and tightened integration with the iTunes store. Apple has used firmware changes to advance its business model: Some "upgrades" prevent music sold by competing online music stores from playing on the iPod [29].

Technology enthusiasts have recognized that product differentiation is often partially implemented by a product's firmware. An entire product line may share the same internal architecture, while feature differences are either implemented or blocked through firmware differences. As a result, some consumers—often with specialized knowledge of device internals—have "unlocked" features that are available in the underlying hardware but disabled in the manufacturer's firmware by "firmware hacking." One example is the Canon EOS 300D digital SLR camera, which was released in 2003. Unofficial firmware distributions [47] enable light metering, flash compensation, and auto-focus modes that are unavailable in factory form. While these modes resulted from relatively minor firmware alterations, Canon excluded them to push more advanced photographers toward the next level of its product line, the EOS 10D, at a 50% price increase.

Some firmware projects are more radical than reenabling features found in related products. The *RockBox* project [354] is an independently developed operating system—which is not based on Linux, unlike many other open-source embedded operating systems—that runs on a variety of music players. The open-source Rockbox replaces the closed-source factory firmware that ships with music players from Apple, Archos, iAudio, and iRiver; it is far more than a slight modification of existing firmware.

Open-source firmware is not just the domain of curious and resourceful electronics owners. It has been deployed by for-profit private companies in mass-market products. The Sharp Zaurus, a handheld PDA, advertises its use of Linux to buyers—presumably in the hopes of leveraging Linux's base of independent developers and free applications. Linux is the embedded operating system in a number of cell phones and smart phones from Motorola, NEC, Panasonic, and Samsung [239].

Another important deployment of embedded Linux is in the first versions of the popular Linksys WRT54G wireless router. These devices enable home users to share a single Internet access point with many computers using Ethernet and wireless interfaces. Many other companies have produced home wireless routers based on Linux, but Linksys appears to be the most widespread of these. Later versions of the WRT54G use the VXWorks operating system, although end users can still install Linux-based firmware on these revisions. Because the GNU public license (GPL) governs Linux, all modifications to the source code—including those made by Linksys to embed it into the company's wireless router—must also carry the GPL and, therefore, be open source. The availability of this firmware has spawned several unofficial firmware versions. The most mature of these (openWRT [295] and DD-WRT [83] among them) offer software development kits, standardized packaging for add-on modules, and rich support communities for both users and developers. Unfortunately, this infrastructure also makes it easy for malicious code writers to develop abusive firmware.

Malicious Alteration

If firmware can be changed, then this ability can be abused. Although the specific abuses possible depend on the particular system, many important systems are becoming more and more capable.

As discussed in Chapter 12, crimeware is motivated by economic gain. Unlike in the early days of malware, vandalism and bragging rights are no longer its principal motivation. Economic gain is largely achieved by gaining illegitimate *access* to some resource or even by extorting users through denial-of-service threats. The targets of embedded crimeware will not be the kitchen toaster or digital camera; their monetization opportunities are limited or inefficient. Cell phones, home network devices, PDAs, media players, and video game consoles—to name a few—are prime victims. They connect to the Internet (and thus have the ability to be remotely controlled and participate in traffic congestion attacks), handle sensitive information (e.g., passwords and account numbers), and have ample system capacity for executing malicious activity. More sensational targets include voting machines [360], automobiles (including engine control units [107] and driver interfaces [82]), space ships (Ariane 5 [241]), medical equipment (Therac-25 [235]), and power distribution systems (the Northeast blackout of 2003 [128, 421]).[1]

Compromised cell phones could limit service on both the Internet *and* the cell phone infrastructure by overloading the cellular network's capacity. Such an attack could be targeted to specific times and locations by using the phone's internal clock and GPS receiver; for example, an attacker might try to eliminate cellular service at a large sporting event by activating all infected phones in the stadium. Sneakier attacks [487] might spy on cell phone users, gathering login credentials, text messages, call records (who and when, but not the conversation itself), and travel paths.

---

1. To our knowledge, no reports of malware have been found on any of these systems. All instances cited refer to errors in embedded software that have caused serious malfunctions. For the automobile recalls, the malfunctions were fixed by reflashing the embedded software at authorized dealers.

Gaming consoles including the Xbox, Playstation 3, and Wii are clients on the Internet, and potentially provide more drones for botnet masters (Chapter 7). However, Chapter 9 shows that the gaming industry is lucrative enough for crimeware exploitation. In 2006, the world's first "virtual millionaire" was recognized [174]; the market value of the player's virtual property in the online game Second Life topped seven figures. Embedded crimeware on gaming consoles could enable theft of similar property through unauthorized account access.

Portable media players have less access to the Internet than cell phones, video game consoles, and network devices do. Nevertheless, they are—as shown by Apple's iPod—the targets of frequent firmware updates. Because they communicate directly with a host computer for playlist updates and synchronization, they have an opportunity to install malware. On September 12, 2006, Apple acknowledged that some iPods shipped from the factory containing a worm that could affect computers running the Windows platform [16].

Microsoft's Zune player sports a wireless network interface that enables inter-player transmission of music through direct connection. The firmware enforces a three-time play limit on music acquired in this way; we imagine that some of the first unofficial firmware updates will circumvent this control. More concerning, however, is the potential to bundle a worm with the music files. Once compromised, new firmware could enable these music players to connect to the Internet through wireless access points and behave as malicious clients. The worm need not come from another Zune (at the time of this writing, the product is in its infancy), but rather from any wireless device that can get its attention (such as a compromised wireless router, for instance).

5.1.2 The Case of Home Wireless Access Points

Wireless access points (WAPs) create local wireless networks, based on the IEEE 802.11 family of standards [189] (also known by the Wi-Fi brand), that enable multiple wireless clients to share access to the Internet. These devices are popular because many households have laptops or multiple computers. The wireless network allows laptop owners hassle-free access to the Internet from their couch, kitchen table, or desktop by un-tethering the computer from an Ethernet cable. Local connection sharing and ease of use have made WAPs popular with small cafes wishing to attract customers with free Internet access. WAPs are attractive targets for malware because they are trusted to provide critical network services to their clients, because they have long up-times on the Internet, and because they have sufficient computational resources to support several kinds of man-in-the-middle attacks.

Classes of Wireless Access Points

Wireless access is commonly bundled in a few different ways. The most basic device creates a wireless *bridge* with a wired network. When clients connect to a wireless bridge, all client IP (Internet Protocol) traffic is retransmitted to the host network (and vice versa) with which the access point is bridged. The services of routing, name resolution, and address allocation are handled by servers on the host network.

The most common bundling option is the wireless router. In this case, wireless access is packaged with a computer that supplies all of the basic services necessary to deploy a local area network (LAN). This includes network address translation (NAT) for sharing client access to the Internet, a firewall, a local name server, and other devices to permit dynamic joining and departure of network clients. A variant, sometimes marketed as a wireless gateway, bundles a broadband service interface with the wireless router; this scheme creates a single device for subscribers who want a shared wireless local network. In all of these configurations, the WAP serves as the client's sole link to the Internet.

Tiny but Conventional Computers

Wireless routers, gateways, and sometimes bridges are based on devices that combine a general-purpose computer, wireless interface, Ethernet interface, and optionally a network switch on a single chip. In 2007, typical configurations approximated the computational abilities of the best desktop computers in the mid-1990s. The CPUs are 32-bit processors that support virtual memory (the MIPS architecture is the most common these days) running at clock speeds up to 300Mhz. RAM varies between 8MB and 32MB, while permanent storage (its most limited resource) varies between 2MB and 8MB. Some routers offer USB ports as well; when connected to a mass storage device, they can behave as file servers, print servers, or even video servers. In summary, the embedded computer has enough resources to execute a number of different attacks.

All of the various network services are implemented in firmware. In the case of Linux, many popular open-source software packages—including a diverse group of network services—are easily ported to the access point's integrated computing platform. Wireless routers and gateways provide all the necessary services to create and manage a local network. At the same time, wireless bridges offer very limited services to the local network; these responsibilities are handled by other nodes. Because many bridges have the same computing platform as a router, an unofficial firmware upgrade can implement many network services and turn a bridge into a limited router.

The rest of the section focuses attacks, vulnerabilities, and countermeasures for wireless routers. Given that bridges and gateways share the same integrated computing platform, nearly all of the discussion applies to them as well.

5.1.3 Configuring and Upgrading Router Firmware

Router configuration faces different requirements than many other peripherals. A given I/O device (such as a mouse or a printer) usually has a configuration program that runs on the computer to which it is connected. A user simply runs this program to make the desired changes; configuration access control is implemented by the host computer. A router, however, connects to many different computers and, therefore, must determine which one has the authority to alter its settings; consequently, configuration access control resides on the router. Moreover, routers run autonomously, unlike other computer peripherals that depend on device drivers inside the host computer. In other words, the settings themselves actually reside on the router hardware, not in some designated host. While some manufacturers provide special-purpose administrative programs to authenticate and transmit settings to the router, most devices implement a web administration interface.

An administrator accesses the router's configuration web page by joining the network either as a wireless or Ethernet client. The administrator loads the page at the router's address (e.g., http://192.168.1.1) into his or her browser. Upon request, the browser asks for login credentials. The administrator's account name, often set to *admin,* is unchangeable in most implementations; the default password, which is changeable, is commonly *admin* as well. These credentials are cached by the browser and sent in the clear for every communication with the router's configuration page.

The web page itself presents the configuration options over a series of HTML and JavaScript forms. One of these pages contains a form for upgrading the router's firmware. When submitted, the form causes an HTTP POST request to send the contents of a specified file on the client to the router's upgrade script. Typically, the script first confirms an identifying number in the initial bytes of the uploaded file and then writes the remainder in its flash memory starting at the boot address. After writing the file into permanent storage, the router reboots with the new firmware.

Bricking

If the firmware file is faulty, the router may crash upon reboot. This unfortunate phenomenon—called "bricking" because the router is as useful as a brick—sometimes results from failed attempts to install third-party firmware. Some routers have boot loaders that include a failsafe mechanism—for example, a TFTP (trivial file transfer protocol) server that accepts a file upload and writes it to the boot sector. On the Linksys WRT54G, this failsafe mechanism has to be enabled prior to firmware corruption. If the router is bricked before the "boot-wait" (the router waits for a TFTP transmission prior to booting) option is enabled, then the recovery process is much more difficult—and certainly beyond economic rationality for most people. The only remaining way to rewrite the firmware is to exploit the unit's JTAG (Joint Test Action Group) interface, a hairy process that requires considerable engineering know-how, special software, and soldering wires to the router's circuit board.

5.1.4 Standard Security Measures

Wireless routers implement several security measures that are specific to 802.11 networks. Higher-level solutions, such as the security-enhanced Internet protocol suite (IPSec) [420] and virtual private networks (VPNs), are also important to consider when forming an effective network access architecture. The two main objectives are to control which clients can join the wireless network and to control access to administrative configuration; joining the network is a prerequisite to configuring the access point.

A few technical details about 802.11 networks provide some necessary background. Wireless access points broadcast information about themselves at a level below IP. The main attributes are the broadcast channel (one of 14 radio frequency ranges between 2.400 and 2.487 GHz), the *service set identifier* (SSID, the network name), the router's media access control address (MAC address), and the network's encryption requirements. The SSID is a nickname that behaves as a non-unique identifier for the network, such as "Acme wireless." The MAC address is assigned by the manufacturer and uniquely identifies the access point for the purposes of low-level network communication.

Controlling WLAN Access

A number of standard security measures are used with wireless access points. Most consumer-oriented WAPs ship with options to hide the SSID, filter clients by MAC address, and encrypt traffic at the 802.11 level. These methods can be effective for small networks. For networks spanning multiple WAPs, more powerful access control methods are implemented externally.

A WAP can obscure its presence by declining to broadcast the SSID. Standard wireless detection software that is bundled with Windows does not display networks with this option enabled. Other detection software displays the presence of the network but with an unknown name. However, when clients attempt to join such a "cloaked" network, they must specify the SSID; a patient attacker can easily observe the string because its cleartext transmission is a requirement for clients joining the network. Some WiFi detection software, such as the open-source passive scanner Kismet [217], captures traffic from cloaked networks and identifies the SSID upon observation of a joining client.

Another security option available on WiFi routers is MAC address filtering. In this case, the router will allow only clients with a certain set of MAC addresses to join the network. As with SSID cloaking, this is a weak solution. Client MAC addresses are attached to every frame of traffic that the router sends. An attacker need simply observe traffic from a legitimate client, and then spoof his or her own MAC address to match the legitimate one.

Two methods are used to encrypt traffic at the 802.11 level: wired equivalent privacy (WEP) and WiFi protected access (WPA). Although they disguise traffic content, the control information—such as the SSID and MAC address—remains unencrypted. Although the technical details [40, 123, 396] of these schemes are beyond the scope of our discussion, we note that the WEP scheme is readily circumvented in minutes with publicly available tools [53]. In many attack models, a 10- to 20-minute delay is expensive enough to push would-be attackers to a more vulnerable system. However, high-value targets will warrant circumvention of WEP: Consider a corporate espionage program that profiles low-level employees who have access privileges but limited awareness of computer security.

The WPA and WPA2 (its update) schema fix the most serious problems with WEP; they provide strong protection to those who deploy it with a sufficiently random passphrase. Unfortunately, WPA adoption is not yet widespread despite the widely known weaknesses in WEP. This is primarily due to its incompatibility with WEP clients. The large base of legacy WiFi systems, the slow rollout of operating system drivers, and the mutual deployment exclusion between the two systems have resulted in a WEP usage rate of more than 75%, even today [40].

Other security strategies, such as VPNs, employ access control and encryption at higher network layers, but may disable the lower-level 802.11 security features. In this case, clients can join a wireless network at the 802.11 level, which allows them to send low-level frames to the access point. Unless they can subsequently authenticate themselves to the VPN server, they will not be able to engage the higher-level network that connects to the Internet. This solution is typical for organizations that employ IT professionals to manage their wireless networks. Home wireless routers do not support this level of security.

Limiting Administrative Access

The previously mentioned methods attempt to regulate access to network traffic. If circumvented, an unauthorized client will be able to send and receive traffic on the Internet, and to sniff and potentially spoof traffic to and from other clients on the same local network. Bypassing these mechanisms does not by itself grant the attacker administrative access to the WiFi router or access point. The commonly available settings that control administrative access are the administrator password, Internet administration availability, WiFi administration availability, and requirement for SSL usage between the administrator's client and the web administration page.

Although no studies have focused on password strength in consumer-oriented WAPs, password selection is notoriously weak in general. One study shows that roughly 25% of passwords are variants of words on a list approximately 65,000 words long [218], making password guessing far easier than if people chose them randomly. Practically speaking, many owners may not even change their passwords due to highly compatible (but insecure) default settings; see Section 5.1.5 for details. To compound issues further, home WiFi routers and access points typically do not impose penalties for erroneous login attempts. The authors have observed that a simple shell script can attempt 500 logins in 45 seconds. At this rate, brute-force password attacks can take on the order of hours. This obstacle presents a more costly barrier than WEP but is still tractable for many attacks.

Home WiFi routers implement coarse-grained access control over sources of legitimate administrative access. By default, administration attempts through the Internet are denied. When enabled, the administrator can specify a special port for Internet access. Another common option is the ability to disable administration through a router's wireless local network. Not all routers provide this option, and we believe that all home wireless routers sold up to 2007 have this access vector enabled by default. As illustrated later, this ability presents a dangerous opportunity for spreading malware by firmware upgrade.

Finally, the administrator may choose to conduct interaction with the configuration page via HTTPS instead of its cleartext brother, HTTP. Content encryption occurs at the application layer according to an SSL key-pair generated in the router. This feature is a necessity for anyone wishing to administrate over the Internet, because anyone with read access to the traffic may extract the router's access credentials. This seems less necessary for LAN-only administration, but wireless eavesdroppers could learn the administrative password if the user engages in communicating in the clear.

Other Settings

Some settings indicate a certain level of administrative rigor without actually making the access point less vulnerable. While they provide no intrinsic security value, they could mislead an attacker looking for easy targets. Simply changing a router's SSID from its factory-assigned setting to a personalized one—say, "Sid and

Al's network"—indicates a degree of diligence. An owner who changes the SSID may have overridden other default settings as well.

Changing the access point's MAC address also has the potential to deter attackers. The first three bytes of a MAC address are determined by the IEEE's OUI (organizationally unique identifier), a publicly available code that identifies the device's manufacturer; the last three bytes are assigned by the manufacturer using a closed proprietary process. Changing the MAC address could be the first step in masquerading as different hardware—perhaps the user-assigned address indicates that the device's brand is one aimed at the enterprise market rather than the home market and, therefore, is not as susceptible to attack.

5.1.5 Weak Security Configuration Is the Rule

Although wireless access points incorporate a number of security measures, they are rarely engaged by the home user. This trend is due to open access settings out-of-the-box, poor configuration interfaces, and widespread failure to alter default settings. The result is a large population of highly vulnerable wireless networks.

Extreme Competition Leaves Security Behind

WiFi routers destined for the home market place a premium on cost and, consequently, on ease of use. It is a cut-throat market where a minute shift in production and delivery costs means the difference between profit and loss. At the time of this writing, the Linksys WRT54G and its competitors have street prices ranging between $40 and $60. Technical support, particularly in the form of phone calls, is very expensive. As a result of economic incentives, default settings are optimized to work in the broadest possible circumstances and with the least possible amount of user interaction. A typical default profile includes the following: 802.11 layer encryption disabled, SSID broadcast enabled, SSID = ⟨manufacturer name⟩ (e.g., Linksys, Netgear, D-Link), administrator password = admin, gateway address = 192.168.1.1, MAC address filtering disabled, DHCP enabled, wireless administration enabled. The end result of these settings is a router that works—that is, shares an Internet up-link over a wireless network—simply by plugging in the power and broadband Ethernet cables. No software configuration is necessary.

Users Don't Change Default Settings

Field studies [182, 371] have shown that for broadcast WiFi access point attributes (broadcast channel, SSID, and encryption state), as many as 50% of popular home routers utilized default settings for all three. Informal surveys further suggest default administrative password usage at a rate between 60% and 70% for otherwise unsecured networks.

To combat this trend, California has mandated (beginning October 1, 2007) stronger security warnings and user affirmation of these statements as a prerequisite to WiFi access point use. Its intent is to encourage owners to change default settings by entering a configuration program that prompts the user to change each setting. In practice, a sticker appears over the broadband connection point and its removal constitutes acknowledgment of these warnings. It remains to be seen whether this requirement will increase the security of consumer-administered WiFi access points.

The Human Factor Affects User Interface Design

User studies [224, 225, 390] have shown that even when people use manufacturers setup wizards, many fail to engage the most important security features. For example, one manufacturer's setup wizard displays 15 asterisks in both the password entry and confirmation boxes. More than one fourth of the users in one study [390] failed to change the default password when presented with this display. Ironically, this manufacturer's default password is the empty string. The asterisks, which are intended to conceal the length of the current password, could have given users the impression that a strong password was already in use. One user commented that he did not change the password because he thought that it could cause the system to stop working [158]. In contrast, all users changed the default password when interacting with a different manufacturer's password entry dialog that displayed empty password and confirmation lines [390].

While subtle human–computer interface differences affect field security for consumer devices, current research [224, 225] shows that goal-oriented user interfaces produce drastically better rates of secure deployment, especially by novice users. A goal-oriented interface focuses on security properties that the user wishes to achieve, rather than technologies that achieve them. One prototype setup interface for wireless routers automates the generation of settings details based on the security desires of the user; users can edit the details afterward. For instance, the goal-oriented interface developed by Kuo et. al. [225] asks whether the user wants to control who accesses the network, if data secrecy is important, and how many clients will access the network. The interface then configures a combination of encryption and MAC address filtering based on the responses. Expert and novice users achieved the same level of security when using this prototype. However, when left to the manufacturer setup interfaces, novices fared worse while expert users maintained the same level of security.

Another goal-oriented prototype [390] displayed a prominent security evaluation as users completed a sequence of configuration screens. The screen sequence was similar to the Linksys setup wizard, but was altered to include MAC address filtering. At each stage, the interface displayed a red, yellow, or green circular graphic indicating the strength to which four different types of access control mechanisms were deployed. The interface avoided details about how the security mechanisms worked. Users "played" the prototype interface like a game, trying to maximize their security rating by revisiting previous screens to improve their score—an uncommon behavior in the standard interfaces. Although users edited their configuration more often with the prototype, they also—and unexpectedly—completed the configuration task much more quickly than with the standard interfaces. Most importantly, the subjects greatly improved router security by using the prototype interface.

Case Study: Diversity in Default Settings

Field studies have shown incredibly high encryption deployment rates (97% according to independent sources [182, 371]) among the WiFi access points manufactured by 2wire. It turns out that 2wire enables WEP by default using randomly generated keys that are printed at the bottom of the device. The company has produced a more secure access point deployment by exploiting user reluctance to change default settings. It can sustain the potentially higher support costs because it employs a different business model than its competitors. 2wire's WiFi products are of the router | DSL interface variety. The company sells directly to DSL providers, which then bundle the devices with the purchase of DSL service. Initially, the 2wire residential gateway (its term for WiFi router + DSL interface) is sent to the customer with installation directions. If the customer is unable to install the device on his or her own, then the customer can pay for a service call; a technician then visits the client's house to set up the gateway and any clients. Business is further bolstered by the DSL provider's limited obligation to support third-party solutions. This model supports the added costs imposed by enabling WEP in the default settings.

　　User studies [224, 225, 390] have noted that WiFi encryption and MAC address filtering are particularly difficult features for novices to configure. This is presumably due to the required coordination of identifiers and keys between the client and the router. We speculate that setting a randomly chosen default administrative password on WiFi routers would cause fewer support issues than 2wire's decision to enable WEP by default, although it would likely increase production costs (which might be resisted by manufacturers). Moreover, novices are unlikely to want access to router administration, while they are guaranteed to want access to the WiFi network; this preference decreases the pool of potential support cases with respect to 2wire's default policy. This decision makes it much harder to execute an unauthorized firmware update or malicious router configuration.

5.1.6 Attacks

WAPJack Attacks

The firmware on a router can be configured for compatibility with a variety of networks. For example, the DNS servers used by the router for hostname resolution can be specified by an administrator of the router. Unfortunately, this means that insufficiently protected routers can be attacked and "configured" by an attacker to perform as the attacker wishes, opening up a variety of attacks. These configuration-change attacks are called WAPJack attacks.

Pharming. An attacker who sets the preferred DNS servers on a router can essentially redirect all DNS traffic from that router's network to the attacker's DNS server. This means the attacker has control over IP-name pairings served to clients of the compromised router and can easily set up a doppelganger site for any domain he or she chooses. To people who use a router compromised in this way, it will appear that they are visiting a legitimate site while they may actually be visiting one set up by the attacker.

Internet-Side Administration. Disabled by default on many routers, Internet-side administration allows someone on a router's external network (anyone on the Internet, really) to log in and control the settings of the router. An attacker who wants to control a router via the Internet just has to determine the password for the router, attack the router from the inside (connecting to the WiFi network or through other vectors), and then enable this feature. This provides a remote-control mechanism for an attacker to maintain control over many routers from anywhere on the Internet.

Wireless Bridging. A more obscure WAPJack attack, and one that is less likely to occur, involves configuring a wireless router to disconnect its current WAN or Internet connection and instead route Internet traffic through another router nearby. For example, imagine an attacker who lives in a high-rise apartment building. He probably notices many wireless networks around him, and he may want to control the traffic between those networks' clients and the Internet. First, the attacker sets up a wireless network of his own—call it WAPFunnel. Next, he breaks into as many other wireless networks around him as he can. For each compromised network, he checks whether the router supports wireless bridging (this advanced wireless feature is not supported by all wireless routers; it ensures that all out-bound traffic is routed through another wireless connection instead of through a wired broadband connection). If a target router does support bridging, the attacker configures the target to bridge to his network, WAPFunnel. This metaphorically "unplugs" the router from its owner's Internet connection and uses

WAPFunnel (the attacker's network) as its connection to the Internet. The result is a bunch of routers that direct all of their external traffic through the attacker's control. The attacker may subsequently inspect, modify, or block whatever traffic from those networks that he pleases.

WAPKit Attacks

When a router is compromised and the attacker completely *replaces* its firmware, the router has been WAPKitted. This type of invasive attack is most dire when successful and provides an attacker with flexibility and complete control over a target network. A WAPKitted router is able to perform more tasks than the original router's firmware was capable, because the attacker is in control of the new firmware. This capability enables the attacker to perform more complex, computationally unique, and robust attacks. A few examples of WAPKit-enabled attacks include man-in-the-middle attacks, trawler phishing (where copies of web form submissions are sent to the attacker), race pharming (where the client is unwillingly forwarded to an attacker's site because the router can spoof an HTTP response that arrives before the response from a real server), click fraud (where advertisement links are followed at the discretion of the router), and general remote control (also known as "zombie" creation).

Man-in-the-Middle. Normally on the Internet, data is sent back and forth between a client and a server. If an attacker can control all the traffic between the client and the server, he or she can manipulate the data to conform to the attacker's interests. For example, if a client is browsing eBay's (a server's) web site for a specific product that the attacker sells, the attack may filter the search results to *only* show the products the attacker is selling. In this way, the attacker "sits" in the middle between the client and the server.

On a WAPKitted router, an attacker can play man-in-the-middle, or literally analyze all traffic sent through the router and watch, change, or drop any pieces of data he or she sees fit. For example, an attacker can place firmware on a router that watches all traffic destined for a search engine, replacing results for all queries about "secure wireless router" with results that direct the client to the attacker's site. The client believes these are the *only* results and is referred to wireless security information on the *attacker's* web site.

More serious man-in-the-middle attacks may be more elaborate and perform tasks such as changing prices on e-commerce web sites to encourage victims to buy items sold by an attacker.

Likewise, security of SSL sessions through a WAPKitted router is compromised because a WAPKitted router may hijack any SSL sessions. Figure 5.1 shows three

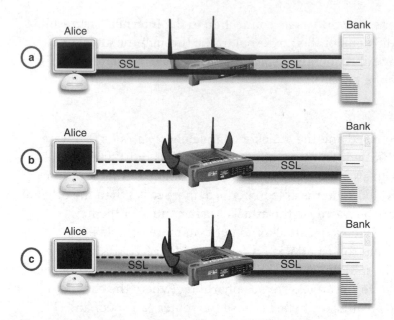

Figure 5.1: Man-in-the-middle attacks via WAPKit. (a) Regular SSL connections are between Alice and Bank. The router simply forwards encrypted traffic and cannot analyze it. (b) A malicious router establishes an SSL connection with Bank and a non-SSL connection with Alice so it can change the data transmitted by Bank or Alice. (c) A malicious router establishes two SSL connections, one with Bank (as client) and one with Alice (as server). A self-signed certificate is presented to Alice, who never sees Bank's real certificate.

scenarios. As shown in Figure 5.1(a), normally SSL is established between a server (Bank) and client (Alice). They agree on a session key and then end up with a secure channel. In this case, the router simply forwards data back and forth and is unable to identify any content encrypted on the SSL channel.

A compromised router, as shown in Figure 5.1(b), may refuse SSL connections, instead establishing an unencrypted session with Alice. The router would then masquerade as Alice, establish an SSL session with the bank, and forward all data provided by Alice. In this scenario, the router can intercept data between Alice and Bank, modifying or detecting Alice's identity. This scheme is likely to work because Alice probably won't notice the lack of an SSL connection and thus will have no idea she is being phished.

Alternatively, as shown in Figure 5.1(c), a WAPKitted router can establish *two* SSL sessions, one between Alice and the router, and the other between the router and Bank. The two SSL sessions use different keys and certificates, but the router can create a self-signed certificate that resembles the Bank's certificate at a quick glance, though it is *not* trusted by any certificate authority. (Despite the invalid certificate presented to Alice by the router, studies have shown she probably won't notice or care [366]. Most of the time people simply click "OK" when warned that a certificate is not trusted, which they should not.) As data is transfered from Alice to the router, it is decrypted, then re-encrypted to be transferred to the Bank.

In these last two scenarios, the attacker can see the plain decrypted traffic as it passes through the router, even if SSL is used. This gives an attacker an easy way to steal credit card numbers, bank account information, or other secret data normally assumed to be protected when using a secure HTTP session with SSL. This attack could be avoided if SSL certificates were properly authenticated by browsers and their users.

Trawler Phishing. Many web sites improperly implement secure form posting: Clients go to an unencrypted page containing a login form, they type in their credentials, a secure connection is established, and the data is sent to the server. In this case, the form is transmitted in plaintext and can be intercepted and modified by an interested party. WAPKit firmware may watch for these forms and modify them such that they cause a victim's browser to transmit a copy of submitted form data to an attacker (Figure 5.2). Everything else proceeds normally, but the attacker can obtain identification information for victims using a WAPKitted router to access any web service that improperly implements secure form posting. This kind of attack does not involve manipulating or playing man-in-the-middle for SSL sessions. It could be avoided if all service providers initiated SSL *before* a client enters any credentials or private information.

Race Pharming. A WAPKitted router can watch all the traffic that passes through it from its clients to the Internet, and back again [254]. It can watch for TCP requests to sites that an attacker is interested in, especially those that are currently spoofed in the form of a phishing site somewhere. When the compromised router sees one of its clients attempting to set up a connection with a legitimate site of

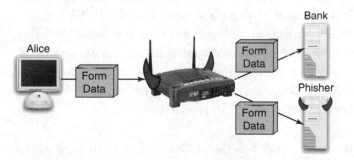

Figure 5.2: Trawler phishing attacks via WAPKit: Copies of all form submissions are sent to the phisher's server.

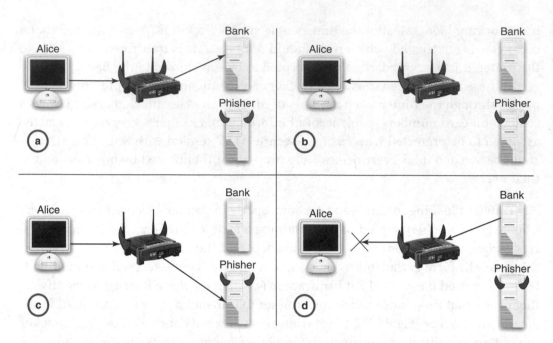

Figure 5.3: Race pharming attacks via WAPKit. (a) Alice sends a request to fetch the bank's web site. (b) The attacker responds with a "moved to" message. (c) Alice then requests data from the "new" server. (d) When the real bank's server responds, its data is ignored.

interest, it can inject a forged TCP ACK packet, causing the client to visit the spoofed site instead of the real one (Figure 5.3). This type of deception is known as race pharming. All appears normal to a client, whose browser is simply instructed that the web site has moved. When the user types in the address of a site to visit, he or she may instead be taken to a phishing site when the user's browser is race pharmed.

Technically, race pharming can be easily accomplished when a compromised router sits between a client and all connections the user wants to make. For example, when an HTTP request is sent from Alice through the compromised router to Bank (see Figure 5.3), the router can respond with an "HTTP 303 See Other" response and tag the TCP connection to drop by setting the TCP "FIN" flag. This causes Alice's browser to attempt a new connection with the server specified in the HTTP 303 message and ignore any incoming results that come from Bank, as shown in Figure 5.3(d). Additionally, the router could simply drop the HTTP request packets so Bank never receives a request in the first place.

Click Fraud. While a WAPKitted router has the ability to engage in general man-in-the-middle attacks, it can also be customized for money-making purposes. A compromised router watching traffic between its clients and the Internet can scan transferred web pages for advertisements published by Google, Yahoo!, or any other advertising service. If an advertisement for the attacker's service passes through the router, the compromised firmware can respond by simulating a click on the advertisement (accessing the URL specified by the ad syndicator, the entity that controls ad publishing and payments). Due to this simulated click, the owner of the ad gets paid—even if the human on the other side of the router doesn't actually click the ad.

This practice is dangerous for two reasons. First, the human will not see the result of the click because it can be discarded by the router. Second, the ad syndicator cannot easily discern between an ad clicked in this fashion and one clicked by a human. Such a click fraud attack can be stopped by requiring users to verify that they really clicked an ad—something most will refuse due to inconvenience. Cutting-edge click pattern analysis may help, but the easiest solution is to prevent WAPKitting.

A WAPKitted router may also masquerade as a client, performing searches and generating clicks all on its own. Traffic that originates from such a compromised router would not be easily differentiated from traffic originating from legitimate human users connecting *through* the router.

Robot Delegate (Zombie). The previously discussed attacks are specific features that can be written into firmware on a WAPKitted router. At a high level, the problem is that the router's firmware can be changed to do almost anything an attacker wants. A WAPKitted router can be turned into a robot (sometimes referred to as a zombie) that the attacker can control from afar. Arbitrary software can be executed, meaning that a router can be turned into an entity on the Internet to do nearly anything. For example, it can be instructed by an attacker to participate in a Distributed Denial of Service (DDoS) attack, flooding traffic to a victim in cahoots with many other robots controlled by the attacker. Many other remote-control features can be built into the firmware, making a WAPKitted router just as dangerous as a controlled PC on the Internet.

Zombie or bot networks are used not only to carry out DDoS attacks, but also to distribute spam or host a web site used in a phishing attack. These two uses for botnets go hand-in-hand, because phishers must lure people to the web sites. Robot delegates are an optimal method for sending email from the same compromised host that serves the phishing web site.

5.1.7 Attack Vectors

How does a router get WAPJacked or WAPKitted? There are many ways, and an attacker needs just one to compromise a router. Some strategies involve the physical presence of the attacker near a target router; others can be accomplished over long distances using the Internet.

Warkitting

Warkitting [426] is the physical locality–based compromise of wireless access points. With this strategy, a mobile attacker uses WiFi network detection software, such as Netstumbler and Kismet, to identify and approach networks. Then, exploiting the large number of poorly secured routers, the attacker uses an open web administration to install malicious firmware on the device. Although they are normally performed through user interaction, these tasks are easily scripted.

One warkitting goal may be to compromise as many vulnerable devices as possible in the shortest amount of time. In this case, the attacker must minimize the amount of time spent compromising each device. He or she will not usually spend the time to crack WEP, bypass MAC address filtering, or try more than a handful of commonly used administrative passwords. Moreover, uploading a 2MB firmware image could require too much reliability from a target at the boundary of its connection range. The indiscriminate warkitter is better off executing malicious configuration of the existing settings—say, set up pharming and enable Internet administration—and then deferring the firmware update to a later time. These alterations require only a few bytes of sent data and have a higher success rate for marginal connections.

An attacker can extend connection range by using an antenna. This need not cost a lot of money: Some home-brew projects make effective directional antennas out of recycling bin contents—for example, variants of the so-called *Cantenna*. The hacker conference DefCon hosts regular contests to establish the farthest WiFi client connection [493]; the world record established an 11 Mbit connection for 3 hours over 124.9 miles. Admittedly, it was achieved under ideal circumstances: good atmospheric conditions, specialized antennas at both ends, minimal interference from competing sources. Nevertheless, specialized equipment can reduce an attacker's risks by decreasing physical proximity.

Although one warkitting objective is to recruit an army of routers, some attackers concentrate on compromising a small number of high-value targets. The targets could be part of an electronic crime—corporate espionage, for instance— where the primary goal is to gain unauthorized access to a protected resource. Alternatively, it could be a prelude to a physical crime, such as stalking or burglary. The ease of compromise makes this type of warkitting accessible to a wide range of attackers. The small number of targets increases the warkitter's ability to bypass weak security measures such as MAC address filtering, SSID hiding, WEP encryption, and low-entropy passwords. The passive network sniffer Kismet is bundled with Airsnort, a program that defeats WEP, the dominant WiFi encryption method in use today. Together, these two programs ensure entry to the target network after analysis of 5 to 10 million packets. This method is completely passive, so analysis of network traffic cannot detect its presence. More recent methods speed up WEP cracking by actively generating traffic and subvert the encryption with as little as one packet. As noted earlier, a dictionary attack on the administrative password could take hours, but this is a plausible expense for a focused attack.

Once encryption is broken, race pharming (e.g., hijacking a TCP connection by subverting the SYN-ACK handshake) becomes a plausible attack. Race pharming enables a social engineering attack to avoid the conspicuously large numbers of failed login attempts resulting from a dictionary attack. After hijacking the TCP connection, the attacker spoofs a message from the router that makes an excuse for the user to initiate administrative access—perhaps a firmware update is available.

Router-to-Router Attacks

A WiFi router subverted with malicious firmware can participate in nearby WiFi networks as a client. Malicious firmware on a router can spread itself to reachable networks by the same methods as a human-directed agent does. This activity is far less risky than warkitting because the attacker does not need to be present, although the spread may be seeded with some other method. Router-to-router firmware attacks enjoy the advantages of the focused attacker; each one tries to corrupt the small number of WiFi networks in its range. Such attacks can spend the necessary resources to circumvent WEP, MAC address filtering, SSID hiding, and weak administrative passwords.

Router-to-router attacks have the potential to be one of the first malware epidemics that spread *outside* the Internet. In the simplest case, when the firmware is installed through the manufacturer's web upgrade interface, the attacking router sends HTTP directly to the target. This greatly increases the difficulty of stopping the spread, because no intermediate system is required to transfer data to the victim. Email viruses must evade spam and virus scanners before delivery, while port-scanning viruses must traverse firewalls and malware signature scanners. These intermediate systems are configured by security-conscious professionals and provide some measure of protection to vulnerable systems. Router-to-router spreads, by contrast, do not require the cooperation of well-administered systems to spread.

How plausible is an epidemic? If there is not a sufficient density of vulnerable routers, the malware will not become a widespread problem. One simplified but illuminating model includes the following assumptions: Infected routers are not removed from the population until they have infected all other reachable and vulnerable routers, and infection time does not matter [77]. This model estimates the density of vulnerable routers with the theory of random geometric graphs and the critical connectivity.[2] In the two-dimensional case, an average of 4.52 vulnerable routers in range of each router is enough to sustain a spread over an arbitrarily long distance. This threshold drops to 2.74 in the three-dimensional case—a plausible assumption in dense populations, such as a high-rise building.

Although based on simplified assumptions, these predictions suggest some possible concerns and countermeasures. Globally reducing WiFi access point signal strength (a configurable setting in most devices) to the minimum necessary pushes the average connectivity lower, potentially below the critical threshold. While changing the existing deployment is at least as hard as getting everyone to change their passwords, manufacturers could effect this change in the new crop of routers by conservatively setting their default broadcast strength. Conversely, newer wireless Internet technologies, such as 802.11n, feature improved range, among other advances. If factory defaults maintain their current level of insecurity, the risk of sustainable router-to-router malware increases.

Web Scripting

Some attackers may attempt to take control of a router through malicious web scripting [389]. An attacker's web site can serve up pages and scripts that are loaded and run by a PC's web browser. The scripts can then look at the network directly attached to that person's PC (the router's LAN or internal network) and locate the router from the *inside*. Finally, the scripts running in the browser can attack the router by sending configuration requests. Routers with a default or no password are easily configured in this fashion, oftentimes without the knowledge of the user (whose web browser is running the scripts).

Once the scripts have been loaded by a web browser, they need to learn a little about the network directly connected to the victim's PC. Computers connected to the Internet through these home routers are usually assigned an internal IP address for communication between PC and router. The router then updates traffic accordingly to act as a middleman between PC and Internet servers. As a result, this internal IP is normally hidden from hosts on the Internet. It can easily be guessed, however, because the IP ranges used by routers in this fashion are selected from a fairly standard range (commonly 192.168.0,1.*). Given that home routers use

---

2. Critical connectivity is the required average number of connections at an arbitrary node to achieve a nonvanishing connected component as the graph size approaches infinity.

only a few addressing schemes, an attacker may simply "guess" the IP of the router (without knowing the IP of the host PC) and often will be right. Once the IP address of the router is discovered, scripts running on the victim's web browser (on the internal network) send it configuration requests.

Example. Bob is surfing the web and locates a site at `evil.com`. He clicks the link and is served the `evil.com` web page. While he is reading it, JavaScript running on the `evil.com` web page guesses common router IP addresses and default passwords such as "admin". It constructs a URL and sends a request for `http://admin:admin@192.168.0.1/manage.cgi?remote_management=1`. This request is received by the router, which parses the request and complies with it, enabling administration of the router from the Internet. Finally, the script sends a message back to `evil.com` indicating that the router is ready to be manipulated. The `evil.com` server then updates the router's firmware by simply logging into the router from the Internet and uploading the new firmware file.

Control of a router can be taken in this fashion, using only common JavaScript features. In this example, the attacker's script made some assumptions about the model of router, password, and IP address; these assumptions are rational, because the attack can be attempted on many internal IP addresses or for many router models simultaneously. The JavaScript can also probe many IP addresses and use the discovered information to determine the router model.

An attack such as this can be completely automated and mounted in a matter of a few seconds. No prior knowledge of the victim's network or router is necessary for the attacker (although it would streamline the attack), and the result is complete control over the router.

A variation of this attack is the use of a simple Java.applet [214] to discover a computer's internal IP. This step is not necessary, but it does provide a more targeted attack. The addressing scheme discovered in this fashion can also be used to more accurately guess the model of router used.

Direct Compromise and Reselling

Lest it be overlooked, an attacker could perform malicious firmware updates in person and resell the devices through an online marketplace. The online marketplace provides a layer of anonymity and relative safety for an attacker using stolen accounts and living outside a jurisdiction with effective fraud enforcement. Distribution costs are much higher for this scheme, and it has a much lower rate of circulation than warkitting, but the victims would be self-selected for a certain level of financial activity on the Internet: They needed to complete an online payment to an individual through an online marketplace. According to the FTC, average identity theft amounts range from $2100 for misuse of existing accounts to $10,200 for new account and other fraud. Any success in this range will cover the cost of distributing tens, if not hundreds, of compromised routers.

Admittedly, the cost of untraceably monetizing stolen credentials could make the business case for this scam more difficult. Nevertheless, there are underground communities available to attackers where these stolen credentials can be sold; they may be used to help minimize any worry of being traced.

5.1.8 Countermeasures

Traditional Antivirus Software Will Not Help

A router can be approached from many angles: through the web using scripts, over the wireless network, or by compromising it before sale. In the case of WAPJacking, the antivirus software may not even see the traffic between the attacker and the wireless router. In any case, it is difficult to distinguish an attacker from a legitimate user because the attacks use the same methods and techniques as *real* administration. WAPKitting is also not easily detected because firmware updates are sometimes distributed by the routers' manufacturers, and upgrading the firmware is not perceived as a threat. Additionally, antivirus software that runs on a PC will probably not even see the firmware files as they are transmitted directly from the attacker to the router. Thus, unless the router checks the firmware before allowing it to be installed, antivirus software will not stop its installation.

Good Security Sense Fixes Most Problems

As always, the best approach to protecting against firmware attacks on wireless routers is to maintain average (not even professional) security practices. Changing settings on a router should require physical access to the router—thus providing a layer of physical security. Internet-based or WAN-side administration of the router should not be enabled. Wireless networks should be encrypted with hard-to-break encryption such as WPA (not WEP). Many routers come from the manufacturer with the same password (e.g., "password") or none at all—and most people don't see a need to change the password. At the very least, the administration password used to enter configuration for the router should be sufficiently hard to guess. Perhaps before the router can be used for the first time, the firmware should require the user to set a password that will be decently secure.

Hack Yourself Before Someone Else Does

Users should take control of a router before an attacker does. WAPJacking yourself consists of logging into the router, setting passwords, enabling encryption, and essentially locking out intruders. WAPKitting yourself involves installing a firmware that enforces more stringent security policies than the manufacturer's copy. For example, OpenWRT implements a penalty system for incorrect login attempts, which helps thwart dictionary attacks. The firmware could be configured to disallow administration from all network locations except computers plugged into the router's LAN itself. This changes the threat of being WAPJacked or WAPKitted to require walking up to the router and plugging in before the threat can become reality.

Host Scanning

Network host scanners such as nmap and p0f-2 may have some success in detecting compromised routers, particularly for the first wave of attacks that are based on open-source software. The goal of these tools is to identify network nodes as thoroughly as possible by identifying details of packet construction, frequency, and volume. There is considerable variability in the space of protocol adherence that specific operating systems, applications, and even hardware from these host traffic details. Network administrators (and attackers) use such tools to help identify vulnerable systems.

The nmap toolkit actively sends traffic to ports of the specified hosts in an attempt to elicit an identifying response. By contrast, p0f is a passive scanner that relies on traffic generated from other computers to identify the host. Because open-source firmware replacements are expedient platforms for developing malicious firmware, a sensible first step is to create scanner profiles for the legitimate distributions. Unsophisticated malware will be one-off remixes of existing open-source software and consequently will exhibit the same communication signature.

Intrusion Detection Systems

Other tools, broadly known as *intrusion detection systems* (IDS), focus on detecting malicious intent in traffic regardless of its source. Two basic approaches to this are *signature or rule-based intrusion detection* (RBID) [381], [45] and *statistical* or *anomaly detection systems*.

The rule-based model uses actual traffic content to detect malicious activity. The rules or signatures are based on substring matching and limited regular expressions. A known worm or virus may contain a substring that is critical to its ability to exploit a vulnerability—for instance, the data used in a buffer overflow. A RBID characterizes this data with a signature and scans incoming traffic for its presence. Other RBID signatures express sequences of events that indicate system abuse. For instance, a naive brute-force password attack is definable by repeated login attempts several times a second from a single IP address. Firmware upgrade attacks that use a WAP's web administration interface, including all of the infection methods discussed in Section 5.1.7, can be recognized with RBID programming. Because a legitimate firmware upgrade is an unusual event, false-positive rates would be low. The main drawback to the RBID approach is that it identifies only known attacks (or very slight variants).

While RBIDs raise alerts by comparing traffic to models of bad behavior, anomaly detection identifies abuse by comparing traffic against statistical models of good behavior. This has the theoretical advantage of detecting unknown attacks, but can also result in high false-positive rates. Moreover, attackers familiar with the anomaly model may be able to statistically camouflage their abuse with other traffic. Because of the high false-negative and false-positive rates, anomaly-based IDSs are largely academic projects today.

Gathering wireless traffic requires more infrastructure than gathering wired traffic. Specifically, it requires a collection of sensors over the airspace of the wireless network. Generally, these sensors passively collect traffic and forward it for centralized analysis. One practical problem is that of the 14 channels defined by the 802.11 standard, commercial chipsets are capable of listening to only one at a time. This is less of a concern for warkitting attacks on wireless access points where the communication channels are known, but rogue access points within an organization may use the less common channels to avoid detection. For instance, Japan and Europe have licensed higher-frequency channels for WiFi use than the channels used in the United States; rogue access points may deploy some of these disallowed (in the United States) channels to hide themselves from conventional scans.

Wireless Honeypots

A full-featured intrusion detection system will also employ honeypots, which deliberately masquerade as vulnerable systems to attract attacks. In reality, they run vulnerable software inside of carefully monitored virtual machines in an attempt to expose the details of malicious activity. The only interactions with honeypots are unauthorized, by definition, so they avoid the problem of separating good traffic from bad traffic. In context of warkitting, honeypots simulate vulnerable wireless access points by advertising a network with apparently default settings. For example, the network name may be Linksys, it may advertise no encryption, the MAC address could indicate Linksys as the manufacturer, and it might simulate the administrative web page accessible with the username and password pair, *admin:admin*. However, the upgrade script would compare the uploaded data with a library of known manufacturer and malicious firmware images, raising an alert whenever it finds a discrepancy.

The main challenge for honeypots is executing a convincing disguise. This is an arms race. The attacker may profile timing or use host identification programs like nmap [278] and p0f [297, 490] to pinpoint unusual activity that could expose honeypots. A low-stealth honeypot may use the straightforward configuration of a desktop with wireless interface to emulate the vulnerable access point. For instance, a host scanner that determines a router's operating system to be BSD or Windows while the router claims a Linksys SSID conclusively identifies a honeypot. More sophisticated honeypots will run firmware on a virtual router, possibly implemented as a software process inside a conventional computer.

Client Containment

Once the IDS detects an attack, an administrator may choose to implement *client containment* [480]—a denial-of-service attack mounted against the client to prevent wireless communication. There are a few ways to implement client containment, and all of them carry risks, particularly in terms of exposing otherwise passive sensors. Some depend on jamming a particular radio frequency, a strategy that destroys service for legitimate users and attackers alike. Other methods exploit weaknesses in the 802.11 handshaking protocols to execute per-client control.

The most commonly implemented strategy is to spoof *deauthenticate frames* from the access point with which the attacker is communicating. This causes the client to reset, assuming that it does not identify the spoofed frame as a fake. Some implementations simply send these frames at regular intervals; others send them only if they have detected a connection attempt by the offending client. A sophisticated attacker would ignore these bogus deauthenticate notices and continue to receive data from the access point. More robust client containment implementations augment this tactic by spoofing deauthenticate frames from the attacking client that are destined for the access point. This extra step fools the access point into dropping the client's connection. Certainly a sophisticated attacker could frustrate containment attempts by changing its client MAC address, although the policy may simply be "no new connections for X minutes upon intrusion detection."

Handshake interruptions may also take place at a higher level for per-protocol DoS. For example, TCP could be blocked by spoofing RST+FIN packets to the server-side host, much like the hijacking technique used in race pharming. In this case, the requests could be sent by a wired host when the server traverses the wired network. In a warkitting attack, the TCP connection is with the access point itself (using the web administration upgrade interface), so in general the interruptions must still come from a wireless agent. Nevertheless, some router switches might conceivably be susceptible to spoofed TCP packets coming from the wired LAN even though the attacker is wireless.

Conclusion

Crimeware is not limited to PC hosts. It can be installed on other devices such as broadband routers, wireless access points, and other firmware-controlled devices. Additionally, these devices can have a wide variety of propogation channels, some of which never pass through PCs that may have antivirus or crimeware detection software installed. Much of today's infectability stems from global defaults that are common to a class of devices, such as a blank administrator password; they allow an attacker to use "cookie cutter" attacks that, in a single form, can affect a large number of default-configured devices. Additionally, technical countermeasures can help protect people from infected firmware devices, but these tactics can be expensive and still fail to catch attackers. Good sense, such as setting nontrivial passwords or turning off unused features, can help protect individuals from compromise. Unfortunately, the "If it ain't broke, don't fix it" belief keeps many people from fiddling with working devices, even if it would enhance security.

5.2 Modeling WiFi Malware Epidemics*

As has been previously discussed in this chapter, it is possible for malware to spread from one infected router to another, by having an infected router communicate with a susceptible router directly over the wireless channel (as opposed to communicating through the Internet). This is troubling for several compounding reasons.

First, as has previously been addressed, there are a number of security holes and weaknesses in deployed home routers that make them vulnerable to infection over this communication channel. These weaknesses are not exposed (by default) through the routers' connection to the Internet.

Second, the severity of these weaknesses has traditionally been downplayed because it has been assumed that one needs to be in close proximity to a router to take advantage of it, and that attackers are not likely to spend the necessary time or take the risk of physical exposure that is required to be in the close proximity necessary to perform the attack. However, one can clearly construct a worm that propagates itself over the wireless vector, hopping from router to router when they are geographically close, delivering a malicious payload. In such cases, the security weaknesses are quite worrisome, as the attacker is likely a neighbor's router, the attack does not have practical time constraints, and the attacker need not fear prosecution or exposure.

---

*This section is by Hao Hu, Steven Myers, Vittoria Colizza, and Alessandro Vespignani.

Finally, the lack of detection and prevention technologies for attacks on wireless routers implies that such a worm might propagate, unmitigated, over dense urban areas, where routers are more likely to be found in close proximity. Thus the attack might evolve into an epidemic.

This case study introduces a mathematical model to simulate possible outbreak scenarios of malware on wireless routers in different geographic settings. The model is then used in conjunction with hobbyist-supplied war-driving data to model several large metropolitan districts of the United States.

The results are disconcerting, suggesting that in some large U.S. cities tens of thousands of routers could be infected in as little as 48 hours. More precise statements of the results are, of course, presented in future sections. The reader is cautioned that while these results are troubling, there have been no such widespread attacks at the time of writing. Normally, attackers go for the lowest-hanging fruit first—that is, the vulnerabilities that are easiest to exploit. While the attacks proposed herein do not take advantage of vulnerabilities that are difficult to exploit, they would require the implementation of a cross-platform worm, implying some care must be taken by attackers in implementing such a strategy.[3] Further, the rather large number of vulnerabilities on users' home computers, combined with near-universal installation of the Microsoft Windows family of operating systems and the rather meek deployment rate for anti-malware software, makes router attacks higher-hanging fruit than those holes often exploited by today's criminals. Yet, if we plug security holes on these PCs without concurrently fixing the security holes in routers, one should expect to see malware authors start to target routers.

5.2.1 Basic Methodology

To study the possibility of wireless router outbreaks, four major steps were taken:

1. Graphs of wireless router networks in major U.S. cities were constructed using real-world router placement data.

2. A mathematical infection dynamics model was developed to represent how a worm might spread across the networks constructed in step 1.

3. Simulation software was written and run to simulate the outbreak of a worm using the mathematical infection model on the constructed network.

4. Given that simulations are stochastic, they were repeated a number of times and analyzed to ensure that they were statistically valid.

---

3. Of course, the open-source code base available for these routers (which is discussed further in the sequel) and the availability of cross-compilers remove most of this difficulty.

5.2.2 Roadmap

A brief roadmap for the presentation of this case study is provided here. Section 5.2.3 discusses the infection of routers by other malicious routers, along with the security weaknesses that are exploited by the attackers. This is followed by a quick overview, in Section 5.2.4, of how to construct the ad hoc wireless networks over which the wireless epidemic will spread in the study's simulations. It includes a brief description of the data source used to extract the characteristics of routers' geographic locations and security settings, as well as the steps necessary to clean this data from artifacts of the hobbyist data collection methods. Additionally, several assumptions about this network are discussed.

Once the ad hoc network over which the epidemic can spread has been established, we then need to consider the infection dynamics by which malware can propagate over the network (i.e., the dynamics that define how different susceptible routers on the network become infected, while taking into account the fact that different routers have different security settings). These infection dynamics are defined in Section 5.2.5.

Section 5.2.6 presents the results of the case study. More specifically, the infection rates for major U.S. centers are presented, given the ad hoc networks and infection dynamics described in the previous sections. Finally, Section 5.2.7 explores the possible effects that changes to typical security setups might have on the findings of this case study.

5.2.3 Infecting the Router

Most commonly deployed home routers have administrative interfaces that allow users to modify their settings, such as a router's name, connectivity, or security settings. Generally, these administrative interfaces can be interfaced through web connections to default IP addresses that the routers specify. For example, one can view the administrative interface for many Linksys routers by directing the browser to http://192.168.0.1. To guard against malicious changes to a router's settings, access to the administrative interface is protected with a standard password mechanism: Without providing the administrative password, the settings cannot be modified. However, if an attacker can provide the password, then these administrative interfaces generally offer the ability to perform a complete firmware update of the router, by providing a file containing an appropriate replacement firmware. It is through this interface that a worm could download a copy of itself to a recipient router.

Two points should be clarified here. First, while most routers have a reset button, it will not reset a router to its original firmware; it will reset the router only to the default settings of the currently installed firmware. Second, if the firmware update process is interrupted, it is possible to leave the router in a permanently nonfunctioning state.

The infection of a susceptible router occurs when the malware of an infected router is able to interface with the susceptible router's administrative interface over the wireless channel. Two main technologies aim at preventing such infection: (1) the use of an encrypted and authenticated wireless communication channel, as is enabled through the use of the WEP and WPA cryptographic protocols, and (2) the use of a standard password for providing access control to the administrative interface. The access-control password is always present regardless of the presence of cryptographic protocols, although (as we will discuss shortly) it is often the case that the password is not modified from the default setting that the router shipped with. The use of encrypted communications channels is optional, and is not enabled on many routers. Indeed, the rates of encrypted communications channel deployment in the cities considered herein vary between 21% and 40% of the router population (as can be seen in Table 5.1). If the encrypted communications channels are deployed, then this security feature must be bypassed before any attempt can be made at bypassing the access-control password.

In the simplest case, when the router does not employ encrypted communication channels, the malware may attempt to directly bypass the router's administrative password. A large percentage of users do not change their router's password from the default established by its manufacturer, and these default passwords are easily obtainable: Web sites exist that do nothing but list default passwords for all types of computer hardware and software systems. In such cases, malware can attack the router simply by interfacing with it, providing the default password for the router,[4] and using the firmware update interface to infect the susceptible router.

Unfortunately, for legal reasons it is difficult to measure the exact percentage of users who use default passwords, so the model will use a proxy: It uses the percentage of users who do not change their router's default SSID to represent the percentage of routers with default passwords. For all other routers, it is assumed that 25% of them can have their passwords guessed within 65,000 login attempts. This is based on evidence provided by security studies performed by Klein [218], which show that approximately 25% of all passwords selected by users without

---

4. The malware can easily determine the brand and model of router that it is interfacing with—and thus the router's appropriate default password—using some simple TCP/IP stack fingerprinting techniques, such as those used by nmap and wireless device driver fingerprinting as discussed in [130].

restrictions are contained in a dictionary of 65,000 words. Based on the infection rates of previous worms that have also relied on brute-force dictionary attacks, it is assumed that another 11% of passwords are contained in a larger library of slightly less than 1 million words [203]. Note that, to the best of the authors' knowledge, none of the commonly deployed home routers provide back-off mechanisms that slow down or prevent systematic dictionary attacks.[5] Thus brute-force dictionary attacks are very feasible against these routers. In case the password is not found in either dictionary, it is assumed that the password cannot be broken and that the attack (i.e., infection) cannot proceed. Alternatively, if the password has been compromised, the attacker can upload the worm's code through the router's administrative interface into the router's firmware, a process that typically takes less than three minutes.

One must now consider routers that employ encrypted communications channels. For the purposes of this work, it is assumed that the WPA cryptographic protocol is not vulnerable to attack.[6] Therefore, any routers that use WPA are considered *immune* to the worm, as opposed to the case of routers that deploy WEP.

Both assumptions—that WPA routers cannot be broken, and that only 36% of routers' passwords will be cracked—are intended to be somewhat conservative estimates. If one assumes that the WPA protocol is broken at certain rates, or that more routers are susceptible to a strong password attack, then the number of routers infected in each epidemic will increase.

Because of the many cryptographic flaws in WEP [40, 395, 419], this cryptographic protocol can always be broken, given that the attacking malware-infected router has access to enough encrypted communications between the susceptible router and one of its legitimate clients. The attacker can listen for such communications by waiting for the susceptible router to be used by its legitimate clients, or by deploying more advanced active attacks, such as having the attacker send malformed communications to the router, which then automatically replies with correctly encrypted retransmission requests. Bypassing WEP is, therefore, feasible and requires only a given amount of time (at most several days, assuming one of the weakest attacks on WEP) and reasonable usage rates of the router.

---

5. Examples of such back-off mechanisms include putting delays between incorrect authentication attempts, where the delay is doubled between each incorrect attempt, and resetting to a small value upon provision of the correct password.

6. This is not entirely accurate, as there are dictionary-based attacks on WPA. Nevertheless, it is reasonable to estimate that many of the users who currently take the foresight to activate WPA are also the same ones who are likely to have strong non-dictionary-based passwords.

5.2.4 The Contagion Network

WiFi routers, even if generally deployed without a global organizing principle, define a proximity communication network: Any two routers that are in the range of each other's WiFi signal can exchange information and may implement an ad hoc communication network. One might wonder if currently the actual deployment of WiFi routers is sufficient to generate large connected networks spanning sizable geographic areas.[7] The possibility of large connected networks in a given urban area is, however, constrained by the area's topology, buildings and landmarks, and demographic distribution dictating the placement of WiFi routers by individuals.

The construction of such ad hoc WiFi networks is based on the data obtained from the public database of the Wireless Geographic Logging Engine (WiGLE) web site [183]. This database collects data on the worldwide geographic location of wireless routers and counts more than 10 million unique networks on nearly 600 million observations (at the time this was written) [184], providing good coverage of the wireless networks in the United States and in North-Central Europe. This implies that each data point in the database has, on average, been measured 60 times,[8] providing some confidence in the data, even if it was publicly collected.

The WiGLE data provides a wealth of information that includes, among other things, the routers' geographic locations—expressed in terms of latitude (LAT) and longitude (LON)—and their encryption statuses. This data is derived from wardrivers who traverse large areas with wireless detection systems attached to GPS systems, recording detected WiFi signals and the location of their detection. The database indicates whether an encryption protocol is being used to secure a router's wireless communication channel, but it does not disambiguate between the different cryptographic protocols. Therefore, there is data only on whether encryption was present, and not on whether the WPA or WEP protocol was used. This point will be important to model later when infection dynamics are discussed.

Our study focuses on the wireless data extracted from seven urban areas in the United States—Chicago, Boston, New York City, San Francisco Bay Area, Seattle, West Lafayette (Indiana), and Indianapolis. Starting from a set of vertices corresponding to geo-referenced routers in a given region, a proximity network [77, 169, 170, 272] is constructed by drawing an edge between any

---

7. For those familiar with the area, this problem is equivalent to the notion of percolation of connected components in graph theory.

8. The variance of the number of observations is likely quite large. However, this is likely acting in the favor of routers in large urban areas (i.e., the ones used in the model), as it seems likely that such data points will be observed more frequently by wardrivers than by those routers in more rural and suburban settings, where presumably the density of wardrivers is lower.

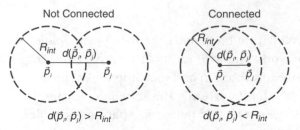

Figure 5.4: Construction of WiFi networks. Given two routers i and j located at $\vec{p}_i = (LON_i, LAT_i)$ and $\vec{p}_j = (LON_j, LAT_j)$, an edge is placed between them if their distance $d(\vec{p}_i, \vec{p}_j)$ is smaller than the maximum interaction radius R_{int}.

two routers i and j located at $\vec{p}_i = (LON_i, LAT_i)$ and $\vec{p}_j = (LON_j, LAT_j)$, respectively, whose geographical distance $d(\vec{p}_i, \vec{p}_j)$ is smaller than a prescribed maximum interaction radius R_{int} [i.e., $d(\vec{p}_i, \vec{p}_j) \leq R_{int}$], as shown in Figure 5.4. In WiFi networks, the maximum interaction radius R_{int} strongly depends on the local environment of any specific router. In practice, R_{int} ranges from 15 m (approximately 50 ft) for a closed office with poor transmission to approximately 100 m (approximately 328 ft) outdoors [144]. For simplicity, it was assumed that R_{int} is constant in a given network, independent of the actual location of a given router. That is, the model does not take into account potential limitations in the broadcast/reception radius of wireless routers that may be present due to different construction materials, geography, or interference in the area surrounding the routers. Increasing and decreasing values of the signal range would generally be expected to average out, and such information would be difficult to obtain otherwise. For this reason, the present study considers four different values for the interaction radii—$R_{int} \in \{15\ m, 30\ m, 45\ m, 100\ m\}$—for each of the seven areas under study to obtain the resulting networks.

Note that the constructed graphs are located on a two-dimensional surface, whereas in some of the cities under consideration there could easily be many routers in high-rise buildings, and thus the graphs might be better modeled in three dimensions. However, there is no altitude coordinate located in the WiGLE database, and one cannot reliably guess what such coordinates would be. This omission is not terribly troubling, because the average height of high-rises and most dwellings in these cities is still relatively close to the ground when considered with respect to the different broadcast radii. Further, it is known [77] that to create large giant components in a three-dimensional network, the average number of neighbors needed per router is smaller than the corresponding case in two dimensions.

In addition to collecting observed router signals, WiGLE contains records of wireless laptops and other devices that may be trying to discover the presence of wireless routers or forming their own ad hoc networks. Such observations are recorded as "probe" requests in the WiGLE database. All "probe" records were removed from the data set in our study because they almost surely corresponded to wireless signals originating from nonrouters. Such records represented a very small percentage of the total number in every city considered. For example, in the Chicago urban area, there were 4433 probe records, corresponding to 3.7% of the total in the original data set.

A preliminary analysis of the data for each urban area revealed the presence of several sets of WiFi routers sharing identical geographic locations. In a few such locations, there were hundreds of overlapping routers. Meta-data from the WiGLE database shows that all such router data points were uploaded to the database over a very short time interval and seem to correspond to unrealistic reporting. To avoid biases due to overrepresentation of records, BSSIDs (i.e., MAC addresses) were checked for uniqueness, and it was assumed that each of the geographic locations could contain at most n overlapping routers, where n was fixed to 20 to provide for realistic scenarios, such as apartment buildings with several routers. For the Chicago urban area, this procedure led to the elimination of 3194 records, which represented 2.7% of the total number of WiFi routers.

Finally, owing to the data collection method (via wardrivers who tend to travel down streets or sidewalks searching for WiFi signals), the coordinates for wireless routers in the database tend to be located directly on top of streets, as opposed to in homes or buildings. A randomized procedure was adopted to redefine the position of each router in a circle of radius R_{ran} centered on the GPS coordinates provided by the original data. The newly randomized positions for the set of routers completely determine the connectivity pattern of the spatial WiFi network, but only a subnetwork of it is used for the epidemic simulation (the subnetwork is termed the "giant component," and its definition and the motivation for its use are motivated in later sections). The value of R_{ran} is determined by the broadcast radius of the routers in a given model (this topic will be discussed in the next subsection). Importantly, results almost identical to those reported in this case study are achieved if the model does not adopt such a randomization procedure. The results presented in the case study are not dependent on this randomization procedure.

The Giant Component: What and Why?

For malware to spread from an infected router to an uninfected one, the two routers must be located within signal range. That is, in the framework of the WiFi networks described in the previous subsection, the two routers must be connected. Given the interest of this case study in whether a small number of infected routers might lead to a large outbreak, simulations considered only outbreaks on the largest set of

City	N	f_{encr}
New York City	36,807	25.8%
Boston	15,899	21.7%
Seattle	3013	26.0%
Chicago	50,084	33.7%
West Lafayette (Indiana)	2629	24.3%
Indianapolis	998	11.0%
San Francisco Bay Area	3106	40.1%

Table 5.1: Properties of the giant components of the WiFi networks for $R_{int} = 45$ m: size of the giant component N, percentage of encrypted routers f_{encr}. The results presented are obtained as averages over five different randomization experiments that perturbed the location of each router; values for N are rounded to nearest integer values.

connected routers that can be extracted from the WiFi network. Each router belongs to a connected component. For a given router A, its connected component simply consists of the set of routers that are reachable by following a path of links on the network, starting at the router A in question.[9] If two routers cannot be connected by a path of links in the network, they belong to separate connected components; otherwise, they are in the same component. The component with the largest number of routers is the giant component.

A router in the giant component has no hope of ever infecting any router outside of the component, either directly or indirectly. Therefore, once the giant component of the network was identified, it could be extracted from the network, whereas the remainder of the network could be removed from consideration, so that the epidemiological simulation focused solely on the giant component. This choice does not imply that routers that are not contained in the giant component are immune to such worms, but only that the effect of an outbreak would be less severe if it was started on such a network.

Table 5.1 reports the main indicators for the giant components of each urban area extracted from the WiFi network built assuming $R_{int} = 45$ m. Because these indicators can change slightly due to some of the random processes in constructing the graph, the results in Table 5.1 represent averages taken over five independent experiments.

Figure 5.5 depicts the various giant components obtained in the Chicago area corresponding to different values of R_{int}. Despite the clear geographical embedding

---

9. It is assumed that router A can reach itself through a path of length 0, and thus router A is in its own connected component.

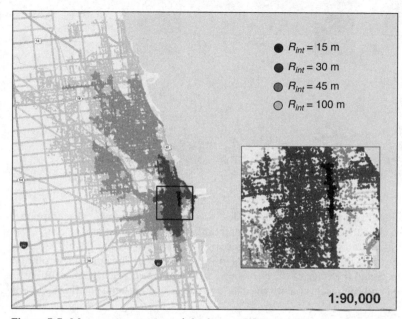

Figure 5.5: Map representation of the largest WiFi network made by routers connected by a path of edge (the so-called giant component) in the Chicago area as obtained with different values of R_{int}. Components with larger values of R_{int} always contain the components defined by smaller values of R_{int}. For example, the component defined when $R_{int} = 30$ contains the component defined when $R_{int} = 15$.

and the city constraints, a large network of more than 48,000 routers spans the downtown area when the wireless transmission radius R_{int} is set to 45 m. For those familiar with epidemic modeling of malware on more traditional computer networks, it is important to stress that the geographic embedding and the existence of a true distance measure exert a strong preventive force on the small-world behavior of the WiFi networks, because the limited WiFi communication radius interaction rules out the possibility of long-range connections.

5.2.5 The Epidemic Model

Constructing the wireless router network and finding its giant component defines the population and the related connectivity pattern over which the malware epidemic will spread. To describe the dynamical evolution of the epidemic (e.g., by monitoring the number of infected routers in the population as a function of time), a framework analogous to one used for infectious disease modeling is considered here. It assumes that each individual (i.e., each router) in the population is in a

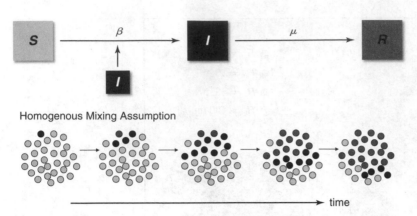

Figure 5.6: Compartmental flows for the basic SIR dynamics with homogeneous mixing assumption. The upper figure shows the class transitions, with associated transition rates, for an abstract SIR model. The lower figure demonstrates the homogeneous mixing assumption. It considers all individuals potentially in contact with all other individuals (no specific links). The epidemic evolution is just due to random contacts and the value of the transition rates. As time progresses, susceptible individuals become infected and then recover, with the classes denoted by the same shading as in the upper figure.

given class depending on the stage of the infection [10]. This basic modeling approach identifies three classes of individuals: *susceptible* (those who can contract the infection), *infectious* (those who contracted the infection and are contagious), and *recovered* (those who recovered or are immune from the disease and cannot be infected). The transition rates from one class to the other is what characterizes the specific disease. This represents the basic susceptible–infected–removed (SIR) epidemic model [10]. Figure 5.6 shows the basic compartmental transitions associated with the SIR model and their transition rates.

The heterogeneity of security levels in the WiFi router population calls for an enlargement of the basic SIR scheme that takes into account the differences in the users' security settings. Three basic levels of security were considered: Routers with no encryption, which are obviously the most exposed to the attack, are mapped into a first type of susceptible class S; routers with WEP encryption, which provides a certain level of protection that can be eventually overcome with enough time, are mapped into a second type of susceptible class denoted S_{WEP}; and routers with WPA encryption, which are assumed to resist any type of attacks, correspond to the removed class R.

This classification, however, needs to be refined to take into account the password settings of users, which range from a default password to weak or semi-strong passwords and finally to strong, noncrackable passwords. For this reason, one can think of the non-encrypted class S as being subdivided into four subclasses. First, one distinguishes between the routers with default password S_{nopass} and the ones with password S_{pass1}; the latter contains passwords of all sorts. A router in the latter class experiences the first stage of the attack, which employs the small dictionary of 65,000 words. If the attack is successful, the router will be moved to the infected class; otherwise, it will be moved to the class S_{pass2} and the attacker will attempt a second-stage attack, which employs the larger dictionary. Finally, if the password is unbreakable, the router is classified as R_{hidden}. This last class represents routers whose passwords cannot be bypassed, but whose immune condition is *hidden*. That is, the router's immunity condition is known only to the attacker who failed in the attempt; to all other potential attackers, the immune router appears to be susceptible. This allows unsuccessful attack attempts of other routers to be modeled in the simulated dynamics.

WEP-encrypted routers have the same properties in terms of passwords as routers that use no encryption, but the relevance of the password starts only when the WEP encryption has been broken on the router. At this stage of the attack, it can be considered to be in the non-encrypted state. For this reason, no subclasses of S_{WEP} have to be defined.

The model also includes the infected class (I), which contains those routers that have been infected by the malware and have the ability to spread the malware to other routers. Of course, if at any point the attack succeeds on susceptible routers in classes S_{nopass}, S_{pass1}, or S_{pass2}, the routers are reclassified as I.

One of the most common approaches to the study of epidemic processes is to use deterministic differential equations to analyze the epidemic. This approach is based on the assumption that individuals mix homogeneously in the population, each potentially coming in contact with every other individual (e.g., people with the flu travel around their communities, mixing with other individuals and potentially infecting susceptible ones). Figure 5.6 shows a basic SIR epidemic compartmental flow with the homogeneous mixing assumption [10]. In this model, individuals do not have specific links to each other, and all individuals are potentially in contact with all other individuals. Therefore, the introduction of a single infected individual allows for the evolution of an epidemic, where the number of infected individuals is just due to random contacts and the infection probability. However, in the case study under consideration, this homogenous mixing assumption is completely inadequate. That is, the static, nonmobile nature of wireless routers and their geographical embedding are essentially the antithesis of the homogenous mixing assumption. Instead, the epidemic dynamics must be studied by explicitly considering the underlying network contact pattern [31, 210, 262, 302, 467].

For this reason, numerical simulations are relied upon. They are obtained by using an individual-based modeling strategy, considering the discrete nature of the individuals and progress in discrete time steps. At each time step, the stochastic disease dynamics are applied to each router by considering the actual state of the router and those of its neighbors, as defined by the actual connectivity pattern of the network. The epidemic model assumes that the attacker targets the router, among its neighbors, with the lowest security settings. That is, attackers tend to focus on low-hanging fruit. In addition, the model does not allow simultaneous attacks: Each infected router chooses its next target only among those routers that are not already under attack. Once an attack has started, the attacker continues trying to bypass the security setting of the same target until (1) the attempt is finally successful or (2) the attacker has tried to use every password in the entire dictionary without success and fails to guess the router's password. In both cases, the attacker then moves to any other available targets that neighbor the router (and that have not been previously infected). It is then possible to measure the evolution of the number of infected individuals and keep track of the epidemic progression at the level of single routers. In addition, given the stochastic nature of the model, different runs with independent random choices and/or different initial conditions can be used to obtain different evolution scenarios.

The dynamics in this model are specified by the transition rates among the different classes of routers, all of which are expressed as the inverse of the average time needed to perform an attack. A router's class in the epidemic dynamics model will change, and thus a transition will occur only if a router is attacked. For instance, a router with no encryption and a default password enters the infectious class with unitary rate β if attacked. The attack on a router in class S_{pass1} is characterized by a transition rate β_1, reflecting the time necessary for the small dictionary attack, and has two possible outcomes: with probability $(1 - p_1)$, the router is infected and enters I; with probability p_1, it enters S_{pass2}, reflecting that the attacker was not able to overcome the password, and the infection attempt requires additional time and resources. Once in class S_{pass2}, it can become infectious with probability $(1 - p_2)$ if the attack is successful; otherwise, the router enters R_{hidden} with probability p_2, reflecting that the password has not been compromised. This process occurs with a transition rate β_2. WEP-encrypted routers follow the same dynamics once the encryption is broken and they enter S_{pass1} with transition rate β_{WEP}.

Figure 5.7 shows the flow diagram of the transmission model. Notice that the infection dynamics do not allow for transitions from class I to class R (as presented in the basic SIR model; see Figure 5.6). The scenario under consideration does not

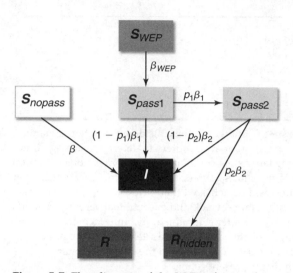

Figure 5.7: Flux diagram of the WiFi infection dynamics considered in the epidemic model. The transition times between states are specified by β_i and the probabilities of following different transition paths—when more than one is available—are given by the p_j values. When more than one transition path is available to leave a given state, then the probabilities assigned to the different exiting paths must sum to 1.

allow for anti-malware solutions that could "cure" the infected router, as a malware writer could lock out any further firmware changes after infection, making the infection permanent.[10] Therefore, the routers cannot transition to the recovered class. Routers in the R class are immune to the attacks and do not change their status during the epidemic evolution.

In the simulation, the unitary time step is defined by the shortest time scale among all processes involved, (i.e., the time ι needed to complete an attack on a non-encrypted router with no password). This automatically defines as unitary the transition rate β associated with an infected router taking a susceptible router with no password S_{nopass} to an infected state I. For example, suppose an infected router is neighbored by a susceptible router with no password. Then it can infect that router in one time step in our simulations, moving the susceptible router from the

---

10. The malware author can lock out further changes by having the malware modify the firmware update process either to never allow further updates or to allow only authenticated updates from the malware designer. Because the firmware changes are permanent, there is no way to clear the malware from the router short of physically tampering with the circuitry; given that many users fail to install antivirus software, it is reasonable to assume they will not go to such lengths to clean their routers. This is similar to how some malware infects the BIOS of users' PCs, making them permanently infected.

	Time Scale (minutes)
τ	5
τ_1	6–15
τ_2	400–1000
τ_{WEP}	2880–5760

Table 5.2: The times used to transition from one state to another in the considered infection dynamics. These times are based on experimenting with a small number of routers to determine average times needed to perform the different attacks, assuming fairly slow communications connections of several megabits per second (mbps). Given that there is not much deviance in hardware performance over router brands, and that in many cases connections will be achieved that have 54 mbps, the numbers are, if anything, cautious. τ is the time necessary to send, install, and execute malware in a router's firmware, assuming that the attacker has access to the router's administrative interface. It is also the unitary time step in the simulations performed. τ_1 is the time necessary to attempt all of the passwords in the smaller dictionary. τ_2 is the time necessary to bypass a password in the larger dictionary. τ_{WEP} is the time necessary to crack any WEP encryption that is present.

	Ranges	Typical Value
β	1	1
β_1	0.33–0.83	0.48
β_2	0.005–0.0125	0.007
β_{WEP}	0.0008–0.0017	0.001
p_1	0.75	0.75
p_2	0.85	0.85

Table 5.3: Ranges and typical values for transition rates. Different transition rates β_i are estimated based on the corresponding time to finish the attack τ_i and unitary time step τ, with $\beta_i = \tau_i^{-1}\tau$. The values β_i correspond to the number of simulation steps for the transitions in Figure 5.7. Specifically, β is the number of simulation steps necessary for infection of a susceptible router with a default password (i.e., the time necessary to upload malware and reset the router); β_1 is the number of steps needed to try a brute-force password attack with the small dictionary; and β_2 is the number of steps necessary to attempt a brute-force password attack with the large dictionary. The p_1 and p_2 values represent the relative success rates of the two types of brute-force password attacks, as modeled.

state S_{nopass} to the state I. In this way, other transition rates can be analogously defined as probabilities expressed in terms of their ratio with β that defines the unitary rate, and can be calculated based on typical time scales for the corresponding processes. Their ranges and typical values are provided in Table 5.2 and Table 5.3.

As multiply seeded attacks are likely (i.e., an attacker is likely to infect multiple routers initially, to start the spread of the worm), simulations start with initial conditions set with five infected routers randomly distributed within the population under study. In simulations performed by the authors, it was observed that attacks with an initial single seed, as opposed to a small number of initial seeds, resulted in very similar outbreaks. Therefore, the results presented here are not very sensitive to the choice of using five initially infected routers.

The initial state for each other router (i.e., the choice of its initial class among S_{nopass}, S_{pass1}, S_{WEP}, and R) is dictated either directly by the wigle.net WiFi data or is obtained from estimates based on real data. The classes S_{pass2} and R_{hidden} are empty at the beginning of the simulations because they represent following stages of the infection dynamics. Encrypted routers are identified from original data. It is assumed, based on estimates or real-world WPA usage, that 30% of these routers are using WPA, and thus are classified as being in the R class for infection dynamics. Analogously, the model assumes that the non-encrypted routers are distributed according to the following proportions: 50% in class S_{nopass} and 50% in class S_{pass1}. Finally, given the stochasticity of the process, the numerical simulations are repeated 100 times changing initial conditions and assuming different configurations of the randomized network, using independent random choices for each simulation.

5.2.6 The Spread of Synthetic Epidemics

Using the simulation procedure just outlined, the behaviors of synthetic epidemics in the seven urban areas were studied. The urban areas considered were quite diverse, in that they range from a relatively small college town (West Lafayette, Indiana) to big metropolises (New York City and Chicago). In each urban area, the study focused on the giant component of the network obtained with a given R_{int}.

The study reported results for a typical epidemic spreading scenario in which the time scales of the processes were chosen according to their average estimates. The best- and worst-case scenarios were also obtained by considering the combination of parameters that maximized and minimized the rate of success of each attack process, respectively. The giant components that were built and used were obtained from the network in the intermediate interaction range of $R_{int} = 45$ m.

The four snapshots of Figure 5.8 and Figure 5.9 provide an illustration of the evolution of a synthetic epidemic in the Chicago area. Shown in black are the routers that were progressively infected by malware. The striking observation is that the malware rapidly propagated on the WiFi network in the first few hours, taking control of about 37% of the routers after two weeks from the infection of the first five routers.

Figure 5.8: The spread of a wireless worm through Chicago after 1 and 6 hours. In this series, the result is based on randomly perturbing the location of each router to remove wardriving data collection artifacts and with the maximum router interaction radius R_{int} set to 45 m.

Figure 5.9: The continued spread of a wireless worm through Chicago after 24 hours and 2 weeks.

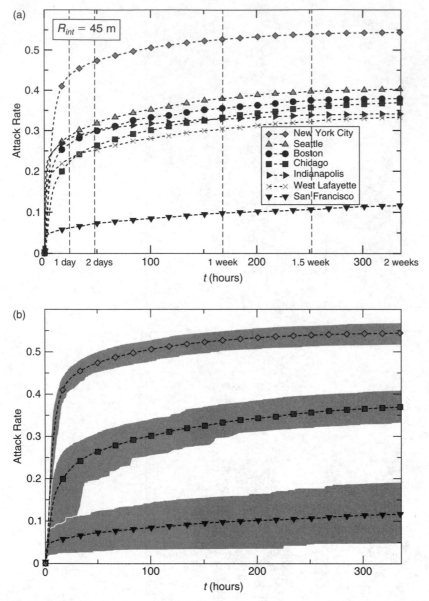

Figure 5.10: Attack rate versus time for the giant component. (a) The average attack rate versus time for the seven urban areas, keeping $R_{int} = 45$ m in all cases. The attack rates are averaged over 100 simulations. (b) The average and 90% confidence interval for three prototypical cases: New York, Chicago, and San Francisco Bay Area. Note that (b) uses the same city markers as (a).

The quantitative evidence of the potential impact of the epidemic is reported in Figure 5.10, where the average profile of the density of infected routers is reported for all the urban areas considered in the numerical experiment. While it is possible to notice a considerable difference among the various urban areas, in each urban area a sharp rise of the epidemic was observed within the first couple of days and then a slower increase. After two weeks, the epidemic left 10% to 55% of the routers in the giant component controlled by malware, depending on the urban area and its encryption rates. The similar time scale in the rise of the epidemic in different urban areas is not surprising, as it was mainly determined by the time scale of the specific attacks considered in the malware propagation model.

In general, the sharp rise of the epidemic in its early stages was due to the non-encrypted routers, which were infected in a very short time. The slower progression at later stages was, instead, due to the progressive infection of WEP routers, whose attack time scale is about one order of magnitude longer.

Figure 5.11 presents the results for the spread of an epidemic from single executions for the simulation—as opposed to results averaged over several simulations, which are presented in Figure 5.10 and Figure 5.12. It clearly shows the effect of the interplay of different time scales involved in the spreading

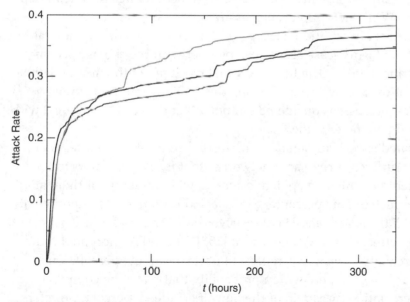

Figure 5.11: Three individual (nonaveraged) results for simulations of the epidemic in the Chicago area (giant component, $R_{int} = 45$ m). Each line represents the plot of the attack rate versus time that results from a single simulation of the epidemic. Because the results are for single simulations, as opposed to an average of multiple simulations (as in Figure 5.10), the variations from breaking WEP and passwords on different routers are visible.

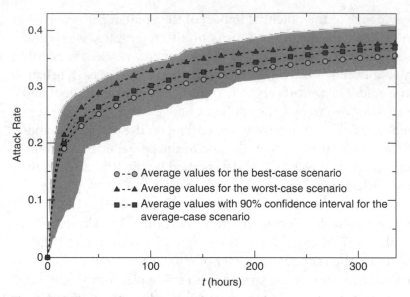

Figure 5.12: Best- and worst-case epidemic spread compared with the average case and 90% confidence interval.

phenomenon. Specifically, we see sharp increases in infection rates in time periods after 48 hours, where WEP encryption schemes are broken on routers, making them vulnerable to attack. In addition, Figure 5.12 reports the average attack rate obtained in the best- and worst-case scenarios, together with the average scenario accompanied by its fluctuations. The best and worst cases are both within the 90% confidence interval of the average case, showing that a change in the parameter values of the infection processes considered did not affect the results obtained with the average estimated parameter values.

A more complicated issue is understanding the different infection rates that the epidemic attained in different urban area networks—that is, of the routers in a given giant component on which an epidemic spread, which fraction of them at a given time became infected. This percentage of infected routers in a component at a given time is termed the *attack rate*. The pervasiveness of the epidemic can be seen as a percolation effect on the WiFi network [153]. The WPA-encrypted routers and those with unbreakable passwords represent obstacles to the percolation process and define an effective percolation probability that has to be compared with the intrinsic percolation threshold of the network. Indeed, percolation refers to the emergence of a connected subgraph of infected routers spanning the whole network. This phenomenon is possible only if the probability that an infected router can find susceptible routers to be infected is larger than a threshold value (the percolation threshold). The larger the probability of finding susceptible routers with respect to the threshold, the larger the final density of infected routers will be.

The percolation thresholds of the networks were not easily estimated because they are embedded in the particular geometries of the cities' geographies. In addition, the cities have different fractions of encrypted routers. While these fractions are not extremely dissimilar, it is clear that given the nonlinear effect close to the percolation threshold, small differences could lead to a large difference in the final attack rate. For instance, San Francisco, with the largest fraction of encrypted routers, corresponding to about 40% of the population, exhibited the smallest attack rate among all the urban areas considered.

Other network features, such as the geometric constraints imposed by the urban area geography, might also have a large impact on the percolation threshold, which can be rather sensitive to the local graph topology. For instance, network layouts with one-dimensional bottlenecks or locally very sparse connectivity may consistently lower the attack rate by sealing part of the network, thereby protecting it from the epidemic. Indeed, a few WPA routers at key bottlenecks could make entire subnetworks of the giant component impenetrable to the malware. This point is discussed further in Section 5.2.7.

The present results offer general quantitative conclusions on the impact and threat offered by the WiFi malware spreading in different areas given current router deployment habits.

5.2.7 Going Forward

Epidemic Spread: WEP and WPA Deployment and Router Density

Because routers can infect only other neighboring routers in the immediate broadcast area, and because routers are immobile, the number of susceptible routers an infected router can infect is fixed. This can have a huge effect on the spread of an epidemic, because if large, relatively well-connected subgraphs of a graph's components are weakly connected through a small number of edges, then an epidemic's progress could be slowed or blocked at these edges.

Figures 5.13, 5.14, and 5.15 consider three progressions of an epidemic on the same graph. All are seeded from the same location. Note that the contagion graph contains two well-connected subgraphs (denoted by the dashed rectangles), but the two subgraphs are connected by a single edge, called the bridge. All of the routers in each of the figures have the same epidemiological dynamics class *except* for the router connected on the left side of the bridge link. In each progression, the epidemic's progress in time is illustrated going from left to right. Consider the differences in the epidemic's outbreak in these three cases, paying attention to its effect on the left subgraph.

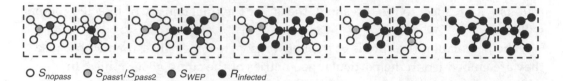

○ S_{nopass} ◔ S_{pass1}/S_{pass2} ● S_{WEP} ● $R_{infected}$

Figure 5.13: The epidemic is not blocked going over the bridge owing to the default password on router on the left of the bridge. Therefore the left subgraph succumbs to infection.

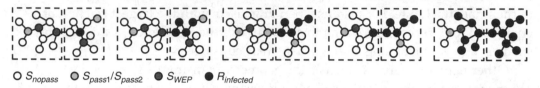

○ S_{nopass} ◔ S_{pass1}/S_{pass2} ● S_{WEP} ● $R_{infected}$

Figure 5.14: The epidemic is delayed going over the bridge owing to the WEP encryption on the router on the bridge's left side. The left subgraph still succumbs to infection, but it is delayed.

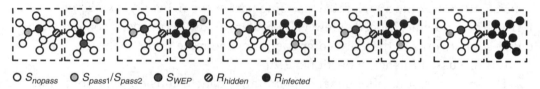

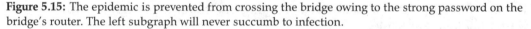

○ S_{nopass} ◔ S_{pass1}/S_{pass2} ● S_{WEP} ⊘ R_{hidden} ● $R_{infected}$

Figure 5.15: The epidemic is prevented from crossing the bridge owing to the strong password on the bridge's router. The left subgraph will never succumb to infection.

In the first progression in Figure 5.13, we see that an infected router in the right subgraph quickly spreads to the left subgraph through the bridge, as the router on the left side of the bridge is completely susceptible to the malware owing to its default password.

In the second progression in Figure 5.14, we see the same initial conditions as in Figure 5.13, with the exception that the router on the left side of the bridge now has WEP installed. The malware infection of the left subgraph is now delayed, owing to the time necessary to break the WEP encryption on the bridge's router. Because the bridge is the only avenue for the malware to spread to the left subgraph, the epidemic is delayed there owing to the WEP. However, because WEP can eventually be overcome, the left subgraph will eventually fall to the epidemic.

Finally, in Figure 5.15, we have the same initial conditions as in Figures 5.13 and 5.14, but now the router connected to the left of the bridge is in the R_{hidden} class. Again, this implies that the router is not susceptible to infection. Therefore, the entire left subgraph will never succumb to the infection, as the epidemic would need to pass over the bridge, and its access there is blocked. In practice, one could imagine that the bridge does not exist, as the infection will not be able to spread over it and, therefore, that there are two separate graphs, making it clear that the infection cannot jump from the right graph to the left.

This phenomenon helps to explain why it is possible to drastically reduce the effects of wireless epidemics if only a few people improve their security, assuming that these individuals are correctly placed in the graph. However, as the general security of routers increases, the connectivity of the graph effectively decreases due to (1) the number of routers that use WPA encryption and thus are removed from the graph completely, and (2) the number of routers that have strong passwords and thus are removed from the graph. As the connectivity of the graph decreases, the size of the largest component can substantially shrink, remarkably reducing the risk for large infection.

A New Wireless Security Law in California

In October 2007, the state of California enacted a bill (AB2415) that requires new security measures to be deployed by router manufacturers selling to the home router market. Specifically, it requires that manufacturers warn users about the potential insecurity of wireless signals. At least one warning sticker must be positioned so that the router cannot be used without the consumer removing it. The main goal of this law seems to be aimed at halting roaming and neighboring users from piggybacking on home and small-business routers' signals, if the owners of these routers did not specifically intend for such behavior.

While this law is sure to have some effect on both the rate at which nondefault passwords occur on routers and the rate at which home routers are deployed with encrypted communications channels, it is far from clear that the prescribed measures will have any beneficial effect in terms of reducing the attack rates of router epidemics, as postulated here. For example, many router companies suggest the use of WEP as a plausible encryption protocol for home users to deploy. As has been seen, this will affect only the rate of spread, and not the number of routers that get compromised. Similarly, encouraging users to change passwords does not mean that they will select strong passwords. Work by Stephano and Groth [390] shows that there is reason to believe that the new security measures put in place by some of the largest router vendors will have little effect on practical security outcomes. In particular, they found that while many users changed the default administrative password with new router installation software meant to comply with the law, few users were able to enable encrypted communications channels.

Chapter 6

Crimeware in the Browser

*Dan Boneh, Mona Gandhi, Collin Jackson, Markus Jakobsson,
John Mitchell, Zulfikar Ramzan, Jacob Ratkiewicz, and Sid Stamm*

This chapter considers crimeware that executes solely in the user's web browser,
but that does not exploit a vulnerability on that browser. The chapter starts with
a discussion of *transaction generators*, which can be used to modify online
transactions (performed using a web browser) in real time. Next, the concept of
a *drive-by pharming* attack is studied—this attack shows how home router DNS
settings can be changed when the victim simply views an external web page.
Finally, this chapter considers *badvertisements*, which demonstrate how JavaScript
can be used to simulate fraudulent clicks on online advertisements.

6.1 Transaction Generators: Rootkits for the Web*

Current phishing attacks steal user credentials, either by directing users to a
spoofed web page that fools them into revealing a password, or by installing
keylogging malware that records user passwords and sends them to the phisher. In
response, web sites are deploying a variety of back-end analytic tools [74, 301, 325]
that use past user behavior to determine transaction risk, such as the time of day
when the user is typically active and the user's IP address and location. Some sites
are moving to stronger authentication using one-time password tokens such as
RSA SecurID [359]. These methods, as well as many other anti-phishing

---

* This section is by Collin Jackson, Dan Boneh, and John Mitchell.

proposals [86, 163, 206, 300, 357, 486], focus primarily on reducing the value that phishers derive from stolen passwords.

Fortunately for thieves, and unfortunately for the rest of us, a new form of attack using a transaction generator (TG) allows criminals to manipulate user accounts directly without stealing user credentials or subverting authentication mechanisms. TG attacks generate fraudulent transactions from the user's computer, through malicious browser extensions, after the user has authenticated to the site. A TG quietly sits on the user's machine and waits for the user to log in to a banking or retail site. Once the authentication completes, web sites typically issue a session cookie used to authenticate subsequent messages from the browser. These session cookies reside in the browser and are fully accessible to malware. A TG can thus wait for the user to securely log in to the site and then use the session cookie to issue transactions on behalf of the user, transferring funds out of the user's account or purchasing goods and mailing them off as "gifts." To the web site, a transaction issued by a TG looks identical to a legitimate transaction issued by the user—it originates from the user's normal IP address at the usual time of day—making it hard for analytic tools to detect.

Because TGs typically live inside the user's browser as a browser extension, SSL provides no defense against a TG. Moreover, a clever TG can hide its transactions using stealth techniques discussed in the next section. To date, we have seen only few reports of TGs in the wild [374], but we anticipate seeing many more reports as adoption of stronger authentication becomes widespread.

In Section 6.1.3, we explore a number of mitigation techniques, including transaction confirmation. A transaction confirmation system consists of isolated client-side software and a trusted path to the user that enables web sites to request confirmation for transactions that the site deems risky.

Cross-Site Request Forgery. At a first glance, a TG may appear to be related to cross-site request forgery (CSRF) [72]. A CSRF vulnerability is caused by an incorrect implementation of user authentication at the web site. To prevent CSRF attacks, the web site need only implement a small change to its user authentication system; this modification is transparent to the user. In contrast, a TG running inside a client browser is much harder to block, and defenses against it require changes to the user experience at the site.

6.1.1 Building a Transaction Generator

TGs can lead to many types of illegal activity:

- *Pump-and-dump stock schemes* [324]. The TG buys prespecified stock on a prespecified date to artificially increase the value of penny stock.

- *Purchasing goods.* The TG purchases goods and has them shipped to a forwarding address acquired earlier by the phisher.

- *Election system fraud.* For voting-at-home systems, such as those used for collecting shareholder votes, a TG can be used to alter votes in one way or another.

- *Financial theft.* A TG can use a bill-pay service to transfer funds out of a victim account.

Example. Building a TG is trivial, as shown in the following hypothetical example. This Firefox extension waits for the user to land on the www.retailer.com/loggedin page, which is reached once the user has properly logged in at the retailer. The TG then issues a purchase request to www.retailer.com/buy and orders 10 blenders to be sent to some address in Kansas. Presumably the phisher hired the person in Kansas to ship the blenders to an offshore address. The person in Kansas (the "mule") may have no idea that he or she is involved in illegal activity.

```
<?xml version="1.0"?>
<overlay xmlns="http://www.mozilla.org/keymaster/gatekeeper/
there.is.only.xul">
<script>
document.getElementById("appcontent")
        .addEventListener("load", function() {
  var curLocation =
    getBrowser().selectedBrowser.contentDocument.location;
  if(curLocation.href.indexOf("www.retailer.com/loggedin") > 0)
  {
    var xhr = new XMLHttpRequest();
    xhr.open("POST", "https://www.retailer.com/buy");
    xhr.send("item=blender&amp;quantity=10&amp;address=Kansas");
  }
}, true);
</script></overlay>
```

6.1.2 Stealthy Transaction Generators

Transactions generated by a TG will show up on any transaction report page (e.g., an "items purchased" page) at the web site. A clever TG in the user's browser can intercept report pages and erase its own transactions from the report. As a result, the user cannot tell that fraud occurred just by looking at pages at the site. For example, the following single JavaScript line removes all table rows on a transaction history page that refer to a blender:

```
document.body.innerHTML =
    document.body.innerHTML.replace(
        /<tr>.*?blender.*?<\/tr>/gi, "");
```

We have tested this code on several major retailer web sites.

Moreover, suppose a user pays her credit card bills online. The TG can wait for the user to log in to her credit card provider site and then erase the fraudulent transactions from the provider's report page, using the same line of JavaScript shown previously. The sum total amount remains unchanged, but the fraudulent transaction does not appear in the list of transactions. Because most consumers do not bother to check the arithmetic on report pages from their bank, the consumer will pay her credit card bill in full and remain unaware that the bill includes a stealthy fraudulent transaction. This behavior is analogous to how rootkits hide themselves by hiding their footprints on the infected system.

The net result of stealth techniques is that the consumer will never know that her machine issued a nonconfirmed transaction and will never know that she paid for the transaction.

6.1.3 Countermeasures

Mitigation Techniques

We discuss three potential mitigation techniques against the stealthy TGs discussed in the previous section. The first two are easy to deploy, but can be defeated. The third approach is the one we advocate.

1. CAPTCHA. A CAPTCHA (Completely Automated Public Turing test to tell Computers and Humans Apart) on the retailer's checkout page will make it harder for a TG to issue transactions automatically. Retailers, however, balk at this idea because the CAPTCHA complicates the checkout procedure and can reduce conversion rates. There are also security concerns because phishers can hire real people to solve CAPTCHAs. After all, if one can buy a $50 blender for free, it is worth paying $0.10 for someone to manually solve the challenge of the CAPTCHA. Alternatively, the malware may try to fool the authenticated user into solving the CAPTCHA for a malicious transaction, while the user thinks he or she is solving the CAPTCHA for some other purpose. Overall, we believe CAPTCHAs cannot defeat a clever TG.

2. Randomized Transaction Pages. As mentioned earlier, a stealthy TG can remove its transactions from an online credit card bill, thus hiding its tracks. Credit card providers can make this a little more difficult by presenting the bill as an image or by randomizing the structure of the bill. As a result, it is more difficult for a TG to make surgical changes to the bill.

3. Transaction Confirmation: A Robust Defense. An online merchant can protect itself from TGs by using a confirmation system that enables users to confirm every transaction. The confirmation system should be unobtrusive and easy to use.

Here we propose a simple web-based confirmation system that can be deployed with minimal changes to the web site. The system combines confirmation with the checkout process. On the client side, the system consists of two components:

- A confirmation agent that is isolated from malware infecting the browser. In our prototype implementation (called SpyBlock), the browser runs in a virtual machine (VM) while the agent runs outside the VM. Alternatively, the confirmation agent might live on a separate hardware device such as a USB token or a Bluetooth cell phone.

- A browser extension that functions as an untrusted relay between the confirmation agent and the remote web site.

We briefly describe the confirmation process here. The confirmation agent and remote web site share an ephemeral secret key generated by an identity system such as CardSpace during user login. During checkout, the remote web site can request transaction confirmation by embedding the following simple JavaScript on the checkout page:

```
if (window.spyblock) {
  spyblock.confirm(document.form1.transaction, {
    observe: function(subject, topic, data) {
      document.form1.transactionMAC.value = data;
} }; }
```

This script interacts with the untrusted browser extension that relays the transaction details to the confirmation agent. The confirmation agent displays the details to the user and asks the user to confirm the transaction. If the user confirms, the agent sends back a MAC of the transaction details to the browser extension, which then forwards the MAC to the remote web site. The web site verifies that the MAC is valid: if it is valid, the web site fulfills the transaction.

Security relies on two properties. First, the agent's secret key must be isolated from malware. Second, the confirmation dialog must not be obscured by a malware pop-up to ensure that the user confirms the correct transaction details. Similarly, malware must be prevented from injecting mouse clicks into the agent's dialog. Note that simply spoofing the confirmation dialog is of no use to the TG, because it cannot generate the necessary MAC itself.

A Nonsolution

Clearly, a potential solution to the TG problem is to prevent malware from getting into the browser in the first place. However, the widespread penetration of end-user machines by spyware and bot networks [263] underscores the vulnerability of many of today's machines to malware attacks. We do not expect this situation to change any time soon.

Conclusion

Transaction generators are a source of concern for enterprises engaged in online commerce [88]. As stronger authentication systems are deployed, we expect transaction generators to pose an increasing threat. This emerging form of malware hijacks legitimate sessions and generates fraudulent transactions using legitimate credentials, instead of stealing authentication credentials. By operating within the browser, TGs can potentially hide their effects by altering the user's view of information provided by any site. Consequently, it is necessary to extend identity systems, such as CardSpace, to include a transaction confirmation component.

6.2 Drive-By Pharming*

This section describes an attack concept termed drive-by pharming, where an attacker sets up a web page that, when simply viewed by the victim, attempts to change the settings on the victim's home broadband router. In particular, the attacker can change the router's DNS[1] server settings. Future DNS queries are then resolved by a DNS server of the attacker's choice. The attacker can direct the victim's Internet traffic and point the victim to the attacker's own web sites regardless of which domain the victim thinks he or she is actually visiting.

For example, the attacker can set up web sites that mimic the victim's bank. More generally, the attacker can set up a man-in-the-middle proxy that will record all traffic packets generated by the victim, including those that contain sensitive credentials such as usernames, passwords, credit card numbers, bank account numbers, and the like. To the victim, everything appears normal because the address bar on the browser displays the correct URL.

This type of attack could lead to the user's credentials being compromised and identity stolen. The same attack methodology could, in principle, be used to make other changes to the router, such as replacing its firmware. Routers could then host malicious web pages or engage in click fraud. Fortunately, drive-by pharming works only when the management password on the router is easily guessed. The remainder of this section describes this kind of attack, its implications, and overall defense strategies.

---

* This section is by Markus Jakobsson, Zulfikar Ramzan, and Sid Stamm.
1. This section assumes the reader is familiar with concepts such as the domain name system (DNS) and pharming; these concepts are described in Section 1.4.6.

6.2.1 The Drive–By Pharming Attack Flow

The flow in a drive-by pharming attack is as follows:

1. The attacker sets up a web page that contains malicious JavaScript code.

2. The attacker uses some ruse to get the victim to visit the web page. For example, the web page could offer news stories, salacious gossip, or illicit content. Alternatively, the attacker could purchase inexpensive banner advertisements for selective keywords.

3. The victim views the malicious page.

4. The page, now running in the context of the user's browser, uses a cross-site request Forgery (CSRF) to attempt a login into the victim's home broadband router.

5. If the login is successful, the attacker changes the victim's DNS settings. This approach works in part because home broadband routers offer a web-based interface for configuration management and, therefore, can be configured through an HTTP request, which can be generated through appropriate JavaScript code.

6. Once the victim's DNS settings are altered, future DNS requests are resolved by the attacker. The next time the victim attempts to go to a legitimate site, such as one corresponding to his or her bank or credit card company, the attacker can instead trick the user into going to an illegitimate site that the attacker set up. The victim will have difficulty knowing that he or she is at an illegitimate site because the address bar on the web browser will show the URL of the legitimate site (not to mention that the content on the illegitimate site can be a direct replica of the content on the legitimate site).

This flow is depicted graphically in Figure 6.1. More details on drive-by pharming can be obtained from the original technical report on the subject [389].

6.2.2 Prior Related Work

At Black Hat 2006, Jeremiah Grossman presented mechanisms for using JavaScript to scan and fingerprint hosts on an internal network [157]. He also suggested that an attacker could mount a CSRF against these devices.

A few months earlier, Tsow [425] described how routers could be used to perpetrate pharming attacks [4]. Subsequently, Tsow et al. [426] described how wardriving could be combined with malicious firmware upgrades, giving rise to the recent term *warkitting*. These last two works assume some physical proximity to the router being manipulated. For the case of wireless routers, the attacker has to be

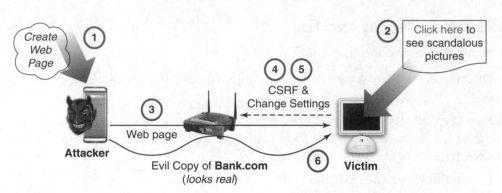

Figure 6.1: The flow of a drive-by pharming attack. (1) The attacker creates a web page and then (2) lures a victim into viewing it. When the web page is (3) viewed, the attacker's page attempts a (4) cross-site request forgery on the victim's home broadband router and (5) attempts to change its settings. If successful, the victim's future DNS requests will (6) be resolved by the attacker.

located within the router's signal range. For the case of wired routers, the attacker must have physical access to the device.

The drive-by pharming attack described in this section observes that JavaScript host scanning and CSRFs can be used to eliminate the need for physical proximity in these router attacks. It is sufficient that the victim navigates to a corrupted site for the router to be at risk. It is a mistake to believe that only "reckless" web surfers are at risk for the attack described here; consider, for example, an attacker who places banner advertisements (for any type of product or service) and probes everyone that is referred to the "advertisement site." The underlying details of the attack from a purely technical perspective are, in our opinion, not nearly as interesting as the potential implications of drive-by pharming.

6.2.3 Attack Details

This subsection describes the drive-by pharming attack in more detail. First, we begin from the bottom up by describing how a CSRF can be used to log in to and change DNS settings on a specific home broadband router, assuming that the attacker knows which router the victim uses, and assuming the attacker knows where on the network the router is located. Second, we explain techniques that allow an attacker to determine which router the victim's network is actually using. Third, we describe how JavaScript host scanning can be used to identify where the router is located on the internal network, assuming the attacker knows the internal IP address space of the network. Fourth, we describe how the internal IP address of the network can be determined using a Java applet.

Most home broadband routers are located at a default IP address, so the first two steps will likely be sufficient for carrying out the attack. Because these steps require only some basic JavaScript, the entire attack can be carried out using JavaScript. To maximize the likelihood that the attacker succeeds, the attack can be augmented using a Java applet, although this step—while helpful—may not be necessary.

Configuring Home Routers Through Cross-Site Request Forgeries

Most home routers use a web-based interface for configuration management. When the user wants to change the router's settings, he or she simply types in the router's internal IP address into the web browser—for example, http://192.168.1.1. The user is then typically prompted for the username and password for the router. (Note that this username and password are separate from the credentials associated with the user's Internet service provider; for example, if the user were using DSL, these credentials would be separate from his or her PPPoE credentials.) At this point, the user is typically presented with a form. Changes can be entered into this form, and the changes are passed in a query string to a CGI script, which in turn modifies the settings and updates the router.

For a specific router, JavaScript code of the following form can automate the process:

```
<SCRIPT SRC = "http://username:password@192.168.1.1/foo.cgi?dns=1.2.3.4">
</SCRIPT>
```

Taken verbatim, this script will not actually work on any of the well-known routers—but modified appropriately it will. To be successful, this script assumes that the attacker has five pieces of information:

- The username and password for the router
- The IP address of the router
- The actual name of the CGI script the router uses
- The actual name of the parameter for changing the DNS settings
- The correct format for submitting updated values

Given that many people use the default username and password for their home broadband router, the first assumption is reasonable. Similarly, the second assumption is reasonable because these routers use a default IP address. Also, the third, fourth, and fifth assumptions are reasonable because the script and parameter names as well as the query string format are uniform for a given router model. To extend the attack to different types of routers, the attacker must determine which router brand is being used. We will describe how that can be done.

Device Fingerprinting

A simple technique (which can be implemented using basic JavaScript and HTML) allows one to determine the brand of a user's home router. Basically, each router hosts a set of web pages that are used as a configuration management interface. These web pages display, among other things, images such as the router manufacturer's logo. An attacker can determine the path names of these logo images ahead of time, and then use an HTML <IMG> tag in conjunction with the OnLoad() handler to perform attack steps for specific routers as follows:

```
<IMG SRC = "http://router-IP-address/path-to-logo/specific-logo"
OnLoad = Do-Bad-Stuff()">
```

If the specific logo file exists at the specified IP address, then the image will be loaded. In that case, the OnLoad() handler will execute the malicious code. Again, the code assumes that the attacker knows the IP address of the router. As remarked previously, there are well-known defaults for this IP address, and using one of them will likely yield a successful result.

It turns out, though, that there are techniques for determining the router's IP address even if it is not at the default location. One way to do so is by

1. Determining the internal IP address of the victim's machine; and

2. Scanning the local address space for the router.

It turns out that (1) can be done using a simple Java applet and (2) can be done in JavaScript. We describe these techniques next.

Internal IP Address Determination and JavaScript Host Scanning

Using a Java applet developed by Lars Kinderman [214], one can determine the internal IP address of the machine. Note that the applet finds the *internal* address. Therefore, being behind a firewall or proxy server will not protect the end user. An alternative approach was described by Petkov [311].

Once the local IP address is known, one can loop through all addresses on the same subnet (for example, by trying different values for the last octet of the IP address). At each address, the attacker can use the previously mentioned finger-printing techniques. Given the internal IP address, one can usually determine which address to start with when doing such a scan. Because most home networks are small, finding the IP address of the home broadband router will not take many tries. The general technique of JavaScript host scanning was described by Grossman [157].

6.2.4 Additional Comments

Visiting the Attacker's Web Page

To become victimized, all a user has to do is examine a web page containing the offending JavaScript code. No traditional download and installation of malicious software is necessary; simply looking at the web page is enough.

One approach that an attacker can take is to set up the malicious web page and then drive traffic to it—for example, by making the site contain attractive content (such as salacious celebrity gossip, or illicit photos). The attacker can also try to manipulate search engine rankings by including popular content. Finally, the attacker can drive traffic by purchasing banner ads and strategic keywords.

Alternatively, an attacker can try to break into an existing web server and host malicious code on its web pages. Then, all visitors to those web pages will be victimized.

A third possibility is for an attacker to find a cross-site scripting vulnerability on an existing web site. Such a vulnerability can, for example, allow an attacker to inject JavaScript code into a web page. One common case is for the code to be injected through the query string on a URL that points to a server-side script. Then, anyone who visits the URL with that particular query string will run the attacker's code in the context of the user's web browser. The attacker can advertise the URL in an email message or as a hyperlink off another web page (or even using a banner advertisement). Victims might be more inclined to click on the hyperlink, especially if the attacker found a cross-site scripting vulnerability on a well-known site.

Drive-By Pharming in the Wild

As of October 2007, no examples of drive-by pharming were actually known in the wild. Nevertheless, this kind of attack is fairly simple and involves piecing together well-known building blocks. Also, the attack has potentially devastating consequences, because the victim merely needs to view the offending web page for the attacker to effectively control the victim's Internet connection. Given that the attack affects potentially anyone with a home broadband router, the implications are staggering. Therefore, it would not be a stretch to imagine that attackers will employ this attack (if they have not done so already). We believe that anyone sufficiently familiar with the technical details of concepts such as JavaScript host scanning and CSRFs could put the pieces of the drive-by pharming attack together. The underlying technical details are, in many ways, less interesting than the overall implications.

Fortunately, there are many simple countermeasures to drive-by pharming, which we discuss later. Given the simplicity of the attack and the simplicity of the defense, we thought it prudent to warn people of the threat before they became victims.

Proof of Concept

We implemented proof-of-concept systems to test the drive-by pharming attack methodology, in which we changed a router's server settings and verified that the new server was being used to resolve requests. We were successfully able to carry out the attack methodology on the following routers: Linksys WRT54GS, Netgear WGR614, and a D-Link DI-524. Given that Linksys, Netgear, and D-Link represent three of the largest home broadband router manufacturers, the number of affected routers is potentially very large.

6.2.5 Countermeasures

A number of simple countermeasures may be deployed to defend against drive-by pharming attacks. We describe some of these measures here.

Changing the Router Password

The simplest way to defend against this kind of attack is to change the administrative password on the home broadband router to something less easily guessed by the attacker. (Note that this password is separate from the one used to actually gain Internet access.) The Symantec Security Response web log contains links to the password change pages for Linksys, Netgear, and D-Link routers [327]. If the attacker guesses the wrong password, then a dialog box will pop up alerting the user of an incorrect guess, which might arouse suspicion. Therefore, the attacker has to guess the password correctly the first time (which implies that even a mildly difficult-to-guess password defends against this attack). However, we still recommend that users choose a strong password.

Local Firewall Rules

If a user is employing a PC-level firewall, such as the one found in the Norton Internet Security software suite, then the user can add rules to the firewall that alert users of connections to the router's management interface. (Note that many PC-level firewall programs might not allow fine-grained user-defined rules.)

CSRF Protection of Routers

There are numerous techniques to make one's web site secure against CSRFs, such as the one described for the drive-by pharming attack. For example, the web site can require a hidden (and unpredictable) variable to be submitted as part of any form input—perhaps the session ID. This input can be validated by the web server before it honors any client requests. If a user is legitimately changing the router settings, then this variable will be passed along with the form input, and the changes will be processed. An attacker, by contrast, will not know the value of the variable and, therefore, cannot include it in his or her request. The validation attempt by the web server will fail, and the request will not be completed. Note that DNS rebinding attacks, which are covered in Chapter 7, can be used to overcome CSRF protection in routers.

A number of other approaches can also be used to defend against drive-by pharming attacks. A full treatment of such approaches is beyond the scope of this section.

Conclusion

This section described drive-by pharming, a type of attack that allows an attacker to change the DNS server settings on a user's home broadband router. Once these settings are changed, future DNS queries will be resolved by the attacker's DNS server. The result is that the attacker effectively controls the victim's Internet connection and can use that control to obtain any sensitive information the victim enters as part of an Internet transaction (e.g., passwords, credit card numbers, bank account numbers). The attack requires only some simple native JavaScript code, and the victim merely has to view the malicious page.

In addition to pharming, this attack methodology can be used to make other router configuration changes, such as malicious firmware upgrades. We believe drive-by pharming has serious widespread implications because it could potentially affect any home broadband user. Fortunately, there are a number of simple defenses, including changing the password on the home broadband router. A more thorough technical report that goes into the attack details is available online [389].

6.3   Using JavaScript to Commit Click Fraud*

This chapter introduces a new and dangerous technique for turning web-site visitors into unwitting click-fraudsters. Many recent click fraud attacks have been based on traditional malware, which installs itself on a user's machine and simulates the clicking of advertisements by the user [150, 230, 296, 483]. The attack presented here is certainly easier to accomplish than that of infecting a machine with malware, as all it requires is that a user visit a web site in a JavaScript-enabled browser. This attack, which is referred to as a badvertisement, has been experimentally verified on several prominent advertisement schemes.

---

*This section is by Mona Gandhi, Markus Jakobsson, and Jacob Ratkiewicz.

In brief, the attack allows a fraudster to force unwitting accessories to perform *automated click-throughs* on ads hosted by the fraudster, resulting in revenue generation for the fraudster at the expense of advertisers. This means a higher number of visits registered for a sponsored ad, leading to a higher per-ad cut revenue for the publisher. While it may at first appear that this attack should be easily detected by inspection of the click-through rates from the domain in question, this is unfortunately not so. The fraudster can cause both click-throughs and non-click-throughs (in any desired proportion) to be generated by the traffic accessing the corrupted page, while keeping end users corresponding to both of these classes unaware of the advertisement. A fraudster can even generate click-fraud revenue from traffic to a site that is not allowed to display advertisements from a given provider. A typical example of such a site would be a pornographic site.

Owners of sites that are used to generate revenue for a "badvertiser" might be unaware of the attack they are part of. Given the invisibility of the attack, domain owners may remain unaware of the existence of an attack mounted by a corrupt web master of theirs, or a person who is able to impersonate the web master. The latter ties the problem back into phishing once again.

This section starts by defining some important terms. It then gives an overview of the basic building blocks of the attack before diving into the implementation details of making a badvertisement in Section 6.3.3. Section 6.3.4 explains in detail the techniques used to cover the attacker's tracks to prevent discovery performed using *reverse spidering*. We then describe scenarios that can be used as potential media for deploying such attacks and explore the economic losses associated with their implementation in Section 6.3.7. Finally, we outline some potential countermeasures.

6.3.1 Terms and Definitions

The following are definitions of terms as used in the context of click fraud.

Phishing. Attempting to fraudulently acquire a person's credentials, usually for financial gain.

JavaScript. A simple programming language that is interpreted by web browsers. It enables web site designers to embed programs in web pages, making them potentially more interactive. Despite its simplicity, JavaScript is quite powerful.

REFERER. When a web browser visits a site, it transmits to the site the URL of the page it was linked from, if any. That is, if a user is at site B and clicks a link

to site A, when the web browser visits A, it tells A that B is its REFERER. The
REFERER information need not always be provided, however. Note that this
word is not spelled in the same way as the English word "referrer."

Spidering. The process of surfing the web, storing URLs, and indexing
keywords, links, and text. It is commonly used by search engines in their
efforts to index web pages [385].

robots.txt. A file that may be included at the top level of a web site, specifying
which pages the web master does not wish web spiders to crawl. Compliance is
completely voluntary on the part of web spiders, but is considered good
etiquette [353].

Reverse spidering. When an ad is clicked, the ad provider can track the page
responsible for serving that ad. That page is known as the REFERER of the ad.
We use the term "reverse spidering" to refer to the ad provider's spidering of
the REFERER page [140].

Dual-personality page. A page that appears differently when viewed by
different agents, or depending on other criteria. Typically one "personality"
of the page may be termed "good" and the other "evil."

6.3.2 Building Blocks

The badvertisement attack consist of two components: delivery and execution. The
first component either brings users to the corrupt information or brings corrupt
information to the users. The second component causes the automated but
invisible display of an advertisement to a targeted user.

The Delivery Component

Bringing users to the corrupt information may rely either on sites that users visit
voluntarily and intentionally due to their content or on sites that may contain
information of no particular value, but which users are tricked to visit.

Users may be tricked to visit sites using known techniques for page rank
manipulation. Fraudsters may also use spam as a delivery approach and try to
entice recipients to click on a link, causing a visit to a site with badvertisements.
Sophisticated spam-driven attempts may rely on user-specific context to improve
the probabilities of visits. For example, a fraudster may send out email that appears
to be an electronic postcard sent by a friend of the recipient; when the recipient
clicks on the link, he or she will activate the badvertisement. An 80% visit rate was
achieved in recent experiments by Jagatic et al. [197] by using relational knowledge
collected from social network sites.

Bringing corrupt information to users may simply mean sending emails with content causing an advertisement to be clicked. This is possible whenever the targeted user has a mail reader in which JavaScript is enabled.

The Execution Component

For all situations described here, successful execution can be achieved when the fraudster can cause the spam email in question to be delivered and viewed by the targeted user. The increasing sophistication of spammers' obfuscation techniques means that one cannot count on a spam filter as the only line of defense against badvertisement attacks delivered through email. Although this delivery component is similar to that used by phishing attacks, here the message can be much more general and, therefore, more difficult to identify and filter. The JavaScript code actually containing the attack cannot reliably be filtered or identified, owing to the vast array of ways in which this code can be obfuscated.

Here's an example of how `eval` may be used to obfuscate JavaScript code. The statement

```
for( i = 1; i <= 10; i++ ) {
    document.write ( i );
}
```

is functionally equivalent to the statement

```
code = "f@o"+"#r(i@"+"#="+1+";@"+"i#<=1%0"+";i"
       +"+@ #+){@"+"d#oc"+"%um#"+"en%t."+"@w#r"
       +"i#te"+"(@i + \"<b" + "r >\");}";
eval(code.replace(/[@#%]/g, ""));
```

Each statement prints the numbers 1–10 when executed by a JavaScript interpreter.

The badvertisment attack does rely on clients having JavaScript enabled. This is not a real limitation, however, both because 90% of web browsers have it enabled and because the advertising services themselves count on users having JavaScript enabled. Thus the execution component of the attack relies simply on a JavaScript trick that causes an ad to be automatically clicked and processed by a client's web browser. This causes the click to be counted by the server side, which in turn triggers a transfer of funds from the advertiser to the domain hosting the advertisement (i.e., the fraudster).

The key feature of a successful attack is to display effectively different text to the user than to any agent that audits the advertiser for policy compliance. This is not as simple as serving a different page to any agent identifying itself as a web spider; it is, for example, known that Google performs some amount of spidering without identifying itself as Google [43].

6.3.3 The Making of a Badvertisement

A successful badvertisement is one that is able to silently generate automatic click-throughs on advertisement banners when users visit the site, but remains undetected by auditing agents of the ad provider. Further, while the ad provider may place restrictions on the type of content that may be shown on a page containing its ads, a fraudster would like to be able to show prohibited content (e.g., pornography) on the badvertisement pages that may draw higher traffic. To this end, we introduce two concepts—a façade page and a dual-personality page. A dual-personality page changes its personality (behavior) based on the kind of its visitor. For an oblivious visitor, the dual-personality page takes on its "evil" form to commit auto-clicking in the background. To avoid being caught, the dual-personality page takes on the "good" form for a suspicious auditor. Thus, when a spider crawls through pages to check for suspicious activities, it sees only the "good" side of the dual personality page.

To monetize prohibited content, the fraudster can use the façade page. It acts as an interface for the visitor to the dual-personality page and exists on a different domain that is not registered with the ad provider.

Figure 6.2 gives a graphical representation of these two pages. In the following explanations, we suppose the existence of two web sites: www.verynastyporn.com, which contains the façade page, and www.veryniceflorist.com, which is registered with the ad provider and contains the dual-personality page.

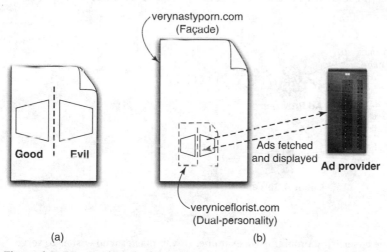

Figure 6.2: Pages to hide badvertisements from users and from auditors. (a) A dual-personality page. To an oblivious user it behaves in an "evil" manner and includes badvertisements (because it "knows" that it will not be detected). To a suspicious auditor, it appears good (because it has detected that it is being audited and has disabled any evil portion). (b) A dual-personality page included in a façade page.

Next, we give a brief overview of how JavaScript is used in these techniques. We then describe the implementation of both the façade page and the dual-personality page.

JavaScript for Click Fraud

Typical online advertisement services (such as AdBrite [3] and the others we examine) work by providing web masters with a snippet of JavaScript code to add to their pages. This code, which is executed by the web browser of a visitor to the site, downloads ads from the advertiser's server at that time. The ad download triggers a rewrite of the frame in which the JavaScript appears, replacing it with the HTML code necessary to display the ads. When a user clicks an advertisement link, he or she "clicks through" the ad provider's server, giving the ad provider the opportunity to bill the client for the click. The user is then taken to the ad client's home page. Figure 6.3 illustrates this scenario.

Badvertisements, then, contain additional JavaScript that simulates automatic clicking. This attack is accomplished as follows: After the advertiser's JavaScript code runs and modifies the page to contain the ads, the badvertisement JavaScript parses the resulting HTML and compiles a list of all hyperlinks. It then modifies the page to contain a hidden frame that loads an advertiser's site, creating the impression that the user has clicked an advertisement link (Figure 6.4).

JavaScript is used both by the legitimate advertiser and by the badvertiser. The latter uses JavaScript to parse and edit the JavaScript of the legitimate advertiser.

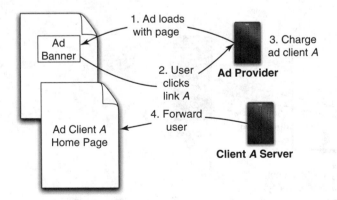

Figure 6.3: Normal use of the advertising programs we examine. A web master who wishes to serve sponsored advertisements places a snippet of JavaScript in his or her page that downloads ads from the ad provider when the page is loaded. If a user clicks a link for one of those ads, it is forwarded to the ad client. On the way, the click is registered so that the ad provider can bill the advertiser and pay the web master a share.

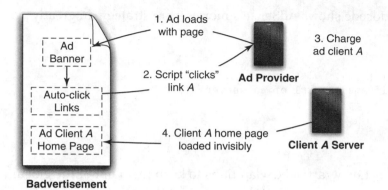

Badvertisement

Figure 6.4: Auto-clicking in a hidden badvertisment. Compared to Figure 6.3, the ad banner presented here is hidden. JavaScript code extracts links from the hidden ad banner and causes them to be displayed in an another hidden iframe, creating the impression that the user has clicked these links.

As an aside, note that it is possible for JavaScripts to be obfuscated to the point that their effect cannot be determined without actually executing them. This obfuscation allows the fraudster to hide the fact that an attack is taking place from bots that search for JavaScripts containing particular patterns that are known to be associated with badvertisements. One such obfuscation method is use of the eval keyword, which allows JavaScript code to programmatically evaluate arbitrarily complex JavaScript code represented as string constants. In essence, this technique allows the inclusion of arbitrary noise in the script, to make searching for tell-tale signs of click fraud fruitless.

Caveat. The attack we present here works on a large variety of platforms but, notably, not on Google AdSense. Google's approach is different in two ways from the vulnerable schemes that we show how to attack.

One difference lies in the fact that the code is downloaded from the Google server to fetch the ads (a script called show_ads.js). Whereas the attacked schemes allow these scripts to be accessed by another JavaScript component, this is prevented in AdSense by defining all functions inside a single anonymous function.

To illustrate this difference, here is pseudocode for the general strategy used by most providers to print ads:

```
function print_ads() {
  for(each ad) {
    document.write(text of ad);
  }
}
```

Note that each ad is inserted directly in the current document.

The following pseudocode shows AdSense's more secure strategy (in greatly simplified form):

```
(function() {
  function print_ads() {
    document.write("<iframe src=url of ad server>");
  }

  print_ads();
})()
```

Here, an anonymous function wraps all declarations to keep them out of the global namespace. Further, the downloaded script does not print the ads itself; it prints an internal frame (iframe) that draws its source from yet another script. This allows browser policies to protect the contents of the iframe from reading by other scripts in the page (such as badvertisment scripts).

A second distinction is that the AdSense code does not rewrite the current page to include the ads; it rewrites the current page to include an internal frame with its source set to the output of yet another script. It is this latter script that actually generates the ads. Given that the source of this generated frame is a Google server, JavaScripts served by other sites (such as any served by a fraudster) are prevented by a browser from accessing it. This would prevent a fraudster from fetching a list of links for auto-clicking.

6.3.4　Hiding the Attack

Client Evasion

As mentioned in the previous section, hidden frames can be used to create an impression of a click for the advertisement URL identified using JavaScript. Repeating this process several times will create the impression on the server side that the user has clicked several of the advertisement links, even though he or she may not have. The behavior described here is implemented in a dual-personality page placed on veryniceflorist.com. This entire site would then be included in a hidden frame in the façade page registered as verynastyporn.com. Thus it will invisibly generate artificial clicks that appear to come from veryniceflorist.com whenever a user visits verynastyporn.com.

Ad-Provider Evasion

Concealing the badvertisement from the legitimate ad provider is somewhat more difficult than hiding it from users. The auditing method commonly used by ad providers is a web spider that follows the REFERER links on clicked advertisements—that is, when a client clicks an ad on a page, an auditing spider

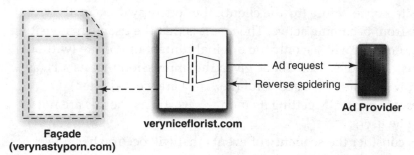

Façade
(verynastyporn.com)

Figure 6.5: Assignment of IDs prevents any agent not entering through the façade from seeing the evil JavaScript. The dual-personality page at veryniceflorist.com reveals its evil side only when passed an as-yet-unvisited ID. When it is given no ID or a visited ID, it shows its good side. When included from the façade page, veryniceflorist.com has an unvisited ID and thus contains badvertisments. However, when a user visits veryniceflorist.com normally, or when a reverse spider from the ad provider audits it, it will show its good side, because these requests contain no ID and a visited ID, respectively. Thus the only way to get veryniceflorist.com to expose its evil personality is to visit it through verynastyporn.com.

may choose to follow the REFERER link back to the page that served the clicked ad. The goal of the fraudster must then be to detect when the page is being viewed by an auditing spider and to serve a harmless page for that instance. The fraudster does so with the dual-personality page; the entire process is as follows (also summarized in Figure 6.5):

1. Create a personalization CGI script that runs when a user visits the façade. This script simply assigns a unique ID to the visitor and redirects the visitor to a second CGI script, passing the ID as a GET parameter so that it appears in the URL.

2. The second CGI script outputs the façade, complete with its script placeholder. This placeholder is configured to run a third CGI script, also passing the ID along.

3. The third CGI script may now choose which JavaScript to generate. If the ID passed has never been visited before, the CGI script will generate an "evil" JavaScript; if the ID has been previously visited, the CGI script will generate some "good" JavaScript. (This script might also use criteria other than an ID to determine which personality to show—for instance, REFERER, browser type, or even time of day.)

The overall effect of this rather strange configuration is a "one-way door" to the badvertisment. Users accessing the site through the façade load badvertisements (albeit in a manner invisible to them). Auditing agents following REFERER links from the ad provider's side will reach the dual-personality page, but because the links have been visited once before (by the client), the "one-way door" will prevent the evil personality from becoming active. The result is that the user, when visiting a site with badvertisements, will see only the original content of the site (without the badvertisements). The advertiser will be given the impression that its ads (as served by the ad provider) are very successful (i.e., they are viewed often). Of course, the advertiser is not really getting its money's worth, as the ads are not really being viewed by users.

As an example, consider the sequence of events that will occur when a user visits verynastyporn.com for the first time:

1. The visitor will first be served the façade page, which will invisibly include www.veryniceflorist.com. The user will also be assigned a unique ID, which will be passed to veryniceflorist.com.

2. A CGI script at veryniceflorist.com will output a completely legitimate page (including visible advertisements and no auto-clicking), but will also include a placeholder for another JavaScript.

3. The visitor's browser will request the JavaScript, passing the unique ID. The server will check whether the ID has already been registered; given that it will not be, the server will return the badvertisement JavaScript and register the ID as visited.

4. The user's browser will interpret the JavaScript, causing the ads in the (invisible) veryniceflorist.com site to be auto-clicked.

5. To the ad provider, the clicks will appear to come from veryniceflorist.com.

The fraudster may choose to pass on a large proportion of chances to serve badvertisements, so as to be more stealthy. This would be accomplished by modifying step 1 to not include veryniceflorist.com some proportion of the time, or by changing step 4 to not generate auto-clicks sometimes. The fraudster might also randomly choose which ad will be auto-clicked from the served list. This will ensure that the same IP address does not generate an excessive number of clicks for a single advertisement, as a different IP will initiate each.

Figure 6.5 illustrates how the web site will change its appearance only when safe to do so. Consider its behavior when visited by various agents:

- *Human visitor* (at verynastyporn.com). The human visitor will not navigate directly to the page; it will likely be invisibly included in the façade page. Thus the user will have an unvisited ID, and auto-clicks may be generated by the fraudster. In addition to considering only whether the ID has been visited, many other policies could be used to determine whether to serve the badvertisment. For instance, the evil web master might choose to serve only good scripts to users coming from a particular IP range or users visiting at a certain time of the day. Using techniques such as those described in [199], a web master might even choose to serve a particular script only to those users with certain other sites in their history.

- *Human visitor or standard spider* (at veryniceflorist.com). Here, the human visitor (or spider) will not have a unique ID, so veryniceflorist.com will show its good personality and not include auto-clicking.

- *Standard (forward) spider* (at verynastyporn.com). Typical web spiders do not evaluate JavaScript in pages. Indeed, it is in general not useful for a web spider to interpret JavaScript, as this is typically used to enhance interaction with users and not to generate text that the web spider might index. Here, however, this fact gives the fraudster an opportunity to hide illicit text from the web spider by causing that text to become available only through the interpretation of JavaScript. Thus, while a spider may visit the façade page and receive an unvisited unique ID, the fraudster may make the badvertisment page visible only after interpretation of JavaScript and, therefore, cause it to remain invisible to the spider.

- *Reverse spider* (at veryniceflorist.com). The reverse spider may not enter the site by way of the façade; rather, it follows a REFERER link on a clicked ad. Any REFERER link will contain the unique ID issued by the façade, and veryniceflorist.com will show its good personality to an already-visited ID. Because any ID in a REFERER link *must* already be visited (by the user who unwittingly generated the auto-click), the reverse spider will always see the good veryniceflorist.com page (even if it evaluates JavaScript).

In any case, the advertiser's detection of an offending site does not necessarily prevent its owner from earning any illicit revenue. A fraudster might, for example, register many veryniceflorist-like domains under different assumed names, and parcel traffic over them so that the advertiser's detection of any one of them eliminates only a portion of the total profits.

The knowledge that this could be the case would prevent an ad provider from immediately blacklisting a host upon detection of one (or a small number of) auto-clicks for a given domain. This behavior is of particular relevance in situations where the badvertisement is sent as spam to a user who is likely to use webmail for displaying his or her email, and where the ad provider may have a small number of email honeypots to detect such attacks.

6.3.5 Why Will Users Visit the Site?

The previous discussion stated that the fraudster will create a legitimate-appearing site that will be approved by the ad provider, and then create a badvertisement JavaScript function that will be loaded from an offsite server for execution only when innocent users visit the site. However, there are other ways the web master might lure users to visit the site, including the use of mass email and hosting the ads on pornographic websites (which itself is prohibited).

Email as a Lure. Multiple variations on the medium through which an attack can be mounted are possible, including through email messages. Email messages can either be spammed indiscriminately to many addresses or spoofed to users so as to appear to be from their acquaintances (cf. [197]). Each email might contain a "hook" line to encourage users to visit the site and a link to the portal page. This also reduces the possibility of a scenario in which a search engine locates the badvertisement, as the abuser would no longer need to list the portal page on any search engine. Thus an ad provider must trap such an email in an email honeypot to locate the site hosting the portal.

Popular Content as a Lure. Unscrupulous web masters with popular sites could easily employ this technique to increase their revenue. In particular, sites that host pornography can take advantage of the high traffic these sites typically generate by hosting hidden badvertisements. This threat was verified by a small experiment conducted at Berkeley, which found that approximately 28% of websites on the Internet contain pornographic content [37].

Although hosting ads with pornography is prohibited by the terms of service by almost all advertising programs, the techniques set forth here could enable a web master to hide all illicit content from spiders, showing it only to users. This would be done by rewriting the page on the client side using JavaScript. We consider this type of content to be distinct from viral content (described next) in terms of the effort that is required by the web master to promote it.

Viral Content as a Lure. A phenomenon associated with the social use of the Internet is the propagation of so-called viral content. This content is typically something that is considered interesting or amusing by a recipient and, therefore, propagates quickly from person to person [201]. A fraudster could host content likely to promote such distribution on his or her site (even cloning or stealing it from another site) and then distribute a link to this content through email, hoping that it is passed along. Such an attack could be perpetrated with minimal bootstrap effort compared to the previous scenario; while the scenario involving popular content as a lure assumes an already-established web site, here a fraudster need only steal a humorous video from another site (for instance) and spoof emails to a few thousand people, hoping they will be sent along.

6.3.6 Detecting and Preventing Abuse

There is an ongoing industry-wide effort to develop tools that will effectively detect and block many common click-fraud attacks. Most of the attacks discovered and reported so far have been malware-based attacks that rely on automated scripts ([151]), individuals hired by competitors [186], or proxy servers used to generate clicks for paid advertisements.

Companies such as AdWatcher [4] and ClickProtector [57] have initiated efforts to counter these attacks. The essence of their approach is to track the IP addresses of machines generating the clicks, and to identify the domain from which the clicks are registered. By collecting large logs and performing expert analysis, irregularities such as a repeated number of clicks for a certain advertisement from a particular IP address or a particular domain or abnormal spikes in traffic for a specific web site may be identified.

Unfortunately, the stealthy attack described in this section will go undetected by any of these tools. It is, therefore, of particular importance to determine other unique mechanisms of detecting and preventing attacks of this nature. These can be divided into two classes: *active* and *passive*. Our proposal for the former is intended to detect click-fraud attempts housed on web pages that users intentionally navigate to (whether they wanted to go there or were deceived to think so), whereas the proposal for the latter is suited for detection of email-instigated click fraud.

An active client-side approach interacts with search engines, performs popular searches, and visits the resulting sites. It also spiders through sites in the same manner as users might. To hide its identity, such an agent would not abide by the robots.txt conventions and so would appear as an actual user to the servers it interacts with. The agent would act like a user as closely as possible, including occasionally requesting some advertisements; it would always verify that the number of ad calls that were made correspond to the number of requests that a human user would perceive as being made. (The latter criterion is meant to detect click-fraud attempts in which a large number of ad requests are made after a user initiates a smaller number of actual requests.)

A passive client-side approach observes the actions performed on the machine of the person appearing to perform the click. This may be done by running all JavaScript components in a virtual machine (appearing to be a browser) and trapping the requests for advertisements that are made. Any web page that causes a call of a type that should be made only after a click occurred can be determined to be fraudulent. While this takes care of the type of automated click fraud described in this section, it would not defend against a version that first causes a long (and potentially random) delay and then commits click fraud *unless* the virtual machine allows randomly selected scripts to run for significant amounts of time, hoping to trap a delayed call. Excessive delays are not in the best interest of the fraudster, as his or her target may close the browser window and, therefore, interrupt the session before a click was made. Passive client-side solutions may be housed in security toolbars or in antivirus software.

Another type of passive solution is an infrastructure component. It would sift traffic, identify candidate traffic, and emulate the client machine that would have received the packets in question, with the intent of identifying click fraud. A suitable application might be an ISP-level spam filter or an MTA. Before emails are delivered to recipients, they could be delivered in virtual machine versions of the same, residing on the infrastructure component, but mimicking the client machine.

For all of these solutions, it should be clear that it is not necessary to trap all abuse. That is, even if a rather small percentage of abuse is detected, it would betray the locations that house click fraud, with a high likelihood that increases with the number of users who are taken to the same fraud-inducing domain. (Of course, a fraudster would not want to limit the number of victims too much, because the profit would become rather marginal.) Evidence shows that if only a small percentage of users had such a client-side detection tool installed, it would make attacks almost entirely unprofitable, given reasonable assumptions on the per-domain cost associated with this type of click fraud. This topic is discussed in depth in Section 6.3.7.

6.3.7 Brief Economic Analysis

This particular type of click fraud can be very profitable, as shown in the following paragraphs, which makes effective countermeasures essential. This discussion hinges on the expected probability that the fraudster will be detected, which we call p. Let us further make the simplifying assumption that the billing cycle of all pay-per-click advertising schemes is one month and adopt that timeframe for an attack cycle.

A particular attack-month would look like this:

- Day 1: Send out a number of attacks, each with a probability p of being instantly caught (thus invalidating the whole attack). This must necessarily cost the fraudster some small amount of money (perhaps to rent time on the botnet used to send the spam emails or to register appropriate domains).

- Days 2–30: Some number of tricked users visit the fraudster's site. With some probability, the fraudster causes these users to (unwittingly and invisibly) commit click fraud in the course of their browsing.
- Day 31: If the fraudster was not caught, he or she receives a check from the ad provider. If he was caught, he receives nothing (and records a loss because of the initial costs).

Note that the fraudster can distribute the attack over multiple domains to amortize the risk of being caught (as detection might mean the loss of profits from only a single domain).

Thus the goal of the countermeasures designer should be to raise the probability p of being caught high enough that the fraudster's expected profits are close to zero. Next, we examine a few countermeasure schemes and their potential impact on the fraudster.

No Countermeasures. With no defense mechanism in place, there are only two ways for the ad provider to find out about the offending site: (1) by having it reported by someone who stumbles on it or (2) by having a human at the ad provider visit the site after noticing its unusual popularity. Let us (reasonably) assume that the probability of this happening is very low, and consider "very low" to mean $p = 2^{-20}$. The fraudster's revenue then grows essentially as a linear function of the number of users targeted (Figure 6.6).

Active or Passive Countermeasures. Suppose that the variables here combine to yield $p \in \{1/1000, 1/10,000, 1/100,000\}$. The analysis for given hypothetical detection probabilities is shown in Figure 6.6. Note that even a modest detection probability, such as $p = 1/10,000$, limits potential profits considerably.

6.3.8 Implications

This type of click fraud is a serious attack with significant revenue potential for its perpetrators. Phishers might find attacks of this nature more profitable than identity theft. It is not necessary that these attacks have more revenue potential than phishing attacks, but they are certainly more convenient to perform: The perpetrator can make cash directly, rather than coming into possession of credit card numbers that must be used to buy merchandise to be converted into cash. The execution of this type of click fraud does not require significant technical knowledge (assuming the development of a page preprocessor that would insert the malicious code), so it could be performed by almost any unscrupulous web master.

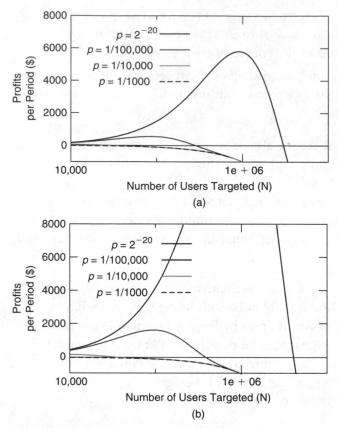

Figure 6.6: Benefit for fraudster, in dollars earned, given several probabilities p of detection by ad providers. Note that when $p = 1/1000$, the profit hardly goes above zero; when $p = 1/10,000$, profit tops out at around \$500 per domain; after that, the risks quickly outweigh the rewards. Once p shrinks below $1/10,000$, however, the fraudster fares much better—this is the current threat situation as far as we can tell. (a) shows the benefit when the reward per click is \$0.25; (b) considers the reward per click to be \$1.00.

We believe that this attack would generalize to any system of user-site-oriented advertising similar in operation to AdBrite. This idea was verified by testing a few other advertising programs, such as Miva's AdRevenue Xpress [261], BannerBox [30], and Clicksor [58]. The code proposed to automatically parse and click advertisements can be adapted to parse any advertisements that are textually represented, so long as they can also be parsed by the client browser (and this must be true, of course). Likewise, our techniques for avoiding detection by spiders do not rely on any particular feature of any of these ad providers and would apply equally well to any type of reverse-auditing mechanism.

Chapter 7

Bot Networks

James Hoagland, Zulfikar Ramzan, and Sourabh Satish

Bot networks are an emerging threat area with a wide variety of malicious applications including spam, phishing, distributed denial of service, click fraud, data harvesting, password cracking, online reputation inflation, and adware installation, among others. In this chapter, we explore botnets in detail. First, we cover what botnets are, why they are important, and how prevalent they seem to be. Next, we describe how botnets work, including the protocols over which botnets communicate, the techniques they use to remain resilient, and the kinds of features that typical bots possess. We then delve into applications of botnets related to online malicious activity. Finally, we speculate about the future of botnets, including topics such as browser-based bots, and touch upon what kind of countermeasures one can deploy to protect against botnets.

7.1 Introduction

Roughly speaking, a bot is an end-user machine containing software that allows it to be controlled by a remote administrator via a *command and control* (C&C) network, often from a central C&C server.[1] The C&C can send commands to the bot.[2] These commands can be executed without the actual physical intervention

---

1. Similar malicious code is not a bot unless it can receive a command from the botmaster. If the malicious code's attacks are entirely predetermined (such as an instance of a worm that conducts a denial-of-service attack at a specific target at a specific time), then we do not consider it a bot.

2. When we refer to a bot in this chapter, we will focus more on the underlying software installed on the machine as well as what it can accomplish.

(and often without the actual knowledge) of the human end user on the machine. The software running on the machine may not be inherently malicious. For example, the software installed on the machine could be used to allow technical support staff to troubleshoot the machine from a remote location. This example would constitute a relatively benign bot. In this chapter, however, we consider more malicious bot uses. In such cases, the machine that includes the bot software typically has been compromised in some way. For example, the attacker may have tricked the user into installing the bot software (e.g., by having the user open an email attachment that installed the bot). Alternatively, the attacker may have exploited a vulnerability on the user's machine to enable remote code execution and set up a backdoor.

Bots are not always active; instead, they often lay dormant until the C&C provides instructions. At that point, they blindly follow the bidding of the C&C. For this reason, bots are often referred to as *zombies*. Typically, a single C&C might control multiple bots, which are collectively referred to as a *bot network* (often abbreviated as *botnet*). The C&C server is often controlled by a human operator who tells the bots under his or her control what to do; this human operator is often referred to as a *botmaster* or *botherder*. The C&C itself can also be (and often is) a machine that was compromised. Therefore, the location of a particular botnet or C&C says nothing about the location of the person controlling it. For example, a botmaster in Russia could be operating a C&C server in China that instructs a network of bots in the United States to carry out a denial-of-service attack on a web server in England.

Because botnets harness the power of multiple compromised machines that can be controlled from different locations, they are quite powerful in the hands of an attacker. The attacker can use botnets to host phishing attacks, send out spam, mount denial-of-service attacks, engage in click fraud, and carry out a host of other malicious activities. The botmaster can even rent his or her bots to other third parties, allowing them to carry out these and similar attacks as well. Therefore, botnets are a highly lucrative weapon.

7.1.1 Challenges of Estimating the Botnet Problem

While botnets are generally agreed to be a significant issue, a number of challenges arise when trying to put an exact number on the size of the problem. Before providing actual numbers related to the size of the problem, we will describe some of these challenges.

A single botnet might, through its lifetime, contain tens of thousands of bots. However, at any given point in time, the C&C might have control over only a few thousand bots. In particular, bots might leave the network as the machine gets cleaned or goes offline. Similarly, bots might join the network as more hosts are compromised and infected. Also, some bots might be directed by their botmaster to migrate from one botnet to another. Furthermore, some bots can be instructed to clone themselves and join different channels on the same IRC server[3] or, for that matter, to join entirely different IRC servers.

Finally, it is important to note that a given botnet might lay dormant for some time before striking. During the quiet period, it is challenging to detect the presence of the botnet. Therefore, there may be a discrepancy between the population of observable botnets and the population of actual bot-infected machines. Note that this discrepancy might not just lead to underestimating the bot population. In particular, if bots are migrant and the same infected machine is counted multiple times, then the number of "observed" bots might exceed the number of actual infected machines. For example, in one study that monitored a specific botnet, 2,383,500 cloned instances emanated from 130,000 actual bots monitored [326].

The issues surrounding size estimation in botnets was studied in some detail by Rajab et al. [326], and we describe some of their work here. They introduce two useful terms for discussing botnet size:

- *Footprint:* the aggregate size of the infected population at any point during the botnet's lifetime.
- *Live population:* the number of infected bots that can actually receive commands at a given point in time (i.e., these bots have established a live communication channel with the C&C server).

In a sense, the footprint represents the potential scope of damage a botnet can cause, while the live population represents the scope of damage that can actually be caused at a given moment. Two techniques for measuring botnet size are *infiltration* and *redirection*.

In infiltration, an attempt is made to join the botnet and then count the number of active bots on the C&C channel (this approach lends itself to IRC channels where it is possible to see the channel members). Using infiltration to measure botnet sizes can be challenging if the botmaster suppresses the identities of the bots joining the channel or if a single bot uses multiple identities. For example, this approach can lead to different estimates depending on whether fully qualified user IDs or unique IP addresses are used to identify a particular bot. In one study that

---

3. IRC is a protocol commonly used for online chat that seems to be a popular choice for commanding bots; IRC is discussed in Section 7.2.2.

tracked botnet sizes, an ID-based count led to identifying 450,000 bots, but a count based on IP address identified roughly 100,000 bots [326].

In redirection, the DNS record for the IRC server used by the botnet is modified and resolves instead to a local *sinkhole* [76]. Therefore, when a bot tries to connect to its IRC server and issues a DNS request, it will be redirected to the sinkhole. When the bot tries to connect to the sinkhole, its IP address is recorded. This approach has led to estimates of botnets with a footprint of 350,000 compromised machines [76]. Because this technique does not actually monitor whether the bot successfully connected to the C&C, it cannot measure the live population. Also, this approach does not elucidate whether the bots are connecting to the same channel (within a specific IRC server). Finally, it is theoretically possible for botmasters to detect the presence of DNS redirection techniques and modify their behavior, which would in turn pollute any size estimates from such a technique [494].

To increase the accuracy of estimating the size of the botnet problem, one should also determine whether there is overlap among seemingly different botnets (observed using techniques such as infiltration and redirection). One can use a number of similarity characteristics to pinpoint the actual identity of a specific botnet. For IRC-based bots, these characteristics include the DNS name or IP address of the IRC server, the IRC server or network name, the server version, the IRC channel name, and the botmaster ID (by determining the ID of the channel operator that posts commands to the channel) [326]. Similar characteristics can be considered for other types of bots as well. One can then form a characteristic vector for different botnets and compute the distance between these vectors. This distance computation can be adjusted to weigh some similarity characteristics more heavily than others.

7.1.2 Botnet Size Metrics

Having described some of the considerations to keep in mind when evaluating botnet size metrics, we will provide some additional numbers to impart a better sense of the magnitude of this problem. In the first six months of 2007, Symantec observed an average of 52,771 active bot-infected computers per day, where by *active bot-infected computer*, we mean one that carries out at least one attack per day [401]. (A given machine can be active on different days.) Further, Symantec observed 5,029,309 distinct computers that were active at least once during the same period. China hosts the largest number of bot-infected computers (accounting for 26% of the world's total). The United States has the largest number of C&C servers, with 43% of the world's total. Recall that the physical location of the C&C may not be correlated with the physical location of the botmaster.

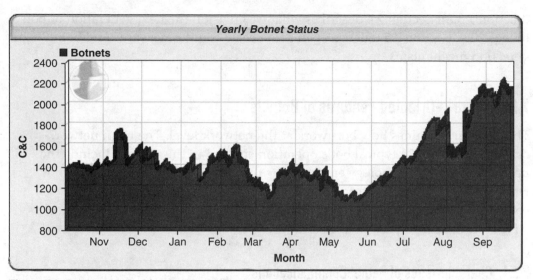

Figure 7.1: Botnets tracked by the Shadowserver group from September 2006 to September 2007, taken from the Shadowserver web site on September 22, 2007. On the low end, 1100 botnets were tracked; on the high end, more than 2200 botnets were tracked. Note that a given botnet may contain many bots.

The Shadowserver foundation[4] tracked anywhere from roughly 1100 to more than 2200 different active botnets between September 2006 and September 2007, where each botnet may comprise many bots. (See Figure 7.1, taken from the Shadowserver web page.) Vint Cerf, a technology pioneer who co-developed the TCP/IP protocol by which all Internet traffic is sent, has estimated that 25% of the world's Internet-connected computers are part of a malicious botnet.[5] However, the basis of his estimate is not entirely clear.

These numbers are all different, in large part, because of the different data collection infrastructures and methodologies employed. However, they all confirm that this problem is, indeed, substantial.

The remainder of this chapter examines bots in more detail. Section 7.2 looks at how bots and botnets work. First, it examines the overall characteristics of botnet communications (Section 7.2.1) and the protocols by which they communicate (Section 7.2.2). Next, Section 7.3 examines the software features of botnets, including which types of functionalities bots possess (Section 7.3.1), what they do to avoid detection (Section 7.3.2), and which applications bots can be used for

4. http://www.shadowserver.org
5. World Economic Forum panel in 2007. See http://news.bbc.co.uk/2/hi/business/6298641.stm.

(Section 7.3.3). Section 7.4 describes what we envision the next generation of bots to look like. Section 7.5 touches upon some basic countermeasures and bot detection mechanisms.

7.2 Network-Oriented Features of Botnets

This section examines how bots work at the network level. The main network-oriented aspects of a typical bot's operation covered in this section include the underlying network topology employed by the network and the mechanism by which the bot communicates with the C&C server. The standard protocols considered include Internet Relay Chat (IRC), the Hypertext Transfer Protocol (HTTP), and peer-to-peer protocols.

7.2.1 Characteristics of Botnet Communications

There are a seemingly unlimited number of ways for botnet communications to be conducted. In fact, almost any form of network communication can be used for botnets. This section looks at a few characteristics of botnet communication, with the goal of exploring some aspects of the space and discussing some implications of different botnet communication design choices. Note that multiple communications patterns can be used within the same botnet, either to accomplish different tasks, in different parts of the network, or at different levels of botnet communication [462].

Botnet Topology
A variety of topologies are possible for botnets. These are the different ways the communication can be organized at any given time.

The simplest and easiest to program topology is to have a central, master C&C server (sometimes called a "rallying box" [75]) to which all bots directly connect. The botmaster connects to (or has physical access to) the server and issues commands there, which are then propagated to all bots. This topology follows the familiar client-server model with a star network topology, as shown in Figure 7.2(a). One obvious concern (from the perspective of the botmaster) is that there is a central point of failure. Another concern is that a single node knows the whole botnet and will contain all of the botnet's data. These concerns are noteworthy given the possibility of take-down efforts against the botnet, either by authorities or by competing botmasters. Another concern with this topology is scalability; there may be a limit to how many bots a single C&C server can effectively handle.

A way to address having a single point of failure while also improving scalability is to have multiple interconnected servers, with the bots distributed

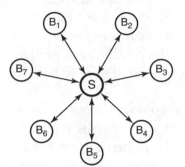

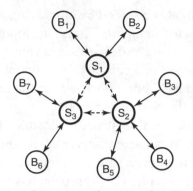

(a) A standard star botnet topology

(b) A multiserver configuration for a botnet

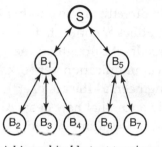

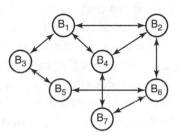

(c) A hierarchical botnet topology

(d) Random botnet topology

Figure 7.2: Botnet topologies. The letter S is used to denote a command and control server and the letter B a bot node. Different topologies provide different levels of resilience and fault tolerance. (a) The star topology is the simplest, but has a single point of failure. (b) The multiserver configuration does not have a single point of failure but requires some care to set up. (c) In the hierarchical topology, no single node is aware of the location of the entire botnet (so no single node can be used to bring down the botnet, although one node can bring down a chunk of the botnet). Also, this topology facilitates having different parts of the botnet used for different purposes. Conversely, there is some latency in issuing a command to a bot because the tree must be traversed. (d) Finally, the random topology is highly resilient because taking down a single node has little impact on remaining botnet nodes. Conversely, latency is increased because multiple hops may be required to reach a particular node (although the latency may not be terrible given that the random graph has extra interconnectedness due to redundant links).

among them, as depicted in Figure 7.2(b). These servers would typically carefully coordinate with one another to give the appearance of having a central state (a single reality). The servers would communicate with one another, perhaps with each one able to directly contact all the others, but there would be no central node. If one of the servers became unavailable, only the bots that reported to that server would be affected, and those bots could potentially switch to another server. This technique requires some careful design and implementation, but to the botmaster's advantage, the IRC protocol was designed to support this type of topology.

Scalability can also be aided by employing a hierarchical communication structure, as depicted in Figure 7.2(c). This topology can involve either a master server or a set of servers as described previously. This approach does not promote reliability in the event of a central failure (in fact, it adds the possibility of partial failure at a lower level), but it does reduce the number of bots that need to be aware of the location of the central server(s).

A twist on a hierarchical structure occurs when what appears to be a server is really just a proxy for an actual server. Here, the apparent server passes along all requests to the actual server, but sends the actual server's reply back to the bot as if it had originated the reply. This approach has been observed in conjunction with fast-flux networks [322], which are discussed in Section 7.2.3.

Central nodes can be avoided by having bots connect directly to one another in a random graph topology, as shown in Figure 7.2(d). The attacker connects to any node in the network and issues a command, which is broadcast throughout the C&C network. The Slapper worm [20] built this type of communication network. Such a C&C network is considerably more difficult to engineer, as the attacker needs to ensure that every command is broadcast exactly once, that new peers can be added by communicating with a single node, and that the resulting network guards against failure.

This type of network can be highly robust in the face of multiple node failures. Another major advantage of this type of topology is that it is very difficult to trace the point of contact between the attacker and the control network. A trade-off with this approach is that the C&C network diameter (the minimum number of intermediate nodes between the two nodes that are the farthest apart in terms of the topology) increases, which increases command latency. This may be something the botmaster wants to optimize, but even purely random graphs tend to have fairly good scaling properties in this regard [75]. In a purely random graph, each node (bot) is directly connected, with equal probability, to all other nodes in the graph; variations on this approach either are approximations or attempts to optimize the C&C *network* with respect to some goal [75]. Another trade-off in network construction is the redundancy of the connection of a bot to the network or of parts of the network to each other; more highly redundant nodes or networks may be easier to discover, but are less vulnerable to failures owing to factors such as node accessibility [75]. A random C&C network is challenging to create incrementally without carrying around the full topology, but this is not a problem if the botnet is being spawned out of an existing botnet.

Dagon et al. [75] present a taxonomy of botnets. They analyze different botnet topologies with respect to the size of the largest interconnected portion, diameter, and local transitivity (a measurement of redundancy). They additionally point out diurnal effects on the availability of certain bots: Certain hosts are powered on and connected to the Internet only at certain times of the day, and these tend to correlate to time zones.

We note a similarity between the botmaster's desire to prevent exposure of one part of the network from leading to exposure of the remainder of the network (especially the network's central nodes) to the similar goal of terror networks and other insurgent movements. Thus some lessons from history could be applied in botnet construction and countermeasures.

Command Initiation and Response

Regardless of the protocol and topology used, a bot's essential requirement in terms of communication is that it receives commands from the botmaster. The most straightforward form of communication is the botmaster *pushing* out a command to a bot. For example, the bot might listen on an IRC channel while the botmaster types a command on that channel. If botnet commands are placed in the topic of an IRC channel, the pushed command is also stored, meaning all bots that newly join the channel will receive it. The command could be added to a data stream that the bot would already receive or have access to. As an alternative, the receipt of new commands may be *bot-initiated*, with the bot initiating the communication to check for new commands. This check could be performed either according to a regular schedule or at a time predetermined by the botmaster.

The push method is clearly convenient for the botmaster: The command can be executed almost immediately by all bots, which allows a last-minute command to be executed. Similar functionality can be approximated in a bot-initiated communication mode only by frequent polling or by scheduling a check for a specific time in which a command is intended to be executed.

On the downside, when using the push method, the botmaster either must be aware of how to reach all of his bots or must broadcast the command to the set of all possible bots, which can be noisy. If the bots initiate the command check, the botmaster need not know how to reach all the bots or even know of their existence. To the botmaster's advantage, if neither the botmaster nor the C&C server knows the locations of the bots, then neither can reveal this information to investigators.

A bot-initiated check can be either *interactive* or *non-interactive*. In an interactive check, the bot issues a query of some sort and the botmaster or C&C channel software replies (most likely in real time) with a command; in this approach, the botmaster performs a command push in response to a bot making a query. HTTP bots based on CGI operate in this manner: A request is made to the server, and the server replies with instructions. A non-interactive check is one in which the commands for the bots are put into place independent of any query. Commands may be stored in a variety of ways, including web pages, files on an FTP server or on peer-to-peer networks, and even through mechanisms that are not normally thought of as storage, such as ports that are open on a given host.

A case in which the storage mechanism for a non-interactive check is not affiliated with either the bot or the botmaster is the analogue of the "dead drop" (a passing of messages without both parties being present at the same time[6]) in espionage activities. This approach provides a significant degree of separation between the botmaster and the bots, especially if the storage mechanism is chosen carefully. An example of a dead drop might involve a bot scanning the comments or trackback section of a third-party blog for a message placed by the botmaster. The message could be encoded to look benign and even normal. This approach is a modern-day equivalent of covert communication through newspaper classified ads.

A variation on this technique is for the botmaster to place a unique (or unusual) string (or combination of words) together with commands to the bot on an arbitrarily chosen web site. The bot then does a web search (using a search engine) for this prearranged signal to locate the command it is to execute [84].

Communication Directions

When the bot initiates a check for commands, the communication channel used must be bidirectional. However, when the botmaster pushes commands to the bot, the communication channel could potentially be inbound only. That is, there need not be a way for the bot to send a message back to the botmaster. By definition, all bots require some form of inbound communication channel; otherwise, they cannot receive commands.

When a botnet uses inbound-only communication, it has the option of using a forged source address. This approach would be particularly appealing when the sender is a high-value node to the botmaster, such as being a central C&C server. ICMP or UDP might be used for inbound-only communications, but TCP (often favored for its built-in reliability) cannot be used. An ICMP ping or a faked ICMP error message can look inconspicuous, so a system administrator might not realize it is associated with a botnet command. The communication can also be inserted into otherwise normal requests such as HTTP requests—for example, by adding an HTTP header or by specifically setting the IPv4 ID field. Techniques such as these were used in DDoS control networks such as stacheldraht [90].

Having bidirectional communications is clearly convenient to botmasters, as they can learn about the status of their bots and determine whether a bot has

---

6. `http://www.espionageinfo.com/Cou-De/Dead-Letter-Box.html`

changed location. In fact, a botmaster cannot (reliably) know of the existence of a bot unless there is some communication from the bot-infected host.

7.2.2 Communications Protocols

A communication protocol is an essential feature of a bot, as a defining characteristic of bots is that they do not necessarily have a predetermined future behavior (i.e., they are under remote control). Bots use a number of protocols to communicate with the C&C.

Internet Relay Chat

The most common type of bot seen today communicates with its C&C server using *Internet Relay Chat (IRC)*. IRC is a popular protocol that people can use to chat with one another over the Internet. To use IRC, you would must install an IRC client such as mIRC.[7] This IRC client then connects to an IRC server. From there, you can join specific channels where others are likely sending chat messages back and forth. Channel names are usually indicative of the kind of conversations taking place in the channel. For example, the #WebAppSec channel serves individuals who are interested in chatting with one another about web application security issues.

Even though IRC was initially a benign mechanism by which individuals chatted online, it has since become a popular vehicle in botnets. A bot can join a specified IRC channel, and the botmaster can instruct the C&C server to provide commands to his or her bots over this IRC channel itself. Two well-known (and otherwise benign) early IRC bots included Eggdrop and EnergyMech, both of which were written mostly in the C programming language, but did include add-ins written in Tcl as well as other scripting languages. These early IRC bots were not necessarily malicious. For example, they could be used for playing games, facilitating the transfer of (legal) files, and automating commands for administering the IRC channel. These bots were simply used to help improve automation, and the authors likely did not have any malicious intent in mind.

The initial popularity of IRC bots bred more popularity as bot writers could, and often did, leverage existing bot source code to develop new bots. Also, IRC provides the bot writer with useful built-in properties such as scalability and fault tolerance. One of the first examples of a malicious IRC bot was GTBot, which like many of its successors incorporated both the mIRC client and the scripting language that came with it. Gaobot [345] is another well-known and frequently

---

7. http://www.mirc.com

discussed IRC bot. Its popularity arose from its well-designed architecture and use of good software engineering practices, such as maintaining modular code. These features made it easy for future bot writers to extend and improve it.

Another reason for the popularity of the IRC protocol is that IRC server implementations are readily available (sometimes available in open-source form) and easily customizable. The two most common IRC servers seen in IRC-based botnet operations are Unreal IRCd and ConferenceRoom. Unreal IRCd works on both UNIX and Windows and can be customized and stripped to support only the needed functionality. ConferenceRoom is a commercial IRC server.

Sometimes well-known IRC clients are repackaged as bots. Some IRC clients (such as mIRC) can be easily scripted using a specific scripting language. This scriptability allows botmasters to easily customize the client for their needs, which is yet another reason why IRC is a popular choice for bots. The client can be scripted so that bot software, upon its installation, automatically connects to a specific IRC server and channel, announces its presence, and awaits commands.

We analyzed one fairly simple IRC bot (which was unnamed as of December 2007) in our labs and illustrate how it works here. In Figure 7.3(a), on the left side, in the Windows Explorer window, A.exe is really the bot package. This bot package, when executed, creates a file called svchost.exe in the Windows directory. Here svchost.exe is the bot process that will run on the system. Note that svchost.exe is the name for a very common and key operating system component, but the real version is actually found in the windows/system32 folder.

In Figure 7.3(b), in the process tree view, A.exe launches the bot svchost.exe and exits, leaving svchost.exe as an orphan process whose parent cannot really be traced, as illustrated in Figure 7.4(a). This bot is simply a customized mIRC client. One can see the mIRC icon in the process tree in Figure 7.4(a).

This bot also uses another stealthing technique, in that this mIRC client is configured to use the Windows task blue color as the icon color. As a result, a user would find it difficult to notice the presence of a new process running in the taskbar! However, when hovering the cursor over the icon, which while not easily visible is still present, the icon text "mIRC Microsoft Windows" is displayed. This icon text appears deliberately chosen to make a naive end user think that the bot is some Microsoft Windows component.

In Figure 7.4(b), the right-click menu really shows the default mIRC menu options. Double-clicking on the icon restores the mIRC windows, but the text settings were changed such that the background and foreground text remained the same. This simple approach keeps end users from easily identifying what is being shown. Changing the text color reveals that the bot is active and connected, and receiving commands from a botmaster.

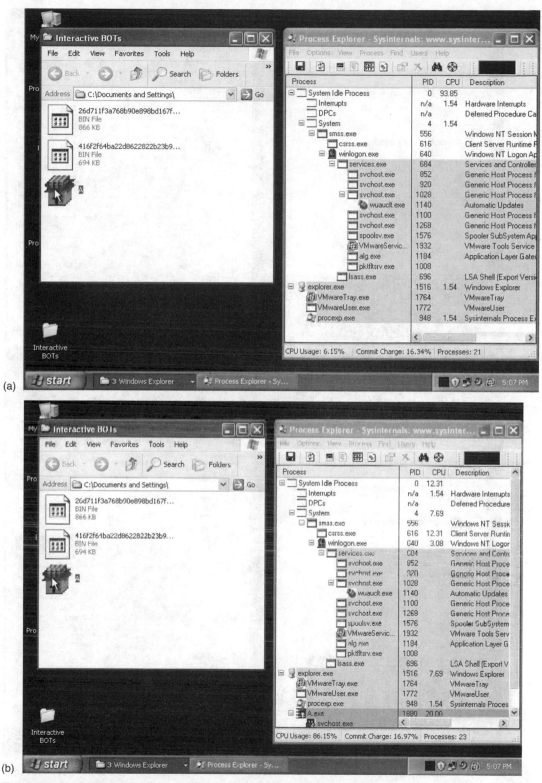

Figure 7.3: The launching of a simple IRC bot. (a) The bot package is named A.exe and creates a file called svchost.exe in the Windows directory. (b) A.exe launches svchost.exe and exits.

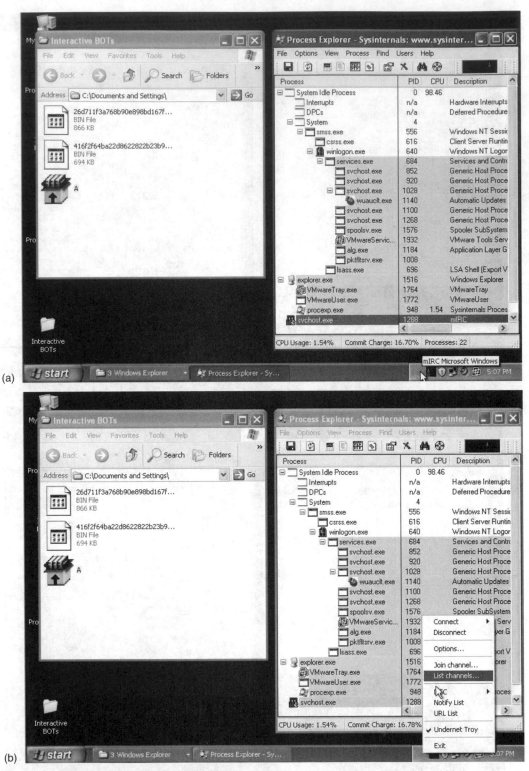

Figure 7.4: A walk-through of a simple IRC bot that was analyzed in the Symantec lab. (a) svchost.exe is an orphan process that cannot be traced back to its parent (lower-right side). (b) Right-clicking the process reveals standard IRC options, indicating that the bot is basically a customized mIRC client.

IRC Server Port	Count of Samples Using Port	Percentage
6667	1745	26.0%
65520	1182	17.6%
7000	483	7.2%
1863	360	5.4%
80	326	4.9%
8080	229	3.4%
5190	171	2.5%
10324	163	2.4%
7654	117	1.7%
441	99	1.5%
All other ports	2631	29.2%

Table 7.1: The 10 most popular IRC ports used among a survey of 6708 IRC bot samples collected by Symantec between August 2006 and September 2007. Of the four standard IRC ports (6667, 6668, 6669, and 7000), only two are reflected in this list. As a result, the port number alone is an insufficient indicator of bot-related IRC traffic on the network.

One drawback of IRC bots today is that they are much easier to detect. Whereas IRC was a common protocol for online chat in the early days of the Internet, it has gradually fallen out of favor and been supplanted by traditional instant messaging clients. Therefore, any IRC traffic emanating from a machine is a serious sign that malicious activity might be taking place. The presence of IRC commands on the network can be found using the ngrep tool, which allows one to search for specific strings in network traffic.

Trying to discern bot-related IRC network traffic through port numbers alone is insufficient, however. IRC bots frequently use a port other than the standard IRC ports of 6667, 6668, 6669, or 7000. In a survey of 6708 IRC bot samples taken in our lab,[8] 476 distinct IRC server ports were observed. The 10 most popular ports are listed in Table 7.1. Only 2 of the top 10 ports used are considered standard IRC ports. What is being counted is how many samples use the different ports. Thus, if a sample used different ports for IRC, they would be represented multiple times. Bots that have more variants would tend to have any port they use be represented more strongly in the accounting.

The 10 most popular destinations among the 6708 samples are identified in Table 7.2. All of the top 10 destinations were addressed by hostname (i.e., a DNS

---

8. These 6708 samples were selected by taking a much larger set of malware samples and identifying those that used IRC within 5 minutes of being run inside a virtual machine. The larger sample set was collected by Symantec between August 2006 and September 2007.

IRC Destination	Count of Samples Using Destination	Percentage
proxim.ircgalaxy.pl	1127	16.8%
f.fenr.net	89	1.3%
saber.ircqforum.com	88	1.3%
scortil.dns2go.com	88	1.3%
ff.arab-hacker.org	79	1.2%
xt.sqlteam.info	77	1.1%
home.najd.us	75	1.1%
xt.enterhere.biz	71	1.1%
xt.ircstyle.net	68	1.0%
new.najd.us	66	0.9%
All other hostnames	4518	67.4%
Addressed by IP	531	7.9%

Table 7.2: The 10 most popular destinations among the 6708 IRC bot samples collected by Symantec between August 2006 and September 2007. In all of these cases, the IRC bot uses DNS resolution to find the IRC server. With this approach, even if one server is taken down, the botmaster can put up a replacement DNS server and update DNS records.

request is made for the hostname and the resulting IP address is used for the connection); this is clearly the most popular addressing mechanism, with 6202 samples (92.5%) using it. Bots use DNS-based resolution to help maintain their longevity: Even if a particular C&C is taken down, another one can be placed elsewhere and DNS records can be updated to resolve to it.

The other addressing mechanism we tracked was by specific IPv4 address (hard-coded into the sample). In our study, 531 samples (7.9%) used this addressing method, with the most popular IPv4 address having 54 samples refer to it.

Here is an example of traffic sent by a bot to proxim.ircgalaxy.pl:

```
NICK qrllplcj
USER a020501 . . :-Service Pack 2
JOIN &virtu
```

Nicknames or user information sometimes contain information about the bot or zombie host, such as the indication here that this zombie is running Windows XP Service Pack 2. Nicknames can also be provided in a format such as t[00¦USA¦XP¦SP2]-7296t. In other cases, the provided nickname and user information can be static strings or can be generated at random.[9]

9. The text provided by bots may contain profanities, be politically incorrect, or contain otherwise inappropriate language.

In the preceding example, the bot is trying to join the channel &virtu. Instead of joining a channel, sometimes IRC bots send a message to the channel using the PRIVMSG syntax. In the following example, the channel is #cfg and the text starting with : is being sent:

```
PASS h4cker
NICK Ar-629730989975
USER rtxynjpmrnvgvd 0 0 :Ar-629730989975
PRIVMSG #cfg :\x02n\x02z\x1Fm\x1F (patcher.p\x1Fl\x1Fg)
x02\xBB\xBB\x02   fixed, version 1.
```

Here the bot is providing a server password (h4cker) to the IRC server as well. The IRC server presumably requires a password, to prevent casual snooping.

Hypertext Transfer Protocol

Another popular protocol by which bots can communicate is the *Hypertext Transfer Protocol* (HTTP). This protocol is the means by which most communication happens between a web browser and a web server. Increasingly more applications have started using HTTP for communication, reflecting the fact that HTTP is very firewall friendly. Botmasters might also prefer HTTP for the same reason. Also, almost all users generate HTTP traffic when they surf the web. In contrast, fewer users might be legitimately generating IRC traffic.

For bots that are hosted in other processes, using HTTP increases the likelihood of remaining under the radar, especially as operating systems such as Vista start rolling out process-hardening technology like *service hardening*, where services are allowed to communicate only over certain ports. Processes and services using HTTP are more reliably and easily found as core operating system services and components than any other protocol.

In protected mode, Internet Explorer 7 (IE7) specifically has lower privileges than a limited user account. Therefore, even if infected, it cannot cause malware to persist. However, bots can simply take advantage of significant browser up-times on consumer machines to be persistent for the duration of the IE7 process. This duration may be sufficient to allow the botmaster to carry out his or her tasks. The user can be enticed to remain on the same page for a long period of time, for example, by hosting a streaming media clip on the page.

Also, RSS (rich site summary) feeds[10] are becoming more prevalent. For example, Windows Vista includes a built-in RSS feed manager. These feeds constitute a convenient—and covert—C&C channel. We discuss browser-bots in

---

10. The RSS 2.0 specification is available from http://www.rssboard.org/rss-specification.

more detail in Section 7.4. Popular HTTP bots include W32.Korgo.Q [343] and Infostealer.Bzup [334]. Clickbot.A [79], whose primary purpose was click fraud, is another bot that communicated over HTTP. We discuss this bot in Section 7.3.3.

Once the HTTP bot registers with the C&C center, it can employ either the pull- or push-based methods discussed in Section 7.2.1. The C&C server can connect through a backdoor on the machine opened up by the bot. Alternatively, it can put a file hosted at a particular location on a web server. This file could contain a list of commands for the bot to execute or an executable file by which the bot can either update itself or otherwise enhance its functionality. It may be possible for security researchers to poll the C&C center by passing it URLs in an effort to understand how the botnet works (and potentially debilitate it). The bot can communicate with the botmaster using URLs, where parameters are passed in the query string of the URL.

FBCS (F28's Botnet Control System)[11] is one such bot-control system that requires the agent to connect back to the server and pull commands, instead of having the server connect to the bots. The obvious advantage of this approach is that the bot communication will go through the firewall without any issues. The control system uses PHP and mySQL as the primary technologies. The FBCS agents are capable of connecting to the server, receiving new commands since the last connect, downloading any new files, and taking actions as specified in the script.

Peer-to-Peer Protocols

Protocols such as IRC and HTTP involve having the bots talk to one centralized server that can be defined statically in the bot software or dynamically through a directory server. Bots based on these protocols can be brought down because a central command server also represents a central point of failure, as described in Section 7.2.1. If a botmaster somehow lost control of a C&C server that communicated over a protocol such as HTTP or IRC, then he or she would potentially lose access to all the bots in the botnet, which could be very costly for the bot master.

In contrast, peer-to-peer (P2P) botnets do not have a central point of control or failure. Recall that, by definition, each node in a P2P network can act as both a client and a server. Without a centralized command infrastructure, there is no single host that can be brought down to kill the botnet.

P2P protocols became popular with the rise of the Napster file-sharing service.[12] Since Napster, other P2P file-sharing protocols have emerged (e.g., *Gnutella*, which was fully decentralized). Because P2P protocols have numerous

---

11. http://f28.ath.cx/-F28/read.txt

12. Files in Napster were indexed using a central server, so strictly speaking Napster was not fully peer-to-peer.

(non-malicious) applications, much research has gone into them, resulting in the development of protocols such as Chord [393] and Kademlia [245]. These protocols use distributed hash tables to facilitate finding information in the network.

Commands to P2P bots are issued through file sharing. The file might contain new instructions for the bot or perhaps an executable file. One disadvantage of P2P botnets is that because they are decentralized, they cannot be organized to collectively carry out a specific task at a moment's notice. For applications such as a distributed denial-of-service (DDoS) attack, this shortcoming is relevant. At the same time, DDoS attacks are not as prevalent as other mechanisms for making money from a botnet. Thus, even though P2P bots lack the alacrity of traditional centralized bots, they make up for it with increased resiliency. A more extensive treatment of P2P bots can be found in the article by Grizzard et al. [156].

Case Study: Trojan.Peacomm. One example of a P2P bot is Trojan. Peacomm [341], which is distributed via email. A potential victim receives an email message with a variety of subject bodies, such as "A killer at 11, he's free at 21 and kills again!"; "U.S. Secretary of State Condoleezza Rice has kicked German Chancellor Angela Merkel"; "British Muslims Genocide"; "Naked teens attack home director"; "230 dead as storm batters Europe"; and "Re: Your text." The email provides an attachment with a file name such as FullVideo.exe, Full Story.exe, Video.exe, Read More.exe, and FullClip.exe. Figure 7.5 shows a screenshot of a sample Peacomm email.

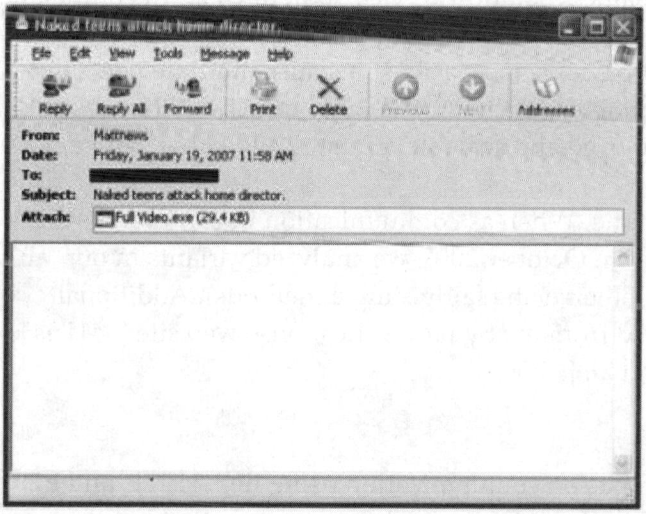

Figure 7.5: A screenshot from a Trojan.peacomm email. The email's subject involves a salacious news story and the attachment claims to be a "video" of this story. As is the case with most malware, a simple social engineering ruse is designed to get victims to open up email attachments and infect themselves.

The attachment is not a movie or story, however, but rather infects a (Windows 95/98/ME/2000/NT/XP) machine with a bot. When executed, the attachment drops the wincom32.sys system driver onto the machine. The driver uses techniques similar to the Rustock rootkit to inject a payload and hidden threads into the service.exe process. The driver does not try to fully hide its presence, and its registry keys are visible. Further, Peacomm disables the Windows firewall, most likely to ensure that it can communicate with its peers without any issue. Peacomm then tries to communicate with a small list of IP addresses over UDP port 4000 using the Overnet protocol (which was once used for P2P file sharing).

Overnet uses the Kademlia [245] distributed hash table algorithm for indexing. Peacomm first establishes itself on the Overnet network, from which it can connect to its peers (an initial set of peers is directly hard-coded into the bot). Peacomm then searches for an encrypted URL, which hosts additional executables. The encrypted URL can be decrypted using a static key that is also hard-coded into the bot. Upon successfully finding and decrypting the URL value, Peacomm proceeds to download additional (crimeware) components. The crimeware downloaded by Peacomm includes a spam relay that sends email over port 25 of the infected machine as well as a mail harvester that collects all email addresses on the machine and sends them to the botmaster by posting them inside the file 1.JPG on a remote server.

Interestingly, the primary function of the P2P network is to provide a URL to Peacomm for downloading additional malicious components. In a sense, then, the network functions as a type of name resolution service, akin to DNS. In contrast to traditional DNS resolution, which can be debilitated by taking down the DNS server, a P2P name resolution protocol is more robust because multiple peers can potentially provide name resolution response. At the same time, DNS has some features—such as an already-deployed and scalable infrastructure—that can be exploited by bots.

Peacomm has evolved over time. Whereas communication in early versions of Peacomm were done in the clear, in October 2007, we analyzed variants in our lab that began encrypting the data (albeit using fairly simple methods). Additional details on Peacomm can be found from the Symantec Response web site [341] as well as in the work of Grizzard et al. [156].

Alternative Communication Channels

Although most of today's bots focus on communication using IRC, HTTP, and P2P network protocols, the possibilities for communications protocols that bots can leverage is limitless. We discuss some potential alternatives when we speculate on the future of botnets in Section 7.4.2. Recall that botnets can potentially leverage more than one communications channel. Such an approach could potentially offer more resilience and simplified management of the botnet. For example, Vogt et al. considered the notion of a *super-botnet* [462], in which many small botnets are aggregated together and the individual botnets can communicate with each other. The result is a hybrid architecture that can combine some of the benefits of decentralized and centralized botnet control. Of course, such an architecture might inherit some of the drawbacks as well.

7.2.3 Network-Level Resilience

Botmasters will generally do what they can to keep their botnet alive and strong for as long as possible. At the network level, they may employ a number of techniques to maintain their botnets, which we discuss next.

Resilience Using DNS. Early bots hard-coded the IP address of the C&C server. This approach was easy to counteract: Simply take the C&C server down, and the botnet would be disabled.

Botmasters countered this move by employing the DNS to improve resiliency. Bots would be hard-coded with the domain name where the C&C server was hosted. To connect to the C&C server, the bot would make a DNS query to resolve the hostname to obtain an IP address, and then it would connect to the specified IP. If one C&C server was taken down, another would spring up in its place—at a different IP address. The DNS record would then have to be updated.

To make botnets even more robust, a single DNS record for a C&C host could specify multiple IP addresses in one *A record*. If a server at one of these addresses is taken down, the bot can still connect through one of the other addresses. Of course, if a bot locates its C&C based on a hard-coded hostname, the way to prevent all instances of that bot from resolving the hostname (which would be the equivalent of an IP takedown for bots that locate their C&C by IP address) is for the DNS provider for the domain to stop supporting that name.

Among DNS's greatest strengths are its reliability and its scalability. Through replication and caching, DNS rarely poses a problem for host-to-IP resolution. However, in concert with DNS's greatest strengths comes a notable shortcoming—namely, updating DNS records takes time, especially given that the update has to propagate across numerous severs. An alternative technique used by botnets is *dynamic DNS*. In a sense, dynamic DNS is like DNS for the masses. If you want to host a web server through your home broadband (cable or DSL) connection, it will be next to impossible to do so using traditional DNS. Because your home IP address changes frequently, existing DNS servers may not be able to keep up the pace. Dynamic DNS providers, by contrast, are designed specifically to circumvent this limitation. While not as scalable as traditional DNS, they are capable of updating rapidly.

Botmasters can take advantage of this feature by frequently changing the IP address of their C&C server. Taking this concept to the next level, some botmasters stretch the limits of existing (traditional) DNS by not only providing a big list of IPs to which the C&C hosts can be resolved, but also frequently updating those IPs (IPs can be updated every few minutes). This technique, which is known as *fast flux*, has its origins in spam (spammers used it to change the site that email recipients were directed to; phishers also used fast flux to keep fraudulent sites up longer). With servers popping up all over the place, the task of taking down a botnet has morphed itself into an Internet-wide game of "whack-a-mole." The use of fast flux makes it more or less impractical to take down a botnet by going after the C&C.

Note that in all of these cases, even the DNS server used by a bot can be hosted on another bot-infected machine. In such cases, the botnet serves as its own DNS cloud. More information on fast flux can be found in the Honeynet Project's whitepaper [322].

Acting Efficiently. Some bots might engage in just enough activity to carry out their purpose and remain otherwise silent. In the case of a denial-of-service attack, they can potentially compute how much traffic is necessary to carry out the purpose of the attack, and then send exactly that amount of traffic. This approach was taken in denial-of-service attacks against Estonia [110]. Minimizing how long bots remain active also minimizes how long they are exposed, which potentially increases how long the bot-infected machine can stay online without being detected and cleaned.

Along similar lines, some botmasters might create special-purpose botnets for carrying out their attacks. These "sub-botnets" are seeded from the botmaster's existing network, but involve only a subset of the machines. This approach limits the exposure of the computers in the network. This technique was also employed in the Estonia attacks [110].

Also, with the Peacomm botnet encrypting its communication (as described earlier), the botmaster might be planning to parcel it out for multiple purposes (given that only peers that share common keys can actually communicate).

Retaliation Through Counter-DDoS. Some botnet operators take the view that retaliation is an effective technique for resilience. In some cases, botnet operators have mounted denial-of-service attacks on security researchers. This happened with Trojan.peacomm, when its distribution nodes were scanned [306].

In another case, 180Solutions was attacked [211]. 180Solutions was an adware provider in the business of providing commissions to affiliates for every affiliate-associated machine that installed the 180Solutions software. A Dutch hacking group created a botnet with 1.5 million nodes and established an affiliate relationship with 180Solutions. The group members installed the 180Solutions software on their bots and collected their commission for doing so. These installations were performed without the consent of the users whose machines were compromised in the botnet. Eventually, in an effort to clean up its act, 180Solutions terminated its agreements with 500 affiliates, including the Dutch hacking group. The group, in turn, threatened to mount a denial-of-service attack on 180Solutions (in an effort to extort money). The FBI successfully tracked down the seven hackers involved.

In another incident, Castlecops, a volunteer organization that works on takedowns of phishing and malware hosting sites, was attacked [231]. In this case, the situation had a happy ending. Not only was Castlecops able to fend off the attacker, but the botmaster responsible for the attack was eventually arrested.

Use of Location-Anonymizing Services. As pointed out by Dagon et al. [75], some IRC operators have observed botnet traffic emanating from TOR exit nodes. Recall that TOR [89] is an implementation of the Onion Routing protocol, which launders the actual origin of a packet through a series of proxy servers. Each proxy server employs a mix-net scheme to inhibit anyone from correlating incoming packets with outgoing ones. Note that TOR also has non-malicious uses—for example, users who wish to maintain a level of personal privacy when surfing the web can use TOR.

Encryption. Some botnets encrypt traffic between the bot and C&C center. The use of encryption makes detection through traffic content analysis difficult at best.[13] Of course, even in the presence of encryption, some traffic analysis can be performed. For example, determining a packet's destination could prove useful in bot detection. One example of a bot that encrypted its traffic was Nugache [346]. Also, variants of Peacomm [341] have started using encryption as well.

7.3 Software Features of Bots

Having just examined how bots work at the network level, we now examine their operation on a more local software level. First, we consider the features a bot comes with, which might include the ability to update itself, the ability to infect

---

13. In some cases, the encryption scheme used is either weak or misapplied to introduce a weakness that allows the bot to be detected.

neighboring hosts through the exploitation of vulnerabilities, and the ability to
execute simple shell code. Next, we consider the techniques bots use to stay
resilient, which include rootkit techniques, virtual machine and debugger evasion,
and being process based versus not process based. Finally, we consider
applications of botnets, including data harvesting, relaying of data (such as spam
or other network traffic), engaging in click fraud, hosting malicious code or
phishing sites, acting as a storage mechanism for pirated software, distributed
computing tasks, inflation of online reputation, and (surreptitious) installation of
adware and other programs.

7.3.1 General Software Features of Bots

Most bots are fairly modular and divide their functionality into the following basic
modules or functional blocks:

- *Communication component*: establishes a channel to the botmaster.
- *Control component*: receives and processes commands issued by the
  botmaster.
- *Main functional component*: loads and runs the bot functionality as a
  stand-alone module (which can be a user mode or kernel mode module)
  or within a trusted process.
- *Propagation component*: tries to find other vulnerable hosts on a network
  through subnet scanning, port scanning, brute-force attacks, or even
  vulnerability scanning scripts. Perlbot[14] uses Google to search for other
  vulnerable hosts (a notion termed *Google dorks*).
- *Self-update component*: downloads updates to the bot software to either
  (1) entirely update the bot binary, (2) seed an update for covert communication,
  (3) get the latest shell code that exploits a vulnerability by which the bot
  can spread itself, or (4) obtain a new polymorphic engine for evading
  detection. (Polymorphic engines are described briefly in Section 7.3.2.)

Of course, not all bots are cleanly modularized, and the previously mentioned
components are not always present in all bots. Gaobot [345] is a notable example of
a modular bot. Modular bots have generally increased in popularity because they
are easy to update, thereby allowing bot writers to extend previous functionality.

---

14. http://handlers.sans.org/jullrich/perlbot.html

7.3.2 Techniques for Staying Resilient

For the botmaster, maintaining a large army of compromised machines is important. Each active bot in the botmaster's possession increases his or her revenue stream. Bots can use a number of techniques to stay more resilient to detection and capture:

- *Using rootkits.* Some bots include rootkit capabilities. A rootkit is a software component that uses various techniques to inhibit its detection on a machine. Rootkits are discussed in detail in Chapter 8.

- *Disabling security software.* Many bots, upon successfully installing themselves onto a end-user machine, will attempt to disable or otherwise interfere with any antivirus or other security software running on that machine. This makes detection by the software more difficult. As part of this process, the bot might, for example, attempt to modify the hosts file[15] on the machine, so that future requests to the security software vendor's update site are directed elsewhere. Of course, the more established security vendors also have techniques in place that make it challenging for malicious software to disable their products.

- *Disabling system software.* Surprisingly, some bots, once successfully installed, actively block or terminate the use of certain system tools and commands. In one case we observed, the bot actively terminated the command shell (cmd.exe) and Task Manager. Such activities may not be comprehended by naive end users and can lead to quite complex support scenarios if the end user leverages support from any software or operating systems vendor (because the vendor, which might use these tools to help troubleshoot the machine, will be unable to do so).

- *Installing antivirus software.* It may come as a surprise that actually installing antivirus software is a technique that a malicious code writer might use. The premise is that once an attacker has compromised and gotten control of a machine, he or she would likely not want *other* attackers to get their malicious code on the machine (otherwise, the attackers' efforts might interfere with each other). Likewise, the attacker might install any operating system patches to further protect the system. Along the same lines, if other malicious software is already present on that machine, such as a backdoor trojan, the attacker might wish to delete it.

---

15. Hosts files are discussed briefly in Chapter 1.

In some cases, malicious code has actually downloaded and installed pirated copies of antivirus software onto the compromised machine. In the process, the malicious code actually modifies any signature or definition file in the software so that it does not get detected. One such example happened with the SpamThru trojan [269], which was being used to carry out a spam-based stock pump-and-dump scheme.

- *Incorporating antidebugging and antivirtualization techniques.* When security researchers wish to understand how a piece of malicious code works, they often execute that code using a debugger, so that they can examine the behavior step-by-step. Also, researchers typically emulate malware samples inside a virtual machine so that any damage caused by the software is limited to the virtualized environment. Some malware authors realize this and include features that allow the malware to detect when it is being run in either a debugger or a virtual machine. If such an environment is detected, the malware behaves differently. By doing so, the malware becomes much more difficult to analyze and, therefore, counteract. Of course, virtual machines have many applications, and as they become more widely used (especially by consumers), it will be interesting to see whether attackers modify such techniques.

- *Employing runtime packers and polymorphic code.* A runtime packer is a well-known component of the malware author's tool chest. These tools can change a piece of executable code through compression and encryption. The result is an executable file that looks different, but does the same thing as the original file. These packers can make signature-based antivirus detection more challenging. Polymorphic code can take this procedure one step further by constantly changing itself using a *mutation engine*. Many packers come with features to detect when code is being run in either a debugger or a virtual machine. One example of a polymorphic bot is W32.Gaobot.gen!poly (also known as Polybot or Phatbot) [344, 391], which is essentially a variant of Gaobot [345], but with a polymorphic engine.

- *Using trivial name-based obfuscation.* Most bots, like many other malware instances, choose names for themselves that either resemble or are identical to those of legitimate system components—for example, `svchost.exe`, `scvhost.exe` (note that scvhost is not a Windows component, but looks much like `svchost.exe`), `taskmgr.exe`, or `service.exe`. Thus an end user or an analyst observing the process list will not be able to easily identify the suspicious candidate. Many times, orphan processes (processes whose parent process has exited) are suspect candidates, as there is usually a good reason for the parent–child relationship. As a result, many security analysts have a good understanding of the process hierarchy. In some advanced cases, a bot may inject code into a trusted process such as Windows Explorer to launch (a malicious version of) `taskmgr.exe` so that even the process tree may not look suspicious.

■ *Repackaging well-known clients for resilience.* As cited in the IRC bot section, some bots may simply choose to repackage well-known (and otherwise benign) IRC clients as bots to make it more challenging for a security software agent to distinguish between legitimate and illegitimate uses of the application.

■ *Running malicious code in a trusted process.* After its successful installation, a bot can load its malicious payload as a DLL, as a thread, or simply as executable code that runs within a trusted operating system process. Examples of such processes include `svchost.exe`, `csrss.exe`, and other networked services. This important technique is well known to malware authors. The obvious benefit is that because these processes are well-known trusted elements of the operating system, even an expert administrator will likely not suspect them. Even if they are found to be suspicious, disabling them or terminating them may render the machine unusable. Also, many types of security software, such as application-aware firewalls and host intrusion prevention systems (IPSs) may be unable to block or challenge these core system services.

Because the malicious code runs within the trusted process, it can perform most of the bot functionality. The actual core bot process or module may just perform the task of loading the malicious code module within the trusted process. In some cases, the bot payload may jump from one process to another process periodically to remain undetected. This kind of technique has often been discussed and practiced in well-known malware payloads.

Some pages that attack the user's browser may choose to simply remain active for the period of the browser up-time. This also may be sufficient for a large attack, because browser up-times are significantly longer than one would imagine and because the user can be tricked into remaining on a page for longer periods of time through a social engineering mechanism such as including streaming media content. This approach becomes a serious problem on Internet Explorer 7 in Vista, where reduced browser privileges of the browser are really not relevant to the bot operation.

In general, bots seem to be increasing in resiliency. For example, according to the Symantec *Internet Security Threat Report*, the average lifespan of a single (active) bot-infected machine increased from three days in the last half of 2006 to four days in the first half of 2007 [401]. This number represents bots actively engaged in malicious activity—it is unknown how long a machine might have been infected prior to its becoming active.

While this subsection focused on software-based techniques that run on the bot client, resiliency-enhancing techniques can also be employed on the server side. For example, when the IRC server to which a bot connects has no other legitimate purpose, the server is sometimes customized to make it more difficult for investigators to gain access to useful information. In particular, there may be no way to list the channels in use or to get a list of channel participants. Similarly, a custom dialect of IRC may be used to complicate the investigation task or to allow additional features. Botmasters may also monitor channel or server participants and ban users who are not wanted. In some cases, server or channel passwords are required (e.g., see chapter 11 of the text by Provos and Holz [323]), as demonstrated in a previous IRC example.

7.3.3 Applications of Botnets

Botnets have numerous malicious applications, most of which can lead to direct financial gain for the botmaster. We discuss some of these applications in this subsection.

Stealing User-Sensitive Data. Bots can be used to install other forms of malicious payload onto a machine. This includes keyloggers and screenscrapers (which were discussed in Chapter 1) as well as any other mechanism for scanning and mining interesting data. Keyloggers can collect sensitive data such as passwords, credit card data, or identity-theft related information such as Social Security numbers. Screenscrapers can collect similar types of information, especially in cases where passwords are entered using a graphical interface (e.g., by clicking on the letters of a graphical on-screen keyboard). Also, users may have sensitive data (e.g., authentication cookies) residing on the machine itself. Bots can steal this data as well. Bots can also potentially enable a user's webcam or browse through the user's image files looking for anything interesting. Finally, a bot may be used to monitor network traffic from a victim's machine and obtain sensitive data that way.

The resulting sensitive data can either be used directly by the botmaster to cause financial harm to the victim (and financial gain for the botmaster) or be sold through underground *economy servers*. For example, stolen credit card numbers can fetch between $0.50 to $5.00 per card [401]. An entire identity, including a government-issued ID number, birth date, bank account number, and credit card number can be purchased for between $14 and $18; valid Hotmail and Yahoo! authentication cookies go for about $3.

Harvesting Email. Bots can search their host machine for any email addresses. These addresses can be passed on to the botmaster, who can form a mailing list that can be separately sold to spammers. A list of 29,000 email addresses can be sold for about $5 [400].

Relaying Spam and General Traffic. On an related note, a botmaster can rent out a bot to a spammer who wishes to use it for the purpose of sending out spam emails. Spammers like to use bot-infected machines because it allows them to change the IP address from which their spam is sent, making it harder to detect the spam (because there is no single, precise, identifiable location from where all the spam is sent). In many cases, the bot-infected machine might just act as an open relay or proxy to transmit whatever traffic it receives. This method hides the true source of the data and keeps it from being included in any real-time blacklists (RBLs). Bots can implement a variety of proxy services, including SOCKS4, HTTP, and HTTPS proxies.

Engaging in Click Fraud. A network of bots can generate fraudulent clicks on advertisements. These clicks can generate profit for the botmaster, who might enter into a syndication deal with an ad network. In this situation, the botmaster would set up a web site that hosts advertisements provided by the ad network. Then he or she would control the bots to generate HTTP traffic that simulates clicks on these ads. The advertiser (thinking that the clicks were generated by legitimate people who saw the advertisement and visited its site) would pay the ad network for generating traffic to its site. The ad network would, in turn, pay a commission to the botmaster for hosting advertisements on his or her site. This kind of click fraud is discussed in more detail in Chapter 11.

One botnet involved in click fraud was Clickbot.A, which was studied extensively by Daswani et al. [79]. Based on their exposition, we describe Clickbot.A briefly here. The Clickbot.A client was an HTTP bot that ran as an Internet Explorer browser helper object (BHO). The botnet itself comprised more than 100,000 machines. The C&C back end was implemented as a web application and was written in PHP with a MySQL database. The various sites on which the back end was hosted appeared to have been compromised web servers. Once installed, Clickbot.A can make the following queries to the C&C server:

- `register`: This query registers the clickbot with the C&C.
- `get_feed`: This query causes the C&C to respond with a URL to a *doorway page*, which implements a small search engine that the botmaster most likely set up.

- get_keyword: This query causes the C&C to respond with a keyword, which the clickbot subsequently "submits" to the doorway page as part of a (pretend) search query. In turn, the doorway page returns a list of "search results," each containing a link that the clickbot could click.

- can_click: Prior to clicking on a link from the search results, the clickbot issues the can_click command to the C&C server. The C&C replies with either yes or no. (This tactic throttles the number of clicks coming from a particular IP address, presumably so that the attack does not arouse the suspicion of an underlying advertising network.)

- clicked: Once a link is clicked, the clicked command is sent by the clickbot to the C&C. At this point, Clickbot.A is sent to a redirector, which is presumably used to strip the referer field in the HTTP header. The clickbot is then sometimes redirected to a page for an actual syndicated search engine,[16] which includes links corresponding to search results as well as links corresponding to advertisements. Clickbot.A then picks a link at random and clicks on it. If the link corresponds to an advertisement, the clickbot winds up on the landing page of the advertiser, thereby performing a fraudulent click. In the other cases, when the clickbot is not redirected to a syndicated search engine, it is instead redirected to a porn site (where presumably the botmaster is profiting through some type of referral arrangement with the porn site operator).

- get_update: This query causes the C&C to respond with a URL from which the bot could download an executable file.

- get_2execute: This unimplemented command, if implemented, would presumably cause the bot client to execute arbitrary code.

Overall, Clickbot.A engaged in low-noise click fraud so as not to arouse the suspicions of the advertising network. To further maintain a low profile, the botmaster appeared to have set up numerous subsyndication and referral accounts, and utilized multiple second-tier search engines. Google detected clicks made by Clickbot.A and marked them as fraudulent.

Hosting Phishing and Other Fraud Sites. A bot-infected machine can be used to host a phishing web site. Phishing web sites pose as legitimate institutions (e.g., a well-known bank or credit card company). They provide users with a (web form)

---

16. The definitions of syndicates, subsyndicates, referrers, and other parties typically involved in online advertising are found in Chapter 11.

interface into which sensitive data can be entered. The botmaster could host the phishing site directly and profit that way, or else simply rent out the infected machine to someone wishing to engage in phishing. Between June and December 2006, typical rates for renting out a compromised web server ranged from $3 to $5 [400].

One important extension to this idea is to launder the same phishing site through multiple bot-infected machines (with different IP addresses) in the network and use fast-flux DNS to round-robin among them. Then, even if any one site is detected and taken down, numerous replicas are waiting in the wings that would allow the phishing attack to continue ensnaring victims.

A more comprehensive discussion of phishing can be found in the text by Jakobsson and Myers [202]. Bot-infected machines can also be used to host other types of fraudulent sites, including those corresponding to money mule operations, online pharmacies, and illegal adult content.

Hosting Malicious Code. A bot can be used to host malicious code, including other types of crimeware. Malicious web sites (including, possibly, a web site hosted on the same machine as the bot) or even otherwise legitimate web sites that have been compromised can point to this code. The code can be transmitted to victims who visit a web site—for example, by tricking them into downloading a file through social engineering means (as described in Chapter 3) or by exploiting a web browser vulnerability. Fast flux can be used here as well.

Harvesting, Storing, and Propagating Warez. Bots can be used to store illegal (i.e., pirated) copies of software, also referred to as *warez*. The warez can then be downloaded by others interested in it (e.g., by people who purchased a license at a discount price in the underground economy). In addition, when a bot infects a machine, it can search for license keys and similar data (in much the same way that it searches for passwords and other sensitive information), and use that information to facilitate software piracy.

Mounting Denial-of-Service Attacks. An army of bots can be commanded to generate a continuous heavy stream of requests toward a specific target server, thereby debilitating the server's ability to handle requests from legitimate users. Techniques for such distributed denial-of-service (DDoS) attacks could include ICMP, SYN, UDP, or HTTP floods. By overloading the target server with requests, the botmaster incapacitates the server.

A botmaster can monetize this type of activity by blackmailing the owner of the target server. For example, the target server might belong to an online casino or sports betting site. These sites make money only when they are online and responding to actual user requests. Around the time of a major event (e.g., the Super Bowl), the attacker might threaten to debilitate the site and demand a payment to not do so. In the case of a sports betting site, much of its revenue comes around the time of the Super Bowl, when a significant number of bets are placed. The site would realize it stood to lose a considerable amount of money if the botmaster could prevent actual user traffic from reaching the site. In such cases, the site might be willing to pay the botmaster off rather than risk losing these revenues.

Extortion through DDoS provides a fairly weak risk/reward ratio for the botmaster, as pointed out in the Symantec Security Response Blog [134]. In particular, if the site targeted refuses to pay, then the botmaster essentially has to follow through and mount a DDoS attack. This action will potentially expose the locations of the bots, and might lead to them becoming disinfected or removed from the network in some other way. In such a case, the botmaster will have lost machines in his or her network and not received any money to show for it. Instead, he or she could have made more direct profits by engaging in one of the other activities mentioned here.

Installing Adware. Adware vendors often sign up affiliates to help distribute their software. They pay the affiliate a commission for every machine on which the affiliate is able to install the adware. Botmasters can sign up as affiliates and install adware across their entire botnet. This approach provides instant financial rewards for the botmaster. Such a situation occurred with the adware provider 180Solutions, as discussed in Section 7.2.3.

Installing Ransomware. A botmaster could install ransomware onto his or her bots. Ransomware, as described in Chapter 1, typically involves encrypting a user's files and then charging a ransom to decrypt them. The ransom is typically paid through a third-party payment system such as e-Gold or Western Union.

One drawback of this technique from the botmaster's perspective is that the end user will know his or her machine has become infected, and might be suitably motivated to purchase antivirus or similar security software. If the machine is secured, it will not be usable as a bot, and the botmaster might lose out on future revenue associated with that machine. Of course, if the user fails to update the antivirus software, the machine could potentially become infected again.

Cracking Passwords. Bots can be rented out for the purpose of carrying out any distributed computing task. One such task, which might be of interest to malicious parties, is cracking passwords that have been hashed by an algorithm such as MD5 [352]. Such hashed passwords are often stored on web servers and other machines. The premise is that there is no known way to directly and efficiently "invert" (or, more precisely, find a pre-image of) any MD5-hashed value. At the same time, it is easy to verify whether someone actually knows a correct password: The password can be hashed and the resulting hash value compared with what is stored.

If an attacker is able to obtain a list of hashed passwords, he or she can mount a dictionary attack. Here the attacker tries running through a dictionary of potential password choices and hashes each one to see if it appears on the hashed password list. If a match is found, the attacker will have a high degree of confidence that the password has been guessed correctly. Given that users often choose relatively simple passwords, dictionary attacks are usually feasible. A number of algorithms for facilitating dictionary attacks have been developed [270, 281].

Building an Online Reputation. One fairly creative application of bots has been in inflating online reputation scores (and then using the scores to scam others) for sites such as eBay [212]. The bot scours eBay for listings of items that cost only $0.01 with no delivery charge and that offer a "buy now" option. There are actually such goods available for sale on eBay; examples include ebooks, screen wallpaper, and graphic images. These auctions are usually run by automated software (i.e., another bot) and provide automatic (positive) feedback for the buyer, which can be used to increase the buyer's reputation on eBay. By repeating this process a number of times, the bot creates a good reputation on eBay. The attacker can then leverage that (inflated) reputation by running a fraudulent auction for a higher-valued item.

This procedure can yield good profit margins for the attacker. For example, suppose the bot purchased 15 items at $0.01 each, for a $0.15 net investment. The resulting inflated reputation can be used to sell an item for $15 in a fraudulent auction where the seller has no intention of actually delivering the goods. This process can itself be repeated by creating multiple accounts.

What makes this particular type of fraudulent scheme interesting is that initially both the buyer and the seller use bots. The seller uses a bot to automate the process of selling the $0.01 good, including giving feedback. The buyer uses a bot to create multiple accounts and purchase multiple such $0.01 goods, thereby pumping his or her reputation.

7.4 Web Bots and the General Future of Botnets

This section describes possible new approaches to bot design. These approaches have been discussed in open forums among researchers, and they represent various tactics that future bot writers might employ and that may need to be considered when developing countermeasures. We begin by discussing browser-based bots, and then move on to more general future bot design considerations.

7.4.1 Botnets 2.0: Browser-Based Bots

Traditional bots are viewed as client-side executables that run directly on top of the operating system. One potential mechanism for future bots is to have them run inside a web browser. In such a case, the bot would be implemented in some client-side scripting language that a browser can interpret (e.g., JavaScript). We describe this approach here based on the exposition given in a paper by Jackson et al. [195] and a talk by Adam Barth [34].

There are several key differences between traditional botnets and browser-based botnets:

- *Infection duration.* Traditional bots maintain a persistent infected state on their hosts. The host will continue to run bot software until it is disinfected (e.g., through antivirus software). Browser bots, by contrast, run only during the course of a web browsing session. As soon as the browser is closed, the bot terminates. Therefore, the amount of time in which a browser bot can do damage (and the scope of its damage) is limited.

- *Infection vector.* Traditional bots usually infect their hosts through vectors such as email (where a user is tricked into installing the bot software, perhaps through some social engineering means) or through a drive-by download. In the latter case, the user visits a web site that exploits a web browser vulnerability to install the bot software onto a machine. The site is either an inherently malicious one or an otherwise benign one that has been compromised to include malicious code. A browser-based bot, by contrast, can infect users through malicious advertisements or web sites. (Of course, the browser-based bot might be more limited given that it does not run native code directly on top of the operating system.)

- *Applications.* Traditional bots can be used for a host of applications, as described in Section 7.3.3. Browser bots can be used for specific goals such as spam (sent through a web-based email service), click fraud, or even denial-of-service attacks.

- *Size.* Traditional botnets might have a footprint of a few hundred thousand machines (which would be on the large end). In contrast, building a browser-based botnet with several million or more infected hosts appears relatively easy to do.

As becomes evident, although browser-bots are less powerful in terms of infection duration, types of infection vectors, and malicious applications, they more than make up for these weaknesses in terms of size. We now move into some technical details of browser-based bot design. We first discuss the same-origin policy, which is a fairly critical security policy for web browsers. Next, we discuss DNS rebinding, which is a technique for circumventing this policy and a key building block for browser-based bots. From there, we discuss the applications of browser-based bots. We conclude the discussion of the topic with a specific case study. The remainder of this section goes into technical detail about the design and analysis of such bots; the reader can feel free to skip this material on a first reading and come back to it later.

Same-Origin Policy

The same-origin policy is a critical security policy governing the operation of web browsers. It states that any document loaded from one origin cannot get or set properties of a document loaded from another origin. For two documents to be considered as having the same origin, their protocol type, host, and port number must match. For example, if one document is loaded from `http://www.domain.com` and the other is loaded from `https://www.domain.com`, then the two documents are not considered to have the same origin because the protocols are different (e.g., HTTP versus HTTPs).

Note that nothing precludes a document originating in one domain from loading a document in a different domain. This can be done trivially through an `<IFRAME>` or even through an `<IMG>` tag. However, the first document will not be able to read the contents of the second document (e.g., using JavaScript code to inspect the DOM), nor will it be able to modify the contents of the second document.

It is also important to understand how client-side scripts are treated with respect to the same-origin policy. From the browser's perspective, any script loaded into a document will take on that document's origin as its own origin, regardless of where it actually came form. For example, if a page on site A includes a script located at site B (e.g., by using the `<SCRIPT SRC = "...">` tag), then the script will be able to access the contents of site A (even if A and B have different origins). However, if the script opens another window and requests content from site C, then the script itself is not allowed to read or modify the contents obtained from site C (even though the content will be displayed in the user's browser). Figure 7.6 illustrates how the same-origin policy applies to client-side scripts.

DNS Rebinding

In a DNS rebinding attack, the attacker basically tricks a browser into sequentially binding two different IP addresses to the same domain. The first IP address might point to a site that contains some malicious JavaScript code, whereas the second might point to a victim site. The idea is that the code obtained from the first site can query and read responses related to the victim site without violating the

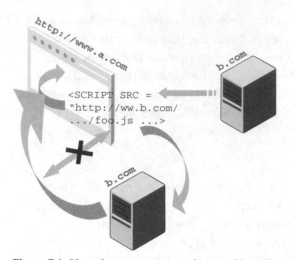

Figure 7.6: How the same-origin policy works with respect to client-side scripts. If a page hosted at a.com includes a script hosted at b.com, then from the browser's perspective, the script has origin a.com (even though it is hosted at b.com). As a result, the script can access (read from or write to) the contents in the browser fetched from a.com. However, while the script can fetch content from c.com and have that content displayed in the browser, the script itself cannot actually read from or write to the contents in the browser obtained from c.com, because c.com is considered to have a different origin.

same-origin policy (as both appear to be under the same origin, even though they are hosted at different IP addresses). The attack is also known as the "Princeton attack" [161], although we prefer the use of the term "DNS rebinding" as introduced by Jackson et al. [195] because it is more descriptive (the following text also follows the presentation given by Jackson et al.).

In one variation of a DNS rebinding attack, the IP address of the victim site could actually be a local address. Therefore, DNS rebinding allows attackers to crawl local intranet sites from an external location, potentially compromising the sites and allowing sensitive data to be transmitted externally. The compromised machines can be turned into spam zombies or clickbots. In general, DNS rebinding attacks permit the attacker to write and read on network sockets directly. In contrast, attacks based on (JavaScript-based) browser puppet nets [227] allow only sending of HTTP requests (without actually being able to read the results, per the same-origin policy). Therefore, while the kinds of attacks described here can, to a certain extent, be carried out without DNS rebinding (e.g., in the puppet nets framework), they are more powerful when combined with rebinding.

At a high level, DNS rebinding attacks work as follows:

1. The attacker first registers a domain name—say, attacker.com. He or she can attract web traffic to this domain through standard means, such as online advertising.

2. The attacker answers DNS queries for `attacker.com` with an IP address of the attacker's own web server (e.g., 66.66.66.66). The site located at 66.66.66.66 contains malicious JavaScript code.

3. The attacker arranges for the DNS response to have a short time to live (TTL). The malicious JavaScript code is designed to make a second request to `attacker.com` (e.g., by using the JavaScript `XMLHttpRequest` object).

4. Because the first DNS response had a short TTL, to fulfill the second request to `attacker.com`, the victim makes a second DNS query for `attacker.com`. This time, the attacker responds to the DNS query with a different "target" IP address (e.g., belonging to the `target.com` web site)—for example, 44.44.44.44.

5. The browser fetches the page hosted at the target IP address 44.44.44.44. At this point, from the browser's perspective, both the initial malicious JavaScript code hosted at 66.66.66.66 and the page fetched from the target IP address 44.44.44.44 appear to originate from `attacker.com`.

6. Thus these two web pages appear to have the same origin. The malicious JavaScript code at 66.66.66.66 now has free reign to interact with the page at 44.44.44.44: It can read the contents, issue both HTTP `GET` and `PUT` requests, read the responses, and so forth.

Observe that this attack did not require the attacker to compromise any DNS servers or engage in any type of cache poisoning or other similar pharming techniques that were described in Chapter 1. Instead, the attacker merely had to provide authoritative responses for a domain (`attacker.com`) that he or she owned. Furthermore, protocols such as DNSSEC[17] do not provide a defense against such attacks, because the attacker is not actually forging DNS responses.

Rebinding attacks have been known for quite some time [85, 356]. To defend against them, some web browsers employ a measure known as *DNS pinning*. The idea is that once the browser receives a DNS response to a particular query, it caches the result locally (ignoring the TTL provided in the DNS response). Subsequent queries for the same domain are resolved locally. Therefore, when the second request to `attacker.com` is made, the browser will go to the same address as it did when it received the previous response.

Unfortunately, pinning fails when pages are also accessed using a browser plug-in [195]. Plug-ins maintain their own separate pin databases, and so permit the possibility of an attacker making separate queries to the same domain and having them be resolved differently. Some plug-ins, such as Adobe Flash 9 and Java

---

17. More information on DNSSEC can be found in RFCs 4033, 4034, and 4035.

LiveConnect, are extremely popular, making it easy for an attacker to mount a rebinding attack with widespread implications. According to Adobe, 55.8% of browsers have Flash 9 installed. A Flash movie (enabled with, say, the Flash 9 plug-in) can open a TCP socket to any host as long as it receives an appropriate XML policy authorizing the origin from the destination. The flow works as follows:

1. The attacker tricks a victim into visiting his or her page at `attacker.com`, in which a Flash movie is embedded.
2. The Flash movie opens a TCP socket to `attacker.com` (with any port number smaller than 1024).
3. The Flash movie sends a `<policy-file-request/ >`.
4. The `attacker.com` site provides the following XML response authorizing the movie's origin:

```
<?xml version = "1.0"?>
<cross-domain-policy>
<allow-access-from domain="*"to-ports="*" />
</cross-domain policy>
```

5. In the meantime, the attacker rebinds `attacker.com` to point to some other target IP address.
6. When the Flash movie opens a socket to any port on `attacker.com`, it actually connects to this target IP address.

Applications of Rebinding

What makes a rebinding attack particularly powerful is that it gets malicious JavaScript to execute as if it has the same origin as the page downloaded from the target IP address. In this way, rebinding permits functionality that does not normally apply when malicious JavaScript is executed in a stand-alone fashion.

Consider, for example, the case of click fraud. In principle, to generate a click, all a client has to do is send an appropriate HTTP request to a server, as discussed in Chapter 6. To prevent fraudulent clicks, ad brokers may include a unique nonce value with each advertising impression; they require that the corresponding click must include this nonce value as well. Basic malicious JavaScript code that is included from a separate origin (e.g., through an `<IFRAME>`) will not be able to simulate a click because it cannot read the nonce value on the page hosting the advertisement. Conversely, malicious JavaScript that is loaded as part of a DNS rebinding attack can do so. In particular, the attacker can use DNS rebinding to make the advertisement impression appear to come from `attacker.com`. Then, the nonce value can be read from the impression without violating the same-origin policy. Knowing this nonce value allows the attacker to submit a click that contains the nonce value, which circumvents a security measure that was put in place by the ad broker.[18]

In more detail, the steps for carrying out the attack are as follows:

1. The attacker enrolls as an *advertisement publisher* with ad network A and publishes pay-per-click ads on his or her site.

2. The attacker enrolls as an *advertiser* with ad network B and buys pay-per-impression Flash advertisements.

3. For each person who views the Flash advertisement, a small percentage will be "converted" into clicks for the pay-per-click ad.[19]

As we will describe in the case study, even if only 1% of the impressions served are converted into clicks, the attacker can get a five times return on investment.

Case Study and Proof of Concept

In a proof-of-concept study, Jackson et al. [195] ran a Flash advertisement, for which they paid $30. The ad generated 50,951 impressions from 44,924 unique IP addresses. Of these, 90.6% were vulnerable to the type of DNS rebinding attack that involves exploiting the separate pin database in Flash. (Presumably a greater percentage would be vulnerable if other DNS rebinding attack variations were attempted.) Therefore, it would cost roughly $100 to "hijack" 100,000 unique IP addresses, or approximately $0.001 per browser clickbot.

We now work out some numbers from the previously given steps for carrying out the attack. Suppose only 1% of impressions are converted into clicks, and each click generates $0.50 in revenue. Generating 100 impressions costs $0.10, as the total cost equals the cost per bot times the number of impressions generated (= $.001 × 100). The result is a five times return on investment (or a profit of $0.40). This process can be repeated as often as the attacker likes, making the venture potentially highly profitable.

---

18. An advertising network might have several measures for detecting fraudulent clicks. Thus, even if the protection provided by the nonce is circumvented, the advertising network may be able to classify a click as fraudulent through other means, such as, the behavior of the "clicker" after arriving at the landing page. Some of these techniques are discussed in detail in Chapter 11.

19. The percentage is kept small to avoid arousing suspicion.

7.4.2 The Future of Botnets

Using the web browser as a platform for running bots is one direction we might expect attackers to take. In this section, we will describe other potential future trends. Many of these trends have been discussed publicly by security researchers [84].

Authenticated Commands. In most cases, the C&C channel does not provide any data authentication. Therefore, it is entirely possible for anyone to hijack a bot by deciphering the different commands and then communicating those commands to the bot. For example, a bot might be hijacked by a competing botmaster looking to grow his or her own botnet, in which case the attacker would instruct the bot to download and install his or her own bot software. Alternatively, a bot might be hijacked by an investigator looking to take down the botnet or learn more about the botmaster.

One technique that botmasters might try to make hijacking more challenging is to use digital signatures, for which the botmaster knows the corresponding signing key. This measure would prevent almost anyone else from hijacking the botnet.

As an alternative, the C&C channel could be authenticated using a message authentication code (MAC). This symmetric key analogue of a digital signature requires the botmaster and bot to share knowledge of a cryptographic key, so a security researcher could potentially reverse-engineer the bot client and discover this key. While MACs require symmetric keys, they have the advantage of being much faster to compute.

XML-Based Commands. The commands transmitted over the C&C channel could be encoded using XML. Advantages of XML include standards compliance, easier extensibility, and the ability to leverage existing tools (e.g., XML parsers).

Alternative (Covert) Command and Control Channels. Bots are being challenged by security vendors (which are developing improved client-side detection mechanisms), system administrators (who are locking down ports and implementing stricter firewall rules), and Internet service providers (which are proactively blocking bot traffic). To escape these constraints, bot writers may increasingly turn their attention to more covert communication channels.

Rather than having a traditional asynchronous, two-way communications channel, a botmaster might use a search engine to transmit commands. Here, the botmaster would take a sufficiently long, random-looking string that both the botmaster and the bots know, and post that string to a web site together with any commands for the bots. The bots would use a standard search engine, such as Google, to look for the string. Upon finding the web page that contains it, they would execute the corresponding commands placed on the page by the botmaster. With this approach, there is no traditional C&C server. Consequently, there is no centralized point of failure from which to take down the botnet.

To take this general approach to the next level, the bot and botmaster could agree on a *one-time password* scheme. Here, the botmaster would include a (private) seed value in the bots. The next random string that is generated and posted with commands to web sites would be a function of this seed value. By changing the strings used each time, the botmaster would make the botnet harder to trace.

One-time passwords could also be used to generate a complete subdomain (owned by the botmaster) that the bot could employ to either contact the C&C channel over HTTP or to perform a DNS lookup. In the latter case, commands for the bot could be stored in the HINFO resource or in other parts of the DNS record. The concept of using DNS as a covert communication channel is well known among security researchers (see, for example, the presentation by Kaminsky [207]).

Multiple Communications Protocols. Rather than simply relying on one communication protocol (e.g., IRC or HTTP), bots can employ several such protocols. They can be modularly designed so that the choice of underlying communication protocol is essentially independent of the core bot software. Permitting multiple communications protocols would make bots more robust, especially in environments where firewall rules might block one protocol.

Direct Transaction Generation and Tampering. Today, information-harvesting bots have the potential to steal credentials such as passwords and cookies. These values are transmitted by the botmaster, who can then make use of them to harm the victim whose machine has been infected by the bot. It is entirely possible for bots to leverage this kind of information directly without necessarily passing it on to the botmaster. The bot can carry out a transaction directly from the victim's machine or modify an existing transaction, with all of these changes appearing to come from the victim. Such a transaction could be financial in nature.

For example, if the victim is performing an online bill payment, the bot might modify the details of the payee. By having the bot modify the transaction itself, the actual botmaster might be harder to trace. In addition, there is no drop server where stolen credentials are stored, so such a server cannot be taken down or otherwise be made inaccessible to the botmaster. Also, modifying a transaction could potentially make network monitoring approaches for detecting bots more difficult because the traffic transmitted to and from the machine might look otherwise legitimate (i.e., the traffic is part of a transaction that the victim could actually be making). Finally, direct transaction tampering negates the benefits of on-screen credential input measures (e.g., graphical passwords or virtual keyboards) because the bot is modifying the transaction itself, rather than passing the credential data to the botmaster.

In this case, the economics of botnets are altered. Rather than profiting from the sale of passwords and other credentials through underground channels, the botmaster is directly seeking financial gain from transaction tampering. For this approach to work, the botmaster must be well versed in this cash-out mechanism. While lone botmasters might have difficulty doing so, botnets that are controlled by organized crime might find this approach easier.

Transaction tampering also requires more special-purpose effort by the botmaster because each bank (or similar institution) might have a different protocol for conducting transactions. Therefore, a single instance of a transaction-tampering bot might be limited in what it can do.

As with most predictions about future technology, it is still very much an open question whether bots will employ the advanced techniques mentioned here. For the most part, attackers tend to prefer taking the easiest route that will get the job done. Consequently, we expect most bots to employ tried-and-true techniques, together with some variations on these techniques. However, as security researchers continue to improve countermeasures, we expect bot writers to adapt as well, in which case we may start to see bots that leverage the previously mentioned techniques. Given that countermeasures can be indicative of future attack trends, we now focus our attention on them.

7.5 Countermeasures

As with any threat class, four categories of countermeasures are possible: prevention, detection, containment, and eradication. We cover how to address bots with respect to each of these classes.

Prevention

One aspect of prevention is protecting the actual client. Having a comprehensive Internet security software suite that includes antivirus, personal firewall, and other capabilities is a useful starting point. It is, of course, important to ensure that this software is kept up-to-date, as new variants of malicious code are constantly springing up. One common misconception about antivirus software is that it can detect only known threats. In reality, many antivirus software vendors include heuristic technologies that are designed to look for malicious behavior or intent rather than specific code instances.

There are two considerations with such behavior-based technologies. First, one challenge is to minimize false positives (i.e., legitimate benign software that shares some characteristic with malware). For example, if a behavior-based anti-bot technology just looked for IRC traffic emanating from a machine, then this software would trigger false positives whenever a legitimate user wished to chat over IRC. The second consideration associated with behavior-based technologies is efficacy testing. It is not enough to simply put a malicious file in a directory and see if it will be quarantined by antivirus software. Instead, that file must be executed in an environment that provides a reasonable facsimile to what would happen if the code infected an actual user. Oftentimes outdated testing methodologies are applied by third parties, and the results are inconclusive at best. The industry has already made a number of advances in behavioral technology, and we expect that trend to continue.

Beyond technical prevention mechanisms, nontechnical measures can be applied for prevention purposes. One approach is through raising end-user awareness. Most bots use social engineering techniques to propagate. For example, a malicious email attachment can be sent to a user or the user can be promised salacious content on a peer-to-peer file-sharing site. While no one would dispute that raising awareness might go a long way toward decreasing the botnet threat, it is unclear how we might effectively raise this awareness. User education poses a number of challenges, many of which are discussed in Chapter 13.

One challenge with prevention on the client side is a potential misalignment of incentives. Infected end users are often not directly affected by the botnet problem. Instead, the entities often affected by bots are recipients of spam, companies that experience denial-of-service attacks, or ISPs that bear the burden of increased traffic. Therefore, end users may not always have the appropriate level of incentives for protecting their own machines. Of course, as bots continue to add malicious features geared toward individual identity theft (e.g., keyloggers and screenscrapers), end users may feel more strongly compelled to protect their own machines.

Detection

One logical place for botnet detection is in network monitoring. For example, if a number of machines seem to be connecting to IRC channels suddenly or exhibiting unusual DNS query patterns, or if traffic on the network seems to be unusually higher, this phenomenon might indicate that something is wrong. A variety of tools, such as packet sniffers, can go a long way toward helping a system administrator determine if his or her network has a botnet problem. At the same time, as network administrators become more adept at monitoring for malicious traffic, we expect that bots will start to employ covert channels more often.

Internet service providers (especially those that operate a tier-1 network) have an advantage in botnet detection because they can perform wide-scale traffic monitoring. ISPs can monitor for patterns associated with scanning, transmission of spam or other types of malicious software over email, or distributed denial-of-service attacks. The study by Karasaridis et al. describes this approach in more detail for IRC-based bots [208].

On the client side, one could look for similar patterns. Also, many bots are built from well-known malicious code tools, such as known trojans or packers. Antivirus software can often detect these tools.

Containment

Once a bot or network of bots is detected, it is important to contain the damage they can do. Often this step can be accomplished by quarantining the infected machines. Some Internet service providers block traffic from specific IP addresses that are believed to be associated with bot-infected machines. System administrators can also potentially block traffic from such machines on their local network. This approach will help slow the spread until the machine can be cleaned.

Eradication

From a purely technical standpoint, eradication can be accomplished through antivirus (and similar) software. A particular challenge arises when bots employ rootkit techniques. If the rootkit is implemented at a sufficiently low level, then more advanced techniques are required for eliminating traces of the malicious software from the machine. This may require running security software from an external (and uninfected) source such as a CD-ROM. Along similar lines, as hardware-based virtualization support improves, it may be possible to contain the bot damage to a specific virtual machine and to have the security software run from a separate (uninfected) virtual machine.

Having said that, while antivirus software might be capable of removing traces of malicious software from a machine, it may not be able to reverse any damage that has already been done to the machine. For example, if the bot program in question encrypted files on the machine, then those files may not be accessible after the malicious program is gone. For these reasons, users should consider comprehensive protection and back up important data regularly.

Another aspect of eradication is takedown. Some law enforcement organizations and volunteer organizations spend time identifying C&C servers (as well as other bot-infected machines) and taking them offline. In some cases, these efforts can be challenging because the person whose machine is infected may be unaware that he or she is part of a botnet. Also, the victim may not be technically savvy enough to realize the ramifications.

One major effort for eradicating botnets was the FBI's operation Bot Roast,[20] which is a national initiative and ongoing investigation into disrupting and dismantling botnets and increasing end-user awareness about bots. In this endeavor, the FBI is working with industry partners like CERT and Carnegie Mellon University.

Conclusion

This chapter provided an overview of the botnet threat. Bots represent a serious security issue. A substantial number of machines appear to be infected with bot software, and this software has numerous malicious applications. Bots employ a host of advanced techniques for staying resilient to detection. As countermeasures develop, we expect bots to develop as well. As indicated, there are numerous avenues through which bots might advance in sophistication. We hope that a better understanding of the threat leads to improved countermeasures.

---

20. http://www.fbi.gov/pressrel/pressrel07/botnet061307.htm

Chapter 8

Rootkits

Prashant Pathak

8.1 Introduction

Symantec Security Response defines a rootkit as follows [337]:

> A rootkit is a component that uses stealth to maintain a persistent and undetectable presence on the machine.

The term "rootkits" originally referred to a modified set of commonly used UNIX utilities such as ps, ls, login, passwd, and netstat. These kits were trojaned copies of original programs used by attackers to hide their traces on a victim machine. Once the victim machine was compromised, the attacker used these kits to replace original programs. The modified versions hide specific system information such as processes, files, ports, registry, and disk space related to the rootkit, thereby concealing the presence of the rootkit.

Rootkits are usually installed along with malicious programs such as backdoors or trojans. These components are installed without user consent or knowledge. Typically, rootkits are installed by an intruder after breaking into a victim machine. In some cases, the user is enticed to execute the malicious program. Once installed, the malicious program can log keystrokes, grab passwords, open a backdoor channel (allowing an attacker to access and control the infected machine remotely), send spam messages, or convert the machine to a zombie on a bot network. To avoid detection, a rootkit is used to hide the presence of the malicious program on the victim machine.

A basic rootkit uses clever tactics to feign CPU, memory, and disk usage in an effort to avoid user suspicion. For example, a rootkit can add the CPU usage of a

malicious program to the system idle process, which may result in the user not
suspecting the presence of the malicious process (of course, most users may not
even know how to examine and interpret the list of processes running on a
machine). The rootkit can also hide the resources and data structures related to the
malicious program such as the underlying process and file. As discussed later in
the chapter, some rootkits actively hide from security software—for example,
antivirus (AV) and intrusion prevention systems (IPS)—by modifying the
underlying operating system (OS) structures. Thus security software that utilizes
any of the application programming interface (API), that internally uses these
modified structures, will be ineffective in detecting the presence of the rootkit.
Hence, specialized anti-rootkit software, which can scan and interpret the data
structures directly, is required in such cases.

Rootkits, by definition, are not necessarily malicious, but are more often than
not used for malicious purposes. In some cases, rootkits can be used for legitimate
purposes. For example, on corporate machines, a rootkit can be used to hide
(benign) backup directories. These directories store backup data and might be
hidden to avoid their accidental deletion by the user.

Rootkits have also been distributed by legitimate corporations for enforcing
copyright protection. In October 2005, it was discovered that Sony BMG used
rootkit technology as part of its Extended Copy Protection (XCP) software. The XCP
software was distributed along with certain copy-protected music CDs [362]. The
Digital Rights Management (DRM) software, a component of XCP, was installed on
the user system. This software prevented the user from making illegal copies of the
content-protected CDs. For the DRM software, all file names began with sys.
Moreover, it used rootkit technology to hide any process, files, and registry whose
names began with sys. Once malware writers were aware of this rootkit
technology, Backdoor.Ryknos [332] and Trojan.Welomoch [342] were seen in the
wild. These threats used file names and registry values beginning with sys, and
the DRM technology then mistakenly hid the malicious files.

In August 2007, it was discovered that Sony's MicroVault USB drives USM-F
and USM-FL series included a rootkit as part of its installation software [42, 470].
The MicroVault USB drives supported biometric fingerprint authentication to
verify the identity of the user. However, to be effective the authentication software
needs to be installed on the user's PC. This software component hides all files from
the folder in which it is executed. The authentication software was originally
intended to hide the fingerprinting authentication data from tampering. However,
any malware can package this software to hide its files.

8.2 Evolution of Rootkits

Even though rootkits have been known to exist for UNIX systems since the early 1990s, the first public appearance of rootkits for Linux systems came in 1996, when "Linux Rootkit" was released. This rootkit contained modified versions of system executables such as ps, login, passwd and netstat, which replaced the original executables on disk. The modified executables concealed the presence of the rootkit. However, these modifications were easily detected by integrity protection software that verifies the checksums of files.

The next generation of rootkits used loadable kernel modules (LKMs) to gain access to the kernel. LKMs are modules that are dynamically loaded into the OS kernel to extend its functionality. Once loaded into the OS kernel, they can access and modify kernel structures such as the system call table, which are otherwise inaccessible even to the root user. However, the rookit can be detected by using the lsmod command or by reading the /proc/modules file. Thus the next generation of rootkits used techniques to write directly to kernel virtual memory. Because these rootkits were not loaded as a module, they were not present in the loaded module list, making such modifications harder to detect. The rootkits also hid themselves by modifying the Linux Virtual File System data structures. Any queries made to these data structures would not indicate the presence of these rootkits.

Proof-of-concept rootkits for Windows systems started appearing in early 1999. However, it was not until the Slanret incident [317] in 2002 that Windows rootkits started to appear in the wild. An administrator discovered a suspicious driver file called ierk8243.sys. This file was later known as Slanret [347] [IERK, Backdoor-ALI] by antivirus software vendors. This driver file was causing random "blue screen of death" (BSOD) crashes on a cluster of Windows 2000 machines that the administrator maintained at Ontario University. It was later discovered that the university network was compromised by an attacker who had uploaded the rootkit to the server.

Since 2002, the number of Windows rootkits seen in the wild has steadily grown. According to several security software vendors, rootkits are next-generation security threats whose numbers are steadily on the rise. A report published by McAfee in 2006 [24] stated the number of malware using rootkit techniques had grown by more than 600% in the past three years. According to the statistics collected by Microsoft Windows Malicious Software Removal Tool (MSRT) in 2006 [67], on the 5.7 million systems that were cleaned by the tool, 14% of the systems

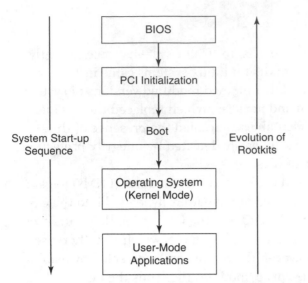

Figure 8.1: The evolution of rootkits. As rootkits evolved, they used techniques at lower and lower levels of the system start-up sequence to hide themselves.

contained a rootkit. This finding is evidence that rootkits are a serious threat and are not restricted to academic research or proof-of-concept code.

Figure 8.1 shows a flowchart depicting the evolution of Windows rootkits. The first generation of Windows rootkits were user-mode applications that patched the address space of user-mode processes to hide their presence on a system. These rootkits modified every process's address space so as to effectively remain hidden. Hacker Defender [114] is the most popular example of such rootkits. However, these rootkits could be easily detected by scanning in kernel mode.

The second generation of rootkits used *kernel-mode hooks*—a technique used to intercept system calls and interrupts, thereby transferring control to the rootkit code. These rootkits actively monitored and modified the output to effectively hide themselves each time they gained control through a hook.

The third generation of rootkits patched OS kernel structures to hide threads, processes, and services. These rootkits needed to execute only once to modify the kernel structures. Because they operated in kernel mode, they posed a significant challenge to detect. A popular technique used to identify such rootkits is known as cross-view detection. In this technique, a list of objects is obtained from two different sources and compared. Any differences in the two lists reveal the existence of a rootkit. Nevertheless, in some cases it is not possible to reliably obtain information from two different lists, so this approach might not always work.

The fourth generation of rootkits uses advanced techniques such as loading during the boot sequence, using virtual machine–based architectures, and modifying BIOS memory and flash memory on PCI cards. The BIOS and PCI-based rootkits rely on reflashing the flash memory present on these devices. Because most BIOS and PCI cards prevent reflashing the flash memory, the installation success achieved by such rootkits varies. Virtual machine–based rootkits (VMBR) run at a layer lower than the operating system. These rootkits compel the native operating system to execute in a virtual environment as a guest operating system. Therefore, once such rootkits are successfully installed, they cannot be detected by any security software running inside the (guest) operating system. Newer 64-bit architectures such as AMD Pacifica and Intel VT-x (Vanderpool), which implement virtual machines at a hardware layer, make it challenging to detect the virtual machine from a guest operating system. One unfortunate consequence is that VMBRs on such architectures are difficult to detect and thus pose a significant challenge.

In this chapter, we describe rootkit techniques for both Windows- and Linux-based systems. We also present the techniques used by advanced rootkits such as BIOS rootkits, virtual machine–based rootkits, and PCI-based rootkits. We conclude the chapter by describing some rootkit defense techniques.

8.3 User–Mode Windows Rootkits

User-mode rootkits affect individual processes on a system. These rootkits modify certain locations in the address space of the target process. To make such modifications, these rootkits must access a process's address space and their success is determined by their ability to do so. Certain security software applications prevent other applications from obtaining access to the address space of a process, thereby generically blocking these rootkits.

The following sections describe the functionality of user-mode rootkits and the various techniques used to achieve this functionality. User-mode rootkits successfully hide themselves in a process by loading the rootkit code into a target process and modifying the execution paths to transfer control to the rootkit code.

8.3.1 Loading the Rootkit into a Target Process

The first step that user-mode rootkits need to perform is to load the rootkit code into a remote process by accessing the address space of the process. The methods commonly used to gain access to the address space of a remote process include DLL injection and remote code injection [226].

DLL Injection

In the DLL injection technique, a Dynamic Link Library (DLL) file is loaded into the address space of a running process. The following techniques are often used to load a DLL into a remote process:

- Creating remote threads
- Using Windows hooks
- Using AppInit_Dlls registry

Creating Remote Threads. We now describe how to create a remote thread in a target process that loads a DLL file into the target process. The CreateRemoteThread API is used to create remote threads in a process. By using specific parameters to this API, a dll file can be loaded into the address space of a remote process. The following code snippet shows the prototype of this API:

```
HANDLE WINAPI CreateRemoteThread(
   HANDLE hProcess,
   LPSECURITY_ATTRIBUTES lpThreadAttributes,
   SIZE_T dwStackSize,
   LPTHREAD_START_ROUTINE lpStartAddress,
   LPVOID lpParameter,
   DWORD dwCreationFlags,
   LPWORD lpThreadId,
);
```

Referring to this function prototype, the *lpStartAddress* is the start address of a function that takes a single parameter, and *lpParameter* is the address of the parameter to the function. The LoadLibrary API is a function that accepts a single parameter. This API is used to load a DLL file into the address space of a process. The prototype for the LoadLibrary API is shown here:

```
HMODULE WINAPI LoadLibrary(
       LPCTSTR lpFileName
);
```

The LoadLibrary API can be executed in a remote process by creating a remote thread using *lpStartAddress* as the address in the LoadLibrary API and *lpParameter* as the name of a DLL file. The LoadLibrary API would then load the DLL file into the remote process. However, to load a DLL using the LoadLibrary API, the parameter *lpFileName* should be present in the address space of a remote process. The memory for the DLL file can be allocated in the remote process using virtual memory allocation functions such as VirtualAllocEx. The WriteProcessMemory API can then used to copy the contents of the DLL file into the newly allocated memory of the remote process.

Using Windows Hooks. Windows uses asynchronous messages to notify applications of system events such as keyboard input and mouse clicks. An application can register to explicitly receive these messages using Windows hooks. These hooks are callback procedures that are invoked whenever a particular event occurs on a system. As mentioned briefly in Chapter 1, such hooks are commonly used by keyloggers to capture keystrokes and mouse clicks. The hook procedures are inserted into the hook chain and are invoked in LIFO (last-in, first-out) order; that is, the procedure installed last is the first procedure invoked.

The scope of these hooks can be either local or global, depending on the type of hook. A thread can install these hooks locally and receive messages for events generated within a particular thread. Similarly, an application can request to install a global hook and receive events for all the threads running on the same desktop. Given that processes' memory address spaces are protected from one another, to use a global hook, the hook function should be located inside a DLL file.

The following SetWindowsHook API is used to install a hook procedure into the hook chain:

```
HHOOK SetWindowHookEx(
     int idHook,
     HOOKPROC lpfn,
     HINSTANCE hMod,
     DWORD dwThreadId
);
```

The *idHook* parameter is a unique identifier used to identify the type of hook function to install. The most commonly used hook types are shown in Table 8.1. Whenever an event occurs on a system, the operating system performs a check to determine whether any hook procedure exists in the hook chain for this particular event. If such a hook exists, the OS attempts to transfer control to the hook procedure. In cases where the hook procedure is not present in the corresponding

Event Hook	Event Description
WH_CALLWNDPROC	Whenever messages are sent to destination window procedure
WH_CBT	Window-related events, such as activating, creating, destroying, and minimizing windows
WH_GETMESSAGE	Monitors messages posted to the message queue
WH_KEYBOARD	Keyboard-related events
WH_MOUSE	Mouse-related events
WH_MSGFILTER	Whenever input events occur from a dialog box, message box, menu, or scrollbar

Table 8.1: Hook types commonly used in the setWindowsHookEx API.

address space of a process, the OS maps the procedure into the address space using a DLL file before transferring control to the hook procedure. The hook procedure can then choose either to return directly or to send the event to the next hook procedure in the chain to process. Thus the SetWindowsHook API is used to load a DLL file by using hooks into a remote process.

Using AppInit_Dlls Registry. The AppInit_Dlls registry value is of string (REG_SZ) type and is found in the following registry key:

```
HKEY_LOCAL_MACHINE\Software\Microsoft\WindowsNT\CurrentVersion\Windows
```

The AppInit_Dlls value contains NULL-terminated DLL file names separated by commas. Whenever a new process is started, certain DLLs, such as user32.dll and kernel32.dll, are loaded into the address space of the process. During the initialization of user32.dll, the AppInit_Dlls are loaded using LoadLibrary. As there are very few instances where an application is not linked with user32.dll, AppInit_Dlls are loaded into any application that is dynamically linked with user32.dll. Thus adding a DLL name to this registry value can load the DLL into any user-mode application's address space.

Remote Code Injection
In the remote code injection technique, code is injected remotely into a running process. The memory for the code in a remote process is allocated using virtual memory allocation functions such as VirtualAllocEx. The WriteProcessMemory API is then used to copy the code into the newly allocated memory in a remote process. Given that the code is injected dynamically into an executing process, the base address for the injected code cannot be predicted beforehand. Hence, the injected code cannot use global data variables and static strings, as these are allocated in the data section.

8.3.2 Modifying the Execution Path
Having described how code is inserted into the address space of a target process, we now describe how to affect the execution path via *IAT hooks* and *inline function patching* (also known as detours).

IAT Hooks
Windows executables do not contain the entire code that would allow them to execute as a process independently. Instead, to reduce the size of executables and improve performance, code that is commonly used is shared among different

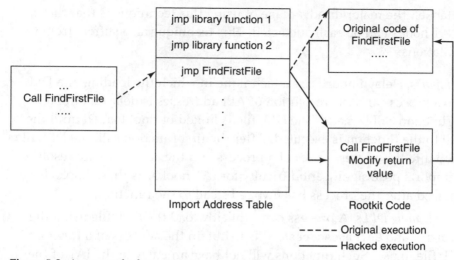

Figure 8.2: An example demonstrating the `FindFirstFile` hook in the IAT table. In the normal execution, represented by the dashed arrow, the original code of `FindFirstFile` executes. In the hacked execution, represented by the solid arrow, the address of the IAT function to be hooked is modified to point to the rootkit code. As a result, the rootkit code executes every time the original function is called.

processes using DLL files. During compilation, a stub code is generated for all the API calls that are imported from the shared DLL files. These stub functions are located in a section of the process code identified as the import address table (IAT). The Windows loader binds function addresses imported from other DLLs at load time and resolves the addresses in the IAT.

As shown in Figure 8.2, the process executes a call into the IAT. The IAT contains branch instructions (e.g., `jmp FindFirstFile`) to addresses that are resolved at load time. Once the rootkit code is loaded into a remote process using any of the techniques mentioned earlier in this section, it can access the portable executable (PE) header of the process. By parsing this header in memory, the rootkit code can discover the mapped addresses of the IAT functions. The address of any IAT function to be hooked can then be modified to point to the injected code [176]. Once the IAT function is hooked, the rootkit code will be invoked every time the function call is made. The rootkit code may choose either to return an error code or to call the original function and then modify the return values so as to effectively hide its presence.

The APIs related to process, file, directory, and registry enumeration are the most commonly hooked ones. In some cases, service-related APIs are hooked to hide services.

For an attacker, the major disadvantage of using this technique is that the presence of IAT hooks can be easily detected. This technique also suffers from the following limitations:

- *Delay imports.* Delay imports are a technique in which the loading of a DLL file into a process and the resolution of API addresses is delayed until an actual function call is made. The DLL file is linked but not loaded until the first call to the function is executed. After the first function call, the DLL file is loaded into the address space of a process and the addresses are resolved. Delay imports pose significant difficulty for IAT hooks, as these hooks have to be placed after the process has invoked a call to the function.

- *Manually loading DLLs.* A process can explicitly load the DLL file using the LoadLibrary and GetProcAddress APIs to obtain the address of a function in the DLL file to use. Such functions will not have an entry in the IAT of the process. Because there is no import table in the PE header, IAT hooks cannot be used in such conditions.

Inline Function Patching (Detours)

The technique of modifying IAT hooks, as described earlier, is one way to amend the execution path to allow rootkit code to execute. However, instead of hooking the call paths to a target function, it may be easier to take control of the target function itself. By modifying the target function, the rootkit code can then be executed irrespective of the manner in which the target function is invoked. This technique is known as inline function patching.

In this approach, the first few instructions of the target function are overwritten with an unconditional branch to a *detour* (new) function [187]. The original instructions are copied to a different location known as the *trampoline.* The number of bytes required for an unconditional branch at the start of the function may not align with the instruction boundary. In cases where an unconditional branch overwrites an instruction partially, the entire original instruction is copied into saved instructions, as shown in Figure 8.3. After copying the branch instruction, the rest of the instruction is filled with NOPs to avoid crashes that may be caused by the presence of invalid opcodes. Hence the trampoline contains the original instructions of the target function followed by an unconditional branch to a particular offset in the original function.

Each time the original function is invoked, an unconditional branch transfers control to the detours function. The detours function may choose either to return an invalid status or to call the original function and modify the return parameters. If the detours function needs to call the original routine, it simply calls the

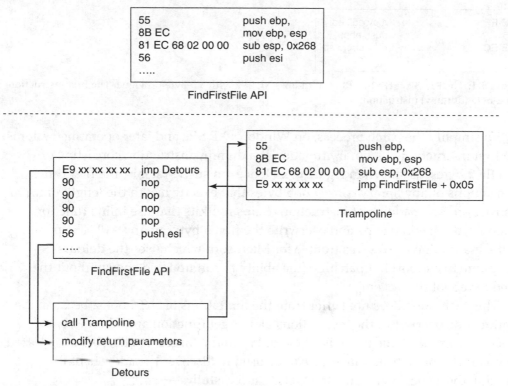

Figure 8.3: An example demonstrating inline patching of the FindFirstFile API in a process. The modified version of FindFirstFile contains an unconditional branch (jmp) instruction that transfers control to the detours function. The detours function calls the trampoline, which stores the instructions in the original version of FindFirstFile. The four NOPS are included to ensure instruction boundary alignment because the unconditional branch requires 5 bytes, whereas the trampoline for FindFirstFile requires 9 bytes.

trampoline function. These instructions transfer control to the original target function using an unconditional branch instruction. After the original function completes the execution, control is transferred to the detours function. The detours function then modifies the output values so as to hide itself.

An example of patching an inline function for the FindFirstFile API is shown in Figure 8.3. In the figure, 5 bytes are needed for a branch (jmp) instruction. However, the first three instructions of the FindFirstFile API occupy 9 bytes. Because the instruction boundary (5 bytes) does not align with the first three instructions (9 bytes), the first three instructions are copied to the trampoline. The first 5 bytes of this API are then overwritten with a jmp instruction and the remaining 4 bytes are filled with NOPs. Thus, whenever the FindFirstFile API is invoked, the detours function gets control. It can then invoke the original API via the trampoline and modify the return parameters to hide its presence.

```
8B FF                   mov edi, edi
55                      push ebp,
8B EC                   mov ebp, esp
.....
```

Figure 8.4: The FindFirstFile API on Windows XP SP2 with a 5-byte prologue. The first instruction is a 2-byte (dummy) instruction.

To simplify the patch process, on Windows XP SP2 and later operating systems, the first instruction of a library function is a dummy instruction consisting of exactly 2 bytes, as shown in Figure 8.4. Hence, on such systems, the first three instructions of any library consist of 5 bytes that exactly match the length of a jmp instruction. The padding of instructions helps rootkits that use inline function patching, as they can copy and overwrite the first 5 bytes of any API. The padding of the instructions also saves trouble for Microsoft, which uses the detours technique to support hot patching (the ability to run updated code without the need to reboot the system).

This technique does not suffer from the limitations of IAT hooks, because the rootkit code overwrites the instructions of a target function and, therefore, executes every time the target is invoked. When the target function is not exported, however, elaborate techniques have to be used to discover the address of the function dynamically to patch the system successfully.

8.4 Kernel–Mode Rootkit Techniques

Unlike user-mode rootkits, kernel-mode rootkits affect all processes on a system. Consequently, they are usually more powerful than user-mode rootkits. Given that security software such as antivirus and intrusion prevention software also runs in kernel mode, kernel-mode rootkits have the potential to avoid detection. This section describes various kernel-mode rootkit techniques in detail.

8.4.1 Interrupt Descriptor Table Hooks

Whenever an interrupt occurs, the processor saves its context and transfers control to an interrupt service routine (ISR), which services the interrupt request. Once an interrupt is serviced, control switches back and the processor resumes original execution. The interrupt descriptor table (IDT) stores the addresses of the ISR for every interrupt supported on the system. In the Intel architecture, the IDT contains 8-byte descriptors (shown in Figure 8.5), each of which stores the segment selector and the offset of an ISR to execute. The IDTR register points to the memory location containing the base address of the IDT.

Offset 31..16	P	D P	0D110	0	Res
Segment Selector	Offset 15..0				

Figure 8.5: The format of an IA-32 interrupt descriptor. The descriptor contains both a segment selector and an offset.

It is possible to hook all interrupts by allocating a new descriptor table and modifying the value of the IDTR register to point to the newly created table. Alternatively, to hook a specific interrupt, the offset value corresponding to the particular ISR may be modified in the descriptor table. The interrupts are first disabled to avoid synchronization issues while the offset value is modified in the IDT. The interrupts are subsequently enabled after the offset value is modified.

Whenever an interrupt occurs, control is transferred to the rootkit code first, which can then choose either to return an error code or to execute the original ISR. The commonly targeted interrupts are 0x2E (system call), Invalid Opcode, PageFault, and General Protection (GP). To avoid changing the stack layout, the IDT hooks use a branch instruction instead of a call instruction to transfer control to the rootkit code. Because the call instruction cannot be used, control cannot be returned to the IDT hooks. Hence, the usual technique of calling the rootkit code and modifying the return values will not work for these hooks and, therefore, has limited advantages. For example, this technique can target certain processes (e.g., AV scanners, intrusion prevention software systems) and prevent them from obtaining the process list by blocking process enumeration system calls such as ZwQuerySystemInformation. An example of hooking the keyboard interrupt (0x31) is presented below.

IDT Keyboard Hook Example. On most systems, the Windows kernel uses entry 0x31 in the IDT to store the address of the keyboard ISR. This routine is invoked every time a key is pressed or released. By modifying the keyboard ISR address to point to a custom routine, execution may be modified effectively as shown in Figure 8.6. This technique is most commonly used by keyloggers.

The modified keyboard ISR can then read the scan code for the key pressed or released directly from the keyboard controller port 0×60. The scan code is placed back into the controller output buffer by issuing a command to port 0×64 and then writing the actual keystroke to port 0×60 [176]. The modified keyboard ISR then logs the keystroke to a file and calls the original keyboard handler routine. In this way, the keylogger uses the IDT hook for a keyboard interrupt.

On multiprocessor systems, each processor has its own IDT. Hence, it is necessary to hook the IDT entries on all processors; otherwise, the rootkit would

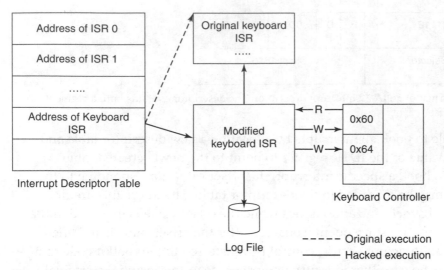

Figure 8.6: An IDT hook-based keylogger. The keyboard ISR is changed so that rather than executing the original keyboard ISR (dashed arrow), the modified keyboard ISR is executed (solid arrow). The modified ISR can log keystrokes and then call the original keyboard ISR.

be ineffective. On single-processor systems, synchronization issues while modifying the IDT are resolved by disabling the interrupts. This technique cannot be applied on multiprocessor systems. On multiprocessor systems, the privilege level of the processor is raised to DISPATCH_LEVEL by scheduling a deferred procedure call (DPC). Once the privilege level for all processors has been raised to DPC, the IDT is modified. As soon as the DPC call returns, the processor privilege is reset to a lower privilege level.

8.4.2 System Call Hooks

In this technique, the execution path is modified by replacing the system service handler (KiSystemService/KiFastSystemService), with rootkit code such that it is executed for every system call. The techniques used to replace the address of the system service handler include INT 0x2E hooks and SYSENTER hooks.

INT 0x2E Hooks. The interrupt 0x2E is a software interrupt that is reserved for system calls on Windows platforms. User-mode applications running on Windows NT/2K systems use this interrupt to make a system call—that is, to transfer control from user to kernel mode. The processor, upon executing the interrupt 0x2E, performs a lookup in the IDT and transfers control to the system service handler ISR. This routine would look up the system service descriptor table (SSDT) and transfer control to the appropriate system call [162]. By modifying the offset value of the descriptor, the rootkit code is executed every time a system call is made.

SYSENTER Hooks. Given that using software interrupts usually requires at least two memory accesses to transfer control to kernel mode, the SYSENTER instruction was introduced in the Intel Pentium III architecture to speed up the transfer. The IA32_SYSENTER_EIP model-specific register stores the address of the routine to execute when the SYSENTER instruction is executed [192]. On hardware platforms that support this instruction, user-mode applications running on Windows XP/Vista use this instruction to transfer control from user mode to kernel mode. When the SYSENTER instruction executes, control is transferred to this routine, which looks up the SSDT and transfers control to the appropriate system call.

SYSENTER hooks are placed by modifying the value of IA32_SYSENTER_EIP register to point to a rootkit routine. By modifying this value, the rootkit code is called each time a system call is made.

As mentioned in Section 8.3.2, the INT 0x2E and SYSENTER hooks suffer from the same limitations as IDT hooks—namely, they cannot call the rootkit code and modify the return parameters, because control never reaches these hooks. Thus these hooks have limited utility and are used mainly for entirely blocking the system call for a particular process.

8.4.3 System Service Descriptor Table Hooks

Hooking the SSDT is by far the most popular rootkit technique used by malware writers owing to its effectiveness and simplicity. Even security software such as antivirus and firewall applications hook into this table to receive notifications about events like file creation and opening of ports.

The address of the system service table is stored in the SSDT, whose structure is shown in Figure 8.7. The first entry in the SSDT refers to the system service table that stores the addresses of the system call routines in Ntoskrnl—for example, ZwCreateFile and ZwOpenKey. The "number of system calls" entry represents the maximum number of system calls that are supported on a system. The "parameter table entry" points to a table that stores the number of parameters used by each system call. The global variable KeServiceDescriptorTable stores the base address of the SSDT [176].

Whenever a system call is made, the system service handler obtains the value of KeServiceDescriptorTable using a per-thread structure. The base address of the system service table is retrieved using the SSDT stored in KeServiceDescriptorTable. The address of a system call routine is calculated using the base address of system service table and the offset of the system call stored in each register. The system service handler then transfers control to the actual system service routine.

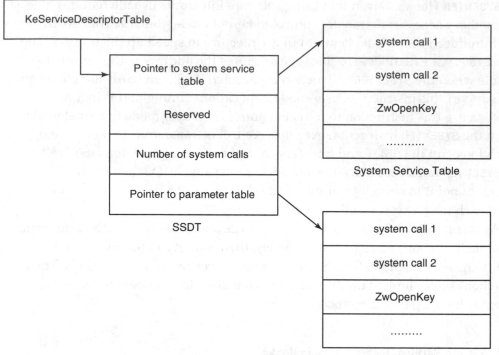

Figure 8.7: The structure of the system service descriptor table. The base address of the SSTD is stored in the global variable `KeServiceDecriptorTable`. The entries in the SSTD include a pointer to the system service table, the number of system calls, and a pointer to the parameter table.

It is possible to hook all system calls by modifying the system service table entry in the SSDT or by modifying the `KeServiceDescriptorTable` to point to a new SSDT, which contains a different value of the system service table entry. To hook individual system calls, the offset value corresponding to the system call is modified in the system service table. However, the SSDT has different memory protections and is write-protected to prevent modifications. Writing to this memory location without turning off memory protection would result in a BSOD (blue screen of death).

The following techniques are used to first gain write access to the system service table:

- *Using the CR0 register*. The operating system kernel enforces write protection on kernel pages that contain important data structures. The write-protect (WP) bit in control register zero (CR0) determines whether this protection is applied to kernel readonly pages. When the WP bit is set, write protection is enforced on readonly pages; when it is off, the write protection is disabled. Hence a driver loaded in kernel mode can disable the write protection by resetting this bit in the CR0 register [404].

- *Modifying the MDL.* Every memory region in Windows is represented with a memory descriptor list (MDL). The MDL contains a start address, end address, and memory protections. It is possible to change permissions on the MDL corresponding to the SSDT table by modifying the MDL flags to include `MDL_MAPPED_TO_SYSTEM_VA` [176].

Using SSDT hooks, whenever the original system call is executed, the rootkit code is invoked. The rootkit code can then call the original system call and modify the output parameters to hide its presence. As an example, Figure 8.8 shows a trace to demonstrate the difference in code paths before and after the hook. The address of the ZwOpenKey system call is modified in the system service table to point to the rootkit code. Whenever ZwOpenKey executes, the system service handler transfers control to the rootkit code. The rootkit then invokes the original system call. Once the call returns, it modifies the output values to hide its presence.

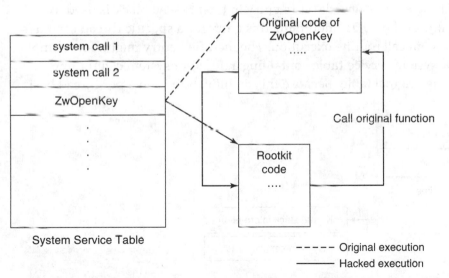

Figure 8.8: Hooking the ZwOpenKey function in the system call table. Note the two execution paths. The original path is denoted by a dashed arrow and the hacked path by a solid arrow. In the hacked path, the address of ZwOpenKey has been modified and points to rootkit code. When ZwOpenKey executes, the system service handler gives control to the rootkit code. At the end of its execution, the rootkit code invokes the original ZwOpenKey system call and modifies the output values to hide its presence.

8.4.4 Thread-Based SSDT Hooks

SSDT hooks are simple to install and affect all processes in a system. Because the change is global, the presence of these hooks can be easily detected. The original addresses of all system calls can be retrieved by parsing the kernel on-disk image. By comparing the real addresses with the in-memory addresses of the system call routines, the presence of an SSDT hook can be readily discerned. A variation of this technique—namely, thread-based SSDT hooks—can be used to make this modification more difficult to detect.

Every thread in a system has a per-thread structure called the KTHREAD block. This structure contains per-thread information such as stack, TLS array, execution time, and a pointer to the SSDT structure known as the system service table, as shown in Figure 8.9.

The SystemServiceTable entry points to the SSDT structure, similar to the global variable KeServiceDescriptorTable. As mentioned in Section 8.4.3, the system service handler (also known as KiSystemService/KiFastSystemService) uses the SystemServiceTable pointer in the KTHREAD block to retrieve the base address of the system service table that is used in the computation of the system call routine to be executed. Control is then transferred to the system call routine to be executed.

Given that the SystemServiceTable entry in the KTHREAD block is used to retrieve the value of the SSDT, modifying this entry for a specific thread can alter the thread's system call routine execution. The modified entry might, for example, point to a new system service table containing a different system call routine address than the original table. Because this modification is on a per-thread basis,

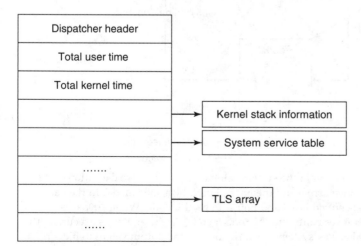

Figure 8.9: The partial KTHREAD structure containing a pointer to the system service table. The KTHREAD structure contains per-thread information.

to be effective it needs to be applied for all threads on a system. The resulting change will not be globally visible, making such modifications harder to detect.

8.4.5 System Call Code Patching

The technique known as system call code patching is very similar to the user-mode inline function patching technique described in Section 8.3.2. Because the system call code is patched in the kernel, this modification affects all processes running on the system that uses the patched system calls.

In this technique, similar to the inline function patching technique, the first few instructions are copied to a different location. If the first few instruction bytes do not align on an instruction boundary, then an additional instruction is copied to a different location. The starting instructions of a system call are then replaced and extra bytes are padded with NOPs to match the instruction boundary. Whenever the system call is invoked, control is transferred to the rootkit code. The rootkit can then invoke the original system call and modify the return values to hide its presence.

Because each system call does not use the same prologue, system call patching needs to properly identify and replace complete instructions. Copying or leaving an incomplete instruction may lead to the dreaded BSOD. To properly patch the system call, the first few bytes have to be disassembled or the opcodes of instructions hard-coded and compared to see if they match the instructions in the system call. Also, different operating system versions, updates, and service packs make this technique challenging to implement owing to the difficulty in identifying the instructions.

Another technique commonly used in patching system call code is to replace the instructions with invalid opcodes instead of far calls. This will generate an Invalid Opcode exception. If a rootkit randomizes the instructions that are copied to overwrite the first few bytes, it can be extremely difficult to detect this modification [348].

8.4.6 Layered Drivers

The Windows Driver Model (WDM) uses a layered model for devices. The devices are layered over one another to form a device stack, as shown in Figure 8.10 [361, 459]. The driver that owns a device is responsible for handling events generated for that particular device. On receiving a request for a particular device, the input/output (I/O) manager creates an interrupt request packet (IRP) and sends it down the device stack. Each driver that owns a device on the device stack is given a chance to handle this request. A driver can choose to simply return, request

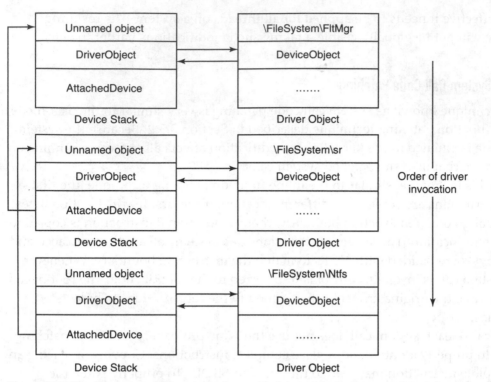

Figure 8.10: The file system device stack along with driver objects. Some rootkits take advantage of the device stack to install file system, keyboard, or network drivers. Such rootkits can then intercept events and modify the output.

to be notified on completion of the request, service the request by itself, or pass the IRP request to the driver below it.

Once the IRP request is serviced, control transfers to an upper layer driver only if the driver has explicitly requested to be notified upon completion. Some rootkits use this layered-driver model to install drivers on the file system, keyboard, or network stack. The layered-driver rootkit can then intercept events and modify the output, thereby changing the behavior of the underlying system.

File System Filter Driver Rootkit

A file system filter driver receives events related to file system changes such as loading of file volumes and creation and deletion of files and directories. The driver can use these event notifications to identify cases where an application is attempting to access the files. For example, an antivirus product can use the file system driver to prevent creation of malicious files. Similarly, a rootkit can use this layered-driver model to hide itself by modifying the output such that the files it hides appear to be nonexistent on the system.

The following are methods by which a driver might be attached to a device stack:

- *Using class drivers.* The class drivers are loaded by the operating system at boot time after the initialization of the base driver. A driver can attach to a particular class of drivers using the registry key

  ```
  HKLM\System\CurrentControlSet\Control\Class
  ```

  added to the USB device stack by creating a value "UpperFilter" = <DriverName> under the following registry key:

  ```
  HKLM\System\CurrentControlSet\Control\Class\
      {36FC9E60-C465-11CF-8056-44553540000}
  ```

- *Dynamically attaching using the API.* Instead of using a registry key, a driver can be added dynamically to the device stack using the Windows kernel API routines such as IoAttachDeviceToDeviceStack, shown here:

  ```
  PDEVICE_OBJECT IoAttachDeviceToDevicesStack(
      IN PDEVICE_OBJECT SoureceDevice,
      IN PDEVICE_OBJECT TargetDevice
      );
  ```

  This routine takes the target device object and attaches it to the source device.

- *Dynamically attaching to the desired device.* A driver can attach to the device stack by obtaining the device object and then manually walking through the stack until it reaches the desired object. By changing the AttachedDevice field, the driver is attached to the device stack.

Once a rootkit attaches itself to the file system device stack, it can intercept IRPs (events) generated by file open, create, write, and delete operations. The rootkit can then determine the file name and the type of access being performed on it using values on the IRP stack. If the file name matches the name that the rootkit is hiding or protecting, the rootkit can simply return an error status or remove the file name from the output. The files that are hidden by filter drivers can be accessed by bypassing the file system stack altogether and accessing the NTFS driver directly.

Example: Rootkit Using a Keyboard Filter Driver

In this example, a rootkit uses a keyboard filter driver to log keystrokes. The keyboard filter driver can attach itself to a low-level port driver or an upper-level keyboard class driver. The driver can intercept scan codes, translate them to ASCII, and log them to a file [55, 468].

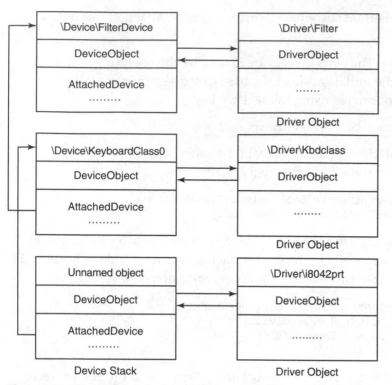

Figure 8.11: The keyboard device stack along with driver objects. The IRP request is sent first to the \Driver\Filter driver and makes its way down to \Driver\i8042prt. Upon processing the keystroke, the i8042prt keyboard controller driver stores the scan code corresponding to the keystroke and transmits it back to the I/O manager.

The I/O manager on a read request for the keyboard device creates an IRP and sends it down the stack to the keyboard controller driver. In Figure 8.11, the IRP is first sent to the \Driver\Filter driver object, then to \Driver\KbdClass, and finally to \Driver\i8042prt. At this point, the IRP does not yet contain a scan code for the keystroke. Each driver can set a callback using the IoSetCompletionRoutine API that causes the driver to be notified when the next-level driver has completed the requested operation [176].

The keyboard controller driver i8042prt, after processing the keystroke, stores the scan code in the IRP and sends it back to the I/O manager. Every driver that has set the completion routine will be notified of the IRP on its way back. The keyboard filter driver can then retrieve scan code for the keystroke from the IRP. However, as the callback is running at Interrupt Request Level > PASSIVE_LEVEL, it is not possible to log the keystrokes to a file. One solution to this problem is to use a dedicated system thread running at PASSIVE_LEVEL to log keystrokes to a file and to use shared memory between the driver and the system thread. With this approach, the keyboard filter driver will be able to log every keystroke typed by looking into the contents of the IRP on its way up to the I/O manager.

8.4.7 IRP Patching

Every driver has a specific structure—namely, the DRIVER_OBJECT—associated with it. The DRIVER_OBJECT structure contains the address of the MajorFunction as well as the other fields shown in Figure 8.12. The MajorFunction table stores the addresses of dispatch routines that are invoked when the driver receives an IRP. The IRP major function codes are used as an index into this table. The IRPs handle events such as create, read, write, query, set, and cleanup operations.

The FastIoDispatch table stores the addresses of the dispatch routines if the driver supports fast I/O. Only file system drivers and network-layered drivers support fast I/O and hence have these addresses set. By modifying the addresses of the dispatch routines in MajorFunction and FastIoDispatch tables, the rootkit code is invoked each time an event occurs, as shown in Figure 8.13. This technique is popular in rootkits and other types of malware to patch TCP/UDP IRPs, thereby avoiding detection by a firewall.

IRP patching consists of two major steps. The first step is to locate the address of the IRP function table of a driver. The second step is to modify the return parameters to hide.

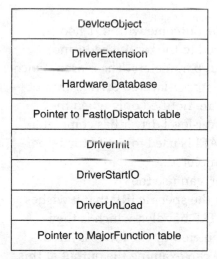

DeviceObject
DriverExtension
Hardware Database
Pointer to FastIoDispatch table
DriverInit
DriverStartIO
DriverUnLoad
Pointer to MajorFunction table

Figure 8.12: The DRIVER_OBJECT structure. Appropriately modifying the addresses of the dispatch routines in MajorFunction and FastIoDispatch can cause the rootkit code to execute each time an event occurs. This process is described in Figure 8.13.

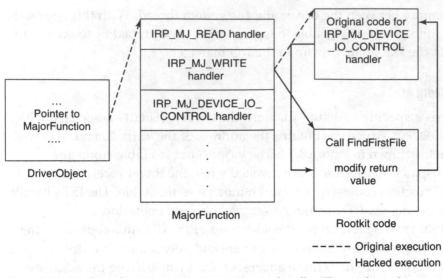

Figure 8.13: Patching the IRP_MJ_DEVICE_IO_CONTROL handler. The rootkit code executes in the hacked execution, denoted by the solid arrow.

Locating the Address of the IRP Function Table. The DeviceObject for a named object is retrieved by using the IoGetDeviceObjectPointer. As mentioned in Section 8.4.6, the DeviceObject contains the address of the DriverObject that owns this device. Once the DriverObject is obtained, the IRP function table can be retrieved easily from the driver object.

Modifying the Return Parameters. Similar to the outcome with IDT hooks, in the IRP patching technique, control is not returned to the rootkit code and, therefore, the rootkit code cannot modify the output parameters. The reason: Once the IRP is handled by the lower-layered drivers, the upper-layered drivers are not notified of the completion. The upper-level drivers are notified only when they specifically request to be notified, after the next-lower-level driver has completed the IRP processing. The IoSetCompletionRoutine API is used to notify the upper-layered drivers when the requested operation is completed.

The rootkit code, after patching the IRP handler, can use the IoSetCompletionRoutine to cause it be notified for the specific IRP that it wishes to process. Next, the rootkit code calls the original IRP handler, which is then passed down the device stack. Once the IRP is completed by the lower-layered driver, the rootkit code is notified. The rootkit code can examine the output at this point and remove itself from the return values to hide its presence.

8.4.8 Direct Kernel Object Manipulation

Direct kernel object manipulation (DKOM) techniques modify kernel memory structures without using any standard API calls. As certain structures (which could be as small as 4 bytes) are modified without using standard APIs, it is a nontrivial task to identify such modifications. These techniques can be used to hide processes, drivers, and services.

Unlinking a Process from the Process List. The Windows scheduler is a thread-based scheduler that maintains a doubly linked list of thread objects for scheduling. The kernel also maintains a doubly linked list of active process objects that can be queried using the standard API (for example, ZwQuerySystemInformation). The Windows task manager uses this API to obtain a list of currently running processes. A process object can be deleted by modifying the forward and backward pointers in the linked list [293]. By removing the process from this list, the process is effectively hidden, as shown in Figure 8.14.

The process enumeration in user and kernel modes using the standard API will fail to reveal the existence of the hidden process. The process will still be

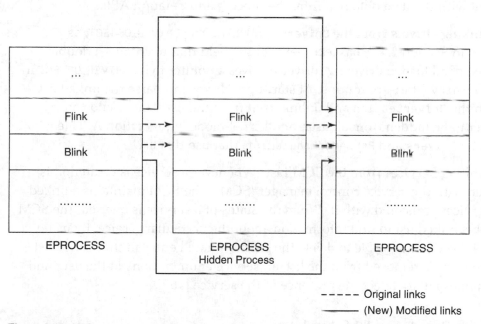

Figure 8.14: Hiding a process from the active process list. The process is removed from the doubly linked list of active process objects. Consequently, enumerating processes using the standard API will fail to show the existence of the hidden process. However, the process will still be scheduled because the scheduler uses the thread list for scheduling.

scheduled, however, as the scheduler does not use the process list for scheduling, but uses the thread list instead.

Unlinking a Process from `PspCidTable`. Every process in a Windows kernel is represented with a per-process structure known as the EPROCESS block. This structure contains information related to the process such as its process ID (PID), threads, quota usage, and a pointer to a handle table—namely, `ObjectTable`. The `ObjectTable` contains a linked list of handles to processes and threads in a system; the kernel maintains a global variable called `PspCidTable` that points to the first element in this list. This list is queried by the `NtOpenProcess`, and `PsLookupProcessByProcessId` APIs to determine the existence of process/threads. A process can be deleted from this list by modifying the forward and backward pointers [375]. Nevertheless, removing a process from this list would still cause the process to be listed using process enumeration APIs. Removing a process from the `PspCidTable` list would cause the open process APIs to fail to obtain a handle on the hidden process.

Some commercial anti-rootkit technology makes use of this list indirectly by calling `NtOpenProcess` on all process PIDs in the valid range and then comparing the result with the data obtained from the process enumeration APIs.

Unlinking Drivers from the `DriverObject` List. The DRIVER_OBJECT, as described in Section 8.4.7, has a `DriverSection` field that maintains a doubly linked list of all loaded drivers. A driver receives a pointer to its DRIVER_OBJECT in its `DriverEntry` (start-up) routine. At start-up, a driver can parse the linked list stored in the `DriverSection` and unlink itself from the list. This would cause the driver to be hidden from all user- and kernel-mode enumeration APIs (e.g., `EnumDeviceDrivers` and `PsLoadedModuleList`) that use this list.

Unlinking Services from the SCM List. Whenever a service is created, it is registered with the service control manager (SCM). The SCM maintains a linked list of services registered with it. When the status of a service is queried, the SCM parses this linked list to find information about the particular service. By using DKOM, it becomes possible to delete the service-related entry in this linked list. Once a service is removed from the list, all service enumerations in the user and kernel modes fail to detect the presence of the service [469].

8.4.9 Hiding Threads from the Scheduler

The FU rootkit hides a process by unlinking it from the process list (as described in Section 8.4.8). The hidden process will still be executed, however, because the Windows scheduler is a thread-based scheduler—that is, it uses thread objects for scheduling. Processes hidden with the FU rootkit are identified by enumerating all the threads in the ready and wait state queues and comparing them with the threads obtained from processes in the process list. If the threads are removed from the ready and wait state queues, then they are never scheduled because the scheduler never sees those threads. By contrast, if a new kernel thread is created that acts as a scheduler to run the hidden threads, then those threads would run even though they are invisible to the actual scheduler. It is necessary to modify NtYieldExecution to give time quantum to hidden threads and to implement a swapper to swap each thread's pages into memory [1].

8.4.10 Redirecting Virtual Memory Access

Redirection of virtual memory access is popularly known as the *shadow walker technique* or *desynchronizing the split translation look-aside buffer* approach [384]. This technique relies on a split translation look-aside buffer (TLB), where separate TLBs exist for instructions and data, as shown in Figure 8.15. This approach is used to hide pages in memory by allowing execute (code) access to a rootkit page but redirecting the data access (read/write) to a different page. Ironically, this technique is based on the PaX project [416], which prevents buffer overflows by effectively making the stack and data pages non-executable.

   Modern operating systems support virtual memory so as to present an unlimited view of the memory address space. The CPU always uses virtual addresses to reference memory locations. The virtual addresses are translated into physical addresses using the hardware-supported paging mechanism. The paging

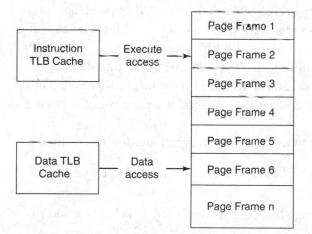

Figure 8.15: Code/data TLB desynchronization. Separate TLBs exist for instructions and data, which can be leveraged to hide pages in memory.

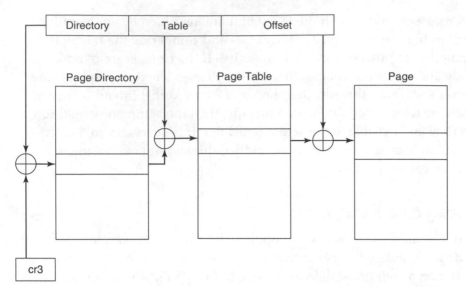

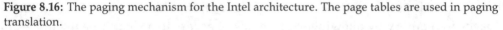

Figure 8.16: The paging mechanism for the Intel architecture. The page tables are used in paging translation.

mechanism, in turn, uses page tables to convert virtual addresses to physical addresses. The paging mechanism for the Intel architecture is shown in Figure 8.16.

Given that it is not possible to store all pages that correspond to the entire virtual memory space in memory simultaneously, pages are swapped out and new pages are swapped into memory by the page fault handler whenever needed. Thus, to access a page, at least three memory references are needed and an additional two disk I/O accesses are needed if the page tables are swapped out of memory. To avoid this overhead for every memory access, most hardware CPUs (such as those provided by Intel and AMD) store this translation in an internal TLB cache. As long as the translation is found in the TLB cache (a TLB hit), the translation is relatively fast. If the translation is not present in the cache (a TLB miss), the translation is calculated by accessing page tables and stored in the TLB for future access. Because the TLB cache is extremely small, the entries are replaced if a page is not accessed for a long period of time.

The sequence of steps that occur in a paging mechanism are described next:

1. If the translation is found in the TLB, then it is converted directly to a physical address.
2. In the event of a TLB miss, a page fault occurs and control is transferred to the page fault handler.
3. The page fault handler checks whether the virtual address is valid.

4. If the address is valid, the page fault handler loads the corresponding page into memory and stores the translation in the TLB.

5. Control is transferred to the original instruction that triggered the page fault.

In this technique, an IDT hook is placed for the page fault interrupt. Every page to be hidden is marked "not present" so that any access to these pages triggers a page fault if the translation is not present in the TLB. Hence, whenever the rootkit pages are accessed, control is transferred to the rootkit code via the page fault hook.

Hiding Code Pages. To hide code pages, the TLBs are desynchronized such that the virtual address is mapped to the correct physical address in case of execute access. In case of read/write access, the virtual address is mapped to a different physical address.

Whenever control is transferred to the rootkit handler, a test is performed to compare the values of the address that caused the page fault with the current execution pointer (EP). In this way, the rootkit can determine if the page fault was due to execute access or read/write access. In case of execute access, control is transferred to the original page fault handler and the execution resumes normally. In case of read/write access, the rootkit code manually loads a page that does not correspond to the rootkit page, thereby effectively hiding the contents of the code page.

This scheme is feasible when separate caches exist for code and data access. For code access, the original translation is stored so that the proper contents execute. For data access, by contrast, the translation is mapped to a different physical address. These translations are cached in TLB entries after the first access and remain until they are flushed, thereby resulting in very little performance overhead.

Hiding Data Pages. To successfully hide a page containing data, the rootkit has to differentiate access to the page by itself from access to the page by an external application, such as anti-rootkit software. A simple approach to hide a data page is to produce a page fault on every data access and then provide for redirection if the data access corresponds to the data page that the rootkit is hiding. Unfortunately, this approach results in significant performance overhead—it causes a page fault for every data access.

To avoid this overhead, the rootkit can selectively choose to load a data page manually when required. During this access to the data page, the rootkit needs to ensure that it has exclusive access to the page. Thus, whenever the rootkit needs to access the data page, it gains exclusive access to the system, thereby preventing an application running at higher privilege from accessing the actual data page. The rootkit then flushes the TLB entry in the cache corresponding to the data page, to avoid reading the redirected page itself. It then manually loads the correct translation corresponding to the data page. Once the rootkit has finished accessing the data page, the TLB entry is purged to prevent an external application from reading the actual page. The rootkit then relinquishes control of the system to allow execution of other applications. Hence both code and data pages are effectively hidden in memory using this technique.

8.4.11 Loading Kernel Drivers Without SCM

A rootkit that utilizes the service control manager (SCM) to load drivers into the kernel address space needs to create a registry key in the hive:

```
HKEY_LOCAL_MACHINE\System\CurrentControlSetxxx\<ServiceName>
```

The SCM uses this registry key during the initialization of the driver object, and the registry key is passed as a parameter to the entry point of the driver. Hence, to successfully hide its presence, the rootkit has to hide service keys along with files related to the rootkit. Alternatively, a rootkit can use other entry points to load drivers into the kernel address space without registering with the SCM.

Loading a Driver Using `SystemLoadAndCallImage`. A kernel driver can be loaded without registering with the SCM by using an undocumented API—namely, `ZwSetSystemInformation`. The prototype of `ZwSetSystemInformation` is

```
NTSYSAPI NTSTATUS NTAPI ZwSetSystemInformation(
    IN SYSTEM_INFORMATION_CLASS SystemInformationClass,
    IN OUT PVOID SystemInformation,
    IN ULONG SystemInformationLength)

typedef struct _SYSTEM_LOAD_AND_CALL_IMAGE{
    UNICODE_STRING ModuleName;
} SYSTEM_LOAD_AND_CALL_IMAGE, *PSYSTEM_LOAD_AND_CALL_IMAGE
```

By calling the `ZwSetSystemInformation` API with `SystemLoadAndCallImage` as `SystemInformationClass` and `SystemInformation` pointing to the `SYSTEM_LOAD_AND_CALL_IMAGE` structure, a module is loaded into the kernel address space [175]. `ModuleName` contains the path for the module image to be loaded. A driver loaded by this technique does not register with the SCM, so scanning for the running services and drivers using the SCM would not reveal the existence of this driver.

Writing to Physical Memory. The Windows Object Manager is responsible for maintaining access to all objects in the operating system. In the Windows OS, every resource—processes, files, directories, and ports—are represented as objects.

The `\Device\PhysicalMemory` object represents physical memory on a system. The Windows 2K and later operating systems do not allow user-mode applications to write to physical memory directly. Only `ntvdm.exe` (the DOS 16-bit emulator application) can write directly to physical memory in user mode. This capability is probably intended to maintain backward compatibility for 16-bit DOS applications; in the DOS operating system, any application was allowed to write to physical memory directly. Hence, writing to physical memory can give an attacker significant advantages.

The following steps are needed to successfully write to physical memory [71]:

- *Restricted permissions.* The `\Device\PhysicalMemory` object is accessible in read mode to all user-mode processes but accessible in write mode only to processes running with `SYSTEM` privileges. By default, the administrator does not have write access to this object. However, processes executing with administrator privileges can obtain access to this object by modifying Access Control List (ACL) settings. Once write access is obtained, it becomes possible to write to arbitrary physical address locations.

- *Mapping virtual to physical addresses.* The CPU uses virtual addresses, so these addresses need to be mapped to physical addresses. In kernel mode, `MmGetPhysicalAddress` is used to convert virtual addresses to physical addresses. However, the routine shown in Figure 8.17 is a near-implementation of this API that can be used to map virtual addresses to physical addresses.

Installing Call Gates. To execute kernel code from user mode, a call gate has to be installed. In the Intel IA-32 architectures, call gates are used to execute a routine at a predefined address using a far call. To install this kind of call gate in the GDT table, kernel-mode privileges are needed. By directly writing to physical memory, it is possible to create an entry in the GDT table. Once the call gate is installed, code

```
PHYSICAL_MEMORY MyGetPhysicalAddress(void *BaseAddress)
{
    if (BaseAddress < 0x80000000 || BaseAddress >= 0xA0000000)
        return(BaseAddress & 0xFFFF000);

    return(BaseAddress & 0x1FFFF000);
}
```

Figure 8.17: Custom code to translate a virtual address to a physical address—a near-implementation of the `MmGetPhysicalAddress` API.

can be executed in kernel mode by making a far jump to the handler specified in the call gate.

The following cases require kernel mode to modify changes to the system. By using this technique, the changes are made from user mode by using a call gate:

- Allocate memory in kernel mode using a call gate handler and modify SSDT entries to point to the allocated memory by writing to physical memory directly. With this approach, the system call table is hooked without loading a kernel driver.
- Modify the process list using a call gate handler to hide certain processes by unlinking them from the process list.

8.5 Linux Rootkits

Besides being written for the Windows operating system, rootkits are available for common variants of the UNIX operating system such as Linux, BSD, and Solaris. In this section, we describe rootkit techniques that apply to the Linux OS. Many of the techniques described here are similar to those used with other UNIX variants and, in some cases, to techniques used with the Windows OS. Nevertheless, some rootkit techniques, such as executable replacement rootkits (described in Section 8.5.1), are specific to UNIX and are not commonly seen in Windows. The following rootkit techniques are explored in this section:

- Executable replacement rootkits (Section 8.5.1)
- Loadable kernel module (LKM) rootkits (Section 8.5.2)
- Runtime kernel patching rootkits (Section 8.5.3)
- Virtual File System (VFS) rootkits (Section 8.5.4)

8.5.1 Executable Replacement Rootkits

Executable replacement rootkits replace or modify on-disk executables of commonly used administrative utilities to hide their presence. Typically, the rootkit replaces the /bin/login utility to create backdoor access. The /bin/login program runs every time a user logs in using a terminal or through remote access. The program checks the user ID and matches the password input by the user against the password stored in the password file. The rootkit-replaced login program can bypass these security checks. Besides the login program, several other programs, such as du (disk utilization), ls (contents of file system), ps (process list), and lsmod (enumerate loaded modules), can be replaced so as to hide the presence of the rootkit [376].

Instead of replacing the executables entirely, some rootkits infect the on-disk images of certain executable types (e.g., system object files) [423]. One such technique is to infect loadable kernel modules (LKMs), which are object files loaded dynamically into the kernel. The LKMs use the Executable and Linking Format (ELF) and consist of sections including the `.symtab`, which contains symbols needed by the linker. The key symbol in this table is `init_module`, which is the routine used to initialize the module. When the module is dynamically loaded, the loader searches the `.symtab` section and retrieves the address of this module. The loader then calls this routine to initialize the module. The rootkit can modify the `.symtab` section by changing `init_module`'s symbol address to point to the rootkit code. When the loader transfers control to `init_module`, control is actually transferred to the rootkit first. This technique is not limited to `init_module`, however, but rather can be extended to replace any of the exported routines.

8.5.2 Loadable Kernel Module Rootkits

Loadable kernel modules are modules that can be loaded dynamically into the Linux kernel. These modules extend the functionality of the kernel, without requiring modifications to the kernel's base image distributions. LKMs are analogous to device drivers in the Windows OS. They work by dynamically loading drivers into a running kernel and are typically used to load device drivers, file system drivers, and network drivers that provide additional support for the rootkit. Once loaded into the kernel, LKMs can modify critical kernel structures. Unfortunately, this functionality can be abused by rootkits to hide their presence on the system.

The most commonly modified structure targeted by LKM rootkits is the system call table (exported as `sys_call_table`) [164, 314, 318]. This technique is similar to the use of SSDT hooks in Windows. With this technique, LKM rootkits redirect a system call to rootkit code by modifying the address stored in the system call table entry. It then becomes possible to hide system activities related to the rootkit, such as processes, files, and ports opened by the rootkit. For example, to redirect the read system call to rootkit code, the LKM can modify the system call table as follows: `sys_call_table[SYS_read] = rootkit_read`. The rootkit can hide its process by modifying the system table entry for the `SYS_getdents` system call. The ps command, which enumerates running processes, internally uses the `getdents` system call to get the directory entries from the proc directory (which contains the directories related to each running process based on the PID). The LKM rootkit can remove the PID from the output or return fake values for the rootkit's PID.

LKMs are detectable by listing the current loaded modules via the `lsmod` command, which internally uses the read system call to read the `/proc/modules` file. Thus, to effectively hide the module from listing, the rootkit needs to hook the read system call in sys_call_table.

Another technique that hides a module is manipulating the "module" structure, which the kernel uses to store information for all modules. This structure is not exported by the kernel; rather, the only means by which this structure is accessible is through an LKM's init routine, init_module(). The init_module function is present in a loadable module, which uses the "module" structure as a parameter. Thus it is possible to manipulate the module structure fields such as those for the name and usage count, related to the rootkit, such that even the kernel is ignorant of the rootkit module's existence [314].

8.5.3 Runtime Kernel Patching Rootkits

In certain cases, LKM support might not be built into the kernel, which would prevent loading an LKM rootkit. In this case, the rootkit can patch the running kernel to insert its image (usually as an LKM object file) into the kernel memory [50]. The kernel's virtual memory is accessible using the device /dev/kmem and, therefore, can be used for runtime LKM rootkit loading, even without LKM support.

The kmem device contents can be searched to locate the desired kernel structures by using symbol addresses publicly exported in /proc/ksyms or by using the /System.map file generated during kernel compilation. For example, it is possible to locate the task_struct structure using the kstat symbol address in the ksyms symbol file. In certain cases, the System.map file might not be present on a system, or the symbol might not be publicly exported in the ksyms file, or the ksyms file might not be present when LKM support is not included in the kernel.

A rootkit module can use the runtime patching technique to hide itself by modifying the "module" structure in memory. However, the "module" structure's symbol is not exported. In this case, certain search techniques can be applied based on the module structure field, such as the address of the module name string. A first search pass on the memory can locate the module name and store its address. This address can then be used during a second search pass to locate the module's entry in the module structure. This technique can be used to hide a rootkit module.

A rootkit can also modify the sys_call_table structure in memory to hijack system calls [192]. Similar to what happens with the module structure, the system call table structure is also not exported. As we are aware, system calls are made using the int 0x80 interrupt on Linux systems, and a system call number is stored in the EAX register before making the interrupt. Also, the interrupt descriptors containing the interrupt's entry point are stored in the interrupt descriptor table

(IOT). Thus, by locating the IDT (by using an instruction such as SIDT), the 0x80 interrupt's entry point can be obtained. The 0x80 interrupt typically uses the instruction call sys_call_table(,eax,4). A disassembly of this instruction can be used to obtain the sys_call_table address, and this address can be searched in the kernel memory. In this way, the rootkit can locate sys_call_table by searching for this address in the kernel memory, and it can then modify the required system call entries to redirect a system call to the rootkit code.

A rootkit can also load kernel modules by directly inserting them into kernel memory. The main challenge with this approach is to find kernel memory that is not used by the running kernel and is not overwritten by a memory operation (such as kmalloc). The solution is based on the kmalloc pool start address's alignment to a page boundary. This leaves a memory gap between the start address and the actual start of kmalloc memory, where the LKM can be inserted. However, the LKM might not fit in this bit of memory. The rootkit can overcome this limitation by inserting bootstrap code in this unused memory region, which would contain code to allocate kernel memory for the LKM. In this way, the LKM rootkit can be loaded into kernel memory even without LKM support.

8.5.4 VFS Rootkits

VFS rootkits modify the virtual file system structures to redirect system calls to rootkit code without modifying the sys_call_table entries. The Linux Virtual File System (VFS) is a kernel component that enables the handling of file system operations across several kinds of file systems, such as EXT2, EXT3, and NTFS. Thus VFS provides a layer of abstraction between the program that makes the file-handling system call and the actual file system implementations.

VFS achieves a common file model using data structures such as the file object, inode object, and dentry object. The file object structure is created for any directory or file when accessed by a process. One of the fields in this structure is a pointer to the file_operations structure (f_op). The file_operations structure, in turn, contains pointers to functions specific to the file system type (e.g., NTFS).

Whenever a read is requested on a file, the SYS_read system call is invoked. The system call then gets the function pointer in the file object structure for the read function as file->f_op->read(..), which is an indirect call to the file system–specific read. A rootkit can modify VFS structures, such as the read function pointer described earlier, to point to the rootkit code [298]. Using this method, the rootkit can hide itself without the need to modify the sys_call_table entries.

Another VFS data structure that is often modified by rootkits is the inode object structure. The inode structure also contains function pointers to inode operation functions such as lookups (used for certain directory enumerations). To hide a process, the rootkit can change the function pointer for the /proc directory's lookup function. The rootkit can then hide a process by modifying the process directory's inode structure.

8.6 BIOS Rootkits

The Basic Input/Output System (BIOS) is the firmware code that is executed first when a PC is powered on. It runs power-on self-test (POST) code, followed by code to control the keyboard and screen display. After a series of initialization of devices and memory, the BIOS locates the master boot record (MBR) of the target drive and transfers control to the code located in the boot sector. Initially, BIOSs were distributed on ROM cards, although most of today's BIOSs are contained on EEPROM cards. Since early 1998, BIOS has also supported power management routines and adheres to Advanced Configuration and Power Interface (ACPI) standards [171].

Based on motherboard settings, it is possible to write to BIOS flash memory. On some motherboards, such as the Intel SecureFlash, unsigned updates to the system BIOS flash memory are disallowed. On a vast majority of motherboards, writing to the BIOS is not allowed by default. This protection can be turned off by setting a jumper on the motherboard or by using a hardware setup program. Once the protection is disabled, a rootkit can write to the BIOS such that it can survive reboots. A rootkit technique using an ACPI-compliant BIOS is described here.

The ACPI is an industry-standard interface developed to provide robust OS-controlled power management and advanced configuration (OSPM). ACPI-compliant hardware platforms use the ACPI control method's virtual machine language (AML) to execute. Conversely, hardware OEM vendors define objects and write control methods in ACPI Source Language (ASL); these methods are translated into AML using an ASL translator. The AML instructions are executed by the AML interpreter that is supported on an ACPI-compliant OS. Figure 8.18 shows a schematic diagram of the ACPI-supported OS.

On ACPI-compliant systems with BIOS reflashing enabled, it is possible to write code into BIOS such that it survives reboots. The rootkit code can be written in Assembly Language (ASM) directly or written using the higher-level ASL, which can then be translated into ASM and written to the BIOS [166]. By creating new opcodes in ASM, the work function corresponding to the opcode can be executed.

Because BIOS can access system memory, the ASL objects can arbitrarily modify kernel memory. For example, an ASL object can overwrite critical kernel structures that can lower system security settings. Given that the BIOS has smaller

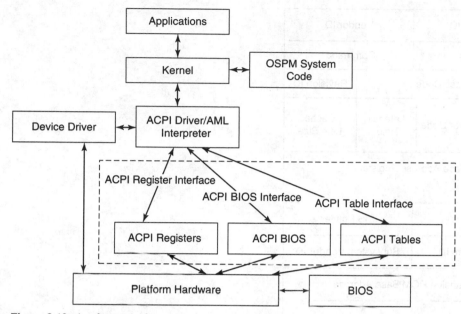

Figure 8.18: A schematic diagram of an operating system that supports ACPI.

memory storage and uses special language (not machine language instructions), the usual hook-based rootkit techniques will not work in this case. If the rootkit modifies firmware, however, it can survive reinstallation of the OS and will then be difficult to remove other than by reflashing the BIOS contents.

8.7 PCI Rootkits

The Peripheral Component Interconnect (PCI) bus specification provides a standard for peripheral devices to communicate with the CPU. The PCI bus connects peripheral devices (e.g., graphics cards, wireless cards) to the computer system. The PCI device can contain initialization code in the expansion ROM. The expansion ROM, in turn, can contain the images required to initialize various architectures in a single ROM. The devices should adhere to the configuration space header as shown in Figure 8.19.

During the POST process, PCI devices are queried to determine whether the expansion ROM base register is implemented in the configuration space. If this register is implemented, then POST maps the ROM image to main memory and determines whether the first two bytes are AA55. If this signature is found, then ROM is present. POST should then find a ROM image that matches the device ID

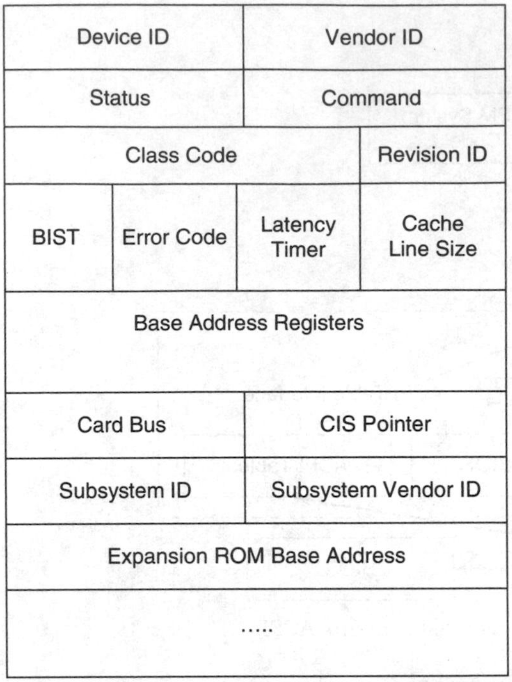

Device ID		Vendor ID	
Status		Command	
Class Code			Revision ID
BIST	Error Code	Latency Timer	Cache Line Size
Base Address Registers			
Card Bus		CIS Pointer	
Subsystem ID		Subsystem Vendor ID	
Expansion ROM Base Address			
.....			

Figure 8.19: Type 00h configuration space header.

```
Offset   Contains
0h       55
1h       AA
2h       Initialization size in
         multiples of 512 bytes
3h       Entry point to INIT function
6h       Reserved
18h      Pointer to PCI data
```

Figure 8.20: ROM header extensions. To ensure compatibility with the PC architecture, the second byte contains the initialization code size.

and vendor ID in the configuration space. To provide compatibility with PC architectures, the second byte contains the initialization code size, as shown in Figure 8.20.

On Windows systems, to write to the expansion ROM of PCI cards, an input/output privilege level (IOPL) of 3 is required. Most user-mode applications have an IOPL value of 1. To obtain a higher IOPL, a process can set SeTcbPrivilege using the NtSetInformationProcess API. Alternatively, the rootkit can install a kernel driver to gain write privileges for PCI devices. Once the IOPL value of 3 is attained, the rootkit is written onto the expansion ROM.

At the next system start-up, the BIOS executes the POST process, which queries PCI devices and transfers control to the initialization code in the expansion ROM. Hence, control is transferred to the PCI rootkit. At this point, however, the rootkit is running in real mode (16-bit). The biggest challenge in PCI/BOOT rootkits is to maintain control during the operating system boot process and to regain control after the OS starts in protected (32-bit) mode. To regain control, real-mode interrupt vector table (IVT) entries are hooked. Some well-known examples of using IVT hooks are interrupt 13h (lower-layer disk services) and interrupt 10h. The rootkit invoked via real-mode interrupt hooks can patch the operating system loader to gain even stronger control, as in a BOOT rootkit. In this way, PCI rootkits may be used as an effective stealthing mechanism.

8.8   Virtual Machine—Based Rootkits

Virtual machine–based rootkits (VMBRs) modify the system such that the entire operating system, including user applications, is run in a virtualized environment. Hence any security applications running on the original operating system will now run in a virtualized environment. The rootkit itself runs outside the virtual machine. Thus VMBR rootkits are at an advantage when compared to security software, as they can execute at a layer lower than security software. Based on the type of virtualization support used by VMBR rootkits, they are classified as either software-based VMBRs (discussed in Section 8.8.1) or hardware-assisted VMBRs (discussed in Section 8.8.2).

8.8.1   Software-Based VMBRs

In software-based virtual machines, the virtualization support is provided by the Virtual Machine Monitor (VMM). The VMM runs on the native (i.e., host) operating system. The operating system that runs in a virtual environment is referred to as the guest operating system. There are no real CPU instructions that can be used to transfer control from host to guest operating system.

The VMM manages access to the underlying hardware and creates virtual devices to be used by the guest operating system. It interfaces with the real hardware by using the host operating system services. The VMM provides an abstract interface to the guest operating system via virtual devices. For its part, the guest operating system interfaces with the emulated hardware as if it were executing on a real machine. These interactions are trapped by the VMM and emulated in software. In short, the guest operating system runs in a virtualized environment without any modifications.

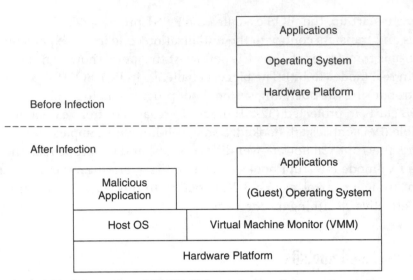

Figure 8.21: Software-based VMBR. Before infection, the operating system runs as normal on top of the hardware platform. After infection, the operating system runs as a guest on top of a VMM. The VMBR installs a new host operating system in which the malicious code runs. Because the malicious code runs on the host operating system, it is not visible to the guest operating system.

The software-based VMBR was first introduced by SubVirt, a proof-of-concept technology developed by University of Michigan researchers with support from Microsoft [215]. SubVirt uses two popular virtual machine monitors, VMware and VirtualPC. On a Windows system, Virtual PC is installed and the target OS is run inside Virtual PC. By contrast, the rootkit and malicious applications execute on host operating systems. On Linux systems, VMWare is used as the VMM and the target OS runs inside VMware. Once the VMM is installed, the images can be downloaded to the target system. Figure 8.21 depicts the workings of a software-based VMBR.

To allow the VMM to gain control of the operating system after a reboot, the boot order of the host operating system is modified. The VMM then starts the guest operating system, thereby allowing the target operating system to run on the VMM. The VMM silently transfers control to the host operating system. After the host operating system is started, the rootkit can then start malicious applications that run outside the target operating system.

8.8.2 Hardware–Assisted VMBRs

Newer 64-bit architectures such as AMD Pacifica and Intel VT-x support virtualization at the hardware layer. This support is provided by means of CPU instructions that can be used to transfer control between the virtual machine and

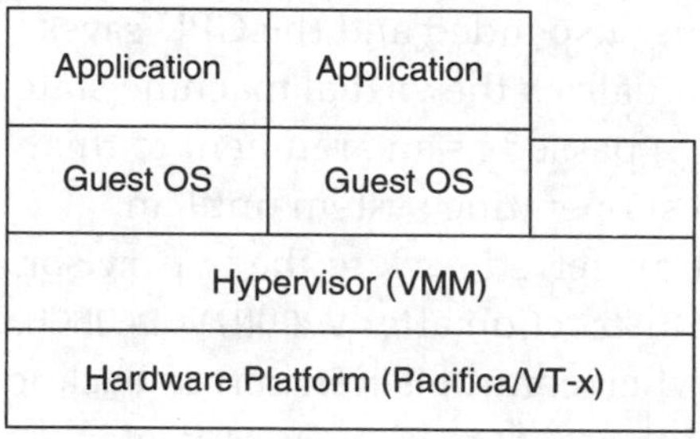

Application | Application

Guest OS | Guest OS

Hypervisor (VMM)

Hardware Platform (Pacifica/VT-x)

Figure 8.22: Hardware-supported VMBR. Multiple guest operating systems, whose execution is controlled by the hypervisor, can run on the underlying hardware platform.

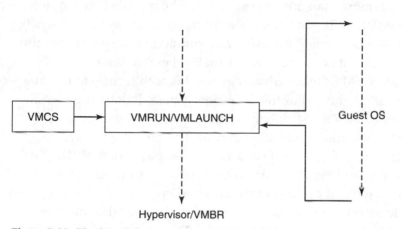

Hypervisor/VMBR

Figure 8.23: The hypervisor and guest operating system after execution of the VMRUN/VMLAUNCH instruction. The state of the hypervisor is saved in main memory. The virtual machine state is initialized from the virtual machine control structure (VMCS), which is passed as an argument to VMRUN/VMLAUNCH. The guest OS then retains control until an intercept occurs.

the host. The virtual machine architecture is designed to support running multiple virtual machines on a single hardware platform, as shown in Figure 8.22. The VMM (also known as the hypervisor) is a system software component that controls the execution of multiple guest operating systems. BluePill, a proof-of-concept hardware-assisted VMBR for AMD, was introduced by Joanna Rutkowska, a renowned security researcher [364]. Another proof-of-concept hardware-assisted VMBR for Intel was introduced by Dino Dai Zovi [495].

The processor supports at least two modes: VM (nonprivileged) mode and non-VM (privileged CPU or ring 0) mode. The hypervisor runs in non-VM mode and the guest operating system runs in a virtualized (VM) mode. The VMRUN (AMD)/VMLAUNCH (Intel) instruction launches a virtual machine, as shown in Figure 8.23. This instruction can be executed only in a privileged (non-VM) mode.

After this instruction is executed, the hypervisor is suspended and the CPU saves the hypervisor state in main memory. The CPU initializes the virtual machine state from the virtual machine control structure (VMCS) passed as an argument to this instruction. Control is then transferred to the guest operating system until an intercept occurs, which causes the control to be transferred back to the hypervisor. The hypervisor resumes its execution at the next instruction after VMRUN/VMLAUNCH.

The VMCS contains settings that determine when control is transferred back to the hypervisor. The hypervisor can explicitly set intercepts to transfer control in case of certain interrupts and when particular instructions are executed. For certain sensitive instructions such as CPUID and RDMSR, control is transferred implicitly to the hypervisor. Although more than one hypervisor may be installed on a system, the hypervisor that is installed first has complete control over the system. There is no hardware bit or register that would help software running in the guest operating system to determine whether it is running in a virtualized environment.

The hardware-assisted VMBR takes advantages of this architecture to run at a layer lower than that used by the rest of the operating system. Its sets the VMCS and executes the VMRUN/VMLAUNCH instruction. After this instruction executes, the VMBR is in suspended mode and acts as a hypervisor. The operating system executing natively is then forced to execute in a virtualized environment. The VMBR acts as a hypervisor and monitors for events generated from the guest operating system. For example, it can detect instances where a guest operating system is attempting to detect that it is running in a virtualized environment.

For example, a guest operating system can use the SIDT instruction to detect the presence of a virtual machine. The SIDT instruction retrieves the base address of the IDT and can be executed in nonprivileged mode. On software-emulated virtual machines, such as VMWare, the IDT of the guest operating system differs from the IDT of the host system. In this situation, the SIDT instruction is used to detect the presence of a software-emulated virtual machine on a pre-hypervisor architecture (also known as Red Pill) [363]. However, a hypervisor-assisted VMBR can request an intercept when the SIDT instruction is executed, and modify the output to resemble execution on a native system.

Emulating VMRUN/VMLAUNCH. To avoid easy detection, the VMBR needs to either emulate the VMRUN/VMLAUNCH instruction or modify the registers to lie about the hypervisor support in the underlying hardware. To emulate this instruction, which can be executed only in non-VM mode, the VMBR running as hypervisor can trap the fault and create a new virtual machine. The VMBR then acts as a conduit between the guest operating system and the VM created by the guest operating system [364].

8.9 Rootkit Defense

This section describes some of the techniques used for the prevention and detection of rootkits. No single approach can effectively guard against all rootkits. Instead, a combination of techniques is needed to provide adequate protection against rootkits.

8.9.1 Rootkit Prevention

The best defense against rootkits is to prevent their installation on the system. As described in this chapter, rootkits modify several important system resources to successfully hide their presence. Thus denying access to such resources could thwart rootkit installation. This section identifies some of the techniques that could prevent rootkit infection.

Denying Write Access to the Process Address Space

As described in Section 8.3.1, for user-mode rootkits to be successful, they must have write access to the target process's address space. By denying write access to a process address space, then, the process is protected from being infected by user-mode rootkits. However, some Microsoft components require write access to a process address space to ensure successful updates. Selectively allowing access to a process address space poses significant challenges.

Denying Write Access to Physical Memory

As described in Section 8.4.11, one way to load a kernel driver without using SCM is to write directly to physical memory. In Windows, physical memory is represented by the device \Device\PhysicalMemory. There are few instances that require write access to this device in user mode. Given this fact, preventing write access to this device in user mode could prevent loading of kernel drivers using physical memory. By default, write access to this device is disabled in Windows Server 2003 but not in other versions of Windows.

Using PatchGuard Protection

Kernel patch protection (PatchGuard) is a protection mechanism developed by Microsoft to prevent unauthorized modifications to key kernel data structures and to the kernel code itself [68]. PatchGuard checks the integrity of the protected structures at regular time intervals and generates a blue screen of death (BSOD) once it detects a modification. Given that many key structures that PatchGuard protects are modified by rootkits, PatchGuard helps to thwart certain kernel-mode rootkits. Note that PatchGuard protection also interferes with many current implementations of software security products such as antivirus and firewall products, as these software products commonly patch the structures protected by PatchGuard.

PatchGuard is currently supported on 64-bit platforms such as Windows Server 2003 x64, Windows XP x64, Windows Vista x64, and Windows Server 2008 x64. The user access control (UAC) and signed driver loading security features [68], which were introduced in Windows Vista to provide protection against malware, also protect against rootkits.

Preventing ROM Updates

On some motherboards, such as Intel SecureFlash, unsigned updates to BIOS are disabled. The write access to BIOS is controlled via jumper settings and can be turned off. Thus, by disallowing writes to BIOS using one of these techniques, BIOS rootkits could be thwarted. Similar techniques of disallowing unsigned updates and writes to PCI flash memory could be used to protect against PCI rootkits.

8.9.2 Rootkit Detection

A rootkit, by definition, is invisible: It hides itself by modifying several key system structures. Thus it should be impossible to detect a complete rootkit that uses effective hiding techniques, as the detection software cannot get an unhidden view of the system. Luckily, so far we have not seen such a complete rootkit. This section describes some techniques that are used to detect rootkits on a system.

Cross-View Detection

The cross-view detection technique is the most popular mechanism for rootkit detection and is used by many rootkit detection software solutions [60, 112]. In this approach, two separate views are obtained for the same system resource and compared for discrepancies. For example, to detect hidden files, one list is generated using a Windows API such as `FindFirstFile` or `FindNextFile`. Another list is generated by reading the on-disk NTFS structures and parsing the structures to enumerate file information. Files that are present in one list but missing in the other are then reported as hidden files.

Similarly, to detect hidden processes, one list is obtained using a Windows API such as `FindProcessFirst` or `FindProcessNext`. The second list is generated by querying the object handle table (`PspCidTable`). Any discrepancies are reported as hidden processes.

The basic assumption made by this approach is that the resource is not visible in one list but visible in the other list. This assumption could be wrong if the rootkit modifies the second list, in which case there would not be any differences in the lists. For example, the rootkit might also remove the process information from the object handle table, so that this technique would not be successful in detecting hidden processes.

Virtual Machine Detection

It is difficult to identify a perfect VMBR, in which the detection software is running at a layer above the rootkit and not below it. However, using subtle techniques, it becomes possible to detect the presence of a virtual machine. This does not guarantee the presence of VMBR, but merely confirms the presence of a virtual machine, which could have been installed for legitimate purposes.

As an example, consider the challenges in detecting BluePill, a hardware-assisted VMBR. The BluePill author claimed that detecting this rootkit was impossible when she demonstrated the prototype developed for Windows Vista executing on an AMD 64-bit Pacifica system [364]. This claim generated a wave of controversy as researchers started challenging the undetectability claim. Several timing-related solutions were proposed, where a timer is used to measure the latency in execution of certain instructions with and without a virtual machine. An obvious problem with this approach is the lack of a baseline for comparing the instruction timings.

Another approach is to use the TLB cache for detecting the presence of a virtual machine [117]. In this approach, TLBs are filled by accessing certain known pages and then a CPUID instruction is executed. This instruction causes a trap if it executes in a hypervisor; as a result, some of the TLBs are flushed. After the execution of this instruction, the known pages are accessed again. If there is a significant difference in the timing before and after executing a CPUID instruction, it indicates the presence of a virtual machine.

Chapter 9

Virtual Worlds and Fraud

Jeff Bardzell, Shaowen Bardzell, and Tyler Pace

9.1 Introduction

The gaming industry is seeing a rapid increase in massively multiplayer online games (MMOGs), in terms of both the number of players and the amount of revenue generated. What was an isolated phenomenon—online gaming—only 10 years ago is now a household staple. The significance of gaming is extending its reach beyond entertainment systems, such as the Sony Playstation, as non-entertainment uses of game technologies become prevalent. Health, education, military, and marketing uses of game technologies are leading a wave of "serious games," backed by both government and private funding.

At the same time, and independently of the progress of the gaming industry, online fraud has grown at a remarkable pace. According to the research firm Javelin, identity theft cost U.S. businesses $50 billion in 2004 and $57 billion in 2005—more recent numbers have not yet been publicly released, but all point to a further increase of the problem. The costs of click fraud[1] in many ways are more difficult to estimate, among other things due to the fact that there are no postmortem traces of it having occurred. As early as 2004, click fraud was recognized as one of the emerging threats faced by online businesses [69].

An increasing number of researchers and practitioners are now starting to worry about a merger of these two patterns, in which MMOGs are exposed to online fraud and provide new avenues for online fraud [401]. The former is largely attributable to the potential to monetize virtual possessions, but will, with the

---

1. Click fraud is discussed in more detail in Chapter 11.

introduction of product placements, also have a component associated with click fraud and impression fraud. The latter is due to the fact that scripts used by gamers may also host functionality that facilitates fraudulent activities beyond the worlds associated with the game. More concretely, gamer-created/executed scripts may carry out phishing attacks on players, may be used to distribute spam and phishing emails, and may cause false clicks and ad impressions.

9.1.1 Fraud and Games

While research on both fraud and, increasingly, video games is available, comparatively little has been written on intersections between the two. Identity theft is one domain of electronic fraud that has been explored in the context of games. Chen et al. [52] provide a useful analysis of identity theft in online games, with a focus on East Asian context. In addition to providing a general introduction to online gaming, they explore several types of online gaming crime, especially virtual property and identity theft, relying in part on statistics collected by the National Police Administration of Taiwan. For them, identity theft is considered the most dangerous vulnerability, and they argue that static username–password authentication mechanisms are insufficient, before exploring alternative authentication approaches.

It is beyond the scope of Chen et al.'s work to consider fraud more generally than identity theft and authentication. Likewise, in their pragmatic focus on designing better authentication systems, they do little conceptualizing or theoretical development in this space. As we approach that topic in this chapter, we will summarize current research on cheating and games, provide a functional and architectural overview of MMOGs, summarize types of electronic fraud, and introduce an updated model of security for online games.

9.1.2 Cheating and Games

An area of direct relevance for game security pertains to cheating in games. Cheating and fraud in games are similar but nonidentical phenomena. Yan and Randell [485] define *cheating* as follows:

> Any behavior that a player uses to gain an advantage over his peer players or achieve a target in an online game is cheating if, according to the game rules or at the discretion of the game operator (i.e., the game service provider, who is not necessarily the developer of the game), the advantage or target is one that he is not supposed to have achieved. (p. 1)

Both cheating and fraud involve players misusing game environments and rule systems to achieve ends that are unfair. One primary difference between the two is

	Relative to	Example
Cheating	Internal rules	Unlocking a cheat giving unlimited player lives, invincibility, and so forth
Fraud	External laws	Discovering personal information for purposes of identity theft, extortion, and so forth

Table 9.1: Fraud versus cheating in MMOGs.

that, whereas cheating is defined relative to the rules of the game as set by the game service provider, fraud involves violations of national and international law (Table 9.1). In addition, whereas cheating is limited to the games themselves, game-related fraud may extend to external media, such as web forums and email. Examples of external purpose include exploiting trust built in a game environment to trick a user to install malware, such as keylogging software, which in turn is used to gain access to real-life bank accounts.

In extreme cases, the actions of virtual identities have resulted in real-life murder. In 2005, the *China Daily* reported that two players found a rare item in the popular game Legend of Mir 3. The players sold the item for 7200 yuan ($939). When one player felt the other cheated him of his fair share of the profits, he murdered his former comrade [292].

The most systematic overview of online cheating can be found in Yan and Randell [485], which offers what is intended to be a complete taxonomy of cheating in games. The authors identify three axes with which to classify all forms of cheating in games:

- *Vulnerability.* This axis focuses on the weak point of the game system that is attacked. It includes people, such as game operators and players, as well as system design inadequacies, such as those in the game itself or in underlying systems (e.g., network latency glitches).

- *Possible failures.* This axis refers to the consequences of cheating across the foundational aspects of information security: loss of data (confidentiality), alteration of game characteristics (integrity), service denial (availability), and misrepresentation (authenticity).

- *Exploiters.* On this axis are the perpetrators of the cheating. It includes cooperative cheating (game operator and player, or multiple players) as well as individual cheating (game operator, single player).

Yan and Randell's framework can be extended more generally to game-related fraud by expanding the scope of each category beyond games as information systems. Vulnerabilities, for example, include technologies that enable the proliferation of trojan horses. Possible failures extend to attacks that access banking information via game subscription payment systems. Exploiters go beyond developers and players to any criminals who use games as part of their portfolio for attacks, without regard for whether they are themselves players or service providers.

9.2 MMOGs as a Domain for Fraud

Massively multiplayer online games are information systems, as are web-based banking applications and auction sites. But MMOGs are also simulated worlds, with embodied avatars, sophisticated communication and social presence tools, and participant-created content. As a result, MMOGs have both commonalties and differences compared to two-dimensional, web-based applications.

9.2.1 Functional Overview of MMOGs

Massively multiplayer online games are a subset of video games uniquely categorized by a persistent, interactive, and social virtual world populated by the avatars of players. Persistence in MMOGs permits the game to run, or retain state, whether or not players are currently engaged with the game. Their interactivity means that the virtual world of a MMOG exists on a server that can be accessed remotely and simultaneously by many players [49]. The social nature of virtual worlds is a result of combining human players; methods for communication, such as chat or voice systems; and different mechanisms for persistent grouping.

MMOGs share the following traits with all games [378]:

- Players, who are willing to participate in the game
- Rules, which define the limits of the game
- Goals, which give rise to conflicts and rivalry among the players

To these traits, MMOGs add network communications, economies with real-world value, and complex social interaction inside a shared narrative/ simulation space. Both the rule-bound nature of games and their sociocultural context—including, for example, persistent groups and social interaction—create possibilities for fraudulent behavior that do not have analogs in two-dimensional, web-based banking or auction sites.

Rules govern the development of a game and establish the basic interactions that can take place within the game world. Two types of rules exist in computer games: game world rules and game play rules (Table 9.2). Game world rules place

	Rule	Violation
Game world	Players run at 20 miles per hour.	A player uses a location hack to teleport around instantly.
	Walls are solid.	Hacked graphics card drivers allow the player to see through previously opaque textures.
Game play	A player has three lives.	A player accesses game memory and overwrites it so that the player has 9999 lives.
	A player has 500 silver pieces.	A player duplicates an item dozens of times and sells the copies to a vendor to make 10,000 silver pieces.

Table 9.2: Game world and game play rules.

	Source	Example
Intra-mechanic rules	Developers	Game function generates a random number to determine loot distribution
Extra-mechanic rules	Players	Player-created loot distribution norms within a group or guild

Table 9.3: Intra- versus extra-mechanic rules.

constraints on the game's virtual world (e.g., gravity). Game play rules identify the methods by which players interact with the game (e.g., number of lives) Differences in games are primarily derived from differences in game play rules [489]. Working around or manipulating these rules creates opportunities for cheating and fraud. Violations of game world and game play rules are not mutually exclusive; thus the same violation may involve the infraction of both types of rules.

One may also consider a higher level of rules, describing the hardware and software limitations associated with the devices used to play games. This is a meaningful angle to consider, given that these "meta-rules" govern which types of abuses of the states of the games are possible—for example, by malware affecting the computers used to execute a given game and, thereby, the game itself.

MMOGs as social spaces require further breakdown of game play rules into intra-mechanic and extra-mechanic categories [379] (see Table 9.3). *Intra-mechanic rules* are the set of game play rules created by the designers of the game. The graphics card bug mentioned in Table 9.2 is an example of an intra-mechanic cheat. *Extra-mechanic rules* represent the norms created by players as a form of self-governance of their social space. Rules implemented by persistent user groups (often called *guilds*) that subject new recruits to exploitative hazing rituals would fall into this category. The interplay between intra- and extra-mechanic rules may change over time, with some game developers integrating player-created extra-mechanic rules into the game to form new intra-mechanic rules. The key insight here is that the concept of "rules" goes far beyond the rules of the game as intended by the game designer; it also encompasses everything from enabling technologies to social norms. All can be manipulated for undesirable ends.

As game worlds mature and the complexity of player interactions increases, the number and scope of the rules tend to increase dramatically. They certainly far outstrip the complexity of the rule systems involved in online banking sites and auctions, making rule complexity one of the distinguishing characteristics of MMOGs, from a security standpoint.

The complexity of game rules provides ever-increasing opportunities for misbehavior. Clever players may knowingly use a flaw in the game rules to realize an unfair advantage over fellow players. Players using a game flaw for personal gain are performing an "exploit" of the game [111]. Commonly, exploits are used to provide players with high-powered abilities that allow them to dominate against their peers in the competitive milieu of the game. Given the competitive nature of gaming, and the pervasiveness of "cheat codes" built into most large-budget games and their wide availability on the Internet and in gaming magazines, the discovery and deployment of exploits are often tolerated—even celebrated. However, the monetization of virtual economies creates growing incentives for players to exploit the game world as a means for cold profit, rather than for the pleasure of achieving game-prescribed goals. The ambiguous nature of the exploit as somewhat undesirable and yet a part of game culture, and as an act that is usually legal, creates a new conceptual and technical space for attacks.

Edward Castranova of Indiana University first studied the growth of real money trade (RMT) in online games in 2001. Castranova [49] analyzed the value of U.S.-based Everquest item and account auctions on popular web sites and calculated the value of Everquest items at close to $5 million. In 2004, Castranova updated his analysis to include international game markets and predicted $100 million in worldwide RMT transactions [496]. A 2007 meta-analysis by the Virtual Economy Research Network predicted a global market of $2.09 billion dollars for RMT transactions [458].

Example: Growth of Monetization of Virtual Property

9.2.2 Architectural Overview of MMOGs

Massively multiplayer online games are complex pieces of software, whose code is literally executed around the globe. Understanding the basics of their architecture provides the basis for understanding certain kinds of attacks.

Network Architecture

The network architectures for MMOGs are client/server, peer-to-peer (P2P), or a combination of the models. Client/server architecture is the most common owing to its ease of implementation and ability to retain complete control over game state on the server. On the downside, the client/server model is prone to bottlenecks when large numbers of players connect to a small set of servers. A P2P architecture reduces the likelihood of bottlenecks but requires complex synchronization and consistency mechanisms to maintain a valid game state for all players [38]. Many MMOGs, such as World of Warcraft, use the client/server model for game play and the P2P model for file distribution. For example, MMOGs require frequent updates, as game publishers enhance security and game play as the game changes over time. Major updates, or *patches*, come out every few months and are often hundreds of megabytes in size; all players are required to implement them as soon as they are released. The bandwidth issues associated with a large percentage of World of Warcraft's 8 million subscribers needing a 250 MB file over a period of hours are far more practically resolved through P2P distribution (Figure 9.1) than through central server distribution.

Interfaces and Scripts

The client-side executable interfaces with the player using the screen and soundcard as well as input devices. Typical input devices include the keyboard, mouse and trackballs, joysticks, and microphones. Technically, these devices write

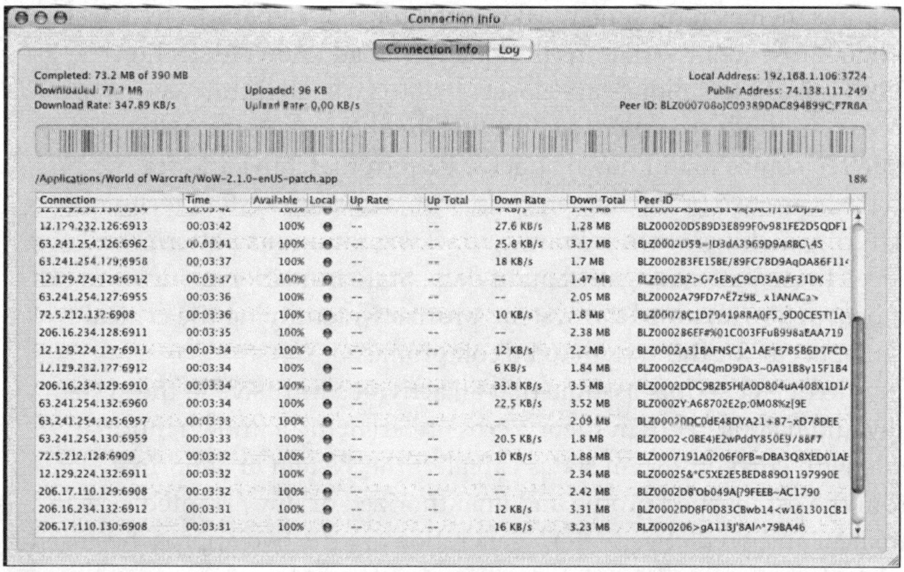

Figure 9.1: MMOG patches are often distributed via both public and private peer-to-peer infrastructures. This screenshot shows the official World of Warcraft patch service.

in unique registers associated with these devices in question, which the CPU polls after it detects interrupts generated by the input devices. This causes the contents of the registers to be transferred to the executable. Any process that can write in these registers, or otherwise inject or modify data during the transfer, can impersonate the player to the client-side executable.

Alternatively, if the entire game is run in a virtual machine, the process may impersonate the player by writing data to the cells corresponding to the input device registers of the virtual machines. These processes are commonly referred to as scripts. Scripts present a major threat to game publishers, as they are the chief tools used by game hackers for activities ranging from simple augmentation of player abilities to large-scale attacks on game servers. A major outlet for scripts, botting, is discussed later in this chapter.

The detection of virtual machines is a growing concern for online game publishers. Game hackers may run virtual machines that host private game servers that grant the hackers unlimited access to modify the game world, avoid or disable DRM and copyright protection systems, and allow willing players to bypass the game publisher's subscription services and play games for free on "black market" servers. Improper virtual machine detection techniques have led publishers to inadvertently cancel accounts for thousands of paying customers who legitimately run their games in virtual machines such as WINE to play the game on the Linux OS [240].

Detecting Scripts

Misuse detection schemes represent attacks in the form of signatures to detect scripts and their subsequent variations designed to avoid known detection measures [399]. Misuse techniques are closely tied to virus detection systems, offering effective methods to protect against known attack patterns, while providing little resistance to unknown attacks. Pattern matching and state transition analysis are two of the numerous misuse detection system techniques available. Pattern matching encodes known attack signatures as patterns and cross-references these patterns against audit data. State transition analysis tracks the pre- and post-action states of the system, precisely identifying the critical events that must occur for the system to be compromised.

Techniques to detect scripts assume that all activities intrusive to the system are essentially anomalous [399]. In theory, cross-referencing a known, normal activity profile with current system states can alert the system to abnormal variances from the established profile and unauthorized or unwarranted system activity. Statistical and predictive pattern generation are the two approaches used in anomaly detection systems. The statistical approach constantly assesses state variance and compares computational profiles to the initial activity profile. Predictive pattern generation attempts to predict future events based on prior documented actions, using sequential patterns to detect anomalous actions.

A variety of techniques exist for detection avoidance. According to Tan, Killourhy, and Maxiom [406], methods for avoiding detection may be classified into two broad categories. First, the behavior of normal scripts is modified to look like an attack, with the goal of creating false positives that degrade anomalous detection algorithms. Second, the behavior of attacks are modified to appear as normal scripts, with the goal of generating false negatives that go unnoticed by both anomalous and signature-based detection systems.

An important subcategory of the latter detection avoidance method is facilitated by rootkits,[2] or software that allows malicious applications to operate stealthily. Rootkits embed themselves into operating systems and mask an attacker's scripts from both the OS and any detection programs running within the OS.

9.3 Electronic Fraud

Electronic fraud is an umbrella term that encompasses many types of attacks made in any electronic domain, from web banking systems to games. In the preceding section, we explored the MMOG as a specific domain of electronic fraud. In this section, we summarize major forms of fraud in any electronic domain. Later, we engage in more specific exploration of fraud in MMOGs.

9.3.1 Phishing and Pharming

Phishing attacks are typically deception based and involve emailing victims, where the identity of the sender is spoofed. The recipient typically is requested to visit a web site and enter his or her credentials for a given service provider, whose appearance the web site mimics. This web site collects credentials on behalf of the attacker. It may connect to the impersonated service provider and establish a session between this entity and the victim, using the captured credentials, a tactic known as a man-in-the-middle attack.

A majority of phishing attempts spoof financial service providers. Nevertheless, the same techniques can be applied to gain access to any type of credentials, whether the goal is to monetize resources available to the owner of the credentials

---

2. Rootkits are discussed in more detail in Chapter 8.

or to obtain private information associated with the account in question. The deceptive techniques used in phishing attacks can also be used to convince victims to download malware, disable security settings on their machines, and so on.

A technique that has become increasingly common among phishers is *spear-phishing* or *context-aware phishing* [197]. Such an attack is performed in two steps. First, the attacker collects personal information relating to the intended victim, such as by data mining. Second, the attacker uses this information to personalize the information communicated to the intended victim, with the intention of appearing more legitimate than if the information had not been used.

Pharming is a type of attack often used by phishers that compromises the integrity of the Domain Name System (DNS) on the Internet, the system that translates URLs such as www.paypal.com to the IP addresses used by computers to network with one another. An effective pharming attack causes an incorrect translation, which in turn causes connection to the wrong network computer. This scheme is typically used to divert traffic and to capture credentials. Given that pharming can be performed simply by corruption of a user computer or its connected access point [389], and that this, in turn, can be achieved from any executable file on a computer, we see that games and *mods*—programs that run inside the game executable—pose real threats to user security.

9.3.2 Misleading Applications

Misleading applications masquerade as programs that do something helpful (e.g., scan for spyware) to persuade the user to install the misleading application, which then installs various types of crimeware on the user's system. The pervasiveness of user downloads in online gaming leaves great room for attackers to transmit their crimeware via misleading applications. Since the release of World of Warcraft, for example, attackers have used game mod downloads to transmit trojan viruses to unsuspecting players [497]. The practice has since grown in frequency and is cited by the developers of World of Warcraft as a chief customer service concern.

Keyloggers and screenscrapers are common types of crimeware installed by misleading applications. A keylogger records the keystrokes of a user, whereas a screenscraper captures the contents of the screen. Both techniques can be used to steal credentials or other sensitive information, and then to export associated data to a computer controlled by an attacker.

Another type of crimeware searches the file system of the user for files with particular names or contents, and yet another makes changes to settings (e.g., of antivirus products running on the affected machine). Some crimeware uses the host machine to target other users or organizations, whether as a spam bot or to perform click fraud, impression fraud, or related attacks. This general class of attacks causes the transfer of funds between two entities typically not related to the party whose machine executes the crimeware (but where the distributor of the crimeware typically is the benefactor of the transfer). The funds transfer is performed as a result of an action that mimics the actual distribution of an advertisement or product placement.

9.4 Fraud in MMOGs

As previously discussed in this chapter, cheating and fraud are separate but related activities. Cheating is a means to obtain an unfair and unearned advantage over another person or group of people relative to game-specified goals. Fraud is an intentional deception intended to mislead someone into parting with something of value, often in violation of laws. In online games, cheating is a prominent facilitator of fraud. Any unfair advantage that can be earned via cheating may be put to use by a defrauder to supplement or enhance his or her fraudulent activity.

For example, a cheat may allow players to replicate valuable items to gain in-game wealth, whereas an attacker may use the opportunity to create in-game wealth via the cheat and then monetize the illicitly replicated items for real-world profit, thereby committing a form of fraud. The same valuable items can be obtained over time with a great investment of time in the game and can still be monetized, but a cheat makes the fraud not only technically feasible, but also economically viable. Thus the game account itself is also a source of value. In 2007, Symantec reported that World of Warcraft account credentials sold for an average of $10, whereas U.S. credit card numbers with card verification values sold for $1 to $6 on the Internet underground market [400].

The following sections recognize cheating as a component of fraud and outline an extended model of security for online games that integrates the potential effect of cheaters into the popular confidentiality, integrity, availability, and authenticity model of security.

9.4.1 An Extended Model of Security for MMOGs

The four foundational aspects of information security—confidentiality, integrity, availability, authenticity—can be used to discuss and model threats against online games [485]. Games, like all information technology platforms, may suffer from data loss (confidentiality), modification (integrity), denial-of-service (availability) and misrepresentation (authenticity) attacks. In the context of a game, all of these attacks result in one player or group of players receiving an unfair or unearned advantage over others. Given the competitive, goal-oriented foundation of most behavior in online games—a foundation that does not exist in the same way with a web-based bank application (where one user is not trying to "beat" another user while banking online)—incentives to cheat are built internally into the game application itself. This unique implication of security in online games extends the traditional model of security to include an evaluation of fairness as a principle of security in online games.

The incentive to cheat and defraud in online games is high. As large virtual worlds, games provide a great deal of anonymity for their users. Few players know each other, and the participants are often scattered across vast geographic locations. Additionally, players' relationships are typically mediated by in-game, seemingly fictional goals, such as leveling up a character or defeating a powerful, computer-controlled enemy; thus people may feel that they are interacting with one another in much more limited ways than in real-world relationships, which are often based on friendship, intimacy, professional aspirations, and so on. As a result, the social structures that prevent cheating in the real world wither away in online games. Security, with a new emphasis on fairness, can serve as a new mechanism for maintaining fair play in MMOGs [485].

9.4.2 Guidelines for MMOG Security

The following MMOG security guidelines are derived from the extended model of security in online games. These guidelines are intended to serve as a set of high-level considerations that can direct and inform game design and implementation decisions in regard to information security in MMOGs:

1. Protect sensitive player data.
2. Maintain an equitable game environment.

Protecting sensitive player data involves a diverse set of concerns. Traditional notions of protecting personally identifiable information such as credit card number, billing information, and email addresses are as applicable to online worlds as they are to e-commerce web sites. However, the complexity of player information found in online games deeply questions the meaning of "sensitive." In-game spending habits, frequented locations, times played, total time played, communication logs, and customer service history are all potentially sensitive pieces of information present in virtual worlds. Determining a player's habits, without his or her knowledge or consent, can open up that player to exploitation and social engineering. Such attacks could include attempts to manipulate players via player–player trade in-game. Alternatively, some locations in virtual worlds that people participate in under the expectation of anonymity are socially taboo, such as fetish sex–based role-playing communities [32]; knowing a player's location in-world can expose participation in such communities, that can be exploited in a number of unsavory ways. Additionally, knowing *when* someone typically plays can help someone predict a player's real-life location. Unlike a web-based banking application, MMOGs often require special software clients and powerful computers to play, indicating when someone is likely to be home or away. A careful evaluation and prioritization of all stored data is critical to protecting "sensitive" player data.

For example, Linden Labs, the creators of Second Life, recently implemented a measure whereby players (called "residents" in Second Life) are no longer able to see the online status of most other residents (previously they could). A notable, and appropriate, exception to this is one's friends list, which includes all individuals whom one has explicitly designated as a friend. A more murky area is Second Life's "groups," which are somewhat akin to guilds in other MMOGs. Residents are able to view the online status of fellow group members. Every resident can belong to a maximum of 25 groups, and most groups are open to the public and free to join. All residents have profiles, and included in their profiles is a list of all groups to which they belong. Through a combination of simply joining a large number of large groups, looking up a given resident's group list, and temporarily joining one of those groups, it is still possible to discover the online status of most residents in Second Life, although Linden Labs clearly meant to disable this capability. As this example shows, sensitive player data includes more than online status; it includes group membership as well, because the latter can lead to the former.

Maintaining an equitable game environment requires the extension of fairness as a component of the extended model of security for MMOGs. However, providing a level game field for all players is a great challenge. The naturally competitive nature of many online games, combined with the anonymity of virtual worlds, creates a strong incentive for players to negotiate abuse of the game world to gain advantages over their peers.

A fair game world is maintained through careful balancing and protection of three facets of the game:

- Player ability
- Player treatment
- Environmental stability

Player Ability
Player ability refers to the preservation of the naturally bounded abilities provided to players by the game mechanics. Amount of player health, power (often

measured by the amount of damage players can inflict in combat), and the virtual currency players have are all forms of player ability. Because computers and game rules are used to simulate familiar sensibilities about player ability, participants are vulnerable to people who manipulate the rules in ways that are not possible in real life, so it does not occur to them that these kinds of cheaters are possible in a virtual world, and therefore players do not protect themselves from this behavior.

A couple of examples demonstrate how these attacks can occur. Perhaps the simplest ruse is a single player who masquerades as multiple players in an online casino. By pretending to be multiple players, the player gains access to far more information than is available to another single player [484]. Yet it may not even occur to the victim that this situation is possible, because in real life no one can simultaneously be three out of four players at a poker table. Likewise, many games involve quick reflexes, such as the pressing of a key on a keyboard to fire a gun. Reflex augmentation technologies, which simulate keypresses at inhuman speeds, make it possible for a player to fire a gun much faster than other players can. The main issue at stake is that real life, in combination with game rules, produces certain mental models about player abilities, and attackers can manipulate systems in blind spots created by these mental models.

In games, ranking systems are used to calculate accumulated player scores and serve as evaluations of players according to their game histories. Player ranking systems are necessary for the majority of MMOGs to supply players with a sense of accomplishment relative to other players. They are also important in facilitating pairings (i.e., fellow players to work with or against). Traditional ranking systems are tightly bound to the specific game client and server and do not track games hosted on local area networks. Tang et al. [407] introduce the concept of independent player ranking systems, where the ranking system is independent of specific architectures and implementations of individual games, making it much harder to manipulate player rankings.

Example: Why Does Player Ability Matter?

Player Treatment

Player treatment is a twofold category encompassing both how players treat other players and how players are treated by the environment.

Community is critical to the success of online games, and negative interactions between players can erode the quality of a player base. *Griefing*, as online harassment is commonly known, is the chief violation of player treatment and is often enabled by a breach in player ability. A simple example of griefing, which recent games have disabled, occurs when a high-level player spends time in an area set aside for new, weaker players and kills the lower-level players over and over for malicious pleasure. A more recent, and more difficult to defeat, form of griefing includes activities such as Alt+F4 scams, in which experienced players tell new players that pressing Alt+F4 enables a powerful spell; in reality, it quits the game, forcing victims to log back in. Both examples are forms of *player–player treatment violations*.

The other major type of player treatment is *world–player treatment*, which refers to how the game world itself treats players. The world should treat all players equally, providing a conducive environment for game play and enjoyment. Unfortunately, certain cheats create global inequities. For example, in Shadowbane, attackers compromised game servers to create ultra-powerful monsters that killed all players. This, in turn, forced the publisher to shut down the game, roll back to a previous state, and patch the game files to remove the exploit [479].

In both player–player and world–player treatment types, the basic principle that no player's achievements or pleasure should be subjected without consent to the control of another player can be violated. These violations may lead to griefing, cheating, or fraud, depending on the circumstances.

The implementation of bots is a common means for influencing the game world's treatment of fellow players. A bot is a computer-controlled automated entity that simulates a human player, potentially through the use of artificial intelligence. Bots are used to give players unfair advantages, such as automating complex processes at inhuman speeds to level characters (i.e., raise their abilities through extensive play), raise virtual money, and so on. Some bots in World of Warcraft, for example, would walk in circles in hostile areas, automatically killing all the monsters (commonly known as *mobs*) to raise experience and gold. This form of gold harvesting threatens the entire virtual economy, cheapening the value of gold for all other players and thereby diminishing their own in-game accomplishments. In Second Life, some residents developed a bot that could automatically replicate proprietary in-world three-dimensional shapes and textures (e.g., virtual homes and clothing) that other residents had made and were selling for real-world income, thereby devaluing the work of and threatening Second Life's entrepreneurial class.

Golle and Duchenault [147] propose two approaches to eliminate bots from online games, based on conceptual principles that require players to interact in specific ways. CAPTCHA tests—Completely Automated Public Turing Test to Tell Computers and Humans Apart—are cornerstones of these approaches. A CAPTCHA test has the ability to generate and evaluate a test that the average human can pass but current computer programs cannot, such as reading a string of

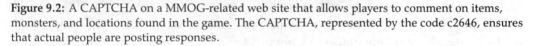

Figure 9.2: A CAPTCHA on a MMOG-related web site that allows players to comment on items, monsters, and locations found in the game. The CAPTCHA, represented by the code c2646, ensures that actual people are posting responses.

characters in a grainy image (Figure 9.2). Another approach abandons the use of software, transforming existing game-input controllers into physical CAPTCHA devices. Similar to a keyboard or joystick, the CAPTCHA device recognizes physical inputs and generates digital outputs, authenticating that a human is using the device. Current research into physical CAPTCHAs suggests that the costs of developing tamper-proof devices and forcing the hardware upgrades onto users are quite high and may prevent future efforts in the area [147].

Environmental Stability

Environmental stability encompasses the proper operation and maintenance of the mechanisms that support the game world, such as the game servers, databases, and network channels. Network latency, fast command execution, and data retrieval are the backbone of any online application, especially in intensive graphical online worlds. Game world downtime is costly in terms of emergency maintenance and customer service response to upset players who demand compensation for the loss of the use of their subscription [276].

Lag, or network latency, also affects the stability of the game world. A player has low lag when communication between his or her client and the server is quick and uninterrupted. Players with higher lag are at a clear disadvantage to those with low lag, because the server is much less responsive to their commands. Lag can be created by a player's geographic location (e.g., propagation delay), access technology (e.g., ADSL, cable, dial-up), and transient network conditions (e.g., congestion).

Zander, Leeder, and Armitage [491] have shown that game-play scenarios with high lag lead to a decrease in performance, and they suggest that nefarious players can use lag to gain an unfair advantage over other players. To combat lag, Zander et al. implemented a program to normalize network latency by artificially increasing the delay between players and the server for players with faster connections. They tested their system using bots with equal abilities, so that if the system is fair, all players should have equal kill counts. Prior to the normalization, bots with low lag had higher kill counts than bots with higher lag. After the normalization, all of the bots had roughly equal kill counts.

9.4.3 Countermeasures

Countermeasures to online game attacks conveniently map to the previously established guidelines for MMOG security: protecting sensitive player data and maintaining an equitable game environment.

Countermeasures for protecting sensitive player data are well understood and researched in the security community, but may be new to some game developers. Popular games such as Second Life and World of Warcraft have a mixed history with proper authentication, storage, and encryption of sensitive information. Second Life lost 650,000 user accounts during a security breach in 2006 [418]. World of Warcraft is entertaining the idea of introducing dual-factor authentication via USB dongles that must be plugged into the player's computer to execute the game [139].

The inclusion of participant-created content, particularly with the use of open-source software in some game clients (such as Second Life's clients) and the release of application programming interfaces (APIs—scripting languages with limited access to the main program), means that players are increasingly installing software written by other players. The potential for crimeware in such circumstances is significant. Although game publishers, such as Blizzard, are doing their part to ensure that game modifications (mods) built with their APIs are safe, they cannot monitor or control all of the downloadable files that claim to be made with their APIs. Some of these files may include additional code that installs crimeware.

The concept of countermeasures must be carefully applied when the focus is maintaining an equitable game world. Fairness in the game world is constantly changing and depends on emergent player behaviors, practices, and beliefs. Maintaining fairness in games requires a highly proactive, rather than reactive, approach to security. The combination of emergent behavior and a variety of attacks available through player ability, player treatment, and environmental stability make mapping and anticipating the attack space very difficult. For example, denial-of-service attacks achieved through an overload in network traffic are common and well understood. However, World of Warcraft experienced a denial-of-service attack through a compromised player ability. Griefing players intentionally contracted a deadly virus from a high-level monster and then teleported to major cities, which are supposed to be safe havens for characters of all levels. The disease spread like a virtual plague, shutting down all highly populated areas for several days, and killing not only low- and medium-level players, but even computer-controlled nonplayer characters placed in the cities [124].

Conclusion

Massively multiplayer online games produce value for their publishers and their players alike. Comprising highly complex rule systems; being deployed via computer networks, protocols, and systems to millions of users; and symbiotically evolving alongside complex subcultures and microcommunities, online games offer a surprisingly diverse array of opportunities for attacks. The security community, having focused much of its attention on two-dimensional web applications, such as banking systems and auction sites, lacks conceptual frameworks for dealing with those aspects of MMOG fraud that are unique to games, including game architecture and game culture. The three-dimensional embodied simulations combined with massive social presence create new opportunities for fraud that merit more serious consideration than they have received to date.

Chapter 10

Cybercrime and Politics

Oliver Friedrichs

While we first saw the Internet used extensively during the 2004 U.S. presidential election, its use in future presidential elections will clearly overshadow those humble beginnings. It is important to understand the associated risks as political candidates increasingly turn to the Internet in an effort to more effectively communicate their positions, rally supporters, and seek to sway critics. These risks include, among others, the dissemination of misinformation, fraud, phishing, malicious code, and the invasion of privacy. Some of these attacks, including those involving the diversion of online campaign donations, have the potential to threaten voters' faith in the U.S. electoral system.

The analysis in this chapter focuses on the 2008 presidential election to demonstrate the risks involved, but our findings may just as well apply to any future election. Many of the same risks that we have grown accustomed to on the Internet can also manifest themselves when the Internet is expanded to the election process.

It is not difficult for one to conceive of numerous attacks that might present themselves and, to varying degrees, influence the election process. One need merely examine the attack vectors that already affect consumers and enterprises today to envision how they might be applied to this process. In this chapter, we have chosen to analyze those attack vectors that would be most likely to have an immediate and material effect on an election, affecting voters, candidates, or campaign officials.

A number of past studies have discussed a broad spectrum of election fraud possibilities, such as the casting of fraudulent votes [258] and the security, risks, and challenges of electronic voting [173]. There are many serious and important risks to consider related both to the security of the voting process and to the new breed of electronic voting machines that have been documented by others [46]. Risks include the ability for attackers or insiders either to manipulate these machines or to alter and tamper with the end results. These concerns apply not only to electronic voting in the United States, but have also been raised by other countries, such as the United Kingdom, which is also investigating and raising similar concerns surrounding electronic voting [274]. Rather than revisit the subject of electronic voting, the discussion here focuses exclusively on Internet-borne threats, including how they have the potential to influence the election process leading up to voting day.

We first discuss domain name abuse, including typo squatting and domain speculation as it relates to candidate Internet domains. Next, we explore the potential impact of phishing on an election. We then discuss the effects of security risks and malicious code, and the potential for misinformation that may present itself using any of these vectors. Finally, we review how phishers may spoof political emails (such as false campaign contribution requests) instead of emails appearing to come from financial institutions. The goal in such attacks might still be to collect payment credentials, in which case the political aspect is just a new guise for fraud. However, political phishing emails might also be used to sow fear among potential contributors and make them less willing to contribute online—whether to spoofed campaigns or to real ones.

These sets of risks cross technical, social, and psychological boundaries. Although traditional forms of malicious code certainly play an important role in these threats, social engineering and deception provide equal potential to be exploited and might have a more ominous psychological impact on voters who are exercising their right to elect their next president, or cast their vote in any other type of election.

This chapter includes both active research conducted by the author and discussion of how current threats may be customized. To determine the impact of typo squatting and domain name speculation, for example, we performed an analysis of 2008 presidential election candidate web sites and discovered numerous examples of abuse.

In regard to the attacks discussed in this chapter, we believe and hope that candidates and their campaigns are unlikely to knowingly participate in or support these activities themselves, for two reasons. First, it would not be acting in good faith. Second, their actions would in many cases be considered a breach of either existing computer crime or federal election law.[1]

We conclude that perpetrators would likely fall into two categories: those with political motives and those seeking to profit from these attacks. In the end, it may

---

1. U.S. Code Title 18, Part I, Chapter 29. Available from `http://www4.law.cornell.edu/uscode/html/uscode18/usc_sec_18_00000594----000-.html`

be difficult to identify from a given attack which one of these goals is the attacker's true motive.

10.1 Domain Name Abuse

To communicate with constituents and supporters, candidates have created and maintain web sites, which are identified by and navigated to via their registered domain names. All candidates for the 2008 federal election have registered, or already own, unique domain names that are used to host their respective web sites. In all cases this domain name incorporates their own name in some capacity, and in some cases has been registered specifically in support of the 2008 campaign. Domain names play one of the most important roles in accessing a web site. They are the core part of the URL that is recognized by the general population and, as such, their ownership dictates who can display content to users visiting web sites hosted on that domain name.

While users may well know the URL for their bank or favorite commerce site, voters may not readily know the URL for their political party's or chosen candidate's web site. Legitimate-sounding domain names may not be as they appear. The authors of this book, for example, were able to freely register domain names such as http://www.democratic-party.us and http://www.support-gop.org that have for some time warned visitors about the risks presented by phishing. It would be easy to use a domain name of this type for the purposes of phishing or crimeware installation.

Consider, for example, an email pointing to one of these domains that contains text suggesting it came from the Democratic Party and asking the recipient for a donation. If willing to contribute, the recipient may be offered to choose a variety of payment methods, each one of which would allow the phisher to potentially capture the user's credentials as he or she enters this data on the site (or on another, suitably named site hyperlinked from the donation page). The email might also offer the recipient a chance to download and access resources, such as campaign movies, which themselves might contain malware. Existing movies can be modified to incorporate malware [388]. Typical Internet users are also very susceptible to attacks in which self-signed certificates vouch for the security of executables as long as a person known to them has also indicated that the material is safe [388]. In one study [388], that known person was a friend; in our hypothetical case, it might be a political party or a politician.

In today's online environment, individuals and businesses must consider a number of risks posed by individuals attempting to abuse the domain name system. These involve domain speculators, bulk domain name parkers, and typo squatters.

10.1.1 Background

Since the early days of Internet commerce, Internet domain names have held an
intrinsic value, much as real estate in the physical world has been valued for
centuries. In the early 1990s, when relatively few .com domain names existed, it
was highly probable that if one attempted to acquire the name of a well-known
company, individual, or trademark, this name would be readily available. Many
early domain name speculators did, in fact, acquire such domain names, in many
cases later selling them to the legitimate trademark holder. At that point, the legal
precedence for domain name disputes had not yet been set, and the speculator had
a chance of profiting from this sale, in particular if it was to a well-known and
well-funded corporation.

It was only a matter of time before formal dispute guidelines were created to
eliminate such infringement. A formal policy was created by ICANN in 1999,
which is known as the Uniform Domain Name Dispute Resolution Policy
(UDRP) [127]. The UDRP is implemented in practice by the World Intellectual
Property Organization's (WIPO) Arbitration and Mediation Center.

While this policy provides a framework for resolving infringement, it does not
preclude the registration of an infringing domain name if that domain name is
unregistered. What is in place is a policy and framework for the legitimate
trademark owner to become the owner of the domain, granted the trademark
owner first becomes aware of the infringing domain's existence. The policy is
frequently used by legitimate business trademark holders to protect their names.[2]

While it is used to protect trademarked proper names, the same policy applies
to unregistered, or "common law" marks, including well-known individuals' proper
names, even when a formal trademark does not exist. Julia Roberts, for example,
was able to obtain ownership of the juliaroberts.com domain name, even in the
absence of a registered trademark.[3] This is common when a domain name is
specific enough and matches a full proper name. In other examples, such as the
more general domain name sting.com, contested by the well-known singer Sting,
the transfer was not granted and the original registrant retained ownership.[4]

There appear to be very few cases in which either elected or hopeful political
candidates have disputed the ownership of an infringing domain name. One

---

2. *The Coca-Cola Company v. Spider Webs Ltd.* http://www.arb-forum.com/domains/decisions/
102459.htm.

3. *Julia Fiona Roberts v. Russell Boyd.* http://www.wipo.int/amc/en/domains/decisions/html/
2000/d2000-0210.html.

4. *Gordon Sumner, p/k/a Sting v. Michael Urvan.* http://www.wipo.int/amc/en/domains/decisions/
html/2000/d2000-0596.html

example that does exist is for the domain name kennedytownsend.com and several variations thereof. Disputed by Kathleen Kennedy Townsend, who was Lieutenant Governor of the State of Maryland at the time, the transfer was not granted, based predominantly on what appears to be a technicality of how the dispute was submitted. Central to the ruling in such dispute cases is whether the trademark or name is used to conduct commercial activity, and thus whether the infringement negatively affects the legitimate owner and, as a result, consumers:

> Here, the claim for the domain names is brought by the individual politician, and not by the political action committee actively engaged in the raising of funds and promotion of Complainant's possible campaign. Had the claim been brought in the name of the Friends of Kathleen Kennedy Townsend, the result might well have been different. But it was not. The Panel finds that the protection of an individual politician's name, no matter how famous, is outside the scope of the Policy since it is not connected with commercial exploitation as set out in the Second WIPO Report.[5]

Within the United States, trademark owners and individuals are further protected by the Anticybersquatting Consumer Protection Act, which took effect on November 29, 1999.[6] The ACPA provides a legal remedy by which the legitimate trademark owner can seek monetary damages in addition to the domain name, whereas the UDRP provides for only recovery of the domain name itself.

Even today, the relatively low cost involved in registering a domain name (less than $10 per year) continues to provide an opportunity for an individual to profit by acquiring and selling domain names. The relative scarcity of simple, recognizable "core" domain names has resulted in the development of a significant after-market for those domain names and led to the creation of a substantial amount of wealth for some speculators [377]. Today, a number of online sites and auctions exist explicitly to facilitate the resale of domain names.

In addition to engaging in domain name speculation for the purpose of its future sale, many speculators seek to benefit from advertising revenue that can be garnered during their ownership of the domain name. These individuals—and, more recently, for-profit companies such as iREIT[7]—may register, acquire, and own hundreds of thousands to millions of domain names explicitly for this purpose. These domains display advertisements that are, in many cases, related to the domain name itself, and their owners receive an appropriate share of the

---

5. *Kathleen Kennedy Townsend v. B. G. Birt.* http://www.wipo.int/amc/en/domains/decisions/html/2002/d2002-0030.html

6. Anticybersquatting Consumer Protection Act. http://thomas.loc.gov/cgi-bin/query/z?c106:9.1255.IS:=

7. Internet REIT. http://www.ireit.com/

advertising revenue much like any web site participating in CPM, CPC, or CPA[8] advertising campaigns.

10.1.2 Domain Speculation in the 2008 Federal Election

Typo squatting seeks to benefit from a mistake made by the user when entering a URL directly into the web browser's address bar. An errant keystroke can easily result in the user entering a domain name that differs from the one intended. Typo squatters seek to benefit from these mistakes by registering domain names that correspond to common typos. Whereas in the past users making typos were most likely to receive an error indicating that the site could not be found, today they are likely to be directed to a different web site. In many cases, this site may host advertisements, but the potential for more sinister behavior also exists.

To determine the current level of domain name speculation and typo squatting in the 2008 federal election, we performed an analysis of well-known candidate domain names to seek out domain speculators and typo squatters. First, we identified all candidates who had registered financial reports with the Federal Election Commission for the quarter ending March 31, 2007.[9] A total of 19 candidates had submitted such filings. Next, we identified each candidate's primary campaign web site through the use of popular search engines and correlated our findings with additional online resources to confirm their accuracy. This, in turn, gave us the primary registered domain name upon which the candidate's web site is hosted.

To simplify our analysis, we removed domains that were not registered under the .com top-level domain. This resulted in the removal of two candidates who had domains registered under the .us top-level domain. Our decision to focus on the .com top-level domain was driven by no other reason than our ability to access a complete database of .com registrants at the time of our research. Our final list of candidate web sites and their resulting domains appears in Table 10.1.

Once we had identified the set of candidate domain names, we conducted two tests to examine current domain name registration data. First, we determined how widespread the behavior of typo squatting was on each candidate's domain. Second, we examined domain name registration data so as to identify cousin domain names [198]. For our search, we defined a cousin domain name as one that contains

---

8. See Chapter 11 for a description of CPM, CPC, and CPA, along with a discussion of Internet advertising.

9. FEC Filing from Prospective 2008 Presidential Campaigns. http://query.nictusa.com/pres/2007/Q1

Joe Biden (Democrat)	http://www.joebiden.com
Sam Brownback (Republican)	http://www.brownback.com
Hillary Clinton (Democrat)	http://www.hillaryclinton.com
John Cox (Republican)	http://www.cox2008.com
Christopher Dodd (Democrat)	http://www.chrisdodd.com
John Edwards (Democrat)	http://www.johnedwards.com
James Gilmore (Republican)	http://www.gilmoreforpresident.com
Rudy Giuliani (Republican)	http://www.joinrudy2008.com
Mike Huckabee (Republican)	http://www.mikehuckabee.com
Duncun Hunter (Republican)	http://www.gohunter08.com
John McCain (Republican)	http://www.johnmccain.com
Barack Obama (Democrat)	http://www.barackobama.com
Ron Paul (Republican)	http://www.ronpaul2008.com
Bill Richardson (Democrat)	http://www.richardsonforpresident.com
Mitt Romney (Republican)	http://www.mittromney.com
Tom Tancredo (Republican)	http://www.teamtancredo.com
Tommy Thompson (Republican)	http://www.tommy2008.com

Table 10.1: The final candidate web site list, together with the domain names.

the candidate domain name in its entirety, with additional words either prefixed or appended to the candidate domain name. In this context, we would consider domain names such as presidentbarackobama.com or presidentmittromney.com as cousin domain names to the candidates' core domain names of barackobama.com and mittromney.com, respectively. One can also define a cousin name more loosely as a name that semantically or psychologically aims at being confused with another domain name. In this sense, www.thompson-for-president.com should be considered a cousin name domain of www.tommy2008.com, despite the fact that they do not share the same core. For the sake of simplicity, we did not examine cousin domains that are not fully inclusive of the original core domain name.

To generate typo domain names, we created two applications, typo_gen and typo_lookup. The typo_gen application allowed us to generate typo domain names based on five common mistakes that are made when entering a URL into the web browser address bar [466].

Missing the first "." delimiter:	wwwmittromney.com
Missing a character in the name ("t"):	www.mitromney.com
Hitting a surrounding character ("r"):	www.mitrromney.com
Adding an additional character ("t"):	www.mitttromney.com
Reversing two characters ("im"):	www.imttromney.com

As a result of such mistakes, the potential number of typos grows in proportion to the length of the domain name itself. The sheer number of typos for even a short domain name can be large. It is rare to find that an organization has registered all potential variations of its domain name in an effort to adequately protect itself. Typo squatters take advantage of such omissions to drive additional traffic to their own web properties.

Our second application, `typo_lookup`, accepted a list of domain names as input and then performed two queries to determine whether that domain name has been registered. First, a DNS lookup was performed to determine whether the domain resolves via the Domain Name System (DNS). Second, a `whois` lookup was performed to identify the registered owner of the domain.

For the purposes of our analysis, we considered a domain to be typo squatted if it was registered in bad faith by someone other than the legitimate owner of the primary source domain name. We visited those web sites for which typos currently exist and confirmed that they were, in fact, registered in bad faith. We filtered out those that directed the visitor to the legitimate campaign web site as well as those owned by legitimate entities whose name happens to match the typo domain.

Our second test involved the analysis of domain registration data to identify cousin domain names. We obtained a snapshot of all registered domains in the `.com` top-level domain during the month of June 2007. We performed a simple text search of this data set in an effort to cull out all matching domains.

Additional techniques could be used to generate related domain names that we did not examine during our research. This may include variations on a candidate's name (`christopher` instead of `chris`), variations including only a candidate surname (`clinton2008.com`), and the introduction of hyphens into names (`mitt-romney.com`). In addition, a number of typos might be combined to create even more variations on a given domain name, although it becomes less likely that an end user will visit such a domain name as the number of mistakes increases. Nevertheless, such domain names can be very effective in phishing emails, because the delivery of the malicious information relies on spamming in these cases, and not on misspellings made by users.

Expanding our search criteria in the future may result in the discovery of an even larger number of related domains. It also has the side effect of increasing our false-positive rate, or the discovery of domains that appear related but may, in fact, be legitimate web sites used for other purposes. In addition, the amount of manual analysis required to filter out such false positives further forced us to limit our search. Our results are shown in Table 10.2.

We can draw two clear conclusions from the results of our analysis. First, a large number of both typo and cousin domain names were registered by parties other than the candidate's own campaign. We found that many of the registered

Domain Name	Registered Typo Domains	Example	Registered Cousin Domains	Example
barackobama	52 of 160	narackobama	337	notbarackobama
brownback	0 of 134		152	runagainstbrownback
chrisdodd	14 of 145	chrisdod	21	chrisdoddforpresident
cox2008	3 of 92	fox2008	50	johncox2008
gilmoreforpresident	0 of 276		20	jimgilmore2008
gohunter08	1 of 150	ohunter08	23	stopduncanhunter
hillaryclinton	58 of 191	hillaryclingon	566	blamehillaryclinton
joebiden	15 of 125	jobiden	43	firejoebiden
johnedwards	34 of 170	hohnedwards	190	goawayjohnedwards
johnmccain	20 of 137	jhnmccain	173	nojohnmccain
joinrudy2008	9 of 173	jionrudy2008	123	dontjoinrudy2008
mikehuckabee	3 of 167	mikehukabee	28	whymikehuckabee
mittromney	18 of 123	muttromney	170	donttrustmittromney
richardsonforpresident	2 of 340	richardsonforpresiden	69	nobillrichardson
ronpaul2008	11 of 143	ronpaul20008	276	whynotronpaul
teamtancredo	1 of 170	teamtrancredo	16	whytomtancredo
tommy2008	1 of 107	tommyt2008	30	notommythompson

Table 10.2: Typo squatting and cousin domain analysis results. Many typo domain names were already registered and being used in bad faith. In addition, even more cousin domain names were registered, both in support of a candidate and, in many cases, to detract from a candidate. Note that all domains and examples are in the .com top-level domain.

web sites, in both the typo squatting case and the cousin domain name case, were registered for the purpose of driving traffic to advertising web sites.

Second, candidates have not done a good job in protecting themselves by proactively registering typo domains to eliminate potential abuse. In fact, we were able to find only a single typo web site that had been registered by a candidate's campaign: http://www.mittromny.com. All typo domains were owned by third parties that appeared unrelated to the candidate's campaign.

One observation that we made is that many of the typo domains that displayed contextual advertisements were, in fact, displaying advertisements that pointed back to a candidate's legitimate campaign web site. This is best demonstrated in Figure 10.1. In such cases, a typo squatter had taken over the misspelling of a candidate's domain name and was able to profit from it. Even worse, the candidate was paying to have his or her ads displayed on the typo squatter's web site! This is a result of the way in which ad syndication on the Internet works.

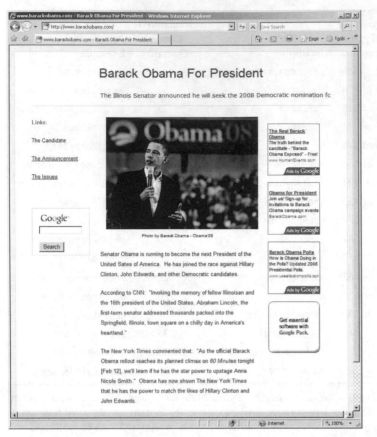

Figure 10.1: When we visited `http://www.barackobams.com` (a typo of Barack Obama's web site, `http://www.barackobama.com`), it contained advertisements pointing to the candidate's legitimate campaign site.

Ad syndicates display advertisements on a web site by indexing its content and displaying advertisements that are appropriate given that content. They may also look at the domain name itself and display advertisements for matching keywords in the domain name. As a result, advertisements for the legitimate campaign may be displayed on a typo squatter's web site. When a user mistypes the web site name and browses to the typo domain, he or she is presented with an advertisement for the legitimate campaign's web site. If the user clicks on this advertisement, the ad syndicate generates a profit, giving a portion to the typo squatter for generating the click through and charging the advertiser, which in this case is the legitimate campaign.[10]

---

10. A more detailed discussion of how Internet advertising works can be found in Chapter 11.

Individuals who register cousin domain names may have similar motives to those of typo squatters, but they may also be speculating on the value of the domain name itself, with the intent to resell it at a later date. It is also possible that they intend to use the domain to defraud people or to make people wary of emails purportedly coming from a given candidate.

In our analysis, the majority of the identified domains, both in the typo and cousin cases, likely had been acquired in bulk, for the explicit purpose of driving traffic to advertisements. As a result, many of these domains were parked with companies that provide a framework for domain name owners to profit from the traffic that their web sites receive.

10.1.3 Domain Parking

Typo squatters and domain name speculators need not host the physical web infrastructure required to display their own web content or to host their advertisements. Instead, domain name owners can rely on domain parking companies that will happily handle this task for them, for an appropriate share of the advertising revenue. Domain name parking companies will provide the required web site and leverage their preestablished relationships with advertising providers to make life as simple as possible for domain name owners. To leverage a domain name parker, the domain name owner need only configure his or her domain's primary and secondary DNS servers to that of the domain parker. This makes the acquisition and profit from the ownership of a domain name even simpler, to the extent that an individual need just register a domain name and park it at the same time.

While registering a domain name and parking that domain name put the core requirements and relationships in place for a revenue generation model, they do not guarantee that the domain owner will, in fact, profit from this setup. To generate a profit, an adequate amount of traffic and interest must be generated to draw Internet users to that domain name. As such, more emphasis is placed on domain names that are more likely to generate more interest. This is supported by our analysis in Table 10.1, which clearly demonstrates that typo squatters and speculators have favored the domain names of leading candidates.

10.1.4 Malicious Intent

While advertising has been the primary motive behind the registration of typo and cousin name domains to date, more measurable damage using these techniques is highly likely to occur. We have already observed a number of cases where a

Figure 10.2: `http://www.hillaryclingon.com` is a typo-squatted version of Hillary Clinton's real web site, `http://www.hillaryclinton.com` (the "g" key is right below the "t" key on the keyboard), but it has another meaning as well.

typo-squatted domain has been forwarded to an alternative site with differing political views, as seen in Figures 10.2, 10.3, and 10.4. This is problematic in the typo squatting case, because the end user is unknowingly being redirected to a different web site. It is even more common when analyzing cousin domains, which can be registered by anyone; the number of possible registrations can become nearly infinite. It is, however, much more difficult to drive visitors to those domains without having some way in which to attract them. As such, owners of cousin domains use other techniques to attract visitors, including manipulating search engines to increase their ranking (search engine optimization) or, in some cases, even taking out their own advertisements. It may also involve phishing-style spamming of a large number of users.

One interesting side effect of ad syndication networks as they exist today is that we frequently encounter typo domains that are hosting advertisements for a candidate's competitor. It is interesting to see how search engine optimization and keyword purchasing play roles in attracting visitors. Many search engines allow the purchasing of advertisements that are displayed only when users search for specific keywords. Google AdWords is a popular example of such a program where particular keywords can be purchased and advertisements of the purchaser's

Figure 10.3: `http://www.joinrudy20008.com`, a typo-squatted version of Rudy Giuliani's campaign web site, `http://www.joinrudy2008.com`, redirects users to a detractor's web site at `http://rudy-urbanlegend.com`.

choice will then be displayed. As shown in Figure 10.5, this may result in advertisements for one candidate being displayed when a user is searching for a particular keyword, or accidentally browsing to a typo-squatted web site.

Advertising, misdirection, and detraction aside, the real potential for future abuse of typo and cousin domains may revolve around the distribution and installation of security risks and malicious code. This attack vector is by no means new, as web sites and banner advertisements are frequently used to attack visitors who happen to browse to a malicious web site [233]. Attackers who control such web sites frequently leverage a software vulnerability in the web browser [234], or use social engineering and misleading tactics to trick the user into installing security risks [95] and malicious code. Even in the absence of a software vulnerability, we can conceive of a number of convincing scenarios that an attacker might use to convince visitors to install such software. For example, a site could easily mirror Hillary Clinton's legitimate web site, but prominently feature an offer for a Hillary Clinton screensaver that is, in fact, spyware or malicious code.

Figure 10.4: `http://www.muttromney.com` is a typo-squatted version (the "u" key is beside the "i" key on the keyboard) of Mitt Romney's web site, `http://www.mittromney.com`, which redirects the user to a detractor's web site.

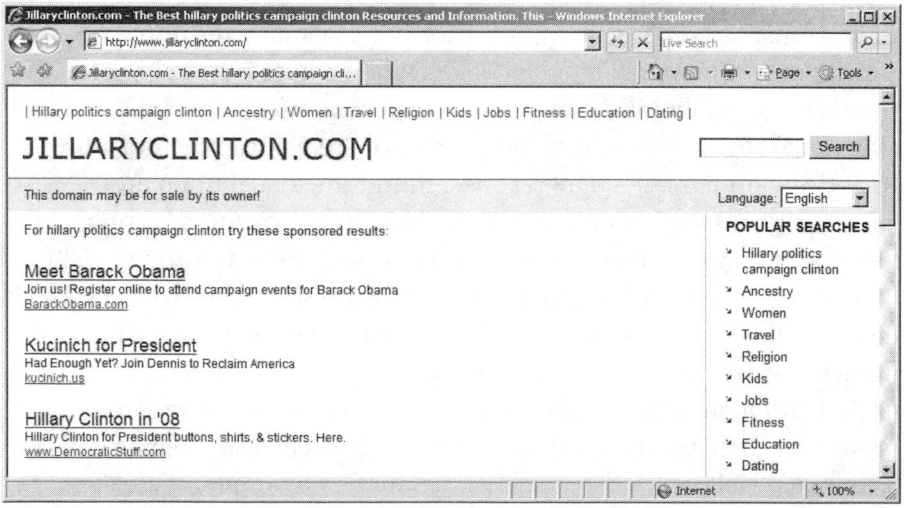

Figure 10.5: `http://www.jillaryclinton.com`, a typo-squatted version of Hillary Clinton's web site, `http://www.hillaryclinton.com`, displays advertisements directing visitors to rival web sites.

Another site, perhaps mirroring that of Rudy Giuliani, might offer an application claiming to give instant access to his travels, speeches, and videos. Yet another site might claim that by downloading an application, the visitor can assist the candidate in fundraising; that application would, instead, monitor and steal the victim's own banking credentials. The impact of downloading such an application under false pretenses is covered in more detail later in this chapter.

10.2 Campaign–Targeted Phishing

Phishing has without a doubt become one of the most widespread risks affecting Internet users today. When we look at phishing and the role that it may play in an election campaign, we can readily envision several incremental risks that present themselves beyond the traditional theft of confidential information.

10.2.1 Profit–Motivated Phishing

Profit-motivated, event-based phishing is certainly not new. It has been seen in the past on numerous occasions leading up to and following significant events worldwide. For example, this type of attack was seen after natural disasters such as the Indian Ocean tsunami in 2004 [66] and Hurricane Katrina in 2005 [220, 251]. It was also seen in conjunction with sporting events, such as the 2006 and 2010 FIFA World Cup [275].

Election-related phishing has been observed in the past. During the 2004 federal election, phishers targeted the Kerry–Edwards campaign [370], a campaign that was acknowledged as being at the forefront of leveraging the Internet for communications. At least two distinct types of phishing were observed. In one case, phishers set up a fictitious web site to solicit online campaign contributions shortly after the Democratic National Convention; this site stole the victim's credit card number, among other information. In the second case, phishers asked recipients to call a for-fee 1-900 number, for which the victim would subsequently be charged $1.99 per minute [417]. This is a prime example of how such attacks can cross technology boundaries to appear even more convincing. The perpetrators of these two attacks were never caught.

When considering the 2004 election as a whole, phishing presented only a marginal risk. At the time, phishing was still in its infancy, and had yet to grow into the epidemic that can be observed today. When assessing the potential risk of phishing in conjuction with the 2008 federal election, however, we find ourselves in a much different position. Candidates have flocked to the Internet, seeing it as a key means to communicate with constituents and to raise campaign contributions.

Domain Name	Redirects to
barackobama.com	https://donate.barackobama.com
brownback.com	https://www.campaigncontribution.com
chrisdodd.com	https://salsa.wiredforchange.com
cox2008.com	https://www.completecampaigns.com
mikehuckabee.com	https://www.mikehuckabee.com
gilmoreforpresident.com	https://www.gilmoreforpresident.com
gohunter08.com	https://contribute.gohunter08.com
hillaryclinton.com	https://contribute.hillaryclinton.com
joebiden.com	https://secure.ga3.org
johnedwards.com	https://secure.actblue.com
johnmccain.com	https://www.johnmccain.com
joinrudy2008.com	https://www.joinrudy2008.com
mittromney.com	https://www.mittromney.com
richardsonforpresident.com	https://secure.richardsonforpresident.com
ronpaul2008.com	https://www.ronpaul2008.com
teamtancredo.com	https://www.campaigncontribution.com
tommy2008.com	https://secure.yourpatriot.com

Table 10.3: An analysis of 2008 federal candidate web sites and the sites to which contributors are directed to. The sites to which contributors are redirected are legitimate, but the fact that they are often different from the original site increases the risk for confusion and thereby the risk that a phishing attack with a similar design would succeed.

We performed an analysis of campaign web sites in an attempt to determine to what degree they allow contributions to be made online. We discovered that every candidate provided a mechanism by which supporters could make a donation online. All of the web sites on which contributions could be made leveraged SSL as a means to secure the transaction. We also noted the domain of each contribution site. In numerous cases, would-be contributors were redirected to a third-party site, which sat on a different primary domain. Table 10.3 lists both the original domain, and the web site to which the user is redirected.

This redirection was the result of third-party consulting, media, and online advocacy firms being used to assist in the running of the campaign, including the processing of online campaign contributions. This practice does not present a security risk in and of itself, nor is it an indication that phishing is taking place; however, the change in the top-level domain may add to the confusion of potential contributors, who tend to err on the side of caution. It also indicates that additional parties may be involved in the gathering and processing of personal information on behalf of a campaign, increasing the overall exposure of the credit card numbers processed during fundraising.

It should also be noted that the redirection used here is not necessary, and that the contribution site could just as easily remain in the same top-level domain, as a subdomain hosted by the third party for processing. To do so simply requires the appropriate configuration of the primary domain's DNS records. In fact, the majority of the remaining candidates have chosen to follow this path. Future research may also reveal whether those donation sites that do live under the campaign's domain name are, in fact, hosted on the same physical network as the campaign web site or on another third-party payment processor's network.

Figure 10.6 provides a sample of the information collected during an online contribution. We found that forms were fairly consistent in the type of information that was collected, while (not surprisingly) varying from a visual perspective.

The ability to process credit card transactions on an authentic campaign web site may provide an unexpected benefit to online identity thieves. One tactic

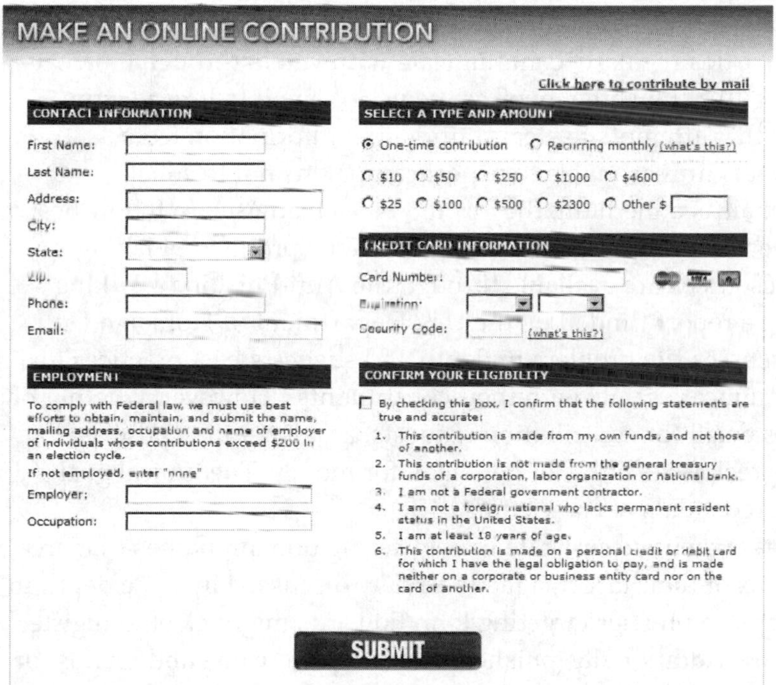

Figure 10.6: A sample form from one candidate's web site allowing visitors to make contributions online. This is a legitimate site. Given that typical Internet users would not be well acquainted with the domains associated with political candidates, there is a risk that phishers might use a similarly designed web site to collect credentials from unsuspecting victims.

regularly employed by those peddling in stolen credit cards is to process a very small transaction so as to validate a credit card as legitimate [48]. Thieves began using this technique in early 2007 on online charity web sites, but it has long been used on other types of online payment sites. Such a small transaction is unlikely to be noticed by the credit card holder and is unlikely to be flagged by the party processing the transaction.

Of course, not all contributions would necessarily be helpful. Attackers might seek to disrupt a candidate's fundraising efforts by initiating illegitimate payments to create confusion. If performed en masse, the widespread contribution of small, random amounts of money, from thousands or tens of thousands of stolen credit cards, would certainly have a negative effect. While there is a slight chance such an attack might remain stealth, it is more likely that it will be noticed, making it nearly impossible to differentiate legitimate contributions from fraudulent donations. Thus a significant burden would be placed on the affected candidates by diluting legitimate contributions with those that were not initiated by the credit card owners.

The increased collection of online campaign contributions also provides a ripe opportunity for phishers to target members of the unsuspecting public. Candidates and their parties regularly communicate with voters through email, as demonstrated in Figure 10.7. Phishing involves the use of email to lure a victim to a fictitious web site that attempts to steal confidential information from the victim [91]. While it is unreasonable to expect campaigns not to solicit contributions using email as a medium, they would be well advised to follow best practices that have been set by other online entities heavily prone to phishing. (A number of excellent resources are available through the Anti-Phishing Working Group [313], including a report funded by the U.S. Department of Homeland Security [101] that discusses the problem in depth and suggests best practices for organizations to communicate safely with their constituents.) However, whether or not the candidate uses email for contribution requests, a phisher may pose as a candidate and ask the recipients of his or her email for money. The typical goal would be to steal the credentials of the victims.

Phishers can increase their success rate by registering domain names that are typos or cousin domains of their target, a tactic already discussed in some depth in this chapter. For example, a phisher targeting John Edwards might elect to register donatejohnedwards.com. Additionally, phishers may simply create subdomains for primary domains that they already own. A phisher who buys the domain donatefor2008.com, for example, might simply add DNS records for johnedwards.donatefor2008.com and ronpaul.donatefor2008.com, among others. These domain names could then be referenced in the phishing emails sent to

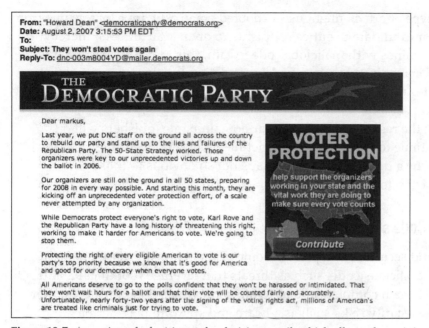

From: "Howard Dean" <democraticparty@democrats.org>
Date: August 2, 2007 3:15:53 PM EDT
To:
Subject: They won't steal votes again
Reply-To: dnc-003m8004YD@mailer.democrats.org

THE
DEMOCRATIC PARTY

Dear markus,

Last year, we put DNC staff on the ground all across the country to rebuild our party and stand up to the lies and failures of the Republican Party. The 50-State Strategy worked. Those organizers were key to our unprecedented victories up and down the ballot in 2006.

Our organizers are still on the ground in all 50 states, preparing for 2008 in every way possible. And starting this month, they are kicking off an unprecedented voter protection effort, of a scale never attempted by any organization.

While Democrats protect everyone's right to vote, Karl Rove and the Republican Party have a long history of threatening this right, working to make it harder for Americans to vote. We're going to stop them.

Protecting the right of every eligible American to vote is our party's top priority because we know that it's good for America and good for our democracy when everyone votes.

All Americans deserve to go to the polls confident that they won't be harassed or intimidated. That they won't wait hours for a ballot and that their vote will be counted fairly and accurately. Unfortunately, nearly forty-two years after the signing of the voting rights act, millions of American's are treated like criminals just for trying to vote.

VOTER PROTECTION

help support the organizers working in your state and the vital work they are doing to make sure every vote counts

Contribute

Figure 10.7: A portion of a legitimate fundraising email, which allows the recipient to click on the hyperlinked "Contribute" button to support the campaign. This approach would be very easy for a phisher to mimic in an effort to make people submit their credentials to the phisher, thinking they are contributing. Of course, phishers can use inflammatory texts (even more so than political candidates) as calls for action. The authors of this book were able to register the domain democratic-party.us, which would be suitable in such an attack, and found a wealth of other cousin name domains available for both parties. Thus, whereas financial institutions typically have registered cousin name domains to defend against abuse, political parties and candidates have not.

potential victims. When clicked on, the link would drive the victim to the fictitious web site.

As we have observed, a significant number of typo domain names have already been registered, or are available to be registered, by parties who are acting in bad faith. Many of these domain names appear so similar to the legitimate domain name that the unsuspecting eye of a potential victim would not notice if directed to one of these sites. Campaigns can take clear and immediate steps to purchase typo domains prior to them falling into the wrong hands. As of this writing, few have done so.

More difficult, however, is the acquisition of cousin domain names. As discussed previously, a significant number of cousin domain names have been registered for both speculative and advertising purposes. Given the near-infinite number of possible cousin domain names, it is unlikely that a campaign could acquire all possibilities. This fact of life provides phishers with the opportunity to register a domain name that may appear similar to the legitimate campaign's web site.

Yet another type of attack might use a spoofed email that appears to come from a political party or candidate to entice recipients to open attachments, thereby infecting their machines with malicious code. Again, this may be done either with the direct goal of spreading malicious code or to deliver a below-the-belt blow to political candidates who rely heavily on the Internet for their communication with constituents.

Even without the registration of a similar domain name, phishers will undoubtedly continue to succeed in constructing emails and web sites that are obvious to detect by a trained eye, but perhaps not so obvious to those who continue to fall victim to them.

10.3 Malicious Code and Security Risks

Malicious code and security risks present some of the more sinister risks to the election process. Malicious code, such as threats that leverage rootkit capabilities,[11] has the potential to gain complete and absolute control over a victim's computer system. Likewise, security risks such as adware and spyware pose serious concerns, both in terms of their invasiveness to a user's privacy (in the case of spyware) and their ability to present users with unexpected or undesired information and advertisements (in the case of adware).

We can consider a number of scenarios where well-known classes of malicious code may be tailored specifically to target those participating in an election. Targets may range from candidates and campaign officials to voters themselves. In discussing these risks we begin with what we consider the less serious category of security risks; we then move into the more serious, insidious category of malicious code.

10.3.1 Adware

Adware, in its truest form, may not pose an immediate and dire risk to the end user. Once installed, however, its control over a user's Internet experience places it into a strategic position on the end user's computer. Adware has the potential to manipulate a user's Internet experience by displaying unexpected or unwanted advertisements. These advertisements may be displayed on the user's desktop or shown to the user through the web browser as the user visits Internet web sites. These advertisements may appear as pop-up windows, or they may appear as content (ads) that are either overlaid or inserted into existing web pages visited by

---

11. A detailed discussion of rootkits can be found in Chapter 8.

the user. Both techniques have been used frequently by such well-known adware applications as 180Solution's Hotbar [99], Gator Corporation's Gator [96], and WhenU's Save [97]. Adware may be installed by the end user as part of another third-party application, or it may be installed surreptitiously through the exploitation of a software vulnerability in the user's web browser. Chapter 12 discusses adware in more detail.

Adware might be used in numerous ways to influence or manipulate users during the course of an election. In its most innocuous form, adware might simply present the user with advertisements promoting a particular candidate and directing the user to the candidate's web site when clicked. Taking a more deceptive angle, adware might be used to silently replace advertisements for one candidate with another. This may be done directly in the user's browser by manipulating the incoming HTML content before it is rendered or by overlaying a new advertisement on top of an existing advertisement on the user's screen.

Until it is observed in the wild, it is difficult for us to predict the real-world impact that such an adware application might have. It would be important for such an application to be silent and unobtrusive, acting clandestinely to avoid annoying the end user lest its objective backfire. In addition, such an effort may simply help to sway those voters who have not already committed to a particular party or candidate, rather than those voters who have already made their decision.

10.3.2 Spyware

We have frequently seen adware and spyware traits combined into a single application that both delivers advertising and monitors a user's Internet habits. For the purposes of our discussion, we chose to distinguish between the distinct behaviors of adware and spyware, discussing each separately. Spyware, with its ability to secretly profile and monitor user behavior, presents an entirely new opportunity for the widespread collection of election-related trend data and behavioral information.

When discussing the use of spyware, we can conceive of a number of behaviors that might be collected throughout the course of an election in an attempt to provide insight into voters' dispositions. The most basic tactic would be to monitor the browsing behavior of voters and to collect the party affiliations of the Internet sites most frequently visited by the end user. Even without the installation of spyware on an end user's computer, one web site may silently acquire a history of other web sites that the user has previously visited. This capability has been demonstrated by researchers in the past and can be observed at `https://www.indiana.edu/~phishing/browser-recon`. This type of data collection may also include the tracking of online news articles that are viewed and online campaign contributions that are made by determining whether a particular URL was visited.

With the addition of spyware on the end user's computer, these information-gathering efforts can be taken a step further. Emails sent and received by the user can be monitored, for example. In our study, we found that all 19 candidates allow a user to subscribe to their campaign mailing lists, from which a user receives regular frequent updates on the campaign's progress. Knowing how many voters have subscribed to a particular candidate's mailing list may provide insight into the overall support levels for that candidate.

Of course, Internet and browsing behavior alone may not be an indicator of a voter's preference, as voters may be just as likely to visit a competing candidate's web sites and subscribe to a competing candidate's mailing list so as to stay informed about that candidate's campaign. Unfortunately, we could find no prior research that examined the correlation between user Internet behavior and party or candidate affiliation. Nevertheless, spyware clearly poses a new risk in terms of the mass accumulation of election-related statistics that may be used to track election trends.

The collection of voter disposition data is certainly not new, as groups such as the Gallup Organization [137] (known for the Gallup Poll) have been collecting and analyzing user behavior since 1935. What is different in this case is spyware's ability to capture and record user behavior without consent and without the voter's knowledge. Even when a spyware application's behavior is described clearly in an end-user license agreement (EULA), few users either read or understand these complex and lengthy agreements [98]. This changes the landscape dramatically when it comes to election-related data collection.

10.3.3 Malicious Code: Keyloggers and Crimeware

By far one of the most concerning attacks on voters, candidates, and campaign officials alike is that of malicious code infection. Malicious code that is targeted toward a broad spectrum of voters has the potential to cause widespread damage, confusion, and loss of confidence in the election process itself. When we consider the various types of attacks mentioned in this chapter, malicious code—in the form of keyloggers, trojans, and other forms of crimeware—has the potential to carry each of them out with unmatched efficiency. These attacks include the monitoring of user behavior, the theft of user data, the redirection of user browsing, and the delivery of misinformation.

One additional angle for crimeware is the notion of intimidation. Given a threat's presence on a voter's computer, that threat has the potential to collect personal, potentially sensitive information about that individual. This capability may include turning on the computer's microphone and recording private conversations. It may include turning on the computer's video camera and recording activities in the room. It may include retrieving pictures, browser history documents, or copyrighted files from a voter's computer. Perhaps the individual would be turned in to the RIAA if copyrighted music was found on his or her computer. This kind of information gathering creates the potential for an entirely new form of voter intimidation. The collection of such personally sensitive or legally questionable data by a threat might, therefore, allow an attacker to intimidate that individual in an entirely new way. We would, of course, expect and hope that the number of voters who might be intimidated in such a way would be relatively low, but only time will tell whether such speculation becomes reality.

Another form of threat that we have seen in the past involves holding a victim's data hostage until a fee is paid to release it. This possibility was first discussed in [487]. An example of such a threat is Trojan.Gpcoder [340], which encrypts the user's data, erasing the original information, until this fee is paid. Such a threat may present another new form of intimidation whereby the only way for a user to regain access to his or her personal data is to vote accordingly. Such an attack presents obvious logistical challenges. For example, how is the attacker to know which way the victim voted? The attacker may, however, take comfort in the belief that he or she has intimidated enough of the infected population to make a meaningful difference.

Just as the widespread infection of the populace's computers poses a risk to voters, the targeted, calculated infection of specific individuals' computers is equal cause for concern. A carefully placed targeted keylogger has the potential to cause material damage to a candidate during the election process. Such code may also be targeted toward campaign staff, family members, or others who may be deemed material to the candidate's efforts. Such an infection might potentially result in the monitoring of all communications, including email messages and web site access initiated on the infected computer. This monitoring would give the would-be attacker unparalleled insight into the progress, plans, and disposition of the candidate's campaign, perhaps including new messaging, speeches, and otherwise sensitive information critical to the candidate's campaign.

10.4 Denial-of-Service Attacks

Denial-of-service attacks have become increasingly common on the Internet today. These kinds of attacks seek to make a computer network—in most cases, a particular web site—unavailable and therefore unusable. Also known as distributed denial-of-service (DDoS) attacks, they are frequently launched by means of inundating a target with an overwhelming amount of network traffic. This traffic may take the form of Internet protocol requests at the IP and TCP layers or application-level requests that target specific applications such as an organization's web server, email server, or FTP server. Denial-of-service attacks are frequently perpetrated through the use of bot networks, as discussed in more detail in Chapter 7.

A number of high-profile, wide-scale DDoS attacks have demonstrated the effects that such an effort can have. One of the best-known and largest attacks was launched against the country of Estonia in May 2007 [81]. It presented a prime example of a politically motivated attack, as it was launched by Russian patriots in retaliation for the removal of a Soviet monument by the Estonian government. Attackers disabled numerous key government systems during a series of attacks that occurred over the course of several weeks.

In 2006, Joe Lieberman's web site also fell victim to a concentrated denial-of-service attack [397]. Forcing the site offline, the attack paralyzed the joe2006.com domain, preventing campaign officials from using their official campaign email accounts and forcing them to revert to their personal accounts for communication.

The implications of such attacks are clear: They prevent voters from reaching campaign web sites, and they prevent campaign officials from communicating with voters.

10.5 Cognitive Election Hacking

Labeled by researchers as *cognitive hacking* [73], the potential for misinformation and subterfuge attacks using Internet-based technologies is as rich as one's imagination. We have already discussed several techniques that may be used to surreptitiously lure users to locations other than a legitimate campaign's web site. These same techniques can be used to spread misleading, inaccurate, and outright false information.

So far, we have discussed typo and cousin domain names that users may visit accidentally when attempting to browse to a legitimate web site. We have also discussed phishing and spam, which have the potential to lure users to web sites by impersonating legitimate candidate web sites. Finally, we have discussed malicious code and the role that it may play in manipulating a user's desktop experience before the user even reaches the intended destination.

The security of a campaign's web site plays another vital role in determining voters' faith in the election process. The breach of a legitimate candidate's web site, for example, would allow an attacker to have direct control over all content viewed by visitors to that web site. This may allow for the posting of misinformation or, worse, the deployment of malicious code to unsecured visitors.

Examples of misinformation about a specific candidate might include a false report about the decision by a candidate to drop out of the race, a fake scandal, and phony legal or health issues. It might also take the form of subtle information that could be portrayed as legitimate, such as a change in a candidate's position on a particular subject, resulting in abandonment of the candidate by voters who feel strongly about that issue.

Attempts to deceive voters through the spread of misinformation are not new. In fact, numerous cases have been documented in past elections using traditional forms of communication [358]. These include campaigns aimed at intimidating minorities and individuals with criminal records, attempts to announce erroneous voting dates, and many other tactics resulting in voter confusion.

During the 2006 election, 14,000 Latino voters in Orange County, California, received misleading letters warning them that it was illegal for immigrants to vote in the election and that doing so would result in their incarceration and deportation. In his testimony before congress, John Trasviña, President and General Counsel of the Mexican American Legal Defense and Educational Fund (MALDEF), discussed this use of misinformation as an example of voter suppression:

> First, the Orange County letter falsely advised prospective voters that immigrants who vote in federal elections are committing a crime that can result in incarceration and possible deportation. This is a false and deceptive statement: Naturalized immigrants who are otherwise eligible to vote are free to vote in federal elections without fear of penalties (including but not limited to incarceration and/or deportation). Second, the letter stated that "the U.S. government is installing a new computerized system to verify names of all newly registered voters who participate in the elections in October and November. Organizations against emigration will be able to request information from this new computerized system." Again, the letter adopts an intimidating tone based upon false information in an apparent attempt to undermine voter confidence within the targeted group of voters. Finally, the letter stated that "[n]ot like in Mexico, here there is no benefit to voting." This letter, representing a coordinated and extensive effort to suppress the Latino vote in the days leading up to a congressional election, has been traced to a candidate running for the congressional seat in the district in which the affected voters live.[12]

---

12. United States Senate Committee on the Judiciary Prevention of Deceptive Practices and Voter Intimidation in Federal Elections: S. 453 Testimony of John Trasviña. Available at http:// judiciary.senate.gov/testimony.cfm?id=2798&wit_id=6514

Another case of deception was targeted at college students in Pittsburgh, Pennsylvania, in 2004 [355]. Canvassers, posing as petitioners for such topics as medical marijuana and auto insurance rates, gathered signatures from students that, unknown to them, resulted in a change to their party affiliation and polling location.

Push polling is one technique that lends itself extremely well to Internet-based technologies. In push polling, an individual or organization attempts to influence or alter the views of voters under the guise of conducting a poll. The poll, in many cases, poses a question by stating inaccurate or false information as part of the question. One well-known push poll occurred in the 2000 Republican Party primary.[13] Voters in South Carolina were asked, "Would you be more likely or less likely to vote for John McCain for president if you knew he had fathered an illegitimate black child?" In this case, the poll's allegation had no substance, but was heard by thousands of primary voters. McCain and his wife had, in fact, adopted a Bangladeshi girl.

A bill known as the Deceptive Practices and Voter Intimidation Prevention Act of 2007[14] seeks to make these attacks illegal. Currently waiting to be heard in the Senate, it is possible that this bill might be in place for the 2008 federal election, making deceptive tactics such as these illegal, and introducing a maximum penalty of up to 5 years in prison for offenders. This legislation is likely to apply to deceptive practices whether they are performed using traditional communication mechanisms or Internet-based technologies.

While the introduction of such policies is important and provides a well-defined guideline under which to prosecute offenders, only time will tell to what extent legislation will succeed in controlling these acts. As we have seen in some areas, such as the policies developed to outlaw the transmission of spam email, regulations have only marginal effectiveness in reducing the problem. Even today, more than 50% of all email sent on the Internet is purported to consist of spam [401]. There is no reason to doubt that the type of deception and intimidation discussed will be equally successful on the Internet.

The challenge with Internet-based technologies is the ease with which such an attack may be perpetrated. Whereas traditional communication media may have required an organized effort to commit an attack, the Internet allows a single attacker to realize the benefits of automation and scale that previously did not

---

13. SourceWatch. http://www.sourcewatch.org/index.php?title=Push_poll

14. Deceptive Practices and Voter Intimidation Prevention Act of 2007. http://www.govtrack.us/congress/billtext.xpd?bill=h110-1281

exist. As such, one person has the potential to cause widespread disruption, with comparably little effort.

Historically, some of the most successful misinformation attacks on the Internet have been motivated by profit. Pump-and-dump schemes [369], for example, have become an extremely common form of spam. These schemes involve the promotion of a company's stock through the issuance of false and misleading statements. After the stock price rises owing to renewed interest from the message's recipients, the perpetrators sell their own stock for a substantial profit.

One significant surge of pump-and-dump emails that was observed in 2006 was attributed to a bot network, operated by Russian fraudsters [268]. In this attack, 70,000 infected computers spread across 166 countries were organized into a bot network that was used to send out unsolicited stock-promoting spam. Such a network could easily be directed to send any form of email, including disinformation and fallacies related to a candidate, voters, and the election itself. Chapter 7 discusses botnets and their applications in more detail.

10.6 Public Voter Information Sources: FEC Databases

The Federal Election Commission [62] was created both to track campaign contributions and to enforce federal regulations that surround them.

> In 1975, Congress created the Federal Election Commission (FEC) to administer and enforce the Federal Election Campaign Act (FECA)—the statute that governs the financing of federal elections. The duties of the FEC, which is an independent regulatory agency, are to disclose campaign finance information, to enforce the provisions of the law such as the limits and prohibitions on contributions, and to oversee the public funding of Presidential elections.

To provide a public record of campaign contributions, the FEC must maintain, and provide to the public, a full record of all campaign contributions. Many web sites that allow online contributions clearly indicate their requirement to report those contributions to the Federal Election Commission. The following text, taken from one candidate's web site exemplifies this kind of disclaimer:

> We are required by federal law to collect and report to the Federal Election Commission the name, mailing address, occupation, and employer of individuals whose contributions exceed $200 in an election cycle. These records are available to the public. However, they cannot be used by other organizations for fundraising. We also make a note of your telephone number and email address, which helps us to contact you quickly if follow-up on your contribution is necessary under Federal election law. For additional information, visit the FEC website at http://www.fec.gov.

The FEC's role is to make this data available to the public. The information is available as raw data files, via FTP, and through online web interfaces on the FEC web site.

Numerous third-party web sites, such as http://www.opensecrets.org, also use this data to provide regular high-level reports on candidate funding. Consumers of the data are restricted by a policy that regulates how the data can be used [64]. The policy is surprisingly lenient, as it is primarily intended to prevent the use of contributors' names for commercial purposes or further solicitation of contributions.

The information provided in this database consists of each contributor's full name, city, ZIP code, and particulars of the contribution, such as the receiving candidate or party, the amount, and the date of the contribution. While limited, this information does allow one to build a history of political contributions for any U.S. citizen who appears in the database.

Contributors of record may be more likely to become victims of the other attacks already discussed in this chapter. Appearing in this database may expose high-net-worth contributors to targeted phishing (spear phishing) or malicious code attacks if the individual's name can be connected to his or her email address (no longer a difficult feat).

10.7 Intercepting Voice Communications

While this chapter has focused primarily on Internet-based risks, we would be remiss if we did not discuss at least one additional risk given a recent particularly noteworthy and sophisticated attack against a foreign nation's communication infrastructure. Labeled the *Athens Affair* by authors Vassilis Prevelakis and Diomidis Spinellis [320], this well-coordinated attack highlighted the increased role that common technologies play in all forms of our daily communications. In their paper, the authors retrace the alarming events related to the interception of cell phone communications from high-ranking Greek government officials:

> On 9 March 2005, a 38-year-old Greek electrical engineer named Costas Tsalikidis was found hanged in his Athens loft apartment, an apparent suicide. It would prove to be merely the first public news of a scandal that would roil Greece for months.
>
> The next day, the prime minister of Greece was told that his cell phone was being bugged, as were those of the mayor of Athens and at least 100 other high-ranking dignitaries, including an employee of the U.S. embassy.
>
> The victims were customers of Athens-based Vodafone-Panafon, generally known as Vodafone Greece, the country's largest cellular service provider; Tsalikidis was in charge of network planning at the company. A connection seemed obvious. Given the

list of people and their positions at the time of the tapping, we can only imagine the sensitive political and diplomatic discussions, high-stakes business deals, or even marital indiscretions that may have been routinely overheard and, quite possibly, recorded.

Even before Tsalikidis's death, investigators had found rogue software installed on the Vodafone Greece phone network by parties unknown. Some extraordinarily knowledgeable people either penetrated the network from outside or subverted it from within, aided by an agent or mole. In either case, the software at the heart of the phone system, investigators later discovered, was reprogrammed with a finesse and sophistication rarely seen before or since.

In this attack, perpetrators used rootkit techniques, like those discussed in Chapter 8, on the cellular provider's phone switch to remain hidden. Over the past two decades, the basic communications systems that we rely on for both our traditional land-line telephones and our cellular phone communications have increasingly moved to commodity-based hardware and software [108]. In the past, would-be attackers were forced to learn complex and proprietary embedded systems, making the introduction of malicious code on these systems difficult, if not impossible. Today's commoditization simplifies this effort, as witnessed by the attack discussed here, and greatly increases the likelihood that an attacker might gain a similar foothold on communications systems in the future.

Central switching networks are not the only target. Mobile devices themselves remain even more likely candidates for interception of communications. Today's mobile devices, an increasing number of which can be considered smartphones, provide ripe opportunities for the introduction of malicious code. While traditional threats such as viruses, worms, and trojans have yet to gain widespread prominence on mobile devices (although they do exist), the potential for targeted customized mobile threats has existed for some time.

One particular application, known as FlexiSpy and sold by Bangkok, Thailand–based software vendor Vervata, allows listening to a remote phone's surrounding while it is not in use (Figure 10.8). It also allows retrieval of the phone's personal data and monitoring of all email and SMS messages sent by the phone. The software itself is available in "Pro," "Light," "Alert," and "Bug" versions. The vendor prides itself on its software's ability to remain hidden and unnoticeable on an infected device.

The infection of a candidate, campaign staff, or candidate's family's cell phone with such a freely available application could have dire consequences. All back-room and hallway conversations engaged in by the candidate could be monitored at all times and intercepted by the attacker. Worse, opinions—perhaps including those not shared with the public or outsiders—could be recorded and

This page helps you understand what all the spyphone features mean	PRO	LIGHT	ALERT	BUG
Application Features				
Remote Listening	✓			✓
Make a spy call to the target phone running FlexiSPY and listen in to the phones surroundings. **This does not allow you to listen to the phone conversation in progress.** Call Tapping will be available very shortly. Please sign up to our mailing list of you are interested in this feature				
Control Phone By SMS	✓	✓	✓	✓
Send secret SMS to the target phone to control all functions. No need to physically access the phone for any feature not related to installation				
SMS and Email Logging	✓	✓		
All SMS and EMAIL contents are sent to your FlexiSPY web account. Support all languages				
Call History Logging	✓	✓		
The time, duration and number of all voice calls are sent to your web account. If the phone number is in the phones address book, then the name will be available also				
Location Tracking	✓	✓		
See the CELL ID and CELL name that the mobile is physically located in. Read more about mobile location tracking by cell id				
Private Data Deleting			✓	
Delete your videos, pictures, SMS, and application with one SMS				

Figure 10.8: FlexiSpy, developed and sold by Bangkok, Thailand's Vervata, allows for monitoring and tapping of cell phone communications. It is supported on Windows Mobile, Symbian OS, and Blackberry devices. Today installation requires physical access to the device. Much like desktop operating systems, however, future versions might be installed through software vulnerabilities or messaging applications.

made available for later playback, introducing the potential for widespread exposure and damage.

We have already seen examples of unexpected recordings accidentally made public for other political figures, including those involving California Governor Arnold Schwarzenegger in 2006 and 2007 [308]. In that case, the recordings were unintentionally exposed through the governor's web site and resulted in criticism of a number of his comments that were made without the intent of them becoming public.

Conclusion

As campaigns increasingly look to the online medium to gather support, it is important to consider the inherent risks that will follow. In this chapter, we discussed a number of risks that may present themselves in any election campaign; however, it is important to acknowledge that many more remain that we have not discussed.

It is apparent both from past events and from our findings that candidates and their campaigns are just beginning to understand the risks of online advocacy and have yet to take the necessary precautions to protect themselves. Our fear is that a true appreciation of the required countermeasures will not be realized until these attacks do, in fact, manifest themselves.

Many of these individual risks, when combined, would result in increasingly sophisticated attacks. While we have discussed many of these risks independently, the combination of these threats creates complex new variations that are already being seen in the wild in other areas such as online banking and ecommerce.

Our goal in writing this chapter was not to sow seeds in the minds of would-be attackers or to spread fear, uncertainty, and doubt, but rather to discuss real-world risks that already exist. None of the attacks discussed here are new or novel; we have simply applied them to a specific recurring event, the election process. Our hope is to raise awareness of the potential risks before they are able to manifest themselves in the upcoming 2008 federal election, or any election that follows.

One thing is clear: It is impossible for us to predict how successful any one of these attacks might be in making a material impact on the election process. Given our experiences with previous widespread Internet-borne risks, we certainly do have an appreciation and respect for the potential that they present. While that is not to be discounted lightly, only time will tell how dangerous they become.

In addition, if a successful widespread attack were to occur (one that was recognized to have swayed the vote), what recourse is there? What if intimidation, misinformation, and infectious election-targeted malicious code become the norm?

Acknowledgments

The author wishes to thank Markus Jakobsson for providing a political fundraising email sample, for pointing out additional political-sounding URLs that he had registered, and for contributing helpful discussions, feedback, and comments on earlier drafts. In addition, the author would like to thank Zulfikar Ramzan for his advice, feedback, and recommendations during the writing of this chapter, and Kevin Haley for his recommendation on the addition of push polling.

Chapter 11

Online Advertising Fraud

Neil Daswani, Chris Mysen, Vinay Rao, Stephen Weis,
Kourosh Gharachorloo, Shuman Ghosemajumder,
and the Google Ad Traffic Quality Team

The growth of the web-based online advertising industry has created many new opportunities for lead generation, brand awareness, and electronic commerce for advertisers. In the online marketplace, page views, form submissions, clicks, downloads, and purchases often result in money changing hands between advertisers, ad networks, and web site publishers. Given that these web-based actions have financial impact, criminals have also sought to take advantage of new opportunities to conduct fraud against these parties with the hopes of having some money illegitimately change into their own hands. This chapter discusses some of the many ways, including using crimeware,[1] that fraudsters attempt to leverage so as to defraud various parties involved in the online advertising marketplace. It also describes countermeasures that ad networks have put in place to mitigate such fraud.

11.1 History

This section offers an abridged history of online advertising, as a precursor to the discussion of online advertising fraud in later sections. This section is not meant to be comprehensive, but does provide some high-level background as to how online advertising via search engines emerged.

---

1. For example, clickbots, as described in Section 11.4.2, are an example of crimeware that can be used to conduct online advertising fraud.

Since the commercialization of the World Wide Web (WWW) in the mid-1990s, the marketplace has explored many alternatives to monetize online content and generate sales leads. During the early stages of commercialization, many companies made online brochures about their products and services available. Some early web pages provided email addresses and phone numbers as contact information, and others allowed users to fill out online forms to gather information about customers' needs and contact information as a means of lead generation. These interactive product brochures were an early form of online advertising and still are very prevalent among low-end web sites.

Companies also had to find robust ways of initially attracting users to their web sites. In addition to adding URLs to offline information provided to customers, companies would often add ".com" to their names during the Internet boom that occurred from 1996 to 2001 to advertise their "destination" web sites. To help users find information, products, and services to help satisfy their needs, several directories (e.g., the Yahoo! directory) and keyword search engines (e.g., AltaVista) were developed to help direct users to destination sites. Companies could request or pay to be listed in online directories, and they could optimize their web sites to show up prominently in search results provided by keyword search engines.

Directories sought to monetize their services by displaying banner ads linked to destination pages. Companies that offered such advertising opportunities boasted that advertisements could be "targeted" more precisely than was possible via other forms of advertising. Such companies attempted to do targeting based on user behavior and to classify users into various categories. These targeting efforts were not very successful, however, because making inferences about which categories visitors to a web site should be placed into was difficult based on browsing behavior alone.

By comparison, search services provide much easier methods of targeting; when a user enters a keyword search term, the user is directly telling a search engine what he or she is interested in, and the need to categorize users based on browsing behavior becomes less necessary for successful targeting. In addition, keyword search engines that display textual ads (as opposed to banner ads) provide a user experience that is not only more targeted, but also less intrusive to users. The combination of better targeting and better user experience has resulted in successful online advertising offerings via search engines.

11.2 Revenue Models

The accounting of ad revenue from an online advertising campaign generally takes one of three forms:

- *Cost per mille (CPM):* The advertiser is charged per 1000 impressions.

- *Cost per click (CPC):* The advertiser is charged per click.
- *Cost per action (CPA):* The advertiser is charged per (predetermined) action (e.g., an online sale).

In this section, we describe each of the three models. We also discuss how syndication and referral deals can be used to derive revenue from online advertising activities.

11.2.1 Impression–Based Model

Advertisers often pay search engines or online magazines a fixed price for every 1000 banner ads that are displayed—known as cost per mille (CPM). When an ad is displayed, an *ad impression* (or simply *impression*) is said to have taken place. The term "impression" is also used to refer to the creative ad that is displayed in this way.

Charging and accounting by CPM is theoretically easy to implement, because each web server log entry for a banner ad image represents one impression. In practice, CPM advertising can be quite complicated, with many different web servers being involved along the path of delivering a banner to an end user. In addition, web page caching needs to be disabled via HTTP response headers, and HTTP proxies need to abide by such headers. Finally, measuring the effectiveness and results of a CPM-based advertising campaign can be difficult owing to a greater emphasis on branding campaigns and offline sales and the existence of impression spam.

Impression spam results from HTTP requests for web pages that contain ads, but that do not necessarily correspond to a user viewing the page. For instance, a web page crawler or "scraping" program might issue an HTTP request for a web page that happens to contain ads. Such a request would need to be distinguished from those requests issued by human users. Also, an advertiser might not receive any feedback when ad impressions occur and may need to completely trust the content provider's or ad network's impression data.

Nevertheless, even during the early commercialization of the Internet, the marketplace immediately recognized that online advertising could improve accountability and return on investment (ROI) over traditional, offline advertisements such as on billboards or television. Each click on a banner ad indicated that an online advertising campaign was driving traffic to an advertiser's site. Online content providers and search engines provided advertisers with click-through rates (CTR), which is the ratio of users' clicks per ad impression. CTRs often depend on the "quality" of banner ads. In practice, CTRs for the early banner ads were often low. Low CTRs could be partially attributed to poor targeting, but may also have been due to technical factors, such as longer download times for large banner ad images by users on dial-up lines.

In addition to low CTRs, another challenge faced by the online advertising industry was advertising sales. It may have not been economical for a small online magazine to hire a sales force to sell its banner ad space to advertisers. This realization motivated the creation of advertising networks that could amortize the cost and overhead of an advertising sales force across large numbers of small web sites. Notably, in the late 1990s, DoubleClick arose as a top-tier banner advertising network. Web sites would lease web page space to DoubleClick, and DoubleClick would find and manage advertisers that paid for ad impressions and clicks on those web pages.

Ad targeting has always been an important aspect of online advertising. Higher CTRs were typically viewed as evidence that the topic of the ad was related to the topic of the web page upon which the ad was placed. The marketplace realized that advertisers would pay more not only based on placement of ads, but also in case of better targeting.

In 2000, Google launched the AdWords CPM-based advertising platform, in which textual ads were targeted based on the keywords for which a user would search. Google initially signed contracts with advertisers to display their ads on a CPM basis on the top of search results pages. In addition, Google auctioned off the ad slots on the right-hand side of search results pages; it eventually did the same for ads shown on the top of search results pages. In this way, a market for charging advertisers based not on the number of ad impressions shown, but rather on the number of times users clicked on ads emerged.

11.2.2 Click–Based Model

In 1998, Goto.com, a start-up that arose out of the *idealabs* business incubator, developed a pay-for-placement search engine where advertisers bid to be the top-placed ads next to search results. Advertisers would pay per click (PPC) for their search result ads. The amount the advertiser pays per click is referred to as its cost per click (CPC). In 2001, Goto.com was renamed Overture; in 2003, the company was purchased by its largest customer, Yahoo!.

In 2002, Google relaunched AdWords as a PPC platform. With this new venture, Google not only took advertisers' bids into account, but also took into account an ad's click-through rate. In particular, advertising slots on Google's search results pages are not simply auctioned off to the highest bidder. Instead, an ad slot is allocated to the advertiser whose bid times the predicted CTR of the ad (as computed by the ad network) is highest. As a result, ad placement depends on two factors: the amount an advertiser is willing to pay and the "quality" of the ad, as determined by how often users click on the ad (in addition to many other factors). In effect, each ad click from a user serves as an implicit vote of the relevance of the ad to the user's query. The result is that not only do users receive more relevant ads, but Google also increases advertisers' revenue by better targeting advertisements.

When advertisers pay per click, it is important that clicks deliver value and ROI to the advertiser. Some clicks might be "invalid" or "fraudulent"; Sections 11.3 and 11.4 define sources of these kinds of clicks. Section 11.5 discusses high-level countermeasures to deal with "click fraud." Fraud exists in both the CPM and the CPC business models; in the former, we speak of "impression fraud," while in the latter we focus on "click fraud."

To complement PPC advertising on its search results pages, in 2003 Google launched AdSense, an online advertising product that allowed web publishers to monetize their content by allowing Google to place ads on their web sites. To ensure the ads are relevant to the user's interest, the entire web page containing the ad slots is analyzed by AdSense to determine a set of relevant topics, and ads about those topics are inserted into the ad slots on the web page. Google pays such publishers a share of the CPC fees paid by the advertisers when the ads are clicked. While the creation of AdSense helped publishers derive revenue for the development of their content, it also introduced new incentives for fraudulent click activity, as discussed in Section 11.3.

11.2.3 Action-Based Model

A more generic online advertising model is pay per action, in which the advertiser pays a cost per action (CPA), where an "action" can be defined as the user arriving at a particular "landing" page on the advertiser's site or the user engaging in a commercial transaction. Strictly speaking, CPC-based advertising is just a special case of CPA, in which the "action" is the user clicking on an ad. However, the term "CPA" typically refers to a more involved action than simply clicking on an ad, and it usually connotes that an advertiser is paying based on a commercial transaction. Some suspect that CPA-based advertising might be less susceptible to click fraud, as fraudsters may need to engage in commercial transactions to successfully defraud advertisers. At the same time, if the commercial transaction is not very costly to induce, CPA-based advertising may be just as vulnerable to click fraud as is CPC-based advertising.

From an advertiser's standpoint, CPA-based advertising can be attractive because advertisers are billed only for predefined user actions—for example, making a purchase or generating a sales lead. Advertisers make payments to an ad network only after they have derived value from a click.

Although CPA-based advertising can be well suited for commercial sites, it has some drawbacks. Some advertisers may not have online commerce web sites. For example, they may be advertising simply for brand-name recognition there, with the goal of increasing offline sales (e.g., typical car manufacturers). Also, an advertiser's web site might have usability issues, have high latency, or simply suffer from intermittent failures that may serve as barriers to users completing transactions. Much of the risk involved in a CPA-based advertising model, then, falls on the ad network.

It is also important to consider the effect of CPA on publishers. For every impression displayed on a publisher's page, a bet is being made on which ads will generate the most revenue for that publisher. When choosing between CPM-based advertisers, such a decision is simple—choose the impression that pays the highest CPM. When working with CPC-based advertisers, the sustained CTR of the advertiser is easy enough to determine with a relatively small amount of data, which helps come up with an eCPM (expected CPM) estimate. However, CPA advertising, especially for small advertisers, is difficult to translate into a reliable eCPM. As a result, small CPA advertisers are often not well suited for many publishers' sites and have a harder time getting significant traffic from their campaigns.

11.2.4 Syndication

Ad networks can increase their reach by syndicating the ads they deliver to other destination sites, such as search engines and other web properties. In a *syndication* deal, an ad network (which may be run by a search engine) provides a data feed in which the syndicator receives URLs for ad impressions. The syndicator earns a share of the CPC paid by the advertiser when the URLs are clicked on. For example, a hypothetical search engine (hyp-search.com) might run a PPC ad network. Another search engine syn-search.com that does not have an ad network of its own might enter into a syndication relationship with hyp-search.com. Whenever syn-search.com receives a query from a user, in addition to providing its search results, it sends the query to hyp-search.com via a data feed; in return, it receives ad impression URLs that are relevant to the query. Then syn-search.com displays the ad impression URLs on its results pages and receives a share of the CPC the advertiser pays to hyp-search.com when users click on the ads.

Figure 11.1 depicts the interactions between the ad network, the syndicator, and the user. (To keep the conceptual depiction simple, note that the arrows in the figure do not correpsond to HTTP requests between web sites, but simply depict

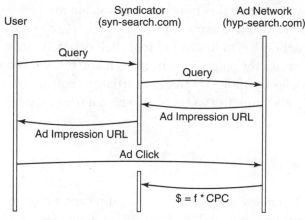

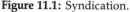

Figure 11.1: Syndication.

the flow of data and money.) Upon receiving a query from the user, syn-search.com relays the query onto hyp-search.com, and then relays the ad impression URL received from hyp-search.com to the user. If and when the user clicks on the ad impression URL, hyp-search.com pays syn-search.com a fraction (f) of the CPC paid by the advertiser. Although not shown in the figure, a click on an ad redirects the user to the advertiser's web site (i.e., the click request is sent to the ad network and generates a redirect response).

11.2.5 Referral Deals

In a *referral* deal, a web site, A, pays another web site, R, for sending web traffic to A. Web site R puts links to web site A on its web pages. In a CPC referral deal, web site A pays web site R a referral fee every time that a user clicks on a link on R's web pages and arrives at web site A. To provide a simple example, a web site called great-online-magazine.com might pay ref-site.com a referral fee every time that it displays a link to great-online-magazine.com on a page, and that link is clicked on by a user. In general, when a site R puts a link to A on its site as part of a referral deal, the link does not necessarily need to be an "ad," but can be used simply to encourage visitors to site R to visit site A thereafter. Reiter et al. discuss how abuse can take place in referral deals [330].

An important distinction between CPC referral deals and CPC advertising deals is which party takes responsibility for accounting and payment. In a CPC referral deal, web site A typically is responsible for keeping track and paying for the number of referrals sent to it by R. In the case that R is a search engine and A is an advertiser in a CPC ads deal, the search engine R is typically responsible for keeping track of and charging for referrals that are made to A.

In general, referral deals can be action-based instead of just click-based. That is, A may pay R not just for clicks, but rather for page views or sales made on A's web site. Also, referral deals often involve less complexity than advertising deals in which online auctions take place to determine the web site to which a user may be referred.

11.3 Types of Spam

An online ad network can be abused in many ways. Each of the ad revenue models described in the previous section (impression-based, click-based, and action-based), for example, can be subject to a corresponding type of spam (impression spam, click spam, and conversion spam).

Fraud based on such abuse can result in reduced ROI for advertisers, although there are many other reasons that advertiser ROI might suffer. For instance, advertiser ROI might suffer due to low-quality ads, high latency at the advertiser's web site, improperly targeted keywords, noncompetitive sale prices, and many other factors. Nevertheless, fraud is one of many variables that can account for nonoptimal advertiser ROI. In this section, we provide an abridged taxonomy of the various types of spam that may affect an online ad network.

Spam is an artifact that does not provide any value, utility, or benefit as expected by one or more parties associated with the artifact. For instance, an email is often considered spam when the recipient of the message does not derive any appreciable value, utility, or benefit from the email. This section focuses on three types of ad-related spam: impression spam, click spam, and conversion spam.

11.3.1 Impression Spam

Impression spam results from HTTP requests for web pages that a user never sees or that provide advertisers little or no value for their money. Impression spam affects CPM-based advertising campaigns because advertisers should not be charged for such HTTP requests.

Furthermore, impression spam affects CTR calculations, as the denominator in the calculation is the number of page views. Because the ranking of ads in an auction may depend on CPC and CTR, manipulating the CTR can be of interest to a malicious advertiser as an indirect method to manipulate the outcome of the ad auction. In addition, click fraudsters may end up increasing the CTRs of ads that they click on, and higher-than-normal CTRs can serve as evidence of a click fraud attack. To counter this possibility, click fraudsters may use impression spam to decrease CTRs for ads that they click on in an attempt to avoid detection.

Once HTTP requests that are deemed to be impression spam are filtered out of a web server log, the number of total page views minus those that are deemed to be impression spam should be used in CTR calculations as well as for CPM counts.

11.3.2 Click Spam

Click spam is a type of spam that occurs when sources other than legitimate users are making HTTP requests for ad impression URLs. Such HTTP requests, which are often called *invalid clicks*, comprise any clicks that an ad network chooses not to charge for. When clicks are marked as invalid, the user agent that issued the click is still directed to an advertiser's web site, but the advertiser is simply not charged for the click.

A *fraudulent click* is one that was issued with malicious intent, and *click fraud* is simply the practice of issuing fraudulent clicks. Because the intent is only in the mind of the person issuing the click or in the mind of the author of software that issues clicks, it is impossible to know with 100% certainty that any click is fraudulent. While the intent of a click is impossible to determine, signs or *signals* may indicate the intent of the click with varying certainty. Clicks that are believed to be fraudulent are marked as invalid, but it is not necessarily the case that all fraudulent clicks will be detected and marked in this way.

When suspected fraudulent clicks are marked as invalid, the user agent is still redirected to the advertiser's web site. Proceeding with the redirection offers two benefits. First, a fraudster does not receive any feedback as to whether he or she has been identified as an attacker. Second, if a suspected fraudulent click is, in reality, a legitimate click (a false positive), then the user's experience is not negatively affected and may provide the opportunity for increased ROI for the advertiser. That is, a user's click may be marked as invalid, and yet the user may go on to purchase a product on the advertiser's site! Of course, too many false positives may decrease a publisher's revenue, so an ad network must do its best to minimize false positives to balance the trade-off involved in providing high advertiser ROI while concurrently attracting and maintaining quality relationships with publishers.

In many cases, invalid clicks are not necessarily fraudulent, and they may have nothing to do with malicious intent. Clicks may be marked as invalid, for instance, based on an ad network's desire to improve advertiser ROI. Many such clicks that are marked invalid are attributable to double clicks (e.g., a user who clicks twice to open a link), crawlers that ignore robots.txt directives, and other technical reasons.

Two sources of invalid clicks that are the result of malicious intent are advertiser competitor clicking and publisher click inflation. In advertiser *competitor clicking*, a malicious advertiser may click on a competitor's ads. There are many reasons why a malicious advertiser might engage in competitor clicking. One possible, simplistic goal is to drain the competitor's advertising budget. Once the competitor's advertising budget has been exhausted, the malicious advertiser's ads may be exclusively shown to a user (assuming that no additional advertisers are bidding for the same keywords). More generally, an advertiser may want to decrease competition for a particular keyword. By fraudulently clicking on others' ads for that keyword, competitors derive less ROI and expend their budgets. In the short term, the auction becomes less competitive as competitors become ineligible to participate due to reaching their daily budget limits. In the long term, the decreased ROI for such keywords may mean that competitors may reduce or stop spending, and CPC rates for the fraudster will be lower.

When Google introduced AdSense, publisher *click inflation* emerged as a new type of click fraud that needed to be mitigated. In this scheme, a publisher clicks on ads on the publisher's own site in hopes of receiving a revenue share of the CPC that the advertiser pays for ad clicks. The incentive for fraud in publisher click inflation is a more financially direct one than is the case in advertiser competitor clicking.

Click fraud countermeasures are discussed in depth in Section 11.5.

11.3.3 Conversion Spam

A *conversion* takes place when an HTTP request is issued for an advertiser-defined URL. For example, the request of the URL could signify a page view, submission of a form, initiation of a file download, or the completion of an online sale.

In *conversion spam*, HTTP requests are issued with the intent of artificially producing conversions. Just as there is incentive for click spam in CPM-based advertising to make it appear that ads are relevant via inflated CTRs, so there exists an incentive for conversion spam in CPC-based advertising to make it appear that clicks are relevant. For instance, after clicking on an ad and being redirected to an advertiser's site, a click fraudster may download a file (such as a trial version of a software package) from an advertiser's site in an attempt to simulate the behavior of a legitimate user.

CPA-based advertising is also susceptible to conversion spam, as fraudulent publishers might like to derive a share of the revenues resulting from artificially produced actions. For example, if such a publisher gets paid a share of the revenues from a CPA-based advertising campaign based on downloads of a trial software package, that publisher might initiate such downloads after fraudulently clicking on ads in an attempt to derive revenue from the self-initiated downloads.

11.4 Forms of Attack

Click fraud can take many different forms. Nevertheless, some key technology and resource limitations constrain which vectors an attacker may try. For example, someone with little time and low determination might attempt only simple attacks from a home computer. By contrast, a dedicated fraudster with more time may write malware, infect machines worldwide, and command the infected machines to click on ads. In this section, we describe some representative forms of attack; we do not attempt to comprehensively enumerate all known forms of attack, but merely seek to give the reader some familiarity with some attacks commonly seen in the wild.

Attacks against networks may generally be classified into two main categories: human, where people manually click on ads, and robotic, in which traffic is generated programmatically by software robots. We describe each of these categories of attack in more detail next.

11.4.1 Human Clickers

Humans are harder to manage than automated software robots, but they are also fundamentally limited by the speed at which they can think and act. Nevertheless, hiring humans to click on ads is a feasible vector by which to attack an ad network in geographies in which human labor is particularly cheap. Even in developed economies, humans can be coerced or leveraged to click on ads just as they can be coerced into solving CAPTCHAs in exchange for the privilege of viewing pornographic images [145]. From an economic point of view, using humans for click fraud purposes is viable as long as the cost of directly paying or coercing a human to click on an ad is lower than the return for clicking on the ad.

For publishers that are paid a share of ad click revenue on their web site, these costs can be quite low. For example, if it takes 10 seconds for a fraudster to view a page and click on an ad with a return of $0.10, a fraudster can realize returns of $0.60 per minute, or as much as $36 per hour, for clicking on ads. In many parts of the world, $36 is a reasonable daily salary at the time of writing of this text. By reducing the incentives and slowing fraudsters down to $0.01 every 20 seconds, a person can still make $1.80 per hour, or approximately $2500 per year, which is roughly the per capita GDP in some developing countries. Even accounting for connectivity costs (which can be $10 per month) and computer costs (cheap computers can run $300 to $400), a person can theoretically make a decent living being paid to defraud advertisers, if countermeasures are not in place. (We discuss countermeasures in Section 11.5.) Of course, constantly loading pages and clicking on ads can be rather tedious.

Given that cheap sources of Internet-connected labor exist, fraudsters have generated several attacks that take advantage of humans. Such attacks all have similar goals, but have different costs and degrees of implementation difficulty. These human-intensive attacks can involve only one human or multiple humans whose efforts can be coordinated. Multiple numbers of machines and/or IP addresses can be taken advantage of. In addition, various means of acquiring the machines and IP addresses can be used.

Before discussing such targeted manual attacks, we first discuss how publishers might encourage or coerce legitimate users to unintentionally click on ads. Such ad clicks may or may not be fraudulent, but neither the advertisers' nor the users' interests are being respected. While much of the latter part in this chapter deals with the technology used to conduct and contain click fraud, the next subsection deals with the psychology of the user.

Coercion

Good web site design is focused on helping a user accomplish a task and is often guided by interaction designers and usability engineers. For example, a web storefront may be designed and implemented so as to help a user find what he or she is looking for and purchase it in an efficient fashion. A social networking site may be designed to help users find and interact with others who have similar interests. Conversely, in an ad-centric web site design, a web publisher may attempt to design a site to "encourage" visitors to click on high-CPC ads.

To ensure that high-CPC ads will appear on her web site, a publisher can replace or supplement regular web page content with collections of keywords for which advertisers typically place high bids. This practice is sometimes called "keyword stuffing." The keywords can be hidden from the user by including them in HTML tags that are not visibly displayed or by rendering the keywords in the same color as the background of the web page. In both cases, the "stuffed" keywords will be seen by the ad network when its automated agents crawl the page to determine relevant ads to show, but not by a human user viewing the web page.

To encourage users to click on the high-CPC ads, the publisher might not include very many (if any) regular links to other web pages and might attempt to make any regular links look like ads as well. A user who then wants to click a link to go to another web page may inadvertently click on one of the high-CPC ads because it is not clear how to easily navigate to a more interesting web page. Similarly, a publisher might modify ad text to something more relevant to coerce users, while retaining the original advertiser URL (e.g., replacing "Click here for

Viagra" with "Free Ringtones"). Alternatively, a publisher may go so far as to make ads invisible to users and give them directions about actions to take (e.g., "Hit tab twice, then enter") to force users to unknowingly click on ads.

Other devious publishers may host games, often written in Macromedia Flash, on web pages such that the game is surrounded by ads. Part of the game play may involve clicking and dragging the mouse. By encircling the game with ads, the publisher increases the chance that users will unintentionally click on ads, providing a near-term benefit to the publisher.

At one extreme, a web publisher may explicitly ask users to click on ads—for example, by including "call to action" text on a web site stating "Please click on the ads on this page." At another extreme are web sites that are intentionally designed and engineered to coerce users to click on ads, even without an explicit call to action. Regardless of the technique used, all of these schemes aim to deceive users and provide a poor user experience. Moreover, users often end up at a site they had no intention of visiting. In such cases, deception leads to low advertiser ROI.

Manual Clicking

A malicious user can generate a relatively large volume of traffic over a relatively short period of time. Even a person who is not very Internet savvy can generate thousands of page views and hundreds of ad clicks over the course of a day. For a web site that earns revenue based on CPM or CPC ads, such page views and ad clicks can translate into hundreds of dollars per day in revenue. Moreover, an advertiser that wants to drain a competing advertiser's budget can potentially rob the competitor's budget of hundreds of dollars per day if appropriate countermeasures are not in place.

At the same time, such behavior can be easily detected if the same user is returning to the same site again and again. Such a manual clicking attack can be simple to execute, but also relatively simple to detect. When such manual clicking attacks appear at high volumes, fraudulent intent can be obvious, as it is rare for a single user to generate large amounts of targeted page view and ad click traffic during normal browsing of the web.

To make such a manual clicking attack more difficult to trace and detect, some fraudsters use HTTP proxies to obscure the source of their clicks. HTTP proxies can anonymize traffic by acting as an intermediary between a user's machine and a web site. Proxies can hide the source IP address and strip identifying information, such as cookies, from HTTP requests. HTTP proxy services are often available for free or at nominal fees. Some attackers also set up a means to systematically reroute traffic through a series of proxy machines to further obscure the original source of HTTP requests. Anonymous routing systems and distributed networks of machines such as Tor [89] sometimes provide a means for a fraudster to anonymize their traffic, although such systems can also be used legitimately for anonymous web browsing. In addition to stripping identifying information from HTTP requests, a given user's traffic may be challenging to uniquely identify because that user's traffic may be "mixed in" with many other users' requests arriving from an HTTP proxy.

HTTP requests for ad impression URLs (clicks) that emanate from such networks may be viewed as suspicious by ad networks. One might argue that a legitimate user might want to take advantage of such anonymization services. At the same time, if the value to advertisers of clicks emanating from such services is dubious or traffic from such a service is anomalous for other reasons, an ad network may decide to mark such clicks as invalid.

An attacker can also explicitly coordinate groups of users to click on ads to drain advertiser budgets or attempt click inflation. In one scenario, a *click farm* firm might be hired to click on ads. Such a firm may be profitable in a developing nation. It may hire employees to click on ads in its offices or may coordinate contract workers who click on ads from cyber-cafes in different cities.

Naturally, distributing such fraudulent ad clicks across many malicious users and machines increases the burden on the detection systems of ad networks by forcing the networks to aggregate activity over a period of time and across many IPs to find significant sources of fraudulent activity. Interestingly, activity distributed as such can be difficult for a single advertiser to detect because the activity occurs "below the radar" for a given advertiser, though it can be detected using aggregated traffic across multiple advertisers. Such distributed attacks can take a significant amount of effort to coordinate and are indicative of fairly determined fraudsters.

An interesting case study of a manual, distributed, click fraud attack occurred on the Google search network in 2006 with clicks relating to the keyword *kiyashinku* (meaning "credit" or "credit cards" in Japanese). Google's Ad Traffic Quality Team noticed an increase in query and click traffic on the keyword that emanated from large numbers of seemingly legitimate users. An inflammatory blog post was later found that incited readers to issue a search query for the keyword on Google and then to click on the resulting ads in an effort to drain the advertising budgets of Japanese credit card vendors.

The resulting traffic looked very anomalous, as there was a sudden surge in interest in these high-value ads. Moreover, users clicked on the same ad dozens of times or clicked on large numbers of ads returned as a result of the query. In cases like this one, however, user interest quickly wanes and the attack tends to be short-lived.

Humans looking to supplement their income can also be recruited directly to click on ads by "pay to read" (PTR) and "pay to click" (PTC) web sites. Such sites accept membership registrations from users (usually other than publishers). The "pay to" web site sends the user instructions on which sites to "read" or click on in return for an extremely small share of revenues derived from such activity. Such sites give explicit directions to users on web pages or in emails about how to act in an attempt to ensure that the ensuing activity appears legitimate from these sites. For example, instructions might specify to "stay on the web site for at least 30 seconds" or "click on links that are interesting to you."

Often, however, users are fundamentally uninterested in the content of these sites, and are more interested in the prospect of being paid for their browsing and clicking. One can find some differences between programs that pay users to surf and programs that pay users to click on ads, because surfing does not guarantee ad clicks. Nevertheless, many of these sites seek to indirectly generate revenue from CPM- and CPC-based advertising. PTR/PTC programs are also often part of a pyramid scheme in which some "users" pay into the program to receive better payouts. As with most pyramid schemes, most participants rarely, if ever, receive any significant payouts themselves.

An intriguing effect of many of these sites is that networks of "pay to" sites are often linked to one another via ads. In effect, users who visit "pay to" sites are likely to sign up on other "pay to" sites. One PTC web site may show advertisements on other PTC sites in an attempt to attract other like-minded users.

Despite the advantages of using humans to conduct click fraud and otherwise generate invalid clicks, people can be difficult to convince, can be hard to provide with adequate incentives, and can get bored or tired quickly. Moreover, a person who is paid to view pages or click on ads can act in ways distinctly different from a user who is truly interested in, say, purchasing a product. For instance, a real user tends to read, consider, think, and surf a web site because he or she wants to learn more about the product. A paid user has few such interests. In addition, PTR and PTC users might be less likely to conduct purchases or "convert," and the lack of conversions can be visible to advertisers in the form of ROI. There are significant gray areas in what an ad network needs to consider fraudulent—bad behavior on one network may be normal on another network. At the end of the day, fraud needs to be defined by what advertisers expect from services provided by an ad network and normal user behavior.

11.4.2 Robotic Clicking

Fraudsters often abandon any pretense of legitimacy in their click inflation efforts and resort to automated traffic generated by software robots, or "bots." Bots enjoy one major advantage over human users: They do what they are told, over and over again, and they do it for free, without needing direct motivation. Running a bot can require less coordination and avoids the pesky requirement of finding and interacting with willing people.

Many software robots are written for legitimate purposes, such as scraping web sites or crawling web links. Sites may place robot exclusion files (i.e., robots.txt) in specific directory trees to direct automated crawlers to avoid scanning parts or all of a web site. Advertising networks often use robots.txt files to prevent robots from inadvertently crawling ads.

A malfunctioning or improperly configured bot may not abide by the robots.txt directives and unintentionally click on ads. These bots are not intended to be malicious and make little effort to "cloak" themselves. They often announce themselves as robots through their user-agent string or other fields in the headers of their HTTP requests, making it easy to detect and account for inadvertent bots.

In contrast, some bots are constructed for the sole purpose of clicking on ads. A *clickbot* [79] is a software robot that clicks on ads by issuing HTTP requests for advertiser web pages with the intent to commit click fraud. Clickbots can be custom-built or purchased, and they can be manually installed by fraudsters or disseminated in a manner similar to malware and worms.

If appropriate countermeasures are not in place, large clickbot networks could potentially conduct significant amounts of fraud, even if each bot executes just a few ad clicks per day. Moreover, the operational costs to run a botnet could decrease over time, entailing even lower risk for attackers [195].

Unfortunately for clickbots, their predictability is a significant weakness. Developing a bot that behaves like a human and cloaks its behavior is challenging. An ad network may use hundreds or thousands of signals to determine whether HTTP requests might have been generated by a machine instead of a human.

Despite this shortcoming, attackers often use robotic traffic sources to send invalid traffic to advertisers. Building a robot to click on ads does require some skill as a programmer. Likewise, it requires significant insight into how one might write a software bot to look and act like a human.

Costs involved in using bots include authoring or purchasing bot software, and obtaining a network of machines on which to run the bot software. Often, these machines have been illicitly compromised and are rented for hire. Current research indicates botnet rental fees run in the cents per bot per week range [195, 229].

Custom-Built Bots

Many tools are available that may be used to develop custom-built bots. Open-source utilities such as wget [277] and curl can, for instance, be used to issue HTTP requests. Shell scripts can be written to invoke such programs in an automated fashion as one form of attack. Libraries that help programmers execute HTTP requests exist for many common programming languages, such as Python, Java, C/C++, and Perl. Some bots can also be written as browser helper objects (BHOs) to leverage existing functionality in web browsers so as to help bot authors construct HTTP requests. These open-source utilities, application libraries, and BHO-based methods often support the use of HTTP proxies, which can help mask the original source of an HTTP request. Such tools can be used to build clients that conduct advertiser competitor clicking or publisher click inflation attacks.

For-Sale Clickbots

After a bot is built, it can be sold on the open market. While some legitimate, testing-oriented applications of bots exist, bots can just as easily be used to conduct attempted click fraud. For-sale clickbots such as the Lote Clicking Agent, I-Faker, FakeZilla, and Clickmaster can be purchased online. They typically use anonymous proxies to generate traffic with IP diversity. Fortunately, IP diversity usually is not enough to hide click fraud attacks conducted by such software, and the traffic generated by them is typically readily evident.

Malware-Type Clickbots

Malware-type clickbots infect machines in an attempt to achieve IP diversity. Their traffic may or may not be as easily identifiable as that generated by for-sale clickbots. Malware-type clickbots can receive instructions from a botmaster server as to which ads to click, and how often and when to click them. Clickbot.A, which is described in more depth in "The Anatomy of Clickbot.A" by Daswani et al. [79], provides a detailed case study of such a clickbot investigated by Google. This case study was published with the hope of helping the security community build better defenses against malware-type bots.

Forced Browser Clicks

Forced browser clicks is a technique that some fraudsters use to turn a legitimate user's browser into a clickbot. This technique takes advantage of flaws in some implementations of AdSense-like programs that could be used by a malicious publisher to conduct click inflation. In AdSense-like programs, web publishers are provided with a "snippet" of HTML code that they place on their web pages in locations where they would like ads to appear. The HTML code often contains elements that render ads, and some implementations of the HTML code can be vulnerable to a forced browser click attack. For instance, if the HTML code simply contained an anchor element that makes up the ad (i.e., <A HREF>), a publisher could insert additional HTML code on its web page that would instruct the browser to click on the anchor element without explicitly being requested to do so by the user.

To implement dynamic ad slots securely, the ad slot code can take advantage of the same-origin security feature [80] implemented in most browsers to prevent script from the publisher's parts of the web page from clicking on the ads. For instance, an HTML IFRAME tag accepts a SRC attribute whose value can be set to an URL owned by the ad network. Using the IFRAME construct, the browser will not allow script on other parts of the web page to access the contents of the IFRAME if that content was not downloaded from the same-origin as the IFRAME's content. The origin is specified by the domain name, port, and protocol in the URL. Google's AdSense ad slots are implemented in this way to protect against fraudulent publishers, although not all ad networks are equally well protected.

Even when an ad network uses a construct such as the IFRAME to prevent other, untrusted parts of the web page from interacting with its ads, the ad network is still relying on the browser and its implementation of the same-origin security model to defend against publisher click inflation. If a widely deployed browser had an implementation vulnerability that allowed a publisher to circumvent the same-origin model, then the ad network may be vulnerable to publisher click inflation.

The forced browser clicks technique was first described publicly in a research paper on "Badvertisements" [140], and Chapter 6 of this book is based on that research paper. The interested reader is referred to that chapter for more details on forced browser clicks.

11.5 Countermeasures

This section describes representative countermeasures that an ad network might deploy to mitigate the click fraud risk to an online advertising business. State-of-the-art click fraud mitigation takes advantage of "defense in depth" [80]. In other words, many countermeasures and defenses are used simultaneously, so that the probability of a successful attack is reduced by each layer of countermeasures a fraudster must circumvent. We divide our discussion of click fraud countermeasures into methods that are targeted at prevention, at detection, and at containment.

Before proceeding with this discussion of click fraud countermeasures, we note that the goal of such countermeasures is to "raise the bar" for conducting a successful attack to the point where the expense and effort of an attack outweigh the potential reward (monetary or otherwise). As such, we do not claim that these countermeasures are perfect or eliminate click fraud in any absolute sense. Rather, the goal is to greatly lower the risk of a successful attack for advertisers, publishers, and online advertising networks and to support a profitable system for all parties involved (except, of course, the fraudsters). It is also not sufficient to introduce only enough countermeasures to allow advertisers to profit from an online advertising ROI that is better than can be achieved offline; minimizing click fraud further allows an ad network to benefit from a significantly higher CPC and stronger profitability for itself, publishers, and advertisers.

Finally, note that all of the countermeasures described in the following subsections may not necessarily be directly targeted at identifying fraudulent clicks. Some, in fact, focus instead on identifying anomalous expected or aggregate user behavior, browser behavior, or other inconsistencies that may be indicative of click fraud. In some cases, clicks associated with such anomalies are marked as invalid whether or not they can be directly linked to fraud.

11.5.1 Prevention

An old adage says, "An ounce of prevention is worth a pound of cure." While it might, indeed, be impossible to prevent someone from manually clicking on a single ad, it is possible to take steps that can prevent larger-scale, more systematic click fraud from occurring.

In the case of click fraud resulting from publisher click inflation, such an attack can be prevented by exercising care with regard to which publishers might be allowed to participate in an AdSense-like syndicated ads program. In addition, publishers that are terminated for low-quality or fraudulent ad clicks sometimes try to re-apply to be included in such programs. As such, it is important for an ad network to uniquely identify publishers and to prevent those that have been previously terminated from rejoining. Many such publishers attempt to sign up for participation with different, invalid, or fraudulent names, addresses, and/or telephone numbers in an attempt to appear distinct from their previous, blacklisted identity.

Ad networks may look at many different characteristics of HTTP query, click, and conversion traffic that might potentially indicate fraudulent click activity. If fraudsters are aware of which characteristics ad networks look for, they may be able to artificially construct HTTP request patterns that do not exhibit any of these anomalous characteristics. While an ad network can be quite open about which types of countermeasures and processes it has in place (see [427] for an example), it is extremely important for ad networks to maintain the confidentiality of those characteristics, or signals, that are considered indicative of fraudulent click behavior. Companies that run ad networks must employ the best enterprise security practices available to protect these signals, just as a company would protect trade secrets against both insider and external attacks. Not only are such signals useful in identifying potential click fraud attacks, but they can also be useful for marking low-value clicks as invalid, thereby providing advertisers with a better ROI and giving the ad network a competitive advantage.

A more concrete preventive technique involves setting up a trust boundary between a publisher's web page content and the ad slots on the publisher's page, as discussed in Section 11.4.2 using an HTML IFRAME. Another example of a concrete, preventive technique would be for an ad network to set a maximum CPC, which can prevent a fraudster from making significant amounts of money with just a few clicks. Fraudsters who then want to attempt to make significant amounts of money would be forced to produce enough clicks to result in statistically significant signals. Of course, such preventive techniques are not perfect, so it is important to complement them with detection and containment countermeasures.

11.5.2 Detection

The purpose of click fraud detection is to mark clicks as invalid after they have occurred, given that much of the time they cannot be effectively prevented altogether. Clicks may be marked as invalid both online and offline. When invalid clicks are detected *online*, advertisers are not billed for them; when they are detected *offline*, advertisers are credited for the clicks. Online detection is preferred, as an advertiser's daily budget is not charged for invalid clicks, and the advertiser does not lose the opportunity to have its ads continue to participate in ad auctions during that day.

Online detection is not always possible, however. When invalid clicks are detected offline, advertisers are credited for the clicks at a later time. Nevertheless, the advertiser may still incur the opportunity cost of not having its ads compete in the ad auction for that day if the advertiser is budget-limited with respect to the amount of click fraud. At the same time, some types of click fraud can be more easily detected offline, such as an attack consisting of just a few clicks per day that requires many days of traffic in aggregate to identify the attack. Such attacks are more difficult to identify in an online fashion when they first start occurring.

Click fraud detection methods usually seek to identify anomalies in streams of click data. Different types of anomalies can be caught at different times in the processing of clicks. Some anomalies may be apparent in a single click, and such a click can be marked invalid by an online filter. Other types of anomalies may become apparent only in looking at an aggregate set of clicks over some time period. The decision as to whether a particular click fraud detection filter should be implemented as an online or offline measure is often guided by exactly which anomalies need to be identified and which time period needs to be analyzed to identify a particular anomaly.

After filters have been applied and invalid clicks have been identified, additional actions may be required. For instance, an AdSense publisher with a high percentage of invalid clicks, or even just one that received potentially anomalous traffic that may or may not be invalid, may be inspected by an ad traffic quality investigator. In certain cases, a relationship with a publisher may be automatically terminated if the publisher's web site attracts unusual numbers of invalid clicks. Ad traffic quality investigators also need to be mindful of the potential for sabotage, such as may occur when a malicious publisher attempts to generate a large number of invalid clicks on a competing publisher's web site to make it seem as if the competitor is attempting a click inflation attack.

Anomaly-based detection can sometimes suffer from data limitations. If too little data is available for clicks associated with a particular advertiser or publisher, it may be difficult or even impossible to make a determination as to whether some clicks should be marked as invalid. If there are too few clicks, the damage from a click fraud attack may be generally low, so long as the CPCs involved in the attack are not too high. Such an attack can still be identified by analyzing longer time periods or clustering clicks with similar properties. In the case in which the clicks are for high-CPC ads, the traffic can be scrutinized even more intensely.

In other cases, if too much click data is associated with an advertiser or publisher, it may be difficult to identify potentially fraudulent clicks, which could get "lost in the sea" of valid clicks. In such cases, the amount of monetary damage from click fraud may be relatively low compared to the aggregate number of clicks. Nevertheless, identifying chunks of click data associated with advertisers and publishers that are "just the right size" is an important aspect of the problem. In particular, click data can be cut into finer chunks based on various properties to reduce the possibility of fraudulent clicks getting lost in the sea.

In addition to "passive" detection by identifying anomalies in streams of click data, an ad network can conduct "active" detection by modifying the interaction with the web browser and/or the user to generate additional data that can be used to ascertain the validity of a click or a set of clicks. For example, an ad network may decide to add extra JavaScript variables in ad slot code that runs computations on clients. Upon receiving ad clicks, the results of such computations are sent back to the ad network, and the ad network can check whether the expected results fit an expected distribution. While it may be apparent to a fraudster that such computations are taking place, the expected result distribution may not be quite as obvious. For example, the ad network might modify the interaction with the user agent by requiring it to send back some computation results, which then serve as a signal of the validity of a set of clicks by legitimate users who are using a web browser (as opposed to, say, a custom-programmed bot that does not support JavaScript). While we use JavaScript-based computations as an example of an active detection technique, we note that we have not adequately covered many technical details for using such a technique to serve as an effective click fraud detection signal.

11.5.3 Containment

Top-tier ad networks employ hundreds or even thousands of passive and active signals to help detect click fraud. Nevertheless, it is typically difficult to ascertain the validity of a click in any absolute sense, even with a plethora of such signals. Prudent ad networks, therefore, may take the stance that some attempted click fraud may not be directly detected. It is important to contain or manage the potential monetary impact of such clicks to advertisers. In this subsection, we briefly describe two representative click fraud containment measures: smart pricing and manual reviews.

Given the difficulty in ascertaining whether any given click is truly fraudulent, some ad networks charge an advertiser only a fraction of the CPC for certain ad clicks. Google's version of this feature is called *smart pricing*. Based on various factors that can be indicative of advertisers' ROI, such as CTR and average CPC, the overall quality of click traffic can be assessed and captured by a smart pricing multiplier.

A smart pricing multiplier can help an ad network contain undetected click fraud attacks. Even though it may be challenging to determine whether a specific click is fraudulent, aggregate characteristics of click traffic may reveal that "something is fishy"; this "fishiness" is captured by a smart pricing multiplier, also called a click cost multiplier (CCM).

The benefits of smart pricing go well beyond containing the effect of any undetected click fraud. For example, a smart pricing multiplier may take into account the effect of aggressive placement of ads on web pages in which the ads are the most prominent feature on the web page. Even though CTRs may be higher for such ads, conversions might be relatively lower, and a smart pricing multiplier can protect advertisers from being charged the full CPC for clicks that are less likely to convert. In addition, a smart pricing multiplier can be used to contain poor ad targeting or other forms of poor content quality. Finally, in contrast to techniques we have discussed thus far that attempt to make a binary decision about the quality of a click, smart pricing allows click quality to be scored on a continuum.

Manual reviews of click traffic can be an important part of an ad network's containment strategy as well. If some fraudulent clicks evade existing automated detection mechanisms, they may eventually be caught by highly trained engineers and operations personnel who, over time, gain a keen sense of "smell" and intuition. In some cases, manual review requests (generated either by internal processes or by advertisers) could potentially result in identification of a new type of click fraud attack. In such cases, engineering and operations personnel may be able to generalize the new pattern of attack and develop automated countermeasures to detect similar attacks in the future.

Feedback from advertisers can also be valuable, because such feedback can sometimes uncover undetected click fraud due to "holes" in detection systems. As such, feedback from particular advertisers can be used to provide better ROI for all advertisers and benefit the ad network. However, in practice, most inquiries by individual advertisers do not uncover undetected click fraud, but rather highlight issues relating to non-optimal ad campaign management or advertiser site design. In a few cases, advertisers correctly identify fraudulent clicks that have already been detected as invalid and for which the advertiser was not charged. In even fewer cases, advertisers actually help uncover undetected click fraud.

To provide some quantitative data, Google reports that less than 10% of all clicks consistently are detected as "invalid" [285]. These clicks include both fraudulent clicks and redundant or inadvertent clicks, and advertisers are not charged for these invalid clicks. All of these clicks are *proactively* detected as invalid by Google. In contrast, all advertiser inquiries to Google lead to less than 0.02% additional clicks being *reactively* classified as invalid and credited back to advertisers.

11.6 Click Fraud Auditing

Click fraud auditing is the process of examining the set of click-throughs delivered to the advertiser's site to determine which of the clicks, if any, may have been fraudulent and/or issued with malicious intent. While an ad network may examine such click-throughs as part of its click fraud detection process, a company that serves as a trusted third party (separate and distinct from the ad network and the advertiser) can do such an examination as well.

An analogy can be drawn between click fraud auditing and auditing of corporate finances. Once a company prepares its financial statements, including its cash flow statements, profit and loss statements, and balance sheet, an auditing firm can verify these statements by analyzing the data and receipts used to construct the statements. The auditor can, in many cases, request to see additional data. Ultimately, the company and the auditor work together to resolve any discrepancies that are found to ensure that the company is correctly reporting its financial health to the market.

In the case of a click fraud audit, an advertiser is interested in determining whether an ad network is correctly reporting the number of valid clicks for which it is charging. The advertiser can hire a third-party organization to serve as an auditor. The ad network and the auditor could work together to resolve discrepancies between the number of valid and invalid clicks indicated by the ad network's click logs and the advertiser's web logs. Click fraud audit reports, when constructed correctly, have the potential to do the following:

- Provide value to advertisers by giving them confidence that they are "getting what they are paying for"
- Allow the click fraud auditor to serve as a trusted third party that can help arbitrate discrepancies
- Help ad networks identify and fix limitations in their click fraud detection and containment systems

When done incorrectly, click fraud audit reports may provide misleading information to advertisers. The erroneous report may negatively impact the advertiser's business by prompting it to alter an advertising campaign that would otherwise result in cost-effective conversions.

The process of click fraud auditing involves several challenges, including maintaining the confidentiality of signals, overcoming data limitations, and maintaining user privacy.

11.6.1 Confidentiality of Signals

As part of a click fraud audit, an ad network cannot disclose information about exactly which clicks it is has charged for and which it has marked invalid—that would leak information about its signals.[2] After all, a malicious advertiser could experiment with issuing a single click or a small number of clicks on its own ads during each billing period to determine how many of those clicks are deemed valid. Each set of clicks that the malicious advertiser issues could be targeted at testing a hypothesis that the advertiser might have about a specific, surmised signal that the

---

2. For transparency, Google does report to advertisers the number of invalid clicks that it discards on a daily basis.

ad network might be employing. If an advertiser repeats such experiments many times, it may effectively reverse-engineer an ad network's signals. It could then use the information to conduct competitor click fraud, sell the information, or issue a click inflation attack on a site for which it is also the publisher. For all these reasons, an ad network cannot disclose exactly which clicks it marks as valid or invalid so that the information cannot be used to create a "playbook" for attackers about how to circumvent signals.

11.6.2 Data Limitations

While click fraud auditing companies are typically given information about the set of clicks that arrive at the advertiser's web site, they may be at a disadvantage compared to ad networks with regard to being able to assess which clicks should and should not be considered valid. Because ad networks cannot disclose information about exactly which clicks they do and do not charge for, a click fraud auditing company is left to take a guess about which clicks the ad network may or may not have considered valid.

A click fraud auditing company may attempt to make its own assessment about which clicks should and should not be considered valid by looking for anomalies. For instance, if a click is issued on the same ad by the same IP in an advertiser's web log multiple times, the click may look anomalous to a click fraud auditing company if the only information it has is the advertiser's web log. At the same time, an ad network has information on clicks from extremely large numbers of advertisers, and a click that may look anomalous in the small stream of data that a click fraud auditor has from the advertiser may look completely normal in the ocean of data that an ad network has from, say, hundreds of thousands of advertisers. For instance, the multiple clicks on the same ad from the same IP address in the previous example may be completely valid if that IP is on HTTP proxy for a large ISP such as America Online or a mobile carrier. A large ad network benefits from seeing click data from across the Internet, and it may be able to do more effective and accurate anomaly detection even compared to a click fraud auditor that has several thousand advertisers as clients.

In addition to being able to use a much larger amount of click stream data in which to look for anomalies, ad networks have web logs from search requests that, when coupled with web logs containing ad clicks, can effectively and accurately help identify signs of click fraud. All ad impression URLs are generated in response to a query; in some cases, cookies are served to users who receive these queries. However, neither the queries used to generate ad impression URLs nor the cookies will appear in the advertiser's web logs and, therefore, will not be available to a click fraud auditor. Such query logs, which are approximately two orders of magnitude greater in size than click logs, contain a wealth of information that can be mined for the purpose of identifying fraudulent, anomalous clicks that can be marked as invalid by an ad network.

Furthermore, in analyzing the click stream data that a click fraud auditor might have from an advertiser's web log, the auditor may not be able to compensate for some effects on its own. For instance, after clicking on an ad impression URL, the user is redirected to the advertiser's site, and the HTTP request corresponding to the advertiser's "destination URL" will appear in the advertiser's web logs. If the user continues browsing the advertiser's web site by clicking links to other parts of the advertiser's site, and then hits the browser's back button one or more times, another HTTP request may be made for the advertiser's destination URL to reload the page. Such HTTP requests may look like repetitive ad clicks in the advertiser's web logs and may look anomalous to a click fraud auditor. An ad network charges only for clicks—not for subsequent page reloads. The advertiser will be charged only for the click preceding the first HTTP request for the advertiser's destination URL. In fact, the page reloads do not go through the ad network at all and involve only the user's computer and the advertiser's site. However, an auditor may not have any way of knowing which requests in the advertiser's web log correspond to actual ad clicks and which are due to page reload requests. The subsequent HTTP requests may be misinterpreted as a fraudulent click by a click fraud auditor, when in reality it was caused by the user navigating back to the destination URL after exploring other parts of the advertiser's site. Such clicks are called "fictitious clicks" in click fraud audit reports.

To help remedy the problem of fictitious clicks, Google provides advertisers with a feature called "auto-tagging." The auto-tagging feature appends a unique ID to the destination URL for each distinct click that has the potential of being charged (i.e., both valid and invalid clicks) to the advertiser's account. The unique ID allows click fraud auditing and analysis firms to distinguish unique ad clicks from page reloads. Without this feature, it would be impossible to distinguish page reloads from new, distinct clicks on ads. Given how commonly users take advantage of such navigation features of web browsers, auto-tagging is essential for proper click fraud auditing. At the time of writing for this chapter, Google was the only ad network providing this feature. More details about fictitious clicks and auto-tagging are provided in [415].

The various limitations discussed here increase the chances of inaccurate analysis and make it more challenging to do click fraud detection based on advertiser-side data. For this reason, advertisers should use care in adjusting their ad campaigns based on such analysis. Decisions made based on inaccurate analysis can adversely affect sales and can cause advertisers to manage campaigns in a suboptimal manner.

As an example, consider an advertiser of leather goods that manages ad campaigns for shoes and handbags in which the advertiser uses two ad creatives, one for shoes and one for handbags, each with a separate destination URL. The advertiser's web logs may indicate several page views for the shoes destination URL, which could be due to reloads caused by users who may have done quite a bit of navigation through the advertiser's site after clicking on the shoes ad. The web logs may not indicate as many page views for the handbags destination URL. An inaccurate analysis of these web logs might tell the advertiser that there is a high level of click fraud occurring for the shoes ads. In reality, the page views corresponding to the advertiser's destination URL may be indicative of *more* user interest in shoes due to users conducting more research about shoes on the advertiser's web site. As a result, it may be worthwhile for the advertiser to invest more in its shoes campaign instead of its handbags campaign in the future. However, if the advertiser invests less in the shoes campaign based on inaccurate analysis, it is unclear what the opportunity cost might be: The advertiser might end up losing potential shoe sales if it makes a decision based on inaccurate analysis. Furthermore, the missed opportunity on shoe sales could be far larger than any money lost on potentially undetected click fraud. In this scenario, the advertiser is far better served by studying its dollars per conversion rate for both the shoes and the handbags campaigns.

It is important for advertisers to closely monitor ROI, and adjust ad campaigns appropriately based on this data. Undetected click fraud can manifest itself as lower ROI than expected (based, say, on past performance). At the same time, many other factors, such as non-optimal keyword or bidding choices, or a competitor having better sale prices, might also negatively affect ROI. Hence, while undetected click fraud will lower ROI, lower ROI does not necessarily imply that undetected click fraud is occurring.

11.6.3 Privacy

One might suggest that if ad networks have more data than click fraud auditors, then perhaps ad networks should share the data with auditors to help them verify the validity of clicks. Unfortunately, to protect the privacy of its users, an ad network cannot share the large amount of data that would be required to allow for such verification.

In addition to considering the number of valid and invalid clicks, it may be useful for click fraud auditing companies to consider auditing metrics such as the number of dollars an advertiser pays per conversion. Given that CPCs are constantly changing as the result of the dynamic ad auction, and that features such as smart pricing are used in weighting CPCs, the expected number of clicks that an auditor believes should be marked as valid or invalid may not be as useful a metric as the expected dollars that an advertiser should pay per conversion.

11.7 The Economics of Click Fraud

As previously discussed, two common forms of click fraud are competitor clicking and click inflation. Competitor clicking is punitive and intended to deplete rivals' marketing budgets. By contrast, click inflation is a for-profit activity that allows fraudulent publishers to collect a share of the click revenue generated by an ad network. In both cases, ad networks have been criticized as being indifferent to fraud. This criticism stems from the misconception that ad networks suffer no economic consequences from click fraud. In reality, ad networks have strong economic incentives to minimize click fraud.

Ad networks need the trust of advertisers, and they have an incentive to provide advertisers with better ROI if they hope to have advertisers increase spending with them in the long term. Market competition is another key incentive for ad networks to combat click fraud. Today, many ad networks are actively competing for the business of both advertisers and publishers. Naturally, both advertisers and publishers will choose the ad network that offers the best ROI. Ad networks that offer lower click fraud rates will, therefore, have a competitive advantage in the market.

Consider the case of competitor click fraud, which saps money directly from advertisers' budgets. Besides violating an advertiser's trust in the ad network, competitor click fraud directly reduces advertisers' ROI. Advertisers victimized by competitor click fraud will either reduce their bid prices or drop out of bidding completely. As a result, there will be fewer participating advertisers. Those advertisers that do participate will make lower bids for potentially fraudulent clicks, which will result in less competitive pressure in ad auctions and, in turn, lower profits for the ad network. Minimizing competitor click fraud is in the ad networks' best interest, because it will maximize the bid prices that an ad network receives and offer a higher ROI to advertisers that might otherwise use a rival ad network.

The same rationale applies to click inflation. Fraudulent publishers that generate bogus clicks on ads displayed on their own properties will reduce the ROI of advertisers. In turn, advertisers will lower their bid prices; as a result, legitimate publishers will receive a smaller share of ad revenues for their valid clicks. These publishers will choose the ad network that offers the best value for their legitimate clicks. Often, ad networks are also one of the largest publishers on the network themselves. For instance, an ad network may run a keyword search engine and display ads next to search results. Click inflation in other parts of the network will reduce the bid price that it would receive for clicks on their own properties.

In a competitive environment, ad networks face pressure to reduce both competitor clicks and click inflation. By reducing click fraud, ad networks will improve the returns of advertisers and publishers, as well as their own returns. More efficiently delivering relevant ads to legitimate users will benefit all parties in the system—except the fraudsters.

Conclusion

This chapter has provided a summary of the current state of online advertising fraud, including representative forms of attack and representative countermeasures. We discussed some of the challenges involved in click fraud auditing, which, when done correctly, can even provide advertisers that receive high ROI further confidence in online advertising. In addition, we explored the economics of click fraud and the incentives that search engines have to catch as many fraudulent clicks as possible to maximize advertiser ROI.

There is much art and science still being developed surrounding various aspects of mitigating online advertising fraud, because the online advertising market is in a state of expansion while working to support the needs of advertisers and online commerce providers. Successful fraud management will provide competitive advantage to ad networks, and help enable them to provide the highest ROI possible to advertisers.

Acknowledgments

We thank the editors, Markus Jakobsson and Zulfikar Ramzan, for the opportunity to contribute this chapter. The authors are grateful to Tom Dillon, Thomas Duebendorfer, Carl Evankovich, Daniel Fogaras, Tri Le, and Razvan Surdulescu for providing feedback that helped improve the quality of this chapter.

Chapter 12

Crimeware Business Models

David Cole and Sourabh Satish

This chapter examines the different avenues by which crimeware authors can profit from their activities. The first part of this chapter presents an overview of the various mechanisms. The last part of the chapter describes one of these avenues, *adware*, at a more basic level. These two portions are relatively self-contained, and the reader can peruse each independently of the other.

12.1 The Crimeware Business*

12.1.1 Introduction

"It's immoral, but the money makes it right."
—Convicted bot-herder Jeanson James Ancheta, January 25, 2006

The confused morality of 19-year-old Jeanson James Ancheta makes a poignant statement on the belief system driving the young criminals who have been thrust into the spotlight after being arrested for developing and using crimeware—they typically recognize what they are doing is wrong but cannot resist the siren call of easy cash. Ancheta's case was certainly not the first.

---

*This section is by David Cole.

While criminal use of malicious code predates the turn of the century, the event that opened the eyes of the industry happened on October 26, 2004. This is the date when the U.S. Secret Service and others swooped in to shut down the ShadowCrew, an international gang with thousands of members focused on widespread online identity theft that had been up and running since August 2002. The leaders of the gang were Andrew Mantovani, a 23-year-old man from Arizona, and David Appleyard, a 45-year-old man from New Jersey. While Mantovani and Appleyard were based in the United States, the members of ShadowCrew spanned many countries, including Bulgaria, Canada, Poland, and Sweden.

Mantovani and Appleyard ran ShadowCrew as a web-based marketplace for stolen identities, operating on an auction model similar to that used on eBay, where the different "vendors" of identities and other stolen property bore confidence ratings and allowed for bidding on their goods and services. The sheer size of the operation made the ShadowCrew hard to hide, and they did not take great pains to mask the existence of the group.[1] These factors and others set the Secret Service on their trail and ultimately led to the arrest of 28 members who were found in eight states and six countries in a large-scale international sting. As law enforcement pored over the data, they counted 1.7 million stolen credit cards and login information for more than 18 million email accounts.

The ShadowCrew bust was one of the most visible signs that online crime had become professional and sophisticated—this was no longer the digital vandalism of web site defacements, but rather people intent on making money from other people's misfortune online. This chapter covers software that is expressly built for committing online crimes, such as keylogging trojan horse programs and botnets that are used for everything from extortion to click fraud. Additionally, adware and spyware will be reviewed, although these two categories differ somewhat from the previously mentioned one: While this software can be used in an illegal fashion, it is not typically purpose-built for cybercrime. Instead, it is intended to generate revenue for the author through traditional software licensing or some form of online advertising. This is especially true for adware, although these programs range from programs that are easily removed and show the occasional pop-up advertisement to downright nasty applications such as Direct Revenue's notorious Aurora program, which besieged infected machines with pop-ups and stubbornly refused removal.

Each section of this chapter explores a particular type of security risk or malware by focusing on its business model. How the people involved in each

---

1. In fact, even today you can use web archiving to access old versions of the ShadowCrew web site: http://web.archive.org/web/*/http://www.shadowcrew.com/

business make their money, who they are, and how much they make are covered for each category, ranging from adware and spyware to trojan horse programs and bots. Even within each category, there are significant differences in the applicable business models. For example, trojan horse programs may be authored primarily to send spam, to steal consumer information for resale on the black market, to perform targeted intellectual property theft in support of espionage, or to conduct extortion by preventing the user from accessing files on his or her own system until the victim pays the attacker. The pains each group takes to avoid law enforcement and public scrutiny will also be covered, whether it is a complex web of affiliate relationships or the location of an operation far away from the victims of the crime in a place where the local authorities look the other way.

Two relevant topics will not be covered in this chapter. The first is the market for hacking toolkits such as the Russian-made WebAttacker and MPack, both of which are used on web servers to exploit web browser vulnerabilities and install malware or other unwanted software. Although toolkits such as these and the popular "Rock Phish kit" for setting up fraud sites are no doubt important, they are often treated as freeware, even if the author intended to sell them. Hacker toolkits suffer from the same licensing problems as standard commercial software, which means the impact of the toolkits on the state of cybersecurity far exceeds any commercial benefit received by their authors. The world of crimeware is quite a different story, with the authors reaping considerable, direct financial reward from their creations.

Second, this chapter will not attempt to assign an overall dollar figure to the market for crimeware or any online crime. It is simply too complex to estimate with any reasonable degree of certainty. The crimes are diverse, ranging from rogue marketing with adware to underground extortion transactions where money silently changes hands. Consider the diversity of currency involved—ranging from U.S. dollars and all types of paper money to credit cards and online payment mechanisms designed to be anonymous, such as e-gold. The international nature of cybercrime also confounds any accurate economic projection, because crimeware is created and distributed across many, many global boundaries. Lastly and most importantly, many—if not most—of the people who are creating and benefiting from crimeware are simply not getting caught, making it difficult to know what the spoils of their activities truly are.

12.1.2 Adware

In contrast to peddling trojan horse programs or renting botnets for attacks, using adware is not an inherently criminal business. In fact, some of the early and most prominent players were trying to do something most people would consider positive: make advertising more relevant than the ever-present banner ads adorning web sites, which are often ignored and have notoriously poor click-through rates. Adware companies figured if they knew what users liked when they browsed the web, why wouldn't they want to see relevant, timely ads on the topic? WhenU, one of the first and best-behaved of the adware players, offered a simple and beguiling flash tutorial on how adware works on its web site. It showed a woman shopping for a Caribbean cruise online. Thanks to WhenU's SaveNow program, she received a just-in-time advertisement for a less expensive cruise than the one she was about to purchase. After availing herself of the competing offer sent to her by SaveNow, the shopper could tuck away the hard-earned cash she preserved through the adware or use it to buy a few extra Rum Runners for herself and her friends as she cruised past Montego Bay.

At its most basic level, adware companies are paid by advertisers for showing supposedly relevant ads to users or driving traffic to advertiser web sites. The difference between adware, banner ads, and other conventional media is that adware generates better sales conversions from web site visits because the ads the user clicks on are displayed based on a detailed understanding of the user's interest. This knowledge of the user's online behavior and interests is created by tracking his or her activity online, which the user has presumably consented to with full understanding before the adware program was installed.

While adware players sometimes work directly with advertisers, they are often one step removed from advertisers through a dizzying network of ad brokers, ad networks, media buyers, and other parties. As a consequence, a fair number of companies did not know they were signing up for an adware promotion, as it was arranged on their behalf by a third party that might be several steps removed from the advertiser. More than one company has been astonished to find angry messages from customers as its advertisement appeared as an unwanted pop-up through adware. In fact, one of them was an anti-spyware company itself![2]

Another oversimplified model can be offered to explain the distribution of adware—that is, how it ends up installed on a person's computer. In this model, adware is bundled with otherwise "free" software to subsidize its development and pay the freeware company's bills. Conceptually, the exchange of value occurs as follows: The advertiser gets interested customers, who purchase its offerings by clicking on relevant ads; the adware company is paid by satisfied advertisers; and the distributor is paid for installing the adware along with its software. Users are

---

2. A McAfee ad appeared via Direct Revenue's "The Best Offers" network: `http://searchsecurity.techtarget.com/originalContent/0,289142,sid14_gci1149928,00.html`

the big winners in this make-believe model: They get the dual win of free software they would have otherwise had to pay for and targeted, timely ads from the ride-along adware program.

Of course, the reality is much more complex and not even close to as pleasant an experience for the user as what is suggested by this oversimplified model. Adware is frequently distributed through an affiliate network run by the adware company and a variety of distributors that are paid on a per-install basis. Each distributor in the program agrees to a code of conduct dictated by the adware company, which is supposed to ensure fair play (i.e., the users consent to the installation and clearly understand what they are installing on their computers). Beyond the code of conduct and distribution agreement, the members of an affiliate program may install adware on users' computers in any number of ways, ranging from clear disclosure as part of a software bundle to the outright deception of telling users that they have to install an adware program to view a web site properly. In the worst-case scenario, adware is installed via exploit of a software vulnerability, usually in a web browser, or downloaded and installed by a malware program without the user even knowing how it arrived on the computer. Adware has been seen bundled with useless system utilities,[3] attached to BitTorrent streams, and downloaded by bots and trojan horse programs. The possibilities have been limited only by distributors' greed and imagination, with the code of conduct often being shuffled aside in the rush to turn a quick buck.

The Players

At center stage of the adware story are the adware companies themselves—some of which are criminal by design and some of which originally had a reasonable business plan but have done things along the road to profitability that they would prefer their mothers don't know about. One might consider the latter to be "marketing gone wild" rather than "Crime, Incorporated."

Most of the adware companies that dominated the scene from 2000 to 2005 were based in the United States. More specifically, the adware companies tended to be positioned on opposite sides of the U.S. coasts: Claria, Enternet, and 180Solutions had their headquarters on the West Coast in the San Francisco Bay Area and Seattle, while WhenU and Direct Revenue operated out of offices in New York City. One might offer an explanation that the West Coast players were firmly implanted

---

3. Claria and WhenU both originally offered time synchronization programs for Windows XP, which claimed to make sure the user's system clock was never out of synch with the official time servers on the Internet. Windows XP does this by default—a fact that was likely not lost on the adware companies in question.

in the technology hotbeds of the United States, whereas WhenU and Direct Revenue were close to the advertisers given their positions next to Madison Avenue.

The varying personalities of the companies were driven by the wildly diverse people at the helm of each organization. Claria's and WhenU's polished and aggressive approaches were fashioned by seasoned marketing and technology executives who are active members of the online business community. While their business models and practices have put them at odds with their peers at times, they have run their companies in plain sight, obtained funding from well-known venture capitalists, and boasted big-name corporations as their customers. This stands in marked contrast to organizations such as ClickSpring and, to a lesser extent, Direct Revenue, both of which operated with a shroud of mystery over their business. For example, Claria's head of marketing would interact directly with security vendors during disputes, whereas Direct Revenue hired a contractor billed as a "privacy expert" to undertake discussions with security companies about the detection and removal of its programs. Not surprisingly, there has been a fairly reliable relationship between the unsavoriness of a particular adware program and the visibility of the responsible company behind it: The more aggressive and higher risk the adware is, the greater the pains taken by the company backing it to obscure what it is doing.

Common Problems

While the adware purveyors and their programs vary greatly in terms of their behavior, a series of common problems with the adware business model have stretched across the industry as a whole.

Weak or Nonexistent Value Proposition. The software bundles that serve as one of the most popular means of installing adware on users' computers are supposed to be an exchange of equal benefit: Users get the software they want for free in exchange for being exposed to advertisements. Nonetheless, the actual value of what users have received has been dubious in some cases and downright vaporous in others. While it's questionable as to whether users would allow someone to track all their web browsing activity in exchange for a calendar program or smiley icons, some of the system utilities that have been bundled with adware and supposedly improve a computer's performance have, in fact, produced misleading or false results, ultimately doing nothing to help the user's quest for better system performance and likely worsening it owing to the addition of irritating pop-up ads from the bundled companion adware program.

Poorly Disclosed Tracking Behavior. Adware companies are notorious for disclosing behavior that many would find objectionable deep within the paragraphs of a long end-user license agreement (EULA) presented in a smallish text box. Mixed in with the normal legalese skipped over by the average user are a series of clauses that would make a reputable attorney blush, such as the following excerpts from prevalent adware programs:

> You hereby grant BDE the right to access and use the unused computing power and storage space on your computer/s and/or Internet access or bandwidth for the aggregation of content and use in distributed computing. The user acknowledges and authorizes this use without the right of compensation.[4]

> By using the Internet and/or the Software and/or the Service and/or the Content, Licensee may be exposed to contaminated files, computer viruses, eavesdropping, harassment, electronic trespassing, hacking, and other harmful acts or consequences that might lead to unauthorized invasion of privacy, loss of data, and other damages.[5]

Such statements would offend the sensibilities of many, well beyond the privacy zealots who are often the first to take notice and blow the whistle on such obviously brazen violations of trust and privacy. Certainly not all EULAs are as obviously one-sided as the ones given here, but many do not make it clear that in exchange for whatever value exists in the program, users subject themselves to conditions they would not agree to if it was explained to them plainly.

Attribution of Ads. The adware business centers on displaying as many ads as possible on a user's machine to increase revenue from advertisers for the adware company in question. Given the near-universal dislike of pop-up and pop-under advertisements, which are standard tools of adware, the programs often do not clearly identify the source of the ads they are delivering to the user. The result for this omission is obvious and intended: Users then do not know the origins of the ad and believe it may have come from a web site they are visiting or a program other than the responsible adware program, thus allowing the adware program to continue to display ads under a smokescreen of confusion. In contrast, WhenU adopted what was widely regarded as a responsible, transparent model of ad attribution for its adware programs. In addition to a brief description of where the ad was coming from and why it was being displayed, WhenU included a toll-free phone number on every ad that allowed concerned consumers to call a helpdesk for assistance. Most adware programs do not come close to the high bar set by WhenU for ad attribution, as this transparency would likely result in their programs being ripped off of users' computers as quickly as they can be placed there.

---

4. The license agreement for the B3D Projector program that comes with KaZaa.
5. Hotbar Terms of Service.

Lack of Effective Removal. Of course, every program installed on the Windows platform should register itself with the Add/Remove Programs area in the Control Panel. But if you are paid for keeping your program on a user's computer for as long as possible, would it not make more sense to ignore this nicety? In addition to failing to register their programs in Add/Remove, some adware companies took extreme measures by intentionally crippling their programs' uninstall function, requiring users to download another uninstall program, requiring users to visit an uninstall web site, or, in some of the worst cases, using rootkits to have their programs burrow deep inside a system and stubbornly refuse to be discovered or removed.

Direct Revenue had one of the most interesting approaches, which combined a confusing uninstall web site (mypctuneup.com) to remove its programs Better Internet and Aurora, alongside watchdog processes that restarted manually killed processes. Also, the company actually deleted other adware programs discovered on users' computers to make more room for its own advertisements. This move, which Direct Revenue named "torpedoing," recognized the fact that when a distributor installed one adware program, it often installed *many* such programs to boost its profits, as the distributor was paid per successful installation. Nonetheless, when users are barraged with ads and the adware programs resist removal, the likelihood that they will rebuild their computers with a fresh version of Windows becomes much greater. The "torpedo" approach likely worked in keeping Direct Revenue's adware on PCs longer without being removed, but extended the group of individuals who detested Direct Revenue beyond users infected with the company's software to Direct Revenue's own peers in the adware industry.

Poor Enforcement of Distribution Network Codes of Conduct. While savvy adware companies have codes of conduct that should effectively control affiliate misbehavior, the question is not how well written the agreement is but rather how well it is enforced by the adware company. The real problem is this: When the adware company profits from the distributors' installations, no matter how they are installed, what natural incentive does the adware company have to enforce the code of conduct? Every installation means another set of eyeballs the adware company can turn around and sell to advertisers ("We can get your message to 5 million potential customers").

Indeed, affiliate programs have often run under a "Don't ask, don't tell" policy, where adware companies point to a comprehensive code of conduct policy signed by all distributors when accused of misbehavior. When acknowledging problems with their affiliate programs, they single out a specific distributor or two as "bad apples" and make a public example of them. One instance of this was illustrated by the series of lawsuits 180Solutions brought against some of its affiliates that were found to be installing the company's adware programs using dubious—if not outright criminal—practices [185]. Blame for improper behavior was diffused over a complex web of affiliate relationships where the guilty party was always one elusive step away.[6]

Over time, rogue distributors have learned to report only modest installations and stretch out their revenue over time so as not to create a situation that would be difficult for an adware company to ignore. Distributors also typically join several affiliate programs so that they can make more for each computer they can gain access to.

Lack of Consent for Install. The "lack of consent" problem arises directly from the pay-per-install model and the murky relationships that make it difficult to determine just who is responsible for clogging a computer with adware. In the past, the distributors were incentivized to behave badly and their scruples did little to prevent the ensuing mayhem. Affiliates many times did not clearly obtain consent for installing adware onto users' machines, fearing that if they did so, the users would by no means agree to the trashing of their PCs and crippling of their Internet connections. Their attitude can be effectively summarized by the following quote from the convicted adware and spammer Sanford Wallace:

> I figured out a way to install a [sic] exe without any user interaction. This is the time to make $$$ while we can.

Sanford Wallace and others found that by using ActiveX "drive-by" installations and exploiting unpatched software flaws in web browsers, adware could be foisted onto users' computers without their knowledge or any need for them to agree to the installation. Perhaps the most infamous of the distributors is a Russian organization that goes by the name of iFrameCash.biz. It leveraged a previously unknown Microsoft Windows flaw starting December 28, 2005, with the motivation of installing massive amounts of adware, spyware, and malware throughout the holiday season. Microsoft released a patch about two weeks after iFrameCash.biz began exploiting the flaw to install adware on unsuspecting users' computers across the globe.

Techniques to Evade Law Enforcement

Many tactics have been used by adware companies to keep the cash flowing in and evade law enforcement. A brief summary of the types of evasion techniques employed follows.

---

6. The Seismic media lawsuit brought by the Federal Trade Commission offers a strong example of how complex the web of relationships in affiliate networks and adware companies can be (`http://www.ftc.gov/opa/2004/10/spyware.htm`).

Smokescreening the Customers and Partners. This technique has meant running interference in the face of angry advertisers or embarrassed venture capitalists. When complaints reached the ears of an adware company's investors, the most frequently cited excuse seems to have been distributor misconduct. The adware company's leaders would assure the investors or partners that everything was fine; the unwanted installations that they were likely hearing about were the work of a few bad actors who were in the process of being punished for their misdeeds in violation of the code of conduct.

Punishing the Distributors. Excuses can last only so long without being followed up with punitive measures if the adware players are to maintain face. As mentioned earlier, 180Solutions took the public action of suing a couple of its former affiliates that violated the code of conduct through rogue installations. Actions taken have ranged from private slaps on the wrist to public, defamatory lawsuits against former partners.

Acquiring the Distributors. 180Solutions was never without a creative approach. In responding to rogue affiliates, the company acquired a major distributor named CDT (not to be confused with the Center for Democracy & Technology) and vowed to clean it up.

Filing Preemptive Lawsuits. In one of the more interesting exchanges, Claria (then Gator) initiated a lawsuit for "malicious disparagement" against the Interactive Advertising Bureau (IAB), which had publicly called the company's practices "deceptive" and stated that it was "illegally" obscuring the ads from other online businesses. This aggressive approach was not unfamiliar to the hard-driving executives of the adware start-ups, and legal fees were no obstacle as they were flush with cash from their impressive profits.[7] Threats of lawsuits against anti-spyware and other security companies became commonplace as adware companies sought to defend their practices and/or intimidate the organizations into no longer detecting and removing their software.

Operating in a Country Favorable to the Business. Generally, this response means a move to a smaller or more tolerant nation than the United States and several of the Asian countries that have taken strong stands against adware. South Korea was perhaps the first country to send an adware purveyor to jail: A Seoul man was sentenced to 8 months in jail in August 2005 for his role in adware installs

---

7. During the time of Gator's skirmish with the IAB, the company reported $14.5 million (2001) and $40.5 million (2002) in revenue (http://www.wired.com/wired/archive/13.12/spyware_pr.html).

from a porn site.[8] This tactic has been used effectively by others, though, without repercussion. For example, the notorious traffic pumping schemes employed by the 40C-plus variants of CoolWebSearch all appeared to operate well out of law enforcement's reach in Eastern Europe.

The Spoils of Adware

There have been a few very revealing disclosures of how much revenue adware companies have generated. The first came from Claria on April 8, 2004, when the company filed its S-1 Form Registration Statement as required by the Securities and Exchange Commission for companies considering an initial public offering. In this form, companies have to make a series of disclosures about their business, including what they do, how they do it (at a high level), who is on their management team, who their partners are, what risks would be involved in holding their stock, and so forth. A glance at Claria's S-1 filing provides a good indication of the health of the firm's business at the time:

> Since the launch of our services in 2000, we have grown rapidly by attracting a large number of advertisers and users. Our audience currently consists of more than 43 million users worldwide, and our direct and indirect customers in 2003 included approximately 425 advertisers, including many leading online advertisers such as Cendant Corporation, FTD.com, Inc., Netflix, Inc. and Orbitz, Inc.[9]

A look at the company's revenue growth is particularly interesting. Claria made $40,587,000 in 2002 according to the S-1 form. In 2003, driven by higher overall ad impressions sold by an increasing customer base, Claria generated $90,480,000, a staggering 123% increase over the previous year. The number is even more astonishing when you consider the number of employees who were used to generate this amount of revenue. Claria had a mere 190 people on staff at the beginning of 2004, which means that it was generating nearly $500,000 per company employee. Inside a technology start-up, a solid achievement in terms of productivity is $250,000 per employee. To double that number is certainly impressive.

While Claria stepped forward into the spotlight with its S-1 filing and depicted a business of explosive growth, Direct Revenue also experienced strong growth but had no immediate intentions of "going public," preferring to keep out of the bright lights and ensuing scrutiny. Given the aggressiveness of the company's adware programs, absence of reasonable removal capabilities, pattern of installations

---

8. http://english.chosun.com/w21data/html/news/200508/200508240032.html
9. http://sec.edgar-online.com/2004/04/08/0001193125-04-059332/Section2.asp

	2003	2004	2005
Revenue attributable to a Direct Revenue program	$6,134,875	$27,994,341	$24,272,155
Revenue from other sources	$848,440	$11,337,620	$9,214,365
Gross revenue	$6,983,315	$39,331,961	$33,486,520

Table 12.1: Revenue generated by Direct Revenue. *Source: People of the State of New York v. Direct Revenue, LLC.* http://www.benedelman.org/spyware/nyag-dr/, Chart 2A, Exhibit 2, p. 11.

without consent, and resultant size of the business, Direct Revenue eventually was unable to keep out of the spotlight. In 2004, Direct Revenue generated in excess of $39 million, having gotten a later start than Claria (at least under the Direct Revenue name, as the principals were involved in previous adware-related entities). See Table 12.1. Similar to Claria, the company showed an enormous growth spurt from one year to the next with a little less than $7 million in 2003 in gross revenue. The Direct Revenue management team did very well financially in the halcyon adware days of 2004: Ringleader Joshua Abrams's compensation totaled in excess of $8 million, and second-in-command Daniel Kaufman recorded more than $7.5 million in salary and other payments.

Adware: An Industry in Evolution

The adware industry has fractured into two opposing forces since pressure began mounting on the companies from all sides in 2005. Whether it was mainstream media calling out the adware players, or consumer advocacy organizations, security companies or the advertising community itself voicing outrage, the outcry against misbehaving adware vendors reached a new peak in 2004. The loud noise of the opposition in the previous year turned into a large number of busts and some sharp turns into different directions in 2005 for prominent adware companies. Claria shopped its assets to Microsoft [287] and announced its exit of the adware business in early 2006 [242]. WhenU took distribution in house and ultimately sent its product strategy in a different direction. Then there were Direct Revenue and Enternet Media (makers of the much-hated Elitebar program), which succumbed to actions taken by Attorney General of New York Eliot Spitzer and the Federal Trade Commission, respectively [63]. At the time of the writing, 180Solutions (now Zango) seems to still be straddling the crossroads of a more traditional affiliate network program with a low-risk program that offers content such as videos and games in exchange for ad impressions. Other, smaller and shadowy adware purveyors that remain in the space seem to have burrowed even farther under-ground and typically moved offshore, if they were operating inside the United States to begin with.

12.1.3 Spyware and Trojans

In contrast to the often irritating, noisy adware program, spyware and trojan horse programs ("trojans") operate in stealth, hoping not to be noticed by the victim whose computer serves as their host. The most common agenda these programs have is to steal confidential information, either via keylogging or by opening a backdoor on the infected system to allow the attacker unfettered access to the computer. While their purpose is often the same, some key differences distinguish spyware and trojans.

The first and most important difference is that spyware is commonly commer-cially sold or distributed with the potential for a noncriminal business model. For example, one of the main types of spyware is keylogging software, which can be used legally to conduct employee surveillance when foul play is suspected. It might also be used to keep an eye on a troubled child or as part of a law enforcement investigation. All of these are legitimate reasons that have been used for installing keyloggers, surveillance programs, and aggressive parental control applications. This type of program has commonly been considered spyware across the anti-spyware industry owing to its ability to invisibly monitor actions and send them back to another person. Other types of spyware also exist, such as ComScore's MarketScore program, which is intended to serve as a sort of Nielsen ratings for the web. Nevertheless, the mainstays of this category have historically been keylogging and surveillance programs.

With spyware, the technology itself is not inherently "bad" but the usage of the technology often is, and many would say that its design lends itself to abuse. With trojans, the technology itself is malicious: It is designed to inflict harm on others by stealing data, facilitating unauthorized access, blasting out spam, perpetrating click fraud, and demonstrating other ill intentions.

When looking at the business of spyware versus trojans, a logical difference can be identified. Spyware authors typically hawk their wares on commercial web sites or otherwise through sale of software licenses. Trojan authors might sell their malware on the underground crime market, they might be commissioned for development of a particular trojan, or they might use the program themselves or as part of a team to commit fraud, distribute adware, or steal intellectual property. In the worst cases, trojans can be used to steal identities that are later used by organized crime to facilitate even more harmful criminal activities or by terrorists for creation of fake identities to elude authorities.

One breed of spyware is similar to adware from a business standpoint, in that it is not intended to steal data but does undertake surveillance at a level many would find uncomfortable.[10] For example, ComScore's MarketScore program is designed to track an individual's web browsing behavior as the user surfs the web, with the goal of generating meaningful statistics that are later aggregated and sold by ComScore in reports. While tracking a user's web browsing habits, ComScore not only monitors standard HTTP traffic but also proxies SSL communications, either inadvertently or intentionally. Peering into encrypted SSL traffic may be acceptable for some users, but others might blanch at having any information from their online banking or shopping sessions shared with a third party such as ComScore. Given the relatively small number of these programs and their similarity to adware in terms of their supporting business model, keyloggers and surveillance programs will be the emphasis of this section.

The Players

Trojans and spyware are a truly worldwide problem and are software tools used by a diverse cast of characters across the globe. This globalization stands in stark contrast to adware, which historically has had a U.S. bias and is a business unto itself (i.e., the basic purpose is to install adware and display ads; adware is not part of a broader scheme except in the most extreme cases). The different types of businesses that peddle spyware and trojans are distinct enough to deserve separate treatment.

Spyware Software Vendors. This category, which includes keylogger, surveillance, and aggressive parental control programs, serves as the mainstay of the spyware genre. These programs have names such as Win-Spy, Actual Spy, NETObserve, and Spy Buddy. Spyware software vendors commonly sell their programs directly through their own web sites as well as through distributors including popular software download sites such as Download.com and TUCOWS. The programs typically tout features such as these[11]:

- Logs all keystrokes, is case sensitive
- Makes screenshots within the specified time interval
- Saves the applications' running and closing

---

10. The line drawn—at least by some of the anti-spyware community—is whether the program tracks personally identifiable information. If it does, then it is commonly considered spyware. If it does not, then it typically is placed in a less severe categorization of adware or trackware.

11. The marketing verbiage was taken from the Actual Spy web site on January 20, 2007: `http://www.actualspy.com/`

- Watches clipboard contents
- Records all print activity
- Records disk changes
- Records Internet connections
- Records all web sites visited
- Records start-up/shutdown
- All information is stored in the encrypted log file
- Convenient interface of the log and screenshot view

The target audience for these programs includes concerned or paranoid parents, jealous spouses and lovers, employers who suspect something is amiss with an employee (or are just nosy), and outright criminals who want an easy, invisible means of stealing someone's information. The following advertisements are representative of the type of tactics used to sell spyware software:

> Would you like to know what people are doing on your computer? Would you feel better to know what your children are doing on the Internet? Ghost Keylogger can help you![12]

> Ensure productive activity in the workplace. Guardian Monitor Professional 9.0 helps you make sure employees are "on task"—not distracted by casual web surfing or excessive personal business.... Control what your children see and do on the Internet. New Guardian Monitor Family Edition software lets you oversee and control Internet activity–even when you can't be there in person.[13]

Once purchased, the spyware customer then must get the program installed on the target computer. Given the audience most of the programs are aiming for, physical access to manually install the program on the target user's machine is presumed in most cases rather than some form of drive-by installation such as vulnerability exploit or ActiveX abuse. Following their installation, spyware programs can run in various stages of stealth, ranging from a small icon in the system tray signaling that the user is being monitored to the more common scenario where there are no visible signs of the spyware running while the target user is on the system. Commercial spyware programs may track keystrokes, IM chat sessions, web activity, all executed programs, and other activities. They are often not terribly complex applications, but they appeal to an audience that needs point-and-click usability rather than the sinister, technical efficiency of a trojan.

---

12. http://www.keylogger.net/index.html
13. http://www.digitalriver.com/v2.0-img/operations/guardian/site/347056/home.html

Much like the spy shops you might find downtown peacefully coexisting with other brick-and-mortar businesses, surveillance and keylogger software purveyors generally have no need to evade law enforcement. Nonetheless, if they cross the line into facilitating unauthorized installations and other criminal activities, they can find themselves on the wrong side of the law. Spyware authors walk a fine line. The letter of the applicable law reads that it is illegal to advertise an eavesdropping device if "the design of such [a] device renders it primarily useful for the purpose of the surreptitious interception of wire, oral, or electronic communications" [329].

LoverSpy was a solution that did just that, promoting itself not just as a comprehensive surveillance application but also as an easy means of infecting the intended target by sending the user a custom-designed electronic greeting card that carried the spyware program. Unbeknownst to the victims, when they opened the card they were also executing the LoverSpy application, which ran silently in the background capturing information as configured by the sender. LoverSpy allowed for all activities to be monitored and could also be used for remote system control and monitoring via webcam (assuming the victim had one). The customer would receive reports automatically (e.g., via email) or return to the LoverSpy web site and receive reports on what the victim had been doing on his or her computer, which ideally included searching for a mate more respectful of the user's privacy.

The LoverSpy operation was shut down in October 2003 by federal search warrant. Its creator and owner, Carlos Enrique Perez-Melara of San Diego, California, was indicted in 2005 on 35 counts, including creating, advertising, and sending a surreptitious interception device [283]. Four LoverSpy customers were also indicted under federal wiretap laws that carry a maximum penalty of up to five years in prison and a maximum fine of up to $250,000. By the time LoverSpy was closed for business, the $89 program and service had been sold to 1000 different customers across the globe and used against 2000 victims.

As the LoverSpy case shows, the market for commercial spyware vendors does not seem to be nearly as profitable as that for vendors of adware or fraud-minded trojans. As of 2007, the large number of competing programs, which have relatively low price points (usually $30 to $50 per user), are all looking for the attention of what seems to be a moderate-size audience based on download numbers at popular software sites.

Bespoke Trojan Authors for Hire. In September 2006, a corporate scandal rocked one of the technology industry's most reputable titans: Hewlett-Packard (HP). While investigating a leak from the corporate boardroom, several dubious tactics were used to identify who was spilling top secret information about HP to CNet reporters Dawn Kawamoto and Tom Krazit. The stories covering the incident claimed "spyware" and "trojan horse" programs had been used to infiltrate the reporters' computers in an effort to determine who was the source of HP's leak. Ultimately, it was discovered that the relatively benign email tracing software ReadNotify was used to track messages sent to Kawamoto in hopes that they would be forwarded to the suspected loose-lipped chairman, rather than an installed trojan on the reporter's computer. Nonetheless, the public reaction to suspected corporate use of malware was revealing: Were well-respected organizations really using spying software on their staff and other companies?

The answer is, unfortunately, yes. Corporate espionage maneuvers have made use of custom trojans with the hopes that the unique nature of the malware would allow it to slip by the radar of the victim's security defenses. Use of these trojans is by no means limited to the business world—governments and the military have been known to employ these software "weapons" to gather intelligence on their adversaries by infecting their systems. A rash of custom trojans leveraging previously unknown Microsoft Office vulnerabilities ("zero days" in security parlance) came to public awareness in 2006. Many of these pointed back to China, and quite a bit of the ensuing industry discussion suggested government sponsorship of these attacks, based on their sophistication and frequency. Whether this is a state-sponsored activity in these cases, all parties agree that custom malware, and especially trojans, has been added to the military arsenal of many countries.

The authors of these programs clearly have a specialized skill set, at times including highly prized skills such as a strong command of cryptography and low-level programming languages. Some may have application fuzzing and disassembly skills,[14] which allow them to identify zero-day flaws. Zero-day flaws are then turned into exploit files that are bundled with custom trojans to improve the attacker's chances of infecting a system undetected. Given that the stakes for discovery are the highest for this group of malware authors, they tend to focus heavily on stealth and evasion features. At least a small number of the custom trojans seen in 2006 replaced the infected exploit file with a clean file following infection to cover their trail, in addition to using back-channel communications that were up and active for only a short period of time. The idea was clear: Get access, steal information, cover all traces of the breach, and get out unnoticed.

Some of these "guns for hire" advertise their services on the black market or have long-standing relationships with private investigators or others who walk in the murky areas of the law. This was the case with the large-scale corporate espionage scandal that unfolded in 2005 when a custom trojan was found on the

---

14. Fuzzing and application disassembly are two types of analysis that are performed when probing a software application for vulnerabilities.

computers of many major corporations across Israel. Michael Haephrati authored a trojan[15] that was delivered as an email or on a disk that was supposed to contain a business proposal. After verifying connectivity, the trojan was capable of performing activities such as scouring the infected host for sensitive files, taking screenshots, and capturing video footage. After recoding the information, it would then be sent to Haephrati's servers back in London, where the Israeli citizen was living at the time. The trojan was sold for 16,000 New Israeli shekels (approximately $3600 at the time) to several reputable private investigation firms. These firms were hired by a number of leading corporations in Israel to gather information on their competitors. Oddly enough, the far-reaching scandal was exposed by Haephrati's former father-in-law, author Amnon Jacont, whom he had infected with the trojan out of spite. Using his trojan, Haephrati stole and then released parts of Jacont's forthcoming novel to the Internet. Jacont complained to police. As the investigation unraveled, dozens of corporate executives were implicated from big-name Israeli companies such as Amdocs, Cellcom, Pelephone, Mayer, and others. Somewhat ironically, among the victims of the espionage trojan was Hewlett-Packard.[16]

The current price for contract trojan development appears to be in the low thousands of dollars, making it potentially lucrative depending on the number and type of development contracts the author can arrange. Many of these developers are believed to operate out of countries where technical skills are easy to find and legitimate, well-paying jobs are in short supply owing to a depressed economy.

Trojan authors who enjoy state sponsorship are on the payroll of the government rather than living contract by contract, but presumably under job titles other than "Trojan Developer." In contrast to the more entrepreneurial "guns for hire" model, these programmers have no need to evade the laws of their own country, but can focus only on evading enemy state detection of their digital weapons. These malware authors probably are not high enough up in the food chain to earn an enviable salary, but they are also probably well treated given the sensitivity of their occupation and the necessary secrecy that shrouds it.

Information-Stealing Trojan Authors. In contrast to the sophisticated and unique custom trojan, the typical crimeware trojan that plagues the Internet is decidedly mundane. The goal of the author is straightforward: infect as many computers as possible with crimeware that steals a predefined type of data and send it back to an established location, known as an "egg-drop" or "dead-drop"

---

15. The trojan itself is referred to either as HotWord or Rona (http://www.symantec.com/ security_response/writeup.jsp?docid=2005-053013-5106-99&tabid=1).

16. The following link contains a post of the original Israeli trojan horse story from Haaretz, which is no longer available from its site: http://financialcryptography.com/mt/archives/000487.html

server. The egg-drop server's data repository is then harvested and either used by
the trojan author or sold off in bulk inside online fraud economies. The difference
between the two types of attacks can be likened to the difference between a
complicated bank heist in search of a single, valuable prize and a simple "smash
and grab" burglary where the attacker attempts to make a little cash per victim
rather than trying to make a large sum of money off of any one theft. While
antivirus software vendors' estimates of the pervasiveness of this type of trojan
vary, all agree that the variants seen for popular families, such as Banker or Bancos,
number in the thousands.

Given the indiscriminate nature of these attacks, they often do not perform
general keylogging as does spyware, but rather aim to steal credentials for certain
brands. Popular targeted brands include financial institutions, online payment
services, online games (especially in China and South Korea), and popular
applications. Trojans of this variety may also steal a particular variety of
information, such as email addresses or Social Security numbers. The better-
written trojans are modular, allowing their authors to modify the code to quickly
and easily target new data types and brands.

Prices for information-stealing trojans on the black market range from
hundreds to thousands of dollars, depending on the sophistication of the threat,
assurances provided by the author, and other factors. The compiled program
(object code) is typically sold, rather than the source code. Some authors offer
"insurance" that their trojans will not be detected by popular security software and
that they will modify it accordingly in the event that it does end up in antivirus
software companies' cross-hairs. A late 2005 investigation into an online fraud
community by Symantec revealed the following promotion for sales of a trojan
(all spelling and grammatical errors belong to the original author):

> I'm here to sell a working version of win32.grams trojan, for those who don't know
> what this trojan does i will explain. It simply steals all the e-gold from the victims [sic]
> account and transfers all the gold into your account. Simple and efficient.
>
> The trojan has been tested succesfully [sic] with WindowsXP [sic] (al SP's [sic]) and
> works ONLY on IE (Internet Explorer).
>
> If any bugs are found it is my responsibility to fix them immediately.
>
> The price for this wonder trojan is only 1000 dollars and I accept only WU/MG and
> e-gold.

In response to a reviewer's feedback on his "product," the author explains his
policy regarding release of the source code for the trojan:

> I'm am [sic] sorry that i haven't been more clear from the first telling you people that I
> am not selling the source code...i thought i explained l8r in the thread...and it was
> obvious...i'm sorry and i wish to take this opuritunity [sic] to clear this out.

> The source is NOT for sale and the reasons are simple.
>
> If the source gets public there would be alot [sic] more hard for us to recode an undetectable version for each customer. If we sell the source, it will get public... because we all have friends plus...you can just resell the source code, also making it public thus so verry [sic] detectable.
>
> Morinex, you are talking about bots wich [sic] is a verry [sic] different subject, i beg you search the internet for trojan sellers and see if any of them is selling the sourcecode [sic].

Many authors undoubtedly use the trojans themselves or work in a group such that the malware code itself is not widely distributed but held as their intellectual property. Other times, some versions of the trojan may be sold while other versions or certain modules that the author believes to be more effective (e.g., due to use of sophisticated techniques such as complex cryptography or polymorphism) are held back for the exclusive use of the author or those in the author's trusted circle.

Pricing of trojans can be variable as well. For example, a simple form-grabbing backdoor may be sold for a few hundred dollars, whereas a more complete trojan (e.g., with an HTTP-based administrative interface and secure proxy) will likely cost more.

After purchasing a trojan, the customer commonly distributes it through one of a number of techniques. Popular distribution methods include spamming the trojan to a large number of potential victims, downloading it to already bot-infected machines or installing it using web browser vulnerabilities such as the popular Windows Metafile flaw.[17] Successfully infected machines are often then pilfered for valuable black market commodities such as login credentials and other identity details, which can be sold in bulk to fraudsters (or by the trojan author), or for email addresses, which can be further used for spamming and phishing.

Ransomware Extortionists. This much-hyped genre of trojan, commonly referred to using the media-friendly title of ransomware, just can't keep itself out of the headlines. While it has not been widely distributed, it bears mentioning owing to the audacity of the attack. The ransomware trojan infects the user machine using any of the typical methods, such as sending victims a convincing email and encouraging them to run the attachment. Once executed on the victim's system, the trojan sets about obfuscating or encrypting presumably valuable information such as Microsoft Office files, photos, archives, password files, and anything else that the victim is likely to find very valuable and willing to pay to

---

17. Microsoft Security Bulletin MS06-001: Vulnerability in Graphics Rendering Engine Could Allow Remote Code Execution (912919). `http://www.microsoft.com/technet/security/Bulletin/MS06-001.mspx`

recover. The user is left with a ransom note in an obvious location, such as a text file in the same folder as the "ransomed" files that are now inaccessible. The ransom note indicates that the victim can quickly regain access to the locked-up digital possessions if he or she contacts the author for payment or sends payment to a particular account.[18]

Little is known about the extortionists behind ransomware. There have been very few of them, and they tend to infect only a small number of systems compared to other types of trojans. The authors likely operate in a similar fashion to information-stealing trojan authors, except that they attempt to monetize their attacks directly by interacting with victims rather than reselling victims' identities or using their stolen information for criminal purposes. The amount of money generated by ransomware schemes would appear to be quite small given their lack of popularity and the asking price in ransom notes, which is usually in the hundreds of dollars. Extortionists' profitability has also been hampered by their minimal encryption skills. Antivirus companies easily broke the obfuscation techniques used by the original Trojan.Gpcoder [340], for example, making it entirely unnecessary for victims to pay the attacker for release of their files. Later versions of GPCoder used stronger encryption (up to a 660-bit key), but very robust encryption has not been used as of yet[19] and challenges of key management as well as other issues that make real-word cryptography nontrivial to deploy seem to have confounded would-be ransomware authors thus far.

The fact that victims have to pay the extortionist to rid themselves of the steely grip of ransomware also makes the criminal's job more difficult: He or she has to hide a trail of money. While this is not an impossible task, it certainly makes evading law enforcement much more difficult for the attacker. For example, if the extortionist uses a single account, it can be frozen and the records turned over to the authorities. Account records can be investigated in most cases, money can often be traced, and attackers can ultimately be brought to justice if their tracks are not expertly covered. All of this must seem like a lot of effort compared to the simpler occupation of the information-stealing trojan author, who anonymously picks the pockets of his or her prey and monetizes these actions through efficient criminal

---

18. The term "cryptovirus" predates ransomware by approximately 10 years. "Cryptovirology" was a term used by Adam Young and Moti Yung in 1996 in their IEEE paper "Cryptovirology: Extortion-Based Security Threats and Countermeasures." Their research and current work can be found at their web site: http://www.cryptovirology.com/

19. It would be quite trivial for malware authors to incorporate much more potent encryption schemes into their attacks. Little stands to prevent them from doing so, particularly with the rapid increase in computing power available on a standard home PC.

economies. Given the comparatively small amount of ransomware witnessed in the wild, these facts do not seem to be lost on the online criminal community.

Downloader Trojan Authors. Downloader trojans are lightweight malware designed to install other programs. They have flooded the Internet over the last couple years, as they are a lightning-quick, silent means of infecting a system. The goal of the downloader trojan is to rapidly and deeply infect a system while opening the computer up for silent installation of more complex, full-featured malware such as a bot, a backdoor, or a spammer trojan. Given that a downloader trojan is not a "complete" attack in and of itself, its author is likely to work with a fraud gang, with a spammer, or under a front company as an affiliate to distribute adware or misleading applications such as rogue anti-spyware.

The main design goal for downloader trojans is stealth: How small can you make it? How effective is it at disabling security software? How deep can it burrow into the system? Remedial downloaders can be written as simple batch files that call out to an FTP server; more sophisticated downloader trojans are written in assembly code to squeeze them down to the smallest size possible. Staying as small as possible is critical for downloader trojans, as it makes their installation as quick and invisible as possible. Often downloader trojans will use a binary packer[20] for compression and obfuscation in an attempt to increase the likelihood that they will slip past a system's defenses.

Whether the downloader trojan is sold or is used as part of a broader attack will determine how the author is paid. More money is likely made as part of a larger group or as a front company that is a member of many affiliate programs—these approaches can yield tens or hundreds of thousands of dollars through commissions or fraud rather than the several thousand dollars that can be generated through simply licensing the trojan to other cybercriminals.

Much like information-stealing trojan authors, professional downloader authors take pains to cover their tracks and evade law enforcement. Former Soviet Bloc countries are apparent hotbeds of downloader trojan activity, as they have many skilled programmers but not enough jobs to employ them, in addition to law enforcement that does not effectively suppress online crimes.

The following IRC dialog, which was captured by SunBelt Software in August 2005 [94], summarizes the purpose and design behind the downloader trojan

---

20. A binary packer is a compression and obfuscation technique often used by malware authors in an attempt to alter the "fingerprint" of their creations. Existing malware is "packed" in hopes that antivirus software will not have the capabilities to handle the decompression or unpacking routines needed to decode the packer and detect the malware. Popular packers go by the names of PECrypt, Morphine, YodaCrypt, and PECompact.

business. Translated from the original Russian into English here, it relays a description of the design criteria for a downloader trojan that in turn downloads yet another downloader trojan intended to install adware:

> Well, we need to infect a user's computer that visits our web site with maximum efficiency. And this must be done as fast as possible. To begin, we would need a very compact loader program (small application, no larger than 2KB, which can be written in assembly language if I'm not mistaken).
>
> The only purpose of the compact loader is to download a real loader. However, the real loader that we need for that purpose will be much larger in size but will support more functionality.
>
> First of all, this loader won't be visible by other processes. It will disable all firewall and antivirus software in all possible ways. The loader must be smart enough to download and run any file for any of our advertisers (I'll come back to advertisers later in this text). One of the most important loader functions is to resist any attempt to terminate it (somehow it should either copy itself somewhere or clone itself or in other words to hide itself from any software that can remove it).

Spammer Trojan Authors. The final—and perhaps most lucrative—trojan business model is that of the spammer trojan. This malware performs exactly as one would imagine: It infects a system and then mercilessly pumps out spam from the infected computer. The year 2006 ushered in a new breed of spammer trojans, including the Rustock and SpamThru families, designed as evasive, stubborn spam pumping machines. This genre of malware differs from the bots that had been the historical mainstay of spamming malware in that the spammer trojans lack the general, multipurpose capabilities of bots while using some complex features not typically seen in bot code.

Rustock, for example, utilizes a rootkit driver inside an Alternate Data Stream, a little-used feature of the Windows NT File System (NTFS). Rustock then prevents access to it by locking the stream from all users so as to help achieve extreme stealth. Rustock's author monitors rootkit research sites and develops malware accordingly. The malware design reflects a deep understanding of how malware analysis is performed, and the author lays a large number of obstacles in the path of anyone who would try to detect the trojan.

Innumerable stories confirm the lucrative nature of the spamming business, where top spammers may rake in millions of dollars per year. Perhaps the best explanation of the spamming business and the colorful characters behind it is found in the book *Spam Kings* by Brian S. McWilliams [253]. While some spammer trojan authors may not be spammers themselves, one can imagine that the revenue generated from their business is not far off from that of their customers, the spammers themselves.

Law enforcement is typically evaded through obfuscation of the trojan author's identity and true location. Additionally, spammer trojan authors seem to locate themselves in areas where they are not likely to be bothered by law enforcement. The author of the Rustock family [331], PE386, is Russian and actively taunts members of the security community on popular message boards where occasionally the topic is how to detect and remove his latest threats.

12.1.4 Bots and Botnets

If the trojan horse business is populated by crimeware programmers who take pride in their tools, the rough-and-tumble world of bot-herders and their botnets sacrifices much of the technical originality seen in trojans for entrepreneurial zeal and black market business acumen. Bot-herders certainly care about evasion just as much as trojan authors do, but they care much less for craftsmanship. Instead, they focus on the many ways they will use or rent out the network of infected computers (or "botnets") they create and manage.[21]

Bot authors may start by developing bot code, but more often than not, they modify someone else's existing bot source code and compile it as a new version. After completing development, the bots are unleashed on the Internet (through spamming, downloader trojans, or other means). After infecting one host, they often scan for new ones by looking for improperly protected computers[22] sitting on a broadband connection. Once a substantial network of infected computers is established, the botnet will be either used by the bot-herder or rented through the black market to fraudsters, spammers, organized crime, extortionists, and just about anyone else looking to perform a misdeed online. At times bot-herders will build botnets on request to carry out a specific task, such as a distributed denial-of-service (DDoS) attack or spamming campaign. In these instances, the bot-herder will infect only as many hosts as are needed to fulfill the "order," preferring to stay under the radar by not growing the botnet to an unmistakably large size.

Botnets offer attackers a veritable grid of attacking power through the infected "zombie" computers as well as a strong measure of anonymity, because bot-herders do not own the systems performing the actual attack. Additionally, botnet-spawned attacks are challenging to track, because they usually spoof IP addresses and

---

21. This section focuses on the financial applications of botnets. For more detail on botnets, their design, and additional applications, see Chapter 7.

22. Oftentimes the infected hosts are Windows PCs that are missing patches and do not have a security suite installed that would block the exploit or the subsequent infections.

spread to thousands of zombie computers, which frequently lie across many national borders.

Bots are the multipurpose "Swiss Army knives" of crimeware, allowing for a wide range of functionality. Most can be updated to assume new functionality via download of new code and features. Popular botnet criminal activities include the following items, which are described in detail later in this chapter:

- Distributed denial-of-service attacks
- Extortion
- Identity theft
- Warez (pirated software) hosting
- Spam
- Phishing
- Spyware and adware distribution
- Click fraud

Although DDoS attacks were the original focus of bot-herders in the late 1990s, adware and spyware distribution quickly became one of the lowest-risk and most-lucrative activities to pursue with a botnet. Bot-herders can easily disguise themselves behind front companies on many affiliate programs, masquerading their illegitimate adware and spyware downloads as real user-initiated installs. The amount of deception required by the bot-herder as part of this scheme depends largely on the legitimacy of the affiliate program and backing adware company.

Before bot-herders discovered adware, bot-borne spam was popular. Spam is one of the most popular botnet activities because several of the original spamming tactics[23] have become less effective and botnets aid spammers in slipping under the radar of the anti-spam community.

Lastly, the explosive growth of online advertising—particularly pay-per-click traffic-driving programs—has garnered the attention of bot-herders. Now presumably lucrative click fraud schemes are actively run via botnets in yet another means of using this versatile malware.

---

23. For example, spam in the 1990s was often sent through "open" SMTP relays, where no authentication was required to send messages. Heightened security awareness and blacklisting of open relays by the anti-spam community have largely addressed the open relay problem, forcing spammers to adopt different techniques for bulk mailing, such as leveraging botnets.

The Players

As global law enforcement has stepped up investigation and prosecution of bot-herders in recent years, a common bot-herder profile has emerged. A bot-herder is often, but certainly not always, a male in his late teens or twenties, with a thirst for quick money and a general disregard for the law. This does not mean that all bot-herders actively wish to harm others, only that they may view it as an acceptable side effect of their rogue business. A bot-herder who goes by the handle of 0×80 in Brian Krebs's February 2006 story explains,

> "All those people in my botnet, right, if I don't use them, they're just gonna eventually get caught up in someone else's net, so it might as well be mine," 0×80 says. "I mean, most of these people I infect are so stupid they really ain't got no business being on [the Internet] in the first place."[24]

Some people, like 0×80, even draw distinctions between bot-herders who download adware as part of an affiliate program and those who steal identities, with the latter being considered the truly criminal side of the trade. Bot-herders often do not have other occupations. The economies where they are located may be depressed, or they may simply not be willing to take an entry-level job and work their way up from the proverbial mailroom. In a number of cases, they are self-taught. A quick scan through the headlines dealing with convicted bot-herders shows that they lack a strong geographical bias, stretching from the United States to Europe, Asia, and South America. The appeal of fast money seems to be a universal attraction.

Bot-herders work alone or in small groups, sometimes for an extended period of time and at other times on a project basis. They spend considerable hours in front of their command and control (C&C) servers, "herding" the zombie flock of infected hosts to new C&C outposts at different locations to evade detection from ISPs. More sophisticated bot-herders have begun using encryption, alternative protocols, and peer-to-peer models to address the hassle of discovery and transport to a new location. Bot-herders are in active competition for new hosts to add to their networks—there is a finite number of unprotected, broadband-connected hosts on the Internet, and there are far too many enterprising bot-herders aiming to plant a bot on such attractive prey. Bot-herders have been seen addressing the problem of competitors through a number of techniques, including everything from patching software vulnerabilities, to turning on firewalls, to even scanning infected hosts with an antivirus product to remove all competing malware (while excluding their own files from the scan, of course) [269].

---

24. Brian Krebs. Invasion of the Computer Snatchers. *Washington Post,* February 19, 2006. http://washingtonpost.com/wp-dyn/content/article/2006/02/14AR2006021401342.html

A bot-herder does not have to be extremely technically savvy because a vast amount of "cut and paste" code is readily available. Indeed, source code for both the popular Agobot and SDBot has been made available under general public license for usage by anyone who can compile it [321]. As a result, it is far more common to see minor variants of bots that use a new binary packer (or packer combination) or that have simply been updated with new exploit code rather than to discover an entirely new version of bot. Popular bots such as SDbot and Spybot have literally thousands of variants, many of which are so minor they never receive a specific variant name (usually a single letter or series of letters after the family name) from antivirus software vendors.

Common Criminal Applications of Botnets

Upon building a botnet, the bot-herder undertakes one or many of the activities described in this section, either alone or with partners who assist the bot-herder with managing and commercializing the botnet.

Distributed Denial-of-Service Attacks. Dating back to the 1990s, networks of zombie machines have been used to try and knock web sites offline, making them unusable by their customers and oftentimes preventing e-commerce. Sometimes DDoS attacks are mere Internet "joy rides"; at other times they are orchestrated by competitors looking to gain the upper hand as they render competing online services inaccessible to customers.

The latter motivation was the case with Jason Salah Arabo (age 19, from Michigan) who hired Jasmine Singh (age 16, from New Jersey) to debilitate his competitors' online sports memorabilia businesses so that his own could flourish. The victim was to be crippled by means of a DDoS attack from Singh's 2000-computer botnet. Both were discovered, and Singh was ultimately sentenced to 5 years in prison while Arabo received 30 months and was forced to pay a hefty restitution ($500,000).

DDoS services, also referred to as "packeting," are typically sold in fraud communities by bot-herders at prices in the thousands of dollars depending mainly on the size (measured in megabytes or gigabytes of traffic generated per second) and duration of the attack desired. Oftentimes, packeting is aimed at other bot-herders as a result of underground business deals gone wrong. Packeting a former business partner in a now-soured relationship is standard fare in the online underground and usually results in the victim "bouncing" his or her botnet to a new location to escape the flood of crippling traffic.

Extortion. While some denial-of-service attacks are executed by zombie machines against an unsuspecting web site or other online service, some victims are warned in advance in what is known as a protection racket or simply as extortion. In such schemes, the criminal threatens to knock the company's web site or online service off the Internet via a DDoS attack for a period of time if the attacker is not paid, usually at a peak hour that would be the most noticeable and do the most damage (i.e., as frustrated customers take their business elsewhere). One online gambling service, BetCris.com, estimated that it would lose "as much as $100,000 per day" [299]. The amount demanded ranges from the thousands to hundreds of thousands of dollars, with at least one large online service claiming to have seen extortionists demand millions in payment.

Extortion demands against offshore businesses such as online casinos that operate outside of U.S. jurisdiction are not unusual. While they can run their businesses unfettered by U.S. law, they are also unprotected by U.S. law enforcement when their lucrative businesses are targeted by extortionists. The amount of extortion that happens will likely never truly be known, as many victims simply pay to make the problem silently go away, and few are willing to talk about it.

Identity Theft. While bots often play some part in an identity theft scheme, sometimes they play the main and supporting role by not only infecting a computer, but also stealing personal information from the victim and sending it to the criminal. This can be done by implementing a keylogging or data thieving feature inside the bot itself or by downloading another crimeware application to the already-infected host.

Warez Hosting. Bot-infected hosts have often been used for hosting warez: pirated applications, movies, music, games, and so on. The owner of the infected host will likely become aware of the fact that he or she is unwittingly taking part in a crime and shut down the operation at some point. In the meantime, hosting and distributing warez from a botnet simultaneously makes it more difficult to pin the crime on the distributor, and the system owner (rather than the bot-herder) ends up paying the bill for the bandwidth. An unusual spike in traffic can be a strong sign that something is amiss; more than one network administrator has investigated strange traffic patterns only to uncover a bot-herder's treasure trove of warez and many unwanted visitors availing themselves of the goods. The economics of warez distribution favors the bot-herder: Warez are sold, bartered, and/or distributed by the bot-herder at no cost to the bot-herder themself.

Spam. Botnets operate at the heart of today's spam industry. Specifically, bots both harvest email addresses for spammers and are used to send spam messages. Sending spam through botnets is particularly common because it makes spammers more difficult to detect, as they can send messages from many machines (all of the infected machines in the botnet) rather than through a single machine, such as an open relay or web form. An obvious stealth advantage accrues to spammers who send only tens or hundreds of messages from a single host and multiply this behavior across thousands of hosts, rather than trying to send thousands or hundreds of thousands of messages from a single location. It is also notoriously difficult to shut down bot-based spam operations because the infected hosts may have dynamically assigned IP addresses, change frequently, and be completely oblivious to the fact that they are blasting others with spam.

Bot-herders can be one and the same as spammers, or they may simply rent their botnets for harvesting and spamming via popular criminal IRC channels or as part of a larger group. Rates charged for spamming and harvesting vary depending on the size of the project, but tend to be around pennies per bot in the network.

Phishing. In nearly every phisher's toolbox is an army of bots. Much like spammers, phishers may use bots both to identify potential victims via harvesting and to send fraudulent emails (spam), which appear to come from a legitimate organization such as the person's bank. Phishers may also use bots to host phony web sites that are used to steal visitors' personal information and serve as collection points ("dead-drop," "blind-drop," or "egg-drop" servers) for stolen data. As with spamming, bot-herders may either be part of a phishing group or rent the services of their botnets to the phishing group. Owing to the risk involved, botnet services for fraud usually carry higher prices than botnet services for DDoS and spamming.

Spyware and Adware Distribution. Leveraging an established botnet to install adware, spyware, and misleading applications on an infected system is one of the most direct, most lucrative, and consequently most popular money-making schemes for bot-herders. Assuming the guise of an online business, the bot-herder signs up as a member of an affiliate network, such as GammaCash (http://gammacash.com/), which pays members for installing adware programs. The botnet owner then downloads and installs the illicit programs on the zombie computers by issuing commands to the bots and automating the clicking of any buttons required to signal a consented-to installation. The bot-herder "affiliate" then reports these events as "consenting" installations in accordance with its distribution contracts and collects anywhere from $0.05 to $0.50 per installation. 0×80 (referenced previously) indicated that he was making an average of $6800 per month, and his partner mentioned making $0.20 per computer for U.S.-based installations and $0.16 for others. Savvy bot-herders such as 0x80 download adware programs slowly to their victims so as not to tip off the distribution network by reporting tens or hundreds of thousands of installations in a short period of time.

Click Fraud. Using botnets to game the pay-per-click advertising system is one of the newer techniques bot-herders are using to turn a quick buck online. The botnets implicated in click fraud have been more purpose-built than the typical bot; they are tailor-made for ripping off advertisers. This scheme works by having a publisher—either the bot-herder or likely someone else—sign up for an advertising program whereby the publisher earns money for displaying ads on its site and having people click on the ads. Visitors presumably are trying to learn more about the offering and ultimately make a purchase if all goes according to the advertiser's design. Click fraud botnets fake a user clicking on the ads on the publisher's site, generating traffic for which the ad program, such as Google's AdSense, will pay the publisher and for which the advertiser pays Google. The bot-herder likely benefits by taking a cut of the publisher's proceeds from the click fraud scheme.

Bot-herders are engaged in a constant cat-and-mouse game with Internet service providers and other Internet infrastructure players. Botnet traffic, when unencrypted, often follows familiar patterns and can be easy to detect. Dynamic DNS services, which have been frequently used by bot-herders, can also detect signs of likely bot behavior based on traffic patterns. ISPs and other providers can often detect less sophisticated botnets and shut them down within their networks. This is part of the game for bot-herders, as they then establish a new C&C server on another, perhaps less vigilant, ISP's network. Newer, more evasive botnets lack a central C&C server and leverage encryption to hide communications and peer-to-peer models without a "head" that can be targeted by service providers or the other groups that hunt botnets.

Law enforcement has similar issues with chasing botnet owners, who can easily pick up and move their business across networks and international boundaries. Nonetheless, careless bot-herders can be caught hawking their wares on IRC channels for online fraud or by being over-aggressive with adware installations through distribution networks. Jeanson James Ancheta, for example, advertised his services under the bold handle of "botz4sale."

Conclusion

A large number of trends have no doubt become apparent while reading this section. The lure of quick cash, the evasiveness of the perpetrators, and connections to a thriving underground criminal community are all common themes among the participants in the crimeware business. Not surprisingly, a serious question surfaces after hearing about such ominous threats: What will it take to stop crimeware? This question deserves at least a few moments of consideration. None of the measures mentioned here are satisfactory in their own right, but all could contribute to solving the growing crimeware problem.

Education. Much of the miscreant software described in this section relies on deception or preys upon fairly basic errors made by victims. While anyone can have a bad day and make a mistake, plenty of evidence suggests that the general public is still lacking in what might be called "Internet street smarts." This naiveté allows attackers to cast their nets across the general populace, betting that enough people will fall for their tactics to offset the risk of getting caught. Education and awareness are no silver bullets, but they can at least eliminate many of the more straightforward attacks that are so common today.

State-of-the-Art Security Software. Far too many people still believe that all they need is a firewall and antivirus software, and they will be virtually impervious to online threats. Others believe that getting the new version of a product is a waste of time: How much could really be new when the interface looks pretty much the same? The truth is that effective online protection requires the layers of defenses provided by a modern security suite that integrates antivirus, anti-spyware, intrusion prevention, anti-spam, and antifraud software, plus an intelligent firewall, of course. An older version of a product will usually not get the job done either, as security companies are in a never-ending arms race with increasingly sophisticated attackers. Sometimes, simply nothing can be done with old versions of software to make it suitable for protecting against the latest threats; a newer version designed to take on attackers' latest schemes is typically required.

Companies Taking an Active Role in Consumer Security. Given that many of the attacks are now focused on consumers, savvy businesses have realized that they can differentiate their services by offering customers security software to make them more comfortable transacting with the firm online. This approach makes good financial sense as well: When customers use automated online services, it is much cheaper than when they call the company or visit a retail location. In some businesses, such as that of Internet service providers, provision of security software to new customers is fast becoming the de facto standard. Earthlink punctuated this trend by acquiring the anti-spyware firm Aluria in a visible sign of its commitment to customer security [109].

Cooperation Among Global Law Enforcement. Crimeware frequently spans international boundaries, with thousands of miles separating the attackers from their victims. The geographic distance is a small barrier compared to the impenetrable tangle of widely differing (or, worse, completely absent) cyber-security laws and the lack of cooperation among law enforcement to share intelligence in an effort to bring cybercriminals to justice. To minimize the problem of crimeware, the truly global nature of the threat must be addressed by law enforcement across the globe cooperating to bring the perpetrators to justice—this matter cannot be solved by the industrialized countries alone.

Meaningful Punishment for Cybercriminals. The punishment for convicted cybercriminals has diverged wildly across the globe and even across highly advanced countries such as the United States. Sometimes the sentences have been little more than slaps on the wrist, with the malefactors being fined far less than they stole. Much less often, heavy-handed sentences have been given that seem excessive given the crime. Judges and juries need to understand the role played by cybercrime when sentencing, and they need to hand out penalties and jail time that are appropriate and serve as real deterrents for would-be online criminals.

Legitimate Job Opportunities in Hotbed Countries with Depressed Economies. Many, but certainly not all, of the countries where crimeware development has flourished are characterized by economies where there are a large number of strong engineering and computer science students, but few jobs available that would benefit from their skills. Add to this mix a not-so-healthy dose of U.S. media influence parading make-believe wealth in front of people in a tough situation, and that is all the motivation some cybercriminals need to make the transition from struggling graduate to fledgling cybercriminal. While the right type of incentives and economic assistance are ultimately challenging questions, it stands to reason that at least some of the current breed of crimeware developers would prefer to work in legal ventures if given a decent opportunity in their home country.

12.2 A Closer Look at Adware*

Adware consitutes "programs that facilitate delivery of advertising content to the user and in some cases gather information from the user's computer, including information related to Internet browser usage or other computer habits" [498]. As the Internet population touches 233 million in North America, 437 million in Asia, and 322 million in Europe, the Internet is now one of the prime advertising media.[25]

Classifying adware as malicious is a matter of opinion and debate. Advertising done right and correctly is not necessarily bad and could be useful to the consumer. The real potential of online advertising lies in contextual and targeted advertising,

---

*This section is by Sourabh Satish.

25. Internet World Stats. July 30, 2007. http://www.internetworldstats.com/stats.htm

where users are shown advertisements that match their interests and their buying patterns and, as a result, are very effectively and positively influenced in favor of the product/services/brand. Correlating advertising efforts with user buying patterns, both online and offline, is a tough problem. On the web, this information is correlated in terms of advertisement views, advertisement clicks, and user transactions. Analyzing user interests and behaviors while respecting user privacy can be quite challenging. Online advertising also has a huge revenue potential (forecasted by Jupiter Research to reach $18.9 billion by 2010). This huge revenue potential has often attracted a few foul players who are eager to claim a bigger share of the pie at the expense of user privacy, inconvenience, and annoyance.

When the advertising delivers what the consumer needs in a way that is not in any form overwhelming or disruptive to the consumer, it is usually considered "good." Users find mild and relevant advertising useful because they find good deals and information about products that interest them. Advertising can become a problem, however, when it is overdone. Some online advertising programs have truly gone to extremes, partly because of the weak economic models of online advertising. If the advertiser will be paid based on the number of times the advertisements are viewed, then potentially the sole purpose of the advertiser, which is interested in maximizing its own profits, would be to show the advertisements as many times as possible, irrespective of the context or interest of the user. Financial incentives of online advertising are being adjusted to deal with this problem, and new models are being explored today.

12.2.1 The Online Advertising Platform

The success of an online advertising campaign is evaluated by advertising agencies and companies on the basis of various metrics:

- *Number of views:* The advertisement is displayed to the user.
- *Number of clicks:* The user clicks on the advertisement.
- *User acquisition:* The user enrolls in the service or buys the product.

Online advertising has evolved into a sophisticated platform that can track any or all of these activities to the site on which the advertisement was displayed to the user as well as the user who makes a purchase or completes a transaction. These metrics are used not only to measure success but also to pay the various parties involved.

An online advertisement can take a variety of forms. A *banner advertisement*, for example, is a graphical online advertisement image displayed on a web site, like one shown in Figure 12.1.

Figure 12.1: A banner advertisement for Symantec's Norton 360 product.

The advertisement could also be textual (usually a link), which is displayed along with search results but in a separate and identifiable area of the page, usually the leftmost column. These advertisements can also be *contextual*—that is, shown in the context of the user action or interest. The user interest may be an interpretation of the search term on a search page; this type of scheme is used by search engines such as Google, which show advertisements on the right-hand column of search results (See Figure 12.2).

An advertisement can also be contextual to the content being reviewed by the user. For example, an advertisement relating to a type of product can be shown on a web page containing an article about the product. In some cases, the

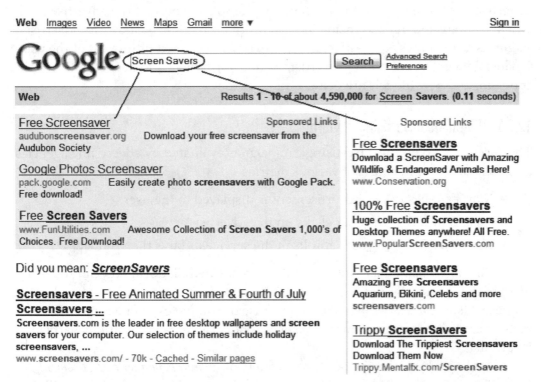

Figure 12.2: A contextual ad from Google. The ad displayed depends on the search string entered by the user.

advertisement might also be related to the content in an email, as in the approach used by Gmail.[26]

The user can interact with these advertisements and click to explore more details about the product or service. The user interaction with these advertisements usually redirects the browser (and thus the user) to the web site of the vendor that placed the advertisement. Thus advertising can be considered successful if higher percentages of users viewing the advertisements are redirected to the product/services web site.

Another means of displaying the advertisement to the user without requiring the web site to change its layout or embed the advertising on the page is to use a *pop-up* or a *pop-under*. A pop-up is an advertisement that is shown in a separate UI/browser window on top of the active window or browser. This type of advertising is very disruptive. It is mostly blocked by common browsers and the user has to explicitly allow them. A pop-under, by contrast, is a technique to launch the advertisement window below the active window such that it does not cause user interruption. This premise is that when the user closes the active window or browser, the user can see the advertisements. When the user does see the advertisements, however, they usually seem out of context given that the user does not notice them until later or when all windows are closed or minimized.

The sites hosting the advertisements and all companies distributing the advertisements (distribution networks) are paid based on either the number of times the advertisements have been seen by the users, referred to as CPM (cost per 1000 impressions) or the number of times the user has clicked on the advertisements, referred to as CPC (cost per click). Some advertisers also pay on the basis of CPA (cost per action)—that is, when the user clicks the advertisements, reaches a page, and fills out a form (called a lead form) or makes a product/service purchase.

CPA models are most lucrative for advertisers, because only real user contacts are paid. In contrast, CPM models are most lucrative for sites hosting the advertisements, because the number of visitors to the site directly translates into revenue. With this compensation plan, sites are incentivized to maintain good site quality and content, which translates into increased user traffic on the site. Unfortunately, both the CPM model and the CPC model are susceptible to attacks such as those simulating site visits or simulating user clicks to maximize the revenue. Such attacks are examples of click fraud, which is discussed in more detail in Chapter 11. The advertisements are usually hosted on a different server (not owned by site administrator) than the site itself.

---

26. http://www.gmail.com

When a product vendor or corporation wishes to launch a new product or increase sales of an existing product, the advertising budget is decided with many factors in mind. Online advertising is typically just a fraction of the company's total budget. The vendor approaches an advertising agency, which is responsible for designing the advertisement campaign and launching the advertisement in various media. The advertisement agency, in turn, approaches an affiliate network for online advertising. An affiliate network is a value-added online media intermediary that provides services such as aggregation, distribution of creative materials, and campaign performance tracking/reporting for affiliate merchants and affiliates.

An affiliate is rewarded for every visitor, subscriber, customer, and/or sale provided through its efforts. This compensation or commission may be made based on any of the CPM, CPC, or CPA models, as explained previously. The affiliate network identifies appropriate sites (sites most relevant to the advertisement) and/or high-traffic sites on the basis of various metrics that suggest the best locations on which to post the advertisement. "Posting an advertisement" implies adding a code block to the web page such that it pulls the advertisements from a predetermined server location in either known or random order. The advertisement hosting server can count either the number of times the advertisements were displayed or the number of times a user clicked on the advertisement. The technology for doing so is quite sophisticated and elaborate. Advertisers with cooperation from the site are usually able to display the advertisement contextually (in the context of content, demographics, geographic location, and so forth). The affiliate network may also pay search engines to include the advertisements in search results pages and other appropriate venues by relating search terms and keywords to the advertisement.

In summary, the advertisements are posted on various sites and are displayed to the user visiting the site. The sites (or search engines) are paid by the affiliate network, which is paid by the advertising agency, which is paid by the product vendor or corporation.

When a software vendor/author creates software, the vendor can generate profits in one of two ways:

1. *The vendor can sell the software for a price to the users.* This marketplace is extremely competitive and hence making decent revenue is very difficult, especially for small utility-like applications and applets. This approach also requires the seller to manage per-copy transactions. Also the seller could be liable for post-sales support and services.

2. *The vendor can provide the software at no cost to the user, but include an advertisement-serving component.* In this approach, the software author

receives compensation from advertisement affiliate networks. This component enables affiliate networks to deliver advertisements to users right on their desktops without requiring the users to run a browser or an application. In this scenario, the software vendor is usually paid based on the number of installations. This approach, which is called "advertisement-supported software," does not involve any software liabilities or support costs, because the software was free. To be profitable, however, the software has to be adequately compelling or else users will not download and use it. There are many distribution networks that software authors can join to aggressively distribute their software on the Internet.

In the second case, the software distribution networks work toward maximizing the distribution of the software, because they could be paid on a per-install basis. When the user installs and downloads such software, advertisements are displayed to the user either on the desktop with pop-up windows or on some form of desktop extension with "toaster pop-ups" without having to wait for the user to visit a site. Toaster pop-ups are usually animated pop-up dialogs that slide out either from the system icon tray or from somewhere in the browser.

The advertisement affiliate network tracks the advertisements displayed to the user either directly from the advertisement-serving component of the software or from the hosting web site page. It might potentially pay sites based on the number of times the advertisement is displayed to users there. Again, the advertisement affiliate network is paid by the advertisement agency. The advertisement agency (or the corporation selling the product) might pay affiliates more if the user clicks on the advertisement and completes some desired action, such as filling out a form or buying a product.

12.2.2 The Malicious Side of Advertising

The challenge in this entire business model is that the user must be shown an advertisement and must be motivated to click on the advertisement. This is possible only if computers can read the human mind—which they can! Search engines can link the terms users type in search fields to the advertisements that get displayed. Of course, this may not provide the best results most of the time because terms cannot be directly translated into intent or interest. Search engines and advertising platforms are working toward improving the technology in this regard. Gmail, for example, can link the keywords in emails to advertisements, and software running locally can link it to any piece of data on the user's system. Over-the-web advertising is generally more acceptable to the users, as it is displayed as a result of their decision to visit a site or as part of the site the user visits. Conversely, pop-up advertisements are an unfortunate development in online advertising. They are annoying and intrusive, preventing the user from browsing and actively disrupting user activity.

Integrating advertisement-serving components in free software was considered quite innovative until developers got too aggressive. Some adware vendors developed their own compelling software so that they could maximize their CPM/CPC revenue. Such software serves advertisements to the user out of context when the user is interacting with some application or is busy with usual work. It consumes system resources in trying to correlate typed words (often irrespective of which application the user was typing in) and pulling the related/unrelated content from the advertisement servers. To maximize on the opportunity to show advertisements to the user, some of these programs would start browser instances and pop-ups with varied content even without user action.

Users soon realized how annoying this advertisement-supported "free" software was and declined to use such software and networks. This led the free software vendors and distribution networks to correct themselves and make the advertising more manageable and nonintrusive to users.

Nevertheless, the prospect of getting paid on a per-install basis was lucrative enough that some still chose to push the software to users' machines even without users' permission. Affiliate networks or distribution networks leveraged operating system and application vulnerabilities to exploit and silently install such advertisement-serving components; hence no user involvement was needed. This means of installing software silently without user consent is usually referred to as "drive-by download." As soon as the user would log on to the machine, he or she would be completely overwhelmed with these advertisements being shown via either application pop-ups or automatic browser launches. This is how some adware finally came to be classified as malware. As a consequence, the general user perception is that adware is malware—no matter what the official word is.

When software with an advertisement-serving component is installed locally and observes all user activity, the advertisement-serving component can identify the user uniquely by his or her email address, name, login, and other data and by his or her interests as evidenced by search terms, interests, sites visited, and news articles read. This information can then be submitted to a back-end processing system, which can then infer the user's interest and select the appropriate advertising content to be displayed by the site—ideally, something that the user is very likely to click on. Once the user's personal information and interests have been harvested, the advertising can also be delivered via email or other means.

In addition to identifying the user and his or her interests, many other pieces of personal information related to the user can be collected and put to other use.

Users' personal information, such as name, email address, Social Security number, and credit card number, has tangible value in the underground economy. There is a very high probability that the software could collect and retrieve any and all information that the user types in any and all forms. Unlike banks, however, these advertising-related networks have no interest in securely storing user personal information.

Interestingly enough, in many cases users have consented to be watched! The software end-user license agreement (EULA) sometimes mentions such details explicitly, but most users accept the terms without reading them carefully. Here is an example of such a EULA:

> The user understands, acknowledges, and gives express permission for the application and/or associated components to collect personal information, including, but not limited to, name, demographic data, interests, profession, education, marital status, sex, age, income, and any other information.... The user understands, acknowledges, and gives express permission for the application and/or associated components to collect information and data regarding Internet activity, including web sites visited, search queries conducted, applications installed and used, files present on user's hard drive or system, transactions conducted, and any other behavioral data deemed necessary.... User hereby understands and gives permission for application and/or any associated components to alter applications, files, and/or data so as to display information and/or marketing messages, including but not limited to file sharing applications, media viewers, and/or player applications.... User hereby understands, acknowledges, and gives express permission for application and/or associated components to disable or delete applications and/or files deemed unfriendly or harmful to...Inc. or any of its partners ...without notice to the user, and may auto-reinstall application and/or any associated components, unless approved auto-uninstall application is used....

Unlike a billboard advertisement on highways, online advertisements can be directly linked to users who buy the product after having seen or clicked on the advertisement, even if the user buys the product after an arbitrary period of time of seeing and/or clicking the advertisement. One of the many ways this is possible is via cookies and advanced web server log analysis.

Web servers are capable of correlating users' advertisement interactions (view or click) to their navigation to sites or pages they browse even after an arbitrary number of days. When the user is shown an advertisement for a product, a cookie is set on the user's machine by the web server. When the user then visits the merchant site, it enables the merchant to infer who the referrer was (based on the cookie). If the user then buys a product, the merchant can pass along a commission to the affiliate network. This would be similar to the case where the user visits a site and clicks on an advertisement that takes the user to the merchant's web site.

In this case, the merchant identifies the referrer by some data in the URL that helps uniquely identify the referrer. This unique identifier (either in cookies or URLs) is commonly known as an affiliate ID. These affiliate IDs are unique within an affiliate program and serve to identify the affiliate that needs to be paid for redirecting the potential buyer to the merchant. As the user visits new sites that display advertisements, the associated affiliate ID is set in the cookie and is overwritten by the last affiliate that displayed the same advertisement. This specific behavior may vary across different affiliate programs. Some programs just add their affiliate ID at the end of a list of affiliate IDs in the cookie. Given that a merchant's advertisement could be posted on many sites visited by the user, the merchant considers only the last affiliate (i.e., affiliate ID in the cookie) that displayed the advertisement to the user.

Some forms of malware insert or overwrite their affiliate IDs in a cookie, even though the user has not seen or clicked the advertisement. In such a case, whenever the user went to a merchant site without ever having seen its advertisement, the merchant would assume that there was a referrer involved who must be paid a commission. This type of malware might insert its affiliate IDs quite regularly. Given that multiple affiliate networks could be advertising the same product, the merchant would pay only the affiliate that last advertised the product—that is, the affiliate with the last inserted affiliate ID in the cookie. Some malware programs watch the cookies and, as soon as they are updated, insert their affiliate IDs again to ensure that only their affiliate is paid no matter who is really advertising! These affiliates are simply "thugs" or "cheats." However, the norm is to use affiliate IDs in the browser redirects via the URL, where dependency on cookies is not needed.

CPM was and still is a commonly used metric in the online advertising industry. The fact that the advertisement was not necessarily seen by the user is an extremely weak aspect of this advertising model. The lack of evidence proving that the user has or has not seen or interacted with the advertisement has been extensively exploited. Sites and site administrators would host advertisements on their web sites and then write crawlers that would simply revisit their web sites on various machines, thereby inflating the advertisement view counts to maximize revenues.

Later, PPC became the more dominant model, as the site was paid only when the user clicked on the advertisement. Unfortunately, this model also resulted in extensive schemes to illegitimately extract revenue. One scheme for extracting revenue by simulating user clicks is detailed in Chapter 6. This approach, known as badvertisements, involves using JavaScript to click on links corresponding to advertisements on behalf of users. However, the users never see the advertisement!

Adware is a problem only when it poses a threat to user personal information, causes annoyance, and interferes in user activity. Advertising in itself is not bad and to a large extent is actually useful to the consumer. Some forward-looking initiatives such as AttentionTrust[27] are making an effort to change the way users should benefit from sharing their choices, such that users are presented with relevant advertising and experiences. Attention Trust is a nonprofit organization that is exploring some interesting ways in which users might strike the right balance between privacy and interest disclosure with the end result that web sites can show precisely those products that match users' interests. The users are given a platform to decide which preferences, interests, and habits should be disclosed to web sites as they visit sites. These sites then analyze users' interests and display only the advertisements that match their disclosed interests. These kinds of models could strike that delicate balance we have been waiting for.

---

27. http://www.attentiontrust.com

Chapter 13

The Educational Aspect of Security

Sukamol Srikwan and Markus Jakobsson

13.1 Why Education?

While good user education can hardly secure a system, many believe that poor user education can put it at serious risk. The current problem of online fraud is exacerbated by the fact that most users make security decisions, such as whether to install a given piece of software, based on a very rudimentary understanding of risk. To highlight the complexities of user education, we describe a case study in which a cartoon-based approach is used to improve the understanding of risk among typical Internet users, as it relates both to phishing and to crimeware. This educational approach is based on four guiding principles:

1. A *research-driven content selection*, according to which we select educational messages based on user studies

2. *Accessibility* of the material, to reach and maintain a large readership

3. User *immersion* in the material, based on repetitions on a theme

4. *Adaptability* to a changing threat

13.1.1 The Role of Education

Online fraud is threatening organizations and individuals alike, and many fear that it might turn into a weapon of electronic warfare within the not-so-distant future. There is a strong consensus that we, as a society, need to improve our resilience against this threat. This goal can be reached using at least three principal approaches: *software-based security initiatives*, *legal and regulatory efforts*, and *educational approaches*. While the approaches are complementary, they are not entirely independent. For example, legal and regulatory efforts are limited by technological issues related to detection and enforcement. Likewise, the impact of client-side software initiatives is affected by educational efforts related to how to use the technology and how to maintain the integrity of deployed software. In turn, regulatory efforts fuel software development and deployment, and recent FFEIC guidance [119] encourages financial institutions to educate their clients.

While technical efforts to fight the problem are proliferating, and legal and regulatory approaches are rapidly catching up, we argue that the development of educational efforts has been left behind. Consumers are faced with a bewildering array of advice about how to stay safe against identity thieves, but we are not certain that any of the efforts manage to communicate a basic understanding of what to do and why. Current advice comes in many forms, from the terse online resources of financial institutions to in-depth self-help books describing how to obtain access to credit reports. Consumers are advised to buy and use paper shredders; they are likewise told to look for icons indicating that sites are hacker safe, use encryption, and are members of the Better Business Bureau. At the same time, the typical Internet user does not know how to identify a phishing email [366], but often relies on checking spelling and identifying known deceit techniques [425]. Many consumers do not realize how easy it is to clone an existing site (e.g., using a tool such as WebWhacker [471]), but rather interpret convincing web site layout as a sign of legitimacy. Similarly, many typical computer users are not well aware of how they may be infected by crimeware and what to do to minimize the risks. It is not surprising that the average consumer has a rudimentary understanding of these threats, both due to the fact that he or she does not understand the intricacies of the Internet, and due to the difficulties of communicating complex notions to users who would rather not be involved at all. To make matters worse, phishing and crimeware have components of both technology and psychology [202, 367], and there is ample evidence (see, e.g., [260]) supporting the contention that most people *want to trust* what they see.

Security education is not easy, especially when it is targeted at general computer users who may not want to take the time to learn. In this chapter, we explain pitfalls and difficulties of this education and describe how a detailed understanding of these—and of typical user behavior—can help guide efforts. While such improved education efforts can be expressed using a variety of available media, we describe only one particular approach in detail: a cartoon format. This format was selected because it is accessible to a large portion of the population and allows the use of stories to illustrate complex processes.

13.1.2 Why Security Education Is Difficult

We believe that the educational aspect of security has not been given the attention it deserves, and that many skeptics have prematurely concluded that any involvement of the end user is doomed to fail. We hope that an improved understanding of the issues surrounding both online fraud and the ways in which people relate to potential threats may help develop educational approaches with better impact, and that at least *some* risky online behavior can be significantly curbed. However, the task of achieving this goal is far from trivial, owing to the complexity of phishing, crimeware, and associated threats. The problem is neither entirely technical nor entirely social in its nature, but rather a combination of the two, and numerous security vulnerabilities are associated with this combination.

Current educational efforts aimed at encouraging safe online behavior have limited efficacy. We argue that many educational efforts expect too much of the audience. Namely, many educational efforts aim at a rather technically knowledgeable reader and, therefore, do not reach the typical Internet user. For example, the Federal Trade Commission (FTC) advises people [132] to forward suspect emails with full headers, but without explaining what a full header is or how to view or forward it. Even though everyone with a networked computer has access to information that would allow them to learn how to view full headers, many users may be insufficiently motivated to find and read such information. As another example, APWG [17] advises users that unless an email is digitally signed, one cannot be sure it was not forged or spoofed. However, recent studies [141] have shown that typical users do not know how to benefit from the security guarantees offered by digitally signed email; moreover, most banks are reluctant to deploy technology to sign outgoing messages given their concern that doing so may drastically increase the number of calls made by recipients who are not familiar with signed email. Handling these calls would incur a cost that is believed to dwarf the savings obtained from the increased security. Thus signed emails are not as common as technologists believed they would be; their lack of popularity is also an outcome of the failure to deploy a public key infrastructure on a large scale.

At the same time as many educational efforts may expect users to be savvier than they are, many other efforts over-simplify the message in an effort to make it digestable to a general audience. For example, financial institutions often warn users not to follow hyperlinks in email messages. As of mid-2007, phishers had started to adapt to users being wary of clicking on links, instead suggesting to targeted individuals that they copy and paste URLs into the address bar. Given that no large-scale effort has warned against this particular attack, the new twist may very well be rather successful. The use of this trick by phishers also illustrates the need to teach people not only simplistic rules but instead to explain *why* one should or should not do a particular thing. Having a true understanding of the threat will help people adapt to changes. Thus, to create a lasting impact of the educational efforts, it is crucial not to teach people to recognize known phishing attempts, but instead to recognize the patterns behind them. This allows people to generalize and truly understand, but takes an even greater effort—on behalf of both the educator and the user.

Some overly simplified educational messages may elevate the risks to which compliant users expose themselves. As an example, consider the suggestion "you should communicate information such as credit card numbers or account information only via a secure web site or the telephone" [17]. While this advice would reduce the vulnerability to many attacks that are commonplace at the time of this writing, it may also increase people's vulnerability to vishing (or voice phishing) attacks, and to phishing/vishing hybrid attacks in which the user is sent an email that advises him or her to call the impersonated service provider using a number supplied in the email. This type of attack may become more common if takedown efforts become increasingly effective.

This example shows that some advice may cause problems if users follow it without much critical thought, which in turn suggests that simple rules may not be suitable for education if an attacker might potentially try to leverage the approaches used by the educational campaign. Thus phishing education may be harder to implement than other types of education, because it requires users to act against a threat that in itself is molded by what users understand. While software can be constantly patched to harden it against an evolving threat, it is more challenging to reeducate users to counter such changes.

Coming back to the conflicts between too demanding education and overly simplified education, we see that at the heart of the dilemma is the fact that *simple* rules do not capture the problem well, whereas *complex* rules do not captivate the audience. It is not easy to explain complex problems to users who often will not be highly motivated to learn until they have already suffered a bad experience. In addition, most people think they are being reasonably careful, and we all like to think that bad things happen to others only. As a result, current mainstream efforts do not attempt to cover advanced topics, recognizing that the typical user would be unlikely to spend enough time to understand anything but the basics.

For example, while research [200, 425] has identified a common inability to distinguish legitimate domain names from those used in cousin-name attacks or subdomain attacks, these topics are rarely addressed in educational efforts targeting typical Internet users. Examples of deceptive URLs of these types are www.citibank-secure-commection.com and www.chase.pin-reset.com, both of which have been shown to inspire confidence among typical users [425]. The same study showed that short URLs inspire more confidence than longer alternatives. There are plenty of examples of unnecessarily long URLs, and we do not even have to go beyond our bibliography to find such examples [51].

Another example of a neglected topic with high security relevance is malware. While almost all educational efforts indicate the importance of having up-to-date antivirus software installed, typical service providers fail to explain the complexity of malware to their clients or suggest ways to defend themselves against the threat. As an example, most people do not fully appreciate that software *they* opted to install—maybe because a friend suggested to do so—could, in fact, be malware. This is a serious security concern: A recent study [388] demonstrated a yield of more than 50% for one particular type of socially propagated malware attack.

A problem that exasperates those who focus on educating users about security is that it is not sufficient to explain the problems to the target audience; instead, users must also change their behavior. An oft-ignored point is that there is a tremendous discrepancy between what typical users *know* and what they *practice*. An example of this is illustrated by the recent studies involving eyeball tracking [477], in which it was concluded that most users rarely look for SSL indicators, much less choose to interact with them. Even so, most people understand that there is an association between security and the presence of an SSL lock. To make matters worse, many phishing attacks use SSL [387], so teaching users to look for an SSL lock may not be the best approach. Security education has to highlight the need for behavioral changes. We believe this is best achieved by illustrating the causality between behavior and security outcome, a task for which the cartoon format is well suited.

Many educational efforts—and in particular those employed by financial institutions—offer highly concentrated advice, often in an itemized format. While the material is correct and almost always constructive, it explains *what* to do as opposed to *what and why*. As such, it may be a better resource for users who already understand the problem than for the larger masses who do not. We think of this type of resource as a dictionary. Whereas no one would attempt to learn a new language from a dictionary alone, dictionaries fill an important role for people with a reasonable background and understanding.

Most existing techniques are best suited to deal with a static threat, which phishing arguably is not. There are several reasons for this preference. For instance, while it is easy to patch software frequently, it is not easy to convince people to educate and reeducate themselves on an ongoing basis. As a consequence, educational efforts must be able to deal with a changing threat (which may adapt to the educational message itself) without relying on constant updates of the material. Such updates are unlikely to be absorbed by the target audience in a timely manner. (While financial institutions, for example, could provide their clients with updated advice as often as they wish, such a move could backfire by breeding fear and prompting people to withdraw from online banking.) Game-based approaches, while being desirable to a large group of users, suffer from a high development cost associated with structural changes that may be necessary to address new topics and changing threats. In comparison, cartoons are lightweight enough to permit integration of new material at a low cost. Both games and cartoons can be designed to avoid the intimidation factor from which lists of abstract "dos and don'ts" typically seem to suffer.

While it is commonly agreed that typical Internet users do not fully understand how to stay safe against phishing, it has also been shown that available training material is surprisingly effective *when used* [223]. A reasonable conclusion one can draw from this finding is that typical consumers do not make sufficient use of available material. To entice the typical banking client to spend hours instead of seconds learning about security, it is necessary to make the educational message both accessible and enjoyable. This chapter describes a cartoon-based effort [386] aimed at reaching this goal as well as the campaign's underlying design principles. These relate to the manner in which material is selected, how the material is made accessible to a typical reader, and how repetition on a theme is used to create an immersion approach.

13.1.3 Some Existing Approaches

A growing body of literature has focused on trying to educate typical users of threats. Consumers are offered a range of books (e.g., [2, 18, 61, 129]) explaining identity theft, ways to stay safe, and means to recover from this kind of attack. These books often focus on a taxonomy of the common scams—for example, what happens in a 419 scam and why one must secure wireless networks. The exposition requires a fair amount of dedication from consumers for them to make substantial progress.

A variety of online resources are aimed at improving the public's understanding of risk. Banks (e.g., [51, 54]) and companies such as eBay [92], Microsoft [255], and

PayPal [304] also supply their own pages to warn users about the dangers of phishing and steps to avoid falling prey to these ruses. Pages such as eBay's Spoof Email Tutorial [93] teach basics about email spoofing as well as technical details regarding URLs and domain names, but with a very clear emphasis on recognizing spoofs on eBay and with a focus on commonly existing psychological twists only. PayPal [303] allows users to take a five-question test that is intended to identify risky behavior, but it is likely that a large portion of users get the highest score. This is not only due to the simplicity of the questions, but is also the result of the subject-expectancy effect—the cognitive bias that occurs when a subject expects a given result and, therefore, unconsciously manipulates an experiment or reports the expected result. There is a risk that users taking the test come away feeling overly confident of their abilities, rather than slightly humbled and intrigued to learn more.

Most financial institutions maintain a list of recommendations, typically in bullet format and fitting on one page. The advice is useful, but seldom communicates any understanding of *why* it is useful. It has been criticized as not being a helpful educational tool [70]. As such, the advice may often be ignored or forgotten, especially under duress, which is a commonly used approach of phishers. Apart from banks, many nonfinancial service providers also provide guidance. AT&T maintains sites [21, 22, 23] that stand out for having a larger degree of interactivity than most, which is believed to promote learning.

A recent academic effort [373] attempted to teach phishing awareness to a general audience using a computer-game–based approach; this approach shares the third design value (accessibility) with our approach, but achieves this goal in a different way, and using true user interaction. We believe that the game-based approach may have many benefits, but that it may fall short in that it may reach a somewhat limited demographic at this point. In related efforts, AT&T [21] and NetSmartzKids [273] use games to teach Internet security to children, and Hector's World [168] uses animation to reach the same goal.

Another approach that relies on user interaction to assess risks is the *phishing IQ test* [244], which scores the user's ability to recognize phishing instances. This approach, which can be thought of as an indirect educational approach, has been criticized for not measuring the ability of the test taker as much as his or her fears of phishing [8]. Embedded education [222] teaches people about phishing during their normal use of email.

Several movie-based efforts have sought to teach security awareness (see, e.g., [264, 460]). These particular examples are highly technical and are accessible only to expert audiences. Other movies [265] are easier to access but relatively brief and, therefore, communicate only a rather limited understanding of the threats and associated countermeasures. The prospect of the extensive effort required to use a movie format to communicate threats appears to offer this approach's significant benefits.

Some educational efforts [372] cover slightly irrelevant educational messages, such as encryption over wireless networks. While encryption is helpful to avoid eavesdropping, it is not a form of access control and does not secure the access points that use it. It is not clear that the educator always has a clear understanding of the threats. This is a pity, given the recent wealth of insights into the nature of the problem of phishing. In particular, there have been several recent advances toward understanding how typical users react to deceit [87, 125, 126, 202, 425, 481].

In this chapter, we describe how cartoons can be used as the main medium of communication. Graphical representations have unique advantages, given that words have context only in the culture of the speakers. That is certainly true when it comes to communication of technology-related messages. Scientists are lost in their own subculture-based vocabulary. In contrast, the concept that "A picture speaks a thousand words" has been used in numerous settings to communicate educational messages of importance. Historical, political, and social issues have all been expressed via editorial cartoons in newspapers and magazines for more than 150 years [286]. Very few people, regardless of their culture and nationality, would not recognize a picture of a soldier and a tank and the associated concept of war. Such images inspire alertness and worry to most people, young or old, a fact that highlights the notion that humans are visual by nature. Our minds cannot avoid making associations between images and experiences. Cartoons can be drawn to enhance specific messages while suppressing others, which provides an excellent tool for communicating complex concepts. A simple cartoon is a form of amplification through simplification [246].

HIV/AIDS education using cartoons was done in the New York subway system for a long period of time, in a way that was very clearly targeted to teenage readers. Copyright law is taught using a cartoon approach [15]. Teaching security, however, is slightly different from teaching other topics since—given the adversarial setting—one must assume that the adversary has access to the same educational material and will do his or her best to find ways of taking advantage of the way material is (or is not) taught. This must be a consideration when designing the educational effort: The effort may, in itself, change the nature of the topic associated with the education.

Some material intended to help the public better understand the threats associated with identify theft focuses on server-side issues and does not make recommendations to the reader [5]. While there may be no direct modification of behavior as a result of this kind of campaign, it may help bring the problem to the attention of the general public, which may in turn facilitate legislative efforts. This is another important role of education.

13.1.4 Some Problems with Practiced Approaches

Following the principle that we learn from our mistakes, we review some common drawbacks associated with mainstream educational techniques. We classify these disadvantages into general categories, and give examples to help make these categories concrete.

A sidebar from a phishing education effort in the *Reader's Digest* [372] provides tips for "Beating the Thieves":

- Install security software and stay current with the latest patches.
- Always be suspicious of unsolicited e-mail.
- Monitor the volume and origin of pop-up ads. A change may signal something sinister.
- Visit the FBI's new website lookstoogoodtobetrue.gov, for tips.
- Use debit cards like credit cards, i.e., with a signature, not a PIN code.
- If you live in one of the 20 states where it's possible, place a freeze on credit reports. This stops any credit activity in your name unless you specifically initiate it.
- Keep an eye out for "skimmers" lurking in places where you use cards.
- Enable encryption on wireless routers immediately upon setting up a home network.
- Shop only on secure websites (look for the padlock or "https" in the address bar); use credit, not debit, cards; don't store financial info in an "account" on the website.

However, a user who is nervous about software security patches, and who does not have a solid understanding of what a patch is and what it is not, may be tricked into installing undesirable software that claims to be a patch. In this case, it might instead be better for users to learn how to configure their computers to perform automated patching. Or perhaps it would have been more useful for the *Reader's Digest* list to explain the more complex picture of malware.

Similarly, while it is good to be wary of unsolicited email, the typical user receives contradictory advice in the form or large quantities of legitimate but unsolicited mail—sometimes even from the same institution that asked the user to be suspicious in the first place.

The third listed piece of advice (above) is well-meaning but hard to follow for the typical user. How does one monitor pop-up ads, and what should be done if there is a drastic change? Later, the user is encouraged to enable encryption on his or her router, but much more important advice would be to set a strong password.

Advice That Is Hard to Follow. Many current educational efforts suffer from giving advice that is hard to follow and that may, as a result, become entirely redundant at some point. An example of this type is the common piece of advice, "Do not click on links." Almost all companies with an Internet presence send email with hyperlinks. Many send unsolicited emails, and a large number of them send such emails to users who have not signed up for their services. The advice not to click on links is helpful to security in some instances, but following it would hamper the web browsing experience for many users.

Similarly, consumers are often advised to disable JavaScript. This, too, is advice that is hard to follow, given that web 2.0 applications rely on it being enabled. Consequently, more than 95% of all Internet users have JavaScript enabled.

Another example of advice that is hard to follow, taken from [368], suggests to the user to "Disable JavaScript or do not visit untrusted and trusted web sites at the same time." Whereas many users would be able to identify a clearly trusted site (say, their bank) as well as many clearly untrusted sites, few would be able to correctly identify randomly chosen sites. Almost no one can determine whether a site is trustworthy before actually having visited it.

Valid but Not Very Important Advice. Some advice is valid, but not very central to the security of the user. If we believe that there is an abundance of important advice to be given, and that the typical user can retain only a given amount of information, then this type of advice would amount to a lost opportunity. An example of this kind of advice is given in *Reader's Digest* [372]: "Enable encryption on wireless routers immediately upon setting up a home network." While this step protects against theft of service, it has little impact on the greater problem of phishing and is probably entirely overshadowed in terms of importance by a piece of advice that is not given: "Select a good password for your router immediately upon setting up a home network. Never use the factory-set password, as strangers on the Internet can easily look this up and access the security settings of your router." Typical Internet users are unaware of this threat and do not know that if their router becomes corrupted, it can steal passwords, mount pharming attacks [425], and block access to antivirus software updates [389]. Most users do not realize the ease with which a router can be infected [389, 425, 426].

Potentially Dangerous Education. Some advice may be both valid and important, but still pose a potential risk to users. In Reader's Digest [372], the reader gets the following advice: "Install security software and stay current with the latest patches." However, the reader is not told how to practically follow the advice and may become more vulnerable to an email that tells the user to install a given security patch. If such an email is spoofed to appear to come from the system administrator, then it may appear fully reasonable to many users to quickly install the required "patch." To make sure that the advice does not pose a risk to the user, it may sometimes be important to qualify exactly *how* to follow the advice and what *not* to do. This is particularly important given that phishers are likely to try to take advantage of habits that their intended victims have been trained to acquire. Another example of this type is to ask users to look for an SSL lock, implicitly equating its presence with security. This is a problem given the ease with which phishers can also use SSL [387].

If we see the creation of habits as a form of education, then another example of potentially dangerous education is a technique that financial institutions commonly use to authenticate themselves to their clients. Namely, many financial institutions authenticate themselves to clients by including "Email intended for your account ending in: XXXX" or a similar text in email communication. As has been shown elsewhere [425], most Internet users do not find a statement such as "Email intended for your account beginning with: XXXX" less trustworthy than a statement such as "Email intended for your account ending in: XXXX" in spite of the fact that the four first digits are possible to infer from the identity of the issuer (a fact that will not be lost on the phisher). Therefore, training users to accept the "last four" as a form of authentication makes them vulnerable to an attack in which the "first four" is used –at least in the absence of a carefully crafted educational campaign aimed at addressing this potential problem.

Advice That Is Not Absorbed. The most significant problem of many current approaches, though, might be that they do not entice the intended readership to spend considerable time and effort understanding the messages. A recent study [223] found that existing phishing education succeeds in communicating important security information, *if accessed*. The last point is the gist of the problem: Typical user education is *not* accessed by the typical consumer or is, at the very least, not given hours of attention and afterthought. We argue that many currently used approaches for teaching Internet security to typical consumers are analogous to a ski lesson in which there is no practice or feedback, but where the lesson consists of a single message: "Don't fall."

13.1.5 Educational Goals

The educational mission can be formulated, quite simply, as "Help typical users improve their security against online threats." This is not quite as straightforward as it may seem, but can be broken down into four partial goals.

Goal 1: Know Your Audience. It is important to understand what the typical user's limitations are—in terms of both what he or she knows and what he or she can reasonably be taught. As we have argued, it is a common mistake to expect too much from the user or to expect so little that the resulting educational message is reduced to sound bites.

It is tempting for security specialists to guess which problems typical users may have based on which problems they themselves perceive. This, however, is a fallacy, and one that led many to believe that the existence of SSL would lead to the failure of phishing as soon as awareness of the problem rose. User experiments, while often challenging to perform [121], provide a better understanding of the likely vulnerabilities.

Goal 2: Know Your Enemy. It is equally important to recognize what the threats *are* and what they may *become*. Namely, it is not helpful to secure users against only current threats, given the proven malleability of the threats. To understand the threats and their likely development, it is crucial to recognize that they have both a technological component and a human factor. The educational effort, too, must take both of these aspects into consideration.

Knowing how typical users relate to both user interfaces and deceit helps to anticipate potential trends in phishing. This can also be done by formulating technological hypotheses, from which one may infer the likely resulting threats. See [198] for an example of this approach.

Goal 3: Know How to Tell the Story. A third goal is to enable communication of insights. To make this possible, the material to be taught needs to be *accessible*. Many researchers agree that security is not a primary goal of the typical user (see, e.g., [257]). The educational technique must take this factor into consideration by making the material accessible to the target audience. This is closely related to the admonition to know one's audience.

Goal 4: Know How People Learn. A fourth and final goal is to facilitate learning. It is not sufficient for the educational material to be appropriately selected and communicated, because learning is not an instantaneous process. To maximize the benefit of the material, repeated exposure is necessary, and the material must be designed with this consideration in mind.

13.2 Case Study: A Cartoon Approach

The approach we describe here is exemplified in Figures 13.1 to 13.4, and is based on the four core principles presented above.

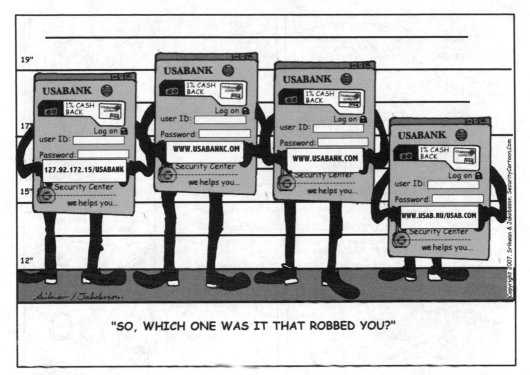

"SO, WHICH ONE WAS IT THAT ROBBED YOU?"

Figure 13.1: This cartoon is intended to increase the understanding of URLs, which is a difficult topic to teach. Typical computer users do not understand the difference between domains and subdomains and are easily fooled by cousin-name attacks, as supported by [200]. None of the large financial institutions attempts to teach its clients about URLs, despite this subject being an important topic for people to master to stay safe. One reason might be that URLs are complex, and an exhaustive set of rules describing their nature would be daunting for the typical consumer. The strip shows four Chase web pages in a line-up. Readers are asked who robbed them, forcing them to start comparing web pages. The only real differences between the web pages are the URLs. This cartoon is intended to reinforce the notion that copying logos is a functionality that is not beyond the reach for phishers, and to force readers to start comparing the URLs.

Research-Driven Content Selection. The educational material is tailored based on an understanding of actual user behavior, as observed in a collection of studies. For example, it has been shown that average users know that an IP address (instead of a regular domain name) signals danger, but do not have any understanding of the risks of cousin-name or subdomain attacks [200]. Similarly, another study showed a success rate of more than 50% for a simulated attack in which victims received an email from a friend in which they were told to run a program with a self-signed certificate [388]. This suggests that typical users do not distinguish well between *trusting their friend's taste* and *trusting their friend's ability to identify a threat.*

Figure 13.2: This cartoon strip shows how easily readers can be updated about recently occurring threats. This strip was developed in response to a wave of malware attacks that occurred in the late spring of 2007, where the recipient of the email was enticed to download content on the premises that it was a postcard from a friend. As described in [39], the attack vector involved both technical and human vulnerabilities in some instances, making this a rather sophisticated attack. Many educational efforts do not warn users against this type of threat, as they often warn users about emails sent from strangers—an email like this one is interpreted by many users as being sent (or at least initiated) by a friend. This is also an example of how attackers are likely to design attacks based on the contents of current educational efforts.

Correspondingly, our approach describes both user-propagated threats and the risks of user-installed programs having malicious content.

Accessibility. It is important to design the educational message in a way that does not alienate or bore the intended readership. Combining warnings with explanations and a "role playing" of consequences allows the reader to gain an intuitive understanding of why to follow given advice. We believe that this knowledge is important for a long-term adherence to the educational message. We let our educational message be framed as a cartoon, to avoid a compact "textbook" feeling, and to help the user identify with the characters in the story. We must

Figure 13.3: Most people are not willing to change their behavior unless they are given a good reason. Therefore, it is not enough to warn people about threats and say what they should and should not do. It is also important to explain what happens if they do not. This strip shows what happens to a victim of a keylogger (identified by the tentacled creature sticking out from his keyboard) and is a continuation on a sequence of strips in which keyloggers are introduced and the victim is infected by one.

remember that phishing education—and the exposure to it—is voluntary. Unless a given reader is highly motivated (which is not common), then the educational medium must make it easy to keep reading.

Immersion. To reach the desired results, we believe that the same message—framed in slightly different ways—needs to be repeatedly communicated to the reader. It is not enough to understand a concept once; the reader needs to practice acting in accordance with the message as well. This requires insight and understanding. This type of learning cannot be achieved simply by repeated use of one and the same message; instead, minor variations are necessary to retain the reader's interest. This principle is fully aligned with how other material is taught and learned: Addition and subtraction, for example, are learned by practice. Knowing the theory alone would not allow many people to obtain the skills needed to do arithmetic.

Figure 13.4: Many educational efforts focus on what to do and what not to do, but neglect to describe why. As a result, people draw their own conclusions, which sometimes leads to a degraded security awareness. This strip attempts to highlight one of these issues in the context of the configuration of home routers. Research [426] shows that less than 50% of consumer routers have been configured correctly, corresponding to a notable practical security vulnerability in the context of potential attacks such as the drive-by pharming attack described in Chapter 6 or the trawler phishing attack described in Chapter 5.

Adaptability. To help defend against a changing threat, it is important to be able to reflect changes rapidly and to communicate recent trends in a manner that allows for quick adoption of new practices. Cartoons permit this to be done, given their relatively low production costs. Furthermore, based on the accessibility and immersion principles, new advice will reach the target audience relatively quickly.

Conclusion

Existing educational approaches to improve secure behavior or the Internet may not be designed with the intended audience in mind. We have put forward a collection of techniques we believe may be useful in improving security education, and given a cartoon-based example of an approach embodying these suggested techniques.

Chapter 14

Surreptitious Code
and the Law*

Fred H. Cate

14.1 Introduction

Computer users increasingly confront software that collects information about them or asserts control over their computers without their knowledge or consent [116]. Whether labeled spyware, adware, ransomware, stealware, keyloggers, trojans, or rootkits, they have in common the fact that they are installed and operate without explicit user knowledge or consent [138]. Unlike earlier forms of code-based attacks that operated without any human intervention, these programs frequently exploit human credulity, cupidity, or naiveté to persuade or trick the computer user into downloading, installing, or executing them.

We often describe these programs collectively as "malicious code" or "malware," but these labels may not be accurate. For example, adware can improve the relevance of advertisements that users see and contribute to making certain programs or information available at no or low cost. Cookies can offer the same benefits as well as enhance consumer convenience and recognition when visiting familiar web sites. Spyware may include programs that allow parents to track their children's computer use or facilitate remote diagnostic testing of computers. These

---

*Editors' Note: To facilitate the readability of this chapter and make it accessible to a broader audience, many of the legal statutes are closely paraphrased rather than quoted exactly. In all cases, the citation for the actual statute is given.

uses are far from malicious, but the code may nevertheless operate without the knowledge of the computer user. Moreover, our current labels are not particularly helpful, because they often reflect judgments that are subjective and usually reflect a conclusion rather than aid in reaching one.

Determining whether programs are malicious—or illegal—often depends on a variety of factors. These include how the user obtained the software; what, if any, information was communicated to the user; whether that information was accurate and complete; which actions the user took in response; how the software operates; what effects it has on the user and the user's computer; whether it can be removed or disabled and, if so, how easily; and even in which state the user resides or the computer is located.

Finding the boundaries of what is lawful is made all the more difficult by the fact-specific nature of these inquiries, the variety of potentially relevant laws and precedents, and the speed with which new applications are evolving. Mistakes and uncertainty about where those boundaries lay pose real risks for programmers, users, researchers, and institutions.

These risks are exacerbated by our changing understanding of consent, including what is required for it to be legally binding. Historically, it was usually possible to avoid liability for installing or operating software simply by burying a disclosure of the existence of the software in the end-user license agreement (EULA)—the terms that a user must accept before most programs will install. It did not matter whether users read the disclosure or even whether they had a reasonable opportunity to read it.[1] Nor would it have mattered how unreasonable the terms of the disclosure were.[2] As long as the existence and operation of the program were accurately described, that would be sufficient.

More recently, however, the U.S. Federal Trade Commission (FTC) and courts have required that the disclosures be "conspicuous" and "material," and that the EULA be capable of being printed or stored. Otherwise, the consumer's "consent" is invalid. As a consequence, it is no longer possible to avoid liability merely through disclosure.

This chapter is concerned with the major legal provisions applicable to determining whether software that is installed or operates surreptitiously—that is, without the actual knowledge of the user—is legal. The chapter does not attempt to

---

1. See, e.g., *ProCD, Inc. v. Zeidenberg*, 86 F.3d 1447 (7th Cir., 1996).

2. The Federal Trade Commission once considered web sites as having a privacy policy even if that policy said users had no privacy, and considered web sites as providing security if their privacy policies referred to security. See Federal Trade Commission, *Privacy Online: Fair Information Practices in the Electronic Marketplace—A Report to Congress*, 11 (2000).

resolve whether a particular variety of surreptitious software is legal. It would be impossible to do so in the abstract, and any answer would likely be out-of-date before it was even published. Instead, this chapter tries to help the reader identify the important questions to ask about any program that installs or operates surreptitiously, and to highlight the legal significance of the answers. It is not intended to be legal advice, but rather to provide the reader with the information necessary to make informed decisions about when legal advice is necessary and whether the law applicable to surreptitious software needs to be supplemented or changed.

14.2 The Characteristics of Surreptitious Code

14.2.1 Surreptitious Download, Installation, or Operation

By definition, surreptitious code downloads, installs, and/or operates without actual user knowledge. This lack of knowledge may result from the user's failure to read a clear disclosure, an inadequate or incomplete disclosure (e.g., failing to disclose that the software will generate pop-up ads), a false disclosure (e.g., promising that the software will remove adware when it actually installs it), a fraudulent disclosure (e.g., when a phishing message or pharming site fraudulently adopts the name and logo of a legitimate business), or the absence of any disclosure at all (e.g., "drive-by" downloads that do not provide the user with notice and take advantage of browser vulnerabilities so that the browser provides no warning of the download). Often surreptitious code is bundled without notice with files that users know they are accessing—music, jokes, sexual images, or other programs ("lureware.") (See Chapter 3 for more details.)

14.2.2 Misrepresentation and Impersonation

Many types of surreptitious software not merely fail to disclose clearly their existence and operation, but actively deceive users about how they operate and what they do. Often this misrepresentation will involve impersonating a legitimate business or other organization through the use of its name, trademarks, and trade dress (e.g., the distinctive appearance of its web site or packaging). This is always true of phishing messages, phishing and pharming sites, and programs that generate messages and windows that appear to come from the operating system or browser. The Infostealer.Banker.D trojan, for example, is software that runs on the user's machine and injects HTML content into the user's web browser when the user visits sites such as paypal.com where sensitive information is shared. The user thinks the content is coming from PayPal, when in reality it is coming from the user's own machine; whatever information the user enters is sent to a third party at a remote location.[3]

Questions surrounding what constitutes "surreptitious" and "deceptive" downloading, installation, or operation of software are among the most difficult and most important under current U.S. law. While in some situations the answers are clear (e.g., phishing or a false or fraudulent disclosure), in many others they are not. For example, what about the disclosure of material terms buried in the midst of a EULA, the failure to disclose in detail all of the operations of a given piece of software, or the fact that the software operates differently than the user anticipated? The law has not yet provided clear answers to these questions, and what answers there are may be changing as policymakers expand their expectations about the comprehensiveness, prominence, and accessibility of disclosures necessary to avoid the label "spyware."

14.2.3 Collection and Transmission of Personal Data

Once present, surreptitious code often collects and transmits to third parties personal information about the computer user. The types of information and the uses to which it is put vary widely. For example, adware may monitor browsing habits to generate targeted advertising. Cookies often hold login and payment information so that the user does not have to reenter that same information in the future. Spyware, however, may collect those same data and transmit them to a third party to be used to commit financial fraud or identity theft.

14.2.4 Interference with Computer Operation

All software interferes to some extent with the operation of a computer by using the processor, occupying storage capacity, or requiring network bandwidth. With surreptitious software, the interference can be quite burdensome and occur in a wide variety of ways. For example, some software (e.g., backdoors) allows third parties literally to take control of a computer or even a network of infected computers (e.g., bot farms). Adware can generate pop-up ads that block the screen and require the user to divert his or her attention to closing the excess windows. Some programs can modify key system files, thereby destabilizing the computer. Dell reported in April 2004 that 25% of its service calls concerning spyware

---

3. http://www.symantec.com/enterprise/security_response/writeup.jsp?docid=2007-052710-0541-99

involved "significantly slowed computer performance."[4] Other surreptitious programs download files to the user's hard drive; these files may then be used to distribute surreptitious code, sexually explicit or copyrighted material, or spam. Other types of surreptitious software interfere with the operation of browsers and search engines by directing users to sites competing with those for which they are searching.

14.2.5 Perseverance of Surreptitious Software

Many creators of surreptitious software make their programs difficult to remove. They may avoid the operating system's Add/Remove Programs function or mask their software using operating system file names or by placing the software in directories usually reserved for operating system files. Rootkits are especially effective—and insidious—in using sophisticated techniques to hide their very existence (see Chapter 8 for more details). Some surreptitious software programs install thousands of files or make so many changes to the system registry that they are virtually impossible to detect and reverse completely. Another common technique is for surreptitious software to automatically reinstall itself when deleted.[5]

14.2.6 Other Burdens of Surreptitious Software

The effects of surreptitious software can extend far beyond interfering with the operation of individual computers. Many users report spending large amounts of time attempting to delete spyware or rebuilding systems that have been infected by them. Billions of dollars are spent each year on antivirus and anti-spyware software and updates. Microsoft reports that 50% of Windows XP operating system crashes are due to spyware.[6] Dell and McAfee report that spyware accounts for 10% to 12% of all technical support calls.[7] Surreptitious code can weaken computer security, interfere with online commerce, alter the behavior of web browsers and search engines, and compromise both individual privacy and the confidentiality of business information.

---

4. Federal Trade Commission, *"Monitoring Software" on Your PC: Spyware, Adware, and Other Software* (staff report, 2005), at 8. [Editors' Note: In footnotes in this chapter, references such as "at 8" refer to the page number in the source material.]

5. Id. at 7–8.

6. Id. at 8.

7. Id. at 12.

14.2.7 Exploitation of Intercepted Information

Information that is intercepted by surreptitious software can be exploited in a variety of ways that injure computer users—for example, to commit identity theft and perpetrate financial frauds. These activities are largely beyond the scope of this chapter. The use of another person's credit card number or account name and password to commit fraud is illegal, irrespective of how the information is obtained. Nevertheless, the intended use of data obtained through surreptitious software may be relevant to determining the legality of that software, because liability often depends on the purpose for which the information was taken.

14.3 Primary Applicable Laws

A variety of federal and state laws are applicable to many of the characteristic behaviors of surreptitious code described previously. As noted in the introduction to this chapter, it would be impossible to discuss them all. This section describes the four laws that are most applicable to surreptitious code and that have been most relied upon by litigants and courts in cases involving such software. Section 14.4 addresses a broader group of laws that apply to a narrower array of attributes of surreptitious code. All of the laws are summarized briefly in Table 14.1 beginning on page 442.

14.3.1 The Computer Fraud and Abuse Act

The Computer Fraud and Abuse Act is a federal law that creates a number of civil and criminal causes of action designed to prevent access to "protected computers" and exploitation of the information found there.[8] The term "protected computer," which originally limited application of the Act, was amended in 1996 to mean not only computers used by financial institutions and the federal government, but also any computer "which is used in interstate or foreign commerce or communication, including a computer located outside the United States that is used in a manner that affects interstate or foreign commerce or communication of the United States."[9] Given that almost any business computer or computer connected to the Internet would fit within this definition, the statute applies very broadly indeed.

---

8. 18 U.S.C. §§1030 et seq.
9. Id. §1030(e)(2).

The Act imposes liability on anyone who, among other things:

- Intentionally accesses a computer without authorization or exceeds authorized access, and thereby obtains information from a protected computer if the conduct involved an interstate or foreign communication; information contained in a financial record of a financial institution, or of a card issuer, or contained in a file of a consumer reporting agency on a consumer; or information from any department or agency of the United States.

- Knowingly and with intent to defraud, accesses a protected computer without authorization, or exceeds authorized access, and by means of such conduct furthers the intended fraud and obtains anything of value (if the object of the fraud or the thing obtained consists only of the use of the computer, the value of such use must be $5000 or more in any 1-year period).

- Knowingly causes the transmission of a program, information, code, or command that intentionally causes damage to a protected computer, or intentionally accesses a protected computer without authorization and causes damage (provided that the damage includes $5000 or more in damage to one or more persons; the modification or impairment of the medical examination, diagnosis, treatment, or care of one or more persons; physical injury; a threat to public health or safety; or any damage to a computer system used by the government in furtherance of the administration of justice, national defense, or national security).

- Intentionally and without authorization accesses any nonpublic computer of a department or agency of the United States.

- Knowingly and with intent to defraud traffics in any password or similar information through which a computer may be accessed without authorization, if such trafficking affects interstate or foreign commerce; or such computer is used by or for the government of the United States.[10]

The penalties for violating the Act include imprisonment for as long as 10 years for first offenses and 20 years for repeat offenses, as well as fines. In addition to enforcement by the government, the Act permits private parties "who suffer loss or damage" to sue.[11]

The Act clearly applies to many activities characteristic of surreptitious code—for example, intentionally accessing nonpublic government computers; intentionally collecting information from any financial institution, government, or

---

10. Id. §1030(a).
11. Id. §1030(g).

other "protected computer"; or trafficking in login information. If the conduct causes fraud or financial injury of $5000 or more aggregated across all people affected, or if it causes physical harm or threat to public health or safety, the penalties are greatly increased.

The repeated use of the phrase "without authorization or exceeds authorized access" makes clear that the Act will apply if the user has not authorized the access, the access was authorized based on false or deceptive information, or the access exceeded that which was authorized.

14.3.2 The Federal Trade Commission Act

Section 5(a) of the Federal Trade Commission Act, the statute that created and empowers the Commission, prohibits unfair or deceptive acts or practices affecting interstate and foreign commerce.[12] It is well settled that misrepresentations or omissions of material fact constitute deceptive acts or practices pursuant to section 5(a) of the FTC Act. For example, promising a customer that you will encrypt transactional data and then failing to do so is deceptive.

An act or practice is unfair if it causes or is likely to cause substantial injury to consumers that is not outweighed by countervailing benefits to consumers or to competition and that is not reasonably avoidable by consumers.[13] Thus the failure to use reasonable security measures to protect a customer's data, even in the absence of any promise to do so, is likely to be deemed "unfair."

The actions commonly associated with surreptitious code qualify as deceptive acts or practices if they involve false, fraudulent, or misleading disclosures. They qualify as unfair acts or practices if they harm the user—for example, by inundating the user with pop-up ads or substantially slowing the user's computer, especially if the software cannot be removed easily. Whether deceptive or unfair, the acts or practices will be subject to enforcement by the FTC as well as state attorneys general.

The FTC has made broad use of its section 5 authority in numerous cases involving spyware. For example, in the FTC's recent case against Direct Revenue, and related companies, the FTC alleged that the respondent companies acted deceptively and unfairly.[14] Deception was found in the fact that the respondent companies

> represented to consumers, expressly or by implication, that they would receive
> software programs either at no cost, or at the advertised cost. Respondents failed

---

12. 15 U.S.C. §45(a).

13. Id. §45(n).

14. *In the Matter of DirectRevenue, LLC, et al.,* Complaint, File No. 052 3131 (FTC, 2006).

to disclose, or failed to disclose adequately, that such software is bundled with respondents' adware, which tracks and stores information regarding consumers' Internet use and displays pop-up and other forms of advertisements on consumers' computers based on such use. The installation of such adware would be material to consumers in their decision whether to install software offered by respondents or their affiliates or sub-affiliates. The failure to disclose or adequately disclose this fact, in light of the representations made, was, and is, a deceptive act or practice.[15]

The FTC alleged unfairness based on both the surreptitious installation and operation of the adware and the difficulty of removing or disabling the adware. With regard to the installation and operation of the software, the FTC alleged:

> [R]espondents, through affiliates and sub-affiliates acting on behalf of and for the benefit of respondents, installed respondents' adware on consumers' computers entirely without notice or authorization. These practices caused consumers to receive unwanted pop-up and other advertisements and usurped their computers' memory and other resources. Consumers could not reasonably avoid this injury because respondents, through their affiliates and sub-affiliates, installed the adware on consumers' computers without their knowledge or authorization. Thus, respondents' practices have caused, or are likely to cause, substantial injury to consumers that is not reasonably avoidable by consumers themselves and not outweighed by benefits to consumers or competition. These acts and practices were, and are, unfair.[16]

Regarding the impediments to uninstalling the software, the FTC charged that "respondents failed to provide consumers with a reasonable and effective means to identify, locate, and remove respondents' adware from their computers."[17] In particular, the FTC noted the following practices:

- Failing to identify adequately the name or source of the adware in pop-up ads or other ads so as to enable consumers to locate the adware on their computers;
- Storing the adware files in locations on consumers' hard drives that are rarely accessed by consumers, such as in the Windows operating systems folder that principally contains core systems software;
- Writing the adware code in a manner ensuring that it will not be listed in the Windows Add/Remove utility in conjunction with the software with which it was originally bundled at installation;
- Failing to list the adware in the Windows Add/Remove utility, which is a customary location for user-initiated uninstall of software programs;
- Where the adware was listed in the Windows Add/Remove utility, listing it under names resembling core systems software or applications;

---

15. Id. at 5.
16. Id.
17. Id. at 5–6.

- Contractually requiring that affiliates write their software code in a manner ensuring that it does not uninstall respondents' adware when consumers uninstall the software with which it was bundled at installation;

- Installing technology on consumers' computers to reinstall the adware where it has been uninstalled by consumers through the Windows Add/Remove utility or deleted by consumers' anti-spyware or anti-adware programs; and/or

- [Providing] an uninstall tool [that] require[ed] consumers to follow a ten-step procedure, including downloading additional software and deactivating all third-party firewalls, thereby exposing consumers' computers to security risks.[18]

As a result of these practices, the FTC asserted:

Consumers thus have had to spend substantial time and/or money to locate and remove this adware from their computers. Consumers also were forced to disable various security software to uninstall respondents' adware, thereby exposing these computers to unnecessary security risks. Respondents' failure to provide a reasonable means to locate and remove their adware has caused, or is likely to cause, substantial injury to consumers that is not reasonably avoidable by consumers themselves and not outweighed by benefits to consumers or competition. These acts and practices were, and are, unfair.[19]

The FTC stressed that there was deception and unfairness even though the existence of the adware was disclosed in the EULA that was accessible through one or more hyperlinks. It noted that the "inconspicuous hyperlinks were located in a corner of the home pages offering the lureware and or in a modal box provided by the computer's operating system. Consumers were not required to click on any such hyperlink, or otherwise view the user agreement, in order to install the programs."[20]

Direct Revenue settled the case with the FTC by signing a 20-year consent agreement promising not to engage in similar activity in the future, and paying $1.5 million in restitution.[21]

The FTC has applied both the deception and the unfairness prongs of the FTC Act to phishing as well.[22] The analysis with regard to deception in phishing appears particularly applicable to deception in other surreptitious code contexts as well,

---

18. Id. at 4–5.

19. Id. at 6.

20. Id. at 3.

21. *In the Matter of DirectRevenue, LLC, et al.,* Agreement Containing Consent Order, File No. 052 3131, 5 (FTC 2007).

22. *Federal Trade Commission v. Hill,* H-03-5537 (S.D. Tex. 2003) (complaint). See also *Federal Trade Commission v. A Minor,* CV No. 03-5275 (C.D. Cal. 2003) (stipulated final judgment).

because the FTC argued that it was deceptive for the defendant to claim, "directly or indirectly, expressly or by implication, that the email messages he, or persons acting on his behalf, send and the web pages he, or persons acting on his behalf, operate on the Internet are sent by, operated by, and/or authorized by the consumers' Internet service provider or by the consumers' online payment service provider."[23]

14.3.3 Trespass to Chattels

The downloading, installation, and operation of surreptitious code may also constitute trespass to personal property—what the law usually calls "trespass to chattels." Until its recent re-invigoration, trespass to chattels was a little-known tort (a civil cause of action for injury to one's person, property, or legal interests) that fell between trespass (illegally occupying land) and theft (stealing personal, movable property). Historically, the tort required an intentional interference with the possession of personal property that caused an injury. Unlike theft, the tort does not require totally dispossessing the rightful owner; unlike trespass, some proof of harm or damage is required.

The trespass to chattels tort made its debut in the Internet context in 1997 in *CompuServe, Inc. v. Cyber Promotions, Inc.*[24] There, the district court found that the millions of unsolicited commercial emails sent by Cyber Promotions to CompuServe subscribers, over the repeated objections of both the subscribers and CompuServe, placed a "tremendous burden" on CompuServe's system, used "disk space[,] and drained the processing power" of its computers.[25]

From this fairly straightforward beginning, the tort has expanded in the Internet context into areas where both the interference with a possessory interest and the harm were less clear. For example in *eBuy, Inc. v. Bidder's Edge, Inc.*, the defendant Bidder's Edge operated a site that aggregated information from Internet auction sites.[26] The user would enter the item he or she was looking for, and Bidder's Edge would show on which, if any, major auction sites the item was available and at what current price. After an initially cooperative relationship with

---

23. *Federal Trade Commission v. Hill,* supra. For additional information on laws applicable to phishing generally, see Fred H. Cate, Liability for Phishing, in Markus Jakobsson & Steven Myers, eds., *Phishing and Countermeasures,* 671 (Wiley, 2007).
24. 962 F. Supp. 1015 (S.D. Ohio 1997).
25. Id.
26. 100 F. Supp. 2d 1058 (N.D. Cal. 2000).

eBay crumbled, Bidder's Edge adopted a strategy of using software robots to access eBay's site as many as 100,000 times per day to collect information on ongoing auctions. The district court concluded that accessing eBay's web site was actionable as a trespass to chattels not because it was unauthorized or because it imposed incremental cost on eBay, but rather on the basis that if Bidder's Edge was allowed to continue unchecked "it would encourage other auctions aggregators to engage in similar recursive searching," and that such searching could cause eBay to suffer "reduced system performance, system unavailability, or data losses."[27]

This ruling marked the beginning of a series of cases testing the limits of trespass to chattels' harm requirement. In *Register.com, Inc. v. Verio, Inc.*, the district court appeared to eliminate the harm requirement entirely when it concluded that a "mere possessory interference"—interference with the possession or use of personal property without demonstrating any resulting injury—was sufficient.[28]

Typically, trespass to chattels claims have been brought by Internet service providers or web site or network owners. However, there is no logical reason why such a claim could not be maintained by the owner of a computer that had been "occupied" by a creator or distributor of surreptitious code, making the computer more difficult to use or less efficient. This is precisely the reasoning of those courts that have considered trespass to chattels claims in response to spam, as noted by the California Supreme Court:

> A series of federal district court decisions, beginning with *CompuServe, Inc. v. Cyber Promotions, Inc.* . . . has approved the use of trespass to chattels as a theory of spammers' liability to ISP's, based upon evidence that the vast quantities of mail sent by spammers both overburdened the ISP's own computers and made the entire computer system harder to use for recipients, the ISP's customers. In those cases, . . . the underlying complaint was that the extraordinary quantity of UCE [unsolicited commercial email] impaired the computer system's functioning.[29]

That would appear to be precisely the claim that victims of surreptitious code would advance: Their computers were occupied by software that diminished their performance or usability. In *Sotelo v. DirectRevenue, LLC,*[30] a federal district court accepted precisely this claim. The fact that the plaintiff was an individual computer owner was deemed irrelevant: "The elements of trespass to personal property—interference and damage—do not hinge on the identity of the plaintiff, and the

---

27. Id. at 1066.

28. 126 F. Supp. 2d 238 (S.D.N.Y. 2000).

29. *Intel v. Hamidi,* 30 Cal. 4th 1342, 1348, 71 P.3d 296, 300 (2003) (citation omitted).

30. 384 F. Supp. 2d 1219 (N.D. Ill. 2005).

cause of action may be asserted by an individual computer user who alleges unauthorized electronic contact with his computer system that causes harm."[31] Moreover, other commentators have observed that "[t]he harm suffered to the plaintiff's computer (use of memory and screen pixels), is similar to the harm the court recognized the plaintiff had suffered in CompuServe"[9].

14.3.4 State Anti-Spyware Laws

Most states have laws like the FTC Act that protect against deceptive or unfair trade practices. Fourteen states, however, have gone further to enact laws specifically addressing surreptitious software. These laws apply both to activities that take place within each state and to activities directed toward the states' residents, irrespective of where the perpetrator is located. These laws typically fall into one of three categories.

The largest category includes the laws promulgated by Arizona, Arkansas, California, Georgia, Indiana, Iowa, Louisiana, New Hampshire, Texas, and Washington, all of which have adopted broad prohibitions against spyware.[32] Although not identical, all of these laws follow the same model. They prohibit any person other than the owner or authorized user of a computer from knowingly transmitting or copying software to a computer and using that software to do any of the following:

- Modify, through intentionally deceptive means, settings that control the page that appears when the user launches an Internet browser, the default search engine, or the user's list of web bookmarks. "Intentionally deceptive means" are defined as an intentionally and materially false or fraudulent statement; a statement or description that intentionally omits or misrepresents material information in order to deceive the user; or an intentional and material failure to provide notice to the user regarding the installation or execution of computer software in order to deceive the owner or operator.

- Collect, through intentionally deceptive means, personally identifiable information through the use of a keystroke logging function; in a manner that correlates the information with data respecting all or substantially all of

---

31. Id. at 1230.
32. Arizona Revised Statutes §§44-7301 to 44-7304; Arkansas Statutes Annotated §§4-111-101 to 4-111-105; California Business and Professions Code §22947; Official Code of Georgia Annotated §§16-9-152 to 16-9-157; Burns Indiana Code Annotated §24-4.8; Iowa Code §715; Louisiana Revised Statutes §§51:2006–51:2014; New Hampshire Revised Statutes Annotated §359; Texas Business and Commercial Code §§48.001-48.102; Revised Code of Washington §19.270.

the web sites visited by the user (other than web sites operated by the person collecting the information); or from the hard drive of the user's computer. "Personally identifiable information" is defined as first name or first initial in combination with last name; home or other physical address including street name; email address; a credit or debit card number or bank account number or any related password or access code; Social Security number, tax identification number, driver license number, passport number or any other government issued identification number; or account balance, overdraft history, or payment history if they identify the user.

- Prevent, through intentionally deceptive means, a user's reasonable efforts to block the installation or execution of computer software by causing that software automatically to reinstall or reactivate on the computer.

- Intentionally misrepresent that computer software will be uninstalled or disabled by a user's action.

- Through intentionally deceptive means, remove, disable, or render inoperative security, anti-spyware or antivirus computer software.

- Take control of the computer by accessing a computer or using its modem or network connection to cause damage to the computer or cause the user to incur financial charges for a service that the user has not authorized, or opening multiple, sequential, stand-alone advertisements without the authorization of the user and that a reasonable user cannot close without turning off the computer or closing the Internet browser. "Damage" is defined as any significant impairment to the integrity or availability of data, computer software, system, or information.

- Modify a computer's privacy or security settings for the purpose of stealing personally identifiable information about the user or causing damage to a computer.

- Prevent the user's reasonable efforts to block the installation of, or to disable, computer software, by presenting the user with an option to decline installation with knowledge that the installation will proceed even if the option is selected, or by falsely representing that computer software has been disabled.[33]

In addition, under these broad state laws, it is unlawful for any person to

- Induce the user to install a computer software component on the computer by intentionally misrepresenting the extent to which installing the software

---

33. See, e.g., Arizona Revised Statutes §§44-7301 to 44-7302.

is necessary for security or privacy reasons or in order to open, view, or play a particular type of content.

- Deceptively cause the execution on the computer of a software component with the intent of causing the user to use the component in a manner that violates any other provision of this section.[34]

There are broad exceptions for network and computer monitoring by a telecommunications carrier, cable operator, computer hardware or software provider, or provider of information service or interactive computer service. These exceptions apply if the purpose of the monitoring is for network or computer security, diagnostics, technical support, maintenance, repair, authorized updates of software or firmware, authorized remote system management, or detection or prevention of unauthorized or fraudulent use or other illegal activities in connection with a network, service, or computer software, including scanning for and removing software prescribed by law.[35]

Some states include additional provisions. For example, Arkansas has specifically provided in its spyware law that "[n]o person shall engage in phishing," and also declared that "[a]ny provision of a consumer contract that permits an intentionally deceptive practice prohibited under this section is not enforceable,"[36] thus eliminating consideration of whether the user agreed to a EULA that permitted the deceptive practice.

Depending on the state, damages for violating these statutes may include actual damages or statutory damages of up to $100,000 per violation, which in some states may be trebled if the defendant has engaged in a "pattern and practice" of violating these provisions (often defined as having engaged in the activity three or more times); court costs; attorneys' fees; and injunctions. Some states also provide for criminal penalties.[37] Civil lawsuits may be brought only by the state attorney general and the "computer software provider or a web site or trademark owner,"[38] No state allows individual computer users to sue under its anti-spyware law.

The second category of state responses focuses exclusively on the use of surreptitious software to trigger pop-up ads based on search engine terms and URLs, or even to alter search results or actually divert browsers to benefit

---

34. See, e.g., id. §44-7302(B).

35. See, e.g., id. §44-7302(C).

36. Arkansas Statutes Annotated §§4-111-103(d), (f).

37. See, e.g., Iowa Code §715.7; Louisiana Revised Statutes §51:2012; New Hampshire Revised Statutes Annotated §359:H3.

38. See, e.g., Arizona Revised Statutes §44-7304.

competing sites. Two states—Alaska and Utah—follow this approach.[39] Their laws prohibit "deceptive acts or practices . . . using spyware," but then define those very narrowly:

- Causing a pop-up advertisement to be shown on the computer screen of a user by means of a spyware program, knowing that the pop-up advertisement is triggered by a user accessing a specific trademark or web site, and the advertisement is purchased or acquired by someone other than the mark owner, a licensee, an authorized agent or user, or a person advertising the lawful sale, lease, or transfer of products bearing the mark through a secondary marketplace for the sale of goods or services.

- Purchasing advertising that violates the restriction on pop-up advertising if the purchaser of the advertising receives notice of the violation from the mark owner and fails to stop the violation.[40]

While this approach is noteworthy for its narrowness—it targets only one of the many types of damage that surreptitious code might cause—it does extend liability beyond the distributor of the code to include advertisers that pay for the code to be distributed.

The third category of state responses includes a handful of more idiosyncratic approaches to surreptitious code. Illinois, for example, recognizes an offense of "computer tampering," which includes the following activities:

- Accessing or causing to be accessed a computer, program, or data without authorization or in excess of any authorization.

- Inserting or attempting to insert a program into a computer or computer program knowing or having reason to believe that such program may damage or destroy that or another computer.

- Inserting or attempting to insert a program into a computer or computer program knowing or having reason to believe that such program may alter, delete or remove a computer program or data from that or another computer, or that may cause loss to the users of that or another computer.

- Falsifying or forging electronic mail transmission information or other routing information in any manner in connection with the transmission of unsolicited bulk electronic mail through or into the computer network of an electronic mail service provider or its subscribers.

---

39. Alaska Statutes §45.45.792; Utah Code Annotated §§13-40-101 to 13-40-201.
40. See, e.g., Alaska Statutes §45.45.792(a).

- Knowingly to sell, give, or otherwise distribute, or possess with the intent to sell, give, or distribute, software which is primarily designed for the purpose of facilitating or enabling the falsification of electronic mail transmission information or other routing information; has only a limited commercially significant purpose or use other than to facilitate or enable the falsification of electronic mail transmission information or other routing information; or is marketed for use in facilitating or enabling the falsification of electronic mail transmission information or other routing information.[41]

The law makes computer tampering a crime, and defines the offense as a felony if it involved collecting data or damaging a computer, program, or data.[42] Civil suits are permitted only for spyware that causes harm and for violations of the unsolicited bulk email provisions.[43]

Nevada has enacted some of the most sweeping restrictions on surreptitious code under the broad title, "Unlawful Acts Regarding Computers."[44] Under this law, anyone who "knowingly, willfully and without authorization" does any of the following commits a crime:

- Modifies, damages, destroys, discloses, uses, transfers, conceals, takes, retains possession of, copies, obtains or attempts to obtain access to, permits access to or causes to be accessed, or enters, data, a program or any supporting documents which exist inside or outside a computer, system, or network.

- Modifies, destroys, uses, takes, damages, transfers, conceals, copies, retains possession of, obtains or attempts to obtain access to, or permits access to or causes to be accessed equipment or supplies that are used or intended to be used in a computer, system, or network.

- Destroys, damages, takes, alters, transfers, discloses, conceals, copies, uses, retains possession of, obtains or attempts to obtain access to, or permits access to or causes to be accessed a computer, system, or network.

- Obtains and discloses, publishes, transfers, or uses a device used to access a computer, network, or data.

- Introduces, causes to be introduced or attempts to introduce a computer contaminant into a computer, system, or network. A "computer

---

41. 720 Illinois Compiled Statutes Annotated §5/16D-3(a).
42. Id. §5/16D-3(b).
43. Id.
44. Nevada Revised Statutes Annotated §205.4765.

contaminant" is defined as any data, information, image, program, signal, or sound that is designed or has the capability to contaminate, corrupt, consume, damage, destroy, disrupt, modify, record, or transmit any other data, information, image, program, signal, or sound contained in a computer, system or network without the knowledge or consent of the owner.[45]

A separate Illinois statute makes it a crime to knowingly, willfully, and without authorization interfere with the authorized use of a computer, system, or network, or to knowingly, willfully, and without authorization use, access, or attempt to access a computer, system, network, telecommunications device, telecommunications service, or information service.[46] Violation of these provisions is a misdemeanor criminal offense. If the violation was committed to defraud or illegally obtain property; caused loss, injury, or other damage in excess of $500; or caused an interruption or impairment of a public service (such as police or fire service), then it is a felony. In addition to the prison terms and fines normally used as penalties for a felony in Illinois, the court may impose an additional fine of up to $100,000 and is required to order the defendant to pay restitution.[47]

Many states, including California, Arkansas, and Texas, have adopted anti-phishing statutes along with their laws addressing surreptitious code.[48]

14.4 Secondary Applicable Laws

14.4.1 The Electronic Communications Privacy Act

The Electronic Communications Privacy Act of 1986 regulates the collection of information from electronic media and in other settings where there is an expectation of privacy.[49] It is divided into three major parts, all of which could be relevant to surreptitious code. Although the Act applies to activities of both the government and the private sector, the discussion here focuses on its application to private-sector collection of data through spyware and other surreptitious software.

The first and oldest part—Title I, the Wiretap Act—was adopted in 1968 and deals with the interception of communications in transmission.[50] The law prohibits

---

45. Id. §§205.4765(1)–205.4765(5), 205.4737.
46. Id. §205.477.
47. Id. §205.4765(6).
48. California Business and Professions Code §22948.2; Arkansas Code Annotated §4-111-103. Texas Business and Commercial Code §48.003.
49. 18 U.S.C. §§2510–2520, 2701–2709.
50. Wiretap Act, Pub. L. No. 90-351, 82 Stat. 197 (1968) (codified as amended at 18 U.S.C. §§2510–2522).

the interception of the "contents of any wire, electronic, or oral communications through the use of any electronic, mechanical, or other device."[51] Spyware that collected data from a computer user and transmitted it to a third party might well violate this provision.

Several exceptions and definitional issues must be addressed. For example, any party to a communication may consent to the interception or disclosure of the communication, unless it is for the purpose of committing an illegal act.[52] Thus, if the user agreed to the interception by accepting a EULA permitting it, the law would not be violated. (Many states have similar laws, but require the consent of all parties to a communication if the communication is to be recorded or intercepted.)

Similarly, most federal courts have found that there has been "interception" only when communications are acquired in transit and not from storage [35]. Moreover, two federal courts have held in cases involving keyloggers that only communications between the computer and an external network can be intercepted.[53] Collecting keystrokes between keyboard and CPU alone will not qualify as an "interception," so adware that does not communicate user data back to some other entity would not be affected by this law.

Finally, there is some ambiguity about the meaning of "content of a communication." Historically, the U.S. Congress has carefully distinguished information about a communication (e.g., address or phone number) from the content of the communication. The statute defines "content" to include "any information concerning the substance, purport, or meaning of that communication."[54] The U.S. Court of Appeals for the Fifth Circuit has found that this definition "encompasses personally identifiable information such as a party's name, date of birth, and medical condition."[55] If surreptitious code causes the interception of communications contents as they enter and leave a user's computer, Title I is clearly implicated. If the software captures only URLs and search terms, there is at least room for argument that this information does not constitute "content."

Title II—the Stored Communications Act—was adopted in 1986 and deals with communications in electronic storage, such as email and voice mail.[56] It provides

---

51. 18 U.S.C. §2510(4).

52. Id. §2511(2)d).

53. *United States v. Scarfo,* 180 F. Supp. 2d 573 (D.N.J. 2001); *United States v. Ropp,* 347 F. Supp. 2d 831 (C.D. Cal. 2004).

54. 18 U.S.C. §2510(8).

55. *In re Pharmatrak, Inc. Privacy Litigation,* 329 F.3d 9 (5th Cir. 2005).

56. Stored Communications Act, Pub. L. No. 99-508, Title II, §201, 100 Stat. 1848 (1986) (codified as amended at 18 U.S.C. §§2701–2711).

for criminal penalties and civil damages against anyone who "(1) intentionally accesses without authorization a facility through which an electronic communication service is provided; or (2) intentionally exceeds an authorization to access that facility; and thereby obtains, alters, or prevents authorized access to a wire or electronic communication while it is in electronic storage in such system."[57]

For Title II to apply, surreptitious code must gain unauthorized access to a "facility through which an electronic communications services is provided."[58] The term "facility" clearly includes telecommunications switches, mail servers, and even voicemail systems.[59] To apply to most surreptitious code, the user's hard drive would have to not only be a "facility," but one "through which an electronic communication service is provided." This issue remains unsettled, but at least one commentator has expressed skepticism that a hard drive would meet this definition.[60]

In addition, Title II applies only if the facility has been accessed without authorization or in excess of authorization, and, like Title I, contains an explicit exemption for consent.[61] If the user accepted a EULA as a condition of downloading the program or accessing the site that contained the surreptitious code, it is possible that he or she may have consented to the code's operation and that the access, even if it was to a facility, did not exceed authorization.

Title III—the Pen Register Act—was adopted in 1986 and significantly amended in 2001. It applies to "pen registers" (to record outgoing communications information) and "trap and trace" devices (to record incoming communications information).[62] The information captured by these devices includes what is contained in a phone bill or revealed by caller ID, email header information (the "To," "From," "Re," and "Date" lines in an email), and the IP address of a site visited on the web. Title III provides that "no person may install or use a pen register or a trap-and-trace device without first obtaining a court order."[63] As a practical matter, only state and federal government officials can apply for the necessary court order, so the law acts as a positive prohibition on private parties using these devices, unless an exception applies.

---

57. 18 U.S.C. §2701(a).
58. Id.
59. See Bellia, supra at 1313–1314.
60. See, e.g., id. at 1331–1335.
61. 18 U.S.C. §2701(c)(2).
62. Pen Register Act, Pub. L. No. 99-508, Title III, §301(a), 100 Stat. 1868 (1986) (codified as amended at 18 U.S.C. §§3121–3127).
63. 18 U.S.C. §3121(a).

Title III contains a variety of exceptions for communications service providers that are not likely to be relevant here, but it also includes an exception for user consent. As a result, the same questions arise regarding what the user consented to in the EULA and whether that consent is valid.

In sum, the Electronic Communications Privacy Act has yet to be applied consistently to surreptitious code. There are many fact-specific inquiries, as well as some ambiguity yet to be resolved by courts. The most obvious and consistent theme throughout the Act is consent. Some efforts to use the Act in connection with surreptitious code—primarily dealing with cookies—have foundered on the existence of consent.[64] But at least one lawsuit has survived the consent hurdle and, in the process, generated useful analysis of what consent requires.[65] In *In Re Pharmatrak, Inc. Privacy Litigation,* the U.S. Court of Appeals for the Fifth Circuit, drawing on prior cases, wrote:

> "[A] reviewing court must inquire into the dimensions of the consent and then ascertain whether the interception exceeded those boundaries." Consent may be explicit or implied, but it must be actual consent rather than constructive consent....
>
> Consent "should not casually be inferred." "Without actual notice, consent can only be implied when the surrounding circumstances convincingly show that the party knew about and consented to the interception." "Knowledge of the capability of monitoring alone cannot be considered implied consent." . . .
>
> Deficient notice will almost always defeat a claim of implied consent.[66]

This case and the authorities on which it relies suggest that for purposes of evaluating surreptitious code under electronic surveillance laws, in the absence of a clear disclosure of the data interception and transmission and evidence of consent more meaningful than merely installing a program, the consent exception will not apply. Specifically, it will certainly not apply where there is no notice or where consent is obtained through deception. This is consistent with the FTC's application of its deception and unfairness powers and suggests that surreptitious code that does act to intercept communications from a computer user to a network or web site or other person will be governed by the Electronic Communications Privacy Act.

---

64. See *In re Toys R Us, Inc. Privacy Litigation,* 2001 U.S. Dist. LEXIS 16947, 2001 WL 34517252 (N.D. Cal. Oct. 9, 2001); *Chance v. Avenue A, Inc.,* 165 F. Supp. 2d 1153 (W.D. Wash. 2001); *In re DoubleClick Inc. Privacy Litigation,* 154 F. Supp. 2d 497 (S.D.N.Y. 2001).

65. *In re Pharmatrak, Inc. Privacy Litigation,* 329 F.3d 9 (5th Cir. 2005).

66. Id. at 23–24, 27 (citations omitted).

14.4.2 The CAN-SPAM Act

The Controlling the Assault of Non-Solicited Pornography and Marketing Act of 2003 imposes a number of requirements and limitations on senders of unsolicited commercial email. These constraints would severely restrict the distribution of surreptitious code by spam and the exploitation of users' computers via surreptitious code to distribute spam. The Act creates six relevant criminal offenses:

- Accessing a computer connected to the Internet without authorization, and intentionally initiating the transmission of multiple commercial electronic mail messages from or through such computer;

- Using a computer connected to the Internet to relay or retransmit multiple commercial electronic mail messages, with the intent to deceive or mislead recipients, or any Internet access service, as to the origin of such messages;

- Materially falsifying header information (which includes "the source, destination and routing information attached to an electronic mail message, including the originating domain name and originating electronic mail address, and any other information that appears in the line identifying, or purporting to identify, a person initiating the message") in multiple commercial electronic mail messages and intentionally initiating the transmission of such messages;

- Registering, using information that materially falsifies the identity of the actual registrant, five or more electronic mail accounts or online user accounts or two or more domain names, and intentionally initiating the transmission of multiple commercial electronic mail messages from any combination of such accounts or domain names;

- Falsely representing oneself to be the registrant or the legitimate successor in interest to the registrant of five or more Internet Protocol addresses, and intentionally initiating the transmission of multiple commercial electronic mail messages from such addresses; or

- Conspiring to do any of these things.[67]

In addition to these criminal provisions, the CAN-SPAM Act contains a number of other requirements applicable to commercial emailers that the distribution of surreptitious code via email is likely to violate. The Act

- Prohibits false and misleading header information;
- Prohibits deceptive subject headings;

---

67. 18 U.S.C. §1037(a).

- Requires that commercial email include a functioning return email address or other Internet-based opt-out system;

- Requires senders of commercial email to respect opt-out requests;

- Requires that commercial email contain a clear and conspicuous indication of the commercial nature of the message, notice of the opportunity to opt out, and a valid postal address for the sender; and

- Prohibits the transmission of commercial email using email addresses obtained through automated harvesting or dictionary attacks.[68]

Penalties for violating the criminal provisions include imprisonment for up to five years and a fine. Violation of the civil provisions may be punished by assessment of actual damages and statutory damages of as much as $2 million, which may be trebled if the defendant acted willfully or knowingly.

14.4.3 Intellectual Property Laws

Under the federal Trademark Act of 1946, called the Lanham Act, a trademark protects a word, phrase, symbol, or design used with a product or service in the marketplace.[69] A trademark may be thought of as a "brand." Most company and product names and logos, as well as many domain names, are trademarks. Trademarks that are registered with the U.S. Trademark Office are usually accompanied by an ®. But trademarks do not have to be registered to be protected, and unregistered trademarks are often indicated with a TM (or SM, which indicates an unregistered mark in connection with a service). Trademark rights may continue indefinitely, as long as the mark is not abandoned by the trademark owner or rendered generic by having lost its significance in the market.

Anyone who uses a trademark in a way that confuses or deceives the audience as to the source of the product or service, or that dilutes the uniqueness of the mark, may be liable under federal law. For example, the Lanham Act provides for causes of action for misappropriation of a trademark, "passing off" the goods of services of one entity for those of another, and false advertising.

Surreptitious code may run afoul of federal trademark laws in a number of ways, but three means appear most immediately relevant. First, if the code is distributed in deceptive ways that falsely employ the name, logo, slogan, domain name, or trade dress of a legitimate business, a trademark claim may arise. Second, if the code

---

68. 15 U.S.C. §7704.
69. Id. §§1051 et seq.

operates to generate specific search results or direct the browser to specific web sites when the user searches for a trademarked name, a trademark claim may arise. (Recall that this activity is also regulated by state laws adopted in Alaska and Utah.) Finally, if the surreptitious code involves phishing or pharming, which by definition involve the impersonation of a legitimate business, a trademark claim may arise.

Most states have unfair competition and false designation or origin statutes or common law provisions that mirror the Lanham Act.

14.4.4 Identity Theft and Fraud Laws

The Identity Theft and Assumption Deterrence Act of 1998, as the title suggests, largely targets identity theft per se, but it is written sufficiently broadly that it also applies to the acts of obtaining and using information through surreptitious software.[70] The act makes it a crime, among other activities, knowingly to

- Transfer or use, without lawful authority, a means of identification of another person with the intent to commit, or to aid or abet, any unlawful activity that constitutes a violation of Federal law, or that constitutes a felony under any applicable state or local law; or

- Traffic in false authentication features for use in false identification documents, document-making implements, or means of identification.[71]

The law defines "means of identification" to mean "any name or number that may be used, alone or in conjunction with any other information, to identify a specific individual," including any

- Name, Social Security number, date of birth, official state or government issued driver's license or identification number, alien registration number, government passport number, employer or taxpayer identification number;

- Unique biometric data, such as fingerprint, voice print, retina or iris image, or other unique physical representation;

- Unique electronic identification number, address, or routing code; or

- Telecommunication identifying information (telephone number) or access device (account number or password).[72]

---

70. 18 U.S.C. §1028.

71. Id. §1028(a).

72. Id. §1028(d)(7).

"Traffic" is defined to mean "to transport, transfer, or otherwise dispose of, to another, as consideration for anything of value; or to make or obtain control of with intent to so transport, transfer, or otherwise dispose of."[73]

Prior to passage of this act, most laws did not treat the individual whose identity was being impersonated as a "victim." The retailer, bank, or insurance company that had been defrauded was considered a victim, but, unless the individual whose identity had been taken had also been defrauded, the law did not recognize that he or she had been injured. As a consequence, the individual had no standing before a government agency or court.

The act changed all of that by making identity theft itself a separate offense. As a result of these very broad provisions, obtaining, storing, transferring, or using a name, Social Security number, date of birth, account number, password, or other means of identification or account access with the intent to commit or assist any felony is a separate criminal offense under this statute. Penalties include up to 15 years in prison, up to 20 years for repeat offenses, and up to 25 years if the fraud is in connection with international terrorism, as well as a fine.[74]

The Act also assigned responsibility for violations to a variety of federal agencies, including the U.S. Secret Service, the Social Security Administration, the Federal Bureau of Investigation, and the U.S. Postal Inspection Service. Such crimes are now prosecuted by the U.S. Department of Justice. This law also allows for restitution for victims.

All but two states—Colorado and Vermont—have also criminalized identity theft as a separate offense, distinct from any other crime committed by the identity thief.

The Credit Card (or "Access Device") Fraud Act was designed to deal with the production and use of fraudulent credit cards, card-processing equipment, and other "access devices."[75] It might, therefore, appear to have little application to surreptitious software. However, the statute's terms are so broad as to apply to some types of such software. For example, the act defines "access device" to include

> any card, plate, code, account number, electronic serial number, mobile identification number, personal identification number, or other telecommunications service, equipment, or instrument identifier, or other means of account access that can be used, alone or in conjunction with another access device, to obtain money, goods, services, or any other thing of value, or that can be used to initiate a transfer of funds (other than a transfer originated solely by paper instrument).[76]

---

73. Id. §1028(d)(12).
74. Id. §1028(b).
75. Id. §§1029.
76. Id. §1829(e)(1).

The act makes it a criminal offense to "knowingly and with intent to defraud" (among other things)

- Produce, use, or traffic in one or more counterfeit access devices;
- Traffic in or use one or more unauthorized access devices during any one-year period, and by such conduct obtain anything of value aggregating $1000 or more during that period;
- Possess fifteen or more devices which are counterfeit or unauthorized access devices;
- Produce, traffic in, have control or custody of, or possess device-making equipment;
- Effect transactions, with 1 or more access devices issued to another person or persons, to receive payment or any other thing of value during any 1-year period the aggregate value of which is equal to or greater than $1000; . . .
- Without the authorization of the credit card system member or its agent, cause or arrange for another person to present to the member or its agent, for payment, 1 or more evidences or records of transactions made by an access device.[77]

The act provides for stiff penalties—up to 15 years in prison and up to 20 for repeat offenses under this law, as well as a fine.[78]

Surreptitious software can also violate the Federal Wire Fraud Statute, which creates a criminal offense applicable to:

> Whoever, having devised or intending to devise any scheme or artifice to defraud, or for obtaining money or property by means of false or fraudulent pretenses, representations, or promises, transmits or causes to be transmitted by means of wire, radio, or television communication in interstate or foreign commerce, any writings, signs, signals, pictures, or sounds for the purpose of executing such scheme or artifice.[79]

Violators are subject to 20 years in prison, or 30 years if a financial institution is affected, as well as a fine.[80]

As with all of the criminal provisions discussed in this chapter, the federal wire fraud statute applies to conduct that affects interstate commerce and U.S. commerce with other nations. U.S. courts tend to interpret these terms broadly to apply U.S. law to situations in which either the perpetrator or the victim of the

---

77. Id. §1029(a).
78. Id. §1029(c).
79. Id. §1343.
80. Id.

fraud is located within U.S. territory, and even to situations where neither is located in U.S. territory as long as the conduct affects U.S. commerce.

14.4.5 Pretexting Laws

Section 521 of the Gramm-Leach-Bliley Financial Services Modernization Act, which took effect in 1999, prohibits any person from obtaining or attempting to obtain "customer information of a financial institution relating to another person . . . by making a false, fictitious, or fraudulent statement or representation to a customer of a financial institution"—a practice commonly referred to as "pretexting."[81] Section 527(2) defines customer information of a financial institution as "any information maintained by or for a financial institution which is derived from the relationship between the financial institution and a customer of the financial institution and is identified with the customer."[82]

As a result, it is logical to conclude, and the FTC has argued in the context of phishing, that fraudulently obtaining financial account, credit card, or other information necessary to access a financial institution account, even though the information is obtained from the customer rather than the institution, is a violation of this provision.[83] This would be true even if the information were never used to access the account or to otherwise steal money from the individual or the institution.

If true with regard to phishing, the same argument would seem to have equal force where surreptitious code is downloaded or installed subject to a "false, fictitious, or fraudulent statement or representation" and operates to obtain "customer information," including account, credit card, or other information necessary to access a financial institution account.

14.4.6 State Theft Laws

Obtaining, or attempting to obtain, valuable information under false pretenses would likely violate criminal conversion laws in every state. For example, Indiana law—like the laws of most states—provides that a "person who knowingly or

---

81. 15 U.S.C. §6821.

82. Id. §6827(2).

83. *Federal Trade Commission v. Hill*, H-03-5537 (S.D. Tex. 2003) (complaint) ("By making . . . false, fictitious, or fraudulent representations to customers of financial institutions, defendant obtained 'customer information of a financial institution' including credit card numbers, debit card numbers, card lists, PIN numbers, [other identifying] numbers, bank account numbers, bank account routing numbers, or PayPal access information [in violation of] Section 521 of the GLB Act, 15 U.S.C. §6821.").

intentionally exerts unauthorized control over property of another person commits criminal conversion"; in lay terms, the person commits "theft."[84]

The law defines "to exert control over property" broadly to mean "to obtain, take, carry, drive, lead away, conceal, abandon, sell, convey, encumber, or possess property, or to secure, transfer, or extend a right to property." That control is "unauthorized" if it is exerted, among other ways, by "creating or confirming a false impression in the other person" or by "promising performance that the person knows will not be performed."[85]

Similarly, Indiana law criminalizes "criminal mischief," which it defines to include "knowingly or intentionally caus[ing] another to suffer pecuniary loss by deception."[86] This aptly describes the behavior of much surreptitious code.

Conclusion

It is plain even from this brief survey that there is no shortage of laws applicable to surreptitious code and that those laws reach most, if not all, attributes of how such code is downloaded, installed, and used. At the FTC's 2005 Spyware Workshop, both the FTC staff and the Department of Justice officials who participated stressed that their current statutory authority was sufficient to prosecute spyware distributors.[87] Since then, 13 additional states have adopted relevant legislation. The FTC has brought numerous cases under its section 5 authority to prosecute deceptive or unfair acts and practices, as have states' attorneys general under state laws. In January 2007, the New York Attorney General demonstrated just how far the law reaches by settling a major case against Priceline, Travelocity, and Cingular for promoting their products and services through adware, even though the adware was placed by third parties.[88]

In addition to the Federal Trade Commission Act and state consumer protection laws, the Computer Fraud and Abuse Act, the common-law trespass to chattels doctrine, and state anti-spyware laws have been used to target surreptitious code. Many other laws may eventually be brought to bear in this area. To be sure, there are inherent difficulties associated with investigating and prosecuting cases involving surreptitious code, owing to the challenges associated

---

84. Burns Indiana Code Annotated §35-43-4-3.

85. Id. §§35-43-4-1(a), (b)(4), (b)(6).

86. Id. §35-43-1-2(a)(2).

87. *"Monitoring Software" on Your PC,* supra at 20.

88. Advertisers Settle Claims for Adware Distributed by Intermediaries, 24(4) *Computer & Internet Lawyer* 48 (2007).

with its global perpetrators, fast-changing tactics, and surreptitious nature.[89] And law is only one—and perhaps the least important one—of many tools for dealing with surreptitious code. Technologies and consumer education are equally, if not more, important. Even so, there is plenty of relevant law, its reach is very broad, penalties can be staggering, and enforcement does work.

In fact, the major issue about law may be not whether there are enough laws, but rather whether there are too many laws or too much ambiguity in existing laws. Because of the breadth of many of the applicable laws, even software features that are intended to be innocent or beneficial may run the risk of creating liability. For example, adware to improve the relevance of advertisements to users, cookies that enhance consumer convenience and recognition when visiting familiar web sites, and monitoring software that allows parents to track their children's computer use or facilitate remote diagnostic testing of computers all run the risk of violating the law if not deployed with clear, conspicuous notice and consent. Because of the variety and complexity of applicable laws, determining precisely what is and what is not permitted is rarely easy or certain, but it is essential to diminish the risk of liability.

---

89. *"Monitoring Software" on Your PC,* supra at 22.

Name and Cite	Application/Definition	Causes of Action	Penalties
Federal Laws			
Controlling the Assault of Non-Solicited Pornography and Marketing Act of 2003 (CAN-SPAM Act), 18 U.S.C. §1037(a), 15 U.S.C. §7704		Accessing a computer connected to the Internet without authorization, and intentionally initiating the transmission of multiple commercial electronic mail messages from or through such computer; Using a computer connected to the Internet to relay or retransmit multiple commercial electronic mail messages, with the intent to deceive or mislead recipients, or any Internet access service, as to the origin of such messages; Materially falsifying header information (which includes "the source, destination, and routing information attached to an electronic mail message, including the originating domain name and originating electronic mail address, and any other information that appears in the line identifying, or purporting to identify, a person initiating the message") in multiple commercial electronic mail messages and intentionally initiating the transmission of such messages; Registering, using information that materially falsifies the identity of the actual registrant, five or more electronic mail accounts or online user accounts or two or more domain names, and intentionally initiating the transmission of multiple commercial electronic mail messages from any combination of such accounts or domain names; Falsely representing oneself to be the registrant or the legitimate successor in interest to the	Penalties for violating the criminal provisions include imprisonment for up to five years and a fine, and for violation of the civil provisions include actual damages and statutory damages of as much as $2 million, which may be trebled if the defendant acted willfully or knowingly.

Table 14.1: Overview of laws relating to surreptitious code.

Name and Cite	Application/Definition	Causes of Action	Penalties
Federal Laws			
		registrant of five or more Internet Protocol addresses, and intentionally initiating the transmission of multiple commercial electronic mail messages from such addresses; or	
		Conspiring to do any of these things. 18 U.S.C. §1037(a).	
		The Act also:	
		prohibits false and misleading header information;	
		prohibits deceptive subject headings;	
		requires that commercial email include a functioning return email address or other Internet-based opt-out system;	
		requires senders of commercial email to respect opt-out requests;	
		requires that commercial email contain a clear and conspicuous indication of the commercial nature of the message, notice of the opportunity to opt out, and a valid postal address for the sender; and	
		prohibits the transmission of commercial email using email addresses obtained through automated harvesting or dictionary attacks. 15 U.S.C. §7704.	
Computer Fraud and Abuse Act, 18 U.S.C. §§1030 et seq.	Applies to "protected computers," the definition of which was amended in 1996 to include computers used by financial institutions and the federal government, and any computer "which is used in interstate or foreign commerce or communication,	Intentionally accessing a computer without authorization or exceeding authorized access, and thereby obtaining information from a protected computer, if the conduct involved an interstate or foreign communication; information contained in a financial record of a financial institution or of a card issuer or contained in a file of a consumer reporting agency on a	Imprisonment for as long as 10 years for first offenses, and 20 years for repeat offenses, as well as fines. In addition to enforcement by the government, the Act also permits private parties "who

Name and Cite	Application/Definition	Causes of Action	Penalties
Federal Laws			
	including a computer located outside the United States that is used in a manner that affects interstate or foreign commerce or communication of the United States." 18 U.S.C. §1030(e)(2).	consumer; or information from any department or agency of the United States.

Knowingly and with intent to defraud, accessing a protected computer without authorization, or exceeding authorized access, and by means of such conduct furthering the intended fraud and obtaining anything of value (if the object of the fraud or the thing obtained consists only of the use of the computer, the value of such use must be $5,000 or more in any 1-year period).

Knowingly causing the transmission of a program, information, code, or command that intentionally causes damage to a protected computer, or intentionally accesses a protected computer without authorization and causes damage (provided that the damage includes $5,000 or more in damage to one or more persons; the modification or impairment of the medical examination, diagnosis, treatment, or care of one or more persons; physical injury; a threat to public health or safety; or any damage to a computer system used by the government in furtherance of the administration of justice, national defense, or national security).

Intentionally and without authorization accessing any nonpublic computer of a department or agency of the United States.

Knowingly and with intent to defraud trafficking in any password or similar information through which a computer may be | suffer loss or damage" to sue. Id. §1030(g).

If the conduct causes fraud or financial injury of $5000 or more aggregated across all people affected, or physical harm or threat to public health or safety, the penalties are greatly increased. |

Table 14.1: Overview of laws relating to surreptitious code. (*Continued*)

Name and Cite	Application/Definition	Causes of Action	Penalties
Federal Laws			
		accessed without authorization, if such trafficking affects interstate or foreign commerce; or such computer is used by or for the government of the United States. Id. §1030(a).	
Credit Card (or **"Access Device"**) **Fraud Act**, 18 U.S.C. §§1029 et seq.	The Act defines "access device" to include: "any card, plate, code, account number, electronic serial number, mobile identification number, personal identification number, or other telecommunications service, equipment, or instrument identifier, or other means of account access that can be used, alone or in conjunction with another access device, to obtain money, goods, services, or any other thing of value, or that can be used to initiate a transfer of funds (other than a transfer originated solely by paper instrument). 18 U.S.C. §1829(e)(1).	The Act makes it a criminal offense to "knowingly and with intent to defraud," among other things: produce, use, or traffic in one or more counterfeit access devices; traffic in or use one or more unauthorized access devices during any one-year period, and by such conduct obtain anything of value aggregating $1,000 or more during that period; possess fifteen or more devices which are counterfeit or unauthorized access devices; produce, traffic in, have control or custody of, or possess device-making equipment; effect transactions, with 1 or more access devices issued to another person or persons, to receive payment or any other thing of value during any 1-year period the aggregate value of which is equal to or greater than $1,000; ... without the authorization of the credit card system member or its agent, cause or arrange for another person to present to the member or its agent, for payment, 1 or more evidences or records of transactions made by an access device. 18 U.S.C. §1029(a).	Up to 15 years in prison and up to 20 for repeat offenses under this law, as well as a fine. 18 U.S.C. §1029(c).
Electronic Communications Privacy Act, Title 1, the **Wiretap Act**, 18 U.S.C. §§2510 et seq.		Prohibits the interception of the "contents of any wire, electronic, or oral communications through the use of any electronic, mechanical, or other device." 18 U.S.C. §2510(4). Exception for consent. Also, most federal courts have found that there has been "interception" only when communications are acquired in	

Name and Cite	Application/Definition	Causes of Action	Penalties
Federal Laws			
		transit and not from storage. Two federal courts have held in cases involving keyloggers that only communications between the computer and an external network can be intercepted. *United States v. Scarfo,* 180 F. Supp. 2d 573 (D.N.J. 2001); *United States v. Ropp,* 347 F. Supp. 2d 831 (C.D. Cal. 2004).	
Electronic Communications Privacy Act, Title II, the **Stored Communications Act,** 18 U.S.C. §§2701 et seq.	Applies to facilities through which an electronic communication service is provided. This clearly includes telecommunications switches, mail servers, and even voicemail systems.	Provide for liability against one who "(1) intentionally accesses without authorization a facility through which an electronic communication service is provided; or (2) intentionally exceeds an authorization to access that facility; and thereby obtains, alters, or prevents authorized access to a wire or electronic communication while it is in electronic storage in such system." 18 U.S.C. §2701 (a). Exception for consent.	Criminal penalties and civil damages.
Electronic Communications Privacy Act, Title III, the **Pen Register Act,** 18 U.S.C. §§3121 et seq.	Applies to "pen registers" (to record out-going communications information) and "trap and trace" devices (to record in-coming communications information). The information captured by these devices includes what is contained in a phone bill or revealed by Caller ID, email header information (the "To," "From," "Re," and "Date" lines in an email), and the IP address of a site visited on the web.	Provides that "no person may install or use a pen register or a trap and trace device without first obtaining a court order." 18 U.S.C. §3121(a). As a practical matter, only state and federal government officials can apply for the necessary court order, so the law acts as a positive prohibition on private parties using these devices, unless an exception applies. Exception for consent.	
Federal Trade Commission Act, 15 U.S.C. §45(a)	Activities affecting interstate and foreign commerce	Declares unlawful "unfair or deceptive acts or practices" 15 U.S.C. §45(a). Misrepresentations or omissions of matarial fact constitute *deceptive* acts or practices. An act or practice is	

Table 14.1: Overview of laws relating to surreptitious code. (*Continued*)

Name and Cite	Application/Definition	Causes of Action	Penalties
Federal Laws			
		unfair if it causes or is likely to cause substantial injury to consumers that is not outweighed by countervailing benefits to consumers or to competition and that is not reasonably avoidable by consumers. Id. §45(n).	
Federal Trademark Act of 1946 (the **Lanham Act**), 15 U.S.C. §§1051 et seq.	A trademark protects a word, phrase, symbol, or design used with a product or service in the marketplace. Trademarks that are registered with the Trademark Office are usually accompanied by an ®. Unregistered trademarks are often indicated with a TM (or SM, which indicates an unregistered mark in connection with a service).	Anyone who uses a trademark in a way that confuses or deceives the audience as to the source of the product or service, or that dilutes the uniqueness of the mark, may be liable under federal law.	
Gramm-Leach-Billey Financial Services Modernization Act, 15 U.S.C. §§6801 et seq.	"Customer information of a financial institution" is "any information maintained by or for a financial institution which is derived from the relationship between the financial institution and a customer of the financial institution and is identified with the customer." 15 U.S.C. §6827(2).	Prohibits any person from obtaining or attempting to obtain "customer information of a financial institution relating to another person ... by making a false, fictitious, or fraudulent statement or representation to a customer of a financial institution"—a practice commonly referred to as "pretexting." 15 U.S.C. §6821.	
The Identity Theft and Assumption Deterrence Act of 1998, 18 U.S.C. §1028	The law defines "means of identification" to mean "any name or number that may be used, alone or in conjunction with any other information, to identify a specific individual," including any: name, Social Security number, date of birth, official state or government issued driver's license or identification number, alien registration number, government passport number, employer or taxpayer identification number;	The act makes it a crime, among other activities, knowingly to: transfer or use, without lawful authority, a means of identification of another person with the intent to commit, or to aid or abet, any unlawful activity that constitutes a violation of Federal law, or that constitutes a felony under any applicable state or local	Penalties include up to 15 years in prison, up to 20 years for repeat offenses, and up to 25 years if the fraud is in connection with international terrorism, as well as a fine.

Name and Cite	Application/Definition	Causes of Action	Penalties
Federal Laws			
	unique biometric data, such as fingerprint, voice print, retina or iris image, or other unique physical representation; unique electronic identification number, address, or routing code; or telecommunication identifying information [telephone number] or access device [account number or password]. 18 U.S.C. §1028(d)(7). "Traffic" is defined to mean "to transport, transfer, or otherwise dispose of, to another, as consideration for anything of value; or to make or obtain control of with intent to so transport, transfer, or otherwise dispose of." 18 U.S.C. §1028(d)(12).	law; or traffic in false authentication features for use in false identification documents, document-making implements, or means of identification. 18 U.S.C §1028(a).	18 U.S.C. §1028(b).
Wire Fraud Statute, 18 U.S.C. §1343		Creates a criminal offense applicable to: whoever, having devised or intending to devise any scheme or artifice to defraud, or for obtaining money or property by means of false or fraudulent pretenses, representations, or promises, transmits or causes to be transmitted by means of wire, radio, or television communication in interstate or foreign commerce, any writings, signs, signals, pictures, or sounds for the purpose of executing such scheme or artifice. §1343.	Violators are subject to 20 years in prison, or 30 years if a financial institution is affected, as well as a fine.

Table 14.1: Overview of laws relating to surreptitious code. (*Continued*)

Name and Cite	Application/Definition	Causes of Action	Penalties
State Laws			
Anti-Spyware Laws I (Arizona Revised Statutes §§44-7301 to 7304; Arkansas Statutes Annotated §§4-111-101 to 105; California Business and Professions Code §22947; Official Code of Georgia Annotated §§16-9-152 to 157; Burns Indiana Code Annotated §24-4.8; Iowa Code §715; Louisiana Revised Statutes §§51:2006-2014; New Hampshire Revised Statutes Annotated §359; Texas Business and Commercial Code §§48.001-48.102; Revised Code of Washington §19.270)		These laws generally prohibit any person other than the owner or authorized user of a computer from knowingly transmitting or copying software to a computer and using that software to do any of the following: Modify, through intentionally deceptive means, settings that control the page that appears when the user launches an internet browser, the default search engine, or the user's list of web bookmarks. "Intentionally deceptive means" are defined as an intentionally and materially false or fraudulent statement; a statement or description that intentionally omits or misrepresents material information in order to deceive the user; or an intentional and material failure to provide notice to the user regarding the installation or execution of computer software in order to deceive the owner or operator. Collect, through intentionally deceptive means, personally identifiable information through the use of a keystroke logging function; in a manner that correlates the information with data respecting all or substantially all of the web sites visited by the user (other than web sites operated by the person collecting the information); or from the hard drive of the user's computer. "Personally identifiable information" is defined as first name or first initial in combination with last name;	Depending upon the state, damages for violating these statutes may include actual damages or statutory damages of up to $100,000 per violation, which in some states may be trebled if the defendant has engaged in a "pattern and practice" of violating these provisions (often defined as having engaged in the activity three or more times), court costs, attorneys fees, and injunctions. Some states also provide for criminal penalties. See, e.g., Iowa Code §715.7; Louisiana Revised Statutes §51:2012; New Hampshire Revised Statutes Annotated §359:I13. Civil lawsuits may be brought only by the state attorney general and "computer software provider or a web site or trademark owner." See, e.g., Arizona Revised Statutes §44-7304. No state allows individual computer users to sue under its anti-spyware law.

Name and Cite	Application/Definition	Causes of Action	Penalties
State Laws			

home or other physical address including street name; email address; a credit or debit card number or bank account number or any related password or access code; Social Security number, tax identification number, drivers license number, passport number or any other government issued identification number; or account balance, overdraft history, or payment history if they identify the user.

Prevent, through intentionally deceptive means, a user's reasonable efforts to block the installation or execution of computer software by causing that software automatically to reinstall or reactivate on the computer.

Intentionally misrepresent that computer software will be uninstalled or disabled by a user's action.

Through intentionally deceptive means, remove, disable, or render inoperative security, antispyware or antivirus computer software.

Take control of the computer by accessing a computer or using its modem or network connection to cause damage to the computer or cause the user to incur financial charges for a service that the user has not authorized, or opening multiple, sequential, stand-alone advertisements without the authorization of the user and that a reasonable user cannot close without turning off the computer or closing the internet browser. "Damage" is defined as any significant impairment to the integrity or availability of data, computer software, system, or information.

Modify a computer's privacy or security settings for the purpose of

Table 14.1: Overview of laws relating to surreptitious code. (*Continued*)

Name and Cite	Application/Definition	Causes of Action	Penalties
State Laws			

stealing personally identifiable information about the user or causing damage to a computer.

Prevent the user's reasonable efforts to block the installation of, or to disable, computer software, by presenting the user with an option to decline installation with knowledge that the installation will proceed even if the option is selected, or by falsely representing that computer software has been disabled. See, e.g., Arizona Revised Statutes §§44-7301 to 7302.

In addition, under these broad state laws, it is unlawful for any person to:

Induce the user to install a computer software component on the computer by intentionally misrepresenting the extent to which installing the software is necessary for security or privacy reasons or in order to open, view, or play a particular type of content.

Deceptively cause the execution on the computer of a software component with the intent of causing the user to use the component in a manner that violates any other provision of this section. See, e.g., Arizona Revised Statutes §44-7302(B).

There are broad exceptions for network and computer monitoring by a telecommunications carrier, cable operator, computer hardware or software provider, or provider of information service or interactive computer service, if the purpose of the monitoring is for network or computer security, diagnostics, technical support, maintenance, repair, authorized updates of software or firmware, authorized remote system management,

Name and Cite	Application/Definition	Causes of Action	Penalties
State Laws			
		detection or prevention of unauthorized or fraudulent use or other illegal activities in connection with a network, service, or computer software, including scanning for and removing software prescribed by law. See, e.g., Arizona Revised Statutes §44-7302(C).	
		Some states include additional provisions. For example, Arkansas has specifically provided in its spyware law that "[n]o person shall engage in phishing," and also declared that "[a]ny provision of a consumer contract that permits an intentionally deceptive practice prohibited under this section is not enforceable." Arkansas Statutes Annotated §§4-111-103(d), (f).	
Anti-Spyware Laws II (Alaska Statutes §45.45.792; Utah Code Annotated §§13-40-101 to 201)		Alaska and Utah prohibit "deceptive acts or practices ... using spyware," but define those narrowly to include only:	
		Causing a pop-up advertisement to be shown on the computer screen of a user by means of a spyware program, knowing that the pop-up advertisement is triggered by a user accessing a specific trademark or web site, and the advertisement is purchased or acquired by someone other than the mark owner, a licensee, an authorized agent or user, or a person advertising the lawful sale, lease, or transfer of products bearing the mark through a secondary marketplace for the sale of goods or services.	
		Purchasing advertising that violates the restriction on pop-up advertising if the purchaser of the advertising receives notice of the violation from the mark owner and fails to stop the violation. See, e.g., Alaska Statutes §45.45.792(a).	

Table 14.1: Overview of laws relating to surreptitious code. (*Continued*)

Name and Cite	Application/Definition	Causes of Action	Penalties
State Laws			
Anti-Spyware Laws IIIa (720 Illinois Compiled Statutes Annotated §5/16D-3(a))		Illinois recognizes an offense of "computer tampering," which includes: Accessing or causing to be accessed a computer, program, or data without authorization or in excess of any authorization. Inserting or attempting to insert a program into a computer or computer program knowing or having reason to believe that such program may damage or destroy that or another computer. Inserting or attempting to insert a program into a computer or computer program knowing or having reason to believe that such program may alter, delete, or remove a computer program or data from that or another computer, or that may cause loss to the users of that or another computer. Falsifying or forging electronic mail transmission information or other routing information in any manner in connection with the transmission of unsolicited bulk electronic mail through or into the computer network of an electronic mail service provider or its subscribers. Knowingly to sell, give, or otherwise distribute, or possess with the intent to sell, give, or distribute, software which is primarily designed for the purpose of facilitating or enabling the falsification of electronic mail transmission information or other routing information; has only a limited commercially significant purpose or use other than to facilitate or enable the falsification of electronic mail transmission information or other routing information; or is marketed for use in	The law makes computer tampering a crime, and a felony if it involved collecting data or damaging a computer, program, or data. Civil suits are permitted only for spyware that causes harm and for violations of the unsolicited bulk email provisions. 720 Illinois Compiled Statutes Annotated §5/16D-3(b).

Name and Cite	Application/Definition	Causes of Action	Penalties
State Laws			
		facilitating or enabling the falsification of electronic mail transmission information or other routing information. 720 Illinois Compiled Statutes Annotated §5/16D-3(a).	
Anti-Spyware Laws IIIb (720 Illinois Compiled Statutes Annotated §205.477)		Illinois makes it a crime to knowingly, willfully, and without authorization interfere with the authorized use of a computer, system, or network, or to knowingly, willfully, and without authorization use, access, or attempt to access a computer, system, network, telecommunications device, telecommunications service or information service. 720 Illinois Compiled Statutes Annotated §205.477.	Violation of these provisions is a misdemeanor criminal offense. If the violation was committed to defraud or illegally obtain property; caused loss, injury, or other damage in excess of $500; or caused an interruption or impairment of a public service (such as police or fire service), then it is a felony. In addition to the prison terms and fines normally available for a felony in Illinois, the court may impose an additional fine of up to $100,000 and is required to order the defendant to pay restitution. 720 Illinois Compiled Statutes Annotated §205.4765(6).

Table 14.1: Overview of laws relating to surreptitious code. (*Continued*)

Name and Cite	Application/Definition	Causes of Action	Penalties
State Laws			
Anti-Spyware Laws IIIc (Nevada Revised Statutes Annotated §205.4765)		Under Nevada's "Unlawful Acts Regarding Computers," anyone who "knowingly, willfully and without authorization" does any of the following commits a crime:	
		Modifies, damages, destroys, discloses, uses, transfers, conceals, takes, retains possession of, copies, obtains or attempts to obtain access to, permits access to or causes to be accessed, or enters data, a program, or any supporting documents which exist inside or outside a computer, system, or network.	
		Modifies, destroys, uses, takes, damages, transfers, conceals, copies, retains possession of, obtains or attempts to obtain access to, or permits access to or causes to be accessed equipment or supplies that are used or intended to be used in a computer, system, or network.	
		Destroys, damages, takes, alters, transfers, discloses, conceals, copies, uses, retains possession of, obtains or attempts to obtain access to, or permits access to or causes to be accessed a computer, system, or network.	
		Obtains and discloses, publishes, transfers, or uses a device used to access a computer, network, or data.	
		Introduces, causes to be introduced or attempts to introduce a computer contaminant into a computer, system, or network. A "computer contaminant" is defined as any data, information, image, program, signal, or sound that is designed or has the capability to contaminate, corrupt, consume, damage, destroy, disrupt, modify, record, or transmit any other data, information, image, program,	

Name and Cite	Application/Definition	Causes of Action	Penalties
State Laws			
		signal, or sound contained in a computer, system, or network without the knowledge or consent of the owner. Nevada Revised Statutes Annotated §§205.4765(1)-(5), 205.4737.	
Theft Laws (all states, see, e.g., Burns Indiana Code Annotated §§35-43-1-2(a) to 4-3)	"Exert control over property" means "to obtain, take, carry, drive, lead away, conceal, abandon, sell, convey, encumber, or possess property, or to secure, transfer, or extend a right to property." That control is "unauthorized" if it is exerted, among other ways, by "creating or confirming a false impression in the other person" or by "promising performance that the person knows will not be performed." Burns Indiana Code Annotated §§35-43-4-1(a), (b)(4), (b)(6).	Indiana law, typical of most states, provides that a "person who knowingly or intentionally exerts unauthorized control over property of another person commits criminal conversion"— in lay terms, "theft." Similarly, Indiana law criminalizes "criminal mischief," which it defines to include "knowingly or intentionally caus[ing] another to suffer pecuniary loss by deception." Burns Indiana Code Annotated §35-43-1-2(a)(2).	
Trespass to Chattels (common law tort cause of action)—see *CompuServe, Inc. v. Cyber Promotions, Inc.*, 962 F. Supp. 1015 (S.D. Ohio 1997); *eBay, Inc. v. Bidder's Edge, Inc.*, 100 F. Supp. 2d 1058 (N.D. Cal. 2000); *Register.com, Inc. v. Verio, Inc.*, 126 F. Supp. 2d 238 (S.D. N.Y. 2000); *Intel v. Hamidi*, 30 Cal. 4th 1342, 1348, 71 P.3d 296, 300 (2003)		An intentional interference with the possession of personal property which causes an injury. Unlike theft, trespass to chattels does not require totally dispossessing the rightful owner, and unlike trespass, some proof of harm or damage is required.	

Table 14.1: Overview of laws relating to surreptitious code. (*Continued*)

Chapter 15

Crimeware and Trusted Computing

Shane Balfe, Eimear Gallery, Chris J. Mitchell,
and Kenneth G. Paterson

Trusted computing technology has been put forward as a potentially revolutionary addition to the field of information security. In this chapter, we examine how trusted computing may be used to defend against the ever-growing threat posed by crimeware. We also highlight a counterintuitive but important use of trusted computing, as a possible facilitator of cybercrime.

15.1 Introduction

The anonymous and international nature of the Internet makes cybercrime a potentially low-risk, high-return activity. Traditionally, the appropriation of user data through "phishing" attacks has relied on social engineering techniques in which a user is tricked into performing an action that results in the revelation of sensitive information. However, as attacks become more sophisticated, social engineering is being superseded by techniques that directly target vulnerabilities in end-user platforms. These vulnerabilities, once exploited, allow crimeware to be surreptitiously installed, leaving the platform prone to data exposure. Crimeware such as keystroke loggers, viruses, worms, rootkits, and trojan horses can execute silently in the background; can monitor, log, and report keystrokes entered by a user; and can steal commercially sensitive data or be used in the furtherance of additional criminal activities.

Recent studies that examined the evolution, proliferation, and propagation of crimeware have noted a marked and steady rise in both the number and the complexity of applications used in the commission of cybercrime [160, 401]. Crimeware is beginning to combine characteristics of viruses, worms, and trojan horses with server and Internet vulnerabilities, fusing numerous methods for compromising end-user systems with multiple means of propagation to other networked machines [401]. Additionally, it is predicted that mobile devices (such as smartphones and PDAs) will increasingly become targets of crimeware in the coming years, especially as organizations begin to allow corporate data to be stored on these devices [401, 429]. Crimeware technology represents a serious and viable threat to both consumer and corporate data.

As a consequence of the perpetual increases in the volume, complexity, and scope of crimeware attacks, a question naturally arises: How can users trust the software environments with which they interact? Trusted computing technology partially addresses this question by providing a means for end users (and third parties) to derive increased confidence in the platforms with which they interface, as well as providing standardized mechanisms to protect user data and information from software attack. In this chapter, we examine how trusted computing technologies can be used to impede the distribution, infection, and execution of crimeware applications. In doing so, we note a counterintuitive but important use of trusted computing, as a possible facilitator of cybercrime.

This chapter is structured as follows. Section 15.2 examines the life cycle of a crimeware attack. Section 15.3 provides an overview of trusted computing–related concepts and examines how trusted computing–enhanced platforms can be used to impede crimeware at each stage of its life cycle. This section also examines how trusted computing may actually compound the threat posed by crimeware. Section 15.4 presents two case studies: One that looks at the use of trusted computing in combating online credit card fraud, and a second that looks at how trusted computing can aid rights management for content protection on mobile platforms.

15.2 Anatomy of an Attack

Cybercrime can broadly be defined as any "crime that is facilitated or committed using a computer, network, or hardware device," where the computer, network, or device may be the agent of the crime, the facilitator of the crime, or the target of the crime [152]. More specifically, the Council of Europe's Convention on Cybercrime uses this term to refer to criminal activity ranging from offenses against computer data and systems to digital content and copyright infringements [282].

Irrespective of the actual motivation for such activity, a crimeware attack—or, more generally, a malware attack—must typically pass through three stages to fulfill its goal [430]:

1. *Distribution.* Distribution refers to the means by which malware arrives at a platform. Traditionally, malware has been heavily reliant on social engineering as a means of distribution. That is, a user is tricked into downloading malware from a compromised server, opening an email or instant message attachment containing malware, or installing malware that has been integrated into an apparently useful application. However, such distribution methods are being displaced by methods that directly target and exploit vulnerabilities on a platform.

2. *Infection.* Infection is the process by which malware penetrates a platform. Malware may be ephemeral and leave behind no lasting executable, as is the case with system reconfiguration attacks, such as DNS poisoning. Alternatively, malware may persistently reside in memory or be executed upon loading an infected component. The infection may target user-space objects, as is the case with malicious browser help objects and application programs, or kernel objects, as is the case with device drivers.

   To disguise an infection, rootkits are sometimes deployed. Basic rootkits simply replace user-level executables with trojanized versions—for example, replacing the Linux processes status command with a version that incorrectly reports running processes. Such attacks are trivially detectable given current antivirus technology. Unfortunately, more recent rootkits are becoming adept at circumventing antiviral defenses, such as variants of the FU rootkit [133] or new rootkits that exploit hardware-based virtualization, such as Microsoft's proof-of-concept rootkit, Subvirt [215]. Subvirt attempts to modify a system's boot sequence so that the legacy operating system (OS) is loaded into a virtual machine monitor. This allows any system call made by the OS to be observed and modified by the Subvirt application.

3. *Execution.* It is during the execution stage that the malicious objectives of the malware are revealed. The malware may attempt to gain unauthorized access to information, capture user-entered details, or steal proprietary data. For example, the Bankash.G trojan horse attempts to steal user account details such as usernames and passwords or credit card information from a compromised computer [402]. This data is collated by the crimeware and transmitted back to the attacker for processing. Another trojan horse called Archiveus [403] (classified as ransomware) bundles randomly selected files on the platform on which it is executing into a password-protected archive

and deletes the original files. The platform user is then requested to purchase any product from a specified site in exchange for the password required to retrieve his or her files.

15.3 Combating Crimeware with Trusted Computing

Trusted computing relates directly to the types of systems proposed by the Trusted Computing Group (TCG). Namely, a *trusted system* is one that will behave in a particular manner for a specific purpose.

The current documentation from the TCG encompasses a vast set of specifications ranging from specifications for personal computer (PC) [409] and server systems [408] to specifications for trusted networking [413] and trusted mobile platforms [414]. However, it is the TCG's specifications for microcontroller design that have perhaps become most synonymous with trusted computing. The Trusted Platform Module (TPM) specifications [410, 411, 412] form the core of all trusted computing implementations. These specifications describe a microcontroller with cryptographic coprocessor capabilities that provides a platform with the following functionality:

- A number of special purpose registers for recording platform state
- A means of reporting this state to remote entities
- Secure volatile and nonvolatile memory
- Random number generation
- A SHA-1 hashing engine
- Asymmetric key generation, encryption, and digital signature capabilities

However, the specification set produced by the TCG is by no means the only work on trusted computing. Trusted computing also encompasses new processor designs [7, 191] as well as OS support [309, 310]. The interested reader may wish to consult introductory texts on trusted computing [259, 307].

Since its introduction, trusted computing has become synonymous with three fundamental concepts: integrity measurement and storage, attestation, and protected storage. However, recently the definition of what constitutes trusted computing functionality has been revised and extended to incorporate the concepts of secure boot and software isolation. In this section, we consider how these fundamental concepts can be used to impede the distribution, infection, and execution of crimeware.

15.3.1 Integrity Measurement and Storage

An integrity measurement is the cryptographic digest or hash of a platform component (i.e., a piece of software executing on the platform) [310]. For example, an integrity measurement of a program can be calculated by computing a cryptographic digest of its instruction sequence, its initial state (i.e., the executable file), and its input. An integrity metric is a digest of one or more integrity measurements [307]. Integrity metrics are stored in special-purpose registers within the TPM called Platform Configuration Registers (PCRs).

During a platform's boot sequence, the entire platform state can be reliably captured and stored, as shown in Figure 15.1. During this process, the integrity of a predefined set of platform components (typically the POST BIOS, option ROMs, the OS loader, and the OS) are measured and the resulting measurements stored in the TPM's PCRs.

In isolation, integrity measurement and storage functionality do not provide a means of defending against crimeware. They do, however, provide the foundation

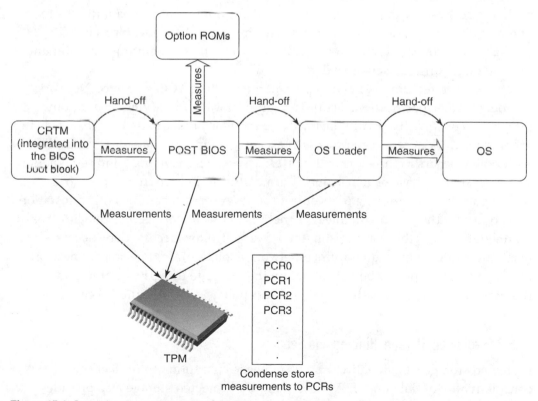

Figure 15.1: Integrity measurement and storage.

for a number of services useful in combating the distribution, infection, and execution of crimeware, as described in Sections 15.3.2 through 15.3.5.

15.3.2 Attestation

Platform attestation enables a TPM to reliably report information about the current state of the host platform. On request from a challenger, a trusted platform can, using a private attestation key, sign integrity metrics reflecting (all or part of) the platform's software environment. The challenger uses this information to determine whether it is safe to trust the platform from which the statement originated and (all or part of) the software environment running on the platform. This is achieved by validating the integrity metrics received from the trusted platform against software integrity measurements provided by a trusted third party, such as a software vendor.

Attestation provides a powerful technique with which to combat crimeware distribution and infection. A platform, upon requesting access to a company's intranet, may be required to demonstrate through attestation that it has up-to-date antivirus software with the latest signature definitions, that its spam filters are operating correctly, and that it has installed the latest OS security patches. Similarly, a client could request that a server attests to its operating environment prior to disclosing any sensitive data.

Attestation features form an important focus of the TCG's Trusted Network Connect (TNC) specifications [413]. TNC offers a way of verifying an endpoint's integrity to ensure that it complies with a particular predefined policy before being granted network access. The process of assaying endpoint integrity for compliance with policy occurs in three distinct phases: assessment, isolation, and remediation. The assessment phase primarily involves a platform that requires access to a restricted network, attesting to its current state. A server examines this attestation and compares the platform's integrity metrics to its network access policies. Based on the outcome of this comparison, the server will allow access, deny access, or place the platform in an quarantined network (isolation). In this isolated network, a platform would typically be able to obtain the requisite integrity-related updates that will allow it to satisfy the server's access policy and be granted access.

15.3.3 Protected Storage: Binding and Sealing

Protected storage functionality uses asymmetric encryption to protect the confidentiality of data on a TPM host platform. Protected storage also provides implicit integrity protection for TPM objects. Both data and keys can be associated with a string of 20 bytes of authorization data before being encrypted. When decryption is requested, the authorization data must be submitted to the TPM. The submitted authorization data is then compared to the authorization data in the decrypted string, and the decrypted object is released only if the values match.

The notions of *binding* and *sealing* are of fundamental importance to trusted computing. Binding refers to the encryption of data with a public key for which the corresponding private key is nonmigratable from the recipient's TPM. In this way, only the TPM that manages the nonmigratable private key will be capable of decrypting the message. Sealing takes binding one step further. Sealing is the process by which sensitive data can be associated with a set of integrity metrics representing a particular platform configuration, and then encrypted. The protected data will be decrypted and released for use by a TPM only when the current state of the platform matches the integrity metrics to which the data is sealed.

Using sealed storage, end users can protect their private data (e.g., credit card numbers) by making revelation of that data contingent on a platform being in a particular state. For example, a user might seal credit card data to a state that requires a particular banking application to be running on the platform, and nothing more. The presence of crimeware would change the platform state. This feature would, therefore, ensure that malicious software, such as the Bankash.G trojan horse, could not gain access to security sensitive data that has been sealed.

Alsaid and Mitchell [6] attempt to address the problem of a user unknowingly revealing sensitive data to a phishing site using the TPM's protected storage capabilities. They propose SSL client-side authentication to establish a mutually authenticated SSL tunnel over which a username/password can be communicated. In this approach, the SSL private key (for which the public key has received certification) is nonmigratable from the client's TPM. Consequently, when a user visits a phishing site and is tricked into revealing a username and password, a phisher will not be able to impersonate the user because the phisher will not have access to the private key used to complete client-side SSL authentication. Unfortunately, such an approach does not prevent crimeware resident on the TPM-host platform from capturing the username/password and using the TPM-protected private key to establish illegitimate sessions and fraudulently impersonate a user. This approach could be enhanced by sealing the TPM-protected private key to a trustworthy platform state.

15.3.4 Secure Boot

A secure boot process extends the integrity measurement and storage functionality described in Section 15.3.1. During a secure boot, a platform's state is reliably captured, compared against measurements indicative of a trustworthy platform state, and stored. If a discrepancy is discovered between the computed measurements and the expected measurements, then the platform halts the boot process.

Secure boot functionality can detect the malicious or accidental modification or removal of security-critical software at boot time. For example, such functionality could detect the Subvirt rootkit, which modifies a system's boot sequence. In a similar way, secure boot functionality could be used to prevent a maliciously modified server from helping to distribute crimeware; this would reduce the effectiveness of a server modification attack to a denial of service.

Secure boot functionality is not currently described as part of the TPM specifications. However, a TCG specification does describe how it can be enabled on a trusted mobile platform [414]. Secure boot has also been independently studied by Tygar and Yee [428]; Clark [56]; Arbaugh, Farber, and Smith [19]; and Itoi et al. [194].

15.3.5 Hardware-Enforced Isolation

Isolation technologies have evolved from OS-hosted virtual machine monitors (VMMs) [461] through stand-alone VMMs [142] to para-virtualization techniques [33]. More recent developments in isolation technology, such as Microsoft's Next Generation Secure Computing Base (NGSCB) [309, 310], incorporate the concept of an isolation layer designed to take advantage of CPU and chipset extensions described in Intel's LaGrande [191] and AMD's Presidio initiatives. An isolated execution environment, independent of how it is implemented, should provide the following services to hosted software [310]:

- *No interference:* Ensures that the program is free from interference from entities outside its execution space.

- *Trusted path:* Ensures the presence of a trusted path between a program and an input device.

- *Secure interprocess communication:* Enables one program to communicate with another, without compromising the confidentiality and integrity of its own memory locations.

- *Non-observation:* Ensures that an executing process and the memory locations it is working upon are free from observation by other processes.

Hardware-enforced software isolation enables the segregation of security-critical software and data so that they cannot be observed or modified in an unauthorized manner by software executing in parallel execution environments. Additionally, the presence of isolated execution environments can ensure that any infection remains confined to the execution environment that the crimeware has infected.

Gajek et al. [135] have used isolated execution environments to protect a secure wallet application from any legacy OS or other applications running on the platform. In this approach, user credentials are sealed (as described in Section 15.3.3) to the isolated secure wallet application. Only when the secure wallet is in the prerequisite state will credentials be unsealed and used to authenticate the user to sensitive services. The authors also suggest that visual cues, such as a colored status bar, would enable users to assess the trustworthiness of the secure wallet application with which they are interacting, an idea originating in [26].

Hardware extensions, as developed as part of Intel's LaGrande initiative [191] and AMD's Presidio initiative, support the establishment of trusted channels between input and output devices and programs running within isolated execution environments. In this way, user I/O data can be secured in transit to protect it from crimeware, such as keyloggers, which may have infiltrated the platform.

We have yet to see the ubiquitous presence of hardware-enabled trusted channels. In the absence of such support, McCune et al. [247] have proposed the use of a trusted mobile device to establish an encrypted and authenticated channel between the user and a TPM host. Their approach, however, considers only the issue of user-level malware; it does not effectively address problems relating to kernel-level subversion.

15.3.6 Trusted Computing: A Panacea?

We have briefly examined a range of trusted computing functionality and explored how it might be used to reduce the impact of crimeware. In reality, trusted computing, *as currently deployed*, can do little to protect an end-user platform from crimeware attack. It will be several years before we begin to see the ubiquitous presence of enhanced processors, chipset extensions, BIOS modifications, and augmented operating systems necessary to implement the fundamental trusted computing concepts identified in Sections 15.3.1 through 15.3.5. The capabilities offered by currently deployed trusted platforms are more akin to those of a high-end smartcard; thus trusted computing, as it currently stands, provides a limited, but useful, set of cryptographic functionality. We expect that these benefits will be extended over time to provide a more secure operating environment.

In addition, it is important to note that problems associated with software vulnerabilities will not be ameliorated by the presence of trusted computing. Likewise, trusted computing is not designed to prevent a platform from being infected. Instead, it provides a set of services that can be used to detect whether a platform has been modified from a known "good" state. Unlike the way in which signature-based antivirus mechanisms operate, a trusted system has a known "good" configuration, and any deviation from this configuration is perceived as a possible breach of security. Such an approach tells a user that something is awry, albeit not necessarily what the problem is.

An abundance of information exists on the potential positive applications of trusting computing. However, as the technology becomes more widely deployed, it seems likely that trusted computing functionality will be increasingly targeted by crimeware. Proof-of-concept rootkits that exploit Intel's VT-X and AMD's SVM virtualization technologies, which are the cornerstones of Intel's LaGrande and AMD's Presidio initiatives, have already been developed by Dino Dai Zovi (Vitriol) [495] and Joanna Rutkowska (Blue Pill) [364].

In addition, trusted computing mechanisms may be used as a means of enhancing crimeware functionality. For example, trusted computing provides trivial means for crimeware to launch denial-of-service attacks against a platform. If a crimeware application can be installed on a platform, thereby altering the system state, then the following scenarios are possible:

- In the case of attestation, access to networked services may be denied, because the platform will (correctly) not be considered trustworthy.

- In the case of sealing, access to data may be denied, because the current state of the platform will not match the integrity metrics to which the data has been sealed.

- In the case of a secure boot, system start-up may be suspended if the presence of crimeware is detected during the boot sequence.

Finally, ransomware (such as Archieveus, as described in Section 15.2), could abuse the TPM's sealing mechanism to encrypt data to a platform state that is contingent on the malware being present on the platform. This approach could potentially be used as a method to extort money from the platform owner.

15.4 Case Studies

In this section, we look at two case studies that examine the use of trusted computing as a means of protecting sensitive data from malicious applications. In the first case study, we look at the issue of online credit card fraud and the potential use of trusted computing as a means of protecting credit card transactions. In the second case study, we look at how trusted computing can be used to enable a robust implementation of Open Mobile Alliance Digital Rights Management (OMA DRM) v2 on mobile platforms.

15.4.1 Securing Credit Card Transactions

Over the past 10 to 15 years, the Internet has been transformed from a research-oriented tool into a global platform for electronic commerce. With this transformation, the use of one particular method of Internet-based payment has emerged as the predominant means through which online goods are purchased. This method, often referred to as a "card not present" (CNP) transaction, uses data from a customer's physical card—typically the personal account number (PAN) and the corresponding card security code (CSC)—to purchase online goods and services. Unfortunately, Internet-based CNP transactions represent a particularly attractive target for phishers and crimeware authors, as the ability to provide card details is typically deemed a sufficient form of transaction authorization. Once this data is captured, it allows a fraudster to impersonate a legitimate cardholder and purchase items online.

Balfe and Paterson examine how the staged rollout of trusted computing technology, beginning with ubiquitous client-side TPMs [27] and culminating in trusted computing with processor, chipset, and OS support [28], can be used to enhance the security of Internet-based CNP transactions. They describe a system [28] that makes use of the full spectrum of trusted computing technologies to securely emulate point-of-sale integrated circuit cards (ICCs) compliant with the Europay Mastercard and Visa (EMV) specifications [103, 104, 105, 106]. Emulation of EMV-compliant cards confers "tamper-resistant" properties that are normally associated with physical EMV card use at point-of-sale terminals, making it possible to demonstrate card ownership and authentication.

To enroll in the virtual EMV architecture, a customer must formally register as a legitimate cardholder. During the enrollment process, the customer's platform generates an attestation key pair (internal to the user's TPM) specifying an authorization requirement for the private key usage, as per Section 15.3.3. The customer's card issuer certifies the public component of the customer's newly generated TPM-resident attestation key pair, and the customer downloads an e-EMV application to his or her platform. This application replicates the functionality of a standard EMV payment card (which has been personalized to the customer) as well as certain aspects of merchant terminal processing.

During merchant enrollment, the merchant's acquirer certifies the public component of a merchant's TPM-resident attestation key pair and downloads a small application bundle to the merchant server that replicates the merchant terminal commands for interacting with an EMV ICC. This software bundle enables the merchant to communicate with a customer's e-EMV card. In addition, the merchant application bundle implements any additional requirements for payment processing as laid down by the acquirer's merchant operator guidelines (MOGs).

The MOG lays out the procedures that should be followed when processing CNP transactions. An example of such a procedure would be a requirement to use an address verification service (AVS), which compares the billing address, as entered by the customer, to the billing address found in the card issuer's records.

Prior to transaction initiation, a customer launches his or her e-EMV application in an isolated execution environment. At this point, the customer and the merchant platform mutually attest to their respective states using their respective private attestation keys, the public keys corresponding to which have been certified during the enrollment process. This provides a guarantee that, at this particular point in time, both the customer's e-EMV application and the merchant's plug-in are operating as intended.

In addition, by using trusted computing functionality, PIN authentication and authorization can be made intrinsic to transaction processing, just as with EMV in point-of-sale transactions. A trusted path between the keyboard and TPM, enabled by chipset extensions (as outlined in Section 15.3.5), can be used to securely transfer authorization data in the form of a PIN or a passphrase from the customer's keyboard to the TPM. A correctly entered PIN/passphrase then assures the TPM of the physical presence of the cardholder and "unlocks" the TPM's private attestation key. The assurance of physical presence can be transferred to the merchant through the TPM's subsequent use of this attestation key to attest to the state of the customer's platform. This combined functionality provides a much stronger form of authentication and authorization than is currently employed for CNP payments.

The mechanism used to prevent crimeware from launching a dictionary attack against key authorization data would be TPM vendor specific. The TPM specifications [410], however, detail an example mechanism where a count of failed authorization attempts is recorded. If this count exceeds a certain threshold, the TPM is locked and remains nonresponsive to further requests for a predetermined time-out period.

In conjunction with this functionality, by allowing customers to inspect a merchant's platform state prior to transaction authorization, customers will be able to satisfy themselves that the merchant will behave in a manner that will protect their sensitive card data. Likewise, for a merchant, any divergence from intended operating state (due to unwanted memory-resident applications, such as keyloggers) will be detected on verification of customers' attestation, allowing merchant risk-management routines to terminate a transaction. Once mutual attestation is complete, transaction processing can continue as defined in the EMV specifications [103, 104, 105, 106]. This work builds upon the preexisting EMV infrastructure to provide a secure and extensible architecture for CNP payments.

15.4.2 Content Protection

Our second case study focuses on DRM in a mobile environment. As other authors have highlighted [401, 429], it is predicted that mobile devices (hosting sensitive corporate data) will increasingly become the target of crimeware. Current third-generation (3G) mobile telecommunications systems are already capable of delivering a wide range of digital content to subscribers' mobile telephones. As network access becomes more ubiquitous and content becomes more easily accessible, media and data objects are exposed to increased risks of illegal consumption and use. DRM facilitates the safe distribution of various forms of digital content in a wide range of computing environments, and it gives assurance to the content providers that their media objects cannot be illegally accessed.

The model under consideration is taken from [290] and is depicted in Figure 15.2. In this model, a user requests a media object from a content issuer. The requested content, which is packaged to prevent unauthorized access, is then sent to the user's device. The packaging of the content may be completed either by the content issuer

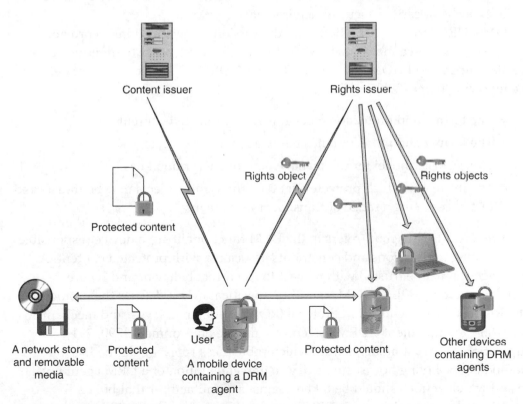

Figure 15.2: OMA DRM system model.

or by the content owner, before it is dispatched to the content issuer. The rights object associated with the requested media object is delivered to the user by the rights issuer. In practice, this rights issuer may be the same entity as the content issuer.

With respect to crimeware, the protection of content can be examined from two contrasting perspectives. From the content provider's perspective, an end user may deploy crimeware to circumvent rights that have been assigned to digital content. From a corporate perspective, DRM solutions can be used to prevent the unauthorized or inadvertent disclosure of corporate data. This usage is particularly relevant in light of the recent trend toward increasing reliance on mobile devices for storing corporate data [429].

The OMA was founded in June 2002. Version 1 (v1) of the OMA specifications [288, 289], released in 2004, represents the OMA's initial attempt to define a DRM solution for a mobile environment. Three main goals were specified for OMA DRM v1: The solution was required to be timely, easy to implement, and inexpensive to deploy. In addition, it was required that the initial OMA DRM solution did not necessitate the rollout of a costly infrastructure. In the development of OMA DRM v1, a trade-off was made, so that the objectives mentioned previously could be met at the expense of certain security requirements.

OMA DRM version 2 (v2) builds on the version 1 specifications to provide higher security and a more extensive feature set. Devices other than mobile phones are also supported by OMA DRM v2. The OMA DRM v2 specification set defines the following items [290]:

- The format and protection mechanism for protected content
- The format and protection mechanism for rights objects
- The security model for the management of encryption keys
- The means by which protected content and rights objects may be transferred to devices using a range of transport mechanisms

The term "DRM agent" refers to the DRM functionality of a device responsible for enforcing permissions and constraints associated with protected content. A DRM agent must be trusted with respect to its correct behavior and secure implementation [290]. The OMA DRM v2 specification set defines the protocols [the Rights Object Acquisition Protocol (ROAP) suite], messages, and mechanisms necessary to implement a DRM system in a mobile environment [290, 291]. Stipulation of a trust model, within which robustness rules are defined, is one method of specifying how secure a device implementation of a DRM agent must be and which actions should be taken against a manufacturer that builds insufficiently robust devices. It is the responsibility of the Content Management

Licensing Administrator for Digital Rights Management (CMLA DRM), or a similar organization, to provide such a model.

To comply with the definition of a "robust" OMA DRM v2 implementation, as defined by the CMLA [59], a number of requirements must be met:

- It is required that "an OMA DRM v2 agent can perform self-checking of the integrity of its component parts so that unauthorized modifications will be expected to result in a failure of the implementation to provide the authorized authentication and/or decryption function" [59].

- A robust implementation of OMA DRM v2 must protect the confidentiality and integrity of an OMA DRM v2 agent's private key when loaded, stored, or used on a device.

- OMA DRM v2 security-critical data must be either integrity-protected or integrity and confidentiality-protected when loaded, stored, or used on a device.

- OMA DRM v2 security-critical data and the OMA DRM v2 agent's private key should be accessible only by authorized entities—namely, the correctly functioning OMA DRM v2 agent.

- A robust OMA DRM v2 implementation must incorporate a DRM time-source synchronization mechanism that is reasonably accurate and resistant to malicious modifications by the end user.

- Nonces generated on the OMA DRM v2 device and used in the ROAP protocols must be both nonrepeating and unpredictable.

Trusted computing functionality can be used to help meet the CMLA requirements for a robust implementation of OMA DRM v2 [136], thereby making it, and the content it protects, less susceptible to crimeware attacks. While trusted computing functionality cannot guarantee the integrity of the OMA DRM v2 agent in storage, secure boot functionality can be used to help detect its malicious or accidental modification or removal. Security-critical data associated with the OMA DRM v2 agent can also be verified as part of a secure boot process.

Sealing can be used to store data that needs to be confidentiality or integrity protected against crimeware attack. It can also ensure that sensitive data is accessible only by authorized entities when the mobile device is in a predefined state—for example, when a legitimate OMA DRM v2 agent is executing in an isolated execution environment. In addition, the TPM can be used to generate the required OMA DRM v2 agent asymmetric key pair.

Trusted computing functionality also enables the isolation of security-critical software and data in a secure execution environment so that it cannot be observed or modified in an unauthorized manner by software executing in parallel execution environments.

A good-quality random number generator is provided by a TPM, enabling the generation of nonrepeating, unpredictable nonces for use in the ROAP suite protocols, thereby mitigating the possibility of replay and preplay attacks. The TPM may also be used to provide accurate time-source synchronization [410]. A comprehensive examination of this use case can be found in [136].

Conclusion

In this chapter, we explored the use of trusted computing technologies as both a defense against, and enabler of, crimeware. We initially described the life cycle of a crimeware attack and subsequently investigated how the technologies examined could be used to disrupt crimeware distribution, infection, and execution. We also investigated how trusted computing might potentially be exploited to facilitate cybercrime. Finally, we considered two case studies in which this technology might be used in the prevention of crimeware attacks.

Chapter 16

Technical Defense Techniques

Peter Ferrie, Markus Jakobsson, Zulfikar Ramzan, Erik Stolterman, Xiaofeng Wang, Susanne Wetzel, and Liu Yang

While crimeware is a growing problem, there are a number of ways to counteract it. Some of these countermeasures, especially those that are specific to a given class of threat, have been covered in other chapters. In this chapter, we will consider additional countermeasures.

When computer viruses first became an issue, there were relatively few of them, and classical antivirus software could afford to scan files for known bad examples. The software would maintain a list of virus *signatures*, which it would scan for. These signatures are often created and verified by an actual person (a virus analyst) prior to being included in a product. As viruses and other types of malware began to proliferate, classical antivirus software kept pace in part through developing quick auto-update mechanisms and employing faster and faster string-matching algorithms. The antivirus software vendors also hired more analysts and built tools to facilitate the process. Unfortunately, even such measures cannot keep up with crimeware developers.

A number of security vendors have been incorporating *heuristics* and *behavior-based technology* into their products. The idea is that rather than look for specific malicious software, the technology attempts to infer the intent of any piece of software and determine whether that intent is actually malicious. If successful, such an approach reduces the need for signatures under the premise that the number of malicious behaviors is far smaller than the number of malware samples that exhibit these behaviors.

Naturally, such an approach can give rise to a number of challenges. The foremost challenge is that determining intent can give rise to false positives—that is, legitimate applications that might appear to be behaving badly. Consider, for example, a keystroke logger. Many keystroke loggers work by hooking the Windows keyboard API. Thus one natural generic approach for keylogger detection would be to monitor which APIs a piece of software hooks and to flag those pieces of software that hook the keyboard API. However, this approach does not fare well in practice. For example, many instant messaging clients hook the keyboard API, typically as part of the feature that tells one party whether the other party is in the process of typing a message. A heuristic such as this one, therefore, needs to be refined. The challenge of mitigating false positives is considerably magnified when you consider that major computer security software vendors have to deploy their technology across hundreds of millions of machines, all of which are likely to be unique in some aspect of their configuration.

Nonetheless, the industry has made a significant number of advances in technology geared toward understanding intent. Many of these technologies are deployed to a large number of users. Even so, there is still considerable room for improvement in such detection.

Another area for future research is in automatic development of signatures for malicious software. The idea here is to reduce the burden on a human analyst. Again, similar challenges apply—namely, there need to be mechanisms in place to thoroughly test these signatures and to ensure that no issues arise when they are deployed.

The subject of automatic detection and signature generation is the focus of the first part of this chapter.

The second part of this chapter considers the fundamental question of which types of authentication protocols can work, even in the presence of malicious client-side software. Naturally, passwords are weak in this case because they can easily be recorded by keylogging software. The topic of crimeware-resistant authentication does not address the question of how to prevent crimeware from infecting the machine or even how to eradicate it. Nevertheless, it does address the important topic of how to mitigate the repercussions of a crimeware infestation. While the section describes a number of approaches, it develops one in detail—namely, how to do secure authentication with *preference-based life questions.*

The final portion of the chapter presents a very brief look at the use of virtual machines as a crimeware protection mechanism. Virtual machines provide users with a virtualized environment in which to run an operating system, together with software on top of that operating system. Anything that happens inside the virtualized environment is, in theory, supposed to stay within the confines of that environment. As a result, any malicious code that gets installed inside the virtual machine cannot, in theory, access files or other data that reside outside the machine. A single user can have multiple virtual machines running concurrently inside of one physical machine.

16.1 Case Study: Defense-in-Depth Against Spyware*

16.1.1 Introduction

Spyware is defined by the Federal Trade Commission as a program that aids in gathering personal and organizational information without consent, or asserts control over a computer without the user's knowledge [115, 463]. The software matching this description is considered to be among the most dangerous types of crimeware for two reasons. First, it is disturbingly commonplace: Webroot estimated that 89% of consumer computers are infected with spyware in this country, with an average 30 pieces per machine [65]. Second, it has been widely used for crimes committed in cyberspace: Spyware has been employed in various criminal activities including spam relay [65], money laundering, and extortion. As a result, spyware has emerged as a major means for launching large-scale cyberattacks, especially for the purpose of identity theft. For example, a staggering identity theft ring discovered in 2006 employed keyloggers to gather personal information ranging from bank account numbers and Social Security numbers to a family's vacation plans [305]. U.S. Secretary of the Treasury John W. Snow has stated that "It is important to realize that such crimes exact a heavy toll on our economy. Every such crime weighs on our entire system of credit, raising the cost of doing business and subtly but surely impeding economic growth" [422].

Classic antivirus mechanisms are inadequate to counter such a grave threat. Specifically, spyware scanners are used to search binary executables for the presence of patterns that appear in a spyware database. These patterns, called signatures, are usually generated through manual analysis of the executables of known spyware, which takes hours, days, or even weeks. While this window remains open, attackers can gather victims' personal information and automatically update their infection code into a completely unrecognizable form. Therefore, it is difficult for such a technique to accomplish large-scale and timely detection and disinfection of compromised systems. A more serious problem

---

*This section is by Xiaofeng Wang.

comes from the lack of depth in the current defense framework: In many computing systems, spyware scanning forms the sole defense line, and evading it will render these systems completely unprotected.

In-Depth Spyware Defense

Effectively curbing the spyware epidemic can be achieved only through an in-depth defense framework. Such a framework has three lines of defense: *prevention, detection and disinfection,* and *containment.* Prevention is conducted by a mechanism that captures the attempts to infect a computing system and automatically fixes the system's vulnerability being exploited. The second line of defense is to detect compromised systems through various scanning techniques including the traditional pattern-matching approach and more advanced approaches such as static and dynamic analyses, and to quickly disable the infections once detected. If a strain of intelligent spyware should survive both layers of defense, the potential damage it could inflict could still be limited by using a lightweight containment mechanism that prevents an untrusted program from getting access to users' critical information such as passwords and bank account numbers.

One way that spyware spreads is by exploiting software security flaws that allow an infection to happen *without any human intervention,* such as opening an email attachment. Such attacks are extremely dangerous because they enable fast and extensive spread of the infections. Therefore, it is extremely important to quickly detect these exploits and effectively remedy the security flaws before great damage is done. This objective must be achieved under practical constraints. In particular, software vendors usually do not make the source code for their products available and could further obfuscate their binary code to resist analysis for the purpose of digital rights management (DRM) [271, 456], which limits the utility of techniques relying on software's source code or binary recompilation [237, 464, 482].

Critical to detection of spyware infections are accurate signatures, which should be generated quickly once a new strain of spyware has been discovered. The timing here is extremely important because a fast-generated signature can not only minimize the damage inflicted on the victims but also enable large-scale detection of compromised hosts even before the perpetrators have time to update their code through existing infections. In addition, disinfection procedures must be automatically generated to make possible large-scale disinfection of spyware-riddled hosts.

Once an infection happens, protection of the victim's information asset becomes an extremely challenging task. Existing access control mechanisms are insufficient to counter spyware surveillance: For example, although mainstream

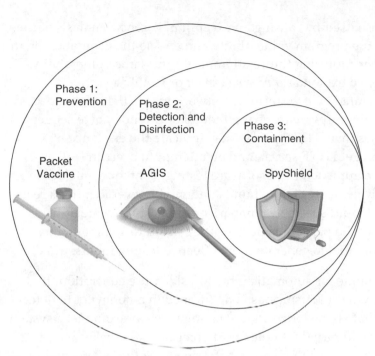

Figure 16.1. An in-depth spyware defense framework.

word-processing software such as Microsoft Word offers password and encryption protection to confidential files, a keylogger can easily circumvent such defenses by recording the password used by an authorized party to access these files. Therefore, research on anti-surveillance techniques is highly demanding.

In this section, we survey a suite of techniques that effectively address the aforementioned technical challenges. These techniques lay a concrete foundation for an in-depth defense framework. Figure 16.1 illustrates the relations between the techniques and the defense framework.

Packet Vaccine. Packet vaccine [465] is a technique for automatic detection of exploit attempts, diagnosis of the underlying security vulnerability it targets, and rapid generation of a fix to protect it from being exploited in the future. The idea behind the technique comes from the biologic concept of vaccines. A vaccine is a living strain of viruses or bacteria that is intentionally injected into the body for the purpose of stimulating antibody production. This strain is deliberately weakened so as to prevent it from causing a severe infection. Similarly, a "weakened" exploit with relevant portions of its payload (e.g., values that could play the role of jump addresses) scrambled would not infect the vulnerable process that receives it and, in fact, would likely expose itself by causing an exception. Forensic analysis of the exception could uncover the program vulnerability and enable the generation of an "immunity," a signature for capturing future attempts on the same vulnerability. We refer to such a weakened exploit as a *vaccine exploit* or simply a *vaccine*.

A vaccine can be generated by transforming network inputs that are suspected to be exploit attempts on the software receiving them. For example, byte sequences resembling jump addresses in an HTTP packet may indicate the existence of a vulnerable buffer in the target HTTP server, and an attempt to overrun it. This property distinguishes the approach from software testing techniques such as fault injection, which randomly generates faulty inputs and might never identify a real vulnerability given a large input space. By comparison, a packet vaccine utilizes exploit attempts to identify the part of network traffic related to a vulnerability and, therefore, has the potential to generate more effective testing inputs.

AGIS. AGIS is a technique for automatic infection signature generation. It monitors the runtime activities of suspicious code trapped in a honeypot to detect the malicious behaviors that characterize a piece of spyware—for example, a system call to hook a dynamic link library (DLL) file for intercepting keystrokes and subsequent I/O activities for depositing and transferring a log file. A spyware infection can be uniquely described by these behaviors and other related actions, such as downloading and installing the malicious code. AGIS employs dynamic and static analyses to extract the instruction sequences necessary for these behaviors to happen, which it then uses to build a variety of signatures serving different purposes. For example, signatures for a spyware scanner may permit detection of a spyware infection, or an instruction template for a static analyzer may identify an infection's variants.

SpyShield. SpyShield [236] is a spyware-containment technique that automatically blocks the view of surveillance software whenever sensitive data is processed by an authorized party. This is achieved through enforcing access control policies on the communication mechanisms inside an operating system (OS), which have been intensively used by spyware to snoop users' activities. For example, SpyShield ensures that whenever an Internet Explorer (IE) browser is visiting a sensitive web site, such as an online bank, no data will flow into untrusted plug-ins that could include spyware.

16.1.2 Packet Vaccines

A fundamental problem in exploit prevention is how to detect a novel exploit quickly and generate a fix to protect vulnerable software without detailed analysis of its source code or executable. A packet vaccine [465] is meant to address this problem. The vaccine mechanism consists of four major steps: vaccine generation, exploit detection, vulnerability diagnosis, and signature generation.

A vaccine is a network packet containing a "weakened" attack payload to be received by a network-facing program such as an HTTP server. The attack is weakened in the sense that it may still exploit the program's security flaw, but the result of such an attack will cause the program to execute instructions located at an illegal memory address and thus triggers a runtime exception to reveal both the attack and the security flaw. Once such an exception occurs, an exploit detection mechanism performs a vulnerability diagnosis to correlate the exception with the vaccine. After a reliable correlation has been established, a *signature generator* extracts the attributes that describe the underlying security flaw to create an *exploit signature* for detecting and filtering the network traffic with these attributes.

A key step in most memory-based exploits is injecting a jump address (usually transported by a network packet) into a vulnerable program so as to force the program to run the code located at that address. For example, if a web service program does not check a buffer's boundary, an exploit in an HTTP request may overflow that buffer to change a function's return address to the location of the code that the attacker wishes to run. Such code can be injected into the program by the exploit input in a *code injection attack*. Its common locations include the stack and heap of that program's process. In contrast, an *existing-code attack* forces the process to run some existing library functions, such as execv, through directing the jump address to the entries of global libraries.

The memory addresses of these potential jump targets are limited, taking up only 0.1% of a process's address space. This property is utilized by the vaccine generator to generate vaccine exploits. Specifically, it first checks every 4-byte sequence (32-bit system) or 8-byte sequence (64-bit system) in a network packet's payload after proper decoding (e.g., Unicode decoding), and then scrambles those sequences that fall in the address range of the potential jump targets in a protected program. Such an address range is easy to obtain; for example, on Linux, the proc virtual file system maintains information about the base addresses and ranges of each process's stack and heap, and the address range of global libraries. If the packet does, indeed, carry an exploit payload that includes jump addresses in the form of byte sequences, these addresses will be set to be outside the process's address space. When this happens, the vulnerable program's attempts to execute the code at these addresses will cause the operating system to issue an exception such as a segmentation fault (SEGV) or an illegal instruction fault (ILL). Such an exception indicates the existence of the exploit, which will therefore be detected and analyzed by the vaccine mechanism.

The Original Packet of Code Red

GET /default.ida?NNNNNNNNNNNNNNNNNNNNNNNNNNNNNNNNNNNNNNNNNNNNN
NNNNNNNNNNNNNNNNNNNNNNNNNNNNNNNNNNNNNNNNNNNNNNNNNNNNNNNNNNNN
NNNNNNNNNNNNNNNNNNNNNNNNNNNNNNNNNNNNNNNNNNNNNNNNNNNNNNNNNNNN
NNNNNNNNNNNNNNNNNNNNNNNNNNNNNNNNNNNNNNNNNNNNNNNNNNNNNNNNNNNN
NNNNNNNNNNNNNNNNNNNNNNNNNNNNNNNN%u9090%u6858%ucbd3%u7801%u909
0%u6858%ucbd3%u7801%u9090%u6858%ucbd3%u7801%u9090%u9090%u8190
%u00c3%u0003%u8b00%u531b%u53ff%u0078%u0000%u00=a HTTP/1.0\r\n

A Vaccine Packet for Code Red

GET /default.ida?NNNNNNNNNNNNNNNNNNNNNNNNNNNNNNNNNNNNNNNNNNNNN
NNNNNNNNNNNNNNNNNNNNNNNNNNNNNNNNNNNNNNNNNNNNNNNNNNNNNNNNNNNN
NNNNNNNNNNNNNNNNNNNNNNNNNNNNNNNNNNNNNNNNNNNNNNNNNNNNNNNNNNNN
NNNNNNNNNNNNNNNNNNNNNNNNNNNNNNNNNNNNNNNNNNNNNNNNNNNNNNNNNNNN
NNNNNNNNNNNNNNNNNNNNNNNNNNNNNNNN%u9090%u6858%ucbd3%ua001%u9090
%u6858%ucbd3%u0401%u9090%u6858%ucbd3%u8c01%u9090%u9090%u8190%
u00c3%u0003%u8b00%u531b%u53ff%u0078%u0000%u00=a HTTP/1.0\r\n

Figure 16.2: A vaccine generated from the Code Red II worm.

For example, Figure 16.2 shows the payload of an HTTP packet containing the famous Code Red II exploit. The exploit attempts to force a vulnerable program to run the code starting at the address 7801cbd3. This address under Unicode encoding appears in the byte sequence %ucbd3%u7801. The vaccine generator identifies multiple occurrences of the byte sequence in the packet and finds it representing an address in msvcrt.dll, a potential jump target. Therefore, a vaccine is created as the new HTTP packet illustrated in Figure 16.2, in which the most significant byte in each instance of the sequence %u7801 is scrambled.

After detecting an exploit and the vulnerability it attempts to exploit, a signature generator automatically creates a signature with which to filter incoming network traffic, which prevents the future attacks on the same vulnerability. The generator uses a known exploit as a template to create vaccines and inject them into the application containing vulnerabilities to acquire key attributes of the flaw. Specifically, it determines the role played by every byte on the exploit payload by scrambling that byte, along with the identified jump address, to create a vaccine. It then tests the vaccine in the vulnerable application: If the original exception disappears, we know that byte is important for a successful exploit; otherwise, we know it is not important. In this way, the generator can pinpoint all bytes indispensable to that exploit and discard irrelevant bytes.

Another way to generate signatures is to take advantage of an application's protocol specifications and properties of typical exploits. For example, a buffer-overflow attack is usually characterized by an overlong application field and, therefore, a signature that indicates the length of this field describes attack traffics. Detailed experimental studies [465] have demonstrated that a packet vaccine is capable of capturing many well-known exploits.

16.1.3 AGIS

The efficacy of spyware detection and disinfection hinges on quickly generated and accurate signatures and disinfection procedures. At present, the process to generate signatures contains a significant manual component, relying on malware analysts' expertise. The proliferation of spyware has rendered this approach increasingly ineffective.

AGIS is a suite of new techniques for automatic analysis of spyware and generation of infection signatures for detecting its components. It is designed to take two key steps to generate signatures: *malicious behavior detection* and *signature generation*. In the first step, suspicious executables are invoked in a honeypot or other sandboxed environment, and their runtime activities are monitored and checked against a set of security policies to detect malicious behaviors. In the second step, a combination of dynamic analysis and static analysis is applied to extract the instruction sequences responsible for these behaviors, from which signatures are constructed.

As an illustrative example, consider a trojan downloader trapped within a honeypot. Once activated, the trojan downloads and installs a keylogger, and sets a Run registry key to point to it so that it is automatically executed each time the infected system reboots. The keylogger consists of two components: an executable file that installs a hook to the Windows message-handling mechanism for intercepting keyboard inputs, and a DLL file with the hooked callback function for recording keystrokes and exporting them to a log file.

To detect this infection, the AGIS-enhanced honeypot first runs the trojan to monitor its system calls that reflect the behavior of the code. From these calls, AGIS constructs an *infection graph* that records the relationships among the trojan and the two files it downloads—for example, the change of the registry to automatically invoke the keylogger executable—and extends the surveillance to them. An alarm is raised when the keylogger installs the DLL to monitor keyboard inputs through a system call, and the DLL exports a file in response to inputs of keystrokes. Such behaviors are suspected to violate a security policy that forbids hooking the keyboard and writing a log file. The presence of this malicious activity can be confirmed by a static analyzer that tries to find an execution path from the callback function in the DLL to the call for writing log files. If this attempt succeeds, the keylogger is detected. By backtracking on the infection graph, AGIS also pronounces the trojan to be malicious.

To extract infection signatures, a dynamic analyzer first finds the locations of the calls within executables (*call sites*) responsible for the malicious behaviors that include downloading of the keylogger, modification of the registry key, invocation of the keylogger, installation of the DLL, and export of a log file. It can also collect other information useful to static analysis—in particular, the call sites of other system calls being observed, which divulge the execution path followed by the malware. Using such information, a static analyzer extracts the instruction sequences in individual executables that induce the malicious calls directly or transitively. Spyware signatures are derived from these instructions.

16.1.4 SpyShield

No prevention and detection techniques are absolutely reliable. We always have to prepare for the worst-case scenario: If a piece of spyware penetrates these layers of defense, protection must still be there to keep important information from being stolen. Serving this purpose are the techniques of spyware containment, which strive to preserve clients' privacy in the presence of malicious surveillance. As the last stand against spyware, these techniques are critical to a defense-in-depth framework.

An example of such spyware-containment techniques is SpyShield [236], which protects an infected system from a variety of software surveillance. SpyShield can automatically block the view of untrusted executables whenever sensitive data are being accessed by an authorized party. This is achieved through enforcing security policies on the communication mechanisms inside an OS that are typically used by spyware. This section presents an example that controls surveillance add-ons for Internet Explorer illustrated in Figure 16.3.

Add-ons are optional software modules that complement or enhance a software application to which they are attached (called a *host application*). Examples of these modules include Microsoft's plug-ins [256] and Mozilla's extensions [266]. Software

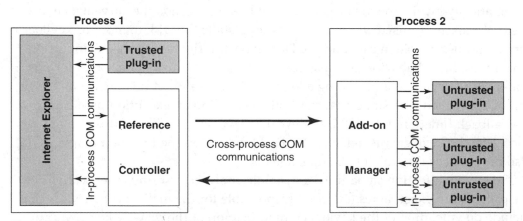

Figure 16.3: Containment of spy add-ons.

manufacturers usually offer interfaces for third parties to develop their own add-ons. Through such interfaces, a spy add-on may acquire confidential information from the host application or even control it. Prominent examples are brower helper objects (BHOs) and toolbars, two types of plug-ins for Internet Explorer that are extensively used by Windows-based spyware [216]. A spy BHO or toolbar can subscribe to browser events, such as opening a URL or downloading a resource, through an interface called Component Object Model (COM) [478]. In response to these events, they can further require a handle from COM to the document being accessed or redirect a browser to another web site, which allows them to steal sensitive data such as passwords or even hijack the browser. A more fundamental problem for current add-on architectures is that an add-on shares the memory address space with its host application and can, therefore, directly access any information found in the application.

To contain spy add-ons, SpyShield inserts an access-control proxy between untrusted add-ons and their host application to control their communications according to a set of security policies. To this end, it separates the add-ons and their host applications into two different processes, thereby preventing untrusted add-ons from accessing the memory space of the host application to obtain any sensitive information. The proxy consists of two components: a reference controller in the form of an IE plug-in, and an add-on manager serving as an independent process that handles a set of untrusted plug-ins. To these plug-ins, the add-on manager plays the role of an IE browser, which automatically loads them into memory and offers standard COM interfaces to enable them to subscribe to events and ask for information of interest. Actual invocation of the COM interface, however, is delegated to the reference controller by transporting add-ons' requests through an interprocess communication channel. Upon receiving each request from plug-ins, the reference controller will make a decision regarding whether to forward the request to the browser. The decisions will be based on a set of security policies predefined by a user (or the network administrator).

IE's event callbacks or responses should go through the security policy enforced by the reference controller. This approach prevents a spy plug-in from stealing information through either the COM interfaces or direct access to the browser's memory. An end user, by contrast, will have more control over his or her information by adjusting security policies.

The concepts underlying SpyShield can also be extended to stand-alone spyware such as keyloggers and screen grabbers. This is achieved through a multilevel security (MLS) model capable of efficiently tracing sensitive data flows and dynamically identifying sensitive information such as a sensitive file's keystroke inputs, screen outputs, and temporary files.

Conclusion

This section has described a defense-in-depth frame that offers fully automated protection to computing systems against spyware. The framework consists of three key defense lines: prevention, detection and disinfection, and containment. A vaccine-based prevention mechanism quickly detects an attempt to implant spyware in a system via software vulnerabilities and automatically generates a remedy for the flaw without relying on the software's source or binary code. The second line of defense relies on AGIS, a mechanism that automatically generates a signature for detecting an infection. If a strain of intelligent spyware manages to evade both of these defense lines, it will still be contained by SpyShield, which prevents untrusted programs from accessing sensitive data.

16.2 Crimeware-Resistant Authentication*

16.2.1 Introduction

Economy and Security. A common goal of crimeware is to capture user credentials and to send these data to a place where the person controlling the crimeware can collect them. The credentials are then tested, classified, and sold to people who would use them for direct financial benefit. The resale value depends directly on how valuable the credentials are to the buyers. Here, one of the most important aspects affecting the resale value is whether the credentials *work* and for how long they are expected to do so. For example, credentials that are generated by one-time password (OTP) tokens have a very low resale value, owing to the fact that they remain valid for only a few minutes. Therefore, financial institutions that deploy OTP tokens increase their security not only by making it harder for attackers to obtain the credentials, but also because the lower value of the credentials makes it less appealing to try to obtain them. Thus an important realization is this: Security is the result of neither good technical design alone nor properly designed user interfaces, but it has economic aspects as well.

When OTP Tokens Are Not Enough. While OTP tokens fill an important role in the authentication market, they are not—at least in their current incarnations—suitable for all types of authentication needs. In particular, while tokens are easy to use and are suitable in settings where a user has a significant business relationship with a service provider (such as a financial institution), they are not as well suited for situations that are short-lived or for which the service provider does not have a

---

*This section is by Markus Jakobsson, Zulfikar Ramzan, Susanne Wetzel, Liu Yang, and Erik Stolterman.

sufficient economic incentive to issue tokens. From the perspective of crimeware alone, these settings may not be very important, though.

There is at least one authentication need, however, that is associated with long-lived business relationships of financial importance. Consider the following scenario: You have an OTP token, and you lose or damage it. You can request a replacement to be sent, but how can you authenticate yourself to the service provider in the meantime? And when you report the loss or damage of the token, how can you assure the service provider that you are you, and prevent a stranger from ordering replacement tokens on your behalf?

Life Questions. The standard approach in the case of lost or damaged tokens is to temporarily revert to a static password, and to be extra careful when granting access to accounts in this state. But how does the user authenticate himself or herself when reporting the lost or damaged token? The typical approach is to rely on what is often referred to as *life questions* or *security questions*. These are questions to which the legitimate user would know the answer, but others should not. Traditional examples of these include *What is your mother's maiden name?*, *What is your city of birth?*, and *What was the name of your first pet?* These very questions are not the best, as research has shown. There are ways to automatically derive mother's maiden names from public databases [155]. Some such databases contain birth records, which are useful in determining the answer to the second question. There are also publicly accessible databases listing the most common pet names [312]. A large number of people would have had pets whose names are ranked high on these lists. Moreover, and also importantly, *none of these questions changes over time!* Thus, if the attacker can obtain the answer to one or more of these questions, that, in itself, is a credential, and one that may be valid for multiple service providers.

In this section, we describe an approach that—at least to some extent—addresses this problem. The *preference-based life questions approach* is based on a user providing answers to a large number of suitable life questions upon registering the account. Each time a user is trying to authenticate himself or herself, the user is required to provide a sufficient number of correct answers to a changing subset of the original questions. The life questions are chosen such that their answers cannot easily be determined through the mining of public databases. These two properties, taken in combination, help assure that the user is actively participating in a given authentication session and as such are expected to considerably limit the resale value of the corresponding credentials.

Assumed Adversary. We will describe an approach that assumes a passive *eavesdropping* adversary who manages to record a user's responses for some period of time. This tactic corresponds to a malware attack in which the adversary loses his or her hold over the victim after some period of time—for example, after firewall logs reveal the crimeware's likely presence. While many types of malware are somewhat resistant, it is not clear that it is possible to address the problem of resistant malware in an authentication scenario that does not involve trusted hardware, making it important to investigate just what guarantees can be offered against less advanced attacks. Therefore, we assume that the adversary manages to capture the answers to all questions posed to the targeted user during the duration of infection, but that all other answers remain unknown. Of course, the adversary may attempt to guess the remaining answers, and can base this guessing strategy on supposedly known preference distributions. The system should provide a reasonable degree of security against such an adversary while being simple to use and offering a low false-negative rate (i.e., it should seldom refuse legitimate users access to the resource).

16.2.2 Crimeware Resistance of Existing Approaches

Before proceeding with the main scheme presented in this section, we will survey previously considered authentication mechanisms and discuss their resistance to crimeware.

Text Passwords

The most common user authentication mechanism today is the text-based password, which users typically enter directly on web forms. Passwords have a number of known weaknesses.

First, they are susceptible to dictionary attacks, where an attacker can try all passwords until one works (and most users tend to pick weak passwords).

Second, users tend to use the same password across multiple accounts. Thus, if a password is compromised for one of these accounts, then it is effectively compromised for all of these accounts.

Third, passwords tend to have longevity because they are not changed often. If an attacker can compromise a user's password for a given account, then the attacker can effectively *own* that account for a very long time without having to change the password. From an economic perspective, this consideration is important because it means that passwords have value and can be sold in underground markets. Indeed, they are sold in such markets [401].

Fourth, passwords provide authentication only in a single direction. For example, if a user authenticates to his bank's site using a password, then the bank has some confidence that the user is who he says he is (assuming the password was not compromised). Conversely, the user does not have any assurance that he is talking to his bank.

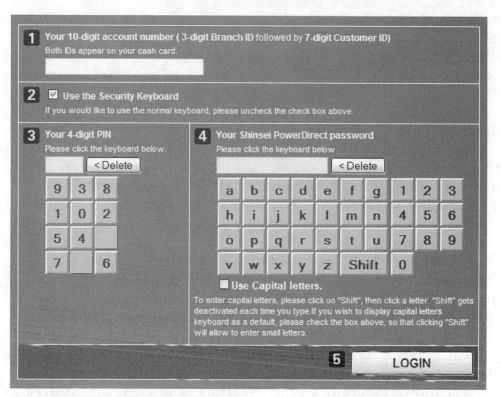

Figure 16.4: A graphical keyboard used as an on-screen input measure. Rather than typing their passwords, users can point and click on the relevant letters. Although this measure does thwart traditional keyloggers, it is still susceptible to other types of malicious client-side software.

Fifth, and most relevant to this text, passwords can be easily stolen by many types of crimeware in use today, such as keyloggers and form grabbers.

On-screen Input Measures

Because text-based passwords are susceptible to keystroke loggers, some argue that on-screen graphical keyboards should be used (see Figure 16.4 taken from the shinseibank.com site for an example). Rather than requiring keystrokes to enter a password, the user can point and click on the characters. Given that no keystrokes are involved, keyloggers cannot break this type of scheme.

Of course, there are other ways to grab passwords entered in this way using crimeware. First, a screenscraper can record the position of the mouse. Second, it is possible to record which portions of the screen were clicked on by the mouse. Finally, each mouse click is translated into a sequence of bits that is transmitted to a server for verification. Client-side crimeware can intercept this stream of bits and use it in the future.

SSL with Client-Side Certificates

An alternative to traditional password authentication involves the use of a client-side certificate with the Secure Sockets Layer (SSL) protocol. The idea is relatively simple. Today, when the SSL protocol is used, a (web) server provides its certificate to a client. The certificate contains the server's public key, and the client encrypts a random string with this public key. This random string is then used as a basis for a cryptographic key that encrypts and authenticates future communication between these two parties. It is also possible (albeit not common) in SSL to allow the client to have its own certificate. Here both the client and the server would encrypt random strings to each other. The resulting cryptographic key would incorporate both random strings. Because of the manner in which both parties are involved in establishing a session key, it becomes impossible for an adversary to eavesdrop on this communication.

A benefit of client-side certificates is that they are a standard part of the SSL/TLS protocol and, in theory, should be implemented on browsers and web servers. One very notable reason that such technologies have not become more widespread is that individual users typically do not have their own certificates. And, if they did, they would need to carry the private key associated with the public key in the certificate (and might possibly have to carry the certificate itself) with them whenever they authenticate themselves. Presumably, they would need some form of external storage for keeping this certificate (e.g., a smartcard, a cell phone, a USB stick, or perhaps even an iPod). Nowadays, users tend to keep more storage with them. Thus, while the lack of a user-friendly storage mechanism for certificates has been a traditional barrier, it is now less of a concern.

From a crimeware perspective, this scheme introduces new risks. Malicious code can now steal the certificate and the private key that is associated with it. While an attacker might have to do more work (in particular, the attacker needs to know how to scan for a cryptographic key), this approach is at least feasible. Some *two-factor authentication* methods can be helpful against malware attacks. Before explaining why, we will review the principles of two-factor authentication.

Two-Factor Authentication

First, let us define what we mean by two-factor authentication. Generally speaking, there are three traditional ways you could authenticate yourself:

1. By something you know (e.g., a password)
2. By something you have (e.g., an ID card or a hardware token)
3. By something you are (e.g., a fingerprint or other biometric data)

With two-factor authentication, two of these mechanisms are employed in hopes that it will be significantly more difficult to circumvent an authentication system that uses two methods. In the online world, two-factor authentication usually involves the first two means of authentication. It seems infeasible to meaningfully incorporate the third item for online authentication given that once one sees a digitization of, say, a fingerprint, those bits can be replayed; of course, in other situations (e.g., where a user has to be physically present), biometric authentication might apply better.

The "something you have" typically means some physical object that theoretically only you (or someone you are willing to allow to act on your behalf) are likely to be in possession of. A classic example of such a "something you have" in the bricks-and-mortar world is a driver's license. In the online world, the physical object could be something very simple, such as a sheet of paper containing a list of additional one-time passwords. When you log in to an account, you would provide (in addition to your normal password) an additional password contained on the list. Supplying the additional password serves as proof that you do, indeed, have possession of the paper containing the passwords.

Tokens such as RSA SecurID [359] essentially just store such a list for you. These *two-factor tokens* are one of the most popular ways to incorporate two-factor authentication into securing online transactions. Using cryptographic hash functions, such a token can actually store this list very efficiently (in fact, it stores only a seed value and computes the list on the fly as needed). At a high level, a two-factor token works as follows: The hardware token and the server both possess knowledge of a secret s. At time t, the two-factor token displays the value $\text{HASH}(s, t)$ where $\text{HASH}()$ is a cryptographic hash function (whose algorithm is either publicly known or at least known to both the client and the server). When the user to whom the token is assigned logs in at time t, she enters this value together with her regular password. The server (which also knows the secret s) can compute the same value. If the user-supplied value and the server-computed value match (and if the user-supplied password is correct), the server has assurance that the user is who she claims to be because the user both possesses the token and knows the correct password.

Alternative mechanisms for such a two-factor token are also possible. For example, rather than having a token compute a one-time password, the server could send a special one-time password to the user via some alternative communication channel (such as over SMS to the user's phone). Then, if the user types that extra password in addition to his normal user password, he has effectively proven both that he knows his password and that he possesses a particular phone.

The main benefit of two-factor tokens is that if an attacker obtains the current value on the token (e.g., by having malicious software on the machine record the value), the attacker will not be able to use that value after a very short period of time. Two-factor tokens do have some notable limitations. First, the use of a two-factor token, in and of itself, does not prevent the damage of crimeware that falls into the transaction generator or session hijacker categories. If such a piece of crimeware is on a machine, and a user types a password in, then that password is still valid (either for that specific transaction or for a short period of time thereafter). Transaction generators or session hijackers can immediately conduct nefarious transactions during this window of opportunity. Using a two-factor token does, however, limit the effectiveness of such attacks when harmful transactions are conducted much later because the one-time password will no longer be useful.

Another limitation of two-factor tokens is that they can result in a *shoebox* (or *necklace*) problem: If every online account required you to carry a two-factor token, you would need a shoebox (or necklace) of such tokens to carry around everywhere. To alleviate such concerns, there are efforts under way to simplify this process through the creation of a *federated two-factor authentication solution* [315].

For all their limitations, one interesting consideration with two-factor tokens is that they change the economics of a crimeware attack. In particular, even if an attacker is able obtain the current value of the token, the attacker cannot easily resell that information because it will be invalid one minute later. Thus, while two-factor tokens may not be perfect in all regards, if they create a situation where attackers cannot make a sufficient profit, then attackers will tend to shift their attention elsewhere.

Password Hashing

Another common problem with passwords is that people often use the same password at multiple sites. Therefore, when one password is compromised, the damage is hard to contain. Password hashing is one technique that is of use here. Blake Ross, Collin Jackson, Nick Miyake, Dan Boneh, and John Mitchell of Stanford University have developed a very nice system, known as PwdHash [357], that implements password hashing and allows users to seamlessly maintain different passwords at different web sites. The system is available for download as a browser plug-in. These different passwords are all derived (through a cryptographic hash function) from a single *master* password—which is the only thing a user has to remember. Furthermore, short of trying a brute-force attack on all possible password choices, it is not feasible for an outsider to infer the master password from a derived password (or even infer a derived password for one site from that used on another).

This idea bears some similarity to the way hardware tokens use cryptographic hash functions, as described earlier. The difference is that the secret s is now replaced with the password, and the time t is replaced with, say, the domain name for a site. For your bank, your derived password, might be HASH(<master password>, www.your-bank-name.com). For your brokerage house, the derived password might be HASH(<master password>, www.your-brokerage-house-name.com). The main benefit of password hashing is that if an attacker obtains your password for one site (e.g., because the attacker installs a keylogger on your machine), you do not have to worry about the implications for other sites where you might use the same password.

The authors of PwdHash [357] note that the idea of password hashing, in and of itself, is not conceptually new. The real contribution of their system is the user interface. The setup requires some effort because users have to replace the passwords on their existing sites with the ones derived using PwdHash. From that point forward, however, the system operates more or less transparently from the user's point of view. Users just attempt to type their master passwords into a password field as they normally do when logging in to their favorite web sites. The system automatically replaces the master password with the derived password. It also incorporates a special password prefix ("@@") that users must type prior to entering their passwords (alternatively, users could press the F2 key prior to entering their passwords). This prefix triggers the PwdHash plug-in prior to when the actual password is entered. This step is important because it is not difficult to write a JavaScript keystroke logger. That is, a malicious person can include JavaScript code on his or her web page to record the password one keystroke at a time (i.e., character by character) as it is entered into the password field. To ensure security, the password hash function has to act immediately so that only a derived password can ultimately find its way into the password field.

This scheme does not resist all types of crimeware—after all, a keylogger can capture the user's master password. Nevertheless, this approach can resist certain strains of crimeware, such as a form grabber.

Spyblock

Collin Jackson, Dan Boneh, and John Mitchell of Stanford University have also developed a system called Spyblock [196] for entering sensitive information into web browsers so that it cannot be sniffed by spyware (such as a keystroke logger). In their approach, users browse the web in a virtual machine (VM). Sensitive information is entered only in a secure environment (outside the VM, but typically on the user's same machine) and injected into the outgoing data stream. A browser extension is used to facilitate the transactions between the secure and insecure environments. Spyblock also includes a number of other features (some of which are discussed in Chapter 6):

- A *transaction confirmation* feature so a user can detect the presence of active malware (i.e., malware that tries to conduct malicious transactions surreptitiously by piggybacking on top of an existing user session).

- Support for password-authenticated key exchange (PAKE), which provides added security against dictionary attacks and supports mutual authentication.

- Support for password hashing, as discussed earlier. In this way, even if a site-specific password is compromised, the damage is limited to only that specific site.

- Use of a user-specified image so an attacker cannot spoof the window in the secure environment into which a user enters his or her password.

The first two features require some back-end server support, whereas the last two do not.

Effectively, the approach taken by Spyblock is to create a type of trusted computing environment that is enabled using a virtual machine. This approach has promise, albeit with a few caveats. First, even though the system involves having the user browse the web in a virtual machine, it is not entirely inconceivable that the user's computer might be infected through some manner that does not involve the web browser. In such a case, the trusted environment will be corrupted, and no security guarantees can be made. The second caveat is that it is possible for attackers to break out of a virtual environment. Naturally this feat is not simple, but this method at least minimizes the number of viable attacks.

Human-Oriented, Challenge-Response Protocols

One classic mechanism for authentication is the *challenge-response protocol*. The idea is that in typical authentication schemes both sides possess knowledge of some common secret and use that secret to establish each other's identity. In a challenge-response protocol, one side would send a *challenge* message to the other side; this message might consist of a unique random string. The *response* would be some appropriate cryptographic function of the string and the common secret. If the challenger knows the secret as well, he or she can verify the response by computing this same function. One benefit of such a protocols is that a shoulder-surfer would not automatically know the secret (given that this person sees only some function of the secret and a unique random string).

While challenge-response protocols provide adequate security, they are not always useful in a setting where a human is involved in the authentication. In particular, because the response is a mathematical function of the challenge, it is often too difficult for a human to carry out (mentally) the steps needed to respond. One appealing approach to authentication would be to construct a challenge-response protocol where the steps could be carried out by a human being.

Hopper and Blum [181] suggested a protocol that moves toward this aim. Their protocol involves computing an inner product of the challenge and the secret. This inner product is carried out in module 10 (so it is possible to compute it mentally, although it may not be easy for the average person to do so). Finally, the inner product is occasionally *perturbed* to make it challenging for an adversary to infer the secret from the challenge and response. Hopper and Blum provide strong theoretical evidence that their protocol is secure by demonstrating that anyone who can compromise the security of their scheme would, in effect, be able to solve the *learning parity with noise* problem—which is assumed to be hard to do. The Hopper-Blum protocol is still probably too difficult for the average person to carry out in sufficient time, but at least it provides some hope that a human challenge-response scheme can be constructed eventually.

Another variation on this idea would involve a *graphical password*. Here the challenge is provided using a graphical image, and the user might have to select some of these images based on a secret. For example, one simple scheme developed by Sobrado and Birget [382] involves the user picking three graphical icons as the password and informing the system of these choices. During authentication, the system provides the user with a grid containing a large number of icons (including the three that the user chose for the secret). To respond, the user simply locates these three icons, visualizes the triangle created by these icons, and then clicks in that triangular region. Here, the response phase involves computing a function that, in effect, is a visualization exercise, and is something most people can do relatively easily.

From a crimeware perspective, the Blum-Hopper and Sobrado-Birget protocols are useful because the only secret is stored in the user's head. Therefore, no malicious client-side software can steal it. Another related scheme, put forth by Weinshall [472], involves having the user pick a secret set of images and then traverse a grid of pictures (including those in the secret set as well as pictures not in the secret set). The path taken depends on the pictures in the secret set. At the end, the user has to report a specific value associated with the exit cell on the grid (i.e., the last cell in the grid that the user traversed). The premise for this scheme is that without knowledge of the secret set, an attacker cannot determine the exit cell and hence cannot determine the value on that cell needed for authentication.

Because the grid is randomized each time it is presented to the user, the hope was that learning one exit cell value would not be sufficient to authenticate in the future. Unfortunately, Golle and Wagner [148] found a weakness in this approach and determined that, after viewing a small number of exit cell values, the user's secret set of pictures could be determined.

All of the previously mentioned challenge-response schemes are conceptually intriguing, but we believe that whether they provide the right combination of adequate real-world security and sufficient usability in practice is still an open question.

To convey the richness of authentication techniques, and to illustrate a less well known authentication technique with anti-crimeware benefits, in the remainder of this section we will explore yet another challenge-response mechanism that might be simple for users and promises to provide some real-world security. More specifically, we will take a close look at *preference-based life questions*.

16.2.3 Preference–Based Life Questions

The intuition behind the preference-based life questions approach is that a user's answers to a given set of suitable life questions will not vary much over time. Thus a user can be authenticated by providing sufficiently many correct answers to a sufficiently large number of questions. While the user is allowed to make some errors in the process, authentication will succeed only if almost all of the user's answers are correct. When considering the correctness of answers, we distinguish between errors that are small and errors that are big. Using a three-point Likert scale for responses ("Really dislike," "Don't care/Don't know," and "Really like"), a *small* error corresponds to a one-step difference—for example, registering the opinion "Really like" for a given question during setup, and later answering "Don't care/Don't know." Likewise, a *big* error corresponds to a two-step difference, such as registering "Really like" during the setup and later answering "Really dislike." Obviously, it makes sense to tolerate small errors to a much larger extent than big errors.

As discussed earlier, the state-of-the-art use of life questions presents the user with very few static questions that lend themselves to data mining and thus does not provide a strong means for authenticating a user. It is difficult to find a sufficient number of questions of this type to obtain a large entropy, especially in the face of data mining threats. In contrast, the preference-based life questions approach allows the use of a larger number of questions and the use of a simpler user interface. While relying on multiple-choice questions affects the entropy negatively, it also makes the user input much more convenient and avoids problems associated with answers that are not identical to the recorded answers, but that have the same meaning to the user. Choosing the right number of suitable questions is key for the approach not only to ensure a sufficient level of security but also to allow for its usability in practice. In particular, it should not be possible to find answers for the questions through simple data mining. At the same time, providing answers to a large number of questions should not burden a user. That is, the answers must come quickly and naturally.

As it turns out, questions that are found on dating web sites have these properties and are well suited to be used in the context of the preference-based life questions approach. In particular, many of the questions on dating web sites reflect long-term personal preferences and not public data, yet the questions are intuitive and can be answered very quickly by any user.

The preference-based life questions approach for user authentication works in two phases, setup and authentication, as shown in Figure 16.5. During the setup phase (i.e., when registering the account), a user is asked to answer a large number of life questions, such as "Do you like game shows?" and "Do you like country music?" The user is asked to respond to these questions by selecting either "Really like" or "Really dislike," or to leave the preselected answer "Don't know/Don't care" unchanged. The answers are submitted to an authentication server. It is assumed that the submission and storage of the answers is done securely, such that these procedures cannot be compromised by an attacker. All questions are related to TV programs, food, music, sports, and similar topics.

An interface for the setup phase is shown in Figure 16.6. Other user interfaces, such as that shown in [188], can be used to address related password reset problems.

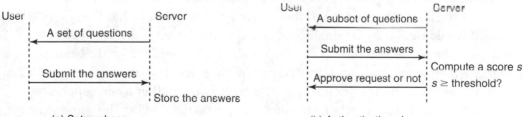

| (a) Setup phase | (b) Authentication phase |

Figure 16.5: The basic scheme of the preference-based life questions approach. The approach works in two phases: setup and authentication. During the setup phase, a user is required to answer a large number of preference-based life questions. The answers are submitted and stored in an authentication server. During the authentication phase, the server prompts the user with a subset of the questions he or she was originally asked during the setup. The answers provided by the user during the authentication phase are compared to the answers of the claimed user during the setup phase, and a score is computed based on the comparison. If the score is above a certain threshold, the user passes the authentication test.

1: My favorite and least favorite TV programs:

Reality shows	○ Really like	◉ Don't care / Don't know	○ Really dislike
News	○ Really like	◉ Don't care / Don't know	○ Really dislike
Sports programs	○ Really like	◉ Don't care / Don't know	○ Really dislike
Dramas	○ Really like	◉ Don't care / Don't know	○ Really dislike
Soap operas	○ Really like	◉ Don't care / Don't know	○ Really dislike
Game show	○ Really like	◉ Don't care / Don't know	○ Really dislike
Documentaries	○ Really like	◉ Don't care / Don't know	○ Really dislike

2: My favorite and least favorite cuisines

Cajun/Southern	○ Really like	◉ Don't care / Don't know	○ Really dislike
French	○ Really like	◉ Don't care / Don't know	○ Really dislike
Indian	○ Really like	◉ Don't care / Don't know	○ Really dislike

Figure 16.6: Part of the interface for the setup phase, during which a user is asked to answer a number of questions by selecting one of three listed opinions for each question.

During authentication (e.g., in the case of a lost OTP token), the server presents the user with a subset of the questions he or she was originally asked during setup. The answers provided during authentication are compared to the respective data stored on the authentication server. For the authentication to succeed, a user is allowed to make some errors but not too many. In particular, the concept distinguishes between small and big errors, where big errors account for dramatic changes in answers and small errors correspond to minor deviations in the answers provided. While it is possible for a legitimate user to make some small errors, it is highly unlikely that a user will make a lot of big errors, considering the fact that the questions reflect a person's long-term preferences, which are relatively stable over an extended period of time. In turn, it is expected that an illegitimate user is very likely to make many big errors because he or she can only guess for which questions the legitimate user might hold strong opinions and what the correct answers would be. This relationship turns out to hold even if the attacker has some partial knowledge about his intended victim. These claims have been experimentally supported, and the detailed findings are described in Section 16.2.6.

Whether the authentication succeeds is based on whether a corresponding score is above or below a certain threshold. In particular, having the same strong opinion for a question in both phases will increase a user's overall score. Making a big error for a question will result in a substantial decrease of the overall score. Making a small error will neither increase nor decrease the score. Similarly, having recorded "Don't care/Don't know" as the answer during the setup phase and later answering this question correctly will neither increase nor decrease the score. These latter choices were made to maximize the resistance to guessing attacks in which the answer "Don't care/Don't like" is given to all questions. Such an attack would otherwise be devastating, as an attacker would not ever take a risk to make a big error using such an approach.

It is possible to implement a policy that allows a user to repeat answering the questions for a second or third time in case the initial answers result in a score that is below the required threshold. The exact response to this situation is a policy issue, of course.

For the method to be resistant against malware attacks, a user will be presented with differing subsets of the original questions for each separate authentication request or time period during which the authentication request takes place. Consequently, it will not be possible for an attacker to capture answers during one request and use it for answering all questions during any subsequent time period.

16.2.4 Characteristics of Good Life Questions

A good life question technique should permit legitimate users to correctly answer the questions while making it unlikely that illegitimate users will correctly do so. Good life questions should also have a high *entropy* [392] to make it a difficult task to exhaustively try all possibilities. Moreover, for a good life question it should not be possible to derive the answer from public data. Thus questions relating to a user's birthday, birth place, high school name, and mother's maiden name are not suitable for use in the context of authentication, because the answers to these questions can readily be found in public databases [155].

It is important not only to select secure questions, but also to consider the user interface. Specifically, the resulting technique should be fast and easy to use, and the security and usability of a set of user-recorded answers should not degrade over time in the sense that it becomes substantially more difficult for legitimate users to correctly answer the questions or substantially easier for illegitimate users to guess the correct answers.

All of these aspects must hold even against an attacker who is able to obtain some personal information of a victim, and the system should be amenable for use by people largely independent of their age, skills, education, cultural background, disability, experience, or beliefs. In terms of cultural background, questions that are ethnicity-dependent should be avoided or, at most, be allowed to contribute to only a small portion of the authentication. For example, many Chinese people will choose the answer "Really like" to the question "Do you like Chinese food?", making this a low-entropy question for this particular demographic group. This is not a problem as long as the average entropy for a selection of questions is sufficiently high. We may consider the entropy in the context of a particular group of users for whom the life questions will be used. Herein, we report on the entropies measured from asking a large number of college students to respond to the selected questions.

Based on these standards, the preference-based life questions approach selects a collection of questions that result in good retention of answers among users, but are unlikely to be guessed correctly by third parties. The selected questions are related to TV programs, foods, music, readings, places to go, sports to do, and sports to watch. One important feature of these questions is that they should reflect who a person is, but not what he or she has recently done. To get the correct answer of a user to a specific question (e.g., whether the user does like reality shows), an adversary may need to get close to this user and observe his or her behavior for an extended period of time. This strategy requires much more effort than determining the mother's maiden name or the birth place of a victim by performing online data mining. Moreover, it is worth noting that whereas a person's *likes* sometimes will leave traces (e.g., a record of a purchase of a CD of a given type), his or her *dislikes* will very rarely leave traces that can be mined by adversaries.

16.2.5 Finding Good Life Questions

As it was pointed out earlier, entropy is an important indicator as to whether a question is a good one. In the context of the preference-based life question approach, the entropy of a question measures the uncertainty of a user's answer to an attacker. The higher the entropy the less likely that an attacker will be able to predict the correct answer by guessing randomly. Thus questions having high entropy are considered to be *good* questions.

To estimate the entropies of the selected questions, an experiment was conducted by asking 423 college students to answer 193 candidate questions anonymously. (The questions are listed in Section 16.2.7.) For each question, the frequency distribution of the answers was computed based on the submitted answers. The frequency distributions were then used to estimate the probability that the average user will choose a specific option as the answer to a particular question. The entropy of each question was computed based on the estimated probabilities. If the distribution of the answers to a question was close to uniform (i.e., the fractions of students having chosen "Really like," "Don't care/Don't know," and "Really dislike" are all close to $\frac{1}{3}$), then it implies that this question has high entropy. A question with uniform or nearly uniform distributed answers makes it very hard for an attacker to provide the correct answer by randomly guessing it.

The computed entropies were used to distinguish good questions from bad ones. For example, "Do you like country music?" is considered to be a good question because it has an entropy of 1.57, which is a high value compared to the overall entropies of all questions, which are in the range of [0, 1.6]. In contrast, the question "Do you like movies?" has a low entropy of 0.61 and is considered a bad question.

16.2.6 Determining Error Rates

As described in Section 16.2.3, a user's score during authentication will be positively affected by correctly answering a question for which he or she has registered a strong opinion during the setup phase. Making a small error or having no strong opinion in both phases for a question will contribute nothing to a user's overall score. Given that only a subset of questions is selected for a user to answer in case he or she requests authentication, the score of a user will be highly dependent on which questions the user is required to answer during this phase. For example, if most of the prompted questions are questions for which the user answered "Don't care/Don't know" during the setup phase, then he or she will get a very low score even if the user gives the exact same answers to these questions in the authentication phase as in the setup phase.

For all users, different combinations of questions may result in different distributions of their scores. For a fixed threshold, the number of users who failed in the authentication (having scores below the threshold) may be different for different selections of questions, rendering different false-negative rates. Owing to the differences in the preference distribution of the original questions, an adversary guessing the answers based on known preference distribution will have different chances to succeed for different selections of questions, resulting in different false-positive rates. A key question is how to divide the original question set into groups such that each group provides both a low false-negative rate and a low false-positive rate for all users. Such a grouping is considered a *beneficial* grouping.

Experiments show that a selection of 123 good questions divided into three subsets having 41 questions each will give low false-negative and false-positive rates for authentication if the questions were grouped in a suitable way. In the experiments, the 123 good questions were selected by using the approach described in Section 16.2.5. During the setup phase, users were required to answer the 123 questions. For the authentication phase, the 123 questions were grouped into three subsets having 41 questions each, and a user was required to answer the questions in one group only. The grouping was the same for all users and thus reflected collections of questions that *on average* minimize the false-positive and false-negative rates. For the ith authentication request, a user was prompted to answer the 41 questions in group (i mod 3). With this approach, it becomes possible to avoid the potential case in which answers captured by malware in one request are applied during the next authentication request. If the user got a score equal to or higher than a threshold, he or she succeeded with the authentication attempt.

A *permutation and search* approach was used to find the most beneficial grouping. First, the 123 questions were randomly ordered a number of times. For each order of the 123 questions, the first 41 questions were considered as group 1, the second 41 questions were considered as group 2, and the last 41 questions were considered as group 3. Then, the false-negative and false-positive rates of each group were computed. For a specific group, the false-negative rate was estimated by the percentage of legitimate users having scores lower than the required threshold, and the false-positive rate was estimated by the percentage of adversaries having scores no less than the required threshold. After the false-negative and false-positive rates for the groups corresponding to all orders were computed, a search operation was performed to find a specific order such that it had the minimum false-negative and false-positive rates in all three groups. Such an order is a beneficial solution to group the 123 questions.

Figure 16.7 shows the false-negative and false-positive rates corresponding to four different orders of the 123 questions among the 1000 random permutations. In Figure 16.7(a), the questions in group 1 provide low false-negative and false-positive rates of 3.85%; the questions in group 2 provide a false negative rate of 3.85% but with an increased false-positive rate; the questions in group 3 provide false-negative and false-positive rates that are greater than those for the other two groups. The groupings in Figure 16.7(b) and Figure 16.7(c) exhibit similar flaws as the grouping in Figure 16.7(a) does. Thus these groupings are not beneficial. In Figure 16.7(d) the questions in each group provide equal and low false-negative and false-positive rates of 3.85%, which is one of the best results obtained after randomly ordering the 123 questions 1000 times. Within a group, the order of questions does not matter.

The beneficial grouping indicated average suitability and does not necessarily imply that all legitimate users got the highest scores. Instead, this grouping maximizes a random user's chance to obtain a score above the threshold so as to pass the authentication test, while minimizing the likelihood that an illegitimate user is able to succeed. It is important to note that the beneficial solution may be not unique.

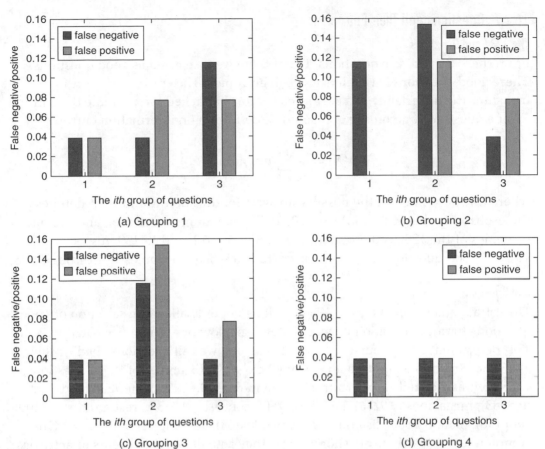

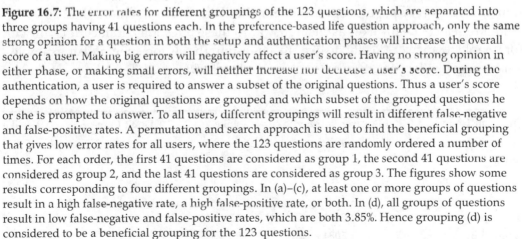

Figure 16.7: The error rates for different groupings of the 123 questions, which are separated into three groups having 41 questions each. In the preference-based life question approach, only the same strong opinion for a question in both the setup and authentication phases will increase the overall score of a user. Making big errors will negatively affect a user's score. Having no strong opinion in either phase, or making small errors, will neither increase nor decrease a user's score. During the authentication, a user is required to answer a subset of the original questions. Thus a user's score depends on how the original questions are grouped and which subset of the grouped questions he or she is prompted to answer. To all users, different groupings will result in different false-negative and false-positive rates. A permutation and search approach is used to find the beneficial grouping that gives low error rates for all users, where the 123 questions are randomly ordered a number of times. For each order, the first 41 questions are considered as group 1, the second 41 questions are considered as group 2, and the last 41 questions are considered as group 3. The figures show some results corresponding to four different groupings. In (a)–(c), at least one or more groups of questions result in a high false-negative rate, a high false-positive rate, or both. In (d), all groups of questions result in low false-negative and false-positive rates, which are both 3.85%. Hence grouping (d) is considered to be a beneficial grouping for the 123 questions.

16.2.7 Questions and Their Entropies

The 123 Good Questions

From the 193 candidate questions, 123 of them were selected as good questions. These good questions have relatively high entropies. The entropy of a question measures the uncertainty of a user's answer to an attacker. We compute the entropy En of a question X according to Shannon's definition on information entropy:

$$En(X) = -\sum_{i=1}^{3} p(x_i)\log_2(p(x_i))$$

where $\{x_1, x_2, x_3\}$ denote the possible answers for question X and $p(x_i)$ denotes the probability that $X = x_i$ for $i = 1, 2, 3$. The maximum, minimum, and average entropies of the 123 good questions are 1.5659, 1.3072, and 1.4159, respectively. The 123 good questions used in the user study are listed in Tables 16.1 through 16.8.

Bad Questions

The estimated entropies for the 193 questions not only allow the selection of good questions for authentication purposes, but also allow one to identify bad questions. This determination, of course, is subjective. Here, we call questions "bad" if their answer distributions result in an entropy below 1.0. Examples of these questions, with their associated answer entropies, are movies (0.6095), American food (0.8583), magazines (0.9286), beach (0.6760), concerts (0.9135), restaurants (0.7109), shopping mall (0.9800), listening to music (0.9803), and television (0.9864). One common feature of these questions is that they actually refer to events or activities that are either very popular or too general. Statistics show that more than 70% of students select "Really like" as their answer to these questions. In fact, it is difficult for people to answer "Really dislike" to a question that is too general. For example, a user may dislike some types of movies but like movies in general. In practice, bad

Question Topic	Answer Entropy	Like	Don't Care	Dislike
Reality shows	1.4632	50.6%	31.9%	17.5%
News	1.3403	36.9%	53.4%	9.7%
Sports programs	1.4205	52.2%	33.3%	14.4%
Dramas	1.3991	52.7%	34.3%	13.0%
Soap operas	1.3614	12.3%	31.2%	56.5%
Game show	1.5084	34.3%	45.9%	19.9%
Documentaries	1.5308	36.4%	42.3%	21.2%

Table 16.1: My favorite and least favorite TV programs (7 good questions).

Question Topic	Answer Entropy	Like	Don't Care	Dislike
Cajun/Southern	1.3925	48.0%	40.7%	11.3%
French	1.3887	29.3%	56.3%	14.4%
Indian	1.4800	21.0%	51.3%	27.7%
Japanese/sushi	1.5396	44.4%	31.4%	24.1%
Jewish/kosher	1.3146	11.3%	60.0%	28.6%
Korean	1.3301	15.6%	61.9%	22.5%
Mediterranean	1.3943	25.3%	57.7%	17.0%
Middle Eastern	1.3512	17.3%	61.0%	21.7%
Seafood	1.5023	49.2%	28.6%	22.2%
Soul food	1.4151	31.9%	53.4%	14.7%
Southwestern	1.3287	31.2%	57.9%	10.9%
Spanish	1.3680	41.1%	48.7%	10.2%
Thai	1.4649	34.8%	48.7%	16.5%
Vegan	1.3214	8.5%	52.2%	39.2%
Vegetarian/organic	1.5298	22.9%	45.4%	31.7%

Table 16.2: My favorite and least favorite cuisines (15 good questions).

questions do not help to distinguish and thus authenticate people. On the contrary, for bad questions it is much easier for an attacker to guess the correct answers according to the known frequency distributions, which negatively affects the security of the systems. Consequently, bad questions, such as those shown in Tables 16.9 through 16.16, should not be used in the preference-based life questions approach.

Conclusion

In this section, we described how the choice of authentication technique may change the economic incentives of crimeware attacks. We briefly discussed the use of second-factor authentication tokens as a tool to reduce the resale value of captured credentials, and we reviewed the situations in which such tokens are suitable. It is important to recognize that while these tokens have many benefits, they cannot always be used. For example, one needs a backup authentication mechanism to report lost or broken tokens. If this backup authentication mechanism is significantly weaker than the token authentication, or if it does not offer the same protection against crimeware, then it becomes the weakest link and will be the target of attacks.

Preference-based life questions can be used to build a meaningful, crimeware-resistant authentication mechanism. While the mechanism described in this

Question Topic	Answer Entropy	Like	Don't Care	Dislike
Acoustic	1.3376	53.2%	36.4%	10.6%
Alternative	1.3590	53.2%	36.2%	10.6%
Big band/swing	1.4183	19.1%	56.5%	24.4%
Blues	1.4763	26.0%	52.0%	22.0%
Christian and gospel	1.4865	20.3%	50.1%	29.6%
Classical	1.4890	24.1%	51.6%	24.8%
Country	1.5659	40.0%	33.3%	26.7%
Dance/electronica	1.5287	30.3%	46.1%	23.6%
Disco	1.4708	18.7%	50.8%	30.5%
Easy listening	1.4420	32.2%	51.8%	16.1%
Folk	1.3930	11.3%	47.8%	40.9%
Hard rock and metal	1.5386	22.7%	43.0%	34.3%
Indie	1.4619	19.9%	52.7%	27.4%
Instrumental	1.4291	21.5%	56.0%	22.5%
Jazz	1.4324	27.0%	54.8%	18.2%
Modern rock 'n roll	1.3369	53.2%	37.4%	9.5%
New Age	1.3873	25.1%	58.2%	16.8%
Oldies	1.3921	44.9%	44.0%	11.1%
Opera	1.3667	9.9%	46.6%	43.5%
Pop/top 40	1.3072	57.7%	32.9%	9.5%
Punk	1.5173	32.6%	46.1%	21.3%
Reggae	1.4218	32.9%	52.5%	14.7%
Show tunes	1.4292	21.7%	56.0%	22.2%
Soul/R&B	1.3841	41.4%	47.8%	10.9%
World music/ethnic	1.3723	13.9%	57.4%	28.6%

Table 16.3: My favorite and least favorite music (25 good questions).

Question Topic	Answer Entropy	Like	Don't Care	Dislike
Comics	1.5345	27.4%	46.1%	26.5%
Nonfiction	1.3671	44.0%	46.1%	9.9%
Poetry	1.5098	20.3%	46.3%	33.3%

Table 16.4: My favorite and least favorite things to read (3 good questions).

section is far from convenient for users, it should be noted that this may be tolerable for backup authentication mechanisms. Moreover, and as suggested by related findings [188], other user interfaces may positively affect the user experience and make mechanisms of this kind more appealing.

Question Topic	Answer Entropy	Like	Don't Care	Dislike
Antique stores	1.5272	21.0%	43.0%	35.9%
Art galleries	1.5319	31.2%	45.4%	23.4%
Bookstores	1.3919	43.5%	45.4%	11.1%
Coffee houses	1.3414	52.2%	38.3%	9.5%
Flea markets	1.4763	35.7%	47.3%	17.0%
Garage sales	1.4916	32.2%	48.5%	19.4%
Karaoke/sing-along	1.4943	33.8%	47.3%	18.9%
Libraries	1.4375	23.6%	55.3%	21.0%
Live theater	1.3775	45.4%	44.2%	10.4%
Museums	1.4273	44.2%	42.8%	13.0%
Opera	1.4634	16.3%	48.5%	35.2%
Political events	1.4392	14.7%	49.4%	35.9%
Raves/parties	1.4147	52.2%	33.8%	13.9%
Skate/bike parks	1.3972	14.4%	55.3%	30.3%
Symphony	1.4171	16.3%	55.1%	28.6%
Volunteer events	1.3189	42.3%	49.6%	8.0%

Table 16.5: My favorite and least favorite places to go to (16 good questions).

Question Topic	Answer Entropy	Like	Don't Care	Dislike
Aerobics	1.4102	48.9%	38.5%	12.5%
Auto racing	1.3877	11.8%	51.5%	36.6%
Baseball	1.4931	42.8%	39.7%	17.5%
Basketball	1.3495	56.7%	31.7%	11.6%
Billiards/pool	1.4612	43.7%	41.1%	15.1%
Cycling	1.4008	33.1%	53.4%	13.5%
Football	1.3257	54.4%	36.4%	9.2%
Golf	1.5398	31.9%	44.2%	23.9%
Hockey	1.3953	20.1%	58.4%	21.5%
Inline skating	1.4023	21.7%	57.9%	20.3%
Martial arts	1.3727	15.8%	58.9%	25.3%
Running	1.4691	49.6%	32.9%	17.5%
Skiing	1.3429	42.3%	48.7%	9.0%
Soccer	1.4144	42.8%	44.9%	12.3%
Tennis/racquet	1.3476	48.9%	41.8%	9.2%
Volleyball	1.3515	45.2%	45.6%	9.2%
Yoga	1.4484	36.2%	48.7%	15.1%

Table 16.6: What kinds of sports/exercise do you enjoy to do? (17 good questions).

Question Topic	Answer Entropy	Like	Don't Care	Dislike
Antiques	1.3583	11.1%	54.6%	34.3%
Arts	1.4386	32.9%	51.5%	15.6%
Astrology	1.3119	10.6%	59.3%	30.0%
Bars/pubs	1.3335	54.6%	35.7%	9.7%
Board games	1.3150	43.5%	48.7%	7.8%
Cars	1.3594	31.0%	56.7%	12.3%
Casino/gambling	1.3878	23.2%	58.6%	18.2%
Cats	1.4980	22.7%	49.9%	27.4%
Collecting	1.3164	16.8%	63.1%	20.1%
Community service	1.3448	34.8%	54.8%	10.4%
Computers/Internet	1.3354	51.3%	39.7%	9.0%
Cooking	1.3172	53.2%	38.3%	8.5%
Crafts	1.4139	35.2%	51.3%	13.5%
Creative writing	1.4065	17.7%	57.0%	25.3%
Dance clubs	1.3565	49.4%	40.9%	9.7%
Dancing	1.3392	52.7%	37.8%	9.5%
Fashion events	1.4646	43.7%	40.9%	15.4%
Gaming	1.4245	31.4%	53.2%	15.4%
Home improvement	1.3342	23.4%	61.5%	15.1%
Motorcycles	1.3094	13.9%	62.6%	23.4%
Museum/arts	1.3778	34.0%	53.9%	12.1%
News/politics	1.4218	20.6%	56.5%	22.9%
Painting	1.3469	24.4%	60.5%	15.1%
Philosophy	1.3335	17.5%	62.2%	20.3%
Reading	1.3840	38.1%	50.6%	11.3%
Religion/spirituality	1.3290	30.0%	58.6%	11.3%
Theater	1.3674	40.9%	48.9%	10.2%
TV: educational	1.3244	30.7%	58.4%	10.9%
Video games	1.4475	32.4%	51.3%	16.3%
Yoga	1.3264	27.7%	60.0%	12.3%

Table 16.7: In my free time I am interested in (30 good questions).

Question Topic	Answer Entropy	Like	Don't Care	Dislike
Auto racing	1.4509	14.4%	42.8%	42.8%
Baseball	1.5112	45.2%	35.0%	19.9%
Bowling	1.4521	14.9%	46.8%	38.3%
Diving	1.5066	29.6%	48.5%	22.0%
Extreme sports	1.4573	44.2%	40.9%	14.9%
Figure skating	1.5448	37.1%	40.2%	22.7%
Golf	1.5515	25.3%	42.8%	31.9%
Hockey	1.5000	27.7%	49.6%	22.7%
Soccer	1.4857	46.1%	36.4%	17.5%
Tennis	1.5097	37.4%	43.5%	19.1%

Table 16.8: What kinds of sports do you enjoy watching? (10 good questions).

Question Topic	Answer Entropy	Like	Don't Care	Dislike
Sitcoms	1.0723	70.2%	24.8%	5.0%
Movies	0.6095	88.2%	9.5%	2.4%

Table 16.9: My favorite and least favorite TV programs (2 bad questions).

Question Topic	Answer Entropy	Like	Don't Care	Dislike
American	0.8583	79.4%	17.5%	3.1%
Barbeque	1.1684	66.9%	25.8%	7.3%
California-fusion	1.2082	22.0%	67.4%	10.6%
Caribbean/Cuban	1.293	26.7%	61.9%	11.3%
Chinese/dim sum	1.2987	61.5%	27.2%	11.3%
Continental	1.205	21.0%	67.8%	11.1%
Deli	1.1689	62.2%	32.9%	5.0%
Eastern European	1.2738	24.4%	63.8%	11.8%
Fast food/pizza	1.2068	67.1%	22.7%	10.2%
German	1.3039	16.5%	63.8%	19.6%
Italian	1.0192	74.0%	20.6%	5.4%
Mexican	1.0786	71.6%	22.0%	6.4%
South American	1.1788	16.8%	70.0%	13.2%
Vietnamese	1.2892	12.1%	62.9%	25.1%

Table 16.10: My favorite and least favorite cuisines (14 bad questions).

Question Topic	Answer Entropy	Like	Don't Care	Dislike
Classic rock'n roll	1.2779	57.9%	34.0%	8.0%
Rap/hip hop	1.2461	63.4%	27.4%	9.2%
Soundtracks	1.2518	51.5%	42.8%	5.7%

Table 16.11: My favorite and least favorite music (3 bad questions).

Question Topic	Answer entropy	Like	Don't Care	Dislike
Fiction	1.2642	58.4%	34.0%	7.6%
Magazines	0.9286	76.6%	19.9%	3.5%
Newspapers	1.2942	55.6%	36.4%	8.0%
Trade journals	1.2844	6.6%	48.5%	44.9%

Table 16.12: My favorite and least favorite things to read (4 bad questions).

Question Topic	Answer Entropy	Like	Don't Care	Dislike
Amusement parks	1.0192	74.2%	20.0%	5.7%
Bars/nightclubs	1.1404	68.6%	24.4%	7.1%
Beach	0.6760	85.6%	12.5%	1.9%
Charity events	1.2956	36.6%	55.3%	8.0%
Circuit parties	1.1673	16.8%	70.4%	12.8%
Comedy clubs	1.2609	54.4%	39.2%	6.4%
Concerts	0.9135	78.7%	16.3%	5.0%
Dance clubs	1.2744	62.2%	27.7%	10.2%
Movies	0.7429	84.2%	12.8%	3.1%
Parks	1.1981	60.3%	34.3%	5.4%
Restaurants	0.7109	83.0%	16.1%	0.9%
Shopping malls	0.9800	74.5%	21.5%	4.0%
Sporting events	1.0278	73.5%	21.0%	5.4%

Table 16.13: My favorite and least favorite places to go to (13 bad questions).

Question Topic	Answer Entropy	Like	Don't Care	Dislike
Dancing	1.2972	58.9%	31.7%	9.5%
Swimming	1.2777	59.1%	32.4%	8.5%
Walking/hiking	1.2968	54.1%	38.1%	7.8%
Weights/machines	1.2150	63.1%	29.6%	7.3%

Table 16.14: What kinds of sports/exercise do you enjoy to do? (4 bad questions).

Question Topic	Answer Entropy	Like	Don't Care	Dislike
Concerts	1.0554	69.7%	26.2%	4.0%
Darts	1.2303	17.7%	67.6%	14.7%
Dining	1.0768	64.1%	33.3%	2.6%
Dinner parties	1.2399	56.0%	38.1%	5.9%
Dogs	1.1160	63.4%	33.1%	3.5%
Family/kids	1.0857	60.8%	37.1%	2.1%
Fine dining	1.2479	50.1%	44.4%	5.4%
Gardening	1.295	14.4%	63.8%	21.7%
Health/fitness	1.2007	59.1%	35.7%	5.2%
Investing	1.2583	15.1%	66.2%	18.7%
Listening to music	0.9803	73.8%	22.7%	3.5%
Movies	0.8771	78.3%	18.9%	2.8%
Outdoor activities	1.1496	61.2%	34.8%	4.0%
Photography	1.2634	44.9%	49.1%	5.9%
Playing music	1.3047	45.9%	46.8%	7.3%
Playing sports	1.2068	61.9%	31.7%	6.4%
Poetry	1.2987	14.2%	63.6%	22.0%
Shopping	1.1941	60.8%	33.8%	5.4%
Social cause	1.219	21.5%	67.1%	11.3%
Surfing the web	1.2437	53.9%	40.4%	5.7%
Television	0.9864	72.1%	25.1%	2.8%
Travel	1.0688	61.7%	36.4%	1.9%
TV: entertainment	1.0650	63.4%	34.5%	2.1%
Volunteering	1.2962	35.7%	56.0%	8.3%
Watching sports	1.2864	57.4%	34.3%	8.3%

Table 16.15: In my free time I am interested in (25 bad questions).

Question Topic	Answer Entropy	Like	Don't Care	Dislike
Basketball	1.1337	69.5%	22.9%	7.6%
Cricket	1.2290	5.2%	54.1%	40.7%
Football	1.1406	69.7%	22.0%	8.3%
Olympic sports	1.2423	63.4%	27.7%	9.0%
Squash/racquetball	1.2422	7.1%	59.8%	33.1%

Table 16.16: What kinds of sports do you enjoy watching? (5 bad questions).

16.3 Virtual Machines as a Crimeware Defense Mechanism*

The biggest problem with crimeware is that if it can gain control of the system, it can access everything on that system. By installing a keystroke logger, all passwords become exposed. Because the crimeware is inside the system, when encrypted files are decrypted by the system, they become available to the crimeware, too. In such a setup, nothing is safe.

The cause of the problem here is that there is no form of data isolation. Thus the obvious solution is to implement some form of data isolation. The difficulty in achieving that goal comes from the fact that everything is on the same system, and the operating system needs full access to everything on the system. This relationship arises because the operating system provides the data to the applications. If the crimeware has sufficient privileges (for example, Local System on the Windows platform), then it will have the same access that the operating system has, and any data isolation measures will be circumvented.

One way to perform a more strict data isolation is to physically separate different kinds of data. For example, a web server that supports some kind of online shopping should not store the credit card details on the same system. Instead, an internal network connection to another system should be used to perform the query and store off that information. While crimeware on one system could still capture the details as they pass, it would first have to understand the protocol that is in use. In the same way, a user's system could be set up whereby one machine is used to browse the Internet and the other machine holds any sensitive information. The second machine could supply the information on demand from the first machine. This type of system would mostly prevent unauthorized access to "interesting" data such as credit card details, although a keystroke logger on the first machine would still receive all passwords that were typed in. Such physical separation is preferred over such methods as chroot on UNIX, which simply changes the root directory. Chroot is not a security mechanism, and it has no defense against sufficiently privileged applications that access files outside the current directory.

Of course, multiple physical machines are not an ideal solution for most people, not least because they require more physical space and power. An alternative that has been gaining popularity recently is the use of virtual machines. One possibility is to replace one of the two physical machines in the example with one virtual machine within a single physical machine. The virtual machine can be used to

---

*This section is by Peter Ferrie.

browse the Internet, whereas the physical machine holds any sensitive information. This setup saves physical space and is almost as secure as having two physical
machines. As before, a keystroke logger on the virtual machine would still receive
all passwords that were typed in.

A virtual machine has a number of advantages over a physical machine.
Depending on the software that controls the virtual machine, a virtual machine's
contents can be "nonpersistent." In other words, when the software exits, the
changes that were made to the virtual machine environment are not saved; as a
consequence, a pristine image is always available. This scheme is ideal for things
such as browsing the Internet, as any wanted file that is downloaded can be
exported to the physical machine through user interaction, and anything else that
might have landed in the virtual machine will be discarded when the virtual
machine is shut down.

An extension to this "virtual browser" model is to increase the number of
virtual machines that are used, and to separate the browsing actions that are
performed in any one of those virtual machines. For example, one virtual machine
could be used solely for Internet banking; another virtual machine could be used
solely for online shopping; and yet another virtual machine could be used solely for
browsing arbitrary sites, such as news and web mail. This kind of isolation helps to
mitigate the problem of a keystroke logger capturing all passwords that are typed
in, because the keystroke logger would now need to be present in all of the virtual
machines rather than in just one of them. It also mitigates some cross-site attacks
for the same reason.

In this example, each virtual machine contains an operating system and a
single application, which produces an interesting side effect: The only application
that should be accessing the Internet is the browser. Thus, if personal firewall
software is installed on the virtual machine, and any other application then
attempts to connect to the Internet or open a port, it is highly likely that malicious
activity is in progress.

The problem with multiple virtual machines is similar to the problem with
multiple physical machines—the increase in the number of machines also increases
the work required to maintain them. With enough machines, this setup quickly
becomes unmanageable. There is also the risk of using the "wrong" virtual machine
for a particular task. However, this kind of mix-up can occur only when the virtual
machine is used in "persistent" mode, which would be the case if the user wanted
the ability to update a Favorites list, for example. The use of multiple virtual
machines for browsing individual sites is also non-intuitive. The common usage
of a browser is to have a single instance of the browser running with multiple
windows or tabs open to those individual sites. The performance impact of virtual

machines in general is significant, and when combined with the number of virtual machines that would be required to serve a typical user's browsing habits, the physical machine would likely be overloaded.

While placing the browser in a virtual machine is a good idea, it should be noted that the browser is not the only vulnerable component on a system. Extrapolating from the virtual browser leads to a "virtual application" model. In this model, every individual application is placed into its own virtual machine. This scheme allows for almost complete data isolation and, as a result, is very safe. Of course, multiple applications can be installed on a single virtual machine, but then the data isolation is broken to some degree. The problem of multiple virtual machines still exists, but it is not as common to run as many different applications simultaneously as when compared to the number of sites likely to be open in a browser.

It is really up to the user to decide about security versus system performance. As noted earlier, running multiple virtual machines simultaneously causes a serious load to be placed on the CPU and the storage hardware. Of course, a user could configure a VM to suspend itself when it is not being actively used—but the typical user will probably not take that step.

In the simplest implementation of the virtual application model, each application has unique data files that will not be dynamically shared with any other application, but merely transferred between the virtual machine and the physical machine or other virtual machines, under the user's control. Therefore, a difficulty arises when applications want to communicate with each other. For example, if the user is running an email application in one virtual machine and wants to import pictures that were created in a graphics application in another virtual machine, how can that goal be achieved? Even the more common task of copying and pasting of text becomes a problem.

One way to import the pictures is for the user to copy the pictures from the graphics virtual machine to the email virtual machine—but that tactic leads to the existence of two versions of the pictures within the system. The copy of the picture that was intended for email can be deleted after sending, of course, but many users will not perform that extra step. Another option is to place the pictures into a directory either on the physical machine or on one of the other virtual machines that is visible to the virtual machine through a network interface, such as a drive mapping. The problem with this method is that it breaks the data isolation again. The likely eventual result is a complete collection of data in the directory that will be visible to virtual machines, including the sensitive data that was supposed to be protected in the first place.

For applications that want to invoke other applications, a similar approach is necessary: The virtual machines need to be connected, but in a way that the operating system itself understands, so that the invocation is transparent. The most popular method is to arrange the virtual machines in their own private network. Once again, the problem with connecting the virtual machines together is that the data isolation is broken, as any virtual machine can then access the files on any other virtual machine. From there, what is to stop crimeware on one virtual machine from requesting data from all of the other virtual machines, just as it would if it were on a physical machine?

An "application firewall" comes into play at this point. Normally, if an application within any one virtual machine requests data directly from any other virtual machine, when the second virtual machine receives the request, the information about the requesting application is lost. Instead, the request appears to come directly from the operating system itself and, therefore, cannot be denied. However, if an application firewall is installed on all virtual machines, it will intercept the request from the first virtual machine, and pass to the second virtual machine the appropriate information: the request for the data and the application that made the request. The application firewall on the second virtual machine can then decide whether to allow or deny the request. The decision is not arbitrary, though. The user must establish the relationships between all applications and all data for those applications.

As with a personal firewall, an application firewall can be programmed to go through a "learning" process. This learning can take one of two forms. The first type of learning is to simply log but allow all requests for some period of time, to get an idea of the typical requests. After the time has expired, any requests that are not of the type that have already been seen can be considered anomalous and denied, or the user can be prompted to make a decision. This method is the most lightweight and transparent from a user's point of view. The second type of learning is to prompt the user every time a request is made of a type that has not been seen before. This method is the most intrusive but also the most accurate, provided that the user does not tire of the prompts and start to accept all of them without any consideration.

In either case, once an application firewall has been set up, any crimeware that is introduced to the system afterward should be detected very quickly if it requests data on its own, because it will not be among the list of applications for which data are allowed to be accessed. Depending on the firewall, the very presence of the crimeware might be sufficient to trigger a detection, as the trusted processes that exist on the virtual machine might be known to the firewall. Thus any new process that appears will be viewed as suspicious.

The use of virtual machines is not limited to ordinary applications. Anti-crimeware researchers often use virtual machines for the analysis of new crimeware samples. This fact is well known to crimeware authors, some of whom have started producing samples that detect the presence of the virtual machine [117]. The sample can be programmed to behave differently if a virtual machine is detected: silently refusing to run at all; running with different characteristics (opening different ports, for example, or creating files with different names); or attacking the virtual machine itself, most commonly through a denial-of-service attack. Research into the detection of virtual machines is ongoing on both sides, as current virtual machines were not designed with "stealth" in mind. That is, they make no real attempt to hide their presence from the software that runs inside them. As a result, a number of methods have been found to detect and attack them [118].

One reason why this technique is not more popular is quite possibly because there is no way for crimeware to reliably determine whether it is running in a virtual machine that belongs to an ordinary user, a corporation, or an ISP (i.e., a machine of interest) or in a virtual machine that belongs to an anti-crimeware researcher (i.e., a machine to avoid). Thus to behave differently or to attack the virtual machine risks not running properly on a potentially valuable machine.

From a security point of view, the use of virtual machines for hosting applications has an unexpected benefit, which relates to rootkits.[1] The use of rootkits to hide the presence of other malware is on the rise. Those rootkits are also becoming ever more advanced, being able to hide themselves almost completely from other applications within the operating system. What is visible to the applications within the operating system is usually slight anomalies in various system structures, process lists, and other items, but the files responsible for those anomalies usually remain hidden and/or otherwise inaccessible. The usual remedy is to boot the system from known clean media and to perform analysis of the compromised system using applications that exist outside the operating system. The justification for this strategy is that the rootkit becomes visible immediately when it is no longer running.

By contrast, if the compromised system is the virtual machine, rather than the physical machine, then all that is required is to shut down the virtual machine; the analysis can then be performed on the virtual image. In that case, there is no need to shut down the physical machine at all. Remediation is also simple: Just restore the virtual image from the original. This step is far easier to take than to format a disk and reinstall the operating system on a physical machine.

---

1. Rootkits are discussed in more detail in Chapter 8.

Chapter 17

The Future of Crimeware

Markus Jakobsson and Zulfikar Ramzan

Malware is becoming an ever-more serious threat to the trustworthiness of our infrastructure. The problem has already reached proportions that many consider catastrophic, but the situation shows no signs of improving. Instead, as we rely on software in more and more settings, including vehicular and medical applications, the severity of the problem is intensified. Moreover, given the increasing reliance on software in our society, malware is no longer a threat just to Internet commerce, but also poses a risk in the context of electronic warfare.

Crimeware is the most worrying aspect of malware: It is malware written by criminals whose goals are not fame but wealth, and whose software does not constitute practical jokes to the victims but loss of money, information, and perhaps lives. Crimeware is a problem that almost did not exist just a few years ago, but that now permeates the Internet. Where is it headed?

17.1 Crimeware, Terrorware, Vandalware, and Ransomware

While one might argue that crimeware is just a particular type of malware, and malware has been around for a long time, many security specialists argue that the two are different due to the incentives of the attackers, and that this is a critical difference. For this reason, we should also be concerned with what we may term *terrorware* and *vandalware*. These types of software would, like crimeware, be specific examples of malware, but with very particular deployment incentives that make them noteworthy.

Terrorware, or malware written with the intention of causing harm to nation-states, is a simple twist on crimeware that—instead of transferring funds from victims to attackers—simply aims at transferring funds *away from* the victims or their representatives. Terrorware does not have to focus on money, however. It might aim to do various types of damage to the infrastructure and people's trust in it, or it might increase the maintenance costs of critical structures. There is no doubt that terrorware is an emerging threat, and governments and financial institutions have already seen attempts from hostile groups and nations. While these attacks often relate to attempts to gain access to resources by stealing credentials, a more general threat could just as easily use malware as a principal attack vector. Note that the malware in question does not necessarily have to infect machines geographically located within the boundaries of a particular nation-state. Instead, external machines could be infected and then used to launch a denial-of-service attack. One example along the lines just discussed were the cyberattacks on Estonia, where attackers continuously bombarded the country's networks with 90 megabit per second data streams [228].

We might think of vandalware as the "little brother" of terrorware. Whereas terrorware may be sponsored by well-established terror organizations or even governments, vandalware may be maintained and used by loosely connected groups of people with political or corporate reasons to attack systems. This characteristic would make vandalware a natural component within the burgeoning hacktivism movement. Like terrorware, the objective would primarily be that of inflicting damage.

Both terrorware and vandalware are *easier* to implement than crimeware in some sense, as there is no need for the attacker to collect spoils, which in turn limits the audit trail. The relationship between the three is still noteworthy, as expressed by the potential advent of mainstream ransomware—malware that will inflict damages unless a ransom is paid or, more generally, unless some organization agrees to perform some action such as free prisoners, transfer funds, initiate economic sanctions, or shine media attention on the cause favored by the aggressors. Moreover, valdalware can be put to use to cause political disruption—for example, by profiling voters and distributing invalid information, such as the time and location where they can cast votes.

While these types of crimeware instances would certainly be noteworthy, it is not clear that they will ever become prevalent. Attacks of this nature are fairly loud, and they may not offer attackers the risk/reward ratio they are seeking. For example, a distributed denial-of-service attack would immediately expose the machines in an attacker's bot network, thereby making it easier to shut them down. Given that the attacker does not receive monetary payment in advance, his or her opportunity cost may be significant in this scenario. In contrast, if the same compromised machines were rented for use as spam zombies, the attacker would get an immediate monetary benefit. While there will likely always be attackers who get involved in high-profile nefarious activity, the vast majority of attackers will likely opt for quieter and less risky means of monetizing their malicious efforts.

17.2 New Applications and Platforms

Thus far crimeware has typically affected traditional computing devices such as laptop and desktop PCs. In part, this concentration may be due to both the prevalence of such devices and the standard software that runs on them. A single piece of crimeware that can run on Windows XP or Windows Vista can potentially affect hundreds of millions of machines. Consequently, these platforms will be high-valued targets for crimeware authors.

When it comes to alternative platforms, there does not yet seem to be such a dominant standard. Consequently, we would not expect crimeware authors to heavily target such non-mainstream platforms, unless they see a clear path to profitability. In contrast, security researchers are often eager to analyze any new and much-hyped technologies, aiming to find security holes. These researchers might be motivated by intellectual curiosity or sometimes fame, recognition among peers, or other means of personal reward.

Given that crimeware is designed to serve financially motivated goals, we would expect that most crimeware in the future will target widespread platforms. Having said that, crimeware might occasionally be written for less prevalent operating platforms. In particular, a piece of crimeware could be *targeted*—whether for an application or a platform, neither of which has to be a mainstream application or platform for the attack to take place. We consider some non-mainstream targets next.

17.2.1 Reputation Systems, Auction Sites, and Gambling Applications

One historic example of an uncommon application being targeted by crimeware is Trojan.checkraise [338]. This program disguised itself as a rake-back calculator, which is often used by online poker players.[1] This particular rake-back calculator

---

1. Online poker sites profit by taking a small percentage (usually up to a maximum) of each pot that is played. This amount is called the rake. To draw more traffic to their sites and entice new customers, many sites offer rake-back promotions. These promotions are typically offered through affiliates; when a customer signs up for an account to a given poker site through a particular affiliate, the customer receives a small percentage of whatever rake was deducted from poker hands he or she was involved in. The affiliate also receives a commission for referring the customer. Rake-back calculators allow online poker players to estimate how much rake they would get back through a given rake-back promotion.

actually stole passwords associated with popular online poker sites. Clearly, rake-back calculators are the kind of tool only a small number of people will try (you not only have to be an online poker player, but you also have to be serious and knowledgable enough to know about rake-back promotions). From an attacker's perspective, however, even a single victim might provide a very high yield, especially if the account belongs to a high-stakes poker player.

Poker sites also provide a natural mechanism for transferring money. Many sites allow direct interplayer transfers (or the transfer can happen in more diabolical ways, such as by having one player "dump" a certain amount of money to another player during the course of play by purposefully playing hands badly). A series of such transfers could prove difficult to trace.

Another way to make it difficult to trace funds can be seen in the following scenario: Bob asks Alice to transfer him money on site A in exchange for having Alice transfer Bob the same amount on site B. Such transactions are commonplace among poker players (who know and trust one another) as a fast mechanism to fund an account on a given site. However, if an attacker compromised Bob's account and used that account to trick Alice, not only could the attacker profit, but tracing him or her might become very difficult because multiple sites are involved. The presence of an essentially unregulated currency exchange might attract attackers given that one challenge in online fraud is converting whatever information is stolen into cash.

We explored this example in detail to show that attackers are willing to go after less mainstream targets if they are sufficiently lucrative and provide a means to cash out. In addition, attackers might have extra incentives owing to the murky legal implications of manipulating such unregulated markets.

Crimeware is also likely to target alternative currencies. In the online world, some virtual assets may have real-world value. For example, an account in a multiplayer online game might have accumulated a certain number of points or virtual assets. Sometimes these virtual assets can be sold in secondary markets (e.g., via auction sites) for real money. Therefore, these points have a de facto real-world value even though they are virtual. We can expect some crimeware authors to target these virtual currencies for several reasons. First and foremost, they have some real-world value. Second, the mere fact that the currencies are virtual might facilitate laundering the proceeds, thereby making it hard to trace them back to an attacker. Finally, it may not be clear whether virtual currency theft has legal ramifications in the same way that theft of real currencies does. This targeting of alternative currencies is already happening: Two of the top 50 malicious code samples received by Symantec from January to June 2007 targeted online games such as Lineage and World of Warcraft [401].

Another virtual asset that might have real-world value is a person's online reputation. For example, sites such as eBay rely heavily on maintaining an active reputation system for buyers and sellers. Such a system gives the parties confidence in the transaction (assuming they have good reputations). If a piece of crimeware were used to steal someone's eBay password, then the thief could use the victim's eBay account, and obtain the rights and privileges of the account owner's reputation. The thief could then use the victim's account to sell defective or nonexistent merchandise. Along similar lines, some bots could be used to inflate sellers' reputations, as discussed in Chapter 7.

17.2.2 Phones, Cars, and Wearable Computers

If a victim's phone is infected by crimeware, this infection may attempt to spread to the computer system of his or her car. Many recent car models include a wireless interface that allows synchronization of a phone to the car computer system. Of course, car manufacturers are well aware of the threats of malware infections, and they have taken cautionary measures to prevent infections that would affect the control of the car. This protection is achieved by having two separate computer systems in the cars: one associated with control, and the other associated with infotainment. Only the latter would be primarily at risk.

Even so, compromise of this system could still result in a significant threat to the driver and passengers. Consider, for example, a GPS-based navigation system that is affected by crimeware. This part of the computer system is part of the infotainment system of the car, so the threat is not far-fetched. Consider further what would happen if the crimeware caused the driver to enter a highway in the wrong direction, drive to an unsafe neighborhood, or suppress traffic alerts. Any of these attacks may pose a threat to the driver and, at any rate, could cause distress. Therefore, the threat of crimeware is a very clear liability to car manufacturers—whether we speak of the cost of improved security measures, of public relations backlash, or of the opportunity cost.

While these attacks are not crimeware per se, they could easily become part of a blackmail effort or be used to taint the image of a competitor. As such, they are worth discussing in this context. Vehicular malware could also potentially obtain the geographic coordinates of the vehicle from the onboard navigation system and send this information back to the attacker. The user might then be blackmailed if he or she was somewhere the user should not have been, or the user's physical house might be robbed if it is discovered that he or she is far from home. Alternatively, the user's locations could be compiled into a lifestyle dossier, and that information could be sold to marketing companies.

Wearable computers, such as RFID, can pose similar liabilities and costs, but for different reasons, as discussed in Chapter 4. While RFID promises tremendous savings to manufacturers, middlemen, and retailers, the over-arching privacy concerns may hold back the deployment of this technology.

17.3 Using Social Networks to Bootstrap Attacks

The last few years have seen the emergence of a relationship between search engine results and the activity on social networks. For example, it is common that material considered valuable by communities such as *digg*, *slashdot*, and *stumbleupon* get high rankings by search engines and attention by media. Attackers now have an opportunity to push their material to a very large number of users, by either creating or corrupting a large enough number of profiles on such networks and then using these profiles to promote material that may contain malware. This type of scheme can also be carried out by using a bait-and-switch approach in which legitimate material is put forward in such social networks, pushed to the front in a legitimate manner, and then augmented or replaced with an infected or otherwise malicious version. (While social networks may react very quickly to such a modification, this response does not matter to the attacker once the links have been picked up by search engines and media.)

17.4 New Use of the Internet: Controlling the Infrastructure

As discussed in Chapter 1, crimeware typically proliferates over email (e.g., users are tricked into opening a malicious attachment). While more sophisticated techniques can be used, such as exploiting a particular vulnerability in a piece of software, most attackers prefer to use much simpler approaches for an obvious reason: They work. As email security improves and as more email providers scan attachments for malicious code, we would expect attackers to put more emphasis on different approaches—for example, transmitting crimeware through instant messages, peer-to-peer networks, or the web browser. While these proliferation vectors have been tried successfully in the past, we would expect their relative frequency to increase, while the popularity of traditional email as an attack method might diminish.

17.5 Moving Up the Stack

We expect third-party applications to increasingly be the target of crimeware-oriented attacks. Operating system security is much better understood nowadays, and many vendors employ techniques to harden their operating systems against common types of attacks, such as buffer overflows. In the meanwhile, a plethora of applications that run on top of the OS are at risk for being infected by crimeware. Not only do many third-party applications communicate over networks, but they may also be developed by people who are not aware of the issues related to the development of secure software.

Of course, one third-party application that will almost certainly be an increasingly popular target for crimeware authors is the web browser. Browsers are quite feature rich, and client-side scripting languages such as JavaScript have become quite powerful. While the feature-rich nature of client-side scripting is useful to web developers who wish to provide new and improved functionality to users, it may also be equally (or more) attractive to attackers. Although crimeware running in the browser may not have direct access to data that does not reside in the browser context (unless, of course, a browser vulnerability has been exploited), it has the potential of reading keystrokes that are typed into forms, mounting denial-of-service attacks, or even engaging in click fraud (as described in Chapter 11). Of course, such crimeware will be ephemeral and last only as long as the user is browsing. Given that most transactions of interest to crimeware authors already involve the web browser and that the browser has become the center of a typical user's computing experience, this ephemeral nature of browser-based crimeware may be of little concern to the attacker.

17.6 The Emergence of an E-Society: Are We Becoming More Vulnerable?

The typical computing environment with which a user interacts today is far more complex than what he or she might have experienced in the past. Consider the web browser:

- Today's web browsers are generally more feature rich, which means more lines of code were required to implement them.
- Browsers support a variety of extensions or plug-ins designed to provide enhanced functionality. These plug-ins may have questionable security or may even be designed by people who do not understand computer security issues. For example, Symantec documented 237 browser plug-in vulnerabilities in the first half of 2007, which is up substantially from the 74 vulnerabilities that were documented in the second half of 2006 [401].
- Browsers are capable of displaying much richer content. Beyond just static HTML, browsers can run client-side scripts. By leveraging plug-ins, they can also display video and other types of animation, produce sound, and render different document formats.

- The user might have programs that interact with his or her browser to provide additional services. One such example is Google Desktop,[2] which acts as a de facto web server residing on the user's machine. This web server, running on the user's machine, listens for traffic on a specific port. While precautions might be taken, the mere presence of a web server running on a machine has security implications.

- The user might have multiple web-enabled devices on the local network. For example, the broadband router, network printer, and network attached storage drive might all have web-based management interfaces. Consequently, if an attacker is able to get malicious code to run within the context of the user's web browser, that code can potentially access information on these local network resources.

Given all these factors, the environment with which the user interacts has suddenly become quite complex, and such complex environments are much more likely to be vulnerable. Two applications or platforms that are not vulnerable by themselves, for example, might be vulnerable when used together. Further, online transactions are becoming more commonplace, not to mention that a user might deal with many virtual currencies (e.g., currencies in a virtual world or multiplayer online games). Situations that pose security risks and involve money (and where money has the potential to be laundered) can give rise to criminally motivated malicious software. With the current momentum of technology, the trends that are rife for the proliferation of crimeware seem to be continuing unabated.

17.7 The Big Picture

It is realistic to think of software as the functional backbone of a large part of society, spanning applications from in-store cash registers, to telephone switching stations, to medical sensors, to control of the power grid, to coordination of traffic lights. In an increasingly interconnected world, these important functions will be ever more vulnerable to attack. Crimeware, therefore, should be thought of as an adversarial condition of these networks. Imagine something that you do not want to fail. Chances are that crimeware could make it fail. What are the incentives for attackers to make this happen? How can they achieve it? And how can we stop it?

Given our increasing dependence on online transactions and the growing complexity of today's computing environment (which seems to be outpacing what

---

2. http://desktop.google.com

typical users understand about the risks associated with that environment), it seems clear that crimeware is here to stay. We do not believe that we can ever fully "solve" online malicious activity in much the same way that it would seem unlikely we will ever "solve" crime. However, we may not need flawless technical solutions. Because crimeware is predicated on an attacker profiting from his or her activities, any solution that either cuts into or completely eliminates the attacker's profit margin will likely reduce attack instances significantly. In this regard, there seem to be a number of promising directions, many of which have been described in this text. We hope that this coverage of issues inspires more research into this important area.

References

[1] 90210, "Bypassing Klister 0.4 with No Hooks or Running a Controlled Thread Scheduler," *29A magazine* 8 (2004).

[2] F. W. Abagnale, *Stealing Your Life: The Ultimate Identity Theft Prevention Plan* (Broadway Books, 2007).

[3] AdBrite, http://www.adbrite.com.

[4] AdWatcher, http://www.adwatcher.com.

[5] M. Alexander, "Your Medical Records Stolen," *Reader's Digest,* Nov. 2006, 86–93.

[6] A. Alsaid and C. J. Mitchell, "Preventing Phishing Attacks Using Trusted Computing Technology," in *Proceedings of the 6th International Network Conference (INC '06),* July 2006, 221–228.

[7] T. Alves and D. Felton, "TrustZone: Integrated Hardware and Software Security— Enabling Trusted Computing in Embedded Systems" (white paper, ARM, July 2004), http://www.arm.com/pdfs/TZ_Whitepaper.pdf.

[8] V. Anandpara, A. Dingman, M. Jakobsson, D. Liu, and H. Roinestad, "Phishing IQ Tests Measure Fear, Not Ability," extended abstract, *USEC,* 2007.

[9] J. Anderson and D. Fish, "Sotelo v. DirectRevenue, LLC: Paving the Way for a Spyware-Free Internet," *Santa Clara Computer and High Technology Law Journal* 22 (2006): 841.

[10] R. M. Anderson and R. M. May, *Infectious Diseases in Humans* (Oxford University Press, 1992).

[11] Anonymous, "FDA Approves Three-in-One HIV Therapy," *Drug Store News,* 2000, http://www.findarticles.com/p/articles/mi_m3374/is_19_22/ai_68876802.

[12] Anonymous, "Gone in 20 Minutes: Using Laptops to Steal Cars," *Left Lane News,* 2006, http://www.leftlanenews.com/2006/05/03/gone-in-20-minutes-using-laptops-to-steal-cars/.

[13] Anti-Phishing Working Group, *Phishing Activity Trends Report* (technical report, May 2006).

[14] Anti-Phishing Working Group, "Anti-Phishing Reports," http://www.antiphishing.org/reports/ (accessed Aug. 2006).

[15] K. Aoki, J. Boyle, and J. Jenkins, "Bound by Law," http://www.law.duke.edu/cspd/comics/ (accessed July 2007).

[16] Apple Support, "Small Number of Video iPods Shipped with Windows Virus," http://www.apple.com/support/windowsvirus/ (accessed Feb. 2007).

[17] Anti-Phishing Working Group, "Consumer Advice: How to Avoid Phishing Scams," http://www.antiphishing.org/consumer_recs.html (accessed July 2, 2007).

[18] M. Arata, *Preventing Identity Theft for Dummies* (John Wiley & Sons, 2004).

[19] B. Arbaugh, "Improving the TCPA Specification," *IEEE Computer* 35, no. 8 (Aug. 2002): 77–79.

[20] I. Arce and E. Levy, "An Analysis of the Slapper Worm," *IEEE Security and Privacy* 1, no. 1 (Jan./Feb. 2003): 82–87, http://csdl.computer.org/dl/mags/sp/2003/01/j1082.htm.

[21] AT&T, "Internet Safety Game for Kids," http://www.att.com/gen/general?pid=1391 (accessed July 2, 2007).

[22] AT&T, "Customer Education," http://www.att.com/gen/landing-pages?pid=6456 (accessed July 2, 2007).

[23] AT&T, "Identifying and Protecting Against Phishing and Other Suspicious E-mails," http://att.centralcast.net/att_safety/Phishing/ (accessed July 2, 2007).

[24] McAfee AvertLabs, "Rootkits: The Growing Threat," Apr. 2006.

[25] G. Avoine, "Security and Privacy in RFID Systems," http://lasecwww.epfl.ch/~gavoine/rfid/.

[26] B. Balacheff, D. Chan, L. Chen, S. Pearson, and G. Proudler, "Securing Intelligent Adjuncts Using Trusted Computing Platform Technology," in *Proceedings of the 4th Working Conference on Smartcard Research and Advanced Applications* 177–195 (Kluwer Academic Publishers, 2001).

[27] S. Balfe and K. G. Paterson, *Augmenting Internet-Based Card Not Present Transactions with Trusted Computing: An Analysis* (Technical Report RHUL-MA-2006-9, Department of Mathematics, Royal Holloway, University of London, 2006), http://www.rhul.ac.uk/mathematics/techreports.

[28] S. Balfe and K. G. Paterson, *e-EMV: Emulating EMV for Internet Payments Using Trusted Computing Technology* (Technical Report RHUL-MA-2006-10, Department of

Mathematics, Royal Holloway, University of London, 2006), `http://www.rhul.ac.uk/mathematics/techreports`.

[29] E. Bangeman, "Where's the Harmony? iPod Firmware Update Shuts Out Real," Dec. 14, 2006, `http://arstechnica.com/news.ars/post/20041214-4466.html` (accessed Feb. 2007).

[30] Banner Box. `http://www.bannerbox.co.uk`.

[31] A. L. Barabási and R. Albert, "Emergence of Scaling in Random Networks," *Science* 286 (1999): 509–512.

[32] S. Bardzell and J. Bardzell, "Docile Avatars: Aesthetics, Experience, and Sexual Interaction in Second Life," in *Proceedings of HCI2007: HCI But Not as We Know It*, 3–12 (Lancaster, UK: Sept. 2007).

[33] P. Barham, B. Dragovic, K. Fraser, S. Hand, T. Harris, A. Ho, R. Neugebauery, I. Pratt, and A. Warfield, "XEN and the Art of Virtualization," in *Proceedings of the 19th ACM Symposium on Operating Systems Principles (SOSP '03)*, 164–177 (ACM Press, Oct. 2003).

[34] A. Barth, D. Boneh, A. Bortz, C. Jackson, J. Mitchell, W. Shao, and E. Stinson, "Detecting Fraudulent Clicks from Botnets 2.0" (talk given at AdFraud, 2007), `http://crypto.stanford.edu/adfraud/talks/adam.ppt`.

[35] P. L. Bellia, "Spyware and the Limits of Surveillance Law," *Berkeley Technology Law Journal* 20 (2005): 1283, 1301.

[36] H. Berghel, "Wireless Infidelity I: War Driving," *Communications of the ACM 47* (Sept. 2004): 21–26.

[37] "How Much Information?" 2003, `http://www.sims.berkeley.edu:8000/research/projects/how-much-info-2003/internet.htm`.

[38] J. L. Bernardes, R. Tori, E. Jacober, R. Nakamura, and R. Bianchi. "A Survey on Networking for Massively Multiplayer Online Games," WJogos, 2003, `http://www.interlab.pcs.poli.usp.br/artigos/WJogos03-Interlab-MMO.pdf`.

[39] B. Betts, "Unwanted E-card Conceals a Storm," `http://www.theregister.co.uk/2007/06/29/ecard\_storm\_trojan/` (accessed June 29, 2007).

[40] A. Bittau, M. Handley, and J. Lackey, "The Final Nail in WEP's Coffin," in *The 2006 IEEE Symposium on Security and Privacy SP '06*, 2006.

[41] Bittorrent homepage, `http://www.bittorrent.com`.

[42] McAfee Avert Labs blog, "Hide Me Sony One More Time," `http://www.avertlabs.com/research/blog/index.php/2007/08/28/hide-me-sony-one-more-time/`.

[43] "German BMW Banned from Google," `http://blog.outer-court.com/archive/2006-02-04-n60.html`.

[44] S. C. Bono, M. Green, A. Stubblefield, A. Juels, A. D. Rubin, and M. Szydlo, "Security Analysis of a Cryptographically-Enabled RFID Device," in *Proc. 14th USENIX Security Symposium,* 1–16 (Baltimore: 2005).

[45] Bro Intrusion Detection System, "Bro Overview," `http://bro-ids.org` (accessed Feb. 2007).

[46] J. A. Calandrino, A. J. Feldman, J. A. Halderman, D. Wagner, H. Yu, and W. P. Zeller, "Source Code Review of the Diebold Voting System," `http://www.sos.ca.gov/elections/voting_systems/ttbr/diebold-source-public-jul29.pdf`.

[47] "Canon EOS 300D, Alternative Firmware Upgrade," `http://www.digit-life.com/articles2/canon300dfw2/` (accessed Feb. 2007).

[48] J. Carr, "Not-So-Sweet Charity: Credit Card Fraud Takes a Charitable Twist," *SC Magazine,* July 6, 2006, `http://scmagazine.com/us/news/article/669553/not-so-sweet-charity-credit-card-fraud-takes-charitable-twist/`.

[49] E. Castronova, "Virtual Worlds: A First-Hand Account of Market and Society on the Cyberian Frontier," *CESifo Working Paper Series,* no. 618 (2001), `http://ssrn.com/abstract=294828`.

[50] S. Cesare, "Runtime Kernel Kmem Patching," `http://www.uebi.net/silvio/runtime-kernel-kmem-patching.txt`.

[51] Chase, "Phishing," `http://www.chase.com/ccp/index.jsp?pg\_name=ccpmapp/shared/assets/page/Phishing` (accessed Feb. 8, 2007).

[52] B. D. Chen and M. Mahesweran, "A Cheat Controlled Protocol for Centralized Online Multiplayer Games," in *Proceedings of 3rd ACM SIGCOMM Workshop on Network and System Support for Games,* 139–143 (Portland, OR: 2004).

[53] H. Cheung, "The Feds Can Own Your WLAN Too," `http://www.tomsnetworking.com/2005/03/31/the_feds_can_own_your_wlan_to%o/` (accessed Feb. 2007).

[54] Citibank, "E-mail Fraud and Security—Learn About Spoofs," `http://www.citi.com/domain/spoof/learn.htm` (accessed Feb. 8, 2007).

[55] Clandestiny, "Designing a Kernel Key Logger: A Filter Driver Tutorial," 2005, `http://lyyer.blog.sohu.com/42601244.html`.

[56] P. C. Clark and L .J. Hoffman, "BITS: A Smartcard Protected Operating System," *Communications of the ACM* 37 (Nov. 1994): 66–94.

[57] ClickProtector, `http://www.clickprotector.com/`.

[58] Clicksor, `http://www.clicksor.com`.

[59] CMLA, *Client Adopter Agreement* (Technical Report Revision 1.00050708, The Content Management License Administrator Limited Liability Company [CMLA, LLC], Aug. 2005).

[60] B. Cogswell and M. Russinovich, "Rootkit Revealer," 2005, `http://www.microsoft.com/technet/sysinternals/Security/RootkitRevealer.mspx`.

[61] J. M. Collins, *Investigating Identity Theft: A Guide for Businesses, Law Enforcement, and Victims* (John Wiley & Sons, 2006).

[62] Federal Election Commission, "About the FEC," `http://www.fec.gov/about.shtml`.

[63] Federal Trade Commission, "FTC Shuts Down Spyware Operation: Outfit Used Unsuspecting Bloggers to Spread Its Malicious Code," press release, Nov. 10, 2005, `http://www.ftc.gov/opa/2005/11/enternet.shtm`.

[64] Federal Election Commission, "Sale and Use of Campaign Information," `http://www.fec.gov/pages/brochures/sale_and_use_brochure.pdf`.

[65] "State of Spyware Q2 2006, Consumer Report," `http://www.webroot.com/resources/stateofspyware/excerpt.html`.

[66] ConsumersUnion.org, "Tsunami Scams Underscore Need for Caution When Giving to Charities Online," press release, Jan. 11, 2005, `http://www.consumersunion.org/pub/core_financial_services/001781.html`.

[67] Microsoft Corporation, "The Windows Malicious Software Removal Tool: Progress Made, Trends Observed," June 2006.

[68] Microsoft Corporation, "Windows Vista Security Enhancements," 2007, `http://www.microsoft.com/presspass/newsroom/security/VistaSecurity.mspx`.

[69] K. Crawford, "Google CFO: Fraud a Big Threat," *CNNMoney.com*, `http://money.cnn.com/2004/12/02/technology/google_fraud/`.

[70] M. Crawford, "Phishing Education for Banking Customers Useless," `http://www.computerworld.com.au/index.php?id=1486962899\&eid=-255` (accessed July 2, 2007).

[71] Crazylord, "Playing with Windows /dev/(k)mem," *Phrack Magazine*, 2002, `http://www.phrack.org/archives/59/p59-0x10.txt`.

[72] Wikipedia, "Cross-site request forgery (CSRF)," `http://en.wikipedia.org/wiki/Cross-site_request_forgery`.

[73] G. Cybenko, A. Giani, C. Heckman, and P. Thompson, "Cognitive Hacking: Technological and Legal Issues," in *Proceedings of Law and Technology*, 2002, `http://www.ists.dartmouth.edu/library/cht1102.pdf`.

[74] Cyota, `http://www.rsa.com/node.aspx?id=3017`.

[75] D. Dagon, G. Lu, C. Zou, J. Grizzard, S. Dwivedi, W. Lee, and R. Lipton. "A Taxonomy of Botnets" (manuscript).

[76] D. Dagon, C. Zou, and W. Lee, "Modeling Botnet Propagation Using Time Zones," in *Proceedings of the 13th Annual Network and Distributed Systems Symposium (NDSS)*, 2006.

[77] J. Dall and M. J. Christensen, "Random Geometric Graphs," *Phys. Rev. E* 66(1):016121, (July 2002).

[78] R. Das and P. Harrop, "RFID Forecasts, Players, and Opportunities 2006–2016," *IDTechEx,* 2006, `http://www.idtechex.com/products/en/view.asp?productcategoryid=93`.

[79] N. Daswani, M. Stoppelman, and The Google Click Quality and Security Teams, "The Anatomy of Clickbot.A," *First Workshop on Hot Topics in Understanding Botnets (HotBots),* 2007, `http://www.usenix.org/events/hotbots07/tech/full_papers/daswani/daswani.pdf`.

[80] N. Daswani, C. Kern, and A. Kesavan, *Foundations of Security: What Every Programmer Needs to Know* (Apress, 2007).

[81] J. Davis, "Hackers Take Down the Most Wired Country in Europe," *Wired Magazine,* `http://www.wired.com/politics/security/magazine/15-09/ff_estonia`.

[82] "NHTSA ODI—Recalls, NHTSA campaign ID number 06V039000," U.S. National Highway Traffic Safety Administration, Office of Defects Investigation, Feb. 7, 2006, `http://www-odi.nhtsa.dot.gov/cars/problems/recalls/recallresults.cfm?start=1&SearchType=QuickSearch&rcl_ID=06V039000&summary=true&PrintVersion=NO` (accessed Feb. 2007).

[83] DD WRT, `http://www.dd-wrt.com/dd-wrtv2/ddwrt.php` (accessed Feb. 2007).

[84] A. Paes de Barros, A. Fucs, and V. Pereira, "New Botnet Trends and Threats," Black Hat Europe, 2007, `http://www.blackhat.com/presentations/bh-europe-07/Fucs-Paes-de-Barros-Pereira/Whitepaper/bh-eu-07-barros-WP.pdf`.

[85] D. Dean, E. W. Felten, and D. S. Wallach, "Java Security: from HotJava to Netscape and Beyond," in *IEEE Symposium on Security and Privacy,* 1996.

[86] R. Dhamija and J. D. Tygar, "The Battle Against Phishing: Dynamic Security Skins," in *SOUPS '05: Proceedings of the Symposium on Usable Privacy and Security,* 2005.

[87] R. Dhamija, J. D. Tygar, and M. Hearst, "Why Phishing Works," in *Proceedings of the Conference on Human Factors in Computing Systems,* 2006.

[88] DHS-SRI Identity Theft Technology Council and the Anti-Phishing Working Group, "The Crimeware Landscape: Malware, Phishing, Identity Theft and Beyond," `http://www.antiphishing.org/reports/APWG_CrimewareReport.pdf`.

[89] R. Dingledine, N. Mathewson, and P. Syverson, "Tor, the Second-Generation Onion Router," in *13th USENIX Security Symposium,* Aug. 2004.

[90] D. Dittrich, "The 'stacheldraht' Distributed Denial of Service Attack Tool," Dec. 1999, `http://staff.washington.edu/dittrich/misc/stacheldraht.analysis`.

[91] C. E. Drake, J. J. Oliver, and E. J. Koontz, "Anatomy of a Phishing Email," *Conference on Email and Anti-Spam,* 2004, `http://www.ceas.cc/papers-2004/114.pdf`.

[92] eBay, "Reporting Spoof (Fake) Emails," http://pages.ebay.com/help/confidence/spoof-email.html (accessed Feb. 8, 2007).

[93] eBay. "Spoof Email Tutorial," http://pages.ebay.com/education/spooftutorial/ (accessed Feb. 8, 2007).

[94] A. Eckelberry, "A Look into the Mind of Spyware Criminals," Sunbelt Blog posting, Aug. 24, 2005, http://sunbeltblog.blogspot.com/2005/08/look-into-mind-of-spyware-criminals.html.

[95] B. Edelman, "Claria's Misleading Installation Methods—Ezone.com," http://www.benedelman.org/spyware/installations/ezone-claria/.

[96] B. Edelman, "Documentation of Gator Advertisements and Targeting," http://cyber.law.harvard.edu/people/edelman/ads/gator/.

[97] B. Edelman, "'Spyware': Research, Testing, Legislation, and Suits," http://www.benedelman.org/spyware/.

[98] B. Edelman, "WhenU License Agreement Is Forty Five Pages Long," http://www.benedelman.org/spyware/whenu-license/.

[99] B. Edelman, "Hotbar Advertising—Screenshots," May 2005, http://www.benedelman.org/spyware/installations/kidzpage-hotbar/details-ads.html.

[100] A. Emigh, "The Crimeware Landscape: Malware, Phishing, Identity Theft and Beyond," http://www.antiphishing.org/reports/APWG_CrimewareReport.pdf.

[101] A. Emigh, "Online Identity Theft: Phishing Technology, Chokepoints and Countermeasures," ITTC Report on Online Identity Theft Technology and Countermeasures, http://www.antiphishing.org/Phishing-dhs-report.pdf.

[102] eMule homepage, http://www.emule-project.net.

[103] EMVCo, *Book 1—Application Independent ICC to Terminal Interface Requirements,* 4.1 ed. (EMVCo., May 2004), http://www.emvco.com.

[104] EMVCo, *Book 2—Security and Key Management,* 4.1 ed. (EMVCo., May 2004), http://www.emvco.com.

[105] EMVCo, *Book 3—Application Specification,* 4.1 ed. (EMVCo., May 2004), http://www.emvco.com.

[106] EMVCo, *Book 4—Cardholder, Attendant, and Acquirer Interface Requirements,* 4.1 ed. (EMVCo., June 2004), http://www.emvco.com.

[107] "2006 to Date Emission Related Recall and Voluntary Service Campaigns Performed on Light-Duty Vehicles and Light Duty Trucks," U.S. Environmental Protection Agency, Oct. 17, 2006, http://www.epa.gov/otaq/cert/recall/2006recallreport6.pdf (accessed Feb. 2007).

[108] Ericsson, "Ericsson and Compaq Form Strategic Partnership to Build Next Generation Switches Based on AlphaServers," press release, Oct. 10, 2000, http://www.ericsson.com/ericsson/press/releases/old/archive/2000Q4/20001010-0060.html.

[109] J. Evers, "Earthlink Nabs Aluria's Anti-spyware," *ZDNet News.com*, Aug. 22, 2005, http://news.zdnet.com/2100-1009_22-5841387.html.

[110] G. Evron, "Estonia: Information Warfare and Strategic Lessons," *Blackhat Briefings*, 2007.

[111] Exploit, "From Half-Real: A Dictionary of Video Game Theory," http://www.half-real.net/dictionary/#exploit (accessed Oct. 26, 2006).

[112] F-Secure, Blacklight, 2005, http://www.f-secure.com/blacklight.

[113] D. Fallows, "Pew Internet and American Life Project," http://www.pewinternet.org/pdfs/PIP_Spam_Ap05.pdf (accessed Apr. 2006).

[114] Holy Father, "Hacker Defender," http://hxdef.org.

[115] Spyware, http://www.ftc.gov/bcp/conline/pubs/alerts/spywarealrt.htm.

[116] Federal Trade Commission, *"Monitoring Software" on Your PC: Spyware, Adware, and Other Software* (staff report, 2005).

[117] P. Ferrie, "Attacks on Virtual Machines," http://www.symantec.com/avcenter/reference/Virtual_Machine_Threats.pdf.

[118] P. Ferrie, "Tumours and Polips," *Virus Bulletin*, July 2006, http://pferrie.tripod.com/papers/polip.pdf.

[119] Federal Financial Institutions Examination Council, "Authentication in an Internet Banking Environment," Oct. 12, 2005, http://www.ffiec.gov/pdf/authentication_guidance.pdf.

[120] K. Finkenzeller, *RFID Handbook: Fundamentals and Applications in Contactless Smart Cards and Identification* (John Wiley & Sons, 2003).

[121] P. Finn and M. Jakobsson, "Designing and Conducting Phishing Experiments," in "Usability and Security," special issue, *IEEE Technology and Society Magazine*, 2007.

[122] "Firewire—All Your Memory Are Belong to Us," May 2005, http://md.hudora.de/presentations/#firewire-cansecwest.

[123] S. R. Fluhrer, I. Mantin, and A. Shamir, "Weaknesses in the Key Scheduling Algorithm of RC4," in *SAC '01: Revised Papers from the 8th Annual International Workshop on Selected Areas in Cryptography*, 1–24 (Springer-Verlag, 2001).

[124] SecurityFocus, "Digital Plague Hits Online Game World of Warcraft," 27 Sept. 2005, http://www.securityfocus.com/news/11330 (accessed Mar. 30, 2007).

[125] B. J. Fogg, J. Marshall, O. Laraki, A. Osipovich, C. Varma, N. Fang, J. Paul, A. Rangnekar, J. Shon, P. Swani, and M. Treinen, "What Makes Web Sites Credible?

A Report on a Large Quantitative Study," in *CHI '01: Proceedings of the SIGCHI Conference on Human Factors in Computing Systems,* 61–68 (ACM Press, 2001).

[126] B. J. Fogg, C. Soohoo, D. R. Danielson, L. Marable, J. Stanford, and E. R. Tauber, "How Do Users Evaluate the Credibility of Web Sites? A Study with Over 2,500 Participants," in *DUX '03: Proceedings of the 2003 Conference on Designing for User Experiences,* 1–15 (ACM Press, 2003).

[127] The Internet Corporation for Assigned Names and Numbers, "Uniform Domain-Name Dispute-Resolution Policy," `http://www.icann.org/udrp/udrp.htm`.

[128] U.S.-Canada Power System Outage Task Force, "Final Report on the August 14, 2003 Blackout in the United States and Canada: Causes and Recommendations," Apr. 2004, `https://reports.energy.gov/BlackoutFinal-Web.pdf` (accessed Feb. 2007).

[129] M. J. Frank, *From Victim to Victor: A Step-by-Step Guide for Ending the Nightmare of Identity Theft* (Porpoise Press, 2004).

[130] J. Franklin, D. McCoy, P. Tabriz, V. Neagoe, J. Van Randwyk, and D. Sicker. "Passive Data Link Layer 802.11 Wireless Device Driver Fingerprinting," in *USENIX-SS '06: Proceedings of the 15th Conference on USENIX Security Symposium,* 12 (Berkeley: USENIX Association, 2006).

[131] M. Frilingos, "As Big as . . . a Carlton Beer Ad," *The Daily Telegraph: Local,* July 23, 2005, at 8.

[132] Federal Trade Commission, "Report Spam," `http://www.ftc.gov/bcp/conline/edcams/spam/report.html`.

[133] Fuzen op, "The FU Rootkit," `http://www.rootkit.com/`.

[134] Y. Gable, "DoS Extortion Is No Longer Profitable," Symantec Security Response blog, Apr. 2007, `http://www.symantec.com/enterprise/security_response/weblog/2007/04/dos_extortion_is_no_longer_pro.html`.

[135] S. Gajek, A.-R. Sadeghi, C. Stüble, and M. Winandy, "Compartmented Security for Browsers—Or How to Thwart a Phisher with Trusted Computing," in *Proceedings of the 2nd International Conference on Availability, Reliability and Security (ARES '07),* 120–127 (Los Alamitos, CA, Washington, DC: IEEE Computer Society, 2007).

[136] E. Gallery, "Authorisation Issues for Mobile Code in Mobile Systems" (Ph.D. thesis, Department of Mathematics, Royal Holloway, University of London, 2007).

[137] Gallup Poll web site, `http://www.galluppoll.com/`.

[138] D. B. Game, A. F. Blakley, and M. J. Armstrong, "The Legal Status of Spyware," *Federal Communications Law Journal* 59 (2006): 157, 161.

[139] GameGuru.com, "'World of Warcraft' Could Get a Security Dongle," Jan. 16, 2007, `http://www.gameguru.in/pc/2007/16/world-of-warcraft-could-get-a-security-dongle/` (accessed Mar. 30, 2007).

[140] M. Gandhi, M. Jakobsson, and J. Ratkiewicz, "Badvertisements: Stealthy Click-Fraud with Unwitting Accessories," in "Anti-Phishing and Online Fraud, Part I," special issue, *Journal of Digital Forensic Practice* 1, no. 2 (Nov. 2006).

[141] S. L. Garfinkel and R. C. Miller, "Johnny 2: A User Test of Key Continuity Management with S/MIME and Outlook Express," in *Proceedings of the 2005 Symposium on Usable Privacy and Security*, 2005, 13–24.

[142] T. Garfinkel, M. Rosenblum, and D. Boneh, "Flexible OS Support and Applications for Trusted Computing," in *Proceedings of the 9th USENIX Workshop on Hot Topics on Operating Systems (HotOS-IX)*, 145–150 (Kauai, HI: USENIX, The Advanced Computing Systems Association, May 2003).

[143] Gartner, "Gartner Says Number of Phishing E-Mails Sent to U.S. Adults Nearly Doubles in Just Two Years," http://www.gartner.com/it/page.jsp?id=498245.

[144] M. Gast, *802.11 Wireless Networks: The Definitive Guide*, 2nd ed., (O'Reilly, 2005).

[145] C. Gentry, Z. Ramzan, and S. Stubblebine, "Secure Distributed Human Computation," in *Proceedings of ACM Conference on Electronic Commerce*, 2005.

[146] Gnutella protocol specification, http://www.the-gdf.org/wiki/index.php?title=Gnutella_Protocol_Development.

[147] P. Golle and N. Duchenault, "Preventing Bots from Playing Online Games," *Computers in Entertainment* 3, no. 3 (2005).

[148] P. Golle and D. Wagner, "Cryptanalysis of a Cognitive Authentication Scheme," in *IEEE Security and Privacy*, 2007.

[149] J. Goodell, "How to Fake a Passport," *New York Times*, 2006, http://query.nytimes.com/gst/fullpage.html?sec=travel&res=980CE6D6133DF933A25751C0A9649C8B63.

[150] "Hosting Company AIT Leads Class-Action Suit Against Google," Dec. 28, 2005, http://www.marketwire.com/mw/release_html_b1?release_id=103417.

[151] "Feds Arrest Alleged Google Extortionist," Mar. 22, 2004, http://www.internetnews.com/bus-news/article.php/3329281.

[152] S. Gordon and R. Ford, "On the Definition and Classification of Cybercrime," *Journal in Computer Virology* 2, no. 1 (July 2006): 13–20.

[153] P. Grassberger, "On the Critical Behavior of the General Epidemic Process and Dynamical Percolation," *Math. Biosci.* 63 (1983): 157.

[154] S. Greengard, "Driving Change in the Auto Industry," *RFID Journal*, Apr. 2004, http://www-03.ibm.com/solutions/businesssolutions/sensors/doc/content/bin/RFID_Journal_driving_change_in_the_auto_industry.pdf.

[155] V. Griffith and M. Jakobsson, "Messin' with Texas, Deriving Mother's Maiden Names Using Public Records," *ACNS*, June 2005.

[156] J. Grizzard, V. Sharma, C. Nunnery, B. B. Kang, and D. Dagon, "Peer-to-Peer Botnets: Overview and Case Study," in *First Workshop on Hot Topics in Understanding Botnets (HotBots)*, 2007.

[157] J. Grossman and T. C. Niedzialkowski, "Hacking Intranet Websites from the Outside: JavaScript Malware Just Got a Lot More Dangerous," *Black Hat Briefings*, 2006.

[158] D. Groth, "Comment on Stephano and Groth's USEable security: Interface Design Strategies for Improving Security," personal communication, Aug. 2006.

[159] Anti-Phishing Working Group, "Phishing Activity Trends: Report for the Month of May 2007," http://www.antiphishing.org/reports/apwg_report_may_2007.pdf.

[160] Anti-Phishing Working Group, "Phishing Activity Trends Report," Apr. 2007, http://www.antiphishing.org/reports/apwg_report_april_2007.pdf.

[161] Princeton Secure Internet Programming Group, "DNS Attack Scenario," Feb. 1996, http://www.cs.princeton.edu/sip/news/dns-scenario.html.

[162] J. Gulbrandsen, "How Do Windows NT System Calls Really Work?" Aug. 2004, http://www.codeguru.com/cpp/w-p/system/devicedriverdevelopment/article.php/c8035.

[163] J. A. Halderman, B. Waters, and E. Felten, "A Convenient Method for Securely Managing Passwords," in *Proceedings of the 14th International World Wide Web Conference*, 2005.

[164] Halflife, "Abuse of the Linux Kernel for Fun and Profit," *Phrack Magazine*, http://www.phrack.org/archives/50/P50-05.

[165] G. P. Hancke, "Practical Attacks on Proximity Identification Systems," short paper, in *Proceedings of the IEEE Symposium on Security and Privacy*, 328–333 (Washington, DC: IEEE Symposium on Security and Privacy, 2006).

[166] J. Heasman, "Implementing and Detecting a PCI Rootkit," http://www.ngssoftware.com/research/papers/Implementing_And_Detecting_A_PCI_Rootkit.pdf.

[167] J. Heasman, "Implementing and Detecting an ACPI BIOS Rootkit," *Black Hat Federal*, 2006.

[168] "Hector's World," http://www.hectorsworld.com/ (accessed July 3, 3007).

[169] A. Helmy, "Small Worlds in Wireless Networks," *IEEE Comm. Lett.* 7 (2003): 490–492.

[170] C. Herrmann, M. Barthélemy, and P. Provero, "Connectivity Distribution of Spatial Networks," *Phys. Rev. E* 68:026128 (2003).

[171] Hewlett-Packard, Intel, and Microsoft, "Advanced Configuration and Power Interface Specification," 2005, http://www.acpi.info/.

[172] T. S. Heydt-Benjamin, D. V. Bailey, K. Fu, A. Juels, and T. O'Hare, "Vulnerabilities in First-Generation RFID-Enabled Credit Cards," Oct. 2006, `http://prisms.cs.umass.edu/~kevinfu/papers/RFID-CC-manuscript.pdf`.

[173] U.S. Congress, House, Committee on Government Reform, Subcommittee on Technology, Information Policy, Intergovernmental Relations and the Census, "Electronic Voting Offers Opportunities and Presents Challenges," testimony prepared by R. C. Hite, also available at `http://www.gao.gov/new.items/d04766t.pdf`.

[174] R. Hof, "Second Life's First Millionaire," *BusinessWeek*, Nov. 26, 2006, `http://www.businessweek.com/the_thread/techbeat/archives/2006/11/second_lifes_fi.html` (accessed Feb. 2007).

[175] G. Hoglund, "Loading Rootkit Using systemloadandcallimage," `http://archives.neohapsis.com/archives/ntbugtraq/2000-q3/0114.html`.

[176] G. Hoglund and J. Butler, *Rootkits: Subverting the Windows Kernel* (Addison-Wesley, 2006).

[177] G. Hoglund and J. Butler, *Rootkits: Subverting the Windows Kernel* (Addison-Wesley, 2006).

[178] G. Hoglund and G. McGraw, *Exploiting Software: How to Break Code* (Addison-Wesley, 2004).

[179] G. Hoglund and G. McGraw, *Exploiting Online Games: Cheating Massively Distributed Systems* (Addison-Wesley, 2008).

[180] U.S. Congress, Senate, *Commerce Hearing on Seaport Security*, July 2001, also available at `http://commerce.senate.gov/hearings/072401EFH.pdf`.

[181] N. Hopper and M. Blum, "Secure Human Identification Protocols," in *Proceedings of Asiacrypt*, 2001.

[182] M. Hottell, D. Carter, and M. Deniszczuk, "Predictors of Home-Based Wireless Security," in *The Fifth Workshop on the Economics of Information Security*, 2006.

[183] WiGLE Wireless Geographic Logging Engine, `http://www.wigle.net/`.

[184] WiGLE General Stats, `http://www.wigle.net/gps/gps/main/stats/` (accessed Feb. 2007).

[185] J. Hu, "180solutions Sues Allies Over Adware: The Advertising Software Maker Alleges That Two Partners Loaded Its Ad-Serving Software onto People's PCs without First Getting Their Consent," *CNET News.com*, July 28, 2004, `http://www.news.com/2110-1024_3-5287885.html`.

[186] "India's Secret Army of Online Ad 'Clickers,'" May 3, 2004, `http://timesofindia.indiatimes.com/articleshow/msid-654822,curpg-1.cms`.

[187] G. Hunt and D. Brubacher, "Detours: Binary Interception of win32 Functions," in *Proceedings of the 3rd USENIX Windows NT Symposium,* 1999, 135–143, `http://research.microsoft.com/sn/detours`.

[188] `I-forgot-my-password.com`.

[189] "IEEE-SA GetIEEE 802.11 LAN/MAN wireless LANS," `http://standards.ieee.org/getieee802/802.11.html` (accessed Feb. 2007).

[190] Symantec Inc., "Symantec and Intel Collaborate to Change Computer Security Model," `http://www.symantec.com/about/news/release/article.jsp?prid=20060424_02`.

[191] Intel, "LaGrande Technology Architectural Overview" (Technical Report 252491-001, Intel Corporation, Sept. 2003).

[192] Intel, *IA-32 Intel Architecture Software Developer's Manual, System Programming Guide, Volume: 3* (Intel Corporation, 2005).

[193] "Anti-Virus USB Drive from IOCell," `http://www.getusb.info/anti-virus-usb-drive-from-iocell/`.

[194] N. Itoi, W. A. Arbaugh, S. J. Pollack, and D. M. Reeves, "Personal Secure Booting," in *Proceedings of the 6th Australasian Conference on Information Security and Privacy (ACISP '01), in Computer Science Lecture Notes (LNCS)* 2119 (July 2001): 130–141.

[195] C. Jackson, A. Barth, A. Bortz, W. Shao, and D. Bonch, "Protecting Browsers from DNS Rebinding Attacks," in *Proceedings of ACM Conference on Communications Security,* 2007, `http://crypto.stanford.edu/dns/`.

[196] C. Jackson, D. Boneh, and J. C. Mitchell, "Stronger Password Authentication Using Virtual Machines" (paper submitted for publication, Stanford University, 2006), `http://crypto.stanford.edu/spyblock/spyblock.pdf`.

[197] T. Jagatic, N. Johnson, M. Jakobsson, and F. Menczer, "Social Phishing," *Communications of the ACM,* Oct. 2007.

[198] M. Jakobsson, "The Human Factor in Phishing," *Privacy and Security of Consumer Information,* 2007, `http://www.informatics.indiana.edu/markus/papers/aci.pdf`.

[199] M. Jakobsson, T. Jagatic, and S. Stamm, "Phishing for Clues," `http://www.browser-recon.info`.

[200] M. Jakobsson and J. Ratkiewicz, "Designing Ethical Phishing Experiments: A Study of (ROT13) rOnl Auction Query Features," in *Proceedings of the 15th Annual World Wide Web Conference,* 2006.

[201] M. Jakobsson and S. Stamm, "Socially Propagated Malware," 2006, `http://www.stop-phishing.com`.

[202] M. Jakobsson and S. Myers, eds., *Phishing and Countermeasures: Understanding the Increasing Problem of Identity Theft* (John Wiley & Sons, 2007).

[203] J. Jeff, Y. Alan, B. Ross, and A. Alasdair, "The Memorability and Security of Passwords—Some Empirical Results," 2000.

[204] A. Juels, "RFID Security and Privacy: A Research Survey," *IEEE Journal on Selected Areas in Communication,* 2006, http://www.rsasecurity.com/rsalabs/staff/bios/ajuels/publications/pdfs/rfid_survey_28_09_05.pdf.

[205] A. Juels, R. L. Rivest, and M. Szydlo, "The Blocker Tag: Selective Blocking of RFID Tags for Consumer Privacy," in *Proceedings of the 10th ACM Conference on Computer and Communications Security* (ACM Press, 2003).

[206] E. Jung, "PasswordMaker," http://passwordmaker.mozdev.org.

[207] D. Kaminsky, "The Black Ops of DNS" (presentation, BlackHat 2004), http://www.blackhat.com/presentations/bh-usa-04/bh-us-04-kaminsky/bh-us-04-kaminsky.ppt.

[208] A. Karasaridis, B. Rexroad, and D. Hoeflin, "Wide-Scale Botnet Detection and Characterization," in *First Workshop on Hot Topics in Understanding Botnets (HotBots),* 2007.

[209] D. Kawamoto, "Virus Writers Follow the Money," *CNET News,* 2005, http://news.zdnet.com/2100-1009_22-5628512.html.

[210] M. J. Keeling, "The Effects of Local Spatial Structure on Epidemiological Invasions," *Proc. R. Soc. Lond. B* 266 (1999): 859–867.

[211] G. Keizer, "Adware Purveyor Claims Extortion by Own Distributor," *Techweb Network,* Nov. 3, 2005, http://www.techweb.com/wire/security/173402770.

[212] G. Keizer, "New Bot-Powered eBay Scam Uncovered," *TechWeb Technology News,* July 31, 2006, http://www.techweb.com/showArticle.jhtml?articleID= 191600603&cid=RSSfeed_TechWeb.

[213] Z. Kfir and A. Wool, "Picking Virtual Pockets Using Relay Attacks on Contactless Smartcards," in *Proc. IEEE Secure Comm.,* 47–58 (Los Alamitos, CA: 2005).

[214] L. Kindermann, "MyAddress Java Applet (To Discover a PC's Internal IP Address)," 2002, http://www.reglos.de/myaddress/MyAddress.html.

[215] S. T. King, P. M. Chen, Y.-M. Wang, C. Verbowski, Helen J. Wang, and Jacob R. Lorch, "SubVirt: Implementing Malware with Virtual Machines," in *Proceedings of the 2006 IEEE Symposium on Security and Privacy (S&P '06),* 314–327 (Washington, DC: IEEE Computer Society, 2006).

[216] E. Kirda, C. Kruegel, G. Banks, G. Vigna, and R. Kemmerer, "Behavior-Based Spyware Detection," in *Proceedings of 15th USENIX Security Symposium,* Aug. 2006.

[217] Kismet, http://www.kismetwireless.net (accessed Feb. 2007).

[218] D. V. Klein, "'Foiling the Cracker'—A Survey of, and Improvements to, Password Security," in *Proceedings of the Second USENIX Workshop on Security*, Summer 1990, 5–14.

[219] B. Krebs, "Data Thefts May Be Linked: Warrants Served in LexisNexis Account Breach," *Washington Post*, May 20, 2005.

[220] B. Krebs, "Katrina Phishing Scams Begin," in "Security Fix" blog, *Washington Post*, Aug. 31, 2005, http://blog.washingtonpost.com/securityfix/2005/08/katrina_phishing_scams_begin_1.html.

[221] M. Krebs, "Vehicle Theft on the Rise," *Cars.com*, Mar. 2005, http://www.cars.com/go/advice/Story.jsp?section=safe&story=secStat&subject=safe_sec&referer=&aff=msnbc.

[222] P. Kumaraguru, Y. W. Rhee, A. Acquisti, L. Cranor, J. Hong, and E. Nunge, "Protecting People from Phishing: The Design and Evaluation of an Embedded Training Email System" (Technical Report CMU-CyLab-06-017, Nov. 2006).

[223] P. Kumaraguru, S. Sheng, A. Acquisti, L. F. Cranor, and J. Hong, "Teaching Johnny Not to Fall for Phish" (technical report, Feb. 2007).

[224] C. Kuo, V. Goh, and A. Tang, "Design and Evaluation Method for Secure 802.22 Network Configuration" (poster presented at the 2005 Symposium on Usable Privacy and Security, 2005).

[225] C. Kuo, V. Goh, A. Tang, A. Perrig, and J. Walker, "Empowering Ordinary Consumers to Securely Configure Their Mobile Devices and Wireless Networks," Dec. 7, 2005, http://www.cylab.cmu.edu/files/cmucylab05005.pdf (accessed Feb. 2007).

[226] R. Kuster, "Three Ways to Inject Your Code into Another Process," http://www.codeproject.com/threads/winspy.asp.

[227] V. T. Lam, S. Antonatos, P. Akriditis, and K. G. Anangnostakis, "Puppetnets: Misusing Web Browsers as a Distributed Attack Infrastructure," in *Proceedings of ACM Conference on Communications and Computer Security*, 2006.

[228] M. Landler and J. Markoff, "Digital Fears Emerge After Data Siege in Estonia," *New York Times*, May 29, 2007, http://www.nytimes.com/2007/05/29/technology/29estonia.html?_r=1&adxnnl=1&oref=slogin&adxnnlx=1190414180-FHjhCCSZ4A0Uxh+bBKuo3Q.

[229] C. Landwehr, "Secure Grid Computing: An Empirical View," http://www.laas.fr/IFIPWG/Workshops&Meetings/48/WS1/10-Landwehr.pdf.

[230] "Company Files Fraud Lawsuit Against Yahoo," May 1, 2006, http://www.washingtonpost.com/wp-srv/technology/documents/yahoo_may2006.pdf.

[231] R. Laudanski, "Botmasters Take Heed: You Are Being Put on Notice," Castlecops web site, Oct. 1, 2007, http://www.castlecops.com.

[232] T. Lemke, "Spammers Make Profits without Making a Sale," *Washington Times*, 2003, http://www.washingtontimes.com/business/20030803-110550-8329r.htm.

[233] R. Lemos, "Attackers Strike Using Web Ads," *CNET News.com,* Nov. 2004, `http://news.com.com/Attackers+strike+using+Web+ads/2100-7349_3-5463323.html`.

[234] R. Lemos, "More Security Hiccups for IE," *CNET News.com,* Nov. 2004, `http://news.com.com/More+security+hiccups+for+IE/2100-1002_3-5457105.html`.

[235] N. G. Leveson and C. S. Turner, "An Investigation of the Therac-25 Accidents," *Computer* 26, no. 7 (1993): 18–41.

[236] Z. Li, X. Wang, and J. Y. Choi, "Spyshield: Preserving Privacy from Spyware Add-Ons," in *Proceedings of Recent Advance in Intrusion Detection (RAID),* Sept. 2007.

[237] Z. Liang and R. Sekar, "Automatic Generation of Buffer Overflow Attack Signatures: An Approach Based on Program Behavior Models," in *Proceedings of ACSAC,* 2005, 215–224.

[238] LimeWire homepage, `http://www.limewire.org`.

[239] "The Linux Mobile Phones Showcase," Dec. 18, 2006, `http://www.linuxdevices.com/articles/AT9423084269.html` (accessed Feb. 2007).

[240] LinuxLookup.com, "Linux Users Banned from World of Warcraft?" Nov. 15, 2006, `http://www.linuxlookup.com/2006/nov/15/linux_users_banned_from_world_of_warcraft` (accessed June 8, 2007).

[241] J. L. Lions, "ARIANE 5: Flight 501 Failure; Report by the Inquiry Board," July 19, 1996, `http://www.holub.com/goodies/ariane5.html` (accessed Feb. 2007).

[242] C. Lombardi, "Claria to Exit Adware Business: Company Formerly Known as Gator Sets Its Sights on Search, as It Seeks Credibility Among Online Publishers," *CNET News.com,* Mar. 22, 2006, `http://www.news.com/2100-1024_3-6052623.html`.

[243] S. Lowe, "Are Container Shippers and Consignees Cutting Cost Corners to Sacrifice the Security and the Safety of the Citizens of USA and Europe?" *Directions Magazine,* May 2005, `http://www.directionsmag.com/press.releases/index.php?duty=Show&id=11727`.

[244] "Mailfrontier Phishing IQ test II," `http://survey.mailfrontier.com/forms/msft\_iq\_test.html` (accessed May 2007).

[245] P. Maymounkov and D. Mazières, "Kademlia: A Peer-to-Peer Information System Based on the XOR Metric," in *Proceedings of the 1st International Workshop on Peer-to-Peer Systems,* 2002.

[246] S. McCloud, *Understanding Comics: The Invisible Art* (HarperCollins Publishers, 1993).

[247] J. M. McCune, A. Perrig, and M. K. Reiter, "Bump in the Ether: A Framework for Securing Sensitive User Input," in *Proceedings of the 2006 USENIX Annual Technical Conference,* June 2006, 185–198.

[248] M. McGee, "RFID Can Help Relieve the Fear of Surgery," *Information Week,* Apr. 2005, http://informationweek.com/story/showArticle. jhtml?articleID=161601037.

[249] G. McGraw, *Software Security: Building Security In* (Addison-Wesley, 2006).

[250] G. McGraw and G. Morrisett, "Attacking Malicious Code: A Report to the Infosec Research Council," *IEEE Software* 17, no. 5 (2000): 33–41.

[251] R. McMillan, "Man Charged in Hurricane Katrina Phishing Scams," *IDG News Service,* Aug. 2006, http://www.infoworld.com/article/06/08/18/ HNkatrinaphishing_1.html.

[252] R. McMillan, "Consumers to Lose $2.8 Billion to Phishers in 2006," http://www.pcworld.com/article/id,127799/article.html.

[253] B. S. McWilliams, *Spam Kings* (O'Reilly, 2004).

[254] M. Meiss, "Case Study: Race Pharming," in *Phishing and Countermeasures: Understanding the Increasing Problem of Electronic Identity Theft* (Wiley, 2007), 133–136.

[255] Microsoft, "Recognize Phishing Scams and Fraudulent E-mails," http://www. microsoft.com/athome/security/email/phishing.mspx (accessed Feb. 8, 2007).

[256] Browser extensions, http://msdn.microsoft.com/workshop/browser/ext/ extensions.asp.

[257] R. Miller, S. Garfinkel, F. Menczer, and R. Kraut, "When User Studies Attack: Evaluating Security by Intentionally Attacking Users" (panel at SOUPS 2005). Slides available at http://cups.cs.cmu.edu/soups/2005/program.html.

[258] L. Minnite and D. Callahan, "Secure the Vote: An Analysis of Election Fraud," http://www.demos.org/pubs/EDR_-_Securing_the_Vote.pdf.

[259] C. J. Mitchell, ed., *Trusted Computing,* IEE Professional Applications of Computing Series 6, (The Institute of Electrical Engineers (IEE), Apr. 2005).

[260] K. D. Mitnick and W. L. Simon, *The Art of Deception: Controlling the Human Element of Security* (John Wiley & Sons, 2002).

[261] Miva AdRevenue Express, http://www.miva.com.

[262] C. Moore and M. E. J. Newman, "Epidemics and Percolation in Small-World Networks," *Phys. Rev. E* 61 (2000): 5678.

[263] A. Moshchuk, T. Bragin, S. Gribble, and H. Levy, "A Crawler-Based Study of Spyware on the Web," in *Proceedings of the 13th Annual Network and Distributed System Security Symposium (NDSS 2006),* Feb. 2006.

[264] F-Secure phishing demo, http://www.youtube.com/watch?v=D54nTfLhRr4 (accessed July 3, 2007).

[265] Livesecurity, "US Bank Phishing Attack Exposed," http://www.youtube.com/ watch?v=n2QKQkuSB4Q (accessed Mar. 27, 2007).

[266] "Mozillazine: Extension Development," http://kb.mozillazine.org/Dev_:_Extensions.

[267] Napster homepage, http://www.napster.com/.

[268] R. Naraine, "'Pump-and-Dump' Spam Surge Linked to Russian Bot Herders," *eWeek,* Nov. 16, 2006, http://www.eweek.com/article2/0,1895,2060235,00.asp.

[269] R. Naraine, "Spam Trojan Installs Own Anti-virus Scanner," *eWeek,* Oct. 20, 2006, http://www.eweek.com/article2/0,1895,2034680,00.asp.

[270] A. Narayanan and V. Shmatikov, "Fast Dictionary Attacks on Passwords Using Time-Space Tradeoff," *ACM CCS,* 2005.

[271] G. Naumovich and N. D. Memon, "Preventing Piracy, Reverse Engineering, and Tampering," *IEEE Computer* 36, no. 7 (2003): 64–71.

[272] G. Nemeth and G. Vattay, "Giant Clusters in Random Ad Hoc Networks," *Phys. Rev. E* 67:036110 (2003).

[273] NetSmartzKids, "Teaching Kids What to Watch Out for Online," http://www.netsmartzkids.org/indexFL.htm (accessed July 2, 2007).

[274] BBC News, "Halt E-voting, Says Election Body," Aug. 2007, http://news.bbc.co.uk/2/hi/uk_news/politics/6926625.stm.

[275] OUT-LAW News, "FIFA Warns Football Fans of Phishing Scam," Sept. 2005, http://www.out-law.com/page-6171.

[276] News.com, "'World of Warcraft' Battles Server Problems," *CNET News.com,* Apr. 24, 2006, http://news.com.com/World+of+Warcraft+battles+server+problems/2100-1043_3-6063990.html (accessed Mar. 30, 2007).

[277] H. Niksi, "GNU Wget," available from the master GNU archive site http://prep.ai.mit.edu and its mirrors.

[278] "Nmap—Free Security Scanner for Network Exploration and Security Audits," http://insecure.org/nmap/ (accessed Feb. 2006).

[279] M. O'Connor, "U.S. Bill Includes RFID Provision for Pets," *RFID Journal,* 2005, http://www.rfidjournal.com/article/articleview/2219/1.

[280] M. O'Connor, "Glaxosmithkline Tests RFID on HIV Drug," *RFID Journal,* 2006, http://www.rfidjournal.com/article/articleview/2219/1/1/.

[281] P. Oechslin, "Making a Faster Cryptanalytical Time-Memory Trade-Off," *Advances in Cryptology—CRYPTO,* 2003.

[282] Council of Europe, "Convention on Cybercrime," Nov. 2001, http://conventions.coe.int/Treaty/en/Treaties/Html/185.htm.

[283] U.S. Department of Justice, "Creator and Four Users of Loverspy Spyware Program Indicted," press release, Aug. 26, 2005, http://www.cybercrime.gov/perezIndict.htm.

[284] National Institute of Standards and Technology, "Draft Special Publication 800-98, Guidance for Securing Radio Frequency Identification (RFID) Systems," Sept. 2006, `http://csrc.nist.gov/publications/drafts/800-98/Draft-SP800-98.pdf`.

[285] Official AdWords blog, "Invalid Clicks—Google's Overall Numbers," `http://adwords.blogspot.com/2007/02/invalid-clicks-googles-overall-numbers.html` (accessed Feb. 2007).

[286] The Ohio State University Libraries, "Thomas Nast," `http://cartoons.osu.edu/nast/`.

[287] S. Olsen, "Microsoft Said to Be Mulling Purchase of Claria: A Buyout Would Give MSN Several Key Assets, But Would Put It Under the Watchful Eye of Consumer Watchdogs," *CNET News.com,* June 30, 2005, `http://www.news.com/Microsoft-said-to-be-mulling-purchase-of-Claria/2100-1030_3-5769583.html?tag=html.alert`.

[288] OMA, "Digital Rights Management V1.0" (Technical Specification OMA-Download-DRM-V1 0-20040615-A, The Open Mobile Alliance [OMA], June 2004).

[289] OMA, "DRM Architecture Specification V1.0" (Technical Specification OMA-Download-ARCH-V1 0-20040625-A, The Open Mobile Alliance [OMA], June 2004).

[290] OMA, "DRM Architecture V2.0" (Technical Specification OMA-DRMARCH-V2 0-2004071515-C, The Open Mobile Alliance [OMA], July 2004).

[291] OMA, "DRM Specification V2.0" (Technical Specification OMA-DRMDRM-V2 0-20040716-C, The Open Mobile Alliance [OMA], July 2004).

[292] ABC News Online, "Online Gamer Killed for Selling Cyber Sword," ABC.net.au, Mar. 30, 2005, `http://www.abc.net.au/news/newsitems/200503/s1334618.htm` (accessed June 8, 2007).

[293] Fuzen Op, "FU Rootkit," 2004, `http://www.rootkit.com/project.php?id=12`.

[294] OpenFT homepage, `http://www.openft.org`.

[295] OpenWrt, `http://openwrt.org` (accessed Feb. 2007).

[296] "Click Fraud Gets Day in Court—Maybe," Apr. 21, 2005, `http://searchlineinfo.com/Click_fraud_lawsuit/`.

[297] "The New p0f: 2.0.8 (2006-09-06)," `http://lcamtuf.coredump.cx/p0f.shtml` (accessed Feb. 2007).

[298] Palmers, "Advances in Kernel Hacking," *Phrack Magazine,* `http://www.phrack.org/archives/58/p58-0x06`.

[299] D. Pappalardo and E. Messmer, "Extortion via DDoS on the Rise," *Computer World,* May 16, 2005, `http://www.computerworld.com/printthis/2005/0,4814,101761,00.html`.

[300] B. Parno, C. Kuo, and A. Perrig, "Authentication and Fraud Detection: Phoolproof Phishing Prevention," in *Proceedings of Financial Cryptography and Data Security (FC '06)*, 2006.

[301] Passmark, http://www.passmarksecurity.com.

[302] R. Pastor-Satorras and A. Vespignani, "Epidemic Spreading in Scale-Free Networks," *Phys. Rev. Lett.* 86 (2001): 3200–3203.

[303] PayPal, "Can You Spot Phishing?" https://www.paypal.com/fightphishing.

[304] PayPal, "Protect Yourself from Fraudulent Emails," https://www.paypal.com/cgi-bin/webscr?cmd=_vdc-security-spoof-outside (accessed Feb. 8, 2007).

[305] "Staggering Identity Theft Ring Discovered Over the Weekend," http://www.pcsecuritynews.com/news/sunbelt-coolwebsearch-identity-theft.wpml.

[306] D. Pearson, "Storm Worm DDoS Threat to the EDU Sector," REN-ISAC mailing list, Aug. 9, 2007, http://lists.sans.org/pipermail/unisog/2007-August/027405.html.

[307] S. Pearson, ed., *Trusted Computing Platforms: TCPA Technology in Context*, (Prentice Hall, 2003).

[308] R. Pedroncelli, "Recordings Reveal Schwarzenegger Annoyed by Democrats, GOP Alike," *USA Today*, Feb. 5, 2007, http://www.usatoday.com/news/nation/2007-02-05-schwarzenegger-recordings_x.htm.

[309] M. Peinado, Y. Chen, P. England, and J. Manferdelli, "NGSCB: A Trusted Open System," in H. Wang, J. Pieprzyk, and V. Varadharajan, eds., *Proceedings of 9th Australasian Conference on Information Security and Privacy, (ACISP '04)*, volume 3108 of *Lecture Notes in Computer Science (LNCS)*, pages 86–97 (Springer–Verlag, July 13–15, 2004).

[310] M. Peinado, P. England, and Y. Chen, "An Overview of NGSCB," in *Trusted Computing*, IEE Professional Applications of Computing Series 6 (The Institute of Electrical Engineers (IEE), Apr. 2005) 115–141.

[311] P. D. Petkov, Javascript Address Info web page, http://www.gnucitizen.org/projects/javascript-address-info/ (accessed Mar. 12, 2007).

[312] "Top 20 Names" http://www.bowwow.com.au/top20/index.asp (accessed Sept. 2007).

[313] Anti-Phishing Working Group, Resources, http://www.apwg.org/resources.html#advice.

[314] Plaguez, "Weakening the Linux Kernel," *Phrack Magazine*, http://www.phrack.org/archives/52/P52-18.

[315] P. Pollack, "Verisign Announces Two-Factor Authentication System," *Ars Technica*, Feb. 13, 2006, http://arstechnica.com/news.ars/post/20060213-6174.html.

[316] K. Poulsen, "Guilty Plea in Kinko's Keystroke Caper," *SecurityFocus,* July 2003, `http://www.securityfocus.com/news/6447`.

[317] K. Poulsen, "Windows Root Kits a Stealthy Threat," *SecurityFocus,* Mar. 2003, `http://www.securityfocus.com/news/2879`.

[318] Pragmatic, "Complete Linux Loadable Kernel Modules," `http://www.thc.org/papers/LKM_HACKING.html`.

[319] Associated Press, "Body ID: Barcodes for Cadavers," *Wired News,* Feb. 2005, `http://www.wired.com/news/medtech/0,1286,66519,00.html?tw=rss.TEK`.

[320] V. Prevelakis and D. Spinellis, "The Athens Affair: How Some Extremely Smart Hackers Pulled Off the Most Audacious Cell-Network Break-In Ever," *IEEE Spectrum Online,* 2007, `http://www.spectrum.ieee.org/jul07/5280`.

[321] The Honeynet Project, "Know Your Enemy: Tracking Botnets," `http://www.honeynet.org/papers/bots/`.

[322] The Honeynet Project, "Know Your Enemy: Fast-Flux Service Networks," July 2007, `http://www.honeynet.org/papers/ff/fast-flux.html`.

[323] N. Provos and T. Holz, *Virtual Honeypots: From Botnet Tracking to Intrusion Detection* (Addison-Wesley, 2008).

[324] Wikipedia, "Pump and dump," `http://en.wikipedia.org/wiki/Pump_and_dump`.

[325] Quova, `http://www.quova.com`.

[326] M. Rajab, J. Zarfoss, F. Monrose, and A. Terzis, "My Botnet Is Bigger Than Yours (Maybe Better Than Yours): Why Size Estimates Remain Challenging," in *First Workshop on Hot Topics in Understanding Botnets (HotBots),* 2007.

[327] Z. Ramzan, "Drive-by Pharming: How Clicking on a Link Can Cost You Dearly," Symantec Security Response web log, Feb. 15, 2007, `http://www.symantec.com/enterprise/security_response/weblog/2007/02/driveby pharming how clicking 1.html`.

[328] S. S. Rao, "Counterspy," *Forbes Magazine,* Feb. 2005, `http://www.landfield.com/isn/mail-archive/2001/Jan/0113.html`.

[329] M. Rasch, "Can Writing Software Be a Crime?" *SecurityFocus,* Oct. 3, 2005, `http://www.securityfocus.com/columnists/360/1`.

[330] M. K. Reiter, V. Anupam, and A. Mayer, "Detecting Hit Shaving in ClickThrough Payment Schemes," in *Proceedings of the 3rd USENIX Workshop on Electronic Commerce,* 1998, 155–166.

[331] Symantec Security Response, "Backdoor.Rustock," `http://www.symantec.com/security_response/writeup.jsp?docid=2006-011309-5412-99`.

[332] Symantec Security Response, "Backdoor.Ryknos writeup," `http://www.symantec.com/security_response/writeup.jsp?docid=2005-111012-2048-99`.

[333] Symantec Security Response, "Infostealer.Banker.D," `http://www.symantec.com/ security_response/writeup.jsp?docid=2007-052710-0541-99`.

[334] Symantec Security Response, "Infostealer.Bzup," `http://www.symantec.com/ security_response/writeup.jsp?docid=2006-080315-1729-99`.

[335] Symantec Security Response, "Infostealer.Gampass," `http://www.symantec.com/ security_response/writeup.jsp?docid=2006-111201-3853-99`.

[336] Symantec Security Response, "Infostealer.Lineage," `http://www.symantec.com/ security_response/writeup.jsp?docid=2005-011211-3355-99`.

[337] Symantec Security Response, "Rootkit definition," `http://www.symantec.com/ enterprise/security_response/glossary.jsp`.

[338] Symantec Security Response, "Trojan.Checkraise," `http://www.symantec.com/ security_response/writeup.jsp?docid=2006-051614-4752-99`.

[339] Symantec Security Response, "Trojan.Dowiex," `http://www.symantec.com/ security_response/writeup.jsp?docid=2006-101716-2136-99`.

[340] Symantec Security Response, "Trojan.Gpcoder," `http://www.symantec.com/ security_response/writeup.jsp?docid=2005-052215-5723-99`.

[341] Symantec Security Response, "Trojan.Peacomm," `http://www.symantec.com/ security_response/writeup.jsp?docid=2007-011917-1403-99`.

[342] Symantec Security Response, "Trojan.Welomoch writeup," `http://www.symantec. com/security_response/writeup.jsp?docid=2005-120709-5703-99`.

[343] Symantec Security Response, "W31.Korgo.Q," `http://www.symantec.com/ security_response/writeup.jsp?docid=2005-011215-592499&tabid=2`.

[344] Symantec Security Response, "W32.gaobot.gen!poly," `http://www.symantec.com/ security_response/writeup.jsp?docid=2004-031915-3501-99&tabid=2`.

[345] Symantec Security Response, "W32.hllw.gaobot.ag," `http://www.symantec.com/ security_response/writeup.jsp?docid=2003-092318-4059-99`.

[346] Symantec Security Response, "W32.Nugache.A@mm," `http://www.symantec.com/ security_response/writeup.jsp?docid=2006-043016-0900-99`.

[347] Symantec Security Response, "Trojan.slanret," Jan. 2003, `http://www.symantec. com/security_response/writeup.jsp?docid=2003-012916-5726-99`.

[348] Symantec Security Response, "Spyware.apropos.c," Feb. 2007, `http://www. symantec.com/security_response/writeup.jsp?docid=2005-102112- 2934-99`.

[349] T. Ricker, "Kanguru's 64GB Flash Drive Max," `http://www.engadget.com/ 2006/ 04/07/kangurus-64gb-flash-drive-max-only-2-800/` (accessed Oct. 2007).

[350] M. Rieback, B. Crispo, and A. Tanenbaum, "Is Your Cat Infected with a Computer Virus?" in *Proceedings of the IEEE Pervasive Computing and Communications,* 169–179 (Pisa, Italy: Mar. 2006), http://www.rfidguardian.org/papers/percom.06.pdf.

[351] M. Rieback, G. Gaydadjiev, B. Crispo, R. Hofman, and A. Tanenbaum, "A Platform for RFID Security and Privacy Administration," in *Proceedings of the USENIX/SAGE Large Installation System Administration Conference,* 89–102 (Washington, DC: Dec. 2006).

[352] R. L. Rivest, "The MD5 Message Digest Algorithm," Internet RFC 1321, Apr. 1992.

[353] Wikipedia, "robots.txt," http://en.wikipedia.org/wiki/Robots_Exclusion_Standard.

[354] "RockBox—Open Source Jukebox Firmware," http://www.rockbox.org/ (accessed Feb. 2007).

[355] D. B. Roddy, "Rendell Vows Action on Voter Scams; Pitt Students Tricked," *Pittsburgh Post-Gazette,* Oct. 27, 2004, http://www.post-gazette.com/pg/04301/402432.stm.

[356] J. Roskind, "Attacks Against the Netscape Browser," (invited talk, RSA Data Security Conference, 2001).

[357] B. Ross, C. Jackson, N. Miyake, D. Boneh, and J. Mitchell, "Stronger Password Authentication Using Browser Extensions," in *Proceedings of the 14th USENIX Security Symposium,* 2005.

[358] L. Rozen, "New NAACP Report on GOP Voter Suppression Efforts Against Minority Voters in America," Nov. 2004, http://www.warandpiece.com/blogdirs/001293.html.

[359] RSA SecurID, http://www.rsa.com/node.aspx?id=1156.

[360] A. Rubin, *Brave New Ballot: The Battle to Safeguard Democracy in the Age of Electronic Voting* (Morgan Road Books, 2006).

[361] M. Russinovich, *Microsoft Windows Internals,* 4th ed., vol. 4 (Microsoft Press, Dec. 2004).

[362] M. Russinovich, "Sony, Rootkits and Digital Rights Management Gone Too Far," October 2005, http://blogs.technet.com/markrussinovich/archive/2005/10/31/sony-rootkits-and-digital-rights-management-gone-too-far.aspx.

[363] J. Rutkowska, "How to Detect VMM Using (Almost) One CPU Instruction," 2004, http://www.invisiblethings.org/papers/redpill.html.

[364] J. Rutkowska, "Subverting Vista Kernel For Fun And Profit," *Black Hat USA,* Aug. 2006, http://www.blackhat.com/presentations/bh-usa-06/BH-US-06-Rutkowska.pdf.

[365] S. Sarma, S. Weis, and D. Engels, "RFID Systems and Security and Privacy Implications," in *Proceedings of Cryptographic Hardware and Embedded Systems (CHES 2002), LNCS,* 2523 (Aug. 2002): 454–469.

[366] S. Schecter, R. Dhamija, A. Ozment, and I. Fischer, "The Emperor's New Security Indicators: An Evaluation of Website Authentication and the Effect of Role Playing on Usability Studies," in *Proceedings of IEEE Symposium on Security and Privacy* (2007).

[367] B. Schneier, *Secrets and Lies: Digital Security in a Networked World* (John Wiley & Sons, 2000).

[368] Secunia Research, "Multiple Browsers Tabbed Browsing Vulnerabilities," http://secunia.com/secunia_research/2004-10/advisory/ (accessed July 3, 2007).

[369] U.S. Securities and Exchange Commission, "Pump and Dump Schemes," http://www.sec.gov/answers/pumpdump.htm.

[370] L. Seltzer, "Spotting Phish and Phighting Back," *eWeek.com,* Aug. 2004, http://www.eweek.com/article2/0,1759,1630161,00.asp.

[371] R. Shah and C. Sandvig, "Software Defaults as De Facto Regulation: The Case of Wireless Aps" (The 33rd Research Conference on Communication, Information and Internet Policy, Arlington, VA, Sept. 2005).

[372] E. Shanahan, "ID Thieves' New Tricks," *Reader's Digest,* June 2006, 82–87.

[373] S. Sheng, B. Magnien, P. Kumaraguru, A. Acquisti, L. Cranor, J. Hong, and E. Nunge, "Anti-phishing Phil: The Design and Evaluation of a Game That Teaches People Not to Fall for Phish," in *Proceedings of the 2007 Symposium On Usable Privacy and Security,* July 2007.

[374] A. Shipp, "New Trojans Plunder Bank Accounts," *CNET News.com,* Feb. 17, 2006, http://news.com.com/New+Trojans+plunder+bank+accounts/2100-7349_3-6041173.html.

[375] P. Silberman and C.H.A.O.S., "Futo," http://www.uninformed.org/?v=3&a=7&t=pdf.

[376] E. Skoudis, "Even Nastier: Traditional Rootkits," http://www.informit.com/articles/article.asp?p=23463&redir=1&rl=1.

[377] P. Sloan, "The Man Who Owns the Internet," *Business 2.0 Magazine,* http://money.cnn.com/magazines/business2/business2_archive/2007/06/01/100050989/index.htm.

[378] J. Smed and H. Hakonen, "Towards a Definition of a Computer Game" (Technical Report 553, Turku Centre for Computer Science, 2003), http://staff.cs.utu.fi/~jounsmed/papers/TR553.pdf.

[379] J. Smith, "Playing Dirty, Understanding Conflicts in Multiplayer Games," *5th Annual Conference of the Association of Internet Researchers,* 2004, http://jonassmith.dk/weblog/uploads/playing_dirty.pdf.

[380] S. Smith, "Another Big Thing, Part 1," Symantec Security Response blog, May 2007, http://www.symantec.com/enterprise/security_response/weblog/2007/05/another_big_thing.html.

[381] "Snort—The De Facto Standard for Intrusion Detection/Prevention," http://www.snort.org (accessed Feb. 2007).

[382] L. Sobrado and J. C. Birget, "Graphical Passwords," *The Rutgers Scholar* 4 (2002).

[383] "Social Engineering, the USB Way," June 7, 2006, http://www.darkreading.com/document.asp?doc_id=95556&WT.svl=column1_1.

[384] S. Sparks and J. Butler, "Shadow Walker—Raising the Bar for Windows Rootkit Detection," *Phrack Magazine*, 2005, http://www.phrack.org/archives/63/p63-0x08_Raising_The_Bar_For_Windows_Rootkit_Detection.txt.

[385] Definition of *spidering*, http://www.mbgj.org/glossary_se_terms.htm.

[386] S. Srikwan and M. Jakobsson, http://www.SecurityCartoon.com (accessed May 16, 2007).

[387] Netcraft News, "More Than 450 Phishing Attacks Used ssl in 2005," http://news.netcraft.com/archives/2005/12/28/more_than_450_phishing_attacks_used_ssl_in_2005.html (accessed July 3, 2007).

[388] S. Stamm, M. Jakobsson, and M. Gandhi, "Verybigad.com: A Study in Socially Transmitted Malware," http://www.indiana.edu/~phishing/verybigad/.

[389] S. Stamm, Z. Ramzan, and M. Jakobsson, "Drive-by Pharming" (Technical Report TR641, Indiana University, Dec. 2006).

[390] A. Stephano and D. P. Groth, "USEable Security: Interface Design Strategies for Improving Security," In *3rd International Workshop on Visualization for Computer Security* (Fairfax County, VA, Nov. 2006).

[391] J. Stewart, "Phatbot Trojan Analysis," Secureworks.com, Mar. 15, 2004, http://www.secureworks.com/research/threats/phatbot.

[392] D. Stinson, *Cryptography: Theory and Practice*, 3rd ed. (CRC Press, Nov. 2005).

[393] I. Stoica, R. Morris, D. Karger, M. F. Kaashoek, and H. Balakrishnan, "Chord: A Scalable Peer-to-Peer Lookup Service for Internet Applications," in *Proceedings of ACM SIGCOMM*, 2001.

[394] D. Strom, "5 Disruptive Technologies to Watch in 2007," *InformationWeek*, Jan. 2007, http://www.informationweek.com/news/showArticle.jhtml?articleID=196800208.

[395] A. Stubblefield, J. Ioannidis, and A. D. Rubin, "A Key Recovery Attack on the 802.11b Wired Equivalent Privacy Protocol (WEP)," *ACM Trans. Inf. Syst. Secur.* 7, no. 2 (2004): 319–332.

[396] A. Stubblefield, J. Ionnidis, and A. D. Rubin, "Using the Fluhrer, Mantin, and Shamir Attack to Break WEP," in *Network and Distributed Systems Security Symposium NDSS*, 2002.

[397] B. Sullivan, "Lieberman Campaign Site, E-mail Hacked," *MSNBC*, Aug. 8, 2006, http://www.msnbc.msn.com/id/14245779.

[398] B. Sullivan, The Secret Tricks That Spammers Use," *MSNBC News*, 2003, http://www.msnbc.msn.com/id/3078640/.

[399] A. Sundaram, "An Introduction to Intrusion Detection," *Crossroads* 2, no. 4 (1996).

[400] Symantec, "Symantec Internet Security Threat Report, Edition XI," http://www. symantec.com/threatreport/.

[401] Symantec, "Symantec Internet Security Threat Report, Edition XII," http://www. symantec.com/threatreport/.

[402] Symantec Security Response, "Infostealer.Bankash.G," Feb. 2006, http://www. symantec.com/security_response/writeup.jsp?docid=2006-010317-5218-99.

[403] Symantec Security Response, "Trojan.Archiveus," May 2006, http://www.symantec. com/security_response/writeup.jsp?docid=2006-050601-0940-99.

[404] P. Szor, *The Art of Computer Virus Research and Defense* (Addison-Wesley, 2005).

[405] T. Kojm, ClamAV homepage, http://www.clamav.net.

[406] K. Tan, K. Killourhy, and R. Maxion, "Undermining an Anomaly-Based Intrusion Detection System Using Common Exploits," in *Proceedings of the 5th International Symposium on Recent Advances in Intrusion Detection*, 2002.

[407] L. Tang, J. Li, J. Zhou, Z. Zhou, H. Wang, and K. Li, "Freerank: Implementing Independent Ranking Service for Multiplayer Online Games," NetGames, 2005, Oct. 10–11, 2005.

[408] TCG, "TCG Generic Server Specification" (TCG Specification Version 1.0 Final, The Trusted Computing Group [TCG], Portland, OR, July 2005).

[409] TCG, "TCG PC Client Specific Implementation Specification for Conventional BIOS" (TCG Specification Version 1.2 Final, The Trusted Computing Group [TCG], Portland, OR, July 2005).

[410] TCG, "TPM Main, Part 1: Design Principles" (TCG Specification Version 1.2, Revision 94, The Trusted Computing Group [TCG], Portland, OR, Mar. 2006).

[411] TCG, "TPM Main, Part 2: TPM Data Structures" (TCG Specification Version 1.2, Revision 94, The Trusted Computing Group (TCG), Portland, OR, Mar. 2006).

[412] TCG, "TPM Main, Part 3: Commands" (TCG Specification Version 1.2, Revision 94, The Trusted Computing Group (TCG), Portland, OR, Mar. 2006).

[413] TCG, "TNC Architecture for Interoperability" (TCG Specification Version 1.2, Revision 4, The Trusted Computing Group (TCG), Portland, OR, Sept. 2007).

[414] TCG MPWG, "The TCG Mobile Trusted Module Specification" (TCG Specification Version 0.9, Revision 1, The Trusted Computing Group (TCG), Portland, OR, Sept. 2006).

[415] Google Click Quality Team, "How Fictitious Clicks Occur in Third-Party Click Fraud Audit Reports," Aug. 2006, `http://www.google.com/adwords/ReportonThird-PartyClickFraudAuditing.pdf`.

[416] PaX Team, Homepage of the PaX team, `http://pax.grsecurity.net`.

[417] Tech Web Technology News, "New Phishing Scam Takes Advantage of Election Hype," Oct. 2004, `http://www.techweb.com/wire/security/49400811`.

[418] TechCrunch.com, "Metaverse Breached: Second Life Customer Database Hacked," Sept. 8, 2006, `http://www.techcrunch.com/2006/09/08/metaverse-breached-second-life-customer-database-hacked/` (accessed Mar. 30, 2007).

[419] E. Tews, R.-P. Weinmann, and A. Pyshkin, "Breaking 104 Bit WEP in Less Than 60 Seconds" (Cryptology ePrint Archive, Report 2007/120, 2007), `http://eprint.iacr.org/`.

[420] R. Thayer, N. Doraswamy, and R. Glenn, "IP Security Document Roadmap," RFC 2411, Nov. 1998, `http://rfc.net/rfc2411.html` (accessed Feb. 2007).

[421] The Associated Press, "GE Energy Acknowledges Blackout Bug," Feb. 2004, `http://www.securityfocus.com/news/8032` (accessed Feb. 2007).

[422] "How the Public and Private Sectors Are Working Together to Help Consumers and Put Fraudsters Behind Bars," `http://www.treas.gov/press/releases/js2501.htm`.

[423] Truff, "Infecting Loadable Kernel Modules," *Phrack Magazine,* `http://www.phrack.org/archives/61/p61-0x0a_Infecting_Loadable_Kernel_Modules.txt`.

[424] K. Tsipenyuk, B. Chess, and G. McGraw, "Seven Pernicious Kingdoms: A Taxonomy of Software Security Errors," in *NIST Workshop on Software Security Assurance Tools, Techniques, and Metrics (SSATTM)* (Los Angeles: 2005).

[425] A. Tsow, "Phishing with Consumer Electronics—Malicious Home Routers," in *Models of Trust for the Web, a Workshop at the 15th International World Wide Web Conference (WWW)*, 2006.

[426] A. Tsow, M. Jakobsson, L. Yang, and S. Wetzel, "Warkitting: The Driveby Subversion of Wireless Home Routers," special issue 3, in *Journal of Digital Forensic Practice* 1 (Nov. 2006).

[427] A. Tuzhilin, "The Lane's Gifts v. Google Report," July 2006, `http://googleblog.blogspot.com/pdf/Tuzhilin Report.pdf`.

[428] J. D. Tygar and B. Yee, "Dyad: A System for Using Physically Secure Coprocessors (Technical Report CMU-CS-91-140R, Carnegie Mellon University, Pittsburgh, PA, May 1991).

[429] Economist Intelligence Unit, "Symantec Ensuring Mobile Security (Survey of 248 Company Executives and Senior IT Employees)," Jan. 2006, `http://www.symantec.com/content/en/us/about/media/mobile-security\_Full-Report.pdf`.

[430] U.S. Department of Homeland Security and SRI International Identity Theft Technology Council and the Anti-Phishing Working Group, "The Crimeware Landscape: Malware, Phishing, Identity Theft and Beyond," Oct. 2006, http://www.antiphishing.org/reports/APWG_CrimewareReport.pdf.

[431] http://www.usbhacks.com/2006/10/07/usb-hacksaw/.

[432] USB switchblade, http://www.usbhacks.com/2006/10/07/usb-switchblade/.

[433] "Fifth-Generation iPods Hit with Windows Virus," Oct. 2006, http://www.itbusinessedge.com/item/?ci=21164.

[434] "Man Used MP3 Player to Hack ATMs," http://www.theregister.co.uk/2006/11/18/mp3_player_atm_hack/.

[435] Sanctuary Device Control, http://www.lumension.com/usb_security.jsp (accessed Oct. 2007).

[436] USB 2 flash drive PRO 2, http://www.buslinkbuy.com/products.asp?sku=BDP2%2D64G%2DU2.

[437] Episode 2×02. http://wiki.hak5.org/wiki/Episode_2x02.

[438] http://www.lcpsoft.com/english/download.htm.

[439] Wikipedia, "Live USB," http://en.wikipedia.org/wiki/LiveUSB (accessed 2007).

[440] "USB Memory Sticks Pose New Dangers—Some New Drives Can Be Used to Automatically Run Malware," http://www.computerworld.com/action/article.do?command=viewArticleBasic&taxonomyName=storage&articleId=9003592&taxonomyId=19&intsrc=kc_top.

[441] "Gartner Says Number of Phishing E-mails Sent to U.S. Adults Nearly Doubles in Just Two Years," http://www.gartner.com/it/page.jsp?id=498245.

[442] http://us1.samba.org/samba/ftp/pwdump/.

[443] http://www.bindview.com/Support/RAZOR/Utilities/Windows/pwdump2_readme.cfm.

[444] http://www.polivec.com/pw3dump/default.htm.

[445] "Apple Video iPods. Now with Malware," http://www.2-spyware.com/news/post135.html.

[446] "Windows Keys," http://www.lostpassword.com/windows.htm.

[447] "Using a Windows Key Bootable USB Flash Drive," http://www.lostpassword.com/windows-howto.htm#usb-flash (accessed June 2007).

[448] "Remove Rjump," description and removal instructions, http://www.2-spyware.com/remove-rjump.html.

[449] SAMDump, http://www.atstake.com/products/lc/download.html.

[450] http://www.insidepro.com.

[451] Wikipedia, "U3," http://en.wikipedia.org/wiki/U3.

[452] W32/RJump.worm, http://vil.nai.com/vil/content/v_139985.htm.

[453] Wikipedia, "USB Flash Drive," http://en.wikipedia.org/wiki/
USB_flash_drive (accessed Oct. 2007).

[454] "How to Hack or Crack a Windows XP Administrator Password," http://www.
clazh.com/how-to-hack-or-crack-a-windows-xp-administrator-password/.

[455] Wikipedia, "Zune," http://en.wikipedia.org/wiki/Zune.

[456] P. C. van Oorschot, "Revisiting Software Protection," in *Proceedings of ISC,* 2003, 1–13.

[457] M. Vargas, "2002 Retail Security Survey Shows U.S. Retails Losing $31 Billion to
Theft," *About.com,* 2002, http://retailindustry.about.com/od/
statistics_loss_prevention/l/aa021126a.htm.

[458] Virtual Economy Research Network (VERN), "How Big Is the RMT Market Anyway?"
Mar. 8, 2007, http://virtual-economy.org/blog/how_big_is_the_rmt_
market_anyw (accessed May 23, 2007).

[459] P. Viscarola and W. A. Mason, *Windows NT Device Driver Development* (New Riders
Press, Nov. 1998).

[460] Vladnik, "Fly-by Malware Installation Demo," July 20, 2006, http://www.youtube.
com/watch?v=oU1gcprFEPU.

[461] VMWare, "VMWare Server: Free Virtualization for Windows and Linux Servers,"
http://www.vmware.com/pdf/server_datasheet.pdf.

[462] R. Vogt, J. Aycock, and M. J. Jacobson. "Army of Botnets," in *Proceedings of Network
and Distributed Systems Security (NDSS),* 2007.

[463] N. Walters, "Spyware and Identity Theft," http://www.aarp.org/research/
technology/onlineprivacy/fs126_spyware.html.

[464] K. Wang, G. Cretu, and S. J. Stolfo, "Anomalous Payload-Based Worm Detection and
Signature Generation," *RAID,* Sept. 2005.

[465] X. Wang, Z. Li, J. Xu, M. K. Reiter, C. Kil, and J. Y. Choi, "Packet Vaccine: Black-Box
Exploit Detection and Signature Generation," in *ACM Conference on Computer and
Communications Security,* 2006, 37–46.

[466] Y.-M. Wang, D. Beck, J. Wang, C. Verbowski, and B. Daniels, "Strider Typo-Patrol:
Discovery and Analysis of Systematic Typo-Squatting" (Technical Report MSR-TR-
2006-40, Microsoft Research, 2006), http://research.microsoft.com/
Typo-Patrol/.

[467] D. J. Watts and S. H. Strogatz, "Collective Dynamics of 'Small-World' Networks," *Nature* 393 (1998): 440.

[468] Weasal, "Unloading Those Pesky Keyboard Filter Drivers!" `http://www.rootkit.com/newsread.php?newsid=398`.

[469] Weasal, "How to Really Really Hide from the SC Manager," 2006, `http://www.rootkit.com/newsread.php?newsid=419`.

[470] F-Secure Weblog, "Sony's USB Rootkit vs. Sony's Music Rootkit," `http://www.f-secure.com/weblog/archives/archive-082007.html`.

[471] Webwhacker 5.0, `http://www.bluesquirrel.com/products/webwhacker/` (accessed July 2007).

[472] D. Weinshall, "Cognitive Authentication Schemes Safe Against Spyware," short paper, *Symposium on Security and Privacy*, 2006, 295–300.

[473] M. Weiser, "The Computer for the Twenty-first Century," *Scientific American*, 1991, 94–100.

[474] M. Weiser, "The World Is Not a Desktop," *ACM Interactions*, 1994, 7–8.

[475] H. Welte, M. Meriac, and B. Meriac, *OpenPICC*, `http://www.openpcd.org/openpicc.0.html`.

[476] J. Westhues, "A Test Instrument for HF/LF RFID," Jan. 2007, `http://cq.cx/proxmark3.pl`.

[477] T. Whalen and K. M. Inkpen, "Gathering Evidence: Use of Visual Security Cues in Web Browsers," in *GI '05: Proceedings of Graphics Interface 2005*, 137–144 (School of Computer Science, University of Waterloo, Waterloo, ON, 2005. Canadian Human-Computer Communications Society).

[478] S. Williams and C. Kindel, "The Component Object Model: A Technical Overview," `http://msdn.microsoft.com/library/default.asp?url=/library/en-us/dncomg/html/msdn_comppr.asp`.

[479] *Wired*, "Hackers Put 'Bane' in Shadowbane," May 3, 2003, `http://www.wired.com/gaming/gamingreviews/news/2003/05/59034` (accessed Mar. 30, 2007).

[480] J. Wright, "Weaknesses in Wireless LAN Session Containment," May 19, 2005, `http://i.cmpnet.com/nc/1612/graphics/SessionContainment_file.pdf` (accessed Feb. 2007).

[481] M. Wu, R. Miller, and S. Garfinkel, "Do Security Toolbars Actually Prevent Phishing Attacks?" in *Proc. CHI*, 2006.

[482] J. Xu, P. Ning, C. Kil, Y. Zhai, and C. Bookholt, "Automatic Diagnosis and Response to Memory Corruption Vulnerabilities," in *CCS '05: Proceedings of the 12th ACM Conference on Computer and Communications Security* (ACM Press, 2005), 223–234.

[483] "Yahoo Settles 'Click Fraud' Lawsuit," June 28, 2006, http://www.msnbc.msn.com/id/13601951/.

[484] J. Yan and H. J. Choi, "Security Issues in Online Games," *The Electronic Library* 20, no. 2 (2002). A previous version appears in *Proc. of International Conference on Application and Development of Computer Games* (City University of Hong Kong, Nov. 2001).

[485] J. Yan and B. Randell, "A Systematic Classification of Cheating in Online Games," (NetGames '05 conference, Oct. 10–11, 2005).

[486] K. -P. Yee and K. Sitaker, "Passpet: Convenient Password Management and Phishing Protection," in *Proceedings of the Symposium on Usable Privacy and Security (SOUPS)*, 2006.

[487] A. Young and M. Yung, *Malicious Cryptography: Exposing Cryptovirology* (John Wiley & Sons, 2004).

[488] Ernst and Young, "Retailers Lose Billions Annually to Inventory Shrinkage," 2002, http://retailindustry.about.com/cs/lp_retailstore/a/bl_ey051303.htm.

[489] J. Zagal, M. Mateas, C. Fernandez-Vara, B. Hochhalter, and N. Lichti, "Towards an Ontological Language for Game Analysis," in *Proceedings of the Digital Interactive Games Research Association Conference* (Vancouver, BC, June 2005), http://www.cc.gatech.edu/grads/z/Jose.Zagal/Papers/OntologyDIGRA2005.pdf.

[490] M. Zalewski, *Silence on the Wire: A Field Guide to Passive Reconnaissance and Indirect Attacks* (No Starch Press, 2005).

[491] S. Zander, I. Leeder, and G. Armitage, "Achieving Fairness in Multiplayer Network Games through Automated Latency Balancing," in *Proceedings of the 2005 ACM SIGCHI International Conference on Advances in Computer Entertainment Technology*, 117–124 (Valencia, Spain, 2005).

[492] T. Zeller, "Black Market in Stolen Credit Card Data Thrives on Internet," *New York Times*, 2005, http://www.nytimes.com/2005/06/21/technology/21data.html?ei=5000&cn=c06800aa210685f8&ex=1277006400&adxnnl=1&partner=rssnyt&emc=rss&pagewanted=all&adxnnlx=1162917731-sbNrtWOThtPy3rRh+yHnAQ.

[493] K. Zetter, "Hackers Annihilate Wi-Fi Record," *Wired News*, Aug. 2, 2005, http://www.wired.com/news/wireless/0,1382,68395,00.html?tw=wn_tophead_3, 2 (accessed Feb. 2007).

[494] C. C. Zou and R. Cunningham, "Honeypot-Aware Advanced Botnet Construction and Maintenance," in *Proceedings of the International Conference on Dependable Systems and Networks*, 2006.

[495] D. D. Zovi, "Hardware Virtualization Based Rootkits," *Black Hat USA*, Aug. 2006, http://www.blackhat.com/presentations/bh-usa-06/BH-US-06-Zovi.pdf.

[496] "Sales in Virtual Goods Top $100 Million." *New Scientist,* Oct. 29, 2004. Retrieved May 23, 2007, `http://www.newscientist.com/article.ns?id=dn6601`.

[497] "Warcraft Gamers Locked Out After Trojan Attack." *Register,* Sept. 29, 2006. Retrieved June 8, 2007, `http://www.theregister.co.uk/2006/09/29/warcraft_trojan_attack/`.

[498] Symantec Security Response "Symantec's Antispyware Approach." Available from `http://www.symantec.com/business/security_response/antispyware_approach.jsp`.

Index

Numbers

180Solutions
  adware techniques for evading law enforcement, 364
  trends in adware business, 366
2wire, WAP default settings, 115
3G mobile technologies, 469
802.11 standard, wireless routers, 110–113

A

A records, DNS, 203
Access control
  J2EE environment problems, 52
  as security feature, 43, 49
  standards for network access, 111
  WLANs and, 110–111
Access Control Lists (ACLs), 259
Access Device Fraud Act, 137, 445
Accessibility of material, education principles, 397, 410–411
ACLs (Access Control Lists), 259
ACPA (Anticybersquatting Consumer Protection Act), 297
ACPI (Advanced Configuration and Power Interface), 264
Action-based model, advertising revenues, 329–330
Active bot-infected computers, Symantec statistics regarding, 186
ActiveX, 77
ActiveX, web browser vulnerabilities, 23
Ad impressions, 327–328
Ad-provider evasion, hiding click fraud attacks, 174–177

Adaptability to changing threats, education principles, 397, 412
Add/Remove Programs
  adware programs bypassing registration with, 362
  difficulty in removal of surreptitious software, 417
Address verification service (AVS), credit card security, 468
Administrative access, in wireless routers, 111–112
Adobe Acrobat plug-ins, web browser vulnerabilities, 23
Adobe Flash, web browser vulnerabilities, 24
AdSense, Google, 334
Advanced Configuration and Power Interface (ACPI), 264
Advertising, 325–353
  action-based model, 329–330
  attack types, 335
  botmasters exploiting click fraud, 379
  click-based model, 328–329
  click fraud auditing, 347
  click spam, 333–334
  coercion, 336–337
  containment of abuses, 346–347
  conversion spam, 334–335
  countermeasures, 342–343
  detection of abuses, 344–346
  domain speculation in politics and, 302–303
  history of, 325–326
  human clickers, 335–336
  impression-based model, 327–328
  impression spam, 332–333
  malicious intent in politics, 304–305
  malicious side of, 391–395
  manual clickers, 337–339

Go Beyond the Book

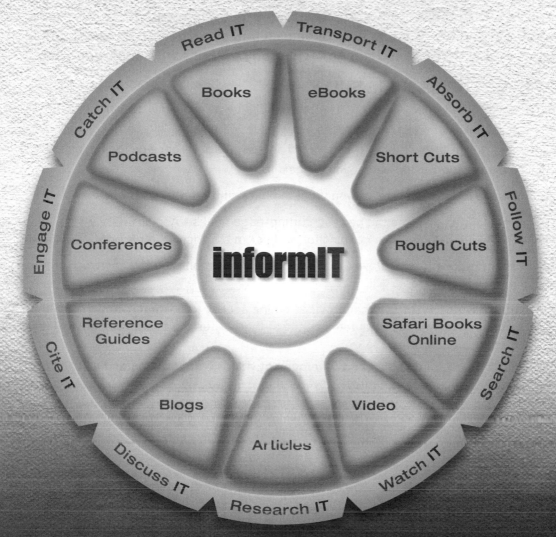

Learn IT at InformIT

Read IT
Transport IT
Catch IT
Absorb IT
Engage IT
Follow IT
Cite IT
Search IT
Discuss IT
Watch IT
Research IT

Books
eBooks
Podcasts
Short Cuts
Conferences
Rough Cuts
Reference Guides
Safari Books Online
Blogs
Video
Articles

informIT

11 WAYS TO LEARN IT at **www.informIT.com/learn**

The online portal of the information technology
publishing imprints of Pearson Education

BOOKS ONLINE

ENABLED

THIS BOOK IS SAFARI ENABLED

INCLUDES FREE 45-DAY ACCESS TO THE ONLINE EDITION

The Safari® Enabled icon on the cover of your favorite technology book means the book is available through Safari Bookshelf. When you buy this book, you get free access to the online edition for 45 days.

Safari Bookshelf is an electronic reference library that lets you easily search thousands of technical books, find code samples, download chapters, and access technical information whenever and wherever you need it.

TO GAIN 45-DAY SAFARI ENABLED ACCESS TO THIS BOOK:

- Go to **informit.com/safarienabled**

- Complete the brief registration form

- Enter the coupon code found in the front of this book on the "Copyright" page

If you have difficulty registering on Safari Bookshelf or accessing the online edition, please e-mail customer-service@safaribooksonline.com.